Iranian Leviathan

A Monumental History of Mithra's Abode

JASON REZA JORJANI

IRANIAN LEVIATHAN

A Monumental History of Mithra's Abode

ARKTOS
LONDON 2019

ISBN 978-1-912975-40-2 (Softcover)
978-1-912975-41-9 (Hardcover)
978-1-912975-42-6 (Ebook)

EDITING AND LAYOUT John Bruce Leonard

COVER Tor Westman

Arktos.com fb.com/Arktos @arktosmedia arktosmedia

Contents

This book is dedicated to my muse and beloved fiancée,
NASSIM NOURI
Who spellbindingly safeguarded my faith, hope, and love
For her mother country and my fatherland.
Iran owes this one to you, Archaeon.

Should sorrow send forth an army that spills the blood of lovers,
Mithra's wine-bearing maiden and I shall conspire to scale the sky,
piercing heaven's dome and drawing down a new design!

— Hafez of Shiraz

INTRODUCTION

A few countries are more than mere nations. They have been translated from the earthly plane into the spectral geography of ideas. As "Rome" is irreducible to Italy, and the modern state of Israel is only a reemergence of "Zion" into the mundane world, "Iran" is far more than the nation-state that foreigners once widely referred to as Persia. Iran is an immortal idea—a terrible thought in the mind of the gods (*devâs, divs*). Iran is destined to reemerge as the Leviathan from amongst all of Earth's great nations.

Until 1935, Iran was referred to internationally as "Persia" (or *La Perse*), and the Iranian people were broadly identified as "Persians." This was the case despite the fact that Persians always referred to themselves as Iranians (*Irâni*) and used the term *Irânshahr* (Old Persian *Aryâna Khashatra*) or "Aryan Imperium" in order to designate what Westerners call the "Persian Empire." The adjective Persian (*Pârsi*) has only been used by Iranians to describe the national language of Iran, which has been spoken, and especially written, by all Iranians regardless of whether it is their mother tongue. The Persian heritage is at the core of Iranian Civilization.

Civilizations are not as narrow as particular cultures in their ideological orientation. Even cultures evolve and are not defined by a single worldview in the way that a political party has a definite ideology. The inner dialectic that drives the historical evolution of Iranian Civilization is based on a tension between rival worldviews. This is comparable to the numerous worldview clashes that have shaped and reshaped Western Civilization, and is more dynamic than the creative tension between the worldviews of Confucianism, Taoism, Buddhism, and Communism and the cultural characters of the Han, the Manchurians, Mongols, and Tibetans in the history of Chinese Civilization.

The phrase "Iranian Civilization" has long been in use by academics in the field of Iranology or Iranian Studies. That there is an entire scholarly field of Iranology at all attests to the world-historical importance of Iran. However, in the public sphere, and even among other academics, Iran has rarely been recognized as a distinct civilization alongside the other major civilizations of world history. Rather, Iran has for the most part been mistakenly amalgamated into the false construct of "Islamic Civilization." We have entered the era of a clash of civilizations rather than a conflict between nation-states. Consequently, the recognition of Iran as a distinct civilization, one that far predates the advent of Islam and is now evolving beyond the Islamic religion, would be of decisive significance for the post-national outcome of a Third World War.

Iran is a civilization that includes a number of different cultures and languages that hang together around a core defined by the Persian language and imperial heritage. Besides the Persian heartland, Iranian Civilization encompasses Kurdistan (including the parts of it in the artificial states of Turkey and Iraq), the Caucasus (especially northern Azerbaijan and Ossetia), Greater Tajikistan (including northern Afghanistan and Eastern Uzbekistan), the Pashtun territories (in the failed state of Afghanistan), and Baluchistan (including the parts of it inside the artificial state of Pakistan). As we shall see, Iranian Civilization deeply impacted Western Civilization, with which it shares common Indo-European roots. There are still a few countries in Europe that are so fundamentally defined by the legacy of the Iranian Alans, Sarmatians, or Scythians that they really belong within the scope of Iranian, rather than European or Western Civilization. These are Ukraine, Bulgaria, Croatia, and, should it ever secede from Spain, Catalonia. The belonging of these European, Caucasian, Middle Eastern, Central Asian, and South Asian ethnicities and territories to an Iranian civilizational sphere is, by analogy, comparable to how Spain, France, Britain, Germany, and Italy are all a part of Western Civilization.

An even closer analogy would be to China, which is also a civilization rather than simply a nation. China, considered as a civilization, includes many cultures and languages other than that of the dominant Han Chinese—for example, the Manchurians, Mongolians, and Tibetans. What is interesting about China, in this regard, is that its current political administration encompasses almost its entire civilizational sphere—with the one exception of Taiwan (and perhaps Singapore). In other words, as it stands, Chinese Civilization has nearly attained maximal political unity. Western Civilization also has a high degree of political unity, albeit not at the level of China. The Western world is bound together by supranational economic and military treaties such as the European Union (EU) and the North Atlantic Treaty Organization (NATO). By contrast, the present political unity of Iranian Civilization is currently near its lowest level in a history spanning at least 3,000 years.

To borrow a term from the Russian philosopher, Alexander Dugin, the Persian ethnicity and language could be described as the *narod* or pith of Iranian Civilization. This would be comparable to the role of the Mandarin language and the Han ethnicity in contemporary Chinese Civilization, or to the role of Latin and the Italian ethnicity in Western Civilization at the zenith of the Roman Empire when Marcus Aurelius had conquered and integrated Britain and Germany. I accept Samuel Huntington's concept of a "clash of civilizations," I reject his distinction between what he calls "Classical Civilization" and Western Civilization. This is a distinction that he adopts from Arnold Toynbee, and perhaps also Oswald Spengler, both of whom see the origins of Western Civilization in Medieval Europe. In my view, Western Civilization begins with Classical Greece and is adopted and adapted by Pagan Rome.

The *narod* of a civilization can change. If Western Civilization were to prove capable of salvaging itself and reasserting its global dominance in the form of a planetary American Empire, this would no doubt involve a shift to the English language and the Anglo-Saxon ethnicity as the Western *narod*. The lack of a clear *narod* in Western Civilization at present is symptomatic of its decline and dissolution following the intra-civilizational war that prevented Greater Germany from becoming the ethno-linguistic core of the entire West. A very strong argument could be made that Germany and the German language were long destined to succeed Italy in this role, which Italy still plays to some extent through the Vatican's patronage of Latin and the Roman Catholic faith. The alliance of Hitler with Mussolini could have prepared for such a transition. If, for whatever reason, Latin America were to one day become the refuge of Europeans and even Anglo-Saxons fleeing Europe and North America, there would be a very good chance that the Spaniard ethnicity and the Spanish language would become the *narod* of Western Civilization following this transformative crisis.

In the three thousand years of Iranian Civilization, the *narod* of the civilization has shifted only once. For the first five hundred years of discernable Iranian history, the Median ethno-linguistic consciousness was at the core of Iran's identity as a civilization that included other non-Median Iranian cultures, such as the Scythians. Actually, for most of this period, the Medes were embattled by the Assyrians and other more entrenched non-Iranian (i.e. non Aryan) cultures, such as the Elamites. It is only for a brief period (on the Iranian scale of history, not the American one) that the Medes established a strong kingdom that included other Iranian cultures and could consequently be considered a standard bearer of an Iranian Civilization rather than a mere culture. This lasted for maybe a couple of hundred years before the revolt of Cyrus the Great in the sixth century BC saw the Persians displace the Medes and expand the boundaries of Iranian Civilization into the borders of the first true empire in history, one that included and integrated many non-Iranian kingdoms, and encompassed almost the entire known world.

For more than a thousand years after Cyrus, and despite the severe disruption of the Alexandrian conquest and colonization of Iran, we saw a succession of the three empires of the Achaemenids, the Parthians, and the Sassanians. The Achaemenid language was Old Persian, while the Parthians and Sassanians spoke and wrote Middle Persian (*Pahlavi*). These languages are direct ancestors of *Pârsi* (or *Dari*), the New Persian language that, in its rudiments, arose at the time of Ferdowsi (tenth century AD) and has remained remarkably stable until the present day.

A Monumental History

For more than 2,500 years, the Persian ethnicity and language have defined the core identity of Iranian Civilization. That was not lost on all of the various Europeans who dealt with Iran as an imperial rival, starting from the days of the classical Greeks and continuing to the pagan Romans, the Byzantines, the British, the French, and the Russians. All of them, without exception, always referred to all of Iran and its entire civilizational sphere as "Persia" or the "Persian Empire." Friedrich Nietzsche wished that the Persians had successfully conquered the Greeks because he believed that they could have gone on to become better guardians of Europe than the Romans proved to be. Nietzsche claimed that "only the Persians have a philosophy of history." He recognized that historical consciousness, of the Hegelian type, begins with Zarathustra's future-oriented evolutionary concept of successive historical epochs leading up to an unprecedented end of history.

In his essay "On the Uses and Abuses of History for Life," which appears in his *Untimely Meditations*, Nietzsche draws a distinction between three types of historiography. Antiquarian history is the historiography of conservatives. They see history as decline from a bygone golden age whose fragments they are trying to conserve and whose grandeur they hope to restore without any innovation. Critical history is the historiography of communists and others on the left. They interpret all of the social structures of various historical cultures as the product of unjust power relations, including and especially economic disparities between classes. Their historiography aims to deconstruct the ideals, symbols, and traditions of any civilization, by disenchanting people with an analysis of the ostensibly oppressive conditions that produced these structures. Finally, there is monumental history, which is Nietzsche's own approach to historiography. Monumental historians recognize that the tree of every living civilization requires a dark and rich soil for its roots if it is to continue to branch out and grow into the sunlight. Metaphorically, this means that myth can never be dispensed with and that the purpose of history is not to arrive at a perfectly accurate representation of the past, whether to reproduce or deconstruct it. Rather, the end or aim of appreciating the past is to attain inspiration for the sake of innovation.

All enduring development requires roots in the living tradition of a certain culture or, in the case of super-cultures like Iran, the historical heritage of a great civilization common to many cultural branches that are still growing. The idea of a repeated rebirth of a culture or civilization, as in the case of the rebirth of Europe through the Italian Renaissance, presupposes something like this monumental conception of history. Nietzsche had the greatest reverence for the Italian Renaissance and the type of human being that it produced. He was not an antiquarian, and would never have mistaken Leonardo da Vinci for an ancient Greek or a pagan Roman. Monumentalizing the past to inspire future development never merely reproduces a past form of culture. A true renaissance is always an evolution beyond what has been achieved before, albeit one firmly rooted in the blood and soil of a concrete community. This book on Iranian Civilization is a monumental history because it aims at an Iranian Renaissance, one that could be as constructive for all of humanity as the Italian Renaissance was for Europe.

The ultimate aim of this monumental history is to provide the basis for the distillation of the principles of an Iranian Renaissance from out of Iran's vast and ancient civilizational heritage. Consequently, the present work does not simply operate in the domain of historiography. It makes sovereign decisions regarding the past and future constitution (*ethos*) of an entire civilization. Moreover, this sovereign decision is not only concerned with Iran and the Iranian people, but with what the institutionalization of an Iranian Renaissance could mean for how the human race faces existential threats in this century. This is, in the end, a book about what conception of the human being we should fight for, and what vision Iranian Civilization has for the human future.

The history of Iranian Civilization has an inner logic, a dialectic driving Iran toward the fulfillment of its destiny on the world stage. The purpose of the present study is to reveal the teleological structure directing the historical development of Iranians, at least from the time of Zarathustra up to the Islamic Republic. Only by discovering the structure that defines this civilization as Iranian rather than Chinese or Western, can we wisely approach the question of Iran's future development. This also means rightly understanding Iran's place in the world and the historical responsibility of Iranians as members of the human community dwelling on this planet.

As in the case of China and the West, Iran is among less than a handful of living world-historical civilizations. Japan is not on this level and, despite Alexander Dugin's Eurasianist ambitions and Samuel Huntington's concept of an Eastern Orthodox Civilization, it is doubtful whether Russia is really at the core of its own civilizational sphere rather than being a lone state with a strong but isolated culture, akin to Japan. This also means that, as a civilization whose imperial sphere once encompassed half of the Earth's population, Iranians have a type of duty to mankind as a whole, which, for example, does not similarly burden the Russians or the Japanese. If Iranians were to mistakenly see Iran merely as a nation, rather than as one of the few great civilizations, and conceive of their concerns only in terms of the "national interest" of Iran, then Iranians would be forfeiting the right to play a determinative role in what promises to be the final phase of human evolution before our species transcends the earthly plane.

All of the Western (especially Anglo) rhetoric about Iran becoming a "responsible" member of the "international community" or a "normal" nation is just that — rhetoric. The tacit aim of such discourse is simply to affirm the dominance of a certain Anglo-American paradigm of power that would be threatened by the reemergence of Iran as an independent pole of cultural, economic, and political influence. Iran's ambitions in a region that has, historically, been that of its own civilization, has been generally supported by Russia, India, and China because these Eastern powers also stand to gain nothing from the perpetuation of the post-1945 Anglo-American geopolitical order.

In his groundbreaking book *The Clash of Civilizations and the Remaking of World Order*, the Harvard political scientist Samuel Huntington argues for a new world order based on a détente of great civilizations rather than perpetual conflict amongst nation-states. In effect, Huntington envisages the end of the Bretton Woods International System put in place from 1945 to 1948 after the Second World War. He advocates for its replacement with a geopolitical paradigm that would be defined by the major world-historical countries. These are the countries that can each be considered the "core state" of a civilization encompassing many peripheral vassal or client states.

The core state of any given civilization can change over the course of history. For example, Italy was the core state of Western Civilization for many centuries, and as the seat of the Roman Catholic Church it still has significant cultural influence over the West — especially in Latin America. Currently, however, the United States of America plays the role of the Western civilizational core state, with the North Atlantic Treaty Organization (NATO) effectively functioning as the superstructure of an American Empire coextensive with the West, with the exception of Latin America, where the United States has been economically and diplomatically dominant at least since the declaration of the Monroe Doctrine.

Huntington identifies less than a handful of surviving world-class civilizations whose interactions would define the post-international world order: Western Civilization, Orthodox Civilization, Chinese Civilization, and Islamic Civilization. The core states of the first three are America, Russia, and China. Within the context of his model a number of major world powers lack civilizational spheres. These "lone states" notably include India and Japan. While it has a high level of culture and deep historical ties to China, Japan is not a part of Chinese Civilization, and yet it lacks a civilizational sphere of its own that would encompass other states. Had the Japanese Empire triumphed in the Second World War, Japan might have become a civilization in its own right — one dominating the Pacific.

India is an interesting case, because in addition to being a "lone state" it also fits Huntington's definition of a "torn state." The latter are nations that are suffering from an identity crisis on account of being torn between two or more civilizations. India has its own Hindu civilization, which once extended to many neighboring states, but which is now more or less confined to India (with the possible exception of Sri Lanka). But India is also the world's largest Muslim country. Despite the fact that Muslims remain, for the moment, a minority in India, the country is still home to more Muslims than Pakistan or any other Islamic nation on Earth. Given current demographic trends, and historical precedents such as the Mughal Empire, the prospect of India becoming a part of Islamic Civilization should be taken seriously.

Of all the major civilizations delineated by Huntington, Islamic Civilization is the only one lacking a clear core state. Huntington considers this one of the reasons for the perpetual strife both within the Islamic world and between Islamic countries and states that are part of other civilizations. In effect, non-Islamic powers are confronted by a situation wherein there is no one to negotiate with, who would have the legitimate authority to enforce a uniform policy within Islamic Civilization in a fashion comparable to America's capability to speak for the West in fundamental conflicts with Russia or China. In such confrontations, European leaders may grumble about hegemonic American decision-making, but when it comes down to it the United States really does make policy for the West. Germany, the strongest and most central state in Europe, is home to numerous American military bases and installations. Italy, historically the most enduring European core state of Western Civilization, also quietly remains under American military occupation.

Since the collapse of the Ottoman Caliphate in 1918, and the Western colonial demarcation of totally artificial national borders across North Africa, the Middle East, and Central Asia, the Islamic World has been without a center. From a historical standpoint, Egypt, Turkey, Iraq, and Saudi Arabia rival each other as artificial nation-states that in a totally incomparable pre-national and pre-modern form once had the legitimacy of being home to the *Khalifa* (or sovereign authority) of the *Ummat* (the worldwide Islamic community). However, when viewed in terms of military and economic power, Pakistan, Malaysia, and Indonesia are more significant geopolitical players within the Islamic world. With a view to assuming leadership of an Islamic civilizational sphere, none of these countries is as well positioned as the Islamic Republic of Iran in terms of its cultural-historical heritage, industrial capability, and strategic location. Of all of the contenders within the Islamic world, Iran alone has the potential to resume its natural historical role, not just as a world power, but as a superpower responsible for securing the Islamic sphere within a new global order.

From an Iranian standpoint, the ultimate aim of this geostrategic project would be to reassert the Iranian character of the core of the Islamic world, thereby dismantling the false construct of Islamic Civilization while forwarding a Renaissance of Iranian Civilization. From a global strategic standpoint, this Greater Iran would be saving the West, India, Russia, and even China (which has an increasingly serious Muslim problem) from the prospect of a late twenty-first century world defined by a global Sunni Caliphate governing a human population demographically dominated by Muslims. This is Iran's cultural and historical responsibility. Only if Iranians themselves admit this, can other major world powers also recognize the fact that Iran's acceptance of this titanic duty is for the good of all mankind. This could be the key to Iran's reemergence as a global superpower.

The twelve chapters of this monumental history of Iran forward several interrelated theses, all of which are revolutionary. These concern the relationship between the different Iranian cultures that form branches of this civilization, the place of Zoroastrianism in this inter-cultural struggle and synthesis, as compared to the role of Mithraism and its antecedents, such as Mazdakism and radical esoteric Shi'ism, in defining the civilizational identity of Iran and determining its historical destiny. Above all, properly understanding the place of Islam in the history of Iranian Civilization is indispensable to constructively envisioning what it would mean for Iranian society to evolve into a post-Islamic epoch that draws on the heritage of Iran's Pre-Islamic period.

Iran as Mithra's Abode

The first revolutionary thesis of this study is that Zoroastrianism can in no way, shape, or form, be considered an uncontested ideological foundation of Iranian Civilization, nor should Zarathustra be seen as the founder of this civilization in anything like the singular sense in which many Chinese would confer upon Confucius the honor of being the father of Chinese Civilization. Rather, if a single religious worldview defined Iranian identity in its formative phase, it was Mithraism, not Zoroastrianism. In Chapter 1, it is argued that Cyrus the Great was not a Zoroastrian, but a worshiper of Mithra and Anahita. Despite the intra-Iranian tribal conflicts between them, the Medes, Persians, Scythians, and Sarmatians were all worshipers of Mithra, the martial god of contracts or covenants, and some form of goddess figure closely associated with him. This goddess figure, variously known as Anahita, Artemis, Satana, or as an arch Gorgon (such as Medusa), was revered as the mother, lover, and initiatrix of Mithra himself or of the Mithraic hero. The opening chapter of this study also discusses how this form of spirituality, in which terrifying sacrifices, ritual intoxication, and the the ordeal by fire, the sacred sword, the holy grail, and lady of the lake played key roles, was transplanted from Caucasian Iran to Europe by the Scythians, Sarmatians, and Alans. Meanwhile, it endured in the Iranian plateau in the Persian tradition of *Jâvânmardi* or *Pahlavâni*, the Chivalric culture of knightly heroes.

This is the culture of Rostam, the Scythian *Pahlavân* who ferociously resists the imposition of Zoroastrianism on Iran by Esfandiyar. The latter is acting effectively as a sword, not only in the hand of his father, Kay Goshtasp or Kavi Vishtaspa, but also at the behest of Zarathustra himself. The teaching and legacy of Zarathustra is the subject matter of Chapter 2. According to Ferdowsi, Zarathustra is alive and well at the court of his patron king during the period in which the latter sends his son on crusades for the faith and, ultimately, on a mission to either force Rostam into submission or assassinate the Scythian warlord. Rostam is only able to defeat Esfandiyar by means of Zal's recourse to the Mithraic shamanic ritual of summoning the magical Simorgh — a chimerical wolf-bird-amphibian that first appears in Scythian and Sarmatian gold crafts.

Just as Cyrus the Great is defeated by a Scythian queen, the "Amazon" Tomyris, on the western side of the Caspian Sea, Zarathustra too is killed in the course of a Scythian invasion of the realm of Goshtasp on the eastern side of the Caspian Sea. This greater Caspian region of northern Iran was known as Hyrcania (Old Persian *Vargkânâ*, Middle Persian *Gorgân*) or "wolf country," with the Caspian Sea itself having been referred to as the "Sea of Hyrcania" (Latin *Mare Hyrcanum*, Persian *Daryâ-ye-Gorgân*) by many ancient sources — in other words, as the "Sea of Wolves." Today the region, which crosses several contemporary Iranian provinces, is most widely known for the Persian caviar-fishing seaside resort town of Râmsar, where Reza Shah built a grand hotel, as well as for the city of Gorgan (Arabic *Jorjan*), its largest metropolis. The Hyrcanian Forest of this region has just been declared a protected site by UNESCO. The wolf was the totemic symbol of the Scythians and is demonized by Zoroastrians as an avatar of Ahriman.

If the historical context of Zarathustra is indeed the Median-Scythian war of the seventh century BC, with Hyrcania, right on the Median border with Scythia, as one of its front lines, then it makes a great deal more sense to see Zarathustra as the first philosopher. A Zarathustra separated from the rest of the history of Philosophy in Greece and India by many hundreds — if not thousands — of years simply does not make sense from the standpoint of psycho-social evolution within the Indo-European community. However, a Zarathustra who is the forerunner of philosophical thought within a century of the Imperial Iranian colonization of Greece, and the rise of Pre-Socratic Greek philosophy in the Iranian colonies of Ionia, makes a great deal of sense. The Iranian origin of Philosophy is the focus of this study's second chapter.

Seeing Zarathustra as the first voice in a philosophical dialogue that ultimately includes such brilliant minds as Pythagoras and Heraclitus, is also to see Zarathustra as fallible. While Pythagoras and Heraclitus were both very closely connected to Imperial Iran — the former studied in its capital for a dozen years and the latter was summoned by Darius to be its court philosopher — these Greeks are not Zoroastrians. They are philosophers, just as Zarathustra was *the first* philosopher. Elements of the Pythagorean and Heraclitean doctrines certainly bear traces of having been influenced by the *Gâthâs*, but there are also ideas in these Pre-Socratic Greek writings — even Iranian ideas — that are most definitely not Zoroastrian, such as Reincarnation. One of the first Pre-Socratic philosophers, who was also considered to be one of the "seven sages" by the Greeks, was Anarcharsis, the Scythian. This Iranian philosopher appears to have taught a doctrine that was opposed to Zoroastrianism.

The Scythian critique of Zoroastrian ideas was, however, far more devastatingly delivered by a certain Gautama Sakamuni. The "Scythain Sage" Gautama, who later came to be known as the Buddha, was an Iranian philosopher who took aim at almost every fundamental concept of Zoroastrianism: one eternal supreme being, the equation of this being with Truth and the absolute opposition of this Truth to all manner of lies and deception, hypostatized as the Lie and conceived of as a really existing Evil entity out to derange the creator's cosmos, a binary moral opposition between these two forces of Good and Evil, the final judgment of an immortal soul who must choose between these two sides in the cosmic war, and the total perfection of the world at the end of history. Gautama's teaching is not a response to Vedic religion, as much as a specific attempt to totally deconstruct every one of these Zoroastrian concepts, among other less significant but related ideas attributed to Zarathustra, such as the categorization of certain animals (for example, snakes, lizards, many insects like spiders) as *khrafstars* — ungodly, demon-spawned vermin — that ought to be exterminated from God's Creation. Gautama teaches that all phenomena are impermanent, variable, and unfixed, and no thing has any self or inherent essence. This means that nothing can be the opposite of anything else, and that everything is interdependent in its origination and dissolution. Fixed and absolute concepts based on polar opposites of the kind that are central to Zoroastrianism, such as Good and Evil, Truth and Lies, Light and Darkness, are deluded abstractions that cause suffering on account of their attempt to approach a world in flux as if reality actually corresponded to these categories.

If this anarchic teaching sounds Taoist, that is not a coincidence. As we shall see in Chapter 3, recent research suggests that Gautama was also the author of the *Tao Te Ching*. In his old age he traveled to northwestern China, where he was known as Lao Tan (*Tzu*, as in Lao Tzu, is an honorific). This name, meaning "old long ears," is a later corruption of the ancient Chinese Gau-Tam-a (which became Kau Tam, then Lao Tan). He taught the Dharma, which the ancient Chinese mispronounced as *Darwa* and which became *Dawa* and then *Dao* or Tao in later Chinese. The Yin-Yang symbol, which is the perfect image to convey the essence of his teaching, was found in Scythian and Sarmatian art. The Buddhist stupas are based on a combination of the Scythian and Sarmatian *kurgans* or burial mounds, surmounted by a representation of the Scythian pointed hat. The stupas of Eastern Iran, which contained relics of the Buddha and various Bodhisattvas, became the basis of the *Imâmzâdeh* pilgrimage culture of Shi'ite Iran. The design of these influenced Iranian architecture in the Islamic period. The largest Buddhist temples in the world were in Eastern Iran, and so were the most colossal carved Buddhas. Buddhism was brought from Iran into China through the Silk Route, and the Parthian missionaries responsible for this left a great deal of Parthian vocabulary in the earliest Buddhist texts that were translated into Chinese by them.

What is even more shocking than the attempted erasure of the history of Buddhism as an Iranian religion, is the highly suggestive evidence pointing to the identity of Gautama, the Scythian sage, with the Magus "Gaumata" of the Behistun Inscription. As will be argued in Chapter 3, Darius the Great's story about having executed Gaumata is not believable given the treatment that rebels against his military takeover of the Persian Empire received. Darius, who invited Heraclitus of Ephesus to become his court philosopher, probably allowed Gautama to go into exile on the fringes of Imperial Iran in northern India, because he identified with certain aspects of his worldview. After all, a comparison of the fragments of Heraclitus with the *Tao Te Ching* or the kind of early Buddhism reconstructed on the basis of Hellenistic travelogues, reveals a largely overlapping metaphysics and epistemology. An examination of Darius' repeated advocacy and use of deception and duplicitous scheming as stratagems in his rise to power, reveals a character that would have believed faking Gautama's death and allowing him to live out his days as a sage was a Noble Lie of the kind that Plato advocates in his *Republic*. However, this does shatter the traditional view of Darius as a zealous Zoroastrian, one who repeatedly emphasizes his opposition to liars and to the Lie in the very same Behistun Inscription in which he tells this colossal lie about killing Gautama.

The conflict between Zoroastrianism and an older Mithraic worldview that evolves in response to Zoroastrianism is not a matter of mere tribalism, it is a fundamental philosophical clash. Zoroastrianism was not only opposed by one single religious or philosophical rival. It was opposed by the Scythian Magic that the message of Zarathustra was directed against. It was opposed by the teaching of the Scythian sage who seized control of the Persian Empire, the man who would go on to become Gautama Buddha after being exiled to Northern India by Darius the Great. It was opposed by certain Pre-Socratic Greek philosophical viewpoints, including and especially that of Heraclitus who, despite his divergence from aspects of Zarathustra's teaching, had a worldview Iranian enough to be invited by Darius the Great to become Iran's court philosopher. Pythagoras, who studied under the Magi in the capital of Achaemenid Iran, also developed a school of thought in which we can see as many ideas that diverge from those of Zarathustra as those that reiterate Zoroastrian doctrine.

The Parthians, who were close cousins of the Scythians and Sarmatians, were Mithraists who took over the mantle of the Persian Empire after centuries of Greek colonization. As explored in Chapter 5, they favored a new, somewhat Hellenized form of Mithraism over Zoroastrianism. Although Ardeshir Babakan fought hard to eradicate this belief system, it survived among the Parthian aristocracy and dissident Mithraic Magi. The Mazdakite movement can be seen as a coup staged by these dissidents and, consequently, the Neo-Mazdakite mystical movements that adopt the "Shi'ite" banner in the epoch after the Arab destruction of the Sassanian state and its Zoroastrian Orthodoxy could also be interpreted as Neo-Mithraic in nature. Suffice it to say that there were many religious and philosophical strands rivaling Zoroastrianism from within the Iranian world, and we have not even mentioned Manichaeism and its Gnostic offshoots, which — although *they* accept Zarathustra — were rejected and persecuted by Zoroastrians.

Yet, despite such a tremendous diversity of thought and belief, this study delineates the cosmological, psychological, and ethical contours of a single, albeit evolving, Mithraic meta-narrative that rivaled Zoroastrianism. This rivalry became especially intense once Zoroastrianism took an orthodox form under Ardeshir Babakan and his Sassanid successors. Its worldview is as "Iranian" as the Zoroastrian worldview that it opposes on certain fundamental points of theological and philosophical outlook.

According to Mithraists, there is no radical opposition between Good and Evil. In Chapter 5, it is argued that Mithra, who is seen as the champion and savior of humanity, is a just and impartial mediator in the cosmic battle between the opposed forces of Ohrmazd (Ahura Mazda) and Ahriman. Moreover, Ahriman and Ohrmazd are twins born of a single mother who is also their father, an androgynous deity called *Zorvân* and sometimes later simply referred to as *Zamân* or "Time." Finally, Ahriman is the firstborn of the two and essentially dominates this world, because *Zorvân* was seduced by *Âz* into unconsciously giving birth to Evil before Good. *Âz* is a female personification of primordial Chaos and a Concupiscence that is the root of all other desirous passions. The supreme God only becomes Good over the course of time, S/he only gives birth to Ohrmazd after attaining self-consciousness by witnessing the exteriorization of His or Her own inner Evil. This process of God transcending unconscious Concupiscence, hypostatized by the feminine arch demon *Âz*, is symbolized by Ohrmazd triumphing over Ahriman at the conclusion of a battle extending through ages of human history.

Without Mithra acting as a mediator, Ohrmazd would not be able to secure this victory — especially at the apocalyptic end of history, where

Mithra has a key role to play as a savior. Salvation consists, not in being Good, but in becoming more conscious of one's Evil. The five demons that are, symbolically, the spawn of *Âz* or primordial Concupiscence, namely Need, Avarice, Lust, Wrath, and Vengeance, must be overcome—not through asceticism, but via an inspired libertine transcendence of possessiveness. This includes both possessiveness with respect to material goods and also with respect to the object of lust. The devotee of Mithra, the perfected human being for whom Mithra is the archetype, practices divine love to overcome the astrologically fatalistic and archontic influences of the stars and planets that move most men through their passions. The Mithraists symbolized this as Mithra overcoming the Gorgon-headed Lord of Time, *Zorvân*, in such a way as to be able to shift the axis of the entire heavens from above the stellar sphere. That powerful cosmic and mythic image lies at the core of Chapter 5. This alternative Iranian worldview is divergent from Zoroastrianism in all of its dimensions—cosmological, psychological, ethical and political.

On a cosmological level, this Mithraic worldview is monistic rather than dualistic. Zoroastrians who, with the hindsight of the modern epoch and in a context of European colonial dominance (especially among the Parsis in India), have attempted to portray their religion as monotheistic are engaging in revisionism. Whether in the Gathas of Zarathustra or the Zoroastrian Orthodoxy established by Ardeshir Babakan, Zoroastrian ontology is dualistic. In Zoroastrian ontology, the Ahrimanic is seen as an entirely negative principle of chaos. Cosmic order (*Ashâ*, *Artâ*) is brought about through *Spentâ Mainyu* or the creative, progressively innovative, bounteous mind at work in Nature. For Zoroastrians, *Angra Mainyu* or Ahriman is nothing more than a deranging force—something akin to static interference (Persian *pârâzit*) that degrades the clarity of a signal. Moreover this "demonic" force emerges from out of a black hole or an abyss that is radically separate from, and unrelated to, the "Good Creation" of Ahura Mazda.

The Mithraic view is totally different. Ahura Mazda shares a common origin with Ahriman, namely the womb of Time (*Zorvân*) and the non-demarcated matrix of Space (*Vay*). Ahriman has priority over Ahura Mazda because chaos is more primordial than cosmic order. This is why, symbolically, *Âz* is capable of seducing *Zorvân* and thereby inducing the birth of Ahriman before that of Ohrmazd. The negative principle is not purely negative from this perspective. Rather, it plays a positive role in creation and the manifestation of our world. In fact, our world is, metaphorically, delivered over to Evil from the start. The Mithraists recognize that cosmic evolution requires the dialectical tension of forces that, although they may appear to be polar opposites, are actually inextricable on an ontological level and equally necessary to Creation.

On this view, from a psychological perspective, just as Order cannot be fundamentally separated from Chaos, the chaotic unconscious always underlies any rational consciousness that appears to be at work in the living world or the universe at large — including and especially in the human mind. That *Âz* is the catalyst for the creation of the cosmos, and at the same time the arch demon whose essential Concupiscence is the root of the demons of Need, Avarice, Lust, Wrath, and Vengeance, means that these passions are not deranging influences from outside of the God-given rational soul of the human being. Rather, the mind of God itself is afflicted by the essence of these passions at the deepest level. God is fundamentally unconscious and therefore also needy, lustful, jealous, wrathful, and vengeful. Creation is driven by God's need to fill a profound sense of want, which, given the feminine aspect of *Zorvân* as an androgynous God, is akin to the sexual desire to be filled. Only by facing the exteriorization of these aspects of its own being does the Creator — or Creatrix — become progressively more conscious and bounteous in a benevolent sense, over vast epochs of time. This means that, from a moral standpoint, the initial impetus for Creation is Evil.

It is precisely because Zoroastrianism is dualistic that theologians have long recognized Zoroastrianism as the only religion that averts the "problem of evil." Ahura Mazda or Ohrmazd is *not* responsible for the evil of the world, and human beings *are* responsible for actions attributable to their own will, because Ohrmazd is neither omniscient nor omnipotent, and Ahriman is a fundamentally distinct principle. The Mithraic view is also divergent from the Zoroastrian one in terms of this ethical dimension. Evil—in its totality—is not only an inseparable part of the Supreme Being, it is a deeper and more originary element of God than Goodness. Free will is not negated through any claim to the omniscience or omnipotence of the Supreme Being. Rather, the Supreme Being is profoundly lacking in knowledge and power, and therefore susceptible to the inadvertent exteriorization of the Evil within Herself, an Evil of which She remains unconscious until it is manifested in a world full of sex and violence. The base passions have a kind of deterministic effect on the natural world, including the human organism—an effect that the ancient Iranians understood in terms of baneful astral influences.

The light and love of rising consciousness, as symbolized by Mithra, can overcome these fatalistic forces. That is why Mithra is also so strongly associated with liberation and free-spiritedness on a symbolic level (the Gorgon-Slaying, the Phrygian Cap, Lady Liberty, the Pirate Flag). This freedom can, however, be attained only by recognizing everything associated with Evil as the shadow side of one's own psyche, not by projecting all of that outside of oneself as the interference of a demonized other in the way that Zoroastrians do. To become Mithra, the mediator between Ohrmazd and Ahriman, in this metaphorical sense, is to transform the Ahrimanic passions within oneself rather than try to exorcise them.

When translated into the social and political sphere, this yields a politics significantly different from that of the Zoroastrian Orthodoxy of those Sassanid monarchs who followed in the footsteps of Ardeshir Babakan. Many did not, including his own son Shapur the Great. However, as will be argued in Chapter 6 of this study, those who did were among the most repressively conservative and puritanical political leaders of all time. As custodians of the totalitarian theocratic vision of Ardeshir Babakan, the likes of Tansar, Kartir, the authors of the *Vendidâd*, Bahram, Azarpad, and Khosrow Anoushiravan suppressed dissident thought and persecuted what they considered deviant religious views, harshly punished perceived perversions or personal vices, and subjugated women on the basis of a horrified disgust at the feminine that ranks among the most vehement expressions of misogynist attitudes in any advanced culture. At the basis of all of this is a view of Evil as something like a contagion that must be zealously guarded against with extreme hygienic measures, lest it infect society as a whole through the contamination of a single careless individual. Women were particularly suspect as potential carriers of this Ahrimanic plague. The aptness of the metaphor of contagion and hygiene can be seen from the Sassanian Orthodoxy's equation of Wisdom (*xerad*) with a being Reasonable or Sensible that is synonymous with Right-conduct (*niki*). The unconscious and irrational is Ahrimanic.

To the extent that *Sraosha* or *Soroush*, namely inspiration, played a significant role in the teachings of Zarathustra, and in the expression of his message in the form of ecstatic poetry—what we see in the Sassanian period is the death of Zarathustra at the hands of Zoroastrianism. However, the problem begins with Zarathustra himself insofar as the Gathas refuse to recognize *Angra Mainyu* as integral to inspiration. Zarathustra was rightly reviled as Evil by those whose culture he challenged with his revolutionary message. Inspiration is *always* blessedly Evil when it threatens a society with revolution! Zarathustra's admonition of the *soma*-intoxicated Scythian shamans is also telling. Although his hymns are clearly ecstatically inspired (and it is to his credit that he did not need any intoxicant other than meditative communion with cosmic consciousness in order to have such poetry pour out of his soul), there is still a streak of puritanism in him. Some of the contemporary characterizations of Zarathustra as a proto-Protestant are not entirely off the mark, even if they are exaggerated and miss his more ecstatic side. The *soma* that he preaches against is the *amanita muscaria*-laced wine that would go on to play a prominent role in Mithraic rituals, the intoxicant that lies behind all of those references to *meyé Moghân* or "Magian wine" in later poets of the Religion of Love.

This Religion of Love, which reemerges in poets such as Rumi and Hafez, actually tried to seize control of the Sassanian state during the Mazdakite Revolution. This revolutionary movement becomes the focus of Chapter 6. It is in this upheaval that the political implications of the

Mithraic worldview can be most clearly discerned by contrast with the political philosophy of the Zoroastrian Orthodoxy. Attempting to blunt the edges of the Mazdakite Revolution by disregarding or downplaying the shocking developments of those days as they are presented by almost every account of Mazdakism that has survived in medieval Persian and Arab writings does a disservice to anyone trying to understand Iran out of a concern for its future. Whether our source is a patriot like Ferdowsi or a hostile Arab-Muslim theologian and heresiarch, we are presented with an extremely radical picture: the abolition of private property and patriarchal marriage in favor of communism and free love, as well as the disestablishment of any organized religious orthodoxy.

Mazdak was not a mere reformer seeking to ameliorate widening class disparities in the distribution of wealth. Mazdak was a Utopian revolutionary backed by Kavad in a bid to bring human history to an end and establish heaven on earth. The transformation of human consciousness demanded by the Mazdakite social policies was impossible, and it was meant to be impossible. We were witnessing the deliberate Mithraic invitation of an Apocalypse ending in Utopia — what the Zoroastrians called *Frashgard* and the Assassins would later refer to as the *Qiyâmat*. Interestingly this Iranian apocalyptic theology of "the end of history" would reemerge in the Hegelian-Marxism of the nineteenth and twentieth centuries, together with the foremost Mazdakite symbol of the Red Flag (*Sorkh Alam*).

Islam Did Not Cause Iran's Decline

It is astonishing that the Mazdakite revolutionary state lasted for an entire generation before being crushed by a brutal conservative coup, one in which as many as 100,000 leading Mazdakites were executed by the restored Sassanian Orthodoxy and their books were all publicly burned. As I suggest in Chapter 7, a likely explanation for this longevity is that the Mazdakite Revolution had the backing of the Parthian feudal houses in the provinces, who wanted to use this revolutionary religious movement in order to shatter and topple the Sassanian central government.

These Parthians were also Mithraists who had never been able to swallow the government-backed Zoroastrian Orthodoxy. The provincial Parthian principalities had secretly retained their own Mithraic magicians, sorcerers, wizards, and witches.

That brings us to the second shocking thesis of this monumental history of Iranian Civilization: namely, that the Islamic Conquest of Iran was engineered by the Parthian elite, as a weapon of last resort against the social and political order of the Sassanids, *and that Islam did not cause the decline of Iranian Civilization*. This engineering was not limited to a refusal on the part of the knights of the Parthian houses to fight to protect the Sassanid state against the Arab invaders. That mutiny did take place, as other scholars have uncovered and extensively documented. But Chapter 7 of this study ventures the view that this sedition ran much deeper than that, and the conspiracy extended into the Arabian peninsula itself. The Mithraic Magus who adopted the identity of "Salman, the Persian" appears to have been sent to Muhammad as a psychological warfare operative. This flesh-and-blood Gabriel "revealed" the Quran and offered Muhammad all kinds of tactical advisement and strategic counsel, making it possible for him to unify the Arabian tribes into a spearhead against the Sassanid state. Salman's backers in the House of Karen even sent their green-clad knights to bail Muhammad out at the Battle of Badr, securing the Army of Islam a "miraculous" victory that would both pave their way to an invasion of Sassanian Iran and also enter the sacred lore at the foundation of their manufactured cult. Only Greater Hyrcania (including Gorgan, Mazandaran or Tabarestan, and Gilan), namely the realm of the House of Karen, was spared in the Arab-Muslim conquest of Iran. Meanwhile, Salman was given the governorship of the Sassanid capital district of Ctesiphon.

What is most significant is the secret aim of this occult conspiracy, which was about far more than a centuries-old Parthian vendetta against the Sassanids. Islam was never supposed to endure in Iran and, had it not been for the invasion of the Turks and the Mongols, Iranian society would have rid itself of Islam together with the Arabian Caliphate. *Islam was the ideological equivalent of a genetically engineered virus designed to inoculate a particular population*, which then enters a group with a different genome, a population for which it had not been tailored. Instead of being inoculated, *this alien population succumbs to and spreads the disease that the virus vector was meant to inoculate the target population against.* The Mithraic Magi and their Parthian feudal lords had designed Islam to work on the Iranian psycho-social system, with the aim of catalyzing an immune response that would manifest as a rebellion against both Islam *and any other form of religious totalitarianism*—such as the Sassanian state orthodoxy. What was supposed to incite Luciferian rebellion in the free-spirited minds of Aryans was swallowed whole by the Turks and Mongols. Exactly those characteristics of Islam that were supposed to trigger the Aryan immune response to oppressive hierarchy, conservative litigiousness, draconian discipline and sadistic punishment, appealed to the despotically oriental souls of these Siberian nomads. "Gabriel" did not foresee that.

That the Parthian or Mithraic conspiracy could have succeeded in its aim without Iran succumbing to Islam can be seen from what actually did take place from the ninth to the eleventh centuries, a Post-Zoroastrian *and Post-Islamic* Iranian Renaissance. I mean "Post-Islamic" in the sense that Zakariyya Razi, Abolqasem Ferdowsi, Fakhruddin Gorgani and Omar Khayyam reject and even mock Islam on the basis of an Iranian identity that is not narrowly restricted to Zoroastrianism. Any Iranian Renaissance that is about to take place will, in actuality, be a Second Renaissance. The first Iranian Renaissance took place from 850–1050 *after the Islamic Conquest of Iran*, and in terms of the level of cultural production in the sciences, arts, and literature it represented *the zenith of Iranian psycho-social evolution up until the present day*. This monumental history identifies that era, the so-called "Golden Age of Islam", as the apex of achievement in Iranian Civilization—not the Achaemenid or Sassanian epochs in the Pre-Islamic period. Reacting against Islam freed the Iranian mind to transcend itself. Although this Renaissance was ultimately destroyed by the Turkic and Mongol conquest of Iran, the transformation that the Iranian consciousness underwent during the course of it yielded the poetry of Hafez. In the *Divân* of Hafez, in particular, we see the pinnacle of Iranian Civilization.

The scientific achievements of the period from the ninth to the twelfth century were extraordinary, not only in the context of Iranian history, but in that of world history. Iranian scientists such as Zakariyya Razi (Rhazes), Abu Rayhan Al-Biruni, Omar Khayyam, Ibn Sina (Avicenna), Musa Al-Khwarazmi, Yahya Ibn Abi Mansur, Haly Abbas, and many others led the world in Astronomy, Mathematics, Physics, Engineering, Biology, and Medicine. There were also major contributions to the human sciences, such as Sociology and History, by the likes of Naser Khosrow and Muhammad al-Tabari. Those who, out of a pathological hatred of Islam, make the claim that this level of scientific achievement had already been reached in the Sassanian period—or for that matter, at any other period of Iran's history before or since—are delusional.

To be sure, Khosrow Anoushiravan took in refugees from the Western academies that were being closed down by an increasingly intolerant Church. However, few of these scientists and scholars could stomach the repressive atmosphere in the court of the Sassanid monarch who had just massacred the Mazdakites. Among the small number who had been invited, most left. They had little impact on the wider scientific culture of Sassanian Iran, and advanced research institutions such as Gondeshapur were few. The situation was not comparable to that of Roman Alexandria, whereas Iran of 850–1050 exceeded the output of Alexandria.

Meanwhile, there was in the same period a renaissance of the Persian language, which evolved beyond Sassanid Middle Persian (i.e. Pahlavi or Parsig) into the much more lyrically expressive New Persian or Dari that remains intelligible today. It was used by Rudaki, Ferdowsi, Gorgani and other romantic and epic poets who laid the groundwork for the literary brilliance that would eventually culminate in Rumi, Sa'adi, and Hafez. Quite to the contrary of those who make the unsupportable and highly hypothetical claim that whatever was in the lost libraries of the Sassanian period must have been the zenith of Iranian literature, the historical reality is that, in terms of the complexity of consciousness and the expansiveness of vision, the literary history of Iran peaks with the *Divân* of Hafez. This Persian literary treasure is contemplated in depth in Chapter 8.

In Hafez we see the culmination of the Religion of Love that had been developing at least since the period of Parthian Mithraism and that seized control of the Sassanian state during the Mazdakite Revolution. The long-standing humanism of Iranian Civilization reaches a point of completion in the postulation of the *rendé qalandar* or mystically inspired libertine as the *ensâné kâmel* or Perfect Man. A close look at Hafez's life will demonstrate that despite his debt to the symbolism and lore of Pre-Islamic Iran, his work would be inconceivable without the Quran and Islam. This is, of course, also true of Rumi, who is the other Persian poet featured in Chapter 8, and who expresses the evolutionary perfection of *Mazhabé Eshq* or *Ayiné Mehr*, the "Religion of Mithra."

Had the Iranian Renaissance of the early Islamic period not met its demise at the hands of the Turkic and Mongol invasions of Iran, the kind of free-spirited Enlightenment reflected in the poetry of Rumi and Hafez would have liberated Iran from every form of dogmatism. It is, in effect, a self-deconstruction of Islam and every other religion and ideology. The Assassins made it fairly clear that this was the esoteric aim of Islam: to destroy *sharia*—not just in the limited sense of "Islamic law" but in the deep psycho-social sense of the need for any law that imposes what is "forbidden" or "permitted" from above or outside of oneself. Hafez knew that "nothing is true; everything is permitted."

The lack of a centralized Iranian state cannot be counted against the glory of the epoch from Razi and Hassan to Rumi and Hafez any more than the greatness of the Renaissance in the history of Italy can be dismissed simply because the Medici clan and other patrons of the arts and sciences were only in control of Florence or Venice and did not govern the whole of Italy as anything even close to a unified nation. In fact, by contrast with the situation of the Italian Renaissance, before the Turks invaded Iran the Buyid dynasty had become so powerful that it had effectively seized control of the Baghdad Caliphate. That is, what was left of the Arabian Caliphate after Neo-Mazdakite rebellions in Azerbaijan, Hyrcania, and Khorasan had shattered its hold on much of Iran. Even after the Turkic invasion, the Order of Assassins was so effective in operating against the Seljuk-revitalized Caliphate that its network of fortresses, *de facto* led by Hassan at Alamut, was laying the groundwork for a Persian-speaking Ismaili state in Iran.

Whether it would have been through the Twelver Shi'ism of the Buyids or the Sevener Shi'ism of the Assassins, before the Mongol invasion of the thirteenth century, the Iranian Renaissance of the ninth through the twelfth century could have continued under the patronage of a centralized Iranian state of the kind that finally did reemerge under the Safavids. This means that all of those scientific treatises that had been written in Arabic would have been penned in the New Persian language that was yielded by the tremendous literary flourishing of the Iranian Renaissance of 850–1050. If the Assassins insisted on using Persian rather than Arabic even as the liturgical language of Shi'ism, they would certainly have mandated its use for the composition of scientific and technical treatises.

What this also means is that Islam was not the cause of the decline of Iranian Civilization and the failure of the Safavid and Afsharid attempt to revitalize Iran. As we see in Chapter 9, this attempt, which began with Shah Ismail Safavid and was resumed by Nader Shah Afshar, succeeded in re-establishing Iran as a vast empire and military superpower. However, this new Iranian Empire ultimately lacked the intellectual, cultural, social, and industrial backbone to rival the rising European colonial powers, including Czarist Russia, which eventually conquered nearly half of Iran's territory. The cause for Iran's catastrophic decline from the late eighteenth century onward is that the genetic impact of the genocidal Turkic and Mongol invasions finally caught up with Iranians.

After 1945 in the Western world it became politically correct to claim that "race" is a social construction that does not correspond to any biological reality. This is essentially a Marxist view that, for reasons having to do with the outcome of the Second World War, became just as culturally predominant in the West as it was among the Soviet allies of the West during the war. We will see how, in the last five years, advances in gene sequencing technology and new archeological finds have destroyed this left-wing myth of human racial equality. This does not mean that Iran will never again produce thinkers on the level of Razi, Avicenna, or Farabi. With the emerging technologies of embryo selection and genetic engineering, it would be possible, with the right leadership and government planning, to restore the pre-Turkic and pre-Mongol genetic character of the majority of the Iranian population within only one or two generations.

Iran as the Leviathan

The third and final thesis of this study, which encompasses the other two, and from which this book as a whole takes its name, is that Iran has been destined to be the Leviathan among nations. One major piece of evidence in favor of the argument that Iran is not fundamentally Zoroastrian is the role that the Achaemenid Emperors played in the world's first Zionist project. As I explain in Chapter 4, if the Achaemenids had really been Zoroastrians they would never have been involved in the creation of Zionism, and of the Jewish religion as we know it today, to the extent that they were. When viewed from a Zoroastrian perspective, Yahweh has all of the qualities of Ahriman — the evil deity that opposes Ahura Mazda and the figure that becomes an Iranian prototype for Satan. Ahura Mazda endeavors to increase human knowledge, he is bounteous, he plans everything in the cosmic creation with his supreme intelligence as best as he can in the face of the assault of Ahriman, he seeks an end to wrathful violence and oppression, and he judges individuals based on their own deeds and through their personal conscience. By contrast, Yahweh enforces human ignorance, he boasts about how jealous he is, he is heedless enough to regret his creation of humanity and to send the great flood to destroy the civilization of Noah, he is a capricious wheeler-dealer and mercurial character amenable to negotiating with prophets over how many people ought to be subject to his vengeance, he deliberately makes individuals act in an evil fashion, as in the case of his hardening Pharaoh's heart, and then he judges people based on the sins of their ancestors and condemns entire communities on the basis of collective guilt. He also orders genocides and holocausts of civilian populations to conquer a "promised land" in the name of a "chosen people."

Despite this fact, Cyrus the Great develops such a close rapport with the Jewish community exiled to Babylon, that after he conquers Babylon he is hailed as the only gentile Messiah in the Jewish scriptures. Cyrus orders the rebuilding of the Jerusalem Temple, at cost to the Persian royal treasury, a project that is completed by his successor, Darius the Great (not his son, but a military officer who marries his daughter). Cyrus also coordinates with the Jewish community to provide them with Achaemenid state support for the project of the resettlement and redevelopment of Israel as a Jewish homeland, the first explicitly Zionist project in history. He is hailed as "the salvation of Zion." Meanwhile, Darius the Great establishes the world's first credit-based private banking system, with the introduction of checks and standardized coinage known as *shekels*, a system through which the Jews of cities such as Susa, Ecbatana, Nippur, and especially Babylon, became the financiers of the first international economic system based on the manipulation of trust and expectations of growth.

As suggested in Chapter 4, the influence of the Jewish community in Imperial Iran must have become so extensive that by the reign of Darius' successor, Xerxes, the Prime Minister hatches a vast plot aimed at persecuting the Jews. Haman may have been reacting to plans for Xerxes' military expedition into continental Europe, which was so gargantuan in scale that he may have believed it would ruin the Achaemenid state, and which he probably suspected was being pushed by the international bankers of Babylon. In any case, Xerxes sides with the Jewish community *by executing no less than 75,000 Iranian officials* and others involved in what was evidently a vast conspiracy to liquidate the Jews. After saving the Jews, this same Xerxes goes forward with his military campaign into Europe, at the outset of which he performs a human sacrifice of virgin girls and boys, together with a Mithraic horse sacrifice. When Xerxes gets to Athens he burns the temples of the Greek idols to the ground. His successor, Artaxerxes makes an exception to the Imperial Iranian policy of not allowing satrapies to have defensive walls by authorizing his cup-bearer, the Jew Nehemiah, to go back to Israel and re-build the fortifications of the city of Jerusalem.

The plot thickens when we consider how many of the defining doctrines of Judaism, as we know it today — doctrines that eventually also became foundational for Christianity — were adopted into Israelite religion under direct Iranian influence. These include: judgment of an individual soul based on his or her own deeds, belief in a heavenly afterlife for the righteous and punishment of the wicked in hell, Satan as an antagonist to God, six arch-demons in the service of Satan and six archangels in the service of God, an eschatological view of history leading up to an apocalyptic end of the world, and the arrival of a Messianic world savior in the lead up to this last judgment. Records of the relationship between Cyrus and the cult of Marduk within the city of Babylon, when taken together with evidence that Cyrus himself met Isaiah, who produced the propaganda depicting him as the Messiah of Zion, suggest that these innovations in Israelite religion did not simply take place by happenstance and as a consequence of Jews living in an Iranian cultural atmosphere. Ezra, who writes the Jewish Bible in the form in which it exists today, was among the Jews supported by the Achaemenid state as part of their very well-organized bureaucratic project of rebuilding Jerusalem and its temple.

In the book of Daniel, a Jewish prophet who is buried in the city of Susa in Iran, we are given the image of a spectral hand that inscribes a prophecy of the rise of the Persians on a plaster wall inside the palace of the last King of Babylon. The proverbial writing on the wall is interpreted to mean: "You have been weighed on the scales and been found wanting, your time is up, and your kingdom shall be given to the Medes and Persians." Taken together with the depiction of Cyrus as the Messiah, and the intervention of Xerxes that is celebrated by the Purim festival to this day, as well as the personal responsibility that Darius assumed to see to the completion of the Second Temple, this writing on the wall effectively declares that Iran is God's Leviathan among the nations. If it is indeed the case that, as we shall see in Chapter 5, Christianity also owes its origin to Iranian Mithraism in the Parthian period, and that, as will be argued in Chapter 7, Mithraic Magi among the Parthian feudal houses designed Islam as a weapon against the Sassanid state, then the history of divine revelation is inextricable from the history of Imperial Iranian political power.

Such a notion would have been very appealing to Thomas Hobbes, who appropriated the image of the Leviathan from the Biblical book of Job as a metaphor for a kind of sovereign authority so absolute that it would be seen as God's viceroy on Earth. When Thomas Hobbes' mother went into labor with him on April 5th of 1588, her birth pangs were induced by shock at the prospect of a Spaniard naval invasion of Britain, such that Hobbes would joke—with a very dark sense of humor indeed—that she "gave birth to twins, myself and fear."[1] Hobbes was a reader of the work of his contemporary, René Descartes, with whom he exchanged barbs over which of them had come up with which of their shared ideas first.[2] Hobbes' friend, Marin Mersenne, was Descartes' publicist, and at one point he asked Hobbes to write a review of Descartes' *Meditations on First Philosophy*; this was published, together with Descartes' replies, in 1641.[3] Hobbes takes Descartes' description of the body as a mechanism and applies it to the social body of the state, with the sovereign as the ghost in the machinery of government.

Hobbes actually says very little about the Book of Job, from which he draws the symbol of the Leviathan (it is more than a mere metaphor). One thing that he does say is that, unlike the historical parts of the Bible, the book is intended less to be a chronicle of events that actually took place than a philosophical treatise on the question of "*why wicked men have often prospered in this world, and good men have been afflicted*."[4] Citing textual analysis by scholars of his time, Hobbes points out that the core "argument" of the book is all in verse, while the narrative Preface and Epilogue are in prose.[5] What this means to him is that an essentially philosophical text has been framed in such a way as it could be incorporated into the Bible.

Hobbes also acknowledges, on stylistic grounds and in terms of its philosophical content, that Job is a relatively late book of the Bible, and he even specifically claims "the Writer must have been of the same time" or "after" the writer of "The History of Queen *Esther* … of the time of the Captivity."[6] In other words, the text is a product of the period of intense Imperial Iranian influence on the formation of Judaism as we know it. Hobbes tries to read the idea of the resurrection back into the book of Job, so as to temper the main philosophical point of the text, namely that God's torture of Job requires no justification. He tries to claim that God only tortures Job's body, without calling into question the resurrection of his righteous soul.[7]

The Leviathan is a monstrous sea creature or, if it is artificial, then it is a titanic submarine machinery of terror. Hobbes remarks on the curious fact that the book of Job is one of the scriptures that, collectively, leave one who has studied the Bible with the impression that Hell is a place underwater in the company of the damned Giants or Heroes whose civilization was drowned by the Flood of Noah.[8] He quotes Job 26:5 as follows: "*Behind the Giants groan under water, and they that dwell with them.*"[9] Hobbes connects this to the idea of "*the congregation of the Giants*" in Proverbs 21:16 and Isaiah 14:9. The latter is fascinating in its reference to the ruler of Babylon as a figure whose place in Hell is to be so prominent that the submarine abode has to be cleared out of Giants in order to make room for him: "*Hell is troubled how to meet thee* [that is, the King of Babylon], *and will displace the Giants for thee…*" Hobbes concludes this quotation by remarking, "and here again the place of the Damned … is to be under water."[10]

Hobbes' *Leviathan* is the most definitive argument for Absolute Monarchy in the history of political philosophy.[11] As we shall see in Chapter 10, the core of *Leviathan* is a critique of that separation of powers which is the aim of every constitutionalist movement.[12] This would include the Persian Constitutional Revolution of 1906–1911, which yielded a parliament (*Majles*) checking the power of the crown and which attempted to establish a constitutional monarchy in Iran. Hobbes saw this kind of limitation and division of the authority of the crown as the consequence of a fundamental misunderstanding of the nature of sovereign power. His defense of Absolute Monarchy is so extreme that he even denies the right of private property and advocates for the suppression of what we would today call "civil society" as a social sphere independent of the political order. Insofar as this social (rather than political) sphere includes the Church, he demands that the latter utterly submit itself to the Sovereign — or, if you prefer, that the Sovereign be seen as God's viceroy. Finally, Hobbes envisions a regime so all-encompassing in its power over human life that the Sovereign would decide even on the meaning of language.[13]

Rather than being praised by monarchists for defending their beloved institution in the strongest terms possible, Hobbes was mercilessly attacked by them.[14] It is not just because they hated the book, but because his masterpiece exposed the deficits of King Charles — a man whom Hobbes saw as too fickle and indecisive to be worthy of the crown as the country slid into civil war. An observer of contemporary Iranian politics cannot help but to notice the similarity to the situation of the monarchist movement among exiled Iranian opposition groups today. Hobbes wrote *Leviathan* during the English Civil War, while he and other royalists were exiled in Paris. In 1642 the tense situation between the King and Parliament erupted into open strife, eventually leading the exiled royalists to Paris. Hobbes was one of these, and by 1646 he found himself employed as the personal mathematics tutor of the sixteen-year-old Prince of Wales.

So Hobbes wrote *Leviathan* at a time when Britain was facing both the prospect of disintegration through Civil War and foreign conquest at the hands of the Spaniards, the main colonial sea power rivaling the nascent British Empire. As the keen reader ought to notice, this is not too dissimilar from the situation faced by the Islamic Republic of Iran today. A nation that, on the one hand, is beginning to carve out an imperial sphere of influence (in Iran's case, unlike in Britain's, for the fifth or sixth time in history) is at the same time facing both the prospect of internal disintegration through civil strife and a potential invasion initiated by foreign powers. The latter are also responsible for manufacturing ethnic separatist movements and stoking dissension so as to divide the country as they conquer it. The balkanization of Iran is, today, a very real impending catastrophe. Ironically, as in the case of Hobbes' Britain, this danger comes on the doorstep of an era of imperial power. If Iran can remain united, it could reemerge not just as a regional hegemon but even as a world power — a role that Iran has played more than several times. Even regaining an imperial power comparable to that of the Achaemenids is achievable. Given the strategic significance of the Islamic world, and the demographic destiny of Islam in the twenty-first century, an Iran that successfully dominates the Muslim heartland could even establish itself as one of several rival superpowers within the foreseeable future.

CHAPTER 1

THE MITHRAIC MOTHER OF IRAN

IRAN, EVEN GREATER IRAN, IS often mistakenly conflated with the Persian Empire, but there was a vast realm of non-Persian Iranians who lived above Persia, in an area stretching from the western edge of the Gobi Desert all the way to the Black Sea. It is only later in history that people of Asian ethnicity migrated into Central Asia or, for that matter, even northwestern China. From about 1000 BC to 500 AD, the entire realm stretching from Southeastern Europe to the Great Wall of China was dominated by a group of Iranians known as Scythians (Old Iranian *Sakâ*). The Chinese built their Great Wall to keep these "Yuezhi" out. Their mummified remains have been found in the deserts around the Tien-Shan mountains, and paintings of them, with the same phenotype as is evident in the mummies, appear in illustrated caves.

The Scythians spent their days on horseback and their nights either in covered wagons or in tents.[1] They drank fermented mare's milk and inhaled cannabis that they threw onto small fires.[2] The most advanced of them had banqueting long halls, similar to those of the Vikings, where they drank *haoma* out of mead horns.[3] Scythian women fought alongside their men. A quarter of all the Scythian tombs that have been discovered to date are those of women warriors who were entombed with their armor.[4]

The broadest confederation of disparate Scythian tribes was known as the Saka Tigrakhauda or "Sakas with Pointed Hats."[5] The Old Iranian name *Tigra-Khauda* refers to very tall conical headgear that begins in an egg shape and then comes to a point.[6] Sometimes, when viewed in profile, the pointed hat with its top tapering backward in a bent fashioned looked like a scythe. It was a status symbol, which was worn only by the Scythian elite — the so-called "royal Scythians" or "Great Scythians" as the Greek writers refer to them.[7] The Saka Tigrakhauda confederation, also known as the *Mâ-Sakâ-Ta* or "Great Scythian Horde," included the Derbices, Dahae, Apasiacae, and those Scythians and Sarmatians who later came to be known in Europe as the "Alans."[8]

The western Iranians, who established the Median Kingdom and then the Persian Empire, were simply domesticated versions of these ferocious Nordic progenitors; they were essentially the same people after long-term exposure to the Elamite and Babylonian civilizations of the Ancient Near East region that they migrated down into and eventually overran.[9] We know this in part because the Median and Persian languages remained close enough to those of the Scythians that the Medes and Persians could still communicate fairly effectively with their northern cousins by simply speaking their own tongues and without requiring the service of translators or interpreters.[10] They also continued to share many of the same myths and legends, which would eventually find their way, centuries later, into the *Shâhnâmeh* of Ferdowsi.[11] Much of the *Shâhnâmeh* concerns war stories that are wrongly described by Ferdowsi as "the battles between Iran and Turan." Turan, or Scythia, is also Iran, and these are battles between two groups of Iranians.

As we shall see at the outset of the next chapter, the rise of Zoroastrianism is somehow inextricable from this Intra-Iranian conflict. Zarathustra's message may have been directed against Scythian warlords who were from "Turan" and were overrunning parts of Iran governed by the Medes (to whom the Persians were then vassals) — i.e. the descendants of Iraj. Then, in turn, the attempt to forcibly convert the Scythians of Turan and Sistan to Zoroastrianism elicited a fierce resistance from them.

Prior to Zarathustra, all branches of Iranians had been worshipers of Mithra, the war god who also presides over the making of oaths, and takes vengeance upon those who break covenants or contracts. Although Mithra had been one of the major gods of the Indo-Iranian pantheon, he is elevated to the status of *bagâ vazrakâ* or the "great god" by the Iranians who break from their Vedic cousins and demonize the *Daevas*. Mithra is an *Ahura*—or, put in Sanskrit, an *Ashura*—part of a class of titans who are depicted in Indo-Iranian mythology as the "demonic" rivals of the gods. The Scythians, and even more so their closest Iranian relatives, the Sarmatians, also worshiped a goddess figure who was viewed as the mother, initiatrix, and consort of Mithra himself or of the Mithraic hero. As we shall see in the first section of this chapter, there is abundant evidence that the figure known to the Medes and Persians as Anahita was seen by these earliest Iranians as the goddess through whom Mithra gives birth to himself by becoming his own father.

In the second section of the chapter we see how this goddess figure was worshiped in the form of an Arch Gorgon by the Scythians, and as Artemis or Satana by the Sarmatians. She was seen, not only as the mother/initiatrix of the Mithraic hero, but as the mother of an entire race of beings known as *Nârts* or, as they come to be known in Europe, "Nords." These chivalric heroes and superhuman progenitors of the Nordic-Iranian race were said to have been trained by the their mother and initiatrix in a secret realm beneath the waters of a lake or sea. Their rituals involved the planted sacred sword, and they drunkenly sang poetic saga songs in long halls that would become the basis for the idea of Valhalla. When the Sarmatians migrate to Europe in large numbers, the Nârt legends and mystical tradition become the prototype for the Arthurian mythos and esoteric cult of the Grail in medieval Europe.

Even before their own mass migration during the collapse of the Roman Empire, Marcus Aurelius had captured a large number of these Sarmatians and then, instead of killing them, incorporated them into the Roman military before stationing them in Britain. Not only does this become the basis for the Arthurian legends, which are Iranian rather than Celtic in origin, but we also find claims among the Scots-Irish that they are Scythian in origin. Their culture may originate in a part of northern Iran, on the Caspian Sea coast where a local tribe speaks a language known as *Gelac* and shares other cultural traits in common with the Celts. The Caucasian side of the Caspian region remains, today, the last stronghold of the Sarmatians as well. The nation of Ossetia, which refers to itself as *Ir-estoon*

("Aryan Province") and to its language as *Iron* (i.e. "Iran," Aryan), retain a cultural memory of being the fountainhead for the "dragon blood" houses of feudal Europe. These Iranians take pride in having invented scale armor, which together with the dragon banners that they raised as they stormed across the European continent, became the basis for their having been mythologized as "reptilians" or "dragon folk."

The ancient Greeks, who gave them this name, were the first Europeans to have encountered them, long before their subsequent colonization of the collapsing Roman Empire. These *Sauromatae* (a false Greek reading of *Sarmat*, to link their name to *Saur*, "dragon" or "reptile," as in Dino*saur*) were also called "Amazons" by the Greeks. Recent excavations in the Black Sea region have uncovered many Sarmatian graves where women are buried with armor, just like male warriors. Later excavations of Medieval European burial grounds have also uncovered female warriors, and remains that are generally almost indistinguishable from those of the Goths — whose culture was fundamentally shaped by both the Sarmatians and, earlier on, by the Scythians. The Greek legends of a society ruled by women warriors, and worshiping the goddess Artemis, has its origins in the northern Iranian culture of the Scythians and Sarmatians. As we shall see, there is some evidence for polyandry and matriarchy in this society.

In fact, it was a matriarch of these northern Iranians who defeated Cyrus the Great and decapitated him on the battlefield. The third section of this chapter focuses on Queen Tomyris, the leader of the Scythian-Sarmatian confederation known as *Tigra-Khauda* or *Mâ-Sakâ-Ta* that stands up against the founder of the Persian Empire. There is no reason to think that Cyrus the Great was a Zoroastrian, but there is plenty of evidence that he was a worshiper of Mithra and that he also promoted the veneration of Anahita. His closest associates are Mithraists, he carries out numerous Mithraic rites and has a distinctly Mithraic and un-Zoroastrian ritual carried out at his tomb after his death, in addition to building numerous cult centers for Anahita throughout the vast empire that he forges. The motivation for the military campaign that cost Cyrus his life was a preemptive strike against a vast Scythian force that had been amassing on the northern borders of the Median Kingdom which he inherited and transformed into the Persian Empire. Cyrus, like any Iranian leader of the time, would have heard much about the barbarically bloody Scythian invasions of the Iranian plateau in the preceding two centuries. Yet, in her interactions with Cyrus preceding their battle, Tomyris made it clear that she considered him to be the aggressor and enjoined him to accept the peaceful co-existence of their respective branches of the Iranian community. When Cyrus refused, what ensued was a battle that entered the annals of the Greeks as the most ferocious battle ever to have been fought by "barbarians."

This is the battle for Iran. Not only does Cyrus lose that battle, but after Tomyris decapitates the inheritor of the Median Kingdom and founder of the Persian Empire, a Mithraic rite is carried out at the tomb of Cyrus the Great that is identical to the chief religious rite of the Scythians who were led by this Amazon Queen. This ought to bring us to the recognition that Iran's foundations are neither religiously Zoroastrian nor ethnically Persian. The mother of Iran was a struggle that took place in a Pre-Zoroastrian and Mithraic context, which involved numerous distinct branches of a vast Iranian community—not just the Medes and Persians, but also the Scythians and Sarmatians. This is as much as to say that, Imperial Iran was, from the outset, not a nation—but an attempt to unify a civilization with multiple branches that influenced each other in complex ways. If these Iranian cultures had one common denominator, it was Mithraism.

1.1 *Mehr* as the Son of *Âbân*

Mithra (Old Persian *Mitra,* Middle Persian *Mehr*) means "sun," "friendship," and "love."[12] The earliest inscription referring to Mithra is in a contract between the Hatti king Shuppiluliuma and the north Mesopotamian Mitanni ruler Kurtiwaza, which dates to circa 1375 BC. Mithra is also apparently depicted as a bull-slayer on a Mittanni royal seal around 1450 BC.[13] The Mitanni were from the Indic branch of the Indo-Iranian group of Indo-Europeans and they entered Mesopotamia as a military elite before invading India.[14] Mithra's name also appears in the earliest of the

Vedas, which are dated to about 1500 BC. In these earliest contexts he appears as the god of oaths and contracts. Mithra mercilessly exacts vengeance upon people who do not abide by contracts or who break their oaths.[15] The original context for Mithra being the lord of contracts may have been protection for livestock, especially cattle, at a time when cattle raids were a common form of a theft, and a serious breach of contract between neighboring tribes.[16] This may be why Mithra is referred to as "lord of the wide pastures" with "a thousand [or ten thousand] eyes and ears … always … awake."[17] Oath breakers may attempt to flee, but no one can outrun his Justice, any more than a person can hide from the sun's light.[18]

To this day, Zoroastrian temples are called *Dar-e Mehr*, "door of Mithra" or "gate to Mithra," because the structure and function of these fire temples was originally Mithraic and was only later appropriated by Zoroastrianism.[19] When they are initiated, Zoroastrian priests receive a bull-headed "mace of Mithra" and, by means of this *gorz*, Mithra sanctifies the ceremonies that they perform.[20] Since Zarathustra does not mention Mithra in the *Gathas*, strictly speaking, Mithra is not a Zoroastrian god. However, the extremely deferential role that he is given in the later *Mehr Yasht*, where Ahura Mazda describes him "as worthy of sacrifice, as worthy of prayer as myself" (10.1.1) and even as "master of the world" (10.23.92) is evidence of a Zoroastrian attempt to assimilate Mithra in order to accommodate what was clearly a dominant cult in the Iranian society that Zoroastrians were proselytizing to.[21]

On the other hand, some of the functions of Mithra were clearly demonized by Zoroastrianism. For example, Zoroastrianism attributes the bull sacrifice to Ahriman rather than to Mithra.[22] The *Mehragân* ceremony, which even in the Achaemenid period remained no less important than *Nowruz*, culminated in the ritual sacrifice of a bull.[23] The Indo-Aryans may have considered Mithrakâna (*Mehragân*) rather than *Nowruz* to be the start of the New Year, much like the Celts with their festival of Samhain.[24] Another connection to Samhain, and the present-day Halloween that is derived from it, is that Mithraists wore animal masks during *Mehregân*.[25] Even today, some Zoroastrian priests omit any reference to Ahura Mazda when officiating at a *Mehragân* ceremony.[26] According to Abu Rayhan Biruni, the ancient Iranians considered *Mehragân* a microcosm of the end of the world, which was to come with the completion of growth to a state of perfection, ready to be harvested.[27] The seventh month of the Iranian calendar, namely *Mehr*, and the sixteenth day of each month, is dedicated to Mithra.[28] The terminology of the month of *Day* also refers to Mithra, since it begins at *Yaldâ*.

Yaldâ was seen as the death and rebirth of Mithra, whom Mithraists would help to be reborn on the following day, namely December 25th, by staying up through the longest night (*shabé yaldâ*) and eating red or "solar" fruits such as watermelons and pomegranates.[29] *Yaldâ* is a term adopted into Persian from Syriac; it means "birth."[30] *Yaldâ* inaugurates a forty-day period known as *chelleh*, which in turn culminates in the fire festival of *Saddeh*. This is echoed at the end of the winter season, on the night of *Chahâr Shanbeh Suri*, the last Wednesday of the year, and the harbinger of *Nowruz*.[31]

The *Mehr Yasht* demarcates a particular geographical realm as the domain of Mithra, a realm bounded by the Indus river in the east and the Tigris in the west.[32] This essentially amounts to a determination of Greater Iran as the abode of Mithra. Since Iranian tribes did not settle along the Tigris river until after the fall of Nineveh in the Median war against the Assyrians, we can date this part of the *Mehr Yasht* to circa 612–590 BC.[33] This is evidence in favor of the hypothesis that the original version of the *Mehr Yasht*, which was later incorporated into the Avesta, was a pre-Zoroastrian hymn belonging to pure Mithraism. Mithra is the guardian of the Aryan Realm, i.e. Iran:

> We sacrifice unto Mithra, the Lord of Wide Pastures … who first of the heavenly gods reaches over Mount Hara, before the undying, swift-horsed sun, and foremost in golden array takes hold of the beautiful summits and from thence looks over the abodes of the Aryans with a beneficent eye, where the valiant chiefs draw up their many troops in array…[34]

This is the realm that is defined by the magical arrow shot by Arash, the bowman. In ancient Iranian mythology, *Ârashé kamângir* or "Ares, the archer" looses an "arrow" or *Tyr* to demarcate the boundaries of the realm of the Aryans. Interestingly, if *Ârash* is indeed Ares, it makes sense that the Nordic god Tyr was syncretized with Mars when the Germans were incorporated into the Roman Empire. *Tyrgân* or the festival of *Tyr*, celebrated during the "dog days of summer," involved the worship of the Dog Star *Tishtriya* as the bringer of rain and lighting storms. Together with the Mehregan and Nowruz, it is one of the explicitly Mithraic holidays that is still celebrated in Iran, where children get into water fights and wear rainbow wristbands on that day.

Eratosthenes, who wrote in Alexandria in the second century BC, describes the Indus river in the east and the mountains of Media in the west as the boundaries of a land that is named *Aryana*.[35] According to Herodotus, the name that the Medes called themselves was *Arioi*, which would be pronounced *Aryai* in Iranian languages.[36] In other words, above and beyond recognition of a unification of the Medes and Persians, or references to other Iranian tribes such as the Scythians, even Westerners in ancient times, such as the classical Greeks, did already grasp the concept of a unified nation of Iran, which they described as *Aryana* or "the Aryan place" populated by the *Aryai* or "Aryan" people.[37]

Of course, this is based on the same descriptions of Iran and Iranians in the Avesta itself. It far precedes the Sassanid designation of their realm as *Irânshahr* or "the Aryan Empire."[38] The Medes venerated Mithra under the title *Khshathrapati*, which in the eighth-century BC Indian *Brahamanas* originally meant "Lord of Power" and in Iran comes to mean "Lord of the Empire."[39] The *Mehr Yasht* suggests that the god of the Median realm was more wrathfully terrifying than merciful.[40] As early as the reign of the Median king, Deioces (*Diâkou*), Mithra was seen as "the clever god who manipulates events with the dominion of an all-powerful tyrant."[41]

Herodotus' description of the Mithraic fortifications that Deioces built for the Median capital of Ecbatana are fascinating. There were apparently seven walls in the form of concentric circles, made of stone and metal that gave each wall the hue of the following colors: white, black, red, blue, orange, silver, and gold.[42] This color scheme was meant to signify the five visible planets, namely Mercury, Mars, Venus, Jupiter, and Saturn, as well as the moon and the sun. The various stages of some Ziggurats were supposedly also painted with such celestial color schemes. As we shall see in Chapter 5, in the form of Mithraism that entered the Roman Empire, it was believed that the initiate's soul had to pass through seven metallic barriers in the heavens, before arriving at the eighth clime.[43] On this view, the gods associated with each of the planets were destructive spirits who had to be propitiated.[44]

Mithra and the Imperial Iranian conception of sovereignty are inseparable. The aforementioned wild boar avatar of Mithra was seen as the bestower of the *Farrnah* or *Farr*, the divine royal glory that confers a kind of mandate of heaven or divine right upon an Iranian leader.[45] *Farr* was also thought to be embodied by birds of prey, such as the eagle that nursed Achaemenes, the patriarch of the Achaemenid clan that includes Cyrus, Darius, and Xerxes.[46] Whether Iranians accepted or rejected a monarch's sovereign authority over them depended on their perception of whether or not that monarch possessed the *Farr*.[47] Ancient Iranians believed that *Farr* could be possessed — or for that matter lost — not only by individuals, but by whole tribes and nations.[48]

The *baga* or "god" to whom the name of Mount *Bagastana* (Behistun, Bisotun) refers is actually Mithra, since he was "the *baga* par excellence."[49] In Sogdian, the festival of *Mithrakana* (Middle Persian *Mehregân*) was simply called *Bagakana*.[50] The seventh month of the pre-Zoroastrian calendar of Iran, in which the festival of *Mithrakana* was celebrated, was called *Bagayadish* or "the Month for Worshipping the *Baga*."[51] When used without further qualification, the term *baga* was understood to refer to *the* "god" — namely Mithra.[52] The emphasis on Ahura Mazda as the "chief of the gods" (*mathishta baganam*) or as "the great god" (*baga vazraka*) in Achaemenid inscriptions from the time of Darius and onward, is a reaction against the predominance of Mithra in the pre-Zoroastrian cultures of the Medes, Persians, Scythians, and Sogdians.[53]

Anahita is the female counterpart of Mithra, and she is invoked together with the war god on Achaemenid inscriptions.[54] Like Mithra, she drives a chariot with four horses into battle against the *daevas*.[55] This also suggests that she is an *Ashura* or *Ahura*, a titan (or titaness). The four horses of her chariot are rain, snow, hail, and wind.[56] The degree to which Mithra and Anahita were conflated, and Mithra himself was seen as a feminine — or at least a hermaphroditic — deity encompassing the qualities of Anahita, is reflected in Herodotus' claim that the Persians worship the "Celestial Aphrodite" under the name of Mithra.[57] At 1.131 in the *Histories*, Herodotus makes the fascinating remark that the Persians worship a goddess who is similar to the Arabian goddess Alilat and the Assyrian goddess Mylitta, and then goes on to name her as "Mitra."[58] This is not an error on his part. To this day, "Mitra" (i.e. Mithra) remains an exclusively female name in Iran. What is being recorded here by Herodotus is a primordial phase of Iranian religion wherein Anahita was not a separate being from Mithra, and where Mithra was believed to be hermaphroditic.[59] It seems that at some point, as Mithra was masculinized, what had been his feminine aspect was split off and worshiped in the form of a goddess figure who was understood to be both his mother and his consort – in other words, the divine feminine matrix through which the god gives birth to himself. The largest Mithraeum in the entire Near East, which was at Kangavar, in Western Iran, bore the following dedication to "Anahita, the Immaculate Virgin Mother of the Lord Mithras."[60]

Anahita was "the great virginal-wanton-motherly-warrior goddess."[61] She is one of those goddess figures who was mysteriously conceived of both as a virgin and as a mother.[62] Anahita was hailed as the "Mother of the Lord," which is the source of the Virgin Mary later being called "the Mother of God."[63] In Lydia, the cult of Anahita was assimilated into that of the great mother goddess Cybele.[64] This is relevant to the belief that Anahita was both the mother and lover of Mithra, since "Cybele is the virgin mother of her consort, Attis" so that "Attis is his own father."[65] Finally, Mithra was identified with Attis by Anatolian Greeks who were familiar with both cults.[66] Cybele means "rock" or "mountain."[67] Mithra overtakes the mountain peaks at daybreak.[68] Mithra was born of the female mountain that he surmounts before the dawn.[69] That Mithra is considered "rock-born" in Roman Mithraism is thus not at all contradictory to his being born of Anahita.[70] The later words for mother and matter, namely *mâter* and *mâteria*, are almost identical.[71] The virginity of the rock calls to mind the "Taoist" image of the uncarved block.[72] The third cycle of the Armenian national epic, *David of Sasun*, features a reference to the birth of Mithra that involves a conflation of the rock birth and lake birth narratives in the imagery of a "milky fountain [that] gushes forth from a great rock."[73]

After Zoroastrianism became dominant in Persia during the Sassanian period, the last stronghold of Mithraism in Greater Iran was Armenia — the princes of which were mainly of Parthian descent.[74] Strabo notes how the Armenians were particularly devoted to Anahita: "the Medes and Armenians honor the same sacred rites [*hiera*] as the Persians; but the Armenians in particular honor those of Anaitis."[75] Consequently, evidence from Armenian historical and theological writings is very relevant in the attempt to reconstruct the characteristics of Anahita in Mithraism.

In his fifth century *History of Vartan*, the Armenian historian Elisaeus Vardapet, also known as Elise or Vardabed, records an exchange between Armenian Christian bishops and Mehr-Narseh, the Prime Minister of the Sassanid Emperor Yazdegerd II (437–458).[76] In response to being mocked for the Christian belief that God could be born of a woman, namely the Virgin Mary, one of the bishops says that the Iranians believe "something more unusual: the god Mehr [Mithra] born of a woman, as if anyone could have intercourse with his own mother."[77] Another version of the same Armenian text, translated by Karabagy Garabed, is even more explicit: "Your god Miher is not only born of a woman but, what is far more ridiculous, he is born of an incestuous intercourse with his own mother."[78] The same passage from the *History of Vartan* also records the bishops mocking the Sassanids for a belief that God and the Devil were both born of a man, namely their father Zurvan.[79] Eznik of Golp, another Armenian writing in the fifth century, also claims that Mithra was born through the intercourse of God with his own mother.[80]

Artaxerxes I, i.e. Ardeshir, was known by the epithet *Deraz Dast*, which was translated into Greek and Latin as *Macroheir* and *Longimanus*.[81] This is likely a reference to the long-handed Mithraic salute, which, after the introduction of Mithraism into the Roman Empire, came to be known as "the Roman salute."[82] Artaxerxes II (404–358 BC) was as ardently devoted to Anahita as he was to Mithra.[83] He set up idols of Anahita at Babylon, Susa, Ecbatana, Persepolis, Bactria, Damascus, and Sardis.[84] We can form some image of what these idols looked like on the basis of an Achaemenid-period seal with an engraving of Anahita riding on the back of a lion, surrounded by a starburst, with a flower in one hand (probably a lotus), and a rod (or *barsom*) in the other.[85] In the *Aban Yasht* or "Hymn to Anahita" that was ultimately incorporated into the Avesta, we meet with the following evocation of the goddess:

> A maid, fair of body, most strong, tall-formed, high-girded, pure, nobly born of a glorious race, wearing along her body a mantle fully embroidered with gold, ever holding the *barsom* [a sacred bundle of twigs] in her hands, according to the rules, wearing square golden earrings on her ears, and a golden necklace around her beautiful neck … and her waist girded tightly, so that her breasts may be well-shaped, that they may be tightly pressed. … Upon her head a golden crown, with a hundred stars, with eight rays, a fine, well-made crown … with fillets streaming down.[86]

From this description we can see that the "rod" on the cylinder seal is actually the *barsom* or "fasces," which is also commonly held by Mithra in ancient Iranian rock carvings. The inscriptions left by Artaxerxes III, also known as Ochus (Old Persian *Vahauka*), show that he continued the Mithraic discourse of Artaxerxes II.[87] This Ardeshir married his own daughter, Homay, in an example of the *xwedodah* that was paradigmatically established by the incestuous relationship between Mithra and his initiatory mother.[88] In fact, before marrying his own daughter, Artaxerxes gave in to the sexual advances of his mother, Parysatis.[89] Philo of Alexandria writes: "Those of the Persians who are in high office marry their own mothers; they consider those who are born from these unions to be of superior birth and, as it is said, think them worthy of the highest sovereignty."[90]

Marriage of one's mother, based on the archetypal relationship of Mithra with his mother and consort (or vice-versa), may be the prototypical example of *xwedodah*. Old Persian *khvaetvadatha* or Middle Persian *xwedodah* was the ancient Iranian practice of incestuous or very close-kin marriage.[91] Some have interpreted this practice as an attempt to ensure that there were no rivals from outside of the royal family who might seek to claim the throne. Bardaisan of Edessa and other Western writers used this Persian practice as a way to claim that there are no universal cultural norms, because even the incest taboo was not accepted by some highly advanced cultures such as that of the Persians.[92] Bardaisan claims that *xwedodah* was practiced across the entire Persian Empire, including Media, Egypt, Phrygia, and Galatia. Clement tells us that, "it is customary among Persians to take mothers and sisters in wedlock, and all Persians under the open heaven marry in this incestuous way."[93] The most famous — or infamous — case of sibling incest among the Persians was Cambyses' marriage to his sister, Atoosa, the daughter of Cyrus.[94] Euripides writes that among "the entire barbarian race the father has intercourse with his daughter, the child with its mother and the girl with her brother."[95]

Contemplating the age differential in such cases is fascinating, since a woman in that era could hardly have been expected to bear a child much after the age of forty. This means that the son who marries her, and fathers a child with her by the age of forty or forty-two at the latest, would have to have been born to her when she was around eighteen or twenty. Persian men were not even allowed to enlist in the military before the age of twenty. So the boy born to a woman when she was twenty, would go on to marry his mother when he was around twenty years of age so as to be able to father a child with her when she was forty — a child that would be both his daughter and sister. He was, in turn, free to marry this daughter/sister after the death of his mother and lover. Intriguing as all this may be, let us not get sidetracked. Suffice it to say that Zoroastrians, who in the modern period have become terribly ashamed of this practice, and often frantically attempt to deny it as a historical fact, can take solace in the likelihood that *xwedodah* predates Zoroastrianism and has Mithraic origins. It was a feature of Persian and other Iranian cultures from very early on.

The *Âbân Yasht* is believed by some to date from the Achaemenid period.[96] However, the hymn describes Anahita wearing a beaver-skin coat.[97] This is significant insofar as beavers are not found in Persia, but they are plentiful in the Caucasus. So one can take this as another piece of evidence for the antiquity of the Iranian veneration for Anahita. It dates from a period prior to the Iranian — i.e., Aryan — migration down from the Pontic Steppe of Eastern Europe and the Caucasus into the plateau that they would name *Aryana* or "Iran" after themselves. It is not a coincidence that the Caucasus was the Scythian and Sarmatian heartland and the worship of Anahita endured most ardently in the Caucasus, to the point where she appears even on contemporary Armenian stamps.[98]

These prototypical Iranians of the Caucasus, who resemble Europeans in every respect, never mixed with the various non-Iranian peoples that some of the Persians interloped with, such as the Elamites and Babylonians. The Cyrus Cylinder draws a racial distinction between Iranians and those governed by them in a way that suggests that black hair was not common in the phenotype of Iranians at the time of Cyrus: "And he [Cyrus] shepherded with justice and righteousness all the black-headed people, over whom he [Marduk] had given him victory."[99] As exemplars of the original Iranian ethnic stock, the Scythians possessed "Caucasian features" including "tall stature," with numerous corpses recovered from *kurgans* being "over six feet tall," as well as "blondish hair, and fierce eyes" that were often blue or green.[100] From the Roman perspective the Scythians were so Germanic in appearance, and so much more "Nordic" in phenotype than the majority of Italians themselves, that it became common for Romans to refer to the Germanic Goths as simply another group of Iranians.[101] The remains found in the graves of Goths are so similar to those found in Scythian burials that anthropologists often cannot tell them apart. It was only much later in their history, especially in the areas near China, that Scythian warlords interbred with their Asian slaves to produce Mongoloid offspring.[102]

The Scythians had a predominately oral culture, so their arts and crafts are key to unlocking their mentality, worldview, and way of life. These northern Iranians loved to work in gold. Their gold-crafted objects, such as hairbrushes or mead horns, are richly decorated with sculptured figures and motifs — including accurate depictions of the people themselves. Scythian gold is full of depictions of both men and women wearing shirts and trousers.[103] As the predominant horseback riders of antiquity, these northern Iranians invented pants. Their fashion of clothing is one of the many cultural elements that they introduced into Europe. A layman untrained in art history would easily mistake most of the imagery on Scythian gold for European artwork. The people look "Germanic," some of the lyrical design elements call to mind Celtic weave patterns, and animals such as griffins and reindeer have an ornate proto-Gothic flare to them that would remind a Westerner of Norse art. Except that all of the Iranian imagery in this style predates the European points of comparison.

The Persian art of the Achaemenid Empire was an imperial style that explicitly aimed at a cosmopolitan synthesis of the art of many non-Iranian (i.e. non-Aryan) peoples who became subjects of the empire, including the Elamites, Babylonians, Assyrians, and ancient Egyptians. So the purest form of ancient Iranian art is actually Scythian. Consequently, to the extent that we want to see the Iranian soul, including that of the earliest Persians, reflected in arts and crafts, we need to look to the north.

Furthermore, since the Parthians eventually branch off of the Scythians and engage in an Iranian Reconquista of the Hellenized territories of what was the Achaemenid Empire (see Chapter 5), Parthian art and architecture must also be considered a development of the Scythian style. It is a terrible mistake on the part of both art historians and Iranologists to consider Parthian sculptures or buildings "European" in style and attribute this solely to the Seleucid legacy. On the contrary, Parthian art is Scythian art elevated to a monumental scale. Parthian sculptures, in particular, are much more Scythian than they are Greek. If they call to mind late Roman or Gothic European art, that is because beginning in late antiquity the European continent was overrun by a group of Scythians or Sarmatians called the Alans.

1.2 The Satanic Dragon Mother of Chivalric Iran

The similarities between the style of Celtic art and the older motifs found on the gold crafts products of the Scythians and Sarmatians are so striking and extensive that, given the massive penetration of northern Iranians into continental Europe, a mere parallel is out of the question.[104] The weave patterns and lyrical depictions of chimerical animals so characteristic of Celtic art are very likely Iranian in origin. It is also noteworthy that this artistic style influenced the rise of "Gothic" art and architecture in Europe precisely in the period when the shattered Roman Empire was inundated by Alans, who represented the last wave of northern Iranians mass-migrating into Europe.[105] The European culture of chivalry would have been inconceivable without the Scythian, Sarmatian, and Alanic influence on the Germanic "barbarians" and Vandals who, only together with these Iranians, conquered large parts of France and established Visi-Gothic and Goth-Alanic Spain.[106]

The Sarmatians not only mixed with the Germanic population of Europe, they also heavily intermixed with various groups of Slavs and shared broad swaths of territory with them. The Serbs (Sorbs) and Croats of the former Yugoslavia are both ethnic groups of northern Iranian origin.[107] *Croat* is an Iranian word that is the origin of *cravat* or neck-tie, an Iranian fashion item that, together with pants, belt, jacket, and all other main elements of "Western" fashion, was brought into Europe by Iranian horseback riders. Poland is Sarmatian, not Slavic, in its ethnic foundation and the Iranian influence on heraldry and the chivalric martial tradition among the Poles remains evident.[108]

When Marcus Aurelius defeated one invading group of Alans in the second century AD, instead of killing them he recruited them as elite guards to defend the empire against "the barbarians." This is quite interesting, since it suggests that Marcus Aurelius, who was a philosopher as well as a Caesar, had sufficient discernment to recognize not only the extraordinary military competence of these Sarmatians, but also the fact that they ought not to be lumped in with savage aliens such as the Germans and Celts, who were threatening the civilized order of imperial Rome. The Alan tribes that invaded Gaul featured horseback-riding women warriors who were both capable archers and who also wielded broadswords.[109] Legends about these women warriors survived in Ferdowsi's *Shâhnâmeh*, as for example the legend of Gordafarid, whose combat with Rostam's son, Sohrab, is famous: "[A]s she was turning in her saddle, [Gordafarid] drew a sharp blade from her waist, struck at his lance, and parted it in two."[110] The Sarmatians or Alans who were settled in Britain by Marcus Aurelius were settled in the area of Chester and Ribchester, with their 5,000 cavalry being given the task of guardian Hadrian's Wall.[111] They were put under the command of a Roman general by the name of Artorius Bastus, whose name, Anglicized to "Arthur," became associated with the legendary king of the Alans.[112]

What the Alans brought with them was the "Arthurian" culture of Chivalry, which is known in Iran as *Javânmardi* or *Farhangé Pahlavâni*. The stories of *Guiw* and of *Kay-Kavus* that have survived in the *Shâhnâmeh* of Ferdowsi are derived from Scythian or Sarmatian legends that were the basis for the development of the legends of "Gawain" and "Kay" in Britain.[113] Batraz had to pull a sacred broadsword out of a tree and the Sarmatians had a ritual of thrusting swords into the earth or into stones piled into a platform on the earth, and then setting up a trial of strength to pull this sword from out of where it had been lodged.[114] *Pahlavâns* or Iranian chivalric knights customarily thrusted their *qamehs* or daggers into the earth before dueling.[115] Batraz asks his comrade Sainag-Alder to throw his sword into the ocean after his death, just as Arthur makes a similar request of Percival that the latter throw Excalibur into the lake. In both cases a goddess figure rises up out of the water to catch the magical sword.[116]

The name "Alan," widely adopted by Europeans, is a variant of *Arân*. In the phonetics of Iranian languages *l* and *r* are interchangeable (think of the way that Japanese people pronounce the word "really"). So *Arâni* or a "person from *Arân*" became *Alâni*. The word *Arân* is simply a different pronunciation of *Irân*, i.e. "Aryan," one local to the Caucasus, which is where Sarmatians lived. Note that white people are referred to as "Caucasians" because many scholars of Indo-European linguistics and anthropology believe the Caucasus region, between the Black Sea and the Caspian Sea, to be the point of origin for the entire Aryan or Indo-European community. So the Sarmatians, close cousins of the Scythians, are the Aryans who remained for much longer in the cradle of the "Indo-European" community while others branched out into northern India, Western Europe, and of course, the "Iranian plateau" (which only then became "Iranian"). Their only remnant today is the nation of Ossetia. Ossetians refer to their language as *Iron*, in other words, "Iranian." That it calls the metal "iron" to mind is also not at all incidental; ironwork may have begun here.

The Sarmatians invented scale armor. Lance-wielding knights in shining armor are Iranian in origin and only became a feature of European cultures much later, through direct Sarmatian or Alanic influence. Actually, the contrived Greek etymology for the name of these people reflects the fact that Europeans had never seen scale armor before, let alone people covered in it from head to toe and riding on horses that were also armored. It reminded the Greeks of snake scale. This, taken together with the fact that the standard or war banner of the Sarmatians was a dragon, compelled the Greeks to refer to the *Sarmat* as *Sauromatae*, a word with the same Greek root as "Dinosaur," which conveys the sense of "lizard people" or reptilians.[117] The whole European lore of people with "dragon blood" begins here, since it is these same "reptilians" who, after the fall of the Roman Empire, assumed leadership of the other "barbarians" and formed the leading aristocratic houses in large parts of Germany, northern Italy, France, and Spain.

Together with the Goths, the Alans formed a kingdom in Spain that was named *Goth-Alania*, the pronunciation of which eventually became "Catalonia." This was the point of origin for the Troubadour culture, which spread throughout the rest of Spain and French Occitan. The bloodline of the Carolingian dynasty traces back to these Iranians, and they also served as top advisors to the Merovingian kings.[118] Alan families settled in Gaul (France) as early as the fifth century and maintained their dominance until the 1200s, and it is in this place, during this period, that the Grail romances were written.[119] The Goths, Franks, and Celts lived under the Alan elite, as village peasantry, and were also employed as shock troops.[120] Together with the Germans, the Alans served as the upper echelon of the Crusader knights, and these Iranians also fought to defeat Attila the Hun so as to protect Europe from non-Aryans.[121] Together with neighboring Bulgaria, so-called "Hungary" was actually part of the core Sarmatian homeland around the Black Sea, before the Turkic Huns invaded this part of Sarmatia and replaced its Indo-European language and Aryan culture with a Finno-Ugric one.[122] In other words, Hungary was more European when it was still solidly Iranian. To this day, the Hungarians and Bulgarians retain the tricolor flag common to other Iranian territories, from Persia and Kurdistan to Tajikistan. Ancient Greek and Roman maps mark the region of Hungary and Bulgaria as inhabited by the *Roxalanoi* or "white Alans."

Sarmatian women are the people mythologized by the ancient Greeks as "Amazons." Excavations around the Black Sea, where Greek heroes were said to have encountered these warrior women, have revealed the graves of Sarmatian women buried with their armor.[123] The origin of the term *Amazon* is debated. Some think that it is a linguistic corruption of the Iranian *Hame-Zan* or "all women." This, however, is debatable, since the Sarmatians were not actually a society consisting only of women. It is just that the patriarchal Greeks were so shocked by a society where women were warriors and even rulers that they mythologized the Sarmatians as a man-hating matriarchal society. Others believe "Amazon" is a Greek word meaning "without breast," coined to describe the alleged Sarmatian practice of cutting the left breast off in order to pull back a bow more effectively. The Sarmatians, together with their Scythian cousins, were the greatest archers in history. Their goddess is also depicted as an archer.

Whether or not it is accurate, the Greek etymology is interesting insofar as Artemis was the chief deity of the Amazons. The majority of Greek writers who refer to Anahita equate her with Artemis.[124] Roman authors also identified Anahita with Artemis/Diana.[125] For example, Tacitus refers to her as the "Persian Diana."[126] The most famous surviving statue of Artemis depicts her with many breasts. These could be the severed breasts of the warrior women being offered to the goddess. Then again, these "breasts" have also been interpreted as testicles, since the castration of males was practiced in the cult of Artemis.[127] This probably terrified the Greeks into telling tall tales about what would happen to men who fell into the hands of the Amazons. The reality is that the males who underwent this ritual were trying to emasculate themselves so as to become fit receptacles for the overpowering force of the divine feminine; they also grew their hair long and wore women's clothing as part of an effort to attain feminine intuition or psychic abilities that were known to be stronger in women than in men.[128]

It is somewhat paradoxical that although she is a virgin goddess, Artemis is also the "child's nurse" (*kourotrophos*) and "nurse of children" (*paidotrophos*), a goddess who presides over childbirth.[129] This seeming paradox can be resolved by taking a closer look at just what is meant by "maiden," which is perhaps falsely assumed to be equivalent to Artemis being a chaste "virgin." Greek myths unambiguously state that Artemis was the most beautiful of all of the female divinities, prompting many men to be attracted to her and to view her as the ultimate trophy to seize and possess.[130] Yet, at the same time, it has been suggested by some researchers that sacred prostitution was ongoing at the Ephesus temple and that her status as "maiden" did not mean so much "virgin" as it meant "unmarried" or not in the possession of any man.[131] This would make a great deal of sense, since the Amazons who worshiped her did have male lovers who were deemed worthy, but they fiercely resisted being claimed as "wives" by any of these men.[132]

This relates in an interesting way to something shocking that Herodotus tells us about Scythian society. He says that whenever Scythian men wanted to have sex with any woman in their tribe, regardless of whether she was "married," they would place their bow beside the door to the woman's tent.[133] Each bow was apparently decorated in a way that identified its owner. If she brought the bow into her tent, it meant she was inviting him in as well. As Reza Zarghamee writes:

> A strong tradition of communal living certainly underlies Herodotus' report, ultimately derived from Persian sources, that each man among the Massagetae married only one woman but had the right to sleep with his neighbor's wife, as long as he signaled his intention to do so by hanging his quiver outside the neighbor's tent. The same custom reportedly existed among the Tapurians, another nomadic tribe from northeastern Iran, as well as in parts of Hyrcania, in the northeastern corner of the Iranian plateau.[134]

Strabo and other Greek authors even saw this Scythian practice as the inspiration for Plato's rationale for common marriage among the warrior caste and philosopher guardians in *Republic*. Like Plato after them, the reason that the Scythian "intercourse with women is promiscuous" is "so that they may be brothers and — as all are kinsfolk to each other — they may neither envy nor hate their fellows."[135]

This kind of promiscuity, when taken together with the prominent role of female leaders such as Tomyris, raises the question of whether the *Saka Tigra-khauda* or *Ma-Saka-Ta* were actually a matriarchal society.[136] Such a practice, which would make cuckolds out of husbands or even male lovers of these women in a patriarchal society, could only be acceptable in an at least quasi-matriarchal society. It is certainly one of the most archaic and unequivocal examples of the Iranian virtue of *Âzâdegi* or free-spiritedness, which we will have occasion to dwell on later in the context of Parthian Mithraism (see Chapter 5) and Sassanian Mazdakism (see Chapter 6). Something of this way of life still survived in the courts of the land-owning and sword-wielding Alan ladies of medieval Europe, who sired the knights sworn to their service and were courted and serenaded by troubadours while their husbands were away on crusades and other quests.

None of this should be misinterpreted as indicative of a permissive society that produces passive and weak men. On the contrary, *Âzâdegi* was a sign of strength and Sarmatian women encouraged the discipline and breeding of the strongest men. The priestesses of Artemis were armed with flagellating whips.[137] This is the origin of the "lasso of Truth" wielded by the American super-heroine, Wonder Woman, who is supposed to be an Amazon princess. In Scythia, the rites of Artemis involved whipping men until blood flowed freely from their wounds and could be smeared onto her altar.[138] This ritual, known as *diamastigosis*, probably made its way down into Persia from the Sarmatians in the Caucasus, since historians of Shi'ite Islam claim that the ritual, which is preserved in Persian Shi'ism, originated in the Azerbaijan province of Iran. The priestesses of Artemis would encourage those who administered the initiation not to be lenient to the boys seeking to enter manhood.[139] They would also be subjected to various other initiation rituals, such as a trial of strength wherein a horseback rider would have to pull a sword up out of earth, where it had been firmly planted. Taken together with the worship of cruciform sacred swords with special names set on stone altars, this is the origin of the chivalric symbol of the "sword in the stone."

The Amazon queen Otrera was the founder of the original Temple of Artemis at Ephesus, which was one of the seven wonders of the ancient world.[140] Recall that this is where Heraclitus took refuge after the anti-Persian coup in Ephesus, instead of accepting Darius the Great's invitation to become the court philosopher of Iran. *Artemis* appears to be an Iranian name meaning "Truth, the Immortal" or the "Undying Right Order," a contraction of *Artâ* (i.e. *Ashâ*), meaning "Truth" or "Right Order" and *Ameshâ* or "immortal" as in the *Ameshâ Spentâs*. As we have seen, Iranians symbolized *Artâ* as an undying fire, and Artemis was also the torch-bearing (*propolos*) "crafty … infernal one" who is a light-bearer or light-bringer (*selasphoros*, *phosphorus*).[141] She brings the light into darkness with the crescent Moon and the planet Venus, also known as "the morning star" or Lucifer. This crescent Moon and "star" was her most widely recognized symbol. The hunting bow of Artemis resembles the new moon; she sometimes wore a lunar crescent as her crown, which, put through her hair, made her appear to have horns; and she was referred to as shooting arrows from her "silver bow."[142]

Like her later Roman adaptation, namely Diana, Artemis is often depicted with a bow and arrow. She was the goddess of the Hunt, in the sense of relentless pursuit, which also made her the avenger and guarantor of victory at war.[143] With a view to the expression, made famous by Shakespeare, "let loose the dogs of war," it is relevant that the sacred animals of Artemis were hunting dogs or even wolves; on some magical charms she was referred to as the "she-wolf."[144] Recall the connection between the Persian *gorg* or "wolf" and the Sarmatian *Gorgons* when considering the fact that Artemis was also associated with gorgons and serpents.[145] According to classical Greeks such as Herodotus, both the Sarmatians and the Scythians worshiped Gorgons. The gorgon entered Greek mythology through the Hellenic encounter with these Iranians in the Black Sea region. Scythian gold features many depictions of Gorgons, and typically two large serpents are sprouting from the shoulders of the goddess. This is rendered in a style that is in some cases identical to the depictions of the serpents growing from Zahhak's shoulders.

As we shall see in Chapter 5, the Greeks claimed that Perseus, who severs the head of the Gorgon Medusa, was the father of *Perses*, patriarch of the Persians. Perseus severs Medusa's head with a harpe sword, which becomes the symbol of the fifth grade of initiation in Mithraism, known as the grade of *Perses*. The word *Gorgon* is indeed of Iranian origin. *Gorg* has become the word for "wolf" in Persian, but the more ancient Iranian meaning of the word *waerg* or *gârg* is to "tear apart" as the fearsome Gorgon goddesses were known to do. In Avestan literature, Ahriman, the father of Zahhak, is sometimes depicted as a wolf. Now, the wolf is the totem of the Scythians or, as Ferdowsi calls them, the Turanians, who are closely related to the Sarmatians and intermixed with them often within overlapping territories.

The actual etymology of the word *Sarmat* can be gleaned from the *Shâhnâmeh* of Ferdowsi. There we have the legend of a prehistoric Iranian (i.e. Aryan) hero named Fereidun whose three daughters are abducted and imprisoned by Zahhak. This king who is demonized for spreading sorcery or black magic, and whose name is derived from the Avestan *azhi dahâkâ* or "dragon," is said to have had a serpent growing from each of his two shoulders. These needed to regularly feast on human brains. During a revolt against his tyrannical rule, led by a blacksmith named Kaveh, Fereidun enters Zahhak's fortress by stealth and smashes his skull with a bull headed mace, thereby liberating his daughters and replacing Zahhak on the throne of Iran.

Toward the end of his life, Fereidun wills his kingdom to be divided between his three sons, Salm, Iraj, and Tur. Iraj inherits Persia and Media, and his descendants can be interpreted as the Persians and Medes. Tur inherits Central Asia, then inhabited by Iranians, so that his realm, Turan, is identifiable as Scythia and his descendants, the Turanians, are the Scythian branch of Iranians. Now recall that *l* and *r* can be phonetically interchangeable in Iranian languages. Salm or Sarm inherits the cold, snowy mountainous realm of the Caucasus. The word for cold in Persian is *sarmâ*. In the Scythian and Sarmatian languages *at* is a plural, so *Sarmat* means the people of Salm (Sarm) or the people of the cold regions. This means that, strictly speaking, the term "Sarmatian" is incorrect usage, because it is a double plural. *Sarmat* in Persian and Ossetian already means "the Sarmatians." Nevertheless, I will defer to common usage.

The serpentine or dragon imagery of the Zahhak story is important because, as in the European mythic tradition, the *Shâhnâmeh* is full of stories of Persian knights slaying dragons. Since the dragon was the war banner of the Sarmatians, I imagine that what is really being depicted in these heroic trials of dragon-slaying are one-to-one combat with Sarmatians clad in their shimmering snake scale-like armor. The question is why the Sarmatians adopted the dragon as their symbol. My guess is that this has to do with Zahhak. The original *Azhi Dahâkâ* or *Ezhdehâ* (i.e. Dragon) certainly was not an Arab, as Ferdowsi anachronistically depicts him to be in order to demonize the Arabs, who become the ultimate villains at the close of the Persian national epic. Some have speculated that he was an Assyrian king whose battle with the Medes or the Scythians in Medea was mythologized in the *Avestâ*. I see no reason why this would be the case. All the *Avestâ* itself says about the lineage of *Azhi Dahâkâ* is that he is the wolf-like son of *Ahriman* himself. Ahriman is, of course, the Great Deceiver.

Zahhak, a black magician and tyrant who feeds on human brains through the serpents growing from his shoulders, had Fereidun's three daughters locked up in his harem, and we are supposed to believe that all the while he did not have sex with them?! Are the Sarmatians, who adopt the dragon as their standard and who come to be known as reptilians, really the descendants of Fereidun's legitimate son Salm/Sarm, or are they the demon-spawn of an illegitimate grandson sired by Zahhak? In that case, what we are seeing in the *Avestâ*, and later in the *Shâhnâmeh*, is a Zoroastrian demonization of the pre- and non-Zoroastrian religion of the northern Iranians, both the *Sarm-at* and *Tur-ân*.

The descriptions of Zahhak as a *jâdoogar* or sorcerer who replaced righteous religion with sorcery and fed on human brains suggests that he is a psychological manipulator. In this connection it is interesting to note that the image of two serpents, who are presumably intertwined inside of Zahhak's body around the central axis of his spinal column, calls to mind the caduceus, the staff of Hermes, the Trickster. In Greek myths, Hermes teaches human beings writing, which is viewed as a departure from the relative sincerity of transmitted tradition in an oral culture. In the *Shâhnâmeh*, *divs* or devils sent by Ahriman teach humanity writing. Recall that Zahhak is, according to the *Avestâ*, the son of Ahriman. Fereidun smites Zahhak with a mace that is bull-headed. Other heroes and kings had maces with different animal symbolism. Is the caduceus a serpentine mace, and is Zahhak the most ancient trickster figure of Iranian mythology? What is the relationship between the wielder of the serpentine mace and Satan, who is depicted in the Bible as a dragon that is turned into a serpent by having his legs removed as a punishment for encouraging human beings to eat from the tree of forbidden knowledge?

The word *Satan* made its way into Hebrew and Arabic but it is actually Iranian in origin. It is the name of a female deity of the Sarmatians. *Satana* is something like the greatest of the Gorgons, and is depicted entwined by serpents or with serpentine limbs. Her cult survives in Ossetia to this day. She is the guardian of a holy grail, the mythical cup of Shah Jamshid (*jâmé jâm*) by staring into whose depths one can observe anything going on in any part of the world (*jâmé jahân-namâ*). Satana dwells under a lake and is responsible for anointing great heroes. It is this goddess figure who travels with the Alans deep into Europe and becomes the "Lady of the Lake" of the Arthurian grail legends. The Sarmatians or Alans believed that Satana emerged, sacred sword in hand, from a realm beneath the waters — whether those of a sea or lake — a realm wherein heroes are raised before being sent as saviors into this world of ours.[146] Like Anahita, Satana wears white garments.[147] Satana and the Dame du Lac are the same goddess figure, and both are northern Iranian versions of Anahita.[148]

The oldest version of the Dame du Lac of "Celtic" Brittany is in fact Anahita or Artemis. Anahita was responsible for carrying out the investiture of the Achaemenid sovereigns.[149] Like Mithra, she is depicted in reliefs bestowing the *farr* to a monarch bearing a broadsword.[150] Bestowing the royal glory upon a broadsword-bearing king, such as Arthur, is also one of the main functions of the Lady of the Lake in the chivalric mysticism that was brought to Britannia by the Alans.[151] The Dame du Lac conferring Excalibur upon King Arthur is an investiture by the bearing of a sacred broadsword, in accordance with the most archaic Iranian tradition.[152] Anahita stands to the left of the sovereign and raises her right hand to him, just as the Dame du Lac does in some depictions of her investiture of King Arthur, such as is preserved in the artwork of Aubrey Vincent Beardsley.[153] *Âbân Yasht*, the fifth Yasht of the Avesta, is devoted to Anahita, who is also known as *Âbân* or "the waters." Therein the goddess is described as "a beautiful, glorious, tall and strong woman, mistress of all waters of the earth and the source of the cosmic ocean," as well as "the sources of fertility for humans, animals, and plants, and the purifier of the seed of all men and the wombs of all women."[154] Similarly, the Lady of the Lake of the Arthurian legends is the guardian of a realm of "eternal spring… eternal joy… eternal youth… eternal health."[155]

A Sarmatian prototype has been found for almost every major theme and symbol in this tradition, from the legend of Lancelot,[156] to the Lady of the Lake,[157] the Sword in the Stone,[158] serpentine and dragon symbolism,[159] the kingly glory of the Holy Grail,[160] and the idea of a Once and Future King.[161] The mistaken attribution of the Arthurian mythos and Grail mysticism to the Celts is understandable considering the intimate kinship of the Celts and the Nordic Iranians, whether Scythians or Sarmatians. The Gaelic text *Lebor Gabala Erenn* claims that the Scots Irish are of Scythian origin.[162] Of the bard and record keeper Fenius Farsaid, it says that his father, a man named Baath Mac Magoc Iathfed, was of "the men of Scythia" and that "from him came the Gael."[163]

This is particularly interesting in light of the fact that on the western side of the Caspian Sea coast in northern Iran, which was an area heavily trafficked by Scythians since the Median period, there are a group of people known as *Gelacs* who speak a language called *Gelac*. A study comparing this northern Iranian language to Gaelic might yield very interesting results. It has already been noted by linguists that despite its (mistaken) classification as a Centrum branch of the Indo-European languages, Gaelic actually has many parallels to the Scythian language, as well as some grammatical features and vocabulary that are shared with Thracian.[164]

Both Scythian and Thracian are part of the Satem branch of Indo-European languages that were spoken in an area of southeastern Europe and the Caucasus dominated by Iranian Scythians and Sarmatians for most of antiquity.[165] Here are just a couple of examples. The word for hen is *cearc* in Gaelic and *kark* in the Ossetian, Kurdish, and Hyrcanian (Gilaki and Mazandarani) languages that are heavily influenced by, or descended from the Scythian language.[166] Then there is the name of Ireland itself, *Erin*, which comes from *Eire* or *Aire*. In both Gaelic and Old Persian this word means "freeman" or, by extension, one not enslaved to or in the service of anyone, "nobleman." In other words, *Eire-an* is *Ir-an*, the land of the free or realm of the noblemen.[167] The *Gelacs* of northern Iran share a number of cultural traits in common with the Irish, including their peculiar wit and sense of humor. They also play the bagpipe or *Nay-anbân*, the origin of which is generally acknowledged by musicologists to be Iranian. Not incidentally, this region of the Caspian coast is very rainy and densely forested. Moreover, *Gelacs* believe their local forests to be inhabited by *paeris* or faeries.

The wisdom goddess Satana was the mother of these *Nârtik* or "Nordic" people.[168] The name *Satana* is a compound of the Old Iranian words *Sat* or "one hundred" (which is still *Sad* in contemporary Persian) and *na* or "mother".[169] This is meant to signify that she is "the mother of a hundred sons," namely the *Narts*.[170] The Narts had great feasting and drinking halls called *Nykhas* that are the same as those of the Scandinavians, which became the basis for the conception of Valhalla in "Nordic" religion. In Iranian *Vâl Hâl* would mean "highest enjoyment" or "loftiest state of being." The Alans would introduce the long-hall banqueting culture to Medieval Europe.[171] Batraz was the leader of this superhuman *Nartik* race.[172] The story of the love affair between Guinevere and Lancelot is based on the romantic rapport of Satana with Batraz, who is her own son in a spiritual as well as a biological sense.[173] The parallels to the "Arthurian" mythos that we find in the Japanese legends of the swordsman Yamato Takeru can most likely be accounted for by a common Scythian origin, since we know that the Scythians reach deep into northern Asia.[174]

The Narts are constantly engaged in combat with the Turks, which makes sense considering the fact that Hun-Turkic invaders from northeastern Siberia eventually poured into the region of Central Asia that had been Iranian, namely Greater Scythia, and ultimately even overran some Sarmatian territories in Eastern Europe such as Hungary (whose the English name reflects its change of language and culture under Turkic or Hun influence).[175] As noted above, the dragon standard of the Arthurian legends is quite simply the Sarmatian war banner.[176] Unlike in both Medieval European Christianity and in Zoroastrian Persia, in China the dragon is an auspicious symbol rather than one of malevolence and destruction. It is associated with power and fortune. Since the Iranian Nords, such as the Scythians, were also on the borderlands of China, as far East as the Tien-Shan mountains and the Western Gobi desert, where they mixed with other closely related Indo-Europeans, such as the Tocharians (*Tokhari*), one has to wonder whether it is Iranians who initially brought the Dragon symbol to China. The most ancient Chinese writings, including the *Tao-te-Ching* of Lao Tzu, make reference to "the Dragon Kings and Phoenix Queens" who ruled China in perfect accordance with the *Tao* in the most distant antiquity.

Some of the massive white stone pyramids that had been buried by time under the "hills" of farmland in Xian, and were re-discovered by aircraft flying over them in the twentieth century, are rumored to contain the remains of these rulers. The Chinese government is hesitant to allow access to the remains within these tombs. Proper archeological and genetic evaluation of them might reveal that, as in the case of the Tarim mummies, they are the remains of Caucasian people and that Chinese Civilization was founded by Aryans who are either closely related to, or even indistinguishable from, the Scythian kings of northern Iran. There is even speculation that the Chinese term *Han* is a corruption of *Hun*, and derives from a confusion of the Scythians with the Huns whose territory the Scythians repeatedly occupied. To this day, a rural northwest part of China on the border with Tajikistan contains the most isolated and purest genetic sample of the original Iranian people. In the *Shâhnameh* of Ferdowsi, this region is referred to as *Turân*—the realm of the descendants of Tur who, as discussed above, was one of the three sons of the primordial Iranian king Fereidun.

The epic war between Iran and Turan in the *Shâhnâmeh* is the Median-Scythian War of the seventh century BC. Once the Median Magi were converted to Zoroastrianism, the war became an ideological crusade of the Medians against Scythian paganism. It is the war in the context of which Esfandiyar distinguishes himself as the leading commander, and the war that eventually claims Zarathustra's life during a Turanian, i.e. Scythian, invasion of the northeastern territory of the Median Kingdom. At the zenith of its expansion to the northeast, the Median Kingdom—or, for a brief period, the Median *Empire*—included the region of Parthia and Hyrcania, in other words, the present-day Khorasan province of Iran, on the border with Turkmenistan.[177] This is where Zarathustra was killed. In the years immediately preceding the rise of Cyrus, the Medes had encroached upon Scythian and Chorasmian territories in Central Asia where Turanian tribes were living.[178] The fact that the thirteenth Yasht of the Avesta includes prayers blessing the souls of righteous Turanians and Dahae, in other words Scythians, suggests that by the Achaemenid period some of these had been (forcibly) converted to Zoroastrianism.[179] Nevertheless, as we can see from the Behistun Inscription, the majority of the Sakas are condemned by Darius for their refusal to accept "the true faith." Darius the Great appears to have been the first Iranian Emperor to adopt Zoroastrianism.

1.3 Queen Tomyris, the Assassin of Cyrus

There is no good evidence that Cyrus the Great was a Zoroastrian, but there is a great deal of evidence in favor of his being a Mithraist — in the original, Pre-Zoroastrian sense of Mithraism as the religion of the Medes and Scythians. In Herodotus' biography of Cyrus, the Persian pastoralist who raises him while concealing his true royal lineage is named Mitradates or "given by Mithra."[180] The closest ally of Cyrus in the Median court, Harpagus, was also a Mithraist.[181] Those Medes who followed Harpagus to Xanthus around 540 BC established a cult of Mithra *Khshathrapati* there while under his command.[182] Those Median priests who accompanied him, and officiated the new cult, even called themselves *karapans* — the same title as the old Indo-Iranian sacrificial priests demonized by Zarathustra in the *Gathas*.[183] Interestingly, while the Aramaic version of an inscription from the Mithraic cult at Xanthus refers to Mithra as *Khshathrapati*, the Greek version of the same inscription refers to Apollo.[184] Cyrus honored many foreign gods, but his exceptionally great respect for the Greek god Apollo has been seen by some scholars as indicative of his recognition of Apollo as a Hellenic equivalent of his own patron solar deity, namely Mithra.[185]

Another major piece of evidence in favor Cyrus not having been a Zoroastrian is that he did not raise his son, Cambyses, to be a Zoroastrian. The often scandalous conduct of the second monarch of the Achaemenid dynasty is most definitely not indicative of any respect whatsoever for the teachings of Zarathustra, or for that matter, even of any awareness of them. Take, for example, the affair of his courtier Perxaspes, who unfortunately made the error of honestly reporting to Cambyses that his fellow Persians consider him to be a drunk. Note that Zarathustra had condemned excessive drinking, which was characteristic of the Mithraic cult. Herodotus recounts the story in the following way:

> [Cambyses] said to Prexaspes — whom he honoured highly and who carried messages for him, and whose son was Cambyses' cup-bearer, a considerable distinction — he is said to have spoken to him as follows: "Prexaspes, what sort of man do the Persians think me to be and what sort of stories do they tell about me?" Prexaspes replied: "My lord, they praise you highly in all respects, except that they say you are too fond of wine." That is what he said about the Persians, at which Cambyses flew into a rage and responded: "So now the Persians say that I am fond of wine and have gone mad and lost my senses! Their previous statement about me was untrue, as well!" For earlier, when some Persians, as well as Croesus, had been sitting with him Cambyses asked them what they thought of him as a man in comparison to his father, Cyrus. They replied that he was better than his father, because he had all the latter's possessions, and had added to them Egypt and the sea. That is what the Persians said, but Croesus, who was there and did not like this answer, said this to Cambyses: "I, son of Cyrus, do not think you are your father's equal. For you have no son such as he left in you." Cambyses was pleased with that response, and practiced Croesus' reply.
>
> That is what he remembered, when he said furiously to Prexaspes: "Now, you see for yourself whether the Persians are telling the truth or whether the ones who say that have not themselves taken leave of their senses. Your son shall stand in the doorway; if I shoot and hit the middle of his heart, the Persians are obviously wrong. If I miss, then the Persians may be telling the truth, and I am not in my right senses." That is what he said, drew the bow and hit the child; when the boy fell, he ordered him to be cut open and his wound examined. When the arrow was found to be in his heart, he said to the boy's father, laughing and pleased: "So, Prexaspes, I am not mad and the Persians are — it is perfectly clear! Now tell me, do you know anybody else in the world, who can hit a bull's eye like that?" Prexaspes saw that the man was out of his mind and, terrified for himself, said: "I don't think, my lord, that

> even the god himself could hit the mark so well." That is what Cambyses did then.[186]

This is not the conduct of a Zoroastrian, and "*the* god" who is an archer that is being referred to by the terrified Prexaspes is undoubtedly the *bagâ vazrakâ*, "the great god," namely Mithra. As noted, there is reason to think that Cambyses was a Mithraist. Two instances from his Egyptian campaign are particularly striking. In one instance, he worships the goddess Neith at her temple and has a great feast set up in her honor because she is considered the mother of Re, the ancient Egyptian solar deity, which Cambyses would have identified with Mithra in a syncretic way.[187] He may have seen Neith as Anahita. When he was crowned Pharaoh of Egypt, Cambyses himself went on to be identified with the Sun God.[188] The second instance is more clear cut. When he arrived in Memphis, he asked the Egyptian priests of the local temple whether they have a sacred bull. When they admitted that they did, the Shah ordered them to bring it to him. When the Apis bull was brought, Cambyses promptly drew his sword and slaughtered it.[189] This is, quite obviously, an example of a Mithraic bull sacrifice. A Zoroastrian would not perform such a ritual, let alone horrify Egyptian priests by doing so. The point is that Cyrus seems to have raised his son as a Mithraist.

Perhaps the single most significant piece of evidence in favor of Cyrus being a Mithraist, and not a Zoroastrian, are the horse sacrifices that were carried out on a monthly basis at his tomb in Pasargadae.[190] Zarathustra vehemently opposed any form of animal sacrifice, and harming horses is considered a particularly heinous offense by Zoroastrians.[191] The floral design engraved on the tomb of Cyrus the Great, which is the only image or motif present on the titanic stone structure, is also Mithraic in nature.[192] It depicts a hybrid of the sun and a lotus flower. A symbol nearly identical to this one shows up in later Iranian rock carvings of Mithra wherein the god is standing on such a solar lotus, while holding a *barsom* or "fasces."[193]

More evidence in favor of Cyrus being a Mithraist is his "punishment" of the Gyndes River in Babylon.[194] According to Herodotus, after one of his sacred white steeds drowned in this river, Cyrus ordered his troops to cut the river up into 360 different channels.[195] The number of channels corresponds to the number of days in the Iranian solar calendar, and the white horse is associated with Mithra and the sun. Mithra guides the sun across the sky in a golden chariot with four white horses.[196] When Cyrus marched into Babylon, his army featured a team of 360 white horses dedicated to Mithra.[197] As we have seen, *Farrnah* is bestowed by an acolyte of Mithra, the war god Verethragna (*Bahram*) in the form of a wild boar.[198] Cyrus was depicted as a mighty boar, meaning that he was seen as an avatar of the Mithraic war god who bestows the *Farrnah* on Mithra's behalf.[199]

As discussed above, Mithra and Anahita were complimentary deities to the point that Anahita was considered both the mother and consort of Mithra.[200] As has already been noted, Anahita may even have been split off of a more primordial conception of Mithra as an androgynous or even a female deity. Several classical sources mention that Cyrus the Great venerated Anahita.[201] Furthermore, sacrifices to Anahita were most un-Zoroastrian in nature. If we are to judge by the *Âbân Yasht*, animals were sacrificed to Anahita in large numbers: "a hundred stallions, a thousand oxen, and ten thousand lambs."[202] Cyrus attributed his victory over some of the Scythians to Anahita, and he ordered the construction of numerous cult centers dedicated to her throughout his nascent empire.[203] Her worship became deeply entrenched in the religious life of the Achaemenid Empire, probably in large part on account of the importance accorded to her by that Empire's founder. Anahita was responsible for carrying out the investiture of the Achaemenid sovereigns.[204] Like Mithra, she is depicted in reliefs bestowing the *farr* to a monarch bearing a broadsword.[205] Plutarch tells us that Artaxerxes II was crowned in the Temple of Anahita, or as he puts it, in the "sanctuary of a warlike goddess, whom one might conjecture to be Athena."[206] In fact, according to Plutarch, the investiture ceremony of every Achaemenid Emperor, which involved donning the robe of Cyrus the Great, was carried out in this temple.[207]

Before the rise of Cyrus there is not a single significant reference to the Persians in Assyrian historical records, which do frequently refer to both the Medes and the Scythians.[208] Scythian worship of Mithra deeply influenced the religious life of Iran when the plateau was overrun by the Saka from about 700—600 BC, just before the Medes subsumed these roving warriors into their kingdom and secured Median supremacy.[209] One example of this can be seen at the Achaemenid-era temple of Anahita at Estakhr in Pars, which was still flourishing a thousand years later in the Sassanian period. It had a trophy room that featured the decapitated heads and flayed skins of the enemies of those devoted to the Mithraic goddess.[210] Herodotus remarks that this trophy room was designed on the basis of Scythian customs, which the Persians had adopted through the Scythian influence on the Medes who formed the backbone of the Achaemenid Empire.[211]

The Median Kings assumed the Scythian style of taking oaths, which involved each kissing an incision that the other had made along the length of his raised right forearm.[212] The Scythian or Saka hordes in the northwest of Iran were the Median Kingdom's most feared subjects.[213] Astyages sent them to Persia with the promise of plundering the land. From the list of nomadic "Persian" tribes that Herodotus provides us with, we see that Scythians such as the Dai (Dahae) and Dropici (Derbices) were transplanted into the heartland of Persia by Astyages.[214] As Reza Zarghamee puts its, "The Median Empire could not escape its Scythian origins…"[215] Much of Media outside of the capital district of Ecbatana was "dominated by roving tribes, many of Scythian or Saka descent."[216] Cyrus likely received combat training from a Scythian, since the Medes at the royal court of Ecbatana had long since put the Scythians in charge of teaching martial arts and horseback riding to the children of the aristocracy.[217]

Defense against a rerun of the Scythian invasion of the Near East was among the priorities of Cyrus, who almost immediately set about constructing seven fortresses on the frontier between his empire and the realm of Scythia.[218] These fortresses in Transoxiana and Bactria also served as a reassurance to the sedentary agricultural population of the region that their farmlands would not be ravaged again by the steppe nomads of "Turan" as they had been a generation or two prior, in the period when Goshtasp ruled in that region (at least as a vassal of the Medes).[219]

From the turrets of these frontier fortresses, Persian Imperial guards would scour the horizon for the wolf- and dragon-shaped standards of the Scythians and Sarmatians.[220]

The most enduring cultural memory of the entirety of the Near East in the two centuries preceding the rise of Cyrus the Great were the Cimmerian and Scythian invasions of this area, which brought the Scythians — in pursuit of the Cimmerians that they defeated — as far as the borders of Greece and Egypt.[221] In other words, there was, in a sense, a very loose Iranian Empire preceding that of the Achaemenids — a Scythian Empire that stretched from the borders of China in Central Asia, all the way to the Eastern Mediterranean, and encompassed nearly all of contemporary Iran. The "heroic" or "epic" parts of the *Shâhnâmeh* are in all likelihood mythologized recollections of this epoch of Scythian dominance of the Iranian world, before the rise of the Medes.

The Massagetae, who were the most important and central of the tribes constituting the Saka Tigrakhauda confederation, were Mithra worshipers.[222] Herodotus tells us this about their religious practices: "The only god they worship is the sun, and to him they offer the horse in sacrifice, under the notion of giving to the swiftest of the gods the swiftest of all mortal creatures."[223] The Scythians in Europe practiced the same kind of sacrifice.[224] The Massagetae also worshiped a green-eyed "Earth Mother" who was the personification of the Haoma plant, and whose characteristics suggest that she is a version of the goddess Anahita.[225]

The Massagetae lived in present day Azerbaijan, north of the Araxes river (Persian *Rudé Aras*) from which they caught fish that supplied the basis of their diet, to the point where Herodotus refers to them as the "Fish-Eaters."[226] Another name that he uses for them is "Apasiacae," which is clearly a corruption of the Old Iranian *Apa-Saka* (Persian *Ab-Saka*), meaning "water Scythians."[227] Such a name suggests more than simply a culture that fishes from a river. It implies a culture that travels through rivers and across seas. After all, the Massagetae were known to live on the banks of the Caspian Sea and to come as far south along the Sea as Hyrcania, which is what warranted the security concerns of Cyrus and his greatest successor, Darius I, over the potential for Scythian incursions into this area whose very name, "wolf country" (Old Iranian *Vargkâna*, Middle Persian *Gorgân*), comes from the symbol on the Scythian war banner. The Greek historians who chronicled the campaigns of Alexander knew the Apasiacae to have been the most formidable foes of Cyrus the Great in his attempt to establish an Imperial Iran governed predominately by Persians and Medes.[228]

In Old Iranian the Massagetae queen's name *Tahma-Rayish* means "Radiant Strength" or "Mighty Radiance."[229] The etymological origin of the Greek term "Massagetae" is the Old Iranian *Mas-Saka-Ta*, which means "Great Scythian Horde."[230] It was not simply the name of another tribe within the confederation, but is an equivalent to the term *Saka Tigra-khauda*.[231] This means that, when she confronted Cyrus on the battlefield, Tomyris was the leader of the entire Scythian sphere of the Iranian world.

It is on the first night after crossing the Araxes river into Scythian territory to meet his eventual death at the hands of Tomyris, that Cyrus the Great has a visionary dream of Darius on the throne of the empire that he has built.[232] He saw his young cousin, who was just then training to enter the Imperial Iranian military, and who was the son of one of his most loyal satraps, Hystaspes, with two wings growing from his shoulders. One of these wings extended outward to cast a shadow over Asia, and the other over Europe.[233] Cyrus believed this dream to be precognitive, and he was concerned that it might portend an attempt by Darius to seize the throne from him, since Darius was not in the royal line of succession.[234] So Cyrus summoned Hystaspes, who was on the Scythian expedition with him, and got a guarantee from Hystaspes that the latter would put his own son to death without hesitation if it were to be discovered that Darius was plotting a coup against Cyrus. The Persian Emperor sent Hystaspes back to Persia on the morning after the dream, so that he could subject his twenty-year-old son to extreme scrutiny and ascertain his loyalty or lack thereof.[235] However, long before Hystaspes could make it back home to Darius, Cyrus was killed at the hands of Tomyris.[236]

Cyrus had Cambyses march all the way to the boundary of the Massagetae territory with him, so that the subject nations along the way would recognize the crown prince as his legitimate heir and successor.[237] That he took the trouble of doing so suggests that Cyrus was aware of the danger posed by the loyalty of many of these people to his younger son, Bardiya, who already governed territories in the northeast, and it also means that Cyrus took seriously the prospect that this may have been his last campaign.[238]

Before engaging the military forces of the Massagetae, Cyrus sends a messenger to their queen, Tomyris, asking for her hand in marriage.[239] The Scythian queen surely recognized that such a union would effectively mean the political subjugation of her realm to the Persian Empire. Tomyris sends the following reply to Cyrus, which interestingly refers to him as a Mede rather than a Persian, and makes reference to the bridge that his forces are building to march their troops across the Araxes river and into Scythian territory:

> King of the Medes, I advise you to abandon this enterprise for you cannot know if in the end it will do you any good. Rule your own people, and try to bear the sight of me ruling mine. But of course, you will refuse my advice, as the last thing you wish for is to live in peace. Listen then — if you are so bent upon trying your strength against the Massagetae, give up the laborious task of building that bridge, and let my army withdraw three days' march from the river, and then come over yourself. Or, if you prefer it, retire the same distance yourselves, and let us meet you on your side of the river.[240]

That Tomyris calls Cyrus "King of the Medes" is evidence in favor of the expansion of the Median Kingdom to the Scythian border with Hyrcania in the century immediately preceding the rise of Cyrus. The Massagetae queen remains more familiar with the Medes than she does with the Persians who have just taken over what was the Median realm at their doorstep.

Croesus alone among Cyrus' top advisors favored engaging the Scythians on their territory rather than allowing them to cross over into Persian territory, and Cyrus took his advice over that of the majority of his leading officers and councilors.[241] Croesus devised an ambush strategy, which Cyrus also accepted and implemented.[242] According to this strategy, the Persians would stage a nighttime banquet after crossing the river into Scythia and leave behind the weakest and most weary of their troops to guard the food and wine as the majority of battle ready soldiers retreated to the river. The Scythians took the bait and, when they slaughtered the weakest troops inside the banquet tent, got drunk off of the plentiful wine that had been left there for them, and gorged themselves on the abandoned feast, the best of the Persian troops ambushed Tomyris' troops and put them to the sword.[243] Those ambushed included Queen Tomyris' own son, Spargapises, who had led the raid. Spargapises requested of the Persians who had bound him as a prisoner to have his fetters removed and when they complied, he seized a weapon from one of the Persian soldiers and promptly killed himself with it.[244]

When news of this got back to Tomyris, she flew into a rage and prepared to launch what Herodotus alleges was the most violent battle ever to have taken place amongst "barbarians."[245] The Scythian forces under the queen's direct command rode out into the battlefield and, after an initial volley of arrows, met the Persians and Medes in close quarters combat and cut them to pieces with spears and swords, before wrestling them to death with daggers.[246] After defeating the Persian imperial forces, Queen Tomyris scoured the battlefield until she found the corpse of Cyrus the Great, whereupon she decapitated the Persian Emperor with her own sword, and plunged his severed head into her wineskin, which she had filled with his blood.[247] Herodotus records her rant to the severed head of Cyrus: "Though I have conquered you and live, yet you have ruined me by treacherously taking my son. See now—I fulfill my threat: you have your fill of blood!"[248]

Once word of the death of Cyrus reached Persia and Media, several weeks after the battle, around late November of 530 BC, the Magi extinguished the fires that had been lit to inaugurate his reign.[249] The remains of Cyrus were retrieved by the Persians, and the emperor's head was reattached to his body when it was embalmed and placed in a gold coffin at his tomb in Pasargadae.[250] Alexander beheld the apparently intact corpse when he visited Pasargadae in 330 BC to pay homage to the man who had been his childhood hero.[251] Interestingly, among the items that Alexander describes as having seen inside the tomb were two Scythian bows.[252] What a thought-provoking and enigmatic statement this is, considering the fact that Cyrus met his demise at the hand of Scythians. Then again, he had also received his training in archery and martial arts at the hands of Scythian teachers in the Median capital of Ecbatana.

The cuneiform inscription that Cyrus had graven onto a separate stela placed at the side of his tomb has been preserved in Greek translations by Plutarch and Strabo. It read, "O man, whoever you are, and from wherever you come — for I know that you will come — here I lie, Cyrus, King of Kings, who founded the empire of the Persians. Grudge me not, therefore, this little earth that covers my body."[253] For the more than two centuries that passed between his funeral and the fall of the Persian Empire to Alexander, the Magi who were attendants of Cyrus' tomb would, once every month, offer a horse up into the fire as a sacrifice to his conquering spirit.[254] As noted above, this is a strong piece of evidence in favor of the view that Cyrus was a Mithraist and not a Zoroastrian. It is quite shocking that his last will and testament included a wish for the very same Mithraic rite to be carried out at his tomb that was the single ritual most clearly identified by ancient writers with the Scythian tribes led by his assassin, Queen Tomyris. As for Tomyris, she apparently went on to live a relatively long life, since the Greek author Polyaenus mentions that a Saka chieftain named "Thamyris" rose up in resistance against Darius when, a generation later, he tried — and also failed — to conquer Scythia.[255]

CHAPTER 2

THE IRANIAN ORIGINS OF PHILOSOPHY

THE EPIC BATTLE BETWEEN THE Scythian Rostam and the crusader Esfandiyar, as it has come down to us in Ferdowsi's *Shâhnâmeh*, is actually an epitome of the struggle between Mithraic Magic and Zoroastrianism. It sets in motion the dialectical forces that go on to define the inner logic of Iranian history. The words "Magic" and "Magician" are Iranian in origin (deriving from the "Magus" or "Magi").[1] The primordial magical tradition in question is that of Mithraism, which was preserved by the Scythians.

Esfandiyar has come to bring Rostam back to the royal court in chains, since the Scythian is in revolt against Esfandiyar's father, the Shah Goshtasp (Avestan *Kâvi Vishtaspâ*). Both Goshtasp and his councilor, Jamasp (Avestan *Jâmaspâ*) are mentioned by Zarathustra in his Gathas, with Goshtasp being clearly identified as the king who became his patron and protector. Meanwhile, in the *Shâhnâmeh* Esfandiyar boasts to Rostam at length about how he has been a crusader in the name of the new faith of Zoroastrianism, even indicating that Zarathustra is still alive and by his father's side back in the royal court of Iran.[2]

The Scythian rebellion against zealous Zoroastrian conversion policies that is the tacit historical context for this epic narrative gives us valuable information toward settling the raging debate over the epoch of Zarathustra, which in the end, is not a mere debate over dates, but a controversy over the cultural matrix of Iranian Civilization as a whole. Using this story as a guiding thread, this chapter comes down on the side of the latest of the three dates usually proposed for Zarathustra. He lived not in 6,000 BC, nor even in 1,500

BC, separated by a vast gulf from the rest of recorded Iranian history, but in 650 BC, about a century before Cyrus the Great integrates the Persian and Median cultures into an Iranian Civilization that is politically unified for the first time.

Specifically, the context for Zarathustra's revolution is a conflict between the Medes and the Scythians, who had helped the Medes defeat the Assyrians but were then betrayed. At this time, the Persians were already vassals of the Medes and for all we know Zarathustra himself was a Persian composing his *Gathas* in a dead language of theological authority — much like a Roman Catholic still writing in Latin during the Renaissance or a Shaivite Brahmin in medieval Kashmir composing a sacred text in Sanskrit. The "mumbling priests" and "plundering princes" that he is preaching against in his Gathic hymns are not Rig Vedic Brahmins. Rather, these antagonists are Scythian Mithraic magicians and semi-nomadic warriors who would terrorize the settled Medes.

Properly placed in this time, the revolutionary message of Zarathustra can be better appreciated against the backdrop of the older Iranian magical Mithraism that the Scythians refused to relinquish. The fundamental principles of the doctrine that would go on to become "Zoroastrianism" are epitomized by the concept of the Bounteous Immortals and Zarathustra's unprecedented insistence on free will or the human capacity to live a life based on conscientious choices. Each of the Bounteous Immortals (*Ameshâ Spentâs*) is examined with a view to its philosophical significance, beginning with metaphysical ideas such as cosmic order (Avestan *Ashâ*, Old Persian *Ârtâ Vahishtâ*, Middle Persian *Ordibehesht*) or the evolutionary mind guiding the life force (Avestan *Spentâ Mainyu*, Middle Persian *Sepandminou*) all the way to the psycho-somatic manifestations of alignment with this order, such as Serenity (Avestan *Armâiti*, Persian *Ârâmesh*), Health or Wholeness (Avestan *Haurvatât*, Middle Persian *Khordâd*), and Vitality (Avestan *Ameretât*, Middle Persian *Amordâd*). The political philosophy of Zarathustra, whose core concept of *Khashathra Vairya* (Middle Persian *Shahrivar*) becomes key to the Achaemenid state under Darius and his successors, is also examined.

The cosmological, psychological, and ethical content of the Gathas is unmistakably philosophical rather than pre-philosophically religious. The closest point of comparison are the compositions — also in poetic style — of the Pre-Socratic Greek philosophers. This first generation of Greek philosophers were writing in the westernmost provinces of the Persian Empire. They were already political subjects of Iran. Consequently, if we place Zarathustra in the Median Kingdom at circa 650 BC, he is the first philosopher in recorded history and, with very solid historical continuity, we can trace the origin of what came to be known as "Philosophy" in the West to the transmission of what Zarathustra calls *Mazda-Yasna* or "Wisdom Worship" to Greece by the Median Magi during the Persian colonization of Western Anatolia. As a point of pride, this is far more valuable to admirers of Iranian Civilization than a Zarathustra who is isolated in the recesses of an inscrutable prehistoric period and whose genius would have to be seen as some freak of nature that was not replicated by anyone for centuries or even millennia. The Median Zarathustra of 650 BC, whose message was brought to Greece by the Persian conquest, made the first "philosophers" out of Pythagoras and Heraclitus.

Eastern Philosophy may also have originated in Iran. Recent research suggests that Gautama *Saka-Muni*, the "Scythian Sage" was not from a region of India near Nepal, but an Iranian whose clan originally ruled "Kapil" or *Kabul*. The Scythian warrior-prince *Sidh-Ârtâ* or "power of Truth" founded the Buddha Dharma. Contrary to what was believed by the old school of scholarship on Buddhism, recent research has revealed that the Hindu philosophical ideas that Buddha was supposedly critiquing do not even predate the lifetime of Gautama. The *Upanishads* with their philosophical outlook on the relationship between Atman and Brahman and so forth are, at the very least, contemporaneous with Gautama if not considerably younger. The Buddha Dharma and Philosophical Hinduism were contemporaneous responses to the introduction of Zoroastrianism into the Indo-Iranian world that included northern India. Not only was Gautama the philosopher whose teachings became the basis of Buddhism, he was also the foreign sage who dictated the *Tao Te Ching* during his travels in the part of China that bordered Scythian Iran. In other words, Lao Tzu and the Buddha were the same man.

2.1 The Scythian Rostam and the Sword of Esfandiyar

In the years immediately preceding the rise of Cyrus, the Medes had encroached upon Scythian and Chorasmian territories in Central Asia where Turanian tribes were living.[3] The fact that the thirteenth Yasht of the Avesta includes prayers blessing the souls of righteous Turanians and Dahae, in other words Scythians, suggests that by the Achaemenid period some of these had been (forcibly) converted to Zoroastrianism.[4] Nevertheless, as we can see from the Behistun Inscription, the majority of the Sakas are condemned by Darius for their refusal to accept 'the true faith.' At the zenith of its expansion to the northeast, the Median Kingdom — or, for a brief period, the Median *Empire* — included the region of Parthia and Hyrcania, in other words, the present-day Golestan and Khorasan provinces of Iran, on the border with Turkmenistan.[5] This is where Zarathustra was killed during a Turanian invasion. Like Cyrus the Great after him, Zarathustra was killed by Scythians in that region of Iran known as Hyrcania.

The legends of the wars between Iran and Turan, which eventually find their way into the *Shâhnâmeh*, are ancestral memories of the Massagetae raids on northeastern Iran during the eighth and seventh centuries BC.[6] By the time of Astyages, the Median Kingdom had begun to impinge on the Scythian territories in what is now the border of Turkmenistan with Iran, on the eastern shores of the Caspian Sea.[7] The *Tur-ân* or "descendants of Tur," i.e. the Turanians, were a tribal group within the greater Scythian confederation known as *Mas-Saka-Ta* or *Tigrakhauda*.[8] Herodotus says that the Massagetae initiated the mass migration of Scythians into the Iranian plateau at the zenith of the Median period.[9] He even reproduces a list of those paying taxes to the Median government during the eighth and seventh centuries BC, which list includes many Scythian migrants that had settled in Media.[10]

The *Saka* tribes of Iranic ethnicity and language, known to Greek and subsequent Western historians as the "Scythians," first appear in written history as the allies of the Assyrians in campaigns that brought these northern Iranians as far to the southwest of their homeland as the Levant and Egypt.[11] Later, the Scythians entered into an alliance with the Medes and, with their forces combined, these Iranians overthrew the Assyrians and established the first kingdom of Iran in the Zagros mountain region.

Around 700 BC, those Scythians who had remained to the north of Media began pursuing the Cimmerians out of the steppes and down into the territory of the Median Kingdom. Having defeated the Cimmerians circa 630 BC, the Scythians went on to conquer and rule the kingdom of their Iranian cousins, the Medes, for a little over a generation.[12] In 585 BC, the Medes rebelled against the Scythians, who were beaten back to their homelands, which stretched from the North Caucasus and the steppe around the Black Sea all the way across Central Asia to the northwest borderlands of China.[13] Dominating trade activities in this region, which would later become the Silk Route, allowed the Scythians to prosper economically and even to gain a reputation for riches despite also being known as fierce, roving barbarians. The Imperial Persian conquest of Bactria and Sogdiana began to threaten this wealth.

Scythian epic traditions were absorbed into the cultures of the Iranian plateau through the large scale settlement of Sakas in Persian or Median regions.[14] The character that Ferdowsi develops as Rostam is essentially the hero who was known to the Greek colonists of this area as the "Scythian Heracles."[15] Herodotus already tells us that some of the nomadic Scythians of the steppe traced their ancestry to this Herculean hero.[16] Sogdian murals in Panjakent that depict Rostam and several knights combating serpentine sorceresses are very similar to descriptions of the trials of the "Scythian Heracles" as recounted by Herodotus.[17]

The Scythians were divided into two groups, the upper Scythians based in Central Asia (Persian *Turân*) and the lower Scythians who had migrated to, and settled in, Kerman, Sistan, and Baluchistan (Old Persian *Kermâniâ* or *Germâniâ*). The greatest hero of the Iranian national epic, Rostam, is one of these lower Scythians and his father, Zal, is a renowned sorcerer who summons the magical Simorgh bird to help Rostam defeat Esfandiyar by occult means. Rostam was from the *Sama*, the plural of which is *Saman*.[18] (In other words, Saman*ian* is redundant.) The *Saman* were the rulers of Sistan or *Sakastana*.[19] This makes sense in that Zaal was a Mithraic Shaman. In Indo-European linguistics *th* is often pronounced *s*, in light of which it becomes clear that Rostam's alternate name, *Th*amtan, is really *Sâm*-tan, designating him as a descendant of the hero Sam, the patriarch of the *Saman* or Shamans, a group of Scythian Mithraic sages. As attested by the *Puranas*, Mithra as a sun god was reintroduced into India in the first century by Saka tribes who invaded and formed the Indo-Scythian Kingdom at the time.[20]

The name of the region currently known as Sistan is actually a contraction in Middle Persian of the Old Iranian *Saka-stana* or "Scythian land."[21] In his *Shâhnâmeh*, Ferdowsi identifies this as the homeland of Rostam and he gives Rostam the epithet *Sagzi* or *Saksi*, in other words, "the Scythian."[22] Just like *r* and *l*, there is a phonetic interchangeability of *g* and *k* in the Iranian languages. *Sag* is the word for "dog." Dogs were highly revered by ancient Iranians because it was believed that they could see evil spirits and warn people of their presence, or even scare them off by barking. The Scythians in particular developed the first thoroughbred hunting dogs, one of the many skills they later passed on to the Germans with whom they intermixed after mass-migrating into Europe. The word "Scythian" comes from *Sakâ*, a variant of *sagâ*. So it means "the dog people." The word *saga*, as in the Nordic-Germanic Sagas, is this same word, and the culture reflected in the

Nibelungenlied and the *Vulsunga Saga* is that of Germanic tribes who were living under the influence of the Iranian elite that had settled in Western Europe.[23]

Ferdowsi tells us that Rostam is from Sistan, which in ancient times was referred to as *Kermâniâ*. Kerman, the largest city in this region of Iran today, preserves this name. Another example of the interchangeability of *k* and *g* is that Kerman or *Kermâniâ* was also referred to, including by European geographers in antiquity, as *Germâniâ* and its inhabitants as *Germâni* (Kermâni) people.[24] "German" is still a common male name in the Iranian enclave of Ossetia in the Caucasus. The branch of the Scythians known as Indo-Scythians had come this far to the south in the Eastern part of Iran. Meanwhile, there were other Scythians in Eastern Europe. When these Scythians in Europe began to invade the Roman Empire in the early second century AD, they settled in large numbers in an area that came to be known as *Saxony*.[25] The word *Saxon* is a contraction of *Saka* or "Scythian" and the word *son*, which means the same thing in Scythian as its Germanic cognate does, namely "heir or descendant of."[26] So the *Saxons* are the "sons of the Scythians" who named the greater region around Saxony after the part of Iran that was the home of the Scythian hero, Rostam, namely *Germâniâ*. To top it off, Rostam wears a helmet with huge horns — long before the Vikings do.

There are no references to Zarathustra or to Zoroastrianism in the *Nârt Sagâ*; it does, however, feature Rostam. This suggests that the lore of the "Scythian Hercules" is pre-Zoroastrian. Furthermore, in the Persian lore that made it to Ferdowsi and that he adapted into the *Shâhnâmeh*, Rostam fights the first evangelical champion of Zoroastrianism, Esfandiyâr, the son of Shah Goshtasp, patron of Zarathustra. This is meant to indicate the Scythian rejection of Zoroastrianism, despite the fact that Ferdowsi also depicts Rostam serving many Zoroastrian kings of Iran. Interpreting the battle of Rostam and Esfandiyar in the context of the Scythian conflict with the Medes also places Zarathustra in history.

In the long debate over the date of Zarathustra, three totally different epochs have been proposed as the period in which he lived. The traditional date, accepted by Zoroastrians themselves until Western scholars began to engage in such debates, was "258 years before Alexander."[27] It has been assumed that the Zoroastrian sources, later quoted by Al-Biruni and other scholars, meant before *the accession of Alexander* to the throne of Iran, not before his birth, and that by the "arrival" of Zarathustra they intended to indicate the beginning of his evangelizing mission at the court of Goshtasp. Accepting the Zoroastrian tradition that Zarathustra was forty-two at this time, we would arrive at 628 BC as the date of Zarathustra's birth.[28] This would place his life during the Median Kingdom and about a century before Cyrus the Great, who is half Median himself by maternal descent, leads a Persian revolt against the Medes and establishes the first integrated Iranian world empire.

The second date proposed for Zarathustra was circa 1500 BC, almost entirely on the basis of an analysis of the "Avestan" language in which he composed the Gathas.[29] This language has also been called "Gathic" because, aside from seven short hymns also thought to originate with Zarathustra, it is the only work that we have in this language. Linguists have assessed its form to be more archaic than what they, by comparison, call "Younger Avestan," named such because it is the language of the Avesta — the Zoroastrian scriptures that were composed in some period subsequent to that of Zarathustra. Since the closest point of comparison to this relatively isolated dialect is the Sanskrit of the Rig Veda, scholars have considered Zarathustra to be a contemporary of the Rig Vedic *rishis* and have interpreted his references to the *karpân* and *kâviân* as a critique of the sacrificial Brahmins and the Kshatriya warlords of early Indo-Iranian society, before the Iranians really even split from the people who became the Hindus.

There are two problems with this argument. The first is that classical languages survive as languages in which theologically or scholastically authoritative texts are composed long after the epoch in which those languages were still living and commonly spoken. Latin is, for example, a language that remained in use for theological and philosophical treatises in Europe for as long as a thousand years after it had effectively become a dead language and devolved into Italian, French, Spanish, and other Romance languages. René Descartes spoke French but, having been a product of the Jesuit academic system, he composed his greatest philosophical work, the *Metaphysical Meditations*, in Latin as late as the seventeenth century. Something like this could have been the case with Zarathustra.

Second, unlike in the case of Latin, where we have extensive examples both from the time that people were composing treatises in it while it was still a living language and, just as extensively or even more so, from the latest era in which it will still being used as a language of scholarship and theology, so-called "Gathic Avestan" or "Old Avestan" is a hypothetical language whose very existence is based on nothing other than the hymns of Zarathustra. Consequently, the similarity to Rig Vedic Sanskrit could simply be on account of the fact that a Mede or Persian living in the seventh century BC, and preaching against sacrificial Scythian paganism, wanted to endow his critique with the same authority as that of the primordial religious tradition shared by him and those whose practices he is condemning.

The Scythians had an annual ceremony wherein they would worship Mithra, their god of war, in the form of a sword planted into an elevated platform.[30] One out of every hundred prisoners of war that they had captured over the past year would be sacrificed in the shadow of this sword, with their blood being poured from a sacrificial vessel onto the blade where it pierced the stone and earthen platform. This is the sacrificial religious culture that Zarathustra preaches against. The Scythians would also mix the blood of their enemies into wine, and drink this from out of goblets that they had crafted from skulls of their enemies that had been dipped into molten metal.[31] The warlord who had collected the most of these blood-drinking vessels was considered foremost among his peers.[32] These Nordic Iranians scalped their foes and used these scalps to decorate both the quiver holding their arrows and also their cloaks.[33] As we have seen, the Norsemen of Europe are the closest cultural relatives of these wild Iranians, whose tribal totem was the wolf.[34]

Mithra's vengeance against oath-breakers is positively blood-lusting and often carried out through the aegis of the Iranian god of victory in war, namely Verethragna or, as he would be later called, Bahram.[35] The latter is an equivalent of the Greco-Roman deity Ares/Mars. Verethragna wreaks havoc on Mithra's enemies in the shape of a wild boar.[36] In the *Mehr Yasht* it is said of this wild boar that he "kills at one stroke, pursuing, wrathful, with blood dripping from his face. … [Verethragna] cuts all the limbs to pieces, and [mashes] together with the earth, the bones, hair, brains, and blood of the men who have lied unto Mithra."[37] From the perspective of the *Gathas*, the wrath of Mithra and his avatar, the wild boar Bahram, epitomizes the sin or vice of *Aeshma*, "wrathful aggression" or the violent passion of relentless vengeance (New Persian *khashm*).[38]

The frenzy of Mithraic berserkers was produced by drinking *Haoma*, the ritual consumption of which is also condemned by Zarathustra in his *Gâthâs*.[39] Haoma was made by grounding the leaves of an ephedrine-containing plant into powder and mixing this with milk.[40] Haoma-drunken devotees of Mithra would express their enthusiasm in an orgiastic fashion as the sacrificial bull was eviscerated.[41] The crazed warlike spirit of Mithraic sacrifice can be sensed through these verses of the longest surviving hymn to Mithra, the *Mehr Yasht*, which was later incorporated into the Avesta:

> We sacrifice unto Mithra, the Lord of Wide Pastures, who is truth-speaking, a chief in assemblies, with a thousand ears, well-shapen, with ten thousand eyes, high, with full knowledge, strong, sleepless, and ever awake; to whom the chiefs of nations offer up sacrifice as they go to the field against havocking hosts, against enemies coming in battle array, in the strife of conflicting nations.[42]

By writing in an archaic language almost identical to the oldest form of Sanskrit, Zarathustra was attempting to imbue his message with the authority of a language that he knew to be ancestral to both his own branch of the Iranian community and to that which he was confronting. What scholars have arbitrarily named "Gathic Avestan" may simply be poor Rig Vedic Sanskrit, the way that French had its origins in improper Latin and bears traces of other languages that had been spoken in Roman Gaul. That is as much as to say that the reason why "Gathic" Avestan is a linguistic isolate, is that Zarathustra, who probably spoke "Young Avestan," was trying to compose in the oldest and most theologically authoritative form of Sanskrit — a language with such authority that it was called *devâ-nagiri* or the "language of the gods." If Zarathustra was going to preach against the *devâs* (*divs*), what better tongue to do that in than their own?

The third date proposed for Zarathustra has only really been argued for by a single scholar, Mary Settegast, with all advocates of this date deferring entirely to her work. Settegast introduces this thesis in her book *Plato Prehistorian*, which is an archeological evaluation of the historical reality of Plato's legend of Atlantis.[43] She then expands upon the thesis of an 8,500 year old Zarathustra in a book titled *When Zarathustra Spoke*, which is devoted solely to making that argument.[44] Settegast notes how several classical Greek authors make the claim that Zarathustra lived circa 6,500 BC. The Lydian historian Xanthus tells us that Zarathustra lived 6,000 years before Xerxes crossed the Hellespont for the conquest of Greece.[45] We also have Eudoxus of Cnidus (404–355 BC) telling us that Zarathustra lived 6,000 years before the death of Plato.[46] Supposedly, this is something that the Magi who attended Plato's funeral mentioned at that ceremony. Aristotle agrees with that date, and then Plutarch (45–120 CE) tells us that Zarathustra's life transpired some 5,000 years before the Trojan War.[47] All of this points to the late Neolithic, about 6,500 BC or 8,500 years before the present time.

Settegast attempts to marshal archeological evidence from transformations in late Neolithic society as evidence for this astoundingly early date by interpreting these remains as corroborative of certain themes in the Gathas. In the Gathas we see that Zarathustra is preaching against a ritualistic, sacrificial religion and against warlords who are allied with the priests of that religion. They would carry out cattle raids and sacrifice cattle that had been captured in those raids. Dwellings of the late Neolithic period in the area of Western Anatolia, an area which later became Kurdistan, are full of bulls horns. Bulls horns are on walls and benches, while there is hardly any trace of agriculture. There are a lot of implements of war and of hunting. All of a sudden, around the date that classical authors give us for Zarathustra, there appears to be a transition to an agricultural society.[48] The bulls horns disappear. The warlike implements disappear. There is the rise of a pottery tradition that involves new firing techniques that produced patterns with a high contrast between light and dark.[49] Settegast takes this to be significant because both fire and light/dark duality are at the core of Zarathustra's teaching, and she suggests that Zarathustra's message inspired an agricultural revolution and is directed against the plundering nomads who threatened the first settled farming population in history.[50] This is all very vague and, unfortunately, Settegast's most explicit textual evidence for agricultural evangelism on the part of Zarathustra comes from the *Vendidad*.[51] This is a late Zoroastrian scripture which, for reasons that will become clear in Chapter 6, we certainly would not want to attribute to Zarathustra himself, and which sound scholarship has no reason to date as older than the second century BC.[52]

From an Iranian standpoint, there are very serious problems with an 8,500 year old Zarathustra. The oldest *historical* records of Iranian Civilization are references to the Medes and Scythians in Assyrian inscriptions that date to no later than 700 or 800 BC. Even a Zarathustra dated to 1,500 BC is separated from the rest of Iranian history by a historical gulf, let alone *a Zarathustra who lived five thousand years before the first verifiable traces of the first Iranian kingdom!* The whole of Iranian history from the time that the Medes and Scythians appear in historical records until the present is less than 3,000 years — and we are supposed to accept a point of origin for Iranian Civilization that lies five thousand years further into the past than those earliest traces?!

Furthermore, if we were to accept a Zarathustra who lived circa 6,500 BC, that would mean that Zarathustra was a teacher in the context of a united Indo-European community that had not yet fractured into the Greeks, the Latins, the Persians, the Hindus, and all of the other various branches that separated from one another and developed their respective historical traditions. Since in the historical branching of evolving (or devolving) languages as analyzed by linguists, the postulated "Avestan" language is distinctly Iranian, and already differentiated from both Sanskrit and Greek, as well as from the Indo-European languages that would transform into the Latinate and Germanic tongues, we would have to accept that the Gathas have reached us in an Iranian translation from an original that Zarathustra composed in Proto-Indo-European.

While this idea is in some ways intriguing, even fascinating, from the standpoint of Indo-European Studies, it means that Zarathustra has no particular relationship with Iran and Iranians. On this view, by some inexplicably mysterious mechanism of historical preservation, his teaching deeply impacted the Iranian branch of the Indo-European world rather than the Western European or Eastern Hindu branches that retained the kind of sacrificial polytheism that he preached against. From an ethnic and historical—rather than an ideological—standpoint, Zarathustra would be just as much an ancestor of the Greeks, Latins, Germans, and Hindus, as he would be of the Iranians.

Leaving aside questions of national or civilizational pride, such an early Zarathustra also does not make sense in terms of the content of the *Gathas*. The vast majority of ancient texts from the period of 1,500 BC—let alone 6,500 BC—are anonymously authored and bear no traces of individual personalities. That is as true of the Indo-European *Vedas* as it is of non Indo-European compositions dated to the same period, for example, the oldest ancient Egyptian texts. Individuals may be mentioned in them, such as Vedic sages and heroes or Egyptian kings and warriors, but these are not well-developed personalities and the composition itself is certainly not a first person narrative marked by autobiographical asides. Zarathustra is very clearly an individual. In his *Gâthâs* or *Gitâ*, his hymns, you see small biographical details of people who were his friends, individuals whose patronage he benefited from, hardships he suffered and harsh words he has for those who burdened him with them, and even a reference to his younger daughter at her wedding. Such a first-person style is much more "modern" than even Homer's *Iliad*.

2.2 The First Philosopher

Zarathustra's teaching left the most enduring impact on Iran through the survival of the *Ameshâ Spentâs* or "Bounteous Immortals" in both the symbolism of the Iranian New Year altar and the nomenclature of the Iranian national calendar. The *Ameshâ Spentâs*, or *Ameshâsepandân*, are the unchanging principles of all progressive change. They are the six rays of the solar light of *Spentâ Mainyu*, or *Sepandminou*, the "Spirit of Progress" or "Progressive Mentality." These six, together with *Sepandminou*, as the seventh of them, are to this day symbolized by items on the *Haft Sin*, the seven "S" spread placed on a *sofreh* (altar cloth) during the Iranian New Year of *Nowruz*, which begins on the Spring Equinox (March 19-21) and lasts for twelve days corresponding to the twelve zodiacal ages. In their *Pahlavi* or Middle Persian forms, the names of the *Ameshâsepandân* remain the names of six out of the twelve months in Iran's calendar year: *Ordibehesht*, *Khordâd*, *Amordâd*, *Shahrivar*, *Bahman*, and *Spandârmad*.

The most important of the *Ameshâ Spentâs* is *Ashâ Vahishtâ* or *Artâ Vahishtâ* in Old Persian. *Artâ* is a variant of the same word as *Ashâ* in the Avestan dialect of Zarathustra.[53] It has two meanings that, from an ontological perspective, are closely connected. Firstly, *Ashâ* or *Artâ* means "Rightness" (New Persian *Râsti*) in the sense of "Truth" (*Haghighat*) or verity, and secondly, *Artâ*, which is a cognate of *Rtâ* in Sanskrit, means things being "in right order."[54] *Vahishtâ*, which becomes *Behesht* in Pahlavi, and is derived from the root *Veh* or *Beh*, signifies "the best" (*behtarin*).[55] The word survives in contemporary usage in Iran through its Middle Persian contraction, *Ordibehesht*.

In view of this etymology, Zarathustra's concept of *Ordibehesht* has to do with how cosmic order is a precondition of any truth (*vâgheiat*). The claim that it is possible to ascertain the truth about some state of affairs, as opposed to being deceived by a semblance or otherwise mistaken as to how things really are, has as its precondition the existence of an order in the world. It presupposes that we are not confronted by mere chaos and that there is actually a cosmos to be comprehended.

This is a simple but profound statement. A world that is entirely random, or one wherein any apparent order is taken to be only a product of our own subjective categories, is not a world wherein anything can be *verifiably* true. Since it would also be devoid of intrinsic meaning, we would be mistaken to refer to it as a "world" at all. The fabric of every world is woven by a network of signifiers and meaningful connections. While the warp and weft of these may change based on time and place, the supposition of some kind of order is the loom without which life would have to be considered absurd. In his inner dialogue with the transcendent intelligence of *Ahura Mazda*, the "Lord of Wisdom," Zarathustra inquires into the meaning of the majestic order at work in the wheelwork of the heavens, ecological processes, and human life:

> This I ask you, tell me truly Lord. Who is the creator of *Ashâ Vahishtâ* (*Ordibehesht*)? Who set the Sun and stars in their paths? By whom does the moon wax and wane? Wise One, I yearn to know all this and more.
>
> This I ask you, tell me truly Lord. Who holds the earth below, who keeps the sky from breaking away? Who creates the waters and who the plants? Who lends the wind and clouds speed? Wise One, who is the creator of consciousness?
>
> This I ask you, tell me truly Lord. Which artist fashioned the light and the darkness? What artist was it that planned sleep and awakening? Who made the dawn, day and dusk that remind the wise of the ultimate goal?
>
> This I ask you, tell me truly Lord. Are the things I speak forth indeed true? Does serenity, by its actions, promote righteousness [or right order]? From whom has dominion been arranged through pure mind? For whom did you fashion this fruitful, joy-bringing world?
>
> This I ask you, tell me truly, Lord. Who fashioned precious serenity with dominion? Who made the child lovingly turn toward the mother's breast?

> It is through these questions, Wise One, that I am able to recognize you as the Creator of all by your progressive mind.[56]

The order of *Ordibehesht* is the best (Old Persian *Vahishtâ*, Middle Persian *Behesht*) order, in other words it is cosmic order, because it is the fundamental basis and precondition for the possibility of any other ordering or making-orderly of things and people. In this connection, it is important to note that in contemporary Persian the word *Behesht* is one of the words used to refer to heaven in the sense of "paradise" (which, as we shall see later, is also a Persian word). Numerous studies have pointed to the Iranian influence on the formation of Christian theology, including both Zoroastrian influence on Judaism and Mithraic influence on Roman culture. Such influences will be discussed at length with respect to Judaism in Chapter 4 and Christianity in Chapters 5 and 6. In the context of such research it is not unreasonable to see *Ordibehesht* as the prototype of the idea of the Kingdom of Heaven, as a standard for bringing earthly affairs in line with the law and order at work in the cosmos. This idea is misinterpreted, or perhaps even deliberately distorted, when we find it in the Gospels in the form of the Lord's prayer, "Thy kingdom come, thy will be done, on Earth as it is in the Heavens." There is a closer parallel in the Indian idea of *Dharma* or the Chinese idea of *Tao*. In what ways the Iranian concept of *Ordibehesht* significantly differs from these can be discerned with a view to just how the Iranians have imagined that the human mind and society as a whole can be brought into attunement with cosmic order.

One difference can already be seen in the imagery that Iranians have used to symbolize *Ordibehesht*. Unlike the *Tao*, which the Chinese usually analogize to flowing water, Iranians compare cosmic order to an eternal fire. The ever-burning fires in Zoroastrian (Parsi) temples and the candle flame on the *Nowruz* altar spread both represent *Ordibehesht*. In the *Gathas*, Zarathustra defines the fire of cosmic order as a pre-existent background and enduring framework for the struggle between the two opposed principles at work in the world, when he sings: "O Ahura, You offer that harmony to each of these two contenders by means of Your hidden Fire and Truth..."[57] This undying fire is constantly changing forms, but whatever shape its flames take, its substrate remains the same. It seems that the ancient Iranians at least intuitively grasped the convertibility of matter into energy and of the fundamental nature of the cosmos as pure, uncreated and indestructible energy.

This brings us to the most defining quality of *Ahurâ Mazdâ*, the innovative spirit. *Sepandminou* is a Pahlavi and New Persian contraction of *Spentâ Mainyu* in Avestan. *Spentâ* comes from the root *spi*, to "increase."[58] It is a cognate of the Sanskrit word *Spandâ*, which means "dynamic impulse" or "reverberating creative burst."[59] *Mainyu* is derived from the root *mano* or "mind" and is the word for "spirit" or "mentality" in the Avestan language spoken by Zarathustra. Witness these beautiful verses from the *Gathas* of Zarathustra: "Ahura Mazda's First Thought blazed into myriads of sparks of light and filled the entire heavens."[60] *Sepandminou* is the progressive or innovative spirit at work in the world, the creative force of cosmic and social evolution that affords us the possibility to "progress from good to greater good."[61] It is in Yasna 43 of the *Gathas* that we see the *Spentâ* or innovative mindedness of Lord Wisdom most clearly emphasized by Zarathustra, especially when he evokes being psychically encompassed and seized by this spirit during his silent meditation:

> I realized you, Wise God, to be progressive when I saw you at the birth of life…
>
> I realized you, Wise God, to be progressive when I was encircled by you through pure mind, and you showed me that silent meditation is the best…
>
> I realized you, Wise God, to be progressive when I was encircled by you through pure mind, and you asked of me "Who are you?! To whom do you belong?! How would you in these days of questioning, explain the directives to the living and to yourself?!
>
> I realized you, Wise God, to be progressive when I was encircled by you through pure mind. To your question: For what purpose do you seek knowledge?" I answered: "With the gift of homage to your fire, I shall meditate, as long as I can, in quest of righteousness [right-ordered-ness, i.e. *Ordibehesht*].[62]

The word *Spentâ* can also be, and often is, translated as "bounteous" in the sense of overflowing. This is particularly the case when discussing the six *Ameshâ Spentâs* (*Ameshâsepandân*) or "Bounteous Immortals" that are emanations or rays of the metaphorical Sun of *Sepandminou*. These eternal and fundamental principles that allow for all innovation or progressive change are what is being represented by the six items on the *Haft Sin* or "Seven S" spread during the Iranian New Year (*Nowruz*), together with their fountainhead in *Spentâ Mainyu* itself as the seventh of them. These principles were eventually anthropomorphized and directly influenced the much later Judeo-Christian development of the idea of the seven archangels.[63] In verses 7 to 12 of Yasna 33 in the *Gathas*, Zarathustra evokes the *Ameshâ Spentâs*, the six aspects of *Spentâ Mainyu*, all at once:

> Come to me in essence and in vision O *Mazdâ*.
> May I be renowned before the Order of the Magi
> By working through *Ordibehesht* and *Bahman*.
> May the solemn promises made to You
> Be understood and fulfilled by us.
>
> O *Mazdâ*, guide my work so that I may continue to worship You
> Through *Bahman*.
> I will sing Your praise and cling to *Ordibehesht*.
> Grant me, therefore, the everlasting blessing
> Of Your *Khordâd* and Your *Amordâd*.
>
> These Twin Powers are Yours, O *Mazdâ*.
> They are constant companions of *Ordibehesht* and dwell
> In the dazzling light of Your Wisdom.
> May Your Supreme Mind bless us with these two
> Whose souls are united.
>
> Everything in the good life is Yours, O *Mazdâ*,
> All which has been, which is, and which shall be.
> You give us our rewards
> In keeping with our actions.
> May the *Amordâd* in man grow
> Through the *Bahman* and *Ordibehesht*
> Under Your *Shahrivar*.

> O *Ahurâ*, You are the most mighty Lord of Wisdom,
> Of Devotion (*Sepandârmad*), and Truth (*Ordibehesht*) which fosters human life.
> It is You who nourish the Best Thinking (*Bahman*) and Just Dominion (*Shahrivar*).
>
> … Arise within me, O *Ahurâ*
> and fulfill my ardent desire for *Khordâd*
> through *Sepandârmad*.[64]

Ordibehesht has already been discussed, but the other five aspects of *Spentâ Mainyu* named here in their Persian forms now need to be defined and elucidated. Contemplation with the aim of understanding, the acquisition of knowledge, or the discernment of truth, only make any sense on the presupposition of a cosmic order like that suggested by the idea of *Ordibehesht*. Zarathustra thinks that a truly human life is one devoted to the cultivation of *Bahman*, the best thinking or intellectual excellence that can discern and bring one into harmony with the cosmic order so that one may contribute to the great work of the creative spirit. *Bahman* is a contraction of the Avestan *Vohu Manah*, which could also be contracted in the form of *human*. This is the prototype of the Latin concept of *humanitas*, which is either an Indo-European cognate or found its way into European civilization through Iranian influence via Mithraism (see Chapter 5). The idea is that one is only a properly human being if one cultivates one's mind. Interestingly, although our intellectual faculty is what separates us from animals, *Bahman* is symbolically associated with the animal kingdom.[65] This is because how we treat animals is a reflection on our own humanity. What separates us from them also makes us responsible for their welfare. There were severe laws against cruelty to animals in the first Persian Empire. For example mistreating a dog was as grievously punished as abusing a human child.

This brings us to the legal and socio-political philosophy of Zarathustra. It is radically utopian. The *Ameshâ Spentâ* that is of most relevance here is *Shahrivar*, a middle Persian contraction of the Avestan *Khashatra Vairya* or the Desirable Dominion.[66] It could also be translated as the Most Choice-worthy Kingship. In other words, it is the ideal form of government, that which one would choose if only one could see it. *Shahrivar* comes into being when *Ordibehesht* is not only discerned by *Bahman* on an individual basis and embodied by a single person, but when an entire political order is rightly guided to bring society as a whole into harmony with cosmic order and the creative divine intellect. *Shahrivar* is elementally associated with the hardest stone or with metal. This has alchemical significance. Imagine the metal sword of the just ruler being forged in the fire of *Ordibehesht*.

Among the Bounteous Immortals of Zoroastrianism, *Spentâ Armâiti* in Avestan or *Sepandârmad* in middle Persian is depicted as a feminine figure — a kind of Mother Earth goddess.[67] The idea that being ever more firmly rooted in the right order also yields an ever increasing serenity, or *Sepandârmad*, is another fundamental idea of Iranian Civilization. This abiding calm that comes over a contemplative and conscientious person is associated with the element of Earth, and in this regard it is one of three closely related principles that demarcate the ecological dimension of Zarathustra's message.

Closely related to *Sepandârmad* is *Khordâd*, or *Haurvatât* in the archaic Avestan dialect of Zarathustra. This *Ameshâ Spentâ* is the spirit of health or wholeness, which is associated with the element of water. The Iranian cult of Anahita, the Lady of the Lake and Virgin mother of Mithra, included baptism rituals with holy water that were intended to make one hale and confer a cleansing spiritual perfection.[68] The idea here is not only that health follows from the intellectual discipline of *Bahman* and the serenity of *Sepandârmad*, so that a disordered mind and a volatile life are unhealthy, but also that proper attention to bodily health and well being is a prerequisite of success in seeking enlightenment.

Zarathustra conceives of the attainment of Enlightenment in terms of *Amordâd*, or *Ameratât* in Avestan. This is often translated as "immortality" but it literally means un-deadness, in the sense of vitality.[69] Intellectual excellence, justice, serenity, and health ultimately lead one to this superhuman or supremely human condition. Zarathustra conceives of this in terms of an alchemical transformation of the human condition that takes place at the end of history. His cosmology was unique in the ancient world for its goal-directed or teleological — rather than cyclical — conception of time and world ages.

On the whole, *Sepandminou* works to progressively and innovatively improve the human condition throughout successive epochs. After a final apocalyptic conflict, which is referred to in the *Gathas* as both "the great event of choice" (namely of choice between the two spirits) and also as the *Frashgard* or the "renewal of existence," all of those who have chosen rightly to be champions of Truth and Justice attain their archetypally perfect form.[70] This *farvahar* acts as one's guardian angel during one's life, enjoining one to become who one really is. Interestingly, in line with the unique reverence for women in Iranian Civilization, in the teaching of Zarathustra, the exteriorization of one's inner conscience or *daena* that one embodies after the apocalypse is feminine in form, whether one is now a man or a woman; she looks like a Valkyrie.[71]

But *Amordâd* does not only refer to personal immortality. It also has another meaning that connects it more closely to the aforementioned ecological principles of Zarathustra's message in order to form the trio of serenity, health, and vitality. In this sense *Amordâd* is associated with the element of vegetation — the lush greenery of trees, plants, fruits, and vegetables.[72] It was considered a sacred duty to propagate agriculture so as to participate in the divine creation and make the living world more bountiful.

The Bounteous Immortals are profoundly interconnected eternal principles, or rather, more than that, they are all aspects of the same essential spirit, namely the "bounteous" or innovative quality that best characterizes the mentality of the Wisdom Lord. These arch-angelic powers are opposed by a spirit or mentality that is the diametric opposite of *Spentâ Mainyu*, namely *Angrâ Mainyu* or *Ahriman*.

The Avestan word *Angrâ* means "constricted" or "constrained."[73] It contains the root of the contemporary Persian word for knot, namely *gereh*, and one might also suspect that it is an Indo-European cognate of the word "angry" in the sense that one is knotted-up inside and constricted or closed-off from the outside when one becomes angry. *Ahriman* is a

Middle Persian contraction of *Angrâ Mainyu*. The idea of *Ahriman* has psychological and ethical dimensions, but it is first and foremost a cosmological principle. We can only fully understand *Sepandminou* when we comprehend how and why the constructive power of *Ahurâ Mazdâ* is limited by a destructive counter-principle or antithetical force.

Zarathustra sometimes uses the term *Druj* or "the Lie" as a synonym of *Ahriman*, as if to suggest that *Ahriman* is the Great Deceiver at the root of all other lies, distortions, and deceptions.[74] From the point of view of cosmology, the significance of *Ahriman* is to clearly indicate that *Ahurâ Mazdâ* is neither omnipotent nor omniscient. Corruption, derangement, and decay are possible because in addition to there being a rationally comprehensible cosmic order there is also an abyss of irrational chaos. In the *Bondaheshn*, we see how *Ahriman* and his demonic spawn emerge from out of this abyss to assault the creation of *Ahurâ Mazdâ*.[75]

If the Lord of Wisdom were all-powerful he would be responsible for all of the evil and imperfection in our world, and if he were all-knowing then that would mean, at present, his mind would be capable of surveying the completed logical structure of all future events. Such a conception is incompatible with the idea of creative evolution that is at the core of the concept of *Spentâ Mainyu*, the "Innovative Spirit." How can there truly be nothing new from God's standpoint if God's chief attribute or essential spirit is the force of innovation at all levels of existence? We see, then, how *Spentâ Mainyu* actually requires an antithetical force to strive against. For *Ahurâ Mazdâ* to be bounteous rather than fatalistically omnipotent, *Sepandminou* must be limited by a niggardly spirit of constraint and constriction. That this is also an agency of deception implies that Truth or *Ordibehesht*, namely cosmic order, is evolutionary. Stagnation or stasis is enforced through manipulating semblances.

2.3 The Iranian Origin of Western Philosophy

In 600 BC, when Zarathustra composed his thought-provoking *Gathas*, thought among the Greeks was still deeply immersed in the world of myth and superstition. Theogonies were being composed, and it seems that which was proposed by Hesiod "had no serious rivals" and held the most sway.[76] It is a genealogical story which sees the world proceed from Chaos and Earth. On the one side, Chaos gives birth to Night and Erebos, which in turn produce Aether and Day. On the other side, Earth produces heaven, mountains and seas, which in turn give rise to a series of gods — Oceanus, Thethys, Theia, Hyperion, Kreios, Eurybie — that in union with each other produce the rivers, sun, moon, and dawn. Finally, the union of Dawn and Astraios (a grandchild of Sea and Earth) engenders the wind and stars.[77] There were other less significant, perhaps more natural cosmological speculations contemporary to the one above that was recounted by Hesiod. However, as M.L. Mills notes, these speculations were very primitive.[78]

For six centuries, from at least the Trojan War in 1230 BC to Hesiod's *Theogony* in 650 BC, we see essentially no change in the mythic worldview of the Greeks. Then, suddenly, in the 500s BC, we have twelve philosophers appearing within just a single century. It must be more than a strange (and suspiciously overlooked) coincidence that the sudden rise of philosophy like a meteor from a Greek mind sunken for millennia in the dark marshes of myth and superstition, coincides precisely with the Persian conquest and colonization of Greece beginning in the sixth century BC and enduring for well over 150 years.

Let us look at Achaemenid society as described by Herodotus, who encountered it first hand as a citizen of Iran. Regarding the religion of the common Persians, he writes:

> They are not wont to establish images or temples or alters at all; indeed, they regard all who do as fools, and this, in my opinion, is because they do not believe in gods of human form, as the Greeks do.[79]

He adds that the Persians do not believe in a God so petty as to entertain prayers asking for an alleviation of the particular problems of any given individual, and so their only lawful prayer is for the well-being of all. Herodotus goes on to explain that the highest value and principle around which their society turns is truthfulness and the condemnation of deceit.

Zarathustra's idea that thoughts, words, and deeds ought to be perfectly aligned is reflected in this observation that Herodotus makes about ancient Persian society:

> Whatsoever things it is not permitted to them to do, of these they must not even speak. Lying is considered among them the very basest thing and, second, indebtedness ... because, as they say, a debtor is bound to lie somewhat.[80]

Apparently, from the age of five and up, Persian children were rigorously disciplined to make a practice of always telling the truth. For Herodotus writes:

> They train their sons from their fifth to their twentieth year in three things only: horsemanship, archery, *and truth-telling*.[81]

One particularly colorful practice that reveals the love of Truth in Achaemenid society is that, according to Herodotus, the Persians would never enter into debates and discussions of serious matters unless they were drunk on wine. The decisions arrived at would later be reviewed in sobriety before being executed:

> They are very addicted to wine ... [and t]hey keep very strictly to this practice, too: that they are wont to debate their most serious concerns when they are drunk. But whatsoever they decide on, drunk, this the master of the house where they are when debating proposes to them again on the next day, when they are sober. And if they like it, too, when sober, they act on it; but if they do not like it so, they let it be. And whatever they debate, in preliminary fashion, sober, they give to final decision drunk.[82]

It seems that they believed the wine would embolden them to drop all false pretenses and get to the heart of the matter.

Yale philologist Stanley Insler has noted a curious feature of Achaemenid society that also attests to its embrace of Zarathustra's principles. Ancient Persian names were always descriptive of a person's qualities and would be chosen by parents as a wish for the kind of person that they would like to see their child become. We have an immense inventory of 1,500 such names inscribed on the many Old Persian tablets surviving from the period. Some of them are: *aspaugura*, "strong as a horse"; *hubaoidi*, "sweet-smelling"; *viraka*, "little hero"; *vsavah*, "having good fame"; *humizda*, "winning a good prize." These express longings for strength, heroism, beauty, fame, and fortune. But what is striking is that the vast majority of names on these tablets do *not* refer to such qualities, but rather incorporate the attribute of Truth (Old Persian *Arta*). For example, we find: *Artapana*, "Protector of Truth"; *Artakama*, "Lover of Truth"; *Artamanah*, "Truth-Minded"; *Artafarnah*, "Possessing the Splendor of Truth"; *Artazusta*, "Delighting in Truth"; *Artastuna*, "Pillar of Truth"; *Artafrida*, "Prospering in Truth"; *Artahunara*, "Having the Nobility of Truth."[83]

Iranian influence on Greek thought began with Cyrus' invasion and occupation of Lydia, whose capital city, Sardis, was the resort of all Greeks inclined toward learning. A short time later, Lampsacus was one of the first Hellenic towns to be conquered by Cyrus and once under the authority of the Pax Achaemenica it became a haven of thinkers persecuted for blaspheming against tradition in Greek mainland cities such as Athens.[84] The channels for influence increased drastically when, by 450 BC, Darius had extended Persian rule beyond the Hellespont to the shores of the Danube in the North, and the Adriatic Sea to the West. Herodotus reports that Darius' conquest brought many Iranian colonists to settle in Greece, particularly in Macedonia and Thrace, in cities such as Abdera and Eion. We know of instances in which Zoroastrian Magi became the tutors of children of Greek aristocrats, one such case being that of Protagoras, whose father Maendrius welcomed and feasted Xerxes.[85]

Two Greeks accused of being Iranian agents were in the inner circle of Pericles of Athens and had a deep influence on him. The first was his mistress, Aspasia of Miletus. Pericles divorced his first wife and the mother of his two children to marry her. According to Plutarch, like the Ionian courtesan Thargelia before her, Aspasia "brought all who had to do with her over to the Persian interest, and by their means, being men of the greatest power and station, sowed the seeds of the Median faction up and down in several cities."[86] In his dialogue *Menexenus*, Plato has Socrates identify her as the true composer of Pericles' famous Funeral Oration.[87] It is likely that it was through Aspasia's role as a social magnet for Greek thinkers of the time, including Socrates, that Pericles became entangled with the other figure that was to exert a tremendous influence on him, Anaxagoras. This philosopher was born and raised as an Iranian subject on the Western coastland of Asia Minor. In his youth he even served in the Persian military. Both Anaxagoras and Aspasia were charged with "impiety and Medism" and sentenced to death by the assembly of Athens.

The charge of "Medism" was tantamount to an accusation that one was under Iranian influence. That this was a codified crime in and of itself, and a crime punishable by the death sentence no less, shows the extent to which the Greeks were terrified of what must have been a tremendous Iranian impact on their culture. That the crime was named "Medism" rather than "Persianism" suggests that this Iranian influence may even have preceded the Persian conquest of the Medes. It may have begun during the Median Kingdom, in the epoch of Zarathustra himself. The entire first generation of Greek philosophers lived, not in mainland Greece, but in colonies that had become a part of Imperial Iran. Thales of Miletus, Anaximander of Miletus, Pythagoras of Samos, and Xenophanes of Colophon — every single one of them was an Iranian subject. Most were from Ionia, the part of Greece that was longest governed by Iran — to the point where, to this day, Iranians refer to all of Greece as *Ionân*. The case of Pythagoras, who was from the island of Samos, is particularly striking — especially since he was the first Greek, and indeed the first Westerner, to call himself a "philosopher."

Pythagoras was studying at the temples in Egypt when he was "arrested" by Cambyses II, the son and heir of Cyrus the Great, and was sent back to Babylon with the Iranian military.[88] Pythagoras becomes a guest of the court of Cambyses and studies with the Magi in Babylon for a dozen years before returning to his native island of Samos.[89] It is noteworthy that he returns to Samos only once the island comes under Persian occupation in 522 BC.[90] After about a decade in Persian-occupied Samos, Pythagoras moves on to southern Italy. Here he establishes a revolutionary school of thought and a secret society that tries to seize political power.[91] Given his pedigree one has to wonder whether the Pythagorean Order was acting as a proxy for the Persian Empire. Pythagoras becomes the first person in Greece to refer to himself as a *philosophos* or "philosopher," a title which reflects the unique rapport of friendship between man and the Lord of Wisdom in Zoroastrianism.[92] *Philosophia* is the literal Greek translation of the older Avestan idea of *Mazdâyasnâ*.

The cosmology of Pythagoras appears to have been influenced by the Zoroastrian idea of archetypes (*Fravashi*) or ideal forms of things pre-existing the physical creation and serving as a model for it. His notion of the dynamic tension between a principle of order and limit on the one hand a negatively unlimited chaos on the other also echoes the kind of Zoroastrian cosmology that leaves room for Ahriman's deranging influence.

In the Zoroastrian scripture *Bondahesh*, we see that before *Ahurâ Mazdâ* creates physical beings he conceives of their archetypes or ideal forms.[93] The ancient Iranian term for such an ideal form is *Fravashi*.[94] The physical creation does not simply follow the conception of the ideal forms in a chronological fashion, because the former exist even without *Ahurâ Mazdâ* having initiated chronological and measurable Time. These forms are consequently motionless and invulnerable to corruption, perfect prototypes of the things and persons who will come to populate the physical world.

The archetypes are internal differentiations within a realm of light that is separated from a realm of darkness by a chasm or void.[95] Both realms are described as infinite in their own dimension, in other words infinitely transcendent light and a bottomless abyss of darkness, except that their meeting place is finite. Leaving aside the logical difficulty of two opposed and mutually exclusive infinities, and focusing on the reconciliation of the description of their common boundary as both a void and also as finite, we would have to conclude that this chasm is a receptacle for the physical creation. In other words, from a primordial standpoint it is a chasm, but in time it comes to be filled with the good creation that is assaulted by the forces of darkness. This is important in terms of understanding what a *Fravashi* is, because the difference between an ideal form and the physical beings that are shaped based on this prototype is on account of the corrupting influence of the realm of darkness and the limiting conditions of the receptacle within which the finite creation is fashioned. Both the good creation and the dark forces deranging it are finite in nature.

The *Bondahesh* makes it clear that the power of *Ahurâ Mazdâ* is limited. The Wise Lord proposes a fixed period of combat with *Ahriman* because he is concerned that if their inevitable struggle were to continue indefinitely, the forces of darkness might actually prevail in destroying the luminous creation.[96] In fact, once the physical creation begins, the constellations and other celestial bodies are described as a "warlike army, which is destined for battle" against the forces of darkness.[97] Then the sky is also created by *Ahura Mazda* as a shining steel egg, a metal "rampart" that is "like a castle or fortress in which every weapon that is needed for the battle is stored … formed so that the adversary should not be able to mingle with" the good creation.[98] In other words, the Zoroastrian cosmos is a gigantic war machine.

Ahurâ Mazdâ's defenses are breached when the Dark Lord "rushed in at noon" and his demonic creatures set about deranging the constellations and setting the Sun and Moon into an unnatural motion "as the sky was shattered and frightened by him, as sheep by a wolf"; *Ahriman* pierces the Earth itself, beneath the water, and at its core.[99] Noxious, biting, and venomous creatures such as snakes, scorpions, and lizards overtake the earth at this point, vegetation is blighted, fires rage and smoke covers the world.[100] But it cannot only have been the smoke that "made the world quite as injured and dark at midday as though it were in dark night."[101] It is worth noting in this regard that the "form of the evil spirit was a log-like lizard body."[102]

All in all, this seems like a description of a meteorite impact, possibly with the fragmentation of a larger meteor that correlates to the demonic army led by the evil spirit himself. The impact disturbed the rotation of the Earth, turning day into night and appearing to disorder the constellations and the movement of the Sun and Moon. Such a prehistoric event witnessed by the most ancient Iranians or Aryans seems to have been projected into the realm of metaphysics and cosmology, thereby becoming fundamental to the Zoroastrian worldview. The belief in eternal and invulnerable archetypes makes a great deal of sense in the context of such a traumatic cultural memory.

This is not meant to be a reductionist explanation. Simply because environmental conditions bring certain people to an idea does not mean that the idea itself is reducible to that experience and does not refer to any reality. Plato claims that archetypes are the absolute standard of the reality of anything else, and he was introduced to this idea through the Pythagorean Order. Plato's argument, in *Republic*, that a just society is one that is ruled by philosophers, was also an idea he absorbed as a Pythagorean initiate.[103] The political philosophy that the Pythagorean Order tried to implement in Greek colonies in southern Italy revolves around the concept of *Khashatrâ Vairyâ* (*Shahrivar*), which harks back to the utopian political doctrine of Zoroastrianism and the relationship between Zarathustra and Kavi Vishtaspa.

Another idea that Plato adopts from the Pythagoreans, which has no precedent in Greek thought, namely the idea of *metempsychosis* or reincarnation, also appears to be an idea that Pythagoras himself learned of from the Magi that he studied under in Imperial Iran. Legends that Pythagoras traveled all the way to India are just that — legends. His only exposure to the idea of reincarnation would have been in Imperial Iran, the eastern borders of which extended into northern India by the time that he was studying in the Achaemenid administrative capital at Babylon.[104] However, this does not mean that the Magi served simply as a conduit for Indian ideas of *karma* and rebirth. As we shall see in the fourth and final section of this chapter, Gautama Buddha was himself an Iranian and, as will be argued in the next chapter, he was actually a Magi in Babylon during the reign of Cambyses, *when Pythagoras was studying there*. Although not a part of Zoroastrian theology, the idea of reincarnation appears to have been a recurrent element in various Mithraic cults and spiritual movements throughout the history of Iran.[105] In fact it is so enduring a feature of such movements, that belief in *tanâsokh* survives well into the Islamic period despite being severely at odds with Islamic orthodoxy. The Khorramis, the cult of Sinbad and Abu Muslim Khorasani, and the Assassins of Alamut all believe in it.

Not everyone appreciated the vast erudition of Pythagoras. Heraclitus of Ephesus penned this scathing critique of him: "Pythagoras son of Mnesarchus pursued inquiry further than all other men and, choosing what he liked from these compositions, made a wisdom of his own: much learning, artful knavery. Pythagoras was the prince of imposters."[106] The fact that the strongest critic of Pythagoras from among the first generation of Greek philosophers was also the most deeply influenced by Iranian ideas is further evidence for the Iranian origin of Western Philosophy. The *Fragments* of Heraclitus are full of parallels to the *Gathas* of Zarathustra. On the face of it, this would appear to be why Darius the Great invited the Ionian to enjoy his patronage at the Persian court. That subject will be explored at length and in depth in the following chapter. For now, it should suffice to point out some of the elements in the writings of Heraclitus that strongly suggest Iranian influence.

Like Zarathustra, Heraclitus attacks the ritual polytheism of his time and calls for us to look at the world with plain sight.[107] Heraclitus is the first Greek to engage in a direct assault on the religious authorities of his own time and the attitudes of their unquestioning adherents.[108] It can hardly be a coincidence that, in what is perhaps his most famous fragment, Heraclitus chooses the very same metaphor as Zarathustra to symbolize the transformation of all phenomena, namely an Eternal Fire.[109] Heraclitus uses the very same words as Zarathustra when he describes the God who is embodied by this cosmic fire as "the Wise One."[110] In a cryptic aside Heraclitus refers to God as "alone" and explains that S/he is not the polytheistic deity Zeus, but God in He/r ineffability is indifferent to whether deluded men call He/r by this name or others.[111] Just as Zarathustra's *Mazdai*, the "Wise One" (*Sophon*) of Heraclitus is an intellect or cosmic consciousness that is co-extensive with Being and thereby directs the right-order of the cosmos through its divine law, which Heraclitus calls *Logos*. This "word" becomes the most fundamental concept of Western Philosophy, and it is first introduced by Heraclitus within a metaphysical context in which it serves almost as a literal translation of Zarathustra's *Asha* or the ancient Persian *Arta*.[112]

Heraclitus expresses the phenomenological understanding of Truth that is at the heart of the *Gathas* almost better than Zarathustra himself, when he conceives of the eternal fire of cosmic transformation as a Sun that never sets.[113] His lofty use of solar imagery is likely another mark of Iranian influence. Like Zarathustra, Heraclitus realizes that we are ever enraptured by the manifestation of divine creation and he asks, "How will one hide from that [i.e., a kind of Sun] which never sets?"[114] His question rings with exasperation and shame at the folly of humanity's deceitfulness. Heraclitus is disgusted by the way in which everyone turns away from the Eternal Sun in fear, trying to hide in a shelter crafted out of their own false thoughts and opinions.[115]

The parallels with the *Gathas* become truly startling when in the same breath Heraclitus prescribes the alignment of thought, speech, and action, through a perfect honesty rooted in self-knowledge, as a means to collapse the illusory cave of the inviolable private self. The authentic selfhood that he calls us to seek is the voice of Conscience. Like Zarathustra, he tells us that through the alignment of thought, speech, and action, the cosmic order of the Wise One's *Logos* will take root in one's life as an inherent Justice that makes "human laws" unnecessary.[116] Heraclitus tells us to "listen not to [him] but to the *Logos*" as the inner voice of our own conscience, and he explicitly distinguishes this practice from the superficial pseudo-scientific and scholastic speculation of his predecessors.[117] It must also be the conscience to which Heraclitus refers in a cryptic fragment where he writes: "To the soul belongs a *Logos* that increases itself."[118] Some translators have rendered *Logos* in this context as "rapport," thereby signifying a relation of oneself to a deeper inner self. This may be the relation between the cognitive executor of thoughts, words, and deeds on the one hand, and the conscience on the other. Its "increase" would then signify the waxing wisdom or deepening burden of greater life experiences that have either been in accord or discord with the voice of conscience. This "increase" could also be a synonym of the Avestan *spentâ*, in which case we see Heraclitus echoing Zarathustra's description of the wise person's soul as having a "progressive mentality." *Spentâ Maynu* has often been badly translated from the Avestan as "Good Thought," and so it may be that Heraclitus means the "progressive mentality" that embraces cosmic creativity when he says "thinking well."[119]

Heraclitus believes that Justice is manifested through conflict and that in the form of the cosmic fire it will punish those who lie.[120] After long ages the world experiences an apocalypse in which final justice is done through a consummation of the earth by purifying fire.[121] This is the *Frashgard* of Zoroastrian theology. No such apocalyptic belief existed among the ancient Greeks before the Persian conquest of Ionia. For the ancient Greeks both good and bad alike descended to the shadow world of *Hades* after death. Heraclitus does not believe in *Hades* and he takes the trouble to emphasize that what awaits man beyond death is inconceivable.[122] He also expresses a view with respect to the disposal of corpses which is unmistakably Zoroastrian.[123] Adherents of Zoroastrianism in ancient Iran viewed a corpse as pollution and they disposed of it immediately by raising it up on a platform or carrying it atop the rocks of mountains where it would be devoured by vultures and other beasts of prey.[124] Eventually enclosures called *dakhmehs* were built for this purpose, namely to prevent the rotting corpse from tainting the sacred purity of the earth and water, while at the same time allowing the flesh of the dead to feed other creatures in nature.

2.4 The Iranian Origin of Eastern Philosophy

Many ancient Greeks themselves made the claim that Philosophy was pioneered by the *barbaroi*, a term that they used almost exclusively to refer to Iranians — especially the Persians and the Scythians.[125] Pyrrho of Elis (355–265 BC) attests to having met Iranian *philosophoi* in the course of his travels.[126] *Philosophoi* or "those who love wisdom" is a plural of the Greek word *philosophos* or "philosopher." So we know that Iranian philosophy existed. According to Diogenes Laertius, Pyrrho developed his own philosophical position in part under the influence of Iranian philosophers in Central Asia and northern India.[127] Pyrrho met Alexander and joined his campaign in 334 BC.[128] The parallels between the school of Sextus Empiricus in the Roman West and that of Nagarjuna in the Buddhist East are really outgrowths rooted in a common origin, namely the teaching of Gautama and its impact on Pyrrho of Elis during his travels in the Indo-Scythian realm of Gandhara.[129]

The "Pali Canon is not a reliable guide to the life and times of Gautama Buddha."[130] The earliest possible dates for the Gandhari scriptures and the Pali canon are no less than *three centuries* after the time of the Buddha's death.[131] We have two Greek sources from the period of the Alexandrian conquest of the Eastern Persian Empire and northern India, which allow us to form a picture of early Buddhism that is more accurate than what we are presented with in the Pali canon. One of these sources is Pyrrho of Elis, who traveled with Alexander himself in Bactria, Gandhara, and Sindh from 330 to 325 BC, and the other is the Greek ambassador Megasthenes who visited Gandhara and Magadha from 305–304 BC.[132]

Two related key terms in Pyrrho's philosophical teachings are *apatheia* and *ataraxia*, with the former meaning to be "without passion" or "beyond suffering" and the latter having the sense of "undisturbedness" or "calm."[133] He argued that on account of the fact that our thought is circular, absolutely objective knowledge is denied to us.[134] Therefore, we should hold "no views" through a suspension of judgment or *epoche* and practice *aklineis* or having "no inclinations" for or against particular matters (*pragmata*).[135] The refusal to decide is also characterized as "determining nothing and withholding assent" with respect to matters or *pragmata*.[136]

The precise meaning of the Greek term *pragma*, of which *pragmata* is the plural form, is "an object of our cogitation or disputation."[137] So the commonplace translation of *pragmata* as "things" is mistaken. "Matters" would be more accurate, and Pyrrho is particularly concerned with "disputed matters," or as Plutarch puts it, the "quarrel about whether the matter [*pragma*] is good or evil or white or not white."[138] *Adiaphora* is the privative of *diaphora* or "differentiated by a logical differentia," so that it means "undifferentiated by a logical differentia" and therefore "without a logical self-identity."[139]

Our minds provide the differentiae that are lacking in things without inherent self-identity.[140] These differentiae usually involve category words or quality descriptors. Our experience of the world is an experience of variation and gradation; uneasy minds project definite types and absolute qualities as criteria for the categorization of what is only relatively gradable and always variable.[141] The idea of "perfection" — any particular ideal of perfection, since there are many — serves the purpose of orienting an aim (*telos*) for a certain endeavor, whether scientific, political, or artistic, by defining a goal that is itself not attainable.[142] One or another ideal of Beauty motivates artists to produce masterpieces. Although they never perfectly instantiate their vaguely imagined ideal, the aim does produce beautiful things. Like all phenomena, Beauty is "varied, imperfect, and ever-changing."[143] In other words, the idea of perfection is an ideal arrived at, and acted on, for *pragmatic* purposes — even if this remains concealed from the person who is blindly driven by such an ideal.

Pragmata are *adiaphorous*. This means that "antilogies" or opposed categories are artificial, subjective, and subject to deconstruction.[144] *Astathmeta* means "unstable, unbalanced" on account of having no "standing place" and, by extension "not measurable" or admitting of being weighed on a scale.[145] It is a privative of the word *stathmos*, which signifies both a balance beam and a scale. As the negative form of *epikrisis* or "determination, judgement," *anepikrita* means "unjudged, undecided, unfixed."[146] The full range of its meaning can be discerned with a view to the verb *epikrino*, namely "to decide, determine; judge; select, pick out, choose," a verb that is in turn derived from *krino*, "to separate, distinguish; choose; decide disputes or contests; judge; prefer," which is the root of the term *kriterion* (English "criterion"), a "standard" that is a "means for judging or trying."[147]

Put in Pyrrho's Greek terminology, Gautama Sakamuni thinks that we ought to be *akradantous* or "unwavering" only in being *adoxastous* or "without views, theories" and *aklineis* or "uninclined."[148] Pyrrho recognized that, despite their appeals to "justice" and denunciation of "injustice" people really manage all matters (*prattein*) on the basis of social custom and political law, which is culturally and historically contingent.[149] In other words, the question is really what is permitted or forbidden according to a certain belief system or customary code of conduct—whether the latter is implicitly or explicitly adhered to by persons within a certain society. Truth and Justice have nothing to do with it, despite self-righteous claims to the contrary.

Greeks of the classical period associated this idea with the Scythians. It is almost always overlooked in the history of Philosophy that the first of the Pre-Socratic thinkers who wrote in the Greek language was an Iranian. Anacharsis the Scythian was actually the brother of the King Caduida of Scythia. He wrote in Greek, and traveled extensively in Greece, because his mother was a Greek.[150] Such was his renown in the age of Solon (592–589 BC) that this Scythian philosopher came to be counted by the Greeks as one of the Seven Sages of Antiquity. Although, tragically, his own works were lost in the course of vicissitudes of history such as the burning of the Library of Alexandria, Anacharsis was so widely read and quoted by other classical Greek and even pagan Roman authors that we are able to reconstruct some key aspects of his teaching—and, by extension, the Scythian worldview.[151]

Anacharsis is remembered as the philosopher who first formulated the Problem of the Criterion.[152] One could summarize it in the following fashion. We are faced with a conundrum when we ask, "Who judges something skillfully?" People who are unskilled are not in any more of a position to judge whether something has been done skillfully, than a blind person can "grasp the workings of sight," or "the deaf person those of hearing." So, suppose we say that only a skilled person can judge whether something has been made in an excellent manner or done in an artful fashion (with *aretê*, virtue in the sense of skill or excellence). Skills or crafts (*techne*) are specialized, so the quality of a particular thing that was crafted, the rightness of a certain decision that was made, or the praiseworthiness or blameworthiness of a particular deed that was done, cannot be properly evaluated by a person with a different expertise than the one that is relevant to what is being judged. In fact, this expert's judgment will not really be worth any more than that of the common man, because his field of expertise is not relevant. This leaves us to conclude that only an expert in the same field as the craftsman who produces a certain craft — the politician who makes a certain decision, the sportsman who is practicing a particular sport, and so forth — is fit to judge whether something was made or done skillfully. However, such a person is biased, since he "has the same pursuits as the one being judged, he will be untrustworthy since he too is being judged" and "it is not possible … to be both judging and judged."[153] The basic idea is that it is impossible to find a perfectly impartial criterion or a truly unbiased and objective judge to devise and apply such a criterion of judgment. "Therefore nothing is a criterion."

Interestingly, this conclusion seems not to have inclined Anacharsis toward democracy, as one might imagine a person would so incline if he believed that anyone's judgment was as good as anyone else's. That is a superficial and false interpretation of what Anacharsis is concerned with in his critique of the criterion, since, according to Diogenes Laertius, the Scythian philosopher also famously "wondered why among the Greeks the experts contend, but the non-experts decide."[154] Such a statement is clearly critical of democracy or the judgment of the mob, as indeed is that part of the criterion argument itself where Anacharsis states that the unskilled are certainly unqualified to judge something skillfully.

The earliest record of the Buddha's personal name as "Gautama" is found in the *Chuangtzu*, which is dated to the late fourth or the third century BC.[155] The tremendous significance of his name first appearing in a Taoist, rather than a Buddhist text, will be revisited below. The earliest attested forms of his epithet are not "Sakyamuni" but "Sakamuni."[156] *Sakyamuni* is a later corrupted Sanskrit transcription of the term *Saka Muni*.[157] The description of Gautama as *Sakamuni* or "the Scythian sage" initially appears in Prakrit texts from the Gandhara region that may date back to the first century BC.[158] If the "Sakya" are the actually the *Saka*, then Siddhartha Gautama would not have been born in northeastern India near Nepal. Rather, he would have been from an area to the northwest of India, in Eastern Iran or Iranian Central Asia.[159] The *Saka* or Scythians were not just to the north of Persia, they were also wedged between Persia and India.[160]

From a scholarly standpoint, the only piece of evidence in favor of the story that Gautama was born in Lumbini, a more eastern part of northern India near the Himalayan border with Nepal, is an inscription that had been attributed to Ashoka but has since been exposed as a much later forgery, perhaps even one made in modern times.[161] Recent scholarship has revealed the Lumbini birth story as a whole to have been fabricated much later than the lifetime of Sakamuni or the Greeks who observed the earliest form of the Buddha Dharma during Alexander's campaign.[162] The name of the legendary hometown of the Buddha, Kapilvastu, means *vastu* or "settlement" of *Kapil*.[163] Where is "Kapil"? There is no "Kapil," but there is a *Kabul* right in the heart of the southeastern Scythian realm that was the matrix of the Buddha Dharma as a cultural-historical phenomenon.[164] The phonetic interchangeability of *p* and *b* in Persian and other Iranian languages is well known. A couple of prominent examples include the names of two of Iran's most well-known rulers in the Sassanian period, the female Shah *Purandokht*, whose name should actually be *Buran-dokht* (i.e. "blond maiden"), and the form of the name of Emperor *Shahpur* the Great that Mani employed when he dedicated a book to him titled *Shaburgan*. So Gautama's Saka clan was probably from Kabul, which was inside Iran's borders until the nineteenth century. It is presently located in Afghanistan, but remains a Persian-speaking city.

The epithet of the Buddha, namely *Sakamuni* or "Sage of the Sakas [Scythians]," must be considered together with the fact that Buddhist stupa architecture is based on the *kurgan* or Scythian-type burial tumulus found throughout Eurasia.[165] The stupa burial practices of Buddhists are modeled on the Scythian and Sarmatian burial of political leaders and war heroes in sacred mounds or *kurgans*.[166] Note the Scythian pointed-hat type shape of the structures. In the context of the fact that Scythian *kings* and conquering heroes were buried in such tombs, we have to revaluate just how literal the early Buddhists may have been when they gave Gautama the epithet "the Conqueror" or described him as a king.[167] An Indian sage or saint would never have been given a foreign epithet if he were not actually a foreigner, in this case a Scythian of Iranian ethnicity.[168] The Buddha and Buddhism are not Indian, but are Iranian in origin.[169]

Persian imperial documents from Central Asia and northern India attest to the introduction of Zoroastrianism into the Gandhara region by the Achaemenids.[170] One of the pieces of evidence for the impact of Zoroastrianism on northern India as early as the fourth century BC are Greek accounts of vultures descending on the deliberately exposed corpses of people in Taxila who refused to bury the deceased.[171] The presence of the Magi as far East as this Achaemenid satrapy was also documented.[172] In recent decades, scholarship has established that the *Upanishads* do not date to a period before Gautama. This requires us to reconsider the traditional view of Buddha's teaching as a critique of Hindu theological concepts. The macrocosm-microcosm relationship between *Brahman* and *atman*, or the aim to be reborn in Heaven due to good karma, are not the ideological backdrop for the Buddha Dharma.[173] There is no evidence that the *Upanishads* are as old as the period of Gautama, the Scythian sage.[174]

The Jains and other wandering ascetic sects did not exist before the time of Gautama, and consequently the Scythian sage knew nothing about them, nor did he encounter them in the course of his own quest for enlightenment.[175] In fact, it has long been argued that the history of India — as compared to its myths and legends — really begins with Gautama Sakamuni, the Scythian sage that would come to be seen, in retrospect, as the founder of the Buddha Dharma.[176] Just as the Upanishads are not older than the time of the Buddha, so the Rig Veda was not composed in India; it was brought there by Aryans. The Jains and other Indian sects manufactured stories regarding their gurus in order to make it appear as if their religions are as old as Buddhism, whereas scholarship has exposed these claims to be fraudulent.[177] The Buddhists themselves eventually accepted these false claims of the Buddha as the contemporary of Mahavira and other sages, so that they could depict Gautama defeating these other gurus in debates.

Buddhism only became "Indian" when, under the Mauryan King Ashoka, "India" expanded northwards into the Iranian territories that are now Afghanistan and Western Pakistan.[178] As we saw in the first chapter, the Persian term "Sistan" for the province of Iran closest to Pakistan and southwestern Afghanistan is a contraction of *Saka-stan* or "Scythian province." It refers to the Lower Scythian realm that was the true matrix of Buddhism. It is also referred to as Baluchistan and is currently home to an Iranian ethno-linguistic group known as the "Baluch" or "Baloch," who extend into Pakistan.[179]

Gautama came from a Scythian tradition of Shamanism wherein the Lion and the Sun were prominent symbols.[180] Clement of Alexandria describes the *Samanaioi* as the "philosophers" of the Bactrians or Kushans.[181] *Sarmana*, *samana*, *shaman* are all variants of the *Sramanâ* that were used throughout Scythian-dominated Central Asia and northern India.[182] The Sogdian, i.e. northeastern Iranian, term *saman* became *shâmen* in Mandarin Chinese.[183] In other words, at its origin, the "Shamanism" of Central Asia *is* the original form of what later came to be known as both 'Buddhism' and 'Taoism.' The Tokharians, who also have the word in their language as *samâne*, may have been a conduit for the spread of this Iranian spiritual tradition from Sogdian and Scythian Central Asia into the region of China that stretches from the Gobi Desert to the Tien-Shan Mountains.[184] There is no concretely datable evidence of "wandering" sages or saints before Sakamuni, and the Scythians were known throughout the ancient world as the quintessential "wanderers." In fact, their pattern of life perfectly fits the precise meaning of the word *nomad* in Greek, namely "wanderers in search of pasture, pastoralists."[185] The Scythians "invented mountain and steppe nomadism," just as their foremost sage, Gautama, was the pioneer of the way of life of the wandering sage.[186]

The archetype of the wandering sage has, for a long time, been epitomized by the putatively "Chinese" sage Lao Tzu. The man referred to as *Lao Tzu* or *Lao Tan* was intercepted by a "border control" official or "border post director" on his way out of China via mountain passes into Central Asia—which at that time, it bears repeating, was inhabited almost exclusively by ethnic Iranians of the Scythian and Sogdian cultures.[187] This border official is the person who compelled him to dictate what became the text of the *Tao Te Ching* before he left. In ancient China it was believed that *Lao Tzu* was a foreigner who, in old age, was leaving China in order to return to his native land so that he could die there.[188]

Tzu or *Tzi* simply means "master, philosopher" as in *Chuang-Tzu* or *Zhuang-Tzi* or even *Kong-Tzu* or *Kong-Tzi* the native Chinese name of Confucius.[189] The actual name of "Lao Tzu" was *Lao Tan*, which means "Old Long-ears" in Chinese.[190] "Lao" means old or aged in Chinese. Chang Chün-hsiang, a Tang Dynasty commentator on the Taoist texts tells us that the master's name was corrupted into *Lao* or "old" in the sense of sagacious so that it would be more familiar in Chinese, whereas his actual name was *K'ao-tan*.[191] He is in turn citing verbatim an earlier text, the *Shuo wen chieh tzu* from circa 100 AD, in support of this etymological claim. Furthermore, what is now pronounced *K'ao* in standard Mandarin was pronounced *Gau* in Early Middle Chinese, while *tan* was pronounced *tem* or *tam*.[192] So *Lao Tan* or *Lao Dan* is actually *Gautam*. Finally, Middle Chinese lost an *-a* that concluded disyllabic morphemes. Restoring this feature of the Chinese language spoken in the time that the *Tao Te Ching* was composed, we arrive at the conclusion that its author's name was *Gautama*.[193]

Now Gautama, the Scythian sage, is depicted almost universally in Buddhist art as having had long ears. Apparently, when this "wanderer"—who we already know traveled long distances like a good *Saka* nomad—spent time in the part of China neighboring Scythian Iran, he was very old. We do not even know if he was intentionally there to teach, since the *Tao Te Ching* was only written down in Chinese under the duress of a Chinese border guard who intercepted the Scythian sage on his way back home.

Add to this the fact that the word *Tao*, which is pronounced—and just as often also transcribed as—*Dao*, is a modern Chinese devolution of the Late Old Chinese word *Darwa*.[194] It devolved from *Darwa* to *Dawa* to *Daw* or *Dao*. *Darwa* sounds awfully close to *Dharma*, the term that Gautama used to describe his "path" or "way."[195] In ancient China, the thinkers and seekers that we now call "Taoists" considered themselves to be followers of the *Darwa* that was pioneered by *Gautama*. *Anâtman*, the denial of antilogies, and all of the other main features of the teaching of Gautama are reflected in the earliest texts that became canonical for Taoism, beginning with the *Tao Te Ching* of the man known to the Chinese by the epithet *Lao Tzu*.[196]

Scholars of Chinese culture have for a long time taken notice of how alien the spirit of "Taoist" ideas are to the mainstream mentality of China.[197] The latter is patriarchal, authoritarian, hierarchical, and collectivistic, whereas the *Tao Te Ching* introduces the spirit of anarchy, implicit matriarchy, egalitarianism, and free-spirited personal spontaneity into Chinese culture. It should be no wonder that this "Taoist" school of thought always remained a fringe phenomenon that was never attractive to more than a small minority of Chinese, as compared to the Confucian majority, who, it is relevant to add, also rejected Buddhism.

If Lao Tzu is Gautama, then the introduction of Buddhism into China—again, mainly by Iranian missionaries traveling the Silk Route from Scythia and Sogdia—is a second introduction of the same ideas into China. So it is no wonder that Taoism and Buddhism were hybridized by these Iranians in China and by an eclectic Chinese minority, such that the synthesis known as *Ch'an* or "Zen" emerged. This northeastern Iranian-infusion was also the matrix for the martial arts traditions of Shao Lin Kung-Fu and Zen Buddhism, which, given the world-renown martial spirit of the Scythians (and of their Parthian cousins), actually makes perfect sense when combined with a philosophical teaching like that of Gautama, which emphasized defense over offense and discouraged the use of weaponry.

Ideas that later concretized into "Taoism" appear in China during the

Warring States period (450–221 BC), shortly after the death of Confucius. Chinese Philosophy as a whole was inspired by Scythian influence, beginning with Gautama Sakamuni or "Lao Tzu."[198] This philosophical tradition is an anomaly against the broader backdrop of Chinese culture, which was then — and remains now — extremely worldly and utilitarian, therefore not given to contemplation of abstract or ethereal ideas, and also not given to philosophical debate on account of its deep conformism, collectivism, and deference to authority. By contrast, Iranian culture was then, and remains now, preoccupied with the ethereal and the unseen to a fault, and Iranians relish heated discussions over various questions, even just for argument's sake.

What Karl Jaspers got wrong in his "Axial Age" theory is that the various contemporaneous flowerings of sagacity are not, as he believed, mere parallels attesting to a parallel evolution of human consciousness in discrete geographical locations. Rather, they all had a common wellspring — the transcontinental phenomenon of Iranian Civilization, which extended into Greece in the West, and both India and China in the East.[199] In the West, it was the Medes and Persians who spearheaded Iranian intellectual and spiritual influence, whereas in the East it was the Scythians and Sogdians. The missing link to the putatively isolated culture of China throughout history is the Scythian and Sogdian part of the Iranian world.[200] This was the matrix of Eastern Philosophy, just as the Persian colonization of Ionia catalyzed Western Philosophy.

CHAPTER 3

EMPEROR OF NOBLE LIES

It is one of the most impressive archeological sites in the world. A massive bas relief carved into the rock cliff of a mountain at *Bagastana*, the name of which means "place of the gods."[1] The erection of monumental inscriptions on mountainsides and such, rather than inside palaces or on the walls of temples, begins with Darius the Great. The Behistun Inscription in the Kurdish region of Iran, near the city of Kermanshah, depicts Darius binding those responsible for regional revolts, including their leader — a certain Magus named "Gaumata" who had seized the throne of the Persian Empire. "Behistun" is a corruption from the Old Persian *Bagastana*, and is pronounced "Be-so-toon" in contemporary Persian.

The Behistun Inscription has been described by archeologists as being to cuneiform what the Rosetta Stone is to deciphering the hieroglyphs of ancient Egypt. That is because the relief features the same proclamation of Darius in three different languages: the Emperor's native Old Persian language, as well as Elamite and Babylonian. It is in this inscription that Darius famously, or infamously, affirms the Aryan racial identity of the Persian people. Darius may have continued the tolerant and benevolent policies of Cyrus toward the many different ethnic groups that he governed over, but he crushed attempts at secession and it is also clear that he saw himself as a paragon of the Aryan race. It is noteworthy that he refers to the language commonly known to scholars as "Old Persian" by naming it the "Aryan" language:

> Darius the King says: By the favor of *Ahurâ Mazdâ* this is the inscription which I made. Besides, it was in Aryan, and on clay tablets and on parchment it was composed…

I am Darius the Great King, King of Kings, King of countries containing all kinds of men, King in this great Earth far and wide, son of Vishtaspa, an Achaemenian, a Persian, son of a Persian, an Aryan, of the Aryan race.[2]

Allied troops of the Anglo-Soviet invasion of Iran during World War II damaged the Behistun Inscription by using it for target practice. Behistun was declared a UNESCO World Heritage Site in 2006.

Whereas the Cyrus Cylinder begins "In the Name of Marduk…," this monumental relief repeatedly describes Darius the Great as the executor of the will of Ahura Mazda. Darius the Great certainly presents himself as a Zoroastrian who rules justly in accordance with right order, reflecting the macrocosm of *Ashâ Vahishta* into this world in the form of the microcosm of *Khashatra Vairya*. Like a chivalrous spiritual aristocrat, Darius takes pride in neither being a rabble-rouser who allows the masses to do injustice to a capable elite, nor in permitting this elite to become drunk on its power to the point where it cruelly oppresses those who are incapable of defending themselves:

> A great god is Ahuramazda, who created this excellent work which is seen, who created happiness for man, who bestowed wisdom and activity upon Darius the King.
>
> Darius the King says: By the favor of Ahuramazda I am of such a sort that I am a friend to the right, I am not a friend to the wrong. It is not my desire that the weak man should have wrong done to him by the mighty; nor is that my desire, that the mighty man should have wrong done to him by the weak.

What is right, that is my desire. I am not a friend to the man who is a Lie-follower. I am not hot-tempered. What things develop in my anger, I hold firmly under control by my thinking power. I am a firm ruler over my Self.[3]

> For this reason Auramazda helped me, and the other gods who are: because I was not disloyal, I was not a follower of the Lie, I was not an evil-doer — neither I nor my family. I acted according to righteousness. Neither to the powerless nor to the powerful did I do wrong.[4]

By the close of this chapter, one ought to be left with a sense of why the Behistun Inscription can be considered the first constitution of Iran. What this also means is that Iran was founded upon lies. This is not any particular indictment of Iran. Every nation is founded upon lies, and that holds especially true of imperial nations. However, this observation is liable to rub many Iranians the wrong way only because Darius the Great places such an emphasis on the opposition to lies and liars in the Behistun Inscription. The rock carving is an impeccable example of the Zoroastrian view that deception is the most definitive hallmark of Ahrimanic forces.

The man who had it carved, namely Darius I, certainly deserves his epithet "the Great." The second of the great monarchs of Imperial Iran solidified the humanistic and free-spirited foundations of Persian culture by formalizing the proto-federal *Satrapy* system of government, which recognized cultural diversity within the limits of promoting human flourishing. The reign of Darius the Great also saw the establishment of the world's first credit-based banking system, standardized coinage, and the first "royal road" or paved highway system, on an intercontinental scale. This infrastructural innovation was used by the first reliable long-distance postal service. Qanats conducting water over vast distances underground allowed for agriculture and settlement in formerly arid lands. Other Achaemenid-period engineering marvels, which reflect the titanic spirit of Zarathustra's injunction to be industrious and earth-transforming, include the Suez Canal and an intercontinental bridge from Asia into Europe across the Bosporus.

Unfortunately for orthodox Zoroastrians, and for those who have idolized Darius the Great without appreciating his true genius as a statesmen, the Behistun Inscription tells the most colossal lie in history. This is the lie that Darius, and a number of co-conspirators, killed a usurper by the name of "Gaumata," a Magus who had seized the throne of Iran while Cambyses was busy conquering Egypt. There is reason to think that this "Gaumata" was actually Gautama Sakamuni, the "Scythian sage" who later came to be known as the Buddha.

The Behistun Inscription recounts how, after the military coup that deposed the Magus, Darius had to secure his rule over the Empire of Iran by putting down numerous secessionist rebellions with brutal force. Given his treatment of the rebels, the accounts that have come down to us of the killing of "Gaumata" are not believable. As we saw in the preceding chapter, recent scholarship places Gautama Buddha in the time and place of Darius the Great. He was an Iranian of Scythian descent who spent most of his life in Gandhara, the southeastern most part of the Persian Empire, not an Indian near Nepal.

What makes the theory that "Gaumata" was the Scythian sage Gautama all the more plausible is that the Buddha's entire teaching is a deconstruction of the core principles of Zoroastrianism. As discussed in Chapter 2, contrary to what was believed by the old school of scholarship on Buddhism, recent research has revealed that the Hindu philosophical ideas that Buddha was supposedly critiquing do not even predate the lifetime of Gautama. The *Upanishads* with their philosophical outlook on the relationship between Atman and Brahman and so forth are, at the very least, contemporaneous with Gautama if not considerably younger. The Buddha Dharma and Philosophical Hinduism were contemporaneous responses to the introduction of Zoroastrianism into the Indo-Iranian world that included northern India. As we shall see, Gautama's teaching is a sustained critique of the absolutist and perfectionist character of Zarathustra's worldview with a particular emphasis on the deconstruction of the idea of an eternal God and an immortal soul destined for Heaven, as well as of thinking in terms of antilogies and polarized moral valuations of binaries such as Light/Dark, Truth/Lies, Good/Evil.

Darius deposed Gautama because he considered the political philosophy that follows from this nihilistic deconstruction of Zoroastrian metaphysics and morality to be ruinous. It certainly borders on anarchism. What is interesting is that instead of executing Gautama, as he claimed to have done in the Behistun Inscription, Darius exiled the Scythian sage to the empire's frontier with India. This noble lie afforded Gautama the opportunity to go on to become a spiritual leader, the founder of the religion now known as Buddhism.

We gain even more insight into the character of Darius the Great when we consider why he would have done this, despite his generally ruthless authoritarianism. The key to unlocking this enigma is the invitation that Darius extended to the Ionian philosopher Heraclitus to come benefit from the patronage of the Persian court. As will be made evident in an exegesis of the *Fragments* of Heraclitus against the backdrop of Gautama's teaching, the worldview of the Ionian philosopher diverges from Zoroastrianism in many of the same ways as the Buddha Dharma. Yet there are a few significant differences that shed light on why Heraclitus received an invitation from Darius whereas Gautama was gifted with exile after a faked death.

3.1 Darius the Great Builder

The Empire of Darius included thirty different ethnic groups, and the Shah himself boasts of the cosmopolitan character of his realm that includes "all nations and languages."[5] However, despite this cosmopolitanism, the Shah of Iran did draw a clear distinction between the *Arya* or Aryans of his realm, which included the Persians, Medes, Bactrians, Sogdians, Scythians, and Sarmatians, and all of the various non-Aryans or *Anarya* who constituted the demographic majority of the Empire's fifty million subjects.[6] Non-Aryans had to pay higher taxes and were not recruited into the military in as large numbers as the Persians and various other Iranian (i.e. Aryan) groups.[7] The contemporary English word "data" comes, via Latin, from the Old Persian word *dâta* that signifies the concept of law and order that became central to the rule of Darius the Great.[8] Darius divided his Empire into twenty satrapies, each with a regional governor responsible for recruiting troops for the imperial military and collecting taxes for the royal treasury.[9]

There were at least five different types of taxes devised by the administrative bureaucracy of Darius.[10] The first was a land tax on properties that included estates, fields, gardens, and mines. The second was a tax on industrial production. The third was a tax on seaports involved in overseas trade and imports. The fourth was a tax on internal, land-based trade activities. The fifth was a sales tax. These taxes were collected by the governments of the satrapies and held in their local coffers before being transferred to the Imperial Treasury at regular intervals. Consequently one form of corruption must have been the withholding of some of the tax revenue from the Empire by regional governors. Evidently, any skimming off the top was so rare or so minimal that this system, the first of its kind on a vast imperial scale, functioned well for hundreds of years.

It is from these tax revenues that the administration would fund infrastructural development, such as the construction of roads and canals, as well as allocate defense spending on the Army and Navy, and, of course, pay the bureaucrats themselves.[11] There was an imperial organization for public works, which, among other things, coordinated the transport of workers over long distances.[12] Public works included bridges, aqueducts, drains, canals and reservoirs.[13] In a pioneering form of government-run social welfare or labor law, the regime of Darius the Great became the first in history to protect the working class from exploitation at the hands of their employers.[14] Tablets discovered at the Treasury of Persepolis reveal a government-imposed minimum wage and guidelines for the compensation of various classes of laborers.[15] Consequently, it could be said that the Achaemenid economy had both capitalistic and socialistic elements to its structure. This description is anachronistic only in the sense that it was the Achaemenid economic system that presaged, or perhaps even suggested, the latter development of both capitalism and socialism as they are practiced today. Skilled female laborers were paid equal wages to men, and women in the workforce who became pregnant were given paid maternity leave.[16] No other society would be so progressive in terms of labor policy until twentieth-century Europe and North America.

Such a progressive labor policy would not have been possible under a barter economy. Darius standardized monetary policy across his vast Empire. This innovation, and the associated development of the first credit based international banking system will be addressed in the next chapter. For now, suffice it to say that the corporate world of private banking begins in Achaemenid Iran under Darius the Great, especially at the administrative capital of the Persian Empire in Babylon. The check, and a credit-based banking system, is a revolutionary development that presumes a maximal trust society and security over intercontinental distances that would deter scammers from running off with real goods by writing an "I owe you" in bad faith.

One of the things that made this possible was Darius' construction of the world's first highway system, a well-planned broad and paved "royal road" (*Shâh Râh*) network that extended from Susa in southwestern Persia to Sardis in Lydian Anatolia.[17] This road system had 111 stations built along it, and it was regularly patrolled by military police who guarded against highway robbers and ensured the safety of travelers.[18] This highway was, in turn, used for the world's first postal system — another innovation attributable to the administrative genius of Darius the Great.[19] The Persian postal system consisted of post stations at regular intervals with fresh horses ready to gallop, so that whenever a horseback postal worker arrived, he would transfer his letters and parcels to another one who would relay them to the next station, and so on.[20] This system extended over an intercontinental scale, making use of the highways also constructed by Darius. The motto of this Persian postal system, that "neither snow nor rain nor heat nor gloom of night stays these couriers from the swift completion of their appointed rounds" was preserved by Herodotus and went on to be adopted as the slogan of the United States Postal Service centuries later. The royal roads were also used by the world's first formal intelligence service, with Darius' agents of espionage being known as the "Eyes and Ears of the King" (*Chasm-o-Goushé Shâh*).[21]

Darius allocated a large part of the imperial budget to the development of a vast system of underground irrigation canals called *qanats* (or *kanât* from the Persian root *kan*, "dig" or "carve").[22] The *qanats* were also means of creating the *paridaeza* in the midst of arid lands.[23] Greek authors of the classical period express their astonishment at all of a sudden discovering elaborate gardens and lush green zoological parks in the midst of arid or even desert terrain, paradises that had been created by the Achaemenids using the *qanat* technology.[24]

Zoroastrians considered plants, together with humans and animals, to be one of three fundamental forms of life that potentially expressed the goodness of the creator.[25] The creation of zoological parks and ornamental gardens was based on the Zoroastrian eschatological view that at the end of history all three of these types of beings would co-exist in perfect harmony, with all harmful creatures and unpleasant 'demonic' aspects of nature removed from their midst.[26] The *paridaeza* or "paradises" created at Pasargadae and elsewhere throughout the empire were intended to be heralds of this post-apocalyptic biosphere.[27] The usage of the term "paradise" to describe the Garden of Eden reflects the editing and finalization of this part of the Bible in a period after the Jews had come under Persian rule in Babylon and Susa.[28] The aromatic quality of carefully selected flowers in the botanical gardens of these paradises was also intended to repel the rank odor characteristic of the demonic beings and aspects of nature engendered by Angra Mainyu.[29] A botanical garden of this kind originally surrounded the tomb of Cyrus the Great at Pasargadae.[30] According to Elamite language tablets unearthed at Persepolis, those heading to pay their respects at the tombs of the Achaemenid Emperors at Naqsh-e Rostam also passed through a paradise that had been cultivated there.[31]

The vast geographical expanse of the Achaemenid Empire meant an equally diverse range of plants and exotic animals could be brought together in these paradises.[32] For example, it is the Persians who named the African giraffe (Old Persian *zaraffe*), which would have been quite a sight at zoos in ancient Iran. Importing bizarre animals also meant transplanting trees that were hitherto unknown to Iran. The skill and sophistication with which gardens were created by the Achaemenids is such that the paradises could even be seen as the first botanical laboratories.[33] To pillage a paradise was a crime on the same level as committing an act of war.[34] However, the Persians used some of their zoological parks as hunting grounds, where the youth of the aristocracy could also be trained to stalk prey on horseback.[35] Parts of these parks were probably also used to play Polo, the "sport of kings," which was invented by the ancient Iranians and, together with backgammon, which they also invented, was one of the favorite pastimes of the Iranian aristocracy.

These paradises are not to be confused with the much simpler Persian *chahar bagh* or fourfold gardens.[36] Such gardens, with their indication of the four cardinal directions of the globe, were incorporated into vastly more complex and sprawling paradises as a kind of compass.[37] The idea of an earthly "paradise" and the design of the bisected quadrangle garden or *Chahâr Bâgh* were both transmitted to the West from Iran, the former via the Greeks and the latter via an Arabian Caliphate that extended into Spain. The Spaniards and Portuguese subsequently brought it into the New World.[38]

Darius the Great was known for the greatest royal construction projects in Iran's history as well. The construction of Persepolis was one of the monumental undertakings that can be attributed to him.[39] The oldest structures on the site date to four years after the start of his reign. While the design of the entire site was his own, some of the key structures of Persepolis were only completed during the reign of Xerxes.[40] From the reign of Darius onwards, the King of Kings and his retinue would spend their winters at Susa, the spring at Persepolis, and summer in the high mountainous clime of Ecbatana (Hamedan).[41] Of course, long royal visits to Babylon were still necessary, since the majority of the administrative bureaucracy remained situated there. While he invented a special script for expressing Old Persian, Darius made the wise move of retaining the Aramaic lingua franca of Babylon as the administrative language of the Empire.[42]

Darius the Great is responsible for the tremendous geo-engineering feat of carving out the Suez Canal in order to connect the Red Sea to the Mediterranean and thereby afford a shorter route for naval forces and mercantile shipping from the Persian Gulf and Indian Ocean to European ports on the Atlantic Ocean.[43] Otherwise, one would have had to circumnavigate the entire African continent. This was not the only transcontinental engineering project of titanic scale that Darius undertook. He also had the first bridge built connecting Asia to Europe at the Bosporus, with two stelae boasting of the greatness of this task erected on each side of the bridge's entrance — one in Greek script and the other in cuneiform.[44] In his *Persica*, Ctesias claims that on his campaign against the Scythians, Darius entered continental Europe across this Bosporus bridge with a military force of nearly a million men marching with their armor.[45]

The Behistun Inscription extensively describes an initial campaign against the *Saka* during the course of which Darius took male and female Scythian captives.[46] After defeating them and their king, Skunkha, who is depicted bound as a prisoner of war in the Behistun Inscription, the "Scythians formed the backbone of the imperial forces together with the Medes and Persians."[47] However, the *Saka Tigrakhuda* or "Scythians with pointed hats" were only one small group of Scythians. A subsequent campaign by Darius the Great to conquer all of Scythia meets with a devastating defeat, which highlights the scale of tensions between the Persian Empire and the northern Iranian culture.

Darius' expedition into Scythia could be interpreted as an attempt to preempt or guard against another Scythian invasion of Persia and Media, comparable to the aforementioned Scythian invasion of the Zagros region that had taken place a century before.[48] One military objective of the Scythian expedition was to fix the Danube (i.e., the Ister) river as the north-western border of Iran.[49] Herodotus refers to the Danube as "the Ister," including when he recounts how Darius camped on the Ister during his Scythian campaign.[50] Of the Ister, he says:

> Darius came to this river and camped there, and because he was delighted with the river, he set up, here too, a stela on which he had engraved an inscription saying: 'The headwaters of the Tearus give water that is the best and most beautiful of all rivers. And to them came, during his campaign to Scythia, the best and most beautiful of all men, Darius, son of Hystaspes, king of the Persians and the whole continent.'[51]

The "Sauromatians," as Herodotus calls them, were part of the coalition of Scythians who fought against Darius.[52] The Persians also crossed "right through the Sauromatian territory" in their pursuit of the Scythians.[53]

Herodotus goes on to specify that the Sauromatians, Geloni, and Budini are subgroups of Amazons, and the only ones who backed the Scythians in their war against Darius, whereas "the Amazons" in general were unwilling to confront the Persians because they saw the Scythians as having brought the war upon themselves.[54]

Herodotus tells us that the "Scythian cavalry always routed the Persian cavalry, and the Persian would then flee for refuge to the infantry, who would help them."[55] At that point the Scythians would feign retreat and make what later came to be known as "the Parthian shot." After Darius taunts the Scythian king for an apparent retreat, Idanthyrsus claims to not be fleeing in fear from Darius, but to simply be engaged in his usual semi-nomadic migrations, seeing as the Scythians have no settled territory or towns to defend. He taunts the Emperor to find the Scythian "ancestral tombs" or *kurgans* if he really wants to come to blows, since the Scythians would fiercely defend the sanctity of these from being violated by the Persians.[56]

Many of the Greek city-states in the Hellespont, Ionia, and surrounding areas supported Darius in this expedition, since they faced a common threat in the Scythian semi-nomads who would occasionally rampage through their territories.[57] In fact, the humiliating defeat that Darius suffered at the hands of the Scythian forces has been seen by some scholars as a potential trigger for the Ionian revolt of 498–499.[58] This Ionian revolt became, in turn, the cause for Darius' vengeful desire to invade continental Europe — a project of imperial hubris taken up by his son and successor, Xerxes, with ultimately disastrous consequences.[59] In other words, the long-term impact of the Persian defeat at the hands of their Scythian cousins is part of the intra-Iranian dialectic that eventually led to the decline and fall of the Achaemenid Empire and the Greek colonization of Iran.

Herodotus portrays the defeat of Darius at the hands of Scythians in a manner consistent with the trope of the triumph of a free people over imperialism.[60] This conflict between the southern and northern Iranians may have had a metaphysical dimension. When Darius waged his unsuccessful war to conquer Scythia he may have been driven by the resistance of one particular Scythian to the Zoroastrian ideology that Darius wanted to turn into the backbone of his Empire. The Scythian campaign is a red thread that unravels the secrets to Darius' success as the ruler of the largest percentage of Earth's population that—to this day—has ever been governed by any Empire.

3.2 Darius the Great Deceiver

The tale that Darius the Great tells us about the rebellion of Gaumata and the conspiracy to dethrone him is featured in paragraphs 10 to 14 of the inscription at Behistun.[61] Some parts of Darius' own account of the rebellions against him that followed his overthrow—and alleged execution—of the magus Gaumata are quite shocking, especially if we are accustomed to thinking of the Persian Empire as founded on the benevolent humanitarianism of Cyrus the Great. For example, note the following sections of the Behistun Inscription, in which Darius appears to boast of his own brutal vengeance while at the same time (perhaps inadvertently) confessing his vast unpopularity, even in central Iran itself—let alone the far-flung provinces of the empire that Cyrus had built:

> (16) Darius the king proclaims: After I had killed Gaumata the magus, a man called Acina, son of Upadarma, rebelled in Elam. To the people, he declared this: "I am king in Elam." After that, the Elamites became rebellious; they went over to that Acina; he became king in Elam. And a man, a Babylonian, called Nadintabaira [Bab. Nidintu-Bel], son of Ainaira [Bab. Kin-zer], rebelled in Babylon; he lied to the people thus: "I am Nebuchadnezzar, son of Nabonidus." Then all the Babylonian people went over to that Nadintabaira; Babylonia became rebellious; he seized the kingship in Babylon.
>
> ...(21) Darius the king proclaims: When I was in Babylon, these are the people/countries who/which became rebellious against me: Persia, Elam, Media, Assyria, Egypt, Parthia, Margiana, Sattagydia, Scythia [Saca].
>
> ...(32) Darius the king proclaims: Then this Fravartish fled with a few horsemen. A place called Raga, in Media—he went there. Then I sent an army in pursuit. Fravartish was seized; he was brought before me. I cut off

> his nose, ears and tongue, and tore out one eye. He was held in fetters at my palace entrance; all the people saw him. After that, I impaled him at Ecbatana; and the men who were his foremost followers, those I hanged at Ecbatana in the fortress.
>
> ...(33) Ahura Mazda helped me; by the favor of Ahura Mazda, my army defeated that rebel army and took Cicantakhma prisoner, brought him to me. After that I cut off his nose, ears, and tore out one eye. He was held in fetters at my palace entrance; all the people saw him. After that, I impaled him at Arbela.
>
> (34) Darius the king proclaims: This [is] what has been done by me in Media.
>
> (35) Darius the king proclaims: Parthia and Hyrcania rebelled against me, called themselves [supporters] of Fravartish. Vishtaspa, my father, was in Parthia; the people abandoned him, became rebellious. Then Vishtaspa went forth with the army which was faithful to him. A place called Vishpauzati, in Parthia — there he joined battle with the Parthians. Ahura Mazda helped me; by the favor of Ahura Mazda, Vishtaspa utterly defeated that rebel army; twelve days of the month Viyakhna had gone [8 March 521 BC]; then the battle was fought by them.
>
> ...(43) Darius the king proclaims: Then, that Vahyazdata and the men who were his foremost followers — a place called Huvadaicaya, in Persia — there I impaled them.
>
> ...(50) I gave the order: that Arakha and the men who were his foremost followers were impaled at Babylon.[62]

Darius even has people executed on the mere suspicion that they might rebel.[63] The emperor also saw it as legitimate to exact vengeance against someone by arresting his entire household and killing innocent members of his family, in addition to executing the person himself. Darius publicly impaled Histiaeus, one of the Persian traitors who helped to organize the Ionian revolt.[64]

The Shah of Iran justifies his merciless crackdown on the rebellions against his military coup in terms that appear strikingly Zoroastrian, with repeated appeals to the authority of Ahura Mazda and characterizations of all of his enemies as promulgators of "the Lie." The tens of times that

Darius references "the lie," rebels "who lied," and his emphatic and repeated denial that he himself is lying, border on being pathological and unconscious admissions of guilt. Another explanation for such phraseology is that many of his contemporaries, whose voices were expunged from the historical record by his imperial power, alleged that Darius was the one who "lied"—and lied big. In any case, this ought to raise doubts about the veracity of the account with which we are being presented. Note paragraphs 52 to 76 of the Behistun Inscription of Darius the Great:

> (52) Darius the king proclaims: This [is] what I have done, by the favor of Ahura Mazda, in one and the same year, after I became king. I have fought nineteen battles. By the favor of Ahura Mazda, I defeated them and took nine kings prisoner. One called Gaumata, a magus, lied, saying: 'I am Bardiya, son of Cyrus'; he made Persia rebellious. One called Acina, an Elamite, lied, saying: 'I am king in Elam'; he made Elam rebellious. One called Nadintabaira, a Babylonian, lied, saying: 'I am Nebuchadnezzar, son of Nabonidus'; he made Babylon rebellious. One called Martiya, a Persian, lied, saying: 'I am Imani, king in Elam'; he made Elam rebellious. One called Fravartish, a Mede, lied, saying: 'I am Khshathrita, of the family of Uvakhshtra'; he made Media rebellious. ... One called Frada, a Margian, lied, saying: 'I am king in Margiana'; he made Margiana rebellious. ... One called Arakha, an Armenian, lied saying: "I am Nebuchadnezzar, son of Nabonidus'; he made Babylonia rebellious.
>
> (53) Darius the king proclaims: These [are] the nine kings whom I took prisoner in these battles.
>
> (54) Darius the king proclaims: These [are] the countries which became rebellious. The Lie made them rebellious, because these [men] lied to the people. After that Ahura Mazda gave them into my hand; as was my desire, so I did unto them.
>
> (55) Darius the king proclaims: You, who shall be king hereafter, be firmly on your guard against the Lie; the man who shall be a follower of the Lie—punish him well, if you think: 'May my country be secure!'
>
> (56) Darius the king proclaims: This that I have done, by the favor of Ahura Mazda, in one and the same year I did. You, who shall read this inscription hereafter, let what (has been) done by me convince you; do not think it a lie.

> (57) Darius the king proclaims: I will take Ahura Mazda's anger upon myself, that I did this truly, not falsely, in one and the same year.
>
> (58) Darius the king proclaims: By the favor of Ahura Mazda, much else has also been done by me, that has not been written in this inscription; it has not been written down for this reason: for fear that, whoever should read this inscription hereafter, it should seem too much for him, [and so] it should not convince him, [but] he think it false. …
>
> (61) Darius the king proclaims: If you conceal this record and do not proclaim it to the people, may Ahura Mazda be your destroyer and may you have no offspring!
>
> (62) Darius the king proclaims: This that I did, by the favor of Ahura Mazda, in one and the same year I did. Ahura Mazda helped me, and the other gods who are.
>
> (63) Darius the king proclaims: For this reason Ahura Mazda helped me, and the other gods who are: because I was not disloyal, I was not a follower of the Lie, I was not an evil-doer—neither I nor my family. I acted according to righteousness. Neither to the powerless nor to the powerful did I do wrong. Him who strove for my house, him I treated well; him who did harm, I punished well.
>
> (64) Darius the king proclaims: You, who shall be king hereafter—the man who shall be a follower of the Lie, or an evil-doer—to those, be not friendly, punish them well.
>
> (65) Darius the king proclaims: You who hereafter shall behold this inscription, which I have inscribed, or these sculptures, do not destroy [them]; as long as you shall have strength, care for them! …
>
> (67) Darius the king proclaims: If you shall behold this inscription or these sculptures, (and) shall destroy them and not, as long as you have strength, care for them, may Ahura Mazda be your destroyer, may you have no offspring, and, whatever you shall do, may Ahura Mazda let it go wrong for you!

As attested by Darius' own treatment of rebels, the established custom for dealing with treasonous usurpers who "lied" was to publicly execute them—sometimes even putting their mutilated or impaled corpses on display. In this context, we have to consider as most curious the account that Darius gives us of having killed the magus Gaumata in a Median fortress with no witnesses other than a handful of his own henchmen.[65] It is noteworthy that Darius admits that all of his loyal co-conspirators in the coup that eventually brought him to power were fellow Persians by ethnicity, with not a single non-Persian Iranian amongst them — whether Mede, Scythian, Sogdian, or otherwise.[66] Darius publicly displays the corpses of all of the regional rulers who revolt in the wake of his overthrow of Gaumata — and in many cases these are grotesque displays of his imperial authority — but he expects us to believe that he simply left Gaumata's corpse in the fortress, with no other witnesses to the magus' execution besides Darius' small band of co-conspirators? Historians of the caliber of Arnold Toynbee, A.T. Olmstead, and T.C. Young have all expressed profound skepticism regarding the account that Darius gives of these events — an account that these scholars agree is royal propaganda.[67]

The very fact that Darius faced no less than nineteen secessionist uprisings in reaction to his overthrow of Gaumata suggests that the so-called "usurper" was actually considered legitimate by all of these provinces and had peacefully held together the empire built by Cyrus the Great. This is confirmed by what Herodotus tells us about Gaumata or, as Herodotus calls, him "Smerdis," who reigned for a period of seven months, enjoying broad popularity:

> They were sure that Smerdis, son of Cyrus, had now come into the kingship, because Prexaspes insisted that he had not killed Smerdis; for, with Cambyses dead, it was not safe for him to say that he had, with his own hands, killed Cyrus' son. So, on Cambyses' death, the magus ruled unafraid for the seven months remaining to make up Cambyses' eight years. During this period, he did great kindness to his subjects, so that when he died, he was greatly missed by the whole of Asia, save the Persians. For the magus sent to all the peoples he ruled over announcing their freedom from military service and tribute for three years.[68]

Certain details of the biography of Darius the Great suggest that, despite his Zoroastrian rhetoric, he was actually quite a trickster. Herodotus relates that Darius was not the instigator of the coup plot against Gaumata. The seven nobles only dealt him into the conspiracy after it was already underway.[69] Otanes, who was apparently the instigator of the plot, was an extremely wealthy Persian aristocrat whose daughter, Phaidymie, had been one of the wives of Cambyses, and was now in the imposter's bed.[70] Darius soon takes the initiative by proposing a bolder and more rapid plan of action than Otanes. As the seven co-conspirators plot the demise of the magus Gaumata, the following exchange takes place between Otanes and Darius. Shockingly, we witness Darius unapologetically advocate the use of cunning deception — not only in this particular case, but in principle and as a legitimate alternative to honest but brute force:

> When Otanes saw Darius' vehemence, he responded: 'Since you are obliging us to move quickly and will not let us delay — come on then, tell us how we are to get into the palace and attack those men. Because, as you know, guards are posted all around; even if you have not seen them, you have heard about them. How are we going to get past them?'
>
> Darius replied as follows: 'Otanes, many things cannot be described in words, yet can be done; others can be described in words, yet no great deed has resulted. You know that it is not so difficult to get past the guardposts. None of them will refuse the likes of us, partly out of respect, partly out of fear. I myself have an excellent reason for getting in — I can say that I have just come from Persia and wish to bring my father's message to the king. When it is necessary to tell a lie, tell it! Whether we are liars or truth-tellers, we are all anxious to achieve the same thing. The liars tell lies in order to gain an advantage by persuading others with their lies; the truth-tellers tell the truth so that they will obtain advantages through their truthfulness and be more trusted. The practices differ, the end is the same. If there were no profit in prospect, the person who tells the truth might lie and the liar tell the truth. Now, whoever of the guards lets us in willingly, will be the gainer in time to come. Whoever blocks our path, let him instantly be declared an enemy; let us push him aside and go in to do our work.'
>
> After this, Gobryas spoke: 'My friends, when will there be a better time to take back power, or if we fail, to die? Seeing that we are Persians being ruled by a Mede, a magus…'[71]

Darius reiterates this philosophical standpoint during the affair of the elimination of Oroites, the governor of Phrygia, Lydia, and Ionia, who had not stood with the Persians against the Medes who had attempted to take back power from the Persians. Recognizing that Oroites had "a thousand Persians in his bodyguard," Darius remarks on the need to sometimes resort to subtly cunning methods rather than forthright force. In a convocation of his fellow aristocrats, he addresses them as follows: "Which of you, Persians, will undertake on my behalf a matter which calls for subtlety rather than force and large numbers. For where subtlety is what is needed, force is not appropriate."[72]

Also relevant in this regard is the account that Herodotus gives us of how Darius attains the kingship by trickery and cunning deception of his co-conspirators:

> Concerning the appointment of a king, they reached the following decision: they would ride out together the next morning into the suburbs of the city, and he whose horse neighed first after the sun rose should have the kingdom.
>
> Now Darius had a groom, a clever man, called Oibares. After the meeting had broken up, Darius said this to him: 'Oibares, this is the way we are going to select the king — we shall mount our horses and he whose horse neighs first, after the sun has risen, will get the kingship. Now, if you have any wit, contrive a way whereby I shall get the prize and not someone else.' Oibares replied, 'Truly, my lord, if that is what you getting the kingship depends on, relax and cheer up, because no one else is going to be king but you; I have a failsafe ruse.' Darius said: 'If you have something like that, then prepare it immediately and don't delay, because the competition is going to take place tomorrow.' Hearing this Oibares did the following: when night fell, he took one of the mares, which was the favourite of the horse ridden by Darius … he stroked the limbs of this mare and then hid his hand in his trousers. As the sun rose and they were letting the horses go, Oibares stretched out his hand and placed it close to the nostrils of Darius' horse; as the horse smelled it, he neighed and whinnied.
>
> Everything was full of Darius' power; and the first thing he did was to make and set up a stone monument. On it was the figure of a man on horseback and the inscription stated: 'Darius, the son of Hystaspes, by means of his horse's excellence (here he gave its name) and that of Oibares, the groom, gained the Persian kingship.'[73]

Clearly, despite his zealous Zoroastrian rhetoric of opposition to the Ahrimanic force of "the Lie" and those who "lied," Darius the Great was not averse to the strategic deployment of deception. Perhaps he considered his own deceptive stratagems to be "noble lies." This is a concept that first explicitly appears in Plato's *Republic*, specifically at 414c and 459d.[74] Plato describes noble lies as a kind of *pharmakon*, a "remedy" or medicine administered by rulers to the population for their own benefit. The concept originates in the practical experience of having to employ deception as a stratagem in warfare. If one tells all of the truth to one's own people, spies for the enemy will be apprised of the same information. Consequently, at least for the sake of defending against one's enemies, it is necessary to lie to one's own people about certain things.

Considering the fact that Plato was a member of the Pythagorean Order, and that the *Republic* argues that noble lies will be necessary to set up the kind of just aristocratic state that the Pythagoreans attempted to establish in Italy, we have to ask ourselves whether the idea of the noble lie originates with Pythagoras. The Pythagoreans certainly made use of strategic deception in order to govern the parts of Sicily where the initiates of their secret society gained influence. As we saw in the preceding chapter, Pythagoras studied with the Magi in Babylon for a dozen years before establishing his esoteric order. Could the noble lie be one of the concepts that he learned from the Magi? Gaumata, the alleged usurper of the throne of Cambyses, was a Magus at Babylon.

Could one of Darius' noble lies — the greatest of them — have been that he let "Gaumata" live in exile rather than actually having executed him as he claims to have done in the Behistun inscription? But why would Darius have done so? Who was this "Gaumata" really — and why was his, albeit brief, rule widely perceived as beneficent? Harvey Kraft has suggested that the deposed Magus-Emperor "Gaumata" of the Behistun Inscription is none other than Gautama, the Scythian sage.[75] Siddhartha Gautama lived from 563–483 BC and Darius the Great's life stretches from 550–486 BC, and so, whether or not they were rivals for the throne of Iran, these two Iranians of royal blood were in fact contemporaries — with Gautama being a mere thirteen years the senior of Darius.[76]

Was the rebel "Gaumata the Magus" really a Mede, as Darius claims in the Akkadian version of the Behistun inscription?[77] Perhaps he was assumed to have been a "Mede" because the majority of the Magi were Medes and the two terms, Mede and Magus, had become somewhat synonymous by the period of Darius — even though, by the same period, non-Medes had entered the Order of the Magi. As we saw in Chapter 1, there was a huge settlement of Scythians in Media in the century preceding Cyrus, and some of these Scythians played key roles in the administrative elite of Media. We know that there was a religious dimension to the rebellion of "Gaumata" and that, during his brief reign, he opposed Zoroastrianism.[78] If the Medes had accepted Zoroastrianism before the Persians adopted it, and if Zoroastrianism was in fact a religion of Median origin, what kind of Median Magus is this who destroys Zoroastrian religious institutions? "Gaumata" was seen as beneficent by most of his subjects, but he destroyed Zoroastrian temples.[79]

This Scythian sage pursued a career as a Magus in Babylon, the administrative capital of the Achaemenid Empire, where he eventually became Chief Magus of the temple complex centered on the Esagila Ziggurat — the main "tower of Babel."[80] Darius the Great describes "Gaumata" as a "stargazer," no doubt with the intention to insult him.[81] This epithet recalls the "House of the Raised Head," the name of the headquarters of the Magi in Babylon, the temple complex of Esagila, which was centered on the main ziggurat of the city.[82] As the tallest tower in a city of towering buildings, the "House of the Raised Head" was used for stargazing among other things.[83]

Gautama was put in power by the Council of Magi and ruled the Persian Empire for three to seven months, until Persian nobles led by Darius organized the coup to overthrow him.[84] The names "Siddhartha Gautama" and of his father "Suddhodana Gautama" appear on personal seals discovered at Persepolis.[85] The name *Sidh-Arta* means "Power of Truth" in ancient Indo-Iranian languages. In his attempt to depict Siddhartha as having a pacifying power even over animals, his canonical biographer, Asvaghosa, distorts Gautama's biography in order to conceal his violent struggle for power and near execution as a usurper of Iran's imperial throne.[86] One way in which Asvaghosa's biography does obliquely reflect reality is in its claim that Siddhartha was of royal descent, that he was a prince, who chose to reject his father's throne in favor of a life devoted to seeking wisdom.[87]

According to canonical biographies, there were nine unsuccessful assassination attempts on the Buddha.[88] This does not fit the biographical profile of a pacifistic wandering sage. However, it does make sense for an exiled Shah of Iran who is living as a fugitive even though, according to state propaganda, he was supposed to have been executed for treason. Perhaps there were those in Darius' retinue who believed his compassionate, noble lie to be a serious liability and who, consequently, took it upon themselves to send assassins in pursuit of Gautama. Maybe this is one of the reasons why he "wandered" so much. One can imagine that there would have been many attempts to finish the job, whether or not these were under Darius' own orders or those of bureaucrats fearing that the official story would be exposed as a lie, with the putatively Lie-punishing Zoroastrian emperor thereby unmasked as a masterful liar himself.

3.3 Gautama's Critique of Zoroastrianism

In the Zoroastrian scripture *Vi-Daeva-datta*, which was probably composed by the Magi late in the Achaemenid period and later came to be known as the *Vendidâd*, the dramatic persona of Zarathustra anachronistically identifies the Buddha as the introducer of an evil and demonic religion.[89] Meanwhile, from Gautama's perspective, the worship of Ahura Mazda was a cult devoted to appeasing a demonic *Ashura* (the Sanskrit version of the Persian *Ahura*) or "titan" whose claim to surpassing "wisdom" (*Mazda*) was intended to justify his vengeful wrath against equally unjust *Daevas*.

Let us consider some of the core teachings of Gautama against the backdrop of the fundamental precepts of Zoroastrianism. There are the "three characteristics" or *Trilakshana* that Gautama Sakamuni attributes to all *dharmas*, with the Sanskrit term *dharma* (or Pali *dhamma*) being equivalent to the Greek term *pragmata* or "thing, (subject) matter."[90] These three characteristics are *anitya*, *duhkha*, and *anâtman*.[91] *Anitya* is the privative of the Sanskrit *nitya* for "eternal, invariant, fixed," so that it means "impermanent, variable, unfixed."[92] *Duhkha* has often been mistranslated as "suffering" or "pain," but "unsatisfactory" is a more precise translation from the Sanskrit. It can be better understood with a view to its opposite, *sukha*, which is used to describe, say, the wheels of a chariot that are turning swiftly or smoothly, in other words, without a hitch. The original form of the word, in Sanskrit, rather than Pali, is *duh-stha* or "standing badly" in the original literal sense of having a bad axle-hole like a wheel that fails to turn properly, resulting in a rickety chariot. By extension it means being "unsteady, disquieted, uneasy."[93] *Anâtman* means "no (innate) self(-identity)," which is in effect a rejection of all absolutes such as good and evil, true and false, light and darkness.[94] This rejection is made explicit in the early Mahayana texts translated into Chinese by Kushan monks between 178 and 189 AD.[95]

If something is lacking in an innate self-identity it cannot be legitimately defined as the opposite of anything else.[96] Furthermore, when things change they always change in a context that involves other things, which means that any thing is not only lacking in self-identity, it is also inextricably interdependent with the things in its context that are defined as "other" than it.[97] This is what the Buddha referred to as "conditioned change" or dependent origination.[98]

Anâtman has the denial of opposites as its corollary.[99] The deployment of negating antilogies is one of the characteristics of the earliest Buddhist texts.[100] Sometimes, as in the *Pratyutpanna Samâdhi Sutra*, this kind of discourse includes an explicit statement about "everything being non-dual."[101] The antilogies can be as extremely amoral, as for instance in the statement, "Do not think of loveliness, do not think of ugliness; do not think of evil, do not think of good."[102] In addition to deconstructing the binary of good and evil, and denying the existence of both radical evil and pure goodness, this line from the *Pratyutpanna Samâdhi Sutra* pulls such a fundamental moral distinction down to the same level as subjective and socially conditioned perceptual distinctions relevant to aesthetic judgment. "Good" and "bad" are relative to context, intentions, and objectives.[103] In actuality, "good" always means "rather good" and "bad" implicitly means "pretty bad" or "not as bad." This psychological and social reality is covered over by the binary opposition of Good and Evil, wherein the absolute term Evil takes the place of what is only relatively bad from a certain perspective.

Gautama teaches that things have no inherent identity or essence that allows any thing to be definitively differentiated from any other thing; they are also unstable, unfixed, and always in a state of flux.[104] Perceptions are dreamlike and do not reflect any objective 'reality.'[105] This means that neither perception of things nor views on matters are absolutely reliable, and so objective knowledge is impossible, even if it is by means of induction, let alone deduction based on induction.[106] Induction, based on perception, is unreliable on account of its subjectivity, and deduction, when independent of induction, is circular in its logical structure, which means that we are left with no means of obtaining "true" knowledge.[107]

Once one has had this insight, the very distinction between "the Truth"—capital *T*—and "the Lie" can no longer be upheld.[108] This is, of course, the fundamental distinction of Zoroastrian doctrine, the opposition of *Asha* (Avestan) or *Arta* (Old Persian) to *Druj*, with the former being an expression of Ahura Mazda and the latter of Ahriman.[109] Zoroastrianism is "permeated with … dualism focused on antilogies, opposed ethical categorizations."[110] Absolute Truth, or putative knowledge of the ultimate nature of reality, is a category contrived by the human mind and imposed on a world of phenomena that can never really conform to such a perfectionist delusion.[111] From Gautama's perspective, the idea—or ideal—of Truth, which we meet with in its most pristine form in Zoroastrianism, is itself the biggest Lie in the history of human thought and spirituality.

Our deductive reasoning is based on inductive perceptions, which are subjectively skewed and perspectival perceptions of a world of things in flux and lacking inherent identities.[112] Our knowledge is so severely limited and imperfect that we cannot even rigorously demonstrate that the world, of which we claim to have knowledge, really exists at all.[113] It may be something like a dream, or hallucination. Even our belief—and it is a mere *belief*—in causality is derived from the experience of a certain effect usually following what we take to be its "cause."[114] If, on the basis of this inference that we make for practical purposes, we project a rational cosmic order including unerring laws of causation that will always produce the same effects, then we are massively deluding ourselves.[115] The current materialistic and mechanistic paradigm of scientific rationalism is based on this delusion. We can only ever imperfectly acquire and analyze imperfect data about an imperfect world.[116] The postulation of a Perfect Being, who in some way could grant us access to His mind, is an attempt to deal with this problem. That is why the Perfect Being appears in Descartes' *Meditations*, the founding text of modern science. The first form of this postulation was Zarathustra's projection of Ahura Mazda as the one true God or, put another way, as the God of Truth. The Zoroastrian idea of God is the background for Gautama's critique of perfectionism.[117]

If all dichotomous criteria, such as good/evil or just/unjust, are human constructs that project perfection onto an ever-changing and imperfect world, then neither does the God's honest "Truth" exist, nor is there any "Lie" so absolute as to not admit of some truth—even implicitly and against the conscious intention of the one who crafted it.[118] There is no criterion that distinguishes perfectly between true and false ideas.[119] Real honesty, authenticity, and integrity begin with recognizing this. One can always endeavor to be more honest with others by being truer to oneself, but not if one remains deluded by mistaking the construct of absolute Truth for an objective reality, in other words, not if one continues to be captivated by the delusion of real objectivity. In a sense, we are always lying to ourselves just by mistaking ourselves to have a stable and unified persona.

The ideas against which Gautama Sakamuni frames his teaching are as foreign to India, and for that matter to China, as the kind of de-constructive critique that he is engaged in.[120] Buddha was reacting against the absolutist and perfectionist ideas of Early Zoroastrianism in ancient Iran, not against the theology of Hindu Brahmanism.[121] Buddhism and philosophical Brahmanism are really parallel responses to the introduction of Zoroastrianism into the civilizational sphere of Greater Iran, including northern India, with the former being an internal Iranian critique of Zoroastrianism and the latter an Indian adoption of Zoroastrian ideas that do not appear in the earlier Vedic religion.[122]

The future resurrection of the human body in a perfected and incorruptibly everlasting form was one of the core teachings of Zoroastrianism.[123] The idea of *karma* and reincarnation in Paradise begins with Zarathustra.[124] All absolute categories and perfect concepts — the self/soul, an external world, even the idea of a Buddha — are imperfect human constructs and projections onto a 'reality' that is unknowable in the *epistemic* sense of knowledge that Persians refer to as *dânesh.*[125] *Dânesh* ought never to be confused with *xerad* or "wisdom." Getting stuck in a worldview based on absolute and perfectionist concepts is actually an obstacle to progress toward enlightenment.[126] Reason, namely *aql* or *manteq* (in Arabic) — what was called *cham* in ancient Iran — is another one of these perfectionist concepts. Just as *xerad* ought not to be conflated with *dânesh*, it should not be confused with reason or constrained by the limits of logic.

Rectilinear logic, the kind that has become definitive of rationality, has as its presupposition the absolute self-identity of the most irreducibly basic terms in any given proposition.[127] For any thing to exist as a discrete entity differentiated from any other entity, that being must possess an absolute and permanently enduring self-identity.[128] For the purposes of the most rigorous logical analysis, it was long assumed that "atoms" in the Greek sense of elementary and indivisible particles were these fundamental building blocks and, therefore, the basic terms of the most elementary logical propositions. One cannot assert that *if* A then B, if A is not A in the first place. That A is A and is not equal to Not-A has, from Aristotle onward, been fundamental to Logic.

Gautama's understanding of the way things are is, consequently, deeper than logic—if not 'illogical,' from the standpoint of a reductive rationalist. The Scythian sage thought that all of our logical argumentation is, in the end, circular rather than linear. This is not a defect. What it points to is the hermeneutic circle as the basic form of human understanding.[129] This circle that wraps us back around on ourselves and into the rounded maze of our persona is what gives us the capacity for introspection. There is no accessible or assessable 'Reality' outside of this circle of understanding that would afford us the opportunity to assess the validity of logical propositions. Nothing exists beyond the phenomena of our perceptions and the subjective thoughts that we have based on these appearances.[130] This also means that there are no *dharmas*, and so there is "in Truth" no Buddha Dharma.[131] Anyone who professes to be a Buddh*ist* or an adherent of Buddh*ism* does not understand the first thing about what Gautama Sakamuni taught.

Buddha taught that we ought to abandon our adherence to any and all dogmatic views.[132] The teaching of "right views" is wrongly attributed to the Buddha.[133] Gautama Sakamuni taught that *there are no right views* and every conception of "the highest knowledge" is indicative of a persistent attachment to "false science."[134] Cultivating the practice of holding no views leads to enlightenment. A true adherent of the Buddha Dharma would never claim to be following a superior *dharma*; he or she would be following a path that is no path at all, and would prefer no way that is opposed to some other way.[135] The significance of the term "Middle Path" is not moderation, let alone mediocrity. Rather, it is radical non-dualism.

Even the Four Noble Truths and the Eightfold Path do not appear to have been taught by Gautama himself.[136] There is no mention of them in Greek descriptions of early Buddhism as it was being practiced in the time of Alexander, and in any case they are too dogmatic and systematic to have been formulated by the Scythian sage. The teaching of Buddha is so negatively stated because it is a reaction against an absolutist and perfectionist worldview, namely Zoroastrianism, not the statement of a doctrine or dogma with positive content of its own.[137] Gautama's aim was a liberating deconstruction of "views," not a replacement of some views with others.

The state of affairs that Gautama deconstructs corresponds precisely to the characteristics that Zoroastrians attribute to both the pre-existent world of archetypes and the earthly realm after it has been purified and perfected by the *Frashgard*. It is a "perfect world, in which everything would necessarily be perfectly differentiated (i.e., self-identified), perfectly balanced, and perfectly fixed (i.e., eternal and unchanging)."[138] There is no reason to believe that such a world of ideas or forms actually exists. Although we have become accustomed to thinking of them as "Platonic" ideals, the concept of these archetypes or *fravashis* (Greek *eidos*, Arabic *mosul*) originates in Zoroastrianism. The point of departure for the entire Dharma of Gautama is a rejection, point for point, of all the core beliefs of Zoroastrianism.[139]

3.4 Darius and the Tao of Heraclitus

So why did Darius let him live? Why was Gautama allowed to go into exile and become "the Buddha" in Northern India instead of facing a death sentence together with all of those who took part in the rebellion led by the Scythian Magus? In order to answer this question, we must ask another: why did Darius the Great invite Heraclitus of Ephesus to philosophize at the Achaemenid court? Answering this question is relevant to addressing the other because the teaching of Heraclitus largely overlaps with that of Gautama. The traditional Persian image of Darius as a zealous Zoroastrian is also called into question by the Emperor's choice of Heraclitus to be his court philosopher.

In his biography of Heraclitus, Diogenes Laertius gives us the following account of the invitation letter that was extended to the Greek philosopher by the Shah of Iran as well as of the scathingly honest reply that Darius received from Heraclitus:

> King Darius, son of Hystaspes, to Heraclitus the wise man of Ephesus, greeting.
>
> You are the author of a treatise *On Nature* that is hard to understand and

> hard to interpret. In certain parts, if it be interpreted word for word, it seems to contain a power of speculation on the whole universe and all that goes on within it, which depends upon motion most divine; but for the most part judgment is suspended, so that even those who are the most conversant with literature are at a loss to know what is the right interpretation of your work. Accordingly King Darius, son of Hystaspes, wishes to enjoy your instruction and Greek culture. Come then with all speed to see me at my palace. For the Greeks as a rule are not prone to mark their wise men; nay, they neglect their excellent precepts which make for good hearing and learning. But at my court there is secured for you every privilege and daily conversation of a good and worthy kind, and a life in keeping with your counsels.

> Heraclitus of Ephesus to King Darius, son of Hystaspes, greeting.
>
> All men upon earth hold aloof from truth and justice, while, by reason of wicked folly, they devote themselves to avarice and thirst for popularity. But I, being forgetful of all wickedness, shunning the general satiety which is closely joined with envy, and because I have a horror of splendor, could not come to Persia, being content with little, when that little is to my mind.[140]

The Ionian philosopher's refusal is particularly poignant in light of his having eventually been reduced to wandering the hillsides of Ephesus and then dying while literally being covered by cow shit in an unsuccessful attempt at a remedy for the dysentery that he had gotten from feeding on grass and herbs.[141] Heraclitus' body was so caked with the manure that it became unrecognizable to wild dogs, who tore him to pieces. This is an ironic death considering his having lived for many years as a hermit in the temple of the goddess Artemis, the huntress who is accompanied by dogs in the wilderness.

As we saw in the previous chapter, there are a number of elements in the enigmatic *Fragments* that suggest Heraclitus was subject to Zoroastrian influence, and that may have given Darius reason to invite the Ionian to philosophize at the court of Iran. There are also political reasons why Darius would have invited Heraclitus to his court, especially after the Ionian revolt. In a textbook on Pre-Platonic Philosophy, Friedrich

Nietzsche writes of his beloved Heraclitus: "He was a merciless opponent of democratic parties; among this herd moved those rebellious to the Persians. Heraclitus, like his friend Hermodorus ... counseled against reckless measures against the Persians, and both were decried as friends of the Persians."[142] Nietzsche goes on to recount how, as a result of his loyalty to the aristocratic rule of the Persian Empire, Hermodorus was exiled, whereupon Heraclitus voluntarily left his home rather than see it ruled by the rabble after their rebellion against the noble Persian rule that he had lived under all his life. Heraclitus writes with utter contempt of his fellow countrymen: "What the Ephesians deserve is to be hanged, every one of them to the last man..."[143] His *Fragments* reveal that Heraclitus had a radically anti-democratic political philosophy that was very much in line with the ideology of Imperial Iran: "What wit or understanding do they have? They believe the poets of the people and take the mob as their teacher, not knowing that 'the many are worthless,' good men are few."[144] Heraclitus upholds the supreme worth of the superior individual: "One man is ten thousand, if he is the best."[145] He even endorses the rule of a single authoritarian sovereign: "It is law also to obey the counsel of one."[146] After abandoning his fellow Ephesians on account of their democratic rebellion, Heraclitus became a recluse in the Temple of Artemis. Although Heraclitus was an exceptionally loyal Persian subject and his *Fragments* appear to echo some of the key principles of Zoroastrianism, a closer look will reveal that the Iranian ideas in the writings of Heraclitus are actually evidence for a worldview substantively divergent from the Zoroastrian one. That this worldview is also Iranian in orientation, and to some extent shares a symbolic lexicon with Zoroastrianism, can lead to confusion. For example, the dialectical tension of opposed polarities is a major theme in the *Fragments* of Heraclitus. So one might assume that passages such as the following are evidence for the Ionian philosopher's acceptance of the Zoroastrian conception of cosmic war between Mazdean and Ahrimanic forces:

> One must realize that war is shared and Conflict is Justice, and that all things come to pass (and are ordained) in accordance with conflict.[147]

Homer was wrong when he said 'Would that Conflict might vanish from among gods and men!' [*Iliad* XVIII.107]. For there would be no attunement without high and low notes nor any animals without male and female, both of which are opposites.[148]

> War is father of all and king of all; and some he has shown as gods, others men; some he has made slaves, others free.[149]

However, setting these fragments in the context of the other references to dialectical tension within the writings of Heraclitus leads us to the conclusion that his thought is actually explicitly anti-Zoroastrian *in much the same way as that of Gautama*. That "Conflict is Justice" does not mean that, through a clash of morally valuated cosmic forces, 'Good' prevails over what we perceive to be 'Evil.' Rather, as Heraclitus sees it, conflict or war — as the proverbial father and king of this world — decides the value of things based on their relative strength. Moreover, any thing or idea that proves itself is entirely indebted to what it prevails against in the perpetual conflict that defines the nature of all things. What proved to be lower and was enslaved to the higher is not on that account an 'Evil' that the 'Good' prevailed over.

"Justice" has absolutely no moral valuation for Heraclitus. As can be seen from the following fragments, human opinions with respect to what is "just" or "unjust" have about the same seriousness as children's toys, when viewed from the perspective of the *Aeon* or highest god of the life force and cosmic time, who is akin to a playing child:

> Human opinions are toys for children.[150] For god all things are fair and good and just, but men have taken some things as unjust, others as just.[151] If it were not for these things, they would not have known the name of Justice.[152] The *Aeon* is a child at play, moving pieces in a game. Kingship belongs to the child.[153]

The literal translation from Greek of the kind of *pesseuon* or "playing" that this *Aeon* is involved in, refers to *pessoi* — a board game involving dice that is an ancient predecessor of backgammon. Persian kings invented backgammon. To be truly sovereign in life is to adopt the attitude of the *Aeon*, to try to see things from the perspective of the life force as it manifests the cosmos from out of primordial chaos over the course of cosmic time. If we were to do so, we would realize that the opinions we form about certain things being "good and just" and others being evil and unjust are not true to the nature of things.

From a cosmic perspective, all those things which we consider injustices inflicted upon us are necessary evils without which we would be incapable of discerning or appreciating everything that we value in positive terms. Moreover, our valuations are all-too-human. Attention to how differently various animals in nature value certain things can disabuse us of our notions of the intrinsic worth of, say, gold, or the intrinsic foulness of mud. Zoroastrianism is full of such intrinsic valuation, with the *Vi-Daeva-datta* (i.e. *Vendidâd*) demonizing entire classes of animals as the filthy, impure creations of evil forces hell-bent on perverting the cosmic order of the "Good Creation."[154] It is actually the duty of a pious Zoroastrian to purify the Creation by exterminating such ungodly creatures as snakes, frogs, and lizards.[155] This is very far from how Heraclitus evaluates the natural world and the variety of beings who populate it with their divergent habits:

> It is not better for human beings to get all they want. It is disease that makes health sweet and good, hunger satiety, weariness rest.[156]
>
> The sea is the purest and foulest water: for fish drinkable and life-sustaining; for men undrinkable and deadly.[157] Asses prefer garbage to gold.[158] Swine delight in mire more than clean water; chickens bathe in dust.[159]

Nevertheless, Heraclitus is not a naïve naturalist. Nowhere does this come across more clearly than in his suggestion that we, human beings, are somehow collectively dreaming the world that we experience every day, i.e. when we believe ourselves to be awake. Interpreting the following fragments, which are among the most cryptic in the surviving corpus of Heraclitus, further calls into question any mistaken identification of his worldview with Zoroastrianism. It also deepens his affinity with the insights of Gautama, the Scythian sage. After all, even those who know very little about it, would come to know Buddhism for the idea that "life is but a dream" woven out of our *karma*.

> [M]en are oblivious of what they do awake, just as they are forgetful of what they do asleep.[160] Although the account is shared, most men live as though their thinking were a private possession.[161] The world of the waking is one and shared, but the sleeping turn aside each into his private world.[162] Thinking [*to phroneein*] is shared by all [things].[163]
>
> Death is all things we see awake; all we see asleep is sleep.[164] A man strikes a light for himself in the night, when his sight is quenched. Living, he touches the dead in his sleep; waking, he touches the sleeper.[165]
>
> Men asleep are laborers and co-workers in what takes place in the world.[166] Immortals are mortal, mortals immortal, living the other's death, dead in the others' life.[167] The same: living and dead, and the waking and the sleeping, and young and old. For these transposed are those, and those transposed again are these.[168]

Interpreting the esoteric meaning of these cryptic sayings is difficult indeed. Here, the notoriously enigmatic Heraclitus is at his most obscure. What he seems to be saying is that when we are literally asleep we are actually very active. The fabric of this world that we experience every day is woven out of our dreams, collectively. "Thinking is shared by all things," means that consciousness — or the collective unconscious — cannot be separated from (what we take to be) the 'physical' world. What we perceive as life is really death, in other words, a realm of transitory phenomena and perpetual decay. We are sleepwalkers in this world — zombies touching other zombies. Ironically, we are more alive and have a greater capacity to be conscious while we are literally asleep. Perhaps Heraclitus has the phenomenon of lucid dreams in mind. We can wake up to the reality of the dreamer, who is actually an immortal dreaming his life as a mortal.

The experience of this immortal, waking state is, moreover, not one of individuated egos. Only when we are, metaphorically "asleep" do people mistakenly "live as though their thinking were a private possession." The individuated ego exists only as part of the illusion of the "private world" or *idios cosmos* of the dreamer — who is an *idiot*, in the literal Greek sense of the word. It covers over the *koinos cosmos* or "world of the waking" that "is one and shared." Heraclitus also seems to refer to the difference between the time frame of waking life and the experience of time in dreams. An old person, when dreaming, can relive her youth, and a young man can dream a whole life through to his old age and death in but a few hours of a single night. If we apply this phenomenological observation concerning dreams to the metaphor of this life as a dream, then it seems that Heraclitus is suggesting that our youth and eventual old age in this world are dreamlike appearances. They are aspects of a death mask concealing the immortal Aeon's face, which we would recognize as our own if we would only wake up.

While it is true that Heraclitus uses the same metaphor as Zoroastrians in order to evoke the ultimate nature of reality, namely an eternal fire, he also uses the metaphor of ever-flowing water. Interestingly, fire and water when taken together as symbols of the divine do evoke an Iranian context, but not a Zoroastrian one. Water is the element of Anahita, the goddess figure that is the feminine counterpart of Mithra who, in the Mithraic tradition preceding Zoroastrianism, was already associated with fire. A closer look at the way in which Heraclitus understands all things to be interchangeable with fire shows that it is precisely in the same way, and for the same reason, as he famously asserts that it is impossible to step into the same river twice. Both fire and water are symbols of perpetual flux in Heraclitus:

> It is wise, listening not to me but to the report [*Logos*], to agree that all things are one.[169] All things are requital [*antamoibe*, exchange; payment; punishment] for fire, and fire for all things, as goods for gold and gold for goods.[170]
>
> As they step into the same rivers, other and still other waters flow upon them.[171] One cannot step twice into the same river, nor can one grasp any mortal substance in a stable condition, but it scatters and again gathers; it forms and dissolves, and approaches and departs.[172] It rests by changing.[173]

The remarks that "all things are one" according to "the report" or *Logos*, the underlying pattern that determines the nature of things, should be considered together with the statement that this One "rests by changing." This is as much as to say that there is a unity of being—not despite, but throughout the course of the transformation of all phenomena. All apparent change is change *in the element of fire*, or to use the symbolism of Mithra's mother and consort, *in the element of water*. Like the fire that is one and the same as its flames twist and turn into a variety of unstable forms, water endures elementally while morphing into all manner of ever-flowing shapes.

This instability is a direct parallel to the *Anitya* concept of Gautama and, as in the case of the Scythian sage's teaching, Heraclitus also sees that the "impermanent, variable, unfixed" character of any given phenomenon is inextricable from both its apparent strife with respect to other phenomena and also its lack of any inherent identity that would definitively demarcate it as a being that is essentially independent of all other beings. What Gautama terms *duhka* and *anâtman* are expressed together with *anitya* in these fragments of Heraclitus:

> The beginning and the end are shared in the circumference of a circle.[174] The way up and down is one and the same.[175] Cold warms up, warm cools off, moist parches, dry dampens.[176]

The counter-thrust brings together, and from tones at variance comes perfect attunement, and all things come to pass through conflict.[177] They do not comprehend how a thing agrees at variance with itself; it is an attunement turning back on itself, like that of the bow and the lyre.[178] The name of the bow is life; its work is death.[179] The hidden attunement is better than the obvious one.[180]

> The god: day and night, winter and summer, war and peace, satiety and hunger. It alters, as [fire] when mingled with perfumes, it gets named according to the pleasure of each one.[181] Graspings: wholes and not wholes, convergent divergent, consonant dissonant, from all things one and from one thing all.[182]

These passages make it perfectly clear that Heraclitus was not a Zoroastrian. What the Ionian philosopher is expressing here is that all states of tension in nature and society, all apparent binary opposition and conflicts based upon the semblance of polarization, are actually manifestations of a dialectical tension that is wholly divine. The unity of being is a "hidden attunement" that Heraclitus calls "the god"—as in the highest god, namely the Aeon compared to a playing child in the quote above. This is an "attunement turning back on itself" in the way that the "beginning and end are shared in the circumference of a circle." All counter currents share a hidden source and end that is the wellspring of all things, whether they are perceived to be Light or Dark, Beautiful or Ugly, Good or Evil.

Recall that Gautama's teaching deconstructs all clear-cut dichotomies between Truth and Lying, Justice and Injustice, Good and Evil, Beautiful and Ugly, or Light and Darkness.[183] That this deconstruction is expressed by Heraclitus in a context that includes the metaphor of ever-flowing water, and of the hidden oneness of other merely apparent polarizations in nature, brings to mind the *Yin-Yang* symbol of the Chinese. Given the speculations in Chapter 1 on the rule of Iranian Dragon Kings in ancient China, and given the fact that the oldest example of the *Yin-Yang* symbol is actually one that has been found on a Roman shield, from the period after the Sarmatians and Scythians began to serve in the Roman military in large numbers, one has to wonder whether the *Taijitu* is also an originally Iranian symbol. For Zoroastrians in Persia, the metaphysical dualism of Light vs. Darkness was absolute and reflected in a moral dualism of Good vs. Evil, whereas for the Amazon devotees of Artemis it seems to have been a relative dualism in the context of which the conflict between opposed forces conceals a deeper harmony, and even war is seen as generative, as an expression of the fiery life force, without any simplistic moral evaluation.

The *Taijitu* or *Yin-Yang* symbol is most commonly associated with Taoism. Much of the *Tao Te Ching* and the *Chuangtzu* concern themselves with the deconstruction of supposed opposites, such as beauty and ugliness or light and dark.[184] Chapter 2 of the *Tao Te Ching* begins with these antilogies: "When the whole world knows beauty as 'beautiful', 'ugly' arises. / When all know 'good', 'evil' arises. 'Existence' and 'nonexistence' are born together."[185] As can be seen from the last of these quoted verses, the deconstructed antilogies are not only ethical in nature but also involve the most fundamental ontological categories. The deconstruction of such categories is often based on the insight that no thing has a self-identity.[186]

So we come back to the question: Why did Darius let Gautama live? The question can now be modified as follows. If the teaching of Gautama—or "Lao Tzu"—has so much in common with the philosophical standpoint of Heraclitus, why did Darius exile the Scythian sage but offer the patronage of the Persian court to the devotee of Artemis? Was Darius so naïve and undiscerning that he mistook Heraclitus for a Zoroastrian? Given his brilliance as an administrator, tactician, and, quite frankly, as a slyly cunning and duplicitous schemer, this is highly unlikely. Darius was many questionable things, but he was no dimwit. The man was a genius, maybe the greatest genius in the entire history of statecraft. So our operative assumption ought to be that he knew exactly what he was doing. He probably had the Magi parse every line of Heraclitus' treatise *On Nature* before dictating that invitation letter to his scribes.

Why would Darius have invited Heraclitus if these Magi came to the conclusion that, superficial symbolic affinities aside, the Ionian philosopher was anti-Zoroastrian? Well, because Darius had just enough respect for the Magi to have slaughtered them as his first sovereign deed, and then, to rub it in, to inaugurate a yearly public holiday celebrating this massacre. It was a day when the Magi had to hide indoors in fear that people, with the backing of Darius, might murder any Zoroastrian priest that they set their eyes on. "The seven" in this passage from Herodotus refers to Darius and his co-conspirators against Gaumata:

> At the same time, they killed every magus they came across. When the Persians discovered from the seven what had gone on and how the magi had deceived them, they did the same: they drew their daggers and killed every magus they found. If night had not fallen, they would not have left any magi alive. This day the Persians celebrate publicly more than any other and hold

> a great festival on it. It is called 'The Killing of the Magi' by the Persians. On that day, no magus dares to go out in daylight, but must spend the day in his house.[187]

What kind of zealous Zoroastrian institutes a national holiday celebrating his mass murder of the Magi? Now, a Zoroastrian might argue that these Magi, like the rebel Magus Gaumata, were not yet Zoroastrians. But if the Magi had *not yet accepted* the message of Zarathustra *even by the time of Darius the Great*, then that makes it unlikely that Zarathustra even lived before the time of Cyrus. The view adopted by the opening chapter was that Zarathustra was a revolutionary figure of the Median Kingdom, and that the predominately Median Magi brought this religion to Persia as part of the unification of Media and Persia. If, on the other hand, Darius the Great is the one who first forces the Median Magi to convert to Zoroastrianism — literally at the point of a sword — then we would have good reason not to so readily dismiss the suggestion that the Vishtaspa named as Darius' father is the very same Vishtaspa who was the patron of Zarathustra. The fact that Zarathustra lived — and died — in a royal court that was situated on the border with Turan, in other words somewhere in present-day Khorasan on Iran's border with Turkmenistan, is not necessarily an objection either.

The Achaemenid clan was known to have ties to Central Asia, and possibly even originated there before migrating to Persia.[188] It is not my intention to seriously advance this as an alternative hypothesis of *a Persian Zarathustra* writing in a much more archaic language than his native Old Persian, for the same reasons having to do with theological authority that were given in Chapter 1. Rather, my point is that any orthodox Zoroastrian insistence that the Magi who were slaughtered, and thereafter ritually intimidated, by Darius the Great were not Zoroastrians, meets with more serious problems for the person who wants to defend an idealized conception of Achaemenid Iran as a Zoroastrian Empire.

If Darius the Great was such a zealous Zoroastrian that he first forcibly converted the Magi to Zoroastrianism, then we have all the more reason to ask: Why did he lie about executing Gautama? Why not actually execute a Scythian sage whose entire teaching revolves around a radical deconstruction of Zoroastrianism? Moreover, why lie about so many other things? Why make systematic use of deception — the highest sin in Zoroastrianism — both in order to come to power and in order to maintain his authority? What kind of zealous Zoroastrian is this consummate con-artist? Finally, to state the question for the third time: if he was *such a zealous Zoroastrian that he converted the Magi himself*, what is the meaning of inviting Heraclitus to philosophize at his court?!

He was not a zealous Zoroastrian. Darius enjoyed celebrating his mass murder of Zoroastrian priests every year, watching them cower in fear that he might publicly impale or dismember them as he did with so many others who refused to bow to his authority. Darius was not some Achaemenid prototype of Ardeshir Babakan, who institutionalized Zoroastrianism as Iran's state religion when he founded the Sassanian Empire. The greatest monarch of the Achaemenid Empire was a thinker who understood the naked reality of imperial power. Zoroastrianism is *useful* to him — useful *to him*. He gets to decide when and in what ways it is useful — not the Magi and not even Ahura Mazda.

Darius invited Heraclitus to the court of Iran because the *Fragments* reveal exactly the same understanding of power and the true nature of "Justice" that the Shah had arrived at himself on the basis of his experience as a soldier and statesman. By contrast, despite its extensive overlap with the metaphysics and epistemology of Heraclitus, when it comes to drawing conclusions about political philosophy from this insight into the nature of the world and the limits of knowledge, the teaching of Gautama is catastrophically naïve. The Scythian sage, who potentially also authored the *Tao Te Ching*, was basically an anarchist — or at least an extreme libertarian. Note these telling verses from the *Tao Te Ching*:

> Trying to govern the world with force / I see this not succeeding / the world is a spiritual thing / it can't be forced / to force it is to harm it / to control it is to lose it[189]

> [T]hose who know how to be perfectly still / are able to govern the world[190]

> Use nonaction to rule the world / how do we know this works / the greater the prohibitions the poorer the people / the sharper their tools / the more chaotic the realm / … the better their possessions / the more numerous the thieves / thus does the sage declare / I make no effort / and the people transform themselves / I stay still / and the people correct themselves / I do no work / and the people enrich themselves.[191]

First of all, these passages are further evidence that "Lao Tan" or *Gau-Tam* was in fact the Scythian sage who, albeit briefly, ruled the Persian Empire. Why would some random Chinese sage be phrasing things in terms of "ruling the world"? In the time when the *Tao Te Ching* was composed, and for a long time afterward, the only nation that had ever come close to ruling the world was Iran. China was provincial by comparison. The problem of administering the entire known world was a uniquely Iranian problem. Considering how brief Alexander's rule was before his heirs broke up the Empire that he inherited from the Achaemenids, world government remained a uniquely Iranian problem until the formation of the British Empire in the early modern period. The Roman Empire and other realms preceding British colonialism never managed to forge a World Order comparable to the one that was established by Darius the Great.

Gautama was going to wreck the Empire of Iran before it even had a chance to crystalize a sense of Iranian national identity. It is true that Gautama was widely seen as a beneficent ruler and that he was able to hold the empire of Cyrus together through this beneficence. However, the secessionist revolts that followed the military coup in which Darius deposed him demonstrate the fundamental flaw of this kind of governance. Many of these secessionist rebellions took place on the basis of ethnic identity. Beneficence does not transform tribalism into national identity. One cannot opt to be a part of a nation, or opt out of being part of it whenever one so chooses. Nations are forged in the fire of war, including and especially civil war, and they are baptized by sacrificial blood.

As was argued in Chapter 1, Cyrus the Great conceived of "Iran" as a nation. But this synthesis of Persian, Median, Scythian, and other hitherto disparate and warring Aryan tribes into a single nation, recognizable to itself as a morally unified community, remained a mere conception. The idea of Iran was suspended in a vulnerable embryonic stage until Darius forged "a more perfect union" in a manner akin to the fascistic Abraham Lincoln during the American Civil War. By refusing the right of secession from the realm, Darius cemented Iran's national identity and secured Iranians a peerless place in world history. Actually, before *his* Iran, there had been only the local histories of diverse peoples. Darius *invented* "world" history. So we call him "Great."

CHAPTER 4

TEKEL TEKEL, MENE SHEKEL

THE GREAT UNFINISHED BUSINESS OF Darius was his invasion of mainland Greece, putatively to punish the Athenians for the burning of Sardis. Darius himself made all of the initial preparations for the military campaign to conquer Greece and march into continental Europe, but he died before being able to carry out the operation under his own command. Herodotus writes:

> The message about the Battle of Marathon came to King Darius, son of Hystaspes, who was already enraged against the Athenians because of their attack on Sardis. So he was now more furious than ever and even more resolved to march against Greece. He immediately sent messengers to each city ordering them to prepare a much larger force than before, as well as ships, horses, grain and vessels. As a result of these demands, Asia was astir for three years, with the best men enrolled for service against Greece and getting ready. In the fourth year the Egyptians, who had been subjugated by Cambyses, revolted from Persia. ... But in the next year after this, and after the revolt of Egypt, when he was in the middle of his preparations, it happened that Darius died after a reign of thirty-six years.[1]

In his *Persica*, Ctesias tells us that Darius the Great died after an illness of thirty days duration, and that his death was followed by that of some of his closest companions.[2] In the end, twelve of Darius' sons, who were brothers and half-brothers of Xerxes, would wind up participating in this military campaign that he planned in the last several years of his reign.[3] One can imagine that being the son of Darius the Great and having a mother who was a daughter of Cyrus the Great would make for pretty big chips on the shoulders of Xerxes, who inherited these war plans from his father.

Xerxes has often been portrayed as mercurial—by turns wrathful, easy to charm, cruel, ostentatiously generous, hedonistically lustful, and deeply mournful.[4] He was given to existential brooding on the tragedy of the human condition, which he seemed hell-bent on defying by reaching for the impossible.[5] Xerxes is the quintessential "mad emperor" of Achaemenid Iran, who was remembered for having defied even the gods of the elements.[6] When the first version of the titanic bridge across the Hellespont was destroyed by a storm, Xerxes not only had the chief engineer executed, he also ordered the sea to be lashed three hundred times and had his men throw a pair of shackles into it.[7] He expected the elements of nature to be as obedient to him as his subjects.

In the course of his retreat from Europe, in November of 480 BC, Xerxes ran out of supplies on land and had to be ferried back to Asia by ship. While still in the northern Aegean Sea, a terrible storm hit and it became necessary to lessen the weight being carried by the vessel so that it did not sink. The captain had allowed the ship to be overloaded and had not taken the seasonal weather under consideration. (Supposedly, even today, that part of the Aegean is prone to bad storms in the late fall season.) Amidst the crisis, Xerxes addressed his fellow passengers in this fashion: "Now you have an opportunity to show how much you care for the safety of your king."[8] Most of the passengers made haste to throw themselves overboard and so drowned to save the emperor. When they reached Asia safely, Xerxes awarded the captain with a gold medal for saving his life. Then, while the captain was basking in such an undeserved honor, Xerxes had him seized and executed for recklessly costing the lives of a boatload of Iranians.[9]

The arrogance—even hubris—of Xerxes was renowned. When he arrived at Thermopylae, Xerxes did not order his forces to attack the Greeks right away. He waited for four days, expecting that the measly Greek force would simply be scared off by the sight of his massive army. This tactical blunder on account of his hubris allowed the 300 Spartans to receive a reinforcement of about 7,000 hoplites.[10] Offended at the insolence of the Greeks, who would dare put up a fight even in the face of such odds, he sent a message to Leonidas instructing him to have the Greeks lay down their weapons. Leonidas' reply has become famous. *Molon labe*, he said — "Come and get them!"[11] Although Xerxes eventually prevailed at Thermopylae, there would have been far fewer Persian casualties if Xerxes had attacked immediately. In the end Xerxes lost 20,000 men, including two of his own brothers.[12] The piles of Iranian bodies were so high that he had to rush to have them buried before allowing the rest of his army and then his navy to advance over the territory of Thermopylae, so that they would not be demoralized by the sight.[13] He left only a thousand Iranian corpses on display, together with the bodies of the dead Spartans — including and especially Leonidas, who was mutilated with his head mounted on a pole.[14]

Both Xerxes and his wife were infamous for sadistically cruel punishments.[15] Xerxes had a disastrous affair with the wife of his brother Masistes, and then with their daughter, his niece Artaynte.[16] Xerxes foolishly gave this niece and lover a shawl that his wife had woven as a birthday gift to him. When the queen saw this she was brimming over with betrayal and jealous wrath, but instead of punishing the niece she decided to take it out on the girl's mother, whom she believed to have been responsible for orchestrating the affair between Xerxes and her daughter so as to deflect her brother-in-law's lust for her.[17] Amestris summoned her personal guard and punished Masistes' wife by having them slice off her breasts and throw them to ravenous dogs. She then cut off the woman's nose, her ears, lips, and tongue before sending her back home to Masistes to live out the rest of her life totally mutilated and disfigured.[18] What kind of man does one have to be to live with a wife who behaves in such a fashion? It says a lot about Xerxes. Afterward, Masistes attempted to flee to Bactria to raise an army in insurrection against his brother, but Xerxes sent assassins after him and they succeeded in eliminating this fratricidal threat to the emperor.

One wonders how such a jealous wife as Amestris was able to put up with the close camaraderie between Xerxes and the woman who was the foremost admiral of the Imperial Iranian Navy. Xerxes' naval commander,

Artemisia, was the ruler of Halicarnassus in Caria, which was the hometown of Herodotus.[19] She was one of Xerxes' most trusted advisors. Artemisia had the distinction of being, not just the satrap, but the Queen of Caria.[20] She was the only one of Xerxes' commanders who had the guts to give him advice that he did not want to hear, and to question his judgment.[21] For example, as an admiral of the Imperial Iranian Navy, she warned strongly against engaging the Greeks in the naval battle of Salamis. Artemisia told Xerxes that he should ignore the Greek navy and continue his land-based campaign.[22] She proved to be right. Although Xerxes was happy with her own performance in the naval battle, and awarded her for it, Salamis was a total disaster for the Iranians. To be fair, Xerxes had engaged the Greeks, and disregarded Artemisia's advice, based on disinformation spread by Themistocles that the Greeks were divided against themselves, that their alliance was beginning to fracture, and so he would find a divided fleet in the straits.[23]

The relationship between Xerxes and Themistocles attests to the fact that Xerxes must also have been a profoundly charismatic man. So charismatic, in fact, that he seduced both of the leading Greek military men *who defeated him* during his invasion of mainland Greece *to eventually come over to his side after the war*. Pausanias, commander of the Spartan forces at the battle of Plataea, eventually adopted Persian customs and even sought the hand of one of Xerxes' daughters in marriage.[24] Following the Persian War, he was implicated in a number of intrigues with the "enemy" of Greece. Finally, after a letter that he had written to Artabazus, a cousin of Xerxes and one of the satraps of Imperial Iran, was seized and leaked, he had to seek asylum in a Temple of Athena where he was blockaded and starved to death.[25] According to his accusers, the seized letter also implicated Themistocles in a plot to establish a Persian fifth column in preparation for a second attempt by Xerxes to seize control of mainland Greece.[26] If true, this would mean that two of the most prominent Greek commanders in the Persian War, one a Spartan army general and the other an Athenian naval admiral, had come over to Xerxes' side.

After being implicated in this pro-Persian conspiracy, Themistocles had to flee Athens for his life. In 471 BC, he began a journey through mountainous territory, disguised as a woman riding in a covered carriage, heading for the court of Xerxes at Susa.[27] When he finally arrived, instead of condemning his former Athenian enemy to death as some had feared, Xerxes was overjoyed. He boasted over celebratory drinks, "I have Themistocles the Athenian!" This reaction is especially shocking in light of the fact that Themistocles had carried out a human sacrifice of three of Xerxes' nephews, the sons of his sister Mandane (some sources record her name as Sandauce), within view of the throne he had set up overlooking the straits of Salamis while contemplating whether to engage the Athenian Navy.[28] We know that, at the time, Xerxes was incensed by this, because it was what finally made it impossible for him to take Admiral Artemesia's advice not to engage the Athenians at Salamis.

As one can imagine, Xerxes' sister Mandane, who had lost all three of her sons in this appalling fashion, demanded the execution of Themistocles. Even though she stormed the palace with her own bodyguard, Xerxes refused to execute the Athenian naval commander without affording him a fair trial. At this trial, Themistocles was able to so effectively defend himself *while speaking fluent Persian* that he was acquitted by a dazzled court and Mandane had to relent.[29] Following the trial, Xerxes treated the former leader of the Athenian Navy exceptionally well, making Themistocles his close hunting companion, giving him large swaths of territory to control—not just one, but several estates together with many servants to cultivate these lands.[30] Themistocles gave his son Cleophantus a Persian education.[31] There are stories to the effect that Themistocles had an affair with the Queen Mother, Atoosa (the daughter of Cyrus the Great) in her old age, and that he also began to study under the Magi.[32]

Themistocles can by no means simply be considered a turncoat. That he spent considerable time and energy trying to have a stolen statue of the Great Mother sent back to Athens demonstrates Themistocles' continued patriotic sentiment toward his hometown.[33] The same conclusion can be drawn from the circumstances of his death. When Themistocles was about sixty-five years old, Xerxes offered him command of a second expedition to conquer mainland Greece.[34] He accepted, but then committed suicide by drinking bull's blood. Nonetheless, that Xerxes was able to garner the loyalty of such an Athenian patriot and Greek war hero in the first place is an astonishing testimony to his charisma.

This is especially the case considering what a horrifically brutal war Xerxes waged in mainland Greece, and particularly in Themistocles' homeland of Attica. When Xerxes attacked Phocis, the only bastion of resistance in northern Greece, the Iranian army plundered the Temple of Apollo at Abae before burning it to the ground. It is reported that during this attack, Iranian soldiers pursued those who had been defeated while attempting to defend their city and temple. When they caught up with the fleeing Greeks, who included civilian women, "some of the women from this party were gang-raped until they died."[35] Xerxes' reputation had preceded him, and so almost all of the inhabitants of Athens had been evacuated before Xerxes set fire to the city and burned the Acropolis to the ground, that is, after looting as many valuables as the Iranian forces could carry away with them.[36] This involved the destruction of the archaic Temple of Athena together with its marble sculptures and pediments, which were smashed.[37] Meanwhile, those bronze sculptures that were considered either too insignificant or too cumbersome to carry away, were melted down for their metal. Xerxes immediately dispatched a message to Sardis informing those back in Iran that the mission of getting revenge for the burning of Sardis in 494 BC had been accomplished.[38]

If Xerxes had stopped there, he might have come home victorious. Yet he insisted on continuing the march into continental Europe, suffering a series of demoralizing defeats — beginning with the Battle of Salamis. Themistocles had convinced the Athenians to engage the Iranians in a naval battle at Salamis, rather than attempting a futile land-based defense of Athens.[39] This meant losing the battle to win the war. In the midst of a heated debate, Themistocles interpreted an ambiguous oracle that included the lines, "Holy Salamis, thou shalt destroy the offspring of women, / When men scatter the seed, or when they gather the harvest."[40] He argued that their oracle would not be referring to Salamis as "holy" if those fated to die there were Greeks.

Part of the problem was that the Greeks were fighting for their lives and their homeland, whereas the Persians — especially the elite guard — were adventurous tourists engaged in a colonial enterprise far from home. The officer corps of "Immortals" were recruited from among the sons of the Persian aristocracy and were provided with their own provision trains of camels, oxen, servants, and concubines in covered wagons.[41] The Immortals were covered in finely crafted gold jewelry, bracelets, armbands, rings, and such, which they kept on even in the heat of battle and that made great spoils for any victorious enemy.[42] They wore yellow-died slippers. Xerxes himself, who cut a dashing figure as the most handsome man in the world of his time, wore fancy blue shoes during the campaign against Greece.[43]

There was also a significant mismatch in military tactics. The Achaemenid military put emphasis on heavy aerial bombardment of the enemy with arrows, in an attempt to devastate them at a distance. After thinning out the enemy forces and throwing them into disarray through this ballistics strike, they would bring in the cavalry.[44] The Greek phalanx presented a problem for this strategy. Tightly bound together as the phalanx was, the Greeks could all raise their shields at once to form a wall blocking the arrows. More problematic was that horses will not charge at a solid object, which is what the wall-like phalanx appeared to them to be.[45] In the end, Xerxes was counting on sheer numbers to prevail over the Greeks. The scale of his military expedition is mind-bending.

The forces marshialed by Xerxes' for his military campaign into continental Europe consisted of a ground force of 2,370,610 men, accompanied by a naval force consisting of 3,000 ships manned by another several hundred thousand sailors, in addition to hundreds of thousands of service and supply train personnel, bringing the total number of enlisted men involved to five million.[46] Experts of ancient warfare estimate that a military force of this size would require 906,066,000 liters of fresh water daily for these men to drink so as not to expire of thirst; they would need to be fed 234,600 tons of grain a day, and would need to feed 127,500 tons of fodder to their warhorses, scout dogs, and other combatant animals.[47] Why would anyone finance a campaign of this size? Just to get revenge for the burning of Sardis? That is simply not credible; and besides, the campaign infamously did not end at that revenge. It was equipped for a conquest of the known territories of continental Europe, and Xerxes proceeded with that titanic military objective despite advice from Artemesia and others to go home triumphant after torching Athens. This chapter begins with the suggestion that we may find an answer to this question by examining the story of Xerxes and his Jewish "queen" Esther, especially when we interpret this story against the backdrop of the rise of the Jewish role in the monetary and banking system established by Darius the Great who, after all, initially planned the European campaign.

The Persian Jewish community is the oldest continuous Jewish diaspora in the world, dating back 2,700 years, since the Assyrian tyrant Shalmaneser V conquered the northern part of the Kingdom of Israel and sent Israeli captives to Iran. Subsequently, the Jews faced even more severe persecution at the hands of the Babylonians, who took them captive in the second major Jewish exile after the one in Egypt. Once Iran gained its political independence from the Assyrians and Cyrus the Great conquered Babylon in 539 BC (the starting point of the Persian Imperial Calendar), the Jews gained a special place within the vast Persian Empire of the Achaemenids (which, based on the population it governed, was the largest empire in world history). Cyrus (Hebrew *Koresh*) not only granted them freedom of religion in Babylon, and allowed Jews who wished to leave the right of return to Israel in peace and security, he also commissioned the building of the Second Temple in Jerusalem at cost to Iran's treasury and at the hands of the Persian corps of engineers. Construction was completed under the reign of Darius the Great, who also endorsed the project. For such deeds, Cyrus is valorized as the "Messiah" of Israel in both the Biblical book of Ezra and that of Second Chronicles. The Jews did not recognize Jesus, one of their own, as a Messiah, nor did they accept the claim to prophet-hood of their fellow Semite, Muhammad. But even today, many Jews await the coming of another *Koresh HaMaschiach* who will build the Third Temple where the Mosque of the Dome of the Rock now stands.

The story of the special historical relationship between Iran and Israel only begins with Cyrus the Great. Many Jews chose to remain in Iran rather than return to Israel. Iranian Studies scholars are familiar with the fact that the Achaemenids first struck silver and gold standard coinage imprinted with a portrait or *shekel*—a Persian word meaning "semblance" or "image"—invented the bank check, and established the world's first banking system based on credit. In Babylon, which became the administrative capital of Iran, the Jews played a key role in this development. Perhaps on account of their growing influence, a court Minister of Xerxes I, named Haman, headed a vast conspiracy planning to liquidate Jews across the Empire. When Xerxes' Israelite Queen, Esther (Hebrew: Hadassah), became aware of this and brought it to her husband's attention, Xerxes instead turned on his own court officials. He executed tens of high-ranking individuals involved in the plot and appointed Mordechai, Esther's godfather, Prime Minister of Iran.

The Purim holiday is a celebration of this second salvation of the Jews by the ancient Persians. Xerxes apparently allowed Mordechai to establish Purim as a holiday celebrated in Susa (Shushan) and other cities. Xerxes is the most respected ancient Persian Emperor after Cyrus and Darius, but unlike them, Xerxes was not known for his tolerance and humanitarianism. He burned Athens to the ground during his invasion of Greece, which makes his treatment of the Jews all the more fascinating and meaningful.

I would ask those allegedly patriotic Iranians who question the historicity of this story to ask themselves whether they believe in the historicity of the Kayanian dynasty that appears in the *Shâhnâmeh*, or for that matter, in the historicity of Zarathustra himself, since his patron, Shah Goshtasp (Kavi Vishtaspa), was a Kayanid monarch. At least in the case of the Esther story, we have numerous supporting accounts and archeological data validating the historicity of Xerxes. There is nothing of the sort for the Kayanids or Zarathustra. All we have are "texts" such as the *Gathas*, other parts of the *Avesta*, and the *Khodai-namag* (Ferdowsi's source for his chronology of Kings) that were handed down through the oral tradition for centuries before being written down, at the earliest, around the same time that Jewish scribes committed the *Tanakh* to writing in its current form (in Imperial Iran, I might add).

Like the *Shâhnâmeh*, or the *Avestâ*, the *Tanakh* is not only a religious scripture. It is also a chronicle and folk history. Mythology that deals in archetypal symbolism has to be differentiated from mythologized accounts of what, based on internal textual evidence, appear to be historical events. One can read these accounts independently of, and even against the grain of, those religious values that they are meant to validate. It may be that instead of some ancestral tribal vendetta on the part of Haman, the plot against the Jews during the reign of Xerxes was motivated by the fact that they controlled the banking system of Babylon, the first credit-based global financial system, established by Imperial Iran during the reign of Darius the Great. This will become the focus of the present chapter — namely, the birth of the first form of Zionism in history: Iranian Zionism.

4.1 Xerxes and Ishtar the Jewess

Xerxes is named as "Ahasuerus" in the Book of Esther, *Axashverosha* being a Hebrew corruption of *Arta-Xashayâr-shâh* or "King Xerxes, the Great." It is said that he "reigned from India even unto Ethiopia" and that "Shushan" or Susa was, in his time, the seat of "the power of Persia and Media" (Esther 1:1–3). The story begins with the disobedience of Xerxes' wife, who is named "Vashti" by the authors of the Biblical book.[48] This could, however, have been an epithet of hers, rather than her actual name, since the Old Persian *Vahishti* means "the best one" or "most excellent." In its Middle and New Persian form *Behesht*, it came by extension to mean something having the quality of paradise. Vashti refuses to sit by her husband's side at the head of a days-long public feast that Xerxes had been hosting.[49]

Some have interpreted this disobedience as a sign of a tension between Iranian traditions and the Semitic customs that were still prevalent in Susa, where the feast was being held. Iranian women customarily appeared in public and joined their husbands in feasting, but Semites considered such behavior on the part of women to be immodest and, at the very least, conduct not befitting an aristocratic woman, let alone a queen, who ought not to become an object for the lust of men other than her husband.[50] If a queen of Xerxes actually disobeyed her husband in such a manner, it would suggest that prolonged settlement of Iranians in Susa, which was an important center of vastly more ancient Semitic and Elamite cultures, had begun to affect Iranian attitudes and mores — to the point where a Zoroastrian woman would be more mindful of Semitic norms than she was of her Iranian husband's wishes, even if he was the emperor himself.

Such an interpretation is bolstered by what happens next. Xerxes considers his wife's behavior to be such an affront that he puts the entire matter before his advisors and judges. They decree that, from henceforth, the emperor is not to be accompanied by his wife at any public function, and that a woman from the harem will take her place at his side.[51] Although the authors of the Esther story tell us that Xerxes eventually voided this judgment, and that his relations with Vashti were fully repaired and restored, the fact that such a judgment was made at all suggests that the king's counsel was subject to the same pressures of Semitic norms at Susa to which Vashti herself had felt beholden.

During the period when the council's judgment was in effect, and Vashti was prohibited from appearing at Xerxes' side, a number of women were recruited into the harem from across the empire and these were vetted for the honor of being the emperor's escorts.[52] One of these was a Jewess named Hadassa or "Myrtle." She was an orphan who had been raised by her uncle, Mordechai, a man already involved in intrigues on the fringes of palace life in Susa. When Mordechai became aware of the counsel's ruling and the recruitment of new courtesans, he volunteered his niece. Hadassa was given the name "Esther" upon entry into the harem, and Mordecai instructed her not to reveal her Jewish origins and true heritage to anyone therein.[53]

Now, "Esther" is simply a mispronunciation of Ishtar or "the star." The so-called "Star of David" or *Mogen David* is actually an ancient Babylonian symbol associated with the goddess Ishtar.[54] Specifically, she was identified with the evening star and the morning star, in other words, the planet Venus (Persian *Zohre*) or Lucifer.[55] After the Iranian conquest of Babylon, the Mithraic goddess Anahita was equated with Ishtar and the planet Venus, the name of which planet in Persian astronomy is *Anâhid*.[56] As another iteration of Ishtar, Anahita was also both the goddess of love and of war.[57] This mirrors the same dual aspect of Mithra. Anahita is not only associated with Venus, but also with the Moon.[58] In other words, her most recognizable standard in the contemporary world is the symbol of the lunar crescent together with the "star" that represents Venus as the "morning star" and the "evening star." This appears on the flags of Turkey, Pakistan, and many other nations that were once a part of Greater Iran.

When we read about Hadassa or "Esther," i.e. Ishtar, being offered up by her uncle Mordechai as a courtesan for Xerxes, we ought to bear in mind that it was expected of every single woman living in Babylon that, married or unmarried, she prostitute herself at the Temple of Ishtar at least once in her lifetime.[59] As late as the time of the Roman Empire, it was reported by Latin authors that women in Babylon were so loose that, although they would show up to dinner parties fully dressed, after some drinking their tops would come off, and a few hours later, they would be traipsing around the party totally naked except for their jewelry.[60] Such lewd conduct was not exclusive to married women, who shamelessly showed their bodies to every man in the gathering regardless of what their husbands may have thought. It was equally characteristic of young, unmarried women who, according to Roman authors, regarded prostitution as simple sociability.[61] What else could one really expect of a city whose temples sponsored "sacred prostitution" and attempted to corner the market for whores in the name of the city's great goddess, Ishtar?[62]

Mordechai, the pimp of his niece and god-daughter "Ishtar," often loitered outside the palace at Susa, awaiting intrigue. One day he heard two eunuch door-keepers at the gate plotting the assassination of Xerxes. Seeing an opportunity to get into the good graces of Xerxes, the Jew revealed this information to his niece. During one of their nights together, Esther informed Xerxes of the potential assassination being planned by Bigthan and Teres, whereupon the emperor had these men seized and hanged.[63] Xerxes recorded this affair in his journal but then put the incident out of his mind.

At that time, the Prime Minister of Iran was a certain Haman, son of Hammedatha.[64] Haman was part of a faction within the Imperial Iranian state that had grown increasingly impatient with, and resentful of, the large number of Israelites who refused to return to their homeland despite the decree of Cyrus and the rebuilding of the Temple of Solomon in Jerusalem, which had been completed by Darius. They were reluctant to leave a comfortable life of relative affluence in major cities of the Persian Empire, such as Babylon, Ecbatana, and Susa, for a hard life rebuilding a relatively barren and desolate Israel.[65] Haman took his place at the head of a plot to liquidate these Israelites and to seize their assets and property in the process of doing so.[66] The Jews were to be arrested and executed on the 13th of Azar.

Word of the plot leaked out to the Jewish community, which was seized by terror. Some covered themselves in sackcloth and ashes to mourn their impending doom.[67] For his part, Mordechai implored his niece to take up the matter with Xerxes. Esther was hesitant to do so. She told her uncle that it had been a month since Xerxes had summoned her, which, not incidentally, is a detail of the story that makes it clear that Esther was not a queen of Xerxes, but a minor concubine who had no right to appear in his presence without a summons. This is also clear from that detail that Xerxes would see her only in her quarters in the harem, and not in his own bedchamber. In any case, Mordechai eventually impresses upon Hadassa the fact that she may have been placed just where she was in order to be an instrument of Jehovah's will to protect his people from being massacred by Haman and his co-conspirators.[68]

After fasting and praying for several days, Esther appears uninvited before Xerxes, beautifully adorned and trembling with anxiety over what his reaction might be to her apparent audacity.[69] Utterly charmed by the secret Jewess, Xerxes pardons her and draws her close to him with his scepter, saying "What do you wish, queen Esther, and what have you come to ask for? If it is half my empire, you shall have it."[70] Esther replies with the seemingly modest request for a private dinner with Xerxes and his Vizier, Haman, which request the Shah readily grants.[71] Unaware of Esther's Jewish background, Haman was initially delighted to hear that he had been invited to a private dinner with the emperor and his favorite concubine; he even brags about it to his wife Zeres and their friends.[72] Yet he continues to prepare his plot against the Jews, which includes setting up an especially high gallows for the particularly influential Mordechai, again without any awareness of the man's relation to Esther.

It just so happened that, the night before the scheduled dinner with Esther and Haman, Xerxes had trouble sleeping and he took to reading his journal as a remedy for insomnia.[73] There he happened upon the passage wherein he had logged the assassination attempt foiled by Mordechai. The Shah summoned his bureaucrats and asked what reward Mordechai had been given, and he was appalled to discover that the answer was none at all.[74] At precisely this moment, Haman arrived with the intention of securing the emperor's permission to execute Mordechai on the gallows that had, unbeknownst to Xerxes, already been prepared for the Jew. Before Haman could get a word out of his mouth about this matter, Xerxes asked him how a man worthy of receiving a particular distinction for his loyalty to the crown ought to be rewarded. Believing this man to be himself, Haman suggested that the favorite of the emperor should be publicly paraded around on the emperor's own horse in a crown and royal garments, while announcers shouted for everyone to hear: "Here is the king's favorite!"[75] Xerxes agreed that this would be a fitting reward and straightaway ordered Haman to have such a honorific parade in the streets of Susa prepared for Mordechai, the Jew.

Haman was mortified, but he suppressed his seething anger as he arrived at the planned private dinner with Esther and Xerxes, who was still unaware that Esther was a Jewess and the niece of Mordechai. It is some time into the dinner that, with Xerxes drunk and thoroughly enchanted by his favorite courtesan, in response to his entreaty for her to reveal to him what she really wanted, and to rest assured that it would be granted no matter what it was, Esther comes out with the truth. She reveals to Xerxes that she is a Jewess and the niece of Mordechai, and that Haman is responsible for a plot to exterminate the Jewish people — her uncle included.[76]

Xerxes is initially so shocked and appalled by his courtesan forcing him to confront his Prime Minister that he gets up and storms out into the garden. When he returns he beholds Haman with his hands all over Esther, and as if he was not incensed enough by this sight, one of the eunuchs in attendance informs Xerxes that Haman has already set up a gallows for Mordechai on his own authority.[77] At this point, Xerxes flies into a rage and has his Vizier seized and executed on the very gallows that the latter had prepared for the Jew.

The emperor proceeds to replace Haman with Mordechai, and he empowers his new Jewish Vizier to take vengeance upon all of those in the vast imperial bureaucracy that had been planning to liquidate the Jews.[78] Dressed in a white robe and purple cloak, with a crown on his head, Mordechai ultimately orders the deaths of no less than 75,000 conspirators, including ten of Haman's sons, thereby securing the place of the Jews in Imperial Iran.[79] The Purim festival was then inaugurated on Xerxes' authority as a yearly commemoration of this salvation of the Jewish people through the agency of Esther.

Dismissing this story out of hand simply because there is no independent corroboration of it from Persian imperial records is unreasonable. If we were to apply such a strict criterion to all our sources, most of what we know about the history of Achaemenid Iran would have to be rejected since it comes from the writings of Greek historians, scholars, and literary figures. There is, moreover, no reason to accept Greek accounts purporting to be history while rejecting Hebrew ones. The Old Testament contains as many "chronicles" as it does stories that are intended for moral instruction. So the Esther narrative has at least the status of folk history. If we were to reject it, we would also have to dismiss out of hand the folk histories that Iranians themselves preserved in the epic tradition that was ultimately shaped into the *Shâhnâmeh* by Ferdowsi. It is more reasonable to assume that there are at least some kernels of truth to this story, which, perhaps for very good reason, may have been deliberately censored by the Achaemenids themselves. After all, Achaemenid records on occasion present us with self-serving and patently false accounts of political and military machinations, which we know, from multiple Greek sources, transpired in a very different fashion.

However, once we admit the potential historical basis for the story of Esther and Xerxes, we do have to ask ourselves: *what could possibly have provoked a conspiracy against the Jews of Imperial Iran so vast that putting down the plotters necessitated the execution of no less than 75,000 Iranians and other subjects of the empire?!* A fascinating, albeit profoundly disturbing, possibility presents itself when we look at one of the most revolutionary reforms implemented under the reign of Xerxes' father, Darius the Great. This reform, namely the issuance of standardized coinage and the creation of a credit-based international banking system, was only briefly touched on in the previous chapter, with the promissory note that it would be addressed here.

The term "shekel," often associated with Jewish financial transactions, actually comes from the Persian word *shekl* or "image, countenance" referring to the portraits of Darius the Great that were stamped on the new, standardized coinage.[80] These were the first coins in history bearing the face of an actual person. The *shekel* was a standard silver coin, and the standardized gold coin was called the *Daric*, which as its name indicates, also bore the image of Darius.[81] To the extent that goods were still used in a continuation of old bartering practices, these were given fixed values in terms of coinage, such as three shekels for a sheep or a shekel for a jar of wine.[82]

The introduction of standardized coinage also facilitated more sophisticated banking activities.[83] Previously banks had been under the direct control of either temples or members of the royal family. Due to Darius' reforms of the monetary system, Achaemenid Iran became the first society in which private banks were established.[84] These banks would be the first to offer loans to individuals for the purpose of affording them sufficient capital for developing their agricultural properties or launching mercantile activities, including shipping, which would eventually be profitable both for the entrepreneur and the lending bank.[85]

Another innovation attributed to Darius the Great is the check.[86] These checks were an integral part of the banking system, as they continue to be today. We even have the names of some of the Achaemenid banks, such as the Bank of Egibi and Sons at Babylon or Murashu and Sons at Nippur.[87] There are surviving records of some of these banks having held land leases and, in some cases, having used their lending activities to secure monopolies on certain industries, such as breweries and fisheries.[88] Who ran these banks? Jews who had married into the local elite.

That the Israelites who wished to return to their homeland were compelled by Ezra to divorce their foreign wives suggests that in Babylon they had married into families of other ethnicities.[89] Such a practice of intermarriage for the sake of increased influence remains characteristic of the moneyed power of International Jewry today.[90] Those who remained in Imperial Iran, not just in Babylon, but also in cities such as Ecbatana and also Susa, where the Esther story takes place, would have continued this practice that was forbidden to those returning to resettle Israel.

The development of their money power began with the issuing of false receipts, in other words the fraudulent creation of credit, based on actual commodities or safe-deposited valuables stored in the warehouses or treasuries of the temple and the state.[91] At a certain point, so many false receipts were in circulation that the resulting credit crisis required a reform of the entire monetary system.[92] This is the aforementioned reform carried out under the reign of Darius. It involves the introduction of *bullion* or standardized coinage minted out of precious metal, whether gold or silver, as a relatively abstract representative of, or token standing for, actual commodities or valued goods. By establishing an exchange equivalence between the former and the latter, the psycho-social value of bullion itself is artificially increased.[93] This also in turn stimulates the growth of the mining and minting industries, which were financed by private banks.

The final step toward the development of the abstract power of money, as we still know it today, involved the creation of credit banking based on checks or promissory notes. These stand, not for actual valued goods, but for the "shekels" that have already come to abstractly represent those goods.[94] As noted above, this feature of the international banking system was also developed under the reign of Darius — the father of Xerxes. What followed was the issuance of far more promissory notes than the actual amount of bullion available in the treasury, which allowed the financial alchemists responsible for this operation to effectively produce wealth from out of nothing.[95] Their influence in the temples and at the royal court of Babylon gave them access to the seals necessary to issue letters authenticating credit that was, in the end, based on nothing other than the sense of confidence that they had instilled in the minds of the empire's subjects.[96]

It is not hard to see how this operation would benefit most from the centralization of both religious and political power. Instead of having to infiltrate many temples of the diverse gods of multiple city-states, such as Ur, Kish, or Lagash, or separately gain favor in the royal courts of Babylon, Sardis, and Susa, the worship of a One True God — the Almighty God of the Shekel — could be enforced by the One World Government. This was the New World Order of Cyrus, Darius, and Xerxes — a vehicle for the already international money power of the former Israelites that had been uprooted by the Assyrians and Babylonians, and forcibly settled, two centuries earlier, in all of the areas that would become the main centers of power of Imperial Iran: Babel (Babylon), Hamedan (Ecbatana), and Shush (Susa).[97]

Can it really be considered a coincidence that the Iranian monarch who takes such a dramatic action against those seeking to liquidate the Jews is the same man who goes on to attempt the conquest of what was left of the known world outside his already long-handed grasp? But who financed that massive Iranian military invasion of Europe? Now the figure of the Vizier Haman, at the head a vast bureaucratic conspiracy against the Jews in Imperial Iran, starts to come into much sharper focus.

Let us take a look back at the numbers that would have been subject to the review of Haman and his fellow bureaucrats, the numbers cited at the outset to this chapter and that delineate the scope of Xerxes' campaign into Europe. Note that the entire world population of the time did not exceed 150 million people. Napoleon Bonaparte's battle of Waterloo involved a force of 200,000 men and Gettysburg, the bloodiest and most ferocious battle in the American Civil War, considerably less than that. Waterloo and Gettysburg took place at a time when the world's population was closer to 750 million. So, scaled to the period between Waterloo and Gettysburg, Xerxes' invasion of Europe involved twenty-five million military men. Scaled to the population of today, we are talking about an armed force of more than 200 million men — in other words, an army and navy comparable to the size of the entire populations of France, Germany, and Italy combined!

Such a force had never been fielded before, and has never been fielded since. It dwarfs even the Allied and Axis forces of the Second World War. Who manufactured this war? Who paid for this war machine? And how?! Could it have been Jewish credit-based private bankers, with spectral money conjured through the manipulation of perceptions and expectations? With what goal? The subjugation of recalcitrant Europe, spearheaded by the mainland Greeks, to the New World Order of Babylon. The front man who founded that New World Order was Cyrus, the Messiah of Israel.

4.2 Cyrus, the Messiah of Israel

Isaiah 46:8–46:13 is about the coming of Cyrus, the *Moschiach* of the Jews. These lines that compare the Shah of Iran and Savior of Zion to a bird of prey are particularly striking, especially considering that the Achaemenid standard was a golden eagle: "From the east I summon a bird of prey; from a far-off land, a man to fulfill my purpose. … I will grant salvation to Zion, my splendor to Israel."[98] Accomplished Judeo-Persian Studies scholars such as Amon Netzer have also interpreted the Servant Song at Isaiah 42:1–42:7 as a reference to Cyrus the Great.[99] The most important passage in the Bible concerning Cyrus as the Messiah of Israel is at Isaiah 45:1–45:7:

> This is what the Lord says to his anointed, to Cyrus, whose right hand I take hold of to subdue nations before him and to strip kings of their armor, to open doors before him so that gates will not be shut: 'I will go before you and will level the mountains; I will break down gates of bronze and cut through bars of iron. I will give you the treasures of darkness, riches stored in secret places, so that you may know that I am the Lord, the God of Israel, who summons you by name. For the sake of Jacob my servant, of Israel my chosen, I summon you by name and bestow on you a title of honor, though you do not acknowledge me. I am the Lord, and there is no other; apart from me there is no God. I will strengthen you, though you have not acknowledged me, so that from the rising of the sun to the place of its setting, men may know there is none besides me. I am the Lord, and there is no other. I form the light and create darkness, I bring prosperity and create disaster; I the Lord do all these things.'[100]

In addition to its spiritual significance, the Hebrew title *Moschiach* (Persian *Massih*) originally signified a man who is the legitimate sovereign of Israel.[101] Such a person had to be not only a Jew, but also someone from the Davidic bloodline. Cyrus is the first person, and thereafter remains the only person ever, who is not descended from the House of David but who is recognized as a legitimate King of Israel and vice-regent of Yahweh.[102]

There is evidence that suggests that Second Isaiah and his circle of Babylonian Jews were in contact with Cyrus before the Iranian Emperor launched his invasion of Babylon.[103] Flavius Josephus, the Jewish historian who wrote in the Roman Empire in the first century AD, claims that Cyrus listened to Second Isaiah's writings being recited to him, and also wept in commiseration with the Jews over the treatment that they had received when Nabuchadrezzar destroyed Jerusalem and forced them into exile at Babylon.[104] Certain passages of Second Isaiah that make reference to Cyrus and the conquest predate the actual Iranian march into Babylon. Their projections of what that seizure would look like, based on Jewish hopes for retribution against their oppressors, do not align all that well with what actually happened.[105]

In particular, instead of humiliating adherents of the cult of Marduk, it seems that Cyrus had coordinated with them at least as closely as with the Jews and he gave the Babylonian god a level of reverence that even Nabonidus had failed to do.[106] Instead of enslaving the people of Babylon, as Isaiah prophesied, Cyrus liberated them just as much as he liberated the Jewish exiles.[107] Had the text been written after the fact, such discrepancies would be unlikely. Rather, the projection was probably formed on the basis of the assurances that Cyrus was giving to the circle of Isaiah in conspiratorial discussions preceding the Iranian conquest of Babylon.[108] This further raises the question of whether, if the political propaganda in Second Isaiah was at least partly of Persian origin, the same is true of the most cosmic character of its theological content.[109]

Any estimation of the extent of the role that Cyrus, the Messiah, may have played in the formation of what we now recognize as Jewish religion must take into consideration the relationship that Cyrus had with the cult of Marduk, which was also a Semitic religion, and his having conspired with the priests of Marduk in his bloodless conquest of Babylon. Numerous passages in the Cyrus Cylinder suggest that there was a collaboration between the cult of Marduk and the forces of Cyrus that paved the way for the latter's conquest of Babylon, including these lines: "Marduk the great lord, guardian of his people, looked with gladness upon his [Cyrus'] good deeds and upright heart. He ordered him to march to his city Babylon. He set him on the road to [Babylon], and like a companion and friend, he went at his side."[110] There is a striking parallel to this passage from the Cyrus Cylinder in the book of Isaiah: "The Lord's chosen ally will carry out his purpose against Babylon. … For your [Israel's] sake I will send [Cyrus] to Babylon. …This is what the Lord says to his anointed, to Cyrus, whose right hand I take hold of to subdue nations before him. … I will go before you." (Isaiah 48:14; 43:14; 45:1–2)[111] In relation to this phrase, "I will go before you," it ought to be noted that Xenophon claimed that the rapidity of Cyrus' military advances was owing to the fact that the army of Cyrus was guided on long night marches by "a heavenly aura" that followed them overhead and illumined the ground around them and the path forward.[112] This is strikingly reminiscent of the account that we are given in the Biblical book of Exodus of the pillar of fire by night that, day after day, is deployed by Yahweh to guide the Israelites through the Sinai, illuminating the desert terrain around and ahead of them.

An inscription on the Babylonian Sippar Cylinder suggests that Cyrus had entered into an alliance with Nabonidus of Babylon as early as 556 BC, even before marching against Astyages and subjugating the former Median overlords of the Persians.[113] The Sippar inscription is particularly interesting insofar as it describes Cyrus as a "little slave" of the god Marduk. It reads:

> The Umman Manda of whom you are speaking, his land, and the kings who march at his side are no more! When the third year comes [553 BCE], [Marduk] will cause Cyrus, King of Anshan, his little slave, to advance against him with his small army. He will overthrow the wide extending Umman Manda; he will capture Astyages, King of the Umman Manda, and take him in bonds to his own land.[114]

On his famous cylinder, Cyrus had this inscribed of his devotion to the Babylonian god Marduk: "When I entered Babylon in a peaceful manner, I took up my lordly residence in the royal palace amid rejoicing and happiness. Marduk, the great lord, caused the magnanimous people of Babylon to love me, and I daily attended to his worship."[115] The Cyrus cylinder goes on to add, "In addition, at the command of Marduk, the great lord, I settled in their habitations, in pleasing abodes, the gods of Sumer and Akkad, whom Nabonidus, to the anger of the lord of the gods, had brought into Babylon."[116]

Cyrus conspired with the priests of Marduk in order to prepare the way for his conquest of the city.[117] The latter had abandoned Nabonidus over his neglect of the rites proper to the cult of Marduk, especially the yearly Akitu festival. The Iranian military under the command of Oebaras, governor of Media, entered the city of Babylon on October 12, 539 BC, facing no resistance.[118] Once the city came under the occupation of Oebaras, Median troops immediately surrounded the Marduk temple complex at Esagila and guarded it in a fashion that allowed all of the rites and festivals dedicated to the Babylonian god to continue uninterrupted.[119] Seventeen days later, on 29 October 539 BC, Cyrus the Great himself entered Babylon.[120] Cyrus was crowned at the Esagila temple complex.[121] Ritual humiliation at the temple involved the king being slapped in the face repeatedly by the priests, hard enough to make him cry, and then forced down on his knees in front of a colossal golden idol of Marduk enthroned.[122] Cyrus submitted to this ritual, before going on to make his address to the people from atop the Tower of Babel.

The Tower of Babel, called *Etemenanki* by locals, was seen as "the house that is the foundation between heaven and earth."[123] It was 300 feet on each side and 305 feet tall, with a large temple surmounting seven stages of the Ziggurat.[124] This temple housed no idol, but it was always occupied by whatever woman of the time was considered the most beautiful and fitting woman to be the consort of Marduk.[125] Herodotus describes the temple as it was in his own time:

> The ascent to the top is on the outside, by a path which winds round all the towers. When one is about half-way up, one finds a resting-place and seats, where persons are wont to sit some time on their way to the summit. On the topmost tower there is a spacious temple, and inside the temple stands a couch of unusual size, richly adorned, with a golden table by its side. There is no statue of any kind set up in the place, nor is the chamber occupied in the night by any one but a single native woman, who as … the priests of this god affirm, is chosen … by the deity out of all the women of the land.[126]

The tallest building in the world, apart from the Great Pyramids of the Egyptians, the Jews claimed that it had been built as a platform from which the antediluvian king Nimrud intended to storm heaven and challenge God for sovereignty over the world.[127]

Cyrus returned from Babylon to Iran as a consequence of the death of his beloved wife, Cassandane, who was entombed at Pasargadae, where Cyrus himself would later be laid to rest.[128] Cyrus instated a period of prolonged public mourning for his departed wife.[129] When he left, he had Cambyses crowned King of Babylon on March 27, 538 BC.[130] Cambyses only managed to maintain this position for nine months before so offending the priests of Marduk that he was removed by Cyrus, who took back the title for himself until his own death. Supposedly, instead of submitting to the aforementioned ritual humiliation that was customary for a king being initiated at Marduk's temple, Cambyses proudly entered the Temple of Marduk wearing splendorous Elamite robes and menacing the priests with a quiver full of arrows.[131]

The two great deities of Babylon, its highest goddess and chief god, were Ishtar and Marduk. If Esther is Ishtar, then could it be that Mordechai is Marduk?[132] Interestingly, the name of the chief deity of Susa was Humban, who was an Elamite god, and Haman's ten sons are named after Elamite demons. If Cyrus had been coordinating with the Marduk cultists before he entered Babylon, was the relatively bloodless conquest of Babylon under the aegis of Cyrus the Great made possible by a conspiracy that also involved the persecuted Israelites within the city?[133] At the very least this would have required intelligence operations, but it may also have extended to raising funds for bribes of Babylonians in high places as well as funding that afforded the Iranian military the best armaments available.[134] Even before the Persians established the sophisticated banking system of Babylon, the Israelite exiles had gotten into the business of money changing in this hub of international trade and finance.[135] Was Cyrus really just repaying a debt to the Israelites exiled in Babylon?

In 2 Chronicles, we have a record of Cyrus' address to the Jews regarding his commissioned reconstruction of the Temple of Solomon at Jerusalem and the repatriation of the Jews to a homeland of "Israel" that is clearly recognized by the Shah of Iran.[136] Second Isaiah 44:24–28 also makes reference to the edict of Cyrus that the Second Temple be built for the Jews in Jerusalem:

> This is what the Lord says — your Redeemer, who formed you in the womb: I am the Lord, who has made all things, who alone stretched out the heavens, who spread out the earth by myself … who says of Jerusalem, 'It shall be inhabited,' of the towns of Judah, 'They shall be built,' and of their ruins, 'I will restore them,' … who says of Cyrus, 'He is my shepherd and will accomplish

> all that I please; he will say of Jerusalem, "Let it be rebuilt," and of the temple, "Let its foundation be laid."'"[137]

One very noteworthy aspect of this passage is the cosmic character evident in the Jewish God's boastful description of himself. Some theologians have argued that the opening of Genesis was written either during or after the period of Second Isaiah and reflects this cosmological shift under Persian influence.[138] The priestly source, or "P," as theologians call him, who authored this part of Genesis together with much of Leviticus, Exodus, and Numbers, was not one man, but a group of Jewish writers who continued to live in Babylon for decades after the death of Cyrus.[139] The polarities of this material are strange in that, on the one hand, we have a more sublime and transcendent Creator god,[140] and on the other, a litigious and even sadistic judge.

Cyrus issued his decree for the restoration of the Jerusalem Temple sometime in the winter of 539–540 BC.[141] This decree was issued both in Aramaic, the administrative language of the Persian Empire, and also in Hebrew. Both versions are preserved in the biblical book of Ezra. The Hebrew version reads as follows:

> This is what Cyrus king of Persia says: The Lord, the God of Heaven, has given me all the kingdoms of the earth and he has appointed me to build a temple for him at Jerusalem in Judah. Anyone of his people among you — may his God be with him, and let him go up to Jerusalem in Judah and build the temple of the Lord, the God of Israel, the God who is in Jerusalem. And the people of any place where survivors may now be living are to provide him with silver and gold, with goods and livestock, and with freewill offerings for the temple of God in Jerusalem.[142]

Cyrus chose the most high-quality and expensive cedar logs from Lebanon for the construction project, and ordered that they be shipped to Jerusalem from Iran's imperial ports in Tyre and Sidon.[143] The temple reconstruction project was only completed in 515 BC after Darius intervened directly in order to finally get the decades-long job done.[144] Cyrus also restored all of the gold and silver vessels that the Babylonians had looted from the Temple of Jerusalem by retrieving them from the pagan shrines in which they had been placed and returning them to the Jews who were headed back home to Israel.[145]

4.3 The Mithraic Mystery of Iranian Zionism

As recorded in the book of Ezra, the Iranian official responsible for the Jewish repatriation program was named "Mithredath the Treasurer."[146] Interestingly, not only is this a Mithraic name, but "Mithredath" or Mithradates (Mehrdad) appoints a Jewish prince named "Sheshbazzar" as the leader of the large and long expedition of migrants returning to Jerusalem. This name "Sheshbazzar" is a Hebrew corruption of the Akkadian *Shamash-apli-usur* or "May Shamash Protect the Son."[147] The Medes had already syncretized Shamash with Mithra.

In Media, Mithra was thus syncretized with two solar Mesopotamian deities, the Babylonian and Assyrian sun god Shamash, as well as the Hittite lord over the kingdom of the dead, Nergal, who was associated with fire, hunting, war, and pestilence.[148] Nergal's animal avatars were the lion, dog, snake, raven, and scorpion, all of which were incorporated into the Median cult of Mithra, as we can see from the iconography associated with Mithra once Mithraism enters the Greco-Roman world.[149] While the dog is considered sacred by Zoroastrians, the rest of these creatures, namely the snake, scorpion, and raven are considered the demon-spawn of Ahriman in Zoroastrianism but are seen as sacred in Mithraism.[150] Even the lion, who together with the Mithraic sun, would go on to become the national standard of Iran, was viewed as an "unholy" and "devlish" creature by the Zoroastrian Magi.[151] Typical depictions of Zahhak in Persian art are very similar to ancient depictions of Nergal, such as on the Hammurabi stela or in carvings at Hatra, where he is depicted with snakes rising from his shoulders.[152] Shamash also sometimes appears with flame-like snakes rising from his shoulders as he rides the winged solar disk.[153] Interestingly, the Babylonian god Marduk was symbolized by a dragon, the same symbol associated with the evil demonic king *Azhi Dahaka* or Zahhak in the Iranian tradition.[154]

The laws of the Torah were only codified and institutionalized across the entire Jewish community under the reign of Artaxerxes I, the most explicitly Mithraist monarch of the Achaemenid dynasty.[155] It was Artaxerxes himself who assigned his scribe, Ezra, with the task of codifying Jewish law.[156] Ezra had been the leader of the Babylonian Jewish community. Jewish scholars have long regarded Ezra as "inferior only to Moses himself." Since the historicity of the at least quasi-mythic figure Moses is very much in question, one could legitimately see Ezra as the true founder of Judaism as we know it from tangible and datable written records reflecting the religion that we still see practiced today.[157] Furthermore, enforcement of the laws of the Pentateuch (the five books of Moses) among the Israelites who returned home — a considerable task, considering how pagan they had become in Babylon — was the responsibility of a certain Nehemiah, who had been the cupbearer of Artaxerxes.[158] This Nehemiah also received permission from the Shah to rebuild the outer defensive wall of Jerusalem, which was a permission generally not given to peoples who had been subjugated by Imperial Iran.[159] The rebuilding of the wall of Jerusalem was symbolic of a certain degree of local autonomy granted by Iran to Israel, and only to Israel, from among all of the imperial satrapies.

Indeed, most scholars admit that Judaism as we know it today is inconceivable without the assimilation of numerous Iranian beliefs that radically restructured the entire Israelite religion. There was hardly any notion of an afterlife in the religion of the Israelites before they were exposed to Iranian culture.[160] There was certainly no Israelite belief that the righteous would be rewarded in a heavenly afterlife.[161] The souls of the good and evil were both thought to wander aimlessly in *Sheol*, the underworld of shadows. The manifest worldly injustice of the Babylonian exile may have inclined those Jews who endured it to be particularly open to Zoroastrian ideas of otherworldly rewards and punishments once they encountered these ideas through the Iranian conquest of Babylon.[162] The replacement of the ancient Israelite conception of the underworld of departed shades, namely Sheol, with a postmortem heaven in which God rewards the good is another clear sign of Iranian influence on the development of what we now recognize as "Judaism."[163] Likewise with the counterpart of heaven, namely a hell wherein the wicked are punished. Ancient Israelite religion had a conception of collective guilt and punishment, not of personal conscience and divine judgment of the individual soul on the basis of whether it has freely chosen to align itself with good or evil.[164]

Ancient Israelite religion did not have any notion of "the devil" either; there were simply other gods besides Jehovah that it was prohibited for Israelites to worship.[165] The figure of Satan is only developed beginning with the Book of Job, which was composed after the Babylonian exile was brought to an end by Cyrus.[166] This Jewish idea of the devil is developed under the direct influence of the Iranian theological idea of Ahriman.[167] That is fairly clear from the fact that the Jews wind up with a theology in which six arch demons serve Satan, just the way that Ahriman has six demonic beings in his service.[168] Likewise, the seven archangels are a theological idea that Jews modeled on the six Amesha Spentas together with Ahura Mazda himself, of which they are an emanation, as the seventh of them.[169] We can find no trace of the elaborate angelology that became a feature of their religion after long-term exposure to Iranian religion, the same angelic hierarchy that was imported into Christianity.[170]

The eschatological conception of time that has, in retrospect, been seen as so characteristic of a prophetic conception of history ending with an apocalyptic judgment and the establishment of heaven's kingdom on earth was utterly lacking in the ancient Israelite religion.[171] The related idea of a messianic savior arriving at the end of the world also only entered the Israelite belief system after prolonged exposure to the religious life of Iran.[172] The Jewish conception of the Messiah as more than just a legitimate King of Israel and vice-regent of God in the present, but as a Coming Savior who would usher in a post-apocalyptic Kingdom of God on Earth, is an idea that mirrors the Zoroastrian belief in the Saoshyant.[173] This idea would, of course, go on to play a key role in the transformation of Judaism into Christianity. It is a gift of the Magi. The ideas of an apocalyptic end of history and savior of the end times begin with the Book of Daniel, which is set in Iran and written after more than a century of Israelite settlement in Iran.[174]

Whereas the final version of the Book of Daniel as we have it today was composed around 167–163 BC, scholars have determined that the original version of it was composed in Achaemenid Babylon.[175] According to Iranologist Ernst Herzfeld, Daniel was born in 602 BC and was taken captive with other Jews who were forced into the Babylonian exile in 597 BC.[176] Jews regard Daniel not as a full-fledged prophet but as a sage who had visions of the future.[177] The biblical book by his name identifies Daniel as having been in the service of "Darius the Mede."[178] The Book of Daniel uses the ancient Persian word *râza* to denote the "mystery" that is going to be revealed at the Apocalypse.[179] Both the river of fire and the idea of a universal savior who arrives at the end of the world are imported into the Book of Daniel from Iranian theology.[180] The Ancient of Days ordains the Son of Man who comes in the clouds of heaven and who is worshiped by people who speak all of the languages of the world, and who establishes an imperishable divine dominion on earth.[181]

The Book of Daniel describes the Persian Empire as a two-horned ram charging to the west, north, and south.[182] Ancient Iranians considered the ram, like the boar and bird of prey, to be a conveyor of the *Farnah*.[183] In fact the idea of royal legitimacy passing from the Babylonians to the Iranians is one of the themes in Daniel. This Biblical book agrees with Xenophon's *Cyropaedia* that Belshazzar died on the night that Babylon fell. Allegedly, he was in the midst of feasting when a spectral hand appeared out of thin air and wrote these words on a plaster wall behind him: *Mene, Mene, Tekel, Upharsin*, which the prophet Daniel interpreted as follows:[184] *Mene* meant "God has numbered the days of your reign and brought it to an end." *Tekel* meant "You have been weighted on the scales and found wanting." Finally, *Upharsin* meant "Your kingdom is divided and given to the Medes and the Persians."

Although scholars admit that the Median and Persian influence on Israelite religion must have been so profound that it essentially produced Judaism as we know it, we are dealing with a situation that is far more complex and nefarious than mere reformation or assimilation. The problem with admitting such a broad and deep restructuring of Israelite religion through Iranian influence is that Jewish theology and ethics is in many ways antithetical to Zoroastrianism. Consequently, if we are to admit that, as suggested above, from Cyrus himself onwards through Darius, Xerxes, and Artaxerxes, Achaemenid sovereigns played a direct role in re-forming the exiled Israelite nation into the Jewish community that we recognize today, this poses another fundamental problem for any claim that the Achaemenids were Zoroastrians. From the perspective of the *Gâthâs* of Zarathustra, the Jewish religion is irredeemably demonic and Yahweh is Ahriman himself.

Zarathustra conceives of Ahura Mazda as a Lord of Wisdom who wishes to enlighten human beings and afford them with every opportunity to increase their wisdom and knowledge. By contrast, Yahweh wants to keep human beings ignorant and he actively denies them knowledge so that they can continue to be his slaves. We see this in the garden of Eden, from Genesis 2–3. This is also a reflection of the fact that while Ahura Mazda is the most beneficent and bounteously generous being, one who wants any given human being to become as much like him as possible, at Exodus 20:5 Yahweh admits to being a murderously jealous God. This jealousy and will to keep human beings subservient is also at the core of the story of the Tower of Babel, where the Lord destroys a unified and co-operative human community by confounding its language and pursuing a policy of divide and conquer to pit nations against each other so that none of them can rise up to heavenly heights.

Ahura Mazda, while not omnipotent, is supposed to be the most awesomely intelligent, discerning, and penetrating mind at work in the cosmos, carefully planning the creative evolution of the cosmos and victory over demonic forces. Meanwhile, in the story of the flood of Noah at Genesis 6:1–8, we see that Yahweh is so heedless that he comes to consider his entire creation a regrettable mistake that needs to be corrected through afflicting humans and other animals with a genocidal cataclysm. In fact, he is so lacking in foresight and so capriciously mercurial, that it is possible to negotiate with him over the number of righteous people in a city that would justify its being spared from destruction on account of its perceived iniquity. This mentality of a petty wheeler-dealer in the bazaar comes across clearly at Genesis 18:22–23, when Abraham is pleading with his Lord to spare the righteous in Sodom.

Zarathustra claims that Ahura Mazda has appointed him to deliver a message whose purpose is to bring wrathful violence and vengeance to an end, so that people can live and let live in peace. Yahweh, on the other hand, repeatedly enjoins his prophets to slaughter civilians, including old men, women, and little children, for doing such harmless things as participating in joyful pagan ceremonies. We see this at Genesis 18:22–32 in the Lord's test of Abraham to prove his unquestioning obedience through his willingness to sacrifice his own son, Isaac. It is evident at Exodus 10:1–2 and 11:3–7 in the Lord's machinations as he deliberately makes Pharaoh recalcitrant just so that he can murder the firstborn children of Egyptians and thereby demonstrate his power. The massacre of everyone worshiping the golden calf by their own brothers, sisters, fathers, uncles, and so forth, at Exodus 32, is another horrific example of this.

Perhaps the worst example is the holocaust carried out by the army of Joshua at Jericho, which, as is made abundantly clear in Joshua 4–5, is a genocide carried out with the explicit approval of the Lord and in coordination with the captain of his heavenly army. At Joshua 6:21–27, we are told that every man, woman, child, and animal in the city was massacred or burnt to death, with the sole exception of a whore who betrayed her own people by facilitating the Israelite extermination of her townsfolk.

We keep on meeting with more and more examples of this throughout the Jewish Bible, such as at Ezekiel 5:5–11 and 9:8–11 where the prophet himself is appalled to learn that the Lord intends to punish Israel's slip back into paganism with a famine that forces people to resort to cannibalism, including parents and offspring eating one another, a pestilence caused by people being forced to eat their own feces, and the murder of old men, women, and little children simply for the sake of establishing ideological purity. In fact, the most distinctive characteristic of this god is probably his willingness to inflict violence, misery, destruction, and death upon everyone who does not offer him unquestioning obedience.

Whereas the core of Zarathustra's entire message in the *Gâthâs* is individual responsibility based on the exercise of free will and personal conscience, Yahweh boasts about punishing generations of innocent people for the sins of their forefathers and rewarding others for no good deed of their own but simply as a repayment for the loyalty of their ancestors. No other conclusion can be drawn from Exodus 20:5–6, where the Lord states his intention to visit the guilt of parents upon their children, punishing them to the fourth generation, while rewarding the descendants of those loyal to him up to the thousandth generation. Judging people as clans and collectives rather than as responsible individuals is also implicit in the very definition of Jews as the Lord's "treasured possession among all the peoples." Compare this to Mazda's universality.

If the Achaemenids had really been Zoroastrians, as some of them claimed to be, they would—at the very least—never have shown the slightest care or concern for the Israelites. A good case could be made that, in line with their worldview, it would even have been justified for them to treat the Jews as demonic enemy combatants. Instead, as we have seen, the Achaemenids went out of their way to support this community and got involved in the details of its reorganization. In the case of those who wished to be repatriated, the Shah handpicked those in leadership roles in the project for the reconstruction of Israel—especially Jerusalem—with funding from Iran's royal treasury. Why would the Achaemenids deliberately re-establish the state of Israel? Perhaps we ought to first ask what exactly "Israel" means.

The key to understanding this is the encounter of Isaac's son Jacob with God, who wrestles with him by the ford of a river. The context for the story is that Jacob, who "steals" the blessing of his brother Essay from his father Isaac, makes a journey to a land by the name of Paddan-aram to work for his uncle Laban. After many years of labor he heads back to Canaan a wealthy man, with Laban's two daughters as his wives (Genesis 27–28). Let it to be noted, if only in passing, that Jacob's interactions with his uncle over these two women are among the most blatant displays of the Israelite view that women are nothing more than property to be handed over from their father to their husband. Jacob works for Rachel instead of for "cash" and Laban shrewdly decides to use Jacob's lust as an opportunity to get rid of Leah as part of the same package-deal, since she is not likely to bring in much on her own in the market for wives (Genesis 29:17–27). Later on, Rachel and Leah define themselves as property when asked by Jacob to seek the monetary aid of their father: "Then Rachel and Leah answered him, saying, 'Have we still a share in the inheritance of our father's house? Surely, he regards us as outsiders, now that he has sold us and has used up our purchase price'" (Genesis 31:14–15). On his way back to Canaan, Jacob sends his wives ahead with his other property across the river Jabbok, some of which is meant to serve as a peace offering to his slighted brother Essau. Earlier in his journeys, Jacob has already had a *dream* of angels ascending and descending a "ramp," "stairway," or "ladder" that he takes to be "the gateway to heaven" from one of the abodes of God on the earth and he has also encountered angels in person (Genesis 28:12–17; 32:2–3).

These events are heralds of the striking vignette that we are presented with at Genesis 32:25–33, when he spends the night alone at the riverbank after having sent his property, including his wives, ahead of him:

> Jacob was left alone. And a man wrestled with him until the break of dawn. When he saw that he had not prevailed against him, he wrenched Jacob's hip at its socket, so that the socket of his hip was strained as he wrestled with him. Then he said, "Let me go, for dawn is breaking." But he answered, "I will not let you go, unless you bless me." Said the other, "What is your name?" He replied, "Jacob." Said he, "Your name shall no longer be Jacob, but Israel [*Yisra-El*], for you have striven with beings divine [*El-ohim*] and humans, and have prevailed." Jacob asked, "Pray tell me your name." But he said, "You must not ask my name!" And he took leave of him there. So Jacob named the place Peni*el*, meaning, "I have seen a divine being face to face [or "I have seen the face of God"], yet my life has been preserved." The sun rose upon him as he passed Penuel, limping on his hip. That is why the children of Israel to this day do not eat the thigh muscle that is on the socket of the hip, since Jacob's hip socket was wrenched at the thigh muscle.

The importance of this event cannot be overestimated. It is the origin of the name of the entire nation of Israel. The word *Israel*, which includes *El* or "a god"—the singular of *elohim*—means "having striven (or wrestled) with a god and come out alive." This feat is all the more remarkable on account of the fact that this god is evidently a dirty wrestler. He dislocates Jacob's hip so that he can have an unfair advantage. Take note of how the god wants to be released before the morning light fully illuminates his face and figure, and remember how he refuses to identify himself by name. To this day, Jews do not pronounce the name of "Yahweh," which they spell out instead, letter by letter: YHWH.

The Roman historian Josephus claims that Xerxes was "pious to Yahweh."[185] Even in light of the Esther story, it is unthinkable that Xerxes was a secret Jew. However, there may have been something underlying such an observation. On his way into Europe, at Nine Ways on the Strymon, in addition to carrying out a Mithraic horse sacrifice, Xerxes sacrificed nine boys and nine virgin girls by burying them alive.[186] No Zoroastrian *would ever* engage in such a human sacrifice of children. Period. The fact that this sacrifice of male youths and maidens was carried out in the context of the well-known Mithraic sacrifice of horses, the same rite carried out at the tomb of Cyrus the Great, suggests some form of Mithraism as the religious context for this grisly propitiation of demonic or archontic forces. As noted above, the Medes had already integrated the worship of Mithra with the cults of the wrathful Shamash and the demonic underworld god Nergal. These were both Semitic deities, similar to Yahweh.

Mithra is not a "good" god. Even as early as the *Mehr Yasht* Mithra is portrayed, on a cosmological level, as the mediator or *miyânchigh* between the forces of Good and Evil.[187] Parts of the *Mehr Yasht* are even older than the *Gâthâs*.[188] The oldest version of the Iranian cosmological myth, which was sanitized by orthodox Zoroastrians, has Mithra presiding over the contract between Ahura Mazda and Ahriman.[189] Mithra is a warrior god who vigilantly enforces covenants.[190] Mithra punishes oath breakers regardless of the contents of the contracts that they broke.[191]

Covenants to Mithra were customarily sworn over or before a fire.[192]

One reason for this is the association between fire and truthfulness in the sense of a "trial by fire," an ordeal that is originally Indo-Iranian.[193] The quintessential trial by fire involved pouring molten metal over the bare chest of an accused person, and determining their innocence on the basis of whether they could survive the ordeal.[194] The image of Siyavash leaping through the flames of a massive bonfire on horseback, which survives in the *Shâhnâmeh* of Ferdowsi, dates back to the Pre-Zoroastrian period of Mithraic fire ordeals.

In contemporary Persian, the expression for "swearing an oath," namely *sogand khordan*, literally translates as "drinking sulphur" and originates in another form of this trial by fire wherein the ordeal involved ingesting a fiery substance.[195] The drinking of sulfur would take place at a *Daré Mehr*.[196] The Zoroastrian sanctification of fire was taken over from Mithraism wherein Mithra was already known as "the Lord of Fire."[197] He was especially associated with the sun. The identification of Mithra with the sun came about as a consequence of the Zoroastrian appropriation of fire as a manifestation of the divine order or *Ashâ/Artâ* of Ahura Mazda.[198]

Xerxes having burned down the temples of the Greek gods in Athens is as consistent with his being a Mithraist as it is with the supposition that he was a Zoroastrian. Mithra is an *Ahura* (or *Ashura* in Sanskrit) not a *Daeva*. Actually, in the *Mehr Yasht* he is portrayed as the greatest enemy and destroyer of the *Daevas*: "Who breaks the skulls of the Daevas, and is most cruel in exacting pains … may smite all the malice of Daevas and Men."[199] The *daeva* temples that Xerxes boasts of having destroyed in his royal inscriptions were quite simply the Greek temples of the Acropolis in Athens, which he subjected to the fire of Mithra.[200]

There is a great deal of evidence in favor of Mithraism, rather than Zoroastrianism, being the *de facto* faith of the Achaemenids. The entrance to the tomb of Cyrus the Great features a solar disc that could well be a Mithraic symbol, and the way in which he secured religious diversity within his realm is more consistent with the ethos of Mithraism than with Zoroastrianism.[201] According to Xenophon, Mithra featured prominently in the royal processions held during the reign of Cyrus.[202] The first

"Mithradata" that we encounter in Iranian history is not a Parthian, but the man who headed the royal treasury of Cyrus.[203] As we saw in Chapter 1, a Mithraic sacrifice of a white horse was carried out at the tomb of Cyrus every month.[204] To repeat what was pointed out in the first chapter, this sacrificial rite is not at all Zoroastrian. Had Cyrus been a Zoroastrian it would have been akin to spitting on Zarathustra's grave.

There are numerous occurrences of the name "Mithrayazna" or Mithra-worshipper preserved in records from the Achaemenid period, particularly among Persian settlers in Mesopotamia and colonized Egypt.[205] Already by the fifth century BC, a temple had been dedicated to Mithra in Memphis by the Persian military colonizers of Egypt.[206] We know from Aramaic tablets recovered at Persepolis that, during the reign of Darius I (550–486 BC), there were more rituals honoring Mithra than Ahura Mazda.[207] Judging by royal inscriptions, Artaxerxes I (465–424 BC), Artaxerxes II (404–358 BC), Artaxerxes III (425–338 BC), and Darius III (380–330 BC) were all devotees of Mithra.[208] Some of their inscriptions also refer to Anahita alongside Mithra. Xenophon (430–354 BC) recounts that Persian rulers of the Achaemenid period in general "swore by Mithra."[209]

Records from Persepolis during the reign of Darius the Great (549–486 BC) have revealed that the majority of Persian names in the Achaemenid period were formed from compounds that included "Mithra," to the extent that Mithraic theophoric names outnumber those honoring Ahura Mazda by a ratio of five to three.[210] In both his *Anabasis* and his *Cyropaedia*, Xenophon tells us that the Achaemenid Emperors swore by Mithra.[211] One conduit for the transmission of Mithraism from Iran into Europe was the Achaemenid period migration of Mithraic Magi into Anatolia and the Eastern Mediterranean, territories that would be incorporated into the Roman Empire.[212] This transmission, which intensified during the Parthian wars with Rome, will be the focus of our next chapter. It will also bring us to the heart of the Mithraic Mystery: why the ancient Iranians would acknowledge and propitiate Ahrimanic forces, such as Yahweh.

CHAPTER 5

THE SKULL AND BONE CROSS

ALEXANDER OF MACEDON INVADED IRAN in 330 BC and his defeat of the Persian Empire ushered in two centuries of Greek colonial rule under the Seleucid dynasty. Iranian Civilization had deeply impacted the culture of Greece for centuries, now the tide turned and Iranians came under Hellenistic influence. This chapter begins by recounting the lore that the Persian people are descendants of the god Perseus through the son born to him by Andromeda, namely Perses. This myth was taken to heart and politically institutionalized by the Parthian dynasty, Iranians from Central Asia who brought two centuries of Greek colonial rule to an end in Iran and who manufactured genealogies to legitimize themselves as heirs to the Persian Emperors. They also claimed Perseus as their patriarch. The Parthians were Mithraists, and an analysis of Mithraic symbolism and ritual suggests that Mithra is none other than Perseus himself.

This claim has sociological, cosmological, and psychological dimensions. On a sociological level, Mithraism or the mystery religion of Perseus was widely understood by classical authors to be "*the* Persian religion" with Perseus himself identified as the arch-magician who made a hearth for the heavenly fire in Persia when he founded the Order of the Magi. On a cosmological level, Mithra qua Perseus was understood to be the agency responsible for the astronomical precession of the equinoxes. As the god above the god who designed the astrological sphere, Mithra overpowers the Gorgon of Fate, namely *Zorvân* (or Chronos), by tilting the axis of heaven and shifting the entire celestial sphere. From a psychological perspective, this signifies a reaffirmation of the free will that was so central to the teaching of Zarathustra, and the ethos of the ancient Iranians, as against the fatalism that had afflicted Iran during two centuries of Hellenistic rule.

At the same time, in the Parthian period, the distinction between Mithraism and Zoroastrianism becomes very clearly defined. Mithra is the mediator between Ohrmazd (Ahura Mazda) and Ahriman, who are twin offspring of the androgynous *Zorvân*. As compared to the explicit ethical dualism, and at least implicit ontological dualism, of Zoroastrianism with its conception of radical evil, "*the* Persian religion" of Mithra is a monist doctrine with a view of Truth and Justice that lies beyond good and evil.

It is this religion that the Parthians deliberately injected into the Roman Empire in a psychological warfare campaign spearheaded by the Cilician pirates, the black ops Navy of Mithradates in the Mediterranean Sea. The Iranian origin of the Skull and Crossbones symbol of pirates (and of poison) as well as the Mithraic significance of Lady Liberty are explored in this chapter with a view to the rites and grades of Mithraic initiation. The chapter concludes by discerning the Mithraic roots of both orthodox Catholic and Gnostic Christianity in the Roman realm. Just like in the case of Judaism, which took its Biblical form under the influence of Cyrus and Xerxes in Achaemenid Iran, Christianity as we know it would not exist but for the Mithraists of Parthian Iran.

5.1 Hellenism, the Parthians, and Rome

In 323 BC Alexander of Macedon died in the capital of the Persian Empire less than a dozen years after having conquered it, and without leaving any explicit instructions regarding secession or the governance of the vast Achaemenid realm after his death. The result was that his commanding officers quickly turned on one another and divided the Persian Empire into several realms, each named after the general who seized it.[1] In 312 BC, Iran came under the control of General Seleucus Nicator who, like his Ptolemaic counterparts in Egypt, set up Hellenistic cultural colonies on the model of the Greek city state or *polis*.[2] Persian and Greek culture had already entered a process of synthesis in the Persian colonies of Greece, now this took place in the Greek colonies of Iran.

Around 300 BC, Seleucus transferred his capital to Antioch — a newly established polis in Syria.[3] This opened a power vacuum to the east, and a group of Iranians from Central Asia that were originally part of the Scythian (*Sakâ*) ethnos exploited this vulnerability. A tribe of these *Pahlavâ* or "heroes" known as the Parni broke off from the greater Scythian community and attempted to appropriate the Persian imperial heritage against both the Scythians to their north and the Greek colonialists to the south and west. The Scythians even allied with the Seleucid Greeks against the Parni breakaways, who were forced to fight a war on two fronts.[4]

The founder of the Parni or "Arsacid" dynasty was a certain *Ashk* (Arsaces) who was crowned in 247 BC in a mountainous area of Khorasan near present-day Quchan.[5] His name identifies him as a Mithraist. The word *Ashk*, which is also part of the name of the Parthian city of Ashkabad (now within the borders of Turkmenistan), was transformed into *eshgh* in Syriac (and later in Arabic). It signifies "love," one of the meanings of *Mehr* or Mithra. The province of Iran in which the Arsacids carved out their autonomy from the Seleucids was known, since Achaemenid times, as Parthava. It is from the appellation of this province that they adopted the name *Pârthi* or "Parthian."

That having been said, given the attempt of the *Ashkânian* (Arsacids) to trace their ancestry to the Achaemenid Persians, it is legitimate to contemplate the possible etymological connection between *Pârthi* and *Pârsi* (Persian). The *th* sound can often be interchangeable with an *s*. It is true that in Sassanian period texts such as the *Dâdestâné Dînîk*, a clear distinction was drawn between *Pahlavik* and *Pârskaden* or "the Parthian and Persian religions."[6] However, this may be less reflective of the way that Parthians really saw themselves, than of a Sassanian attempt to maliciously dismiss the Parthians as "not real Persians" on account of their being Mithraists rather than Zoroastrians. After all, the term *Pahlavi* comes to be the name of the Middle Persian language, which the Sassanids adopt and adapt from the Parthians. Parthava or Khorasan would ultimately become the second greatest bastion of Persian culture after Pars (Fars) itself. The roots of this may go all the way back to the Arsacids.

By 170 BC, the Arsacids or Parthians had put an end to Greek colonial rule in areas around the Caspian Sea adjacent to Khorasan, i.e. Hyrcania (Greater Gorgan) — including Tabarestan (Mazandaran).[7] This will go on to become significant to the present study, since it is in these three closely related regions of northern and eastern Iran, namely Khorasan, Gorgan, and Mazandaran, that the great Parthian feudal houses such as Suren-Pahlav, Kâren, Ispahbudhân, and Mehrân would deeply entrench themselves, and remain entrenched for many centuries after the Parthians are defeated by the Sassanids.[8] Shortly thereafter they pushed on toward Media (Azerbaijan and Kurdistan), seizing Rayy (Tehran) in the process and making it an important cultural center.[9]

It is not from Pars (Fars) but from this greater area around the Caspian Sea that the majority of violent Iranian revolts against the Baghdad-based Caliphate are staged. A literary renaissance of the Persian language eventually emerges in this north and northeastern realm, where several generations of Iranian scientists and inventors also set the standard for research and engineering on the planet. Let us not get a thousand years ahead of ourselves, except with a view to understanding that the feudal houses and their knights, who bring two hundred years of Greek colonial rule in this area to an end by the late second century BC, manage to endure for that long.

The predominant concern of this chapter will be to delve into the worldview of such a resilient group of people, with a focus on their metaphysical cosmology and how it grounded their ethos. It was a worldview most definitely subject to Greek influences, which were assimilated by Iranian Mithraism in order to produce a religion that the Parthians ultimately used for an almost totally successful social infiltration and psychological warfare campaign against the Roman Empire.

By the time Mehrdâd or Mithradates I (171–138 BC), whose name means "Mithra's Justice" or "Given by Mithra," was crowned king of the Parthians, the Romans had displaced the Hellenistic heirs of Alexander and emerged as the great power of the Western world. The Parthians became the greatest rival of pagan Rome.[10] The Roman General Crassus, emboldened by having made a name for himself while putting down the revolt of Spartacus, led an ill-advised military campaign against the Parthians in 53 BC.[11] His soldiers were unprepared for the unorthodox military tactics of the Parthian horseback archers, who with their long-distance rain of arrows and their "Parthian shots," fired during feigned retreats, cut the Romans to pieces.[12] Crassus himself was beheaded and, as the story goes, his severed head was delivered to the Parthian Shah Orodes while the latter was appreciating a performance of Euripides's Dionysian tragedy, *The Bacchae*.[13] The Parthian general who defeated Crassus went down in the annals of Iran's history as one of the most patriotic and ruthlessly effective military commanders of the time. His name, Surena, suggests some connection to the House of Suren-Pahlav, which like the other Parthian feudal houses, will become more significant as this study progresses.[14]

The famous Roman armor of overlapping plates (*lorica segmentata*) was eventually designed in response to the threat of Parthian arrows, and the Romans also developed a tactic of slowly advancing toward the Parthians in close formation under a domed roof formed by a wall of shields, known as "the tortoise" (*testudo*).[15] Despite these innovations, the Romans under the command of Mark Antony suffered further humiliations in the face of Parthian forces, to the point that Augustus Caesar eventually settled on a policy of superpower stalemate with Iran.[16] Augustus's successor, Nero, and the Parthian Shah Vologases (Valkash) I set up the Kingdom of Armenia as a buffer state in the cold war between Rome and Iran.[17]

There was another front in this rivalry between the two world superpowers of the epoch: psychological warfare. On that front, the Parthians were overwhelmingly dominant and, by the first century BC, had managed to thoroughly infiltrate Rome with the Iranian religion of Mithraism. The cosmological worldview and sociopolitical doctrine of this revolutionary religion will be the focus of the present chapter. The chapter will conclude with some remarks on how it, rather than Christianity, almost became the dominant religion of Rome, along with reflections on how many Mithraic ideas, symbols, and rituals were adopted by Christianity—whether in its orthodox Catholic or its Gnostic form.

5.2 Perseus and the Persian Religion

Perseus was believed to be the patriarch of the Persian nation. This myth had already been opportunistically exploited by the Achaemenids in their attempts to incorporate mainland Greece.[18] Many Greeks of the Achaemenid period relate this heroic genealogy of the Persian people. Skylax of Caryanda, Aeschylus, Hellanikos, and Herodotus all connected Perseus with Persia, with Herodotus claiming that his son by Andromeda, Perses, was patriarch of the Persian nation.[19] According to his Greco-Persian devotees, Perseus founded the order of the Magi, having brought the celestial fire to the Earth, and entrusted it to the descendants of his son by Andromeda, namely Perses — the first Persian. The Byzantine historian Gregorius Cedrenus preserves the legend that

> Perseus, they say, brought to Persia initiation and magic, which by his secrets made the fire of the sky descend; with the aid of this art he brought the celestial fire to the earth, and he had it preserved in a temple under the name of the sacred immortal fire; he chose virtuous men as ministers of a new cult, and established the Magi as the depositors and guardians of this fire which they were charged to protect.[20]

In the wake of the Hellenization of Persia during the Seleucid period, the Parthians really embraced this idea. Mithradates II had himself depicted as Perseus on some of his coinage, which also featured the harpe sword as well as the crescent and star.[21] The harpe sword was given to Perseus by Hermes.[22] The harpe together with the crescent moon and star is the symbol of the fifth grade of initiation in Mithraism, the grade of *Perses* or "the Persian," and the symbol of the seventh grade of "the Father" — which refers to Perseus or Mithra himself — is a curved knife next to a Phrygian cap with a staff and bowl.[23] This Parthian king, who is the first person to describe himself on his coins as "*Shahanshah* of Iran," had the epithet *Philhellenes* or "lover of the Greeks" struck on the same coinage, thereby reconciling both the Achaemenids and the Greeks who defeated them, as part of his legacy.[24] He also referred to himself as *Epiphanes* or the manifestation of god. Which god did he consider himself to be an embodiment of? Mithra. Mithradates I believed that the Parthian dynasty were descended from Perseus, via his son Perses.[25] Given that he also traced his lineage to the Achaemenids, via Darius III, this means that Mehrdâd wanted to see himself and his heirs as Persians, whether or not they actually were as a matter of ethnographic fact. The Gorgon and Pegasus are also depicted on his coins, as well as those of Mithradates III and IV.[26]

In the Parthian Mithraism that nearly conquered the soul of the Roman Empire, Mithra is none other than Perseus himself and the bull-sacrifice or *tauroctony* imagery at the heart of the Mithraic mystery is an astrologically encoded version of his heroic Gorgon-slaying. *Mithras* is simply the Greek pronunciation of the name "Mithra" (or *Mitra*). The original Iranian version of the god's name will be used here. Mithra is a youth wearing a tunic and a Phrygian cap. He stabs the bull with a small dagger in his right hand while holding its head up with his left hand. He looks away from the bull as he stabs it in the neck.[27] He is atop the bull, with his left knee bent and his right leg extended. It has been noted by art historians that the looking-away of Mithra from his aim and deed is not at all consistent with classical art, and has only one precedent: Perseus averting his eyes from Medusa as he decapitates her.[28] The constellation of Perseus is directly above the constellation of Taurus.[29] The most ancient depictions of Perseus show him wearing a Phrygian cap just as Mithra does. It is the cap of Hades, which renders the wearer *invisible*. It was given to him by the nymphs as a tool to use in the task of slaying the gorgon Medusa.[30] Mithraea or temples to Mithra were built underground, and an underground cavern was believed to be the birthplace of Perseus.[31]

The Gorgan is the androgynous deity of Time known as *Zorvân* in Persian and *Chronos* in Greek. The leontocephalic (lion-headed) god in Mithraic iconography is a reference to the Gorgon archetype. The most archaic Gorgon images have leonine animalistic faces, with snakes emerging from the hair and entwining the body as in the case of the Mithraic leontocephalic god.[32] Some Mithraic sculptures even feature a lion on one side and a Gorgon on the other.[33] This was also the case in the colonnades of buildings associated with Mithraism, whose marble columns sometimes had alternating lion and Gorgon heads depicted on their upper ledges. While the Gorgon is female and the leontocephalic Zorvan is assumed to be male, the latter's genitals are covered by the serpents entwining its body so that its sex is in question.[34] Zorvan is hermaphroditic. The lion-headed god of Mithraism is to Mithra as the Gorgon is to Perseus.[35]

Mithra takes the power of the Gorgon and thus becomes lion-headed himself.[36] Some classical sculptures depict this.[37] The Orphic Phanes, entwined by the serpent Chronos, breaks out of the cosmic egg, and on his chest he bears the lion-head symbol of Mithra.[38] Some classical inscriptions suggest an identification or syncretization of Mithra and Phanes.[39] Likewise with Mithra and Aion, a youth who turns the zodiac in Greek mythological images.[40] The ultimate legacy of this idea is the heraldic standard of the Iranian people (*mellaté Irân*), the harpe-sword-wielding lion with the sun rising behind him. The lion and sun symbol, especially considering the harpe sword in the lion's hand, represents Mithra having conquered Zorvan or Fate — as in the expression: "fortune favors the bold." As we shall see, this heraldry combines the symbols for the fourth, fifth, and sixth grades of initiation in Mithraism, the grades of Leo, the Persian, and the Solar Charioteer.

Before dismissing the idea that Perses, the son of Perseus, is the patriarch of the Persians as a Greek myth and a legacy of the Hellenistic Seleucid period, we would do well to consider the exceedingly ancient and even pre-historic relationship between the Persians and the Scythians, their Iranian cousins and adversaries to the north. As we saw in the last chapter, the Scythians worshiped Gorgons. Even before the Persians displaced the Medes as the dominant Iranians, Scythian invasions of predominately Persian territories were commonplace. Later, as the *Shâhnâmeh* records, Scythia — or Turan, as Ferdowsi calls it — becomes the main rival of Persia. Could the rivalry between these two ancient Iranian ethnic groups have become the basis for the imagery of the grandfather of the Persians slaying the deity of the Scythians and appropriating her power — a symbol that later, in mature Mithraism, developed cosmological significance? Moreover, as would-be "Persians" (via Darius III) who were coming from the borderlands of the Scythian realm, the Parthians would be most insistent on defining themselves against their closest Iranian relatives so as to appropriate the prestigious imperial heritage of their more distant Persian cousins.

Under the influence of Greek fatalism, the battle between the forces of Ahura Mazda or "Ohrmazd" (Middle Persian for Ahura Mazda) and Ahriman was recast as a gigantomachy whose main protagonists, the Lord of Light and the Lord of Darkness, are twins born of Time and controlled by fate. The twelve constellations of Ohrmazd and the seven planets of Ahriman are part of a heartless celestial machinery, *Sepehr*, whose turning wheels mercilessly deal out fortune and, more often, grave misfortune to the men at their mercy. Zorvan, the progenitor of both Ohrmazd and Ahriman is the god of earthly birth, death, and decay in Mithraism.[41] Some residues of this remain in references to Zorvan that were not expunged from the Middle Persian scriptures of the Sassanian period. "Zorvan is the god of death," and, as the *Shikandé Gomâni Vazâr* puts it, this god is "nearer to man than the jugular vein."[42] That is quite clear from this striking passage in Chapter 1 of the Middle Persian text *Bundahishn*:

> Time is mightier than both creations, — the creation of Ohrmazd and that of the Destructive Spirit. Time understands action and order [the law, *dâtastân*]. Time understands more than those who understand. Time is better informed than the well informed; for through Time must the decision be made. By Time are houses overturned — doom is through Time — and things graven shattered. From it no single mortal man escapes, not though he fly above, not though he dig a pit below and settle therein, not though he hide beneath a well of cold waters.[43]

Another Pahlavi text warns: "For Zorvan there is no remedy. From death there is no escape."[44] The heavens are a machinery of death. *Sepehr*, the celestial sphere or firmament, is the body of Zorvan and it dispenses both good and bad fortune, being alternatively called "the good Spihr" and "the evil Spihr."[45] It is through *Sepehr* that destiny is apportioned on earth.[46] The *Sepehr* is viewed as having begun as a seed into which finite Time enters before it grows through all the stages of an embryo and ultimately becomes the material Cosmos.[47]

It can be no coincidence that the 3,000 years for creation of the ideal world and 9,000 years of conflict after it is attacked by Ahriman come to 12,000 years; there are twelve signs of the Zodiac and Zorvan is the lord of the firmament and the cycle of time.[48] But this suggests that the cycle is really not one of 12,000 years but of twelve zodiacal ages of 2,160 years each, or approximately 26,000 years in total. The term *hezâr* in Persian still often refers not necessarily to 1,000 but to "many many" as in *hezâr-pâ,* the name of a centipede. So twelve *hezâres* really means something like a dozen epochs of long duration. That was misunderstood by orthodox Zoroastrians who were unfamiliar with the Mithraic mystery of precession. In Mithraism, the struggle that takes place between Ohrmazd and Ahriman over the course of these twelve zodiacal epochs is characterized, in Greek terms, as a *gigantomachy.*[49] Mithraic iconography includes depictions of the *Gigantomachia*, which is essentially a story about the overthrow of Chronos.[50] These include a depiction of Saturn handing over his thunderbolt and scepter to Jupiter, marking the passage out of the golden age.[51] The mutability of the reign of the god-father is in evidence here. Astrological and sexual symbolism pervade the Mithraic account of this cosmic war between the gods and titans.

Plutarch describes Mithra as the mediator who arbitrates the contract defining the terms of engagement between Ohrmazd and Ahriman during the cosmic war.[52] Mithra was the god of contracts, oaths, truth and trust. The handshake, as a sign of trust (indicating that one is not carrying a weapon) in greeting a friend or closing a business deal, originated within the Mithraic order.[53] There is no evidence for it as a common custom in Europe prior to the spread of Mithraism. Its earliest depiction is a first-century relief of Mithra shaking right hands with the Parthian Shah Antiochus.[54] The Mithraic handshake was referred to as *dexiosis* and so initiates of the Order were called *syndexioi*, "those who have been united by a handshake" (with the Father).[55] The colossal tomb of Antiochus I of Commagene (69-34 BC), known as *Epiphanes*, at Nemrood Dagh in the Taurus mountain range, with a distant view of the Euphrates valley, is one of the most impressive Mithraic architectural sites that survives.[56] The Nemrood Dagh bas-relief of King Antiochus shaking hands with Mithra is one piece of evidence in favor of the Mithraic origin of the handshake.[57]

In his capacity as the lord of oaths, Mithra is judge over the oaths that each of the two parties swears in their agreement to abide by the terms of the treaty governing the cosmic battle.[58] One of the Middle Persian titles of Mihr is *harvisp-patmân*, "he who deals with all treaties."[59] In the *Zandi Xvartak Apastâk*, we read,

> We praise and invoke the creator, Ohrmazd ... in that he fashioned thee forth, O right-dealing Mihr [Mithra] of wide pastures, for thou art a just judge and wakeful, for thou dost work justice and just *mediation* among spiritual and material creatures.[60]

Eznik confirms that the Magi believed that "the Sun acts as mediator between Ohrmazd and Ahriman" and as the judge over them.[61] This cannot be the actual sun, since the Sun was produced through the incestuous intercourse between Ohrmazd and his mother, the hermaphroditic Zorvan.[62] Eznik is confusing the Sun with Mithra, the Unconquerable Sun. The sun god (*Helios*) kneels before Mithra in submission, since as *Sol Invictus* Mithra is superior to the *sol* that can be conquered by night and darkness.[63] Mithra is the light that shines amidst the darkness in an inextinguishable and enduring fashion.[64]

Conclusive confirmation of the role of Mithra as mediator between Ohrmazd and Ahriman, and judge over both of them, can be found in a passage of the *Bahman Yasht* that, somewhat shockingly from an orthodox Zoroastrian standpoint, admits that Ahriman has breached the terms of the contract without Ohrmazd being able to do anything about it. Consequently, Mithra must retroactively take remedial action:

> The accursed Destructive Spirit cries out to Mihr of wide pastures saying,

> 'Rise up in righteousness, O Mihr of wide pastures.' Then Mihr of wide pastures cries out saying, 'Of those nine thousand years which were agreed upon, up till now Dahâk of evil religion and Frâshyâß, the Turanian and Alexander the Macedonian and the demons with leather belts and disheveled hair have ruled for a thousand years more than the treaty [allowed for].' The accursed Destructive Spirit is laid low when he hears these words.[65]

The *Bundahishn* has sanitized an older and more original narrative in which Zorvan, not Ohrmazd, is the creator of Mithra the Judge over the two brothers who are her twin sons.[66]

The bull in the tauroctony iconography of Mithraism symbolizes the constellation Taurus, while Mithra or Perseus, progenitor of the Persians, is Aries bringing the former zodiacal age to an end and inaugurating a new age, the epoch when, in all likelihood, Zarathustra composed his *Gathas*. The precession of the equinoxes was discovered by Hipparchus in the second century AD, contemporaneous with the formation of this belief system, and what the Mithraists were suggesting is that Mithra is the Lord of Precession.[67] By comparison to the Earth's rapid rotation, precession is a slow wobble in the Earth's rotation on its axis. The poles of the Earth trace out a circle over 25,920 years, causing a change in the stars that appear on the celestial equator, including the constellation in the night's sky at the point on the horizon where the sun is going to rise on the equinoxes and the solstices. Over the full cycle of the Great Year, the twelve signs of the zodiac each spend 2,160 years as the constellation that the sun rises into at dawn on the Spring Equinox. That constellation is currently Pisces and is about to yield to Aquarius as we complete one Great Year and enter another cycle.[68] Mithra slaying the bull is the Age of Taurus giving way to the Age of Aries (or Mars, who some Romans equated with Mithra).[69]

Mithra as *kosmokrator* (ruler of the cosmos) is depicted holding a sphere marked by the intersection of the circle of the zodiac and circumference of the terrestrial equator.[70] Sometimes he is even depicted in the guise of Atlas, bearing such a sphere on his shoulder.[71] The identification of Mithra with Atlas makes sense in terms of the former's power over the celestial sphere and its cruel creator.[72] According to Ovid, there is also a connection between Perseus and Atlas insofar as it is Perseus who, by showing the titan the head of a Gorgon, turned Atlas into stone.[73] That the starry sky appears on the inside of Mithra's billowing cape is another reference to him as the *kosmokrator*.[74]

At least by the Parthian period, as a reaction to Greek fatalism, Mithra becomes a being capable of moving the entire sphere of the fixed stars, a being more powerful than the planets and the Sun. Most importantly, Mithra would on this basis be viewed as even more powerful than the creator of the Cosmos — the being symbolized by the leontocephalic Lord Time, namely Chronos or Zorvan.[75] He stands outside of the celestial sphere, which is both the creation and embodiment of the cruel demiurge, and so he is in a position to change fate by shifting the axis of the heavens. In a world where the movement of stars and planets were believed to determine one's fate, "the lord of the precession" would have the power to change fate or, to put it in positive rather than negative terms, to grant the human being a free will that overpowers the cruel stellar machinations of the demiurge who created the Cosmos.[76] This was conceived of as holding a royal scepter over the heavens and sovereignty over the fates.[77] Perhaps this is why the Swastika, a symbol of "good fortune," is the "wheel of Mithra" (*gardâne-ye Mehr*). It is the handle he uses to move the heavens. The celestial bears or Arktoi (singular *Arktos*) are the symbol and instrument of the *kosmokrator* at the pole.[78]

According to classical thought, the fixed stars rotated around the fixed polar axis, beginning with "the shining Bears" (*Arktoi* or Ursa Major and Ursa Minor). In works such as Aristotle's *On the Heavens* this stability is taken to be a symbol of the eternal perfection of the Unmoved Mover. Cicero, Manilius, and Aratos all agree. So precession was conceived of as a de-stabilization of the axis of the Cosmos, the heavenly Logos of which was supposed to be mirrored in the Nomos of earthly law and order.[79] This is a very dangerous idea with social, religious, and political implications.

By overpowering the creator, Mithra is capable of bringing a New Age.[80] This was envisioned as a shifting of the basic structure of the Cosmos itself. In accordance with the ancient Hermetic idea of "as above, so below" such a shifting of cosmic order ought to also yield a New World Order, an epochal reorganization of socio-political systems. When we combine this astrological metaphor with the view that Mithra is the "mediator" between Ohrmazd and Ahriman, as well as the "judge" over them (or umpire in their cosmic competition), we arrive at the view that Parthian Mithraism was about reclaiming — on the far side of Hellenistic fatalism — the conscientious free will and individual self-determination that was at the heart of Zarathustra's own teaching.

5.3 The Crossed Bones and Lady Liberty

The "Persian religion" of Mithraism was deliberately injected into the continental European Empire of the Romans by their Parthian rivals as a means of psychological warfare and social engineering. One of the main instruments for this was an ostensibly pirate navy based in Cilicia. The pirates of Cilicia were no ordinary pirates. At the zenith of their power, having established particularly close relationships with the aristocracy and intellectual elite of the port cities of the Roman Empire, they controlled the entire Mediterranean.[81] They were known for their strange mix of scientifico-intellectual erudition and cut-throat enterprise. The inviolable oath of loyalty taken by Mithraists, and enforced by a merciless lord of contracts, would have been appealing to pirates, bands of thieves, or mercenary soldiers.[82]

It is also not hard to understand that a deity thought to control the stars would be revered by mariners, who are most dependent on the stars for navigation. According to Apian, the Cilician pirates were actually a black ops or false flag Parthian navy established by Mithradates II, who ruled from 88–66 BC (when he was defeated by Pompey).[83] Whenever he was in danger of shipwreck, Mithradates had no hesitation in transferring himself to the Cilician pirate fleet, who would safely sail him to his destination.[84] In his book *Piracy in the Ancient World*, H.J. Ormerod claims that the Romans considered the war against Mithradates equivalent to the crackdown on Cilician piracy in the Mediterranean.[85] Franz Cumont was one of the first scholars to note that the pirates of Cilicia played a significant role in introducing the Persian mystery religion to the Roman Empire.[86] Cumont colorfully remarks: "Supported by its bellicose religion, this republic of adventurers dared to dispute the supremacy of the seas with the Roman colossus."[87] By the time they were somewhat restrained by Pompey, the pirates of Mithra had already done their work.[88]

The "Jolly Roger" or skull and crossed-bones pirate flag is Mithraic in origin.[89] The crossed bones represent the Greek letter *chi* or the X of the intersecting zodiacal circle and celestial equator, and the skull designates this earthly plane of astrologically marked time as the realm of fateful death. The mock interment rituals of the Skull and Bones fraternity can be traced back through Freemasonry all the way to the ordeals of being buried alive that the initiate into the first grade of Mithraism, the grade of the Raven, had to undergo in order to transcend this realm of death.

In ancient Iran ravens were used for the removal of flesh from an exposed corpse before its bones were placed in an ossuary.[90] The "raven's head" was the black sediment left at the bottom of an alchemical distillation.[91] It symbolizes the blackness of both putrefaction and primordial chaos. The initiate is made to ingest this putrefaction.[92] The candidates for the grade of *Corax* in Mithraic initiation wore raven masks as they flapped their wings in the center isle between the reclining benches of the Mithraeum.[93] They were stripped naked, their eyes were blindfolded, and their hands were bound behind their backs with chicken guts, as they were guided over trenches filled with water.[94] Ravens are perpetually thirsty, and this was taken to be a metaphor for the sinful desire for the wetness of human existence that caused the soul's fall from the astral plane.[95] The grade of Raven symbolizes the trauma of incarnation into the wetness of worldly existence, which is at the same time a spiritual death.[96]

The initiate was subjected to intense verbal abuse and intimidation by jeering spectators, according to the script of a *legomena* ("things said") that was prepared for this ceremony.[97] Such hazing and humiliation rituals were common, and continue to be common, as part of induction into fraternal societies—especially warrior brotherhoods.[98] The Raven was lain down on the floor and forced to prostrate, threatened with a burning torch that at least briefly touched him, and a bizarre double-edged blade designed to sever the initiate's body in two at the waist.[99] A successful initiation was concluded by the Father severing the Raven initiate's bonds with his sword and removing his blindfold.[100] People put in such situations in Mithraea were occasionally actually murdered, so that the initiate could never be entirely sure whether he would come out of this ordeal alive. Both the Caesars Commodus and Julian were accused of performing human sacrifices during Mithraic rites.[101] The ritual sacrifice usually took the form of a Magus playing the role of the Father drawing his bow and shooting an arrow at the blindfolded and bound initiate, resulting (hopefully) in a very near miss.[102] The ritual sacrifice was followed by a mock interment, the one still practiced by the Skull and Bones society.

The exact angle formed by the two intersecting bands symbolized by the crossed bones is 23°, the same angle formed by the ecliptic's intersection of the celestial equator. It is the Cilician pirates who first raised it as their black or stateless banner, in a mockery of the heraldry of any and every nation and culture controlled by Chronos or Zorvan. In this connection it is relevant that another variant of it are the crossed keys, which in the Vatican came to symbolize the *inter regnum* between the death of one Pope and the appointment of another — in other words, the fact that the throne is vacant.[103] It is by means of the Mithraic emphasis on the uses of poisons for assassinations and the development of antidotes to them that the skull and bones became a symbol of poisons and drugs (*pharmakea*).[104] Mithradates VI was known as "the poison king" for his extensive experimentation with concocting various poisons both for use in assassinations of his enemies and also for his own ingestion, in controlled doses, to build his resistance to being poisoned.[105]

The skull and bones symbolizes the initiatory death of the Raven and the initiate of the Raven grade who serves the raven's bread or circular bread marked with an X or cross at the Eucharistic supper that Christians adopted from Mithraists.[106] They were also the cup bearers or *hyperetountes* ("waiters") who served the sacred wine.[107] The symbol of the Raven grade is the raven together with a cup and a caduceus.[108] In his *Refutation of All Heresies*, the Church father Hippolytus quotes from a lost exegesis of Aratos' *Phaenomena*: "Perseus is the winged axis which pierces both poles through the center of the earth and rotates the cosmos."[109] This winged axis is obviously the Caduceus.

In what way is Mithra associated with the Caduceus? The Caduceus is the magical staff of Hermes, or Mercury, and Mercury is the astrological symbol for the Raven grade of initiation in Mithraism.[110] The twin serpents copulating around the rod is a symbol of hermaphroditic union, and in alchemical lore it is the hermaphroditic union of the Sun and the Moon that produces the raven. But there is a deeper meaning here. Mithra, like Hermes, is the thief of cattle (Hermes stole his brother Apollo's cattle).[111] In fact, the Christians used to chide Mithraists for worshiping a thief. Furthermore, inscriptions in Mithraea identify Mithra in the form of the Raven as Hermes—Mercury, the thief and trickster.[112] There is, however, an even more disturbing implication of this.

In the *Shâhnâmeh* of Ferdowsi we encounter the classic description of the "demon king" Zahhak with the two serpents emerging from each of his two shoulders. They are presumably intertwined inside of Zahhak's body around the central axis of his spinal column. This clearly calls to mind the caduceus, the staff of Hermes or Mercury, the Trickster who, as we have just seen, is identical to Mithra as the divinity manifests himself to the initiate of the first grade in Mithraism. In the *Shâhnâmeh*, Ferdowsi has Satan promise Zahhak that, "Your head will rise in heaven, like the Sun."[113]

The descriptions of Zahhak as a *jâdoogar* or sorcerer who replaced righteous religion with sorcery and fed on human brains suggests that he is, from an orthodox Zoroastrian standpoint, a psychological manipulator. Ferdowsi tells us that after capturing Jamshid's daughters: "Zahhak trained them in magic and taught them evil ways..."[114] In Greek myths, Hermes teaches human beings writing, which is viewed as a departure from the relative sincerity of transmitted tradition in an oral culture. In the *Shâhnâmeh*, it is the *divs* or devils sent by Ahriman who teach humanity writing.[115] Zahhak is, according to the *Avestâ*, the son of Ahriman. Fereidun smites

Zahhak with a bull-headed mace. Other heroes and kings had maces with different animal symbolism. Seen in this light, the caduceus is a serpentine mace. *Mehragân* or the "festival of Mithra" commemorates the defeat of the Dragon King Azhi-Dahhaka or Zahhak at the hands of the hero Fereidun, in revenge for Zahhak's slaying of Jamshid who had inaugurated *Nowruz*.[116] As in the case of the Gorgon-slaying, where Perseus does not just kill Medusa but appropriates her power (her *Shakti*) as a weapon against his own enemies, the fact that Mithra wields what was Zahhak's scepter suggests that he is an ancient Iranian iteration of the trickster archetype.

How the god of oaths and enforcer of contracts, who is invoked when one swears to tell the truth, could also be seen as a manipulative deceiver is at the very heart of the Mithraic mystery. At this relatively preliminary stage in our study, we still remain a long way from being fully prepared to fathom what such a diabolical idea was meant to suggest. Chapters 3 and 4 ought, however, to have been preparatory in this regard.

The form of Mithraism practiced by the Cilician pirates, with their skull and crossbones banner, likely accorded a particularly significant role to Anahita. The initiation rites that they introduced into the Roman Empire through the port cities of the Mediterranean certainly incorporated an embodiment of the divine feminine. The symbol for the second grade of initiation is the crescent diadem of the goddess together with a torch and an oil lamp to guide the way to the bridal chamber.[117] The astrological archetype associated with this grade of initiation is the planet Venus or Aphrodite, which is referred to as Lucifer in Latin when it rises as the morning star. Mithra was the bringer of dawn. Here one must recall that from the most ancient times until the present day, the Iranian name *Mitra* is predominately used for females and, according to Herodotus, the ancient Persians used to translate the name of the Greek goddess Aphrodite as *Mitra*.[118] So the god Mithra is also the goddess of Love.

At this stage, the initiate was forced to become a transvestite. He was made to dress in female attire and wear a bridal veil that hid his face, so that the grade was sometimes also called *Kryptos*, "the Occult, or Hidden."[119] At the end of the ritual, the neophyte's veil was totally removed.[120]

The initiatory rite involved his being married to the Father, in the course of which it was expected that he "pours out the cup of his heart" upon a statue of Mithra.[121] Part of this mystical marriage of the bridegroom to the Father included kissing him on the mouth, the navel, the lower spine (or even the anus), as well as on the phallus.[122] The marriage culminated with the bridegroom being sodomized.[123]

Orthodox Zoroastrians consider sodomy to be the worst of all vices.[124] Yet traces remain in Middle Persian scriptures of a doctrine according to which the planets are very powerful demons that Ahriman brings into being by sodomizing himself.[125] It was believed that

> All welfare and adversity that come to man and other creatures, come through the Seven and the Twelve. The twelve Signs of the Zodiac, as the Religion says, are the twelve commanders on the side of Ohrmazd; and the seven planets are said to be the seven commanders on the side of Ahriman. And the seven planets oppress all creation and deliver it over to death and all manner of evil; for the twelve Signs of the Zodiac and the seven planets rule the fate of the world and direct it.[126]

The *Minouyé Kherad* quite frankly admits that, in conjunction with the planets, the constellations determine the fate of the world.[127] The planets intercept the beneficence bestowed by the constellations and use these stellar influences for their own demonic purposes.[128] The planets accompanied Ahriman in his attack on the creation. Chapter 4 of *Shikand Gomâni Vazâr* and Chapter 5 of the *Greater Bundahishn* both describe the countermeasures taken by the forces of light on this occasion.[129]

Various planets are described as attacking various stellar constellations, for example, Saturn, the commander-in-chief of the planetary forces attacks the Pole Star, who is the supreme commander of the Zodiac.[130] The "war in heaven" was a mythical explanation for the irregular motion of the planets, which, having been bound by the forces of light, are pulled back once they reach the end of their rope.[131] Despite being bound, the planets are the "Rulers of the World" deputized by Ahriman.[132] The heavenly sphere is divided into seven grades or seven heavens, with the uppermost ruled by Saturn (*Kayvân*).[133] According to the *Bundahishn*, the two most powerful planets, Saturn (*Kayvân*) and Mars (*Bahrâm*), are triumphant over their adversaries in "the astral battle."[134] In other words, as in the most pessimistic types of Gnosticism, this world is predominately governed by the forces of evil.[135] In this context, the sodomy endured by the Mithraic initiate of the second grade can be seen as a symbolic recognition of the Ahrimanic power of the planetary bodies, with a view to overcoming their influences.

Such a transcendence would mean rising above the earthly plane itself, and this brings us to the sixth grade of initiation in Mithraism, which is known as *Heliodromus*. In Greek *Dromos* means astronomical orbit, so *Heliodromus* is the charioteer in the orbit of the Sun. His symbols are a solar whip, a crown with seven rays standing for the seven grades of initiation, and a torch.[136] These last two implements offer a clue to the hidden Mithraic symbolism of the Statue of Liberty, which was designed by Freemason Bartholdi, with the assistance of his fellow Masonic brother Gustav Eiffel. They were initiates of the same lodge, and clearly familiar with Mithraic symbolism.[137] The crescent diadem of Nymphus looks like the lower part of the crown of the Statue of Liberty in New York with the windows carved into it, and the oil lamp carried by the initiate of this grade is like that which originally lit the fire in the statue's torch. The cornerstone of the colossal statue's pedestal was lain by the Masonic Grand Master of New York in 1884.[138] She is a synthesis of Mithra as *Nymphus* and as *Heliodromus*. The "liberty cap," which became a symbol of freed slaves in the Roman Empire, and of liberty during the French and American revolutions, is originally the Phrygian cap of the Mithraists.[139] In Lady Liberty, Mithra's Liberty cap has been replaced by the crescent diadem and solar rays.

In the guise of *Sol*, or the Sun, the Heliodromus initiate would participate in a banquet with the Father, sitting on the hide of a slaughtered bull.[140] The wine consumed at this banquet was not ordinary wine. It was that wine which, according to Iranian mythology, is the blood of the giants who attempted to scale and storm heaven.[141] This wine is still produced by Kurdish tribes in the area of Kermanshah today, where both the Yezidis and the Ahl-e-Haq preserve Mithraic traditions.[142] The women of the tribe gather mushrooms that are referred to as *mehrgiah* or "Mithra's vegetation." As one informant, a Kurd named Siamak, reports, "This is not like normal wine… You drink a little bit and you feel like you can fly."[143] The flight is that of the charioteer who ascends above the Earth and into the orbit of the Sun. Certain Roman accounts suggest that this actually produced an out of body experience or "astral travel," which allowed those who experienced it to come back and describe the Earth as if from space.[144]

The fiery fall of Phaëton, the son of the Sun, in his father's solar chariot, sets the Earth ablaze with droplets of solar fire of red and amber color, in other words, the psychedelic *Amanita muscaria* mushrooms.[145] These are the mushrooms that, after being dried and ground, are used to lace or spike the wine of the Mithraic Eucharist. Mithra is identified as "Phaëton in Persia" by the fifth-century poet Nonnos.[146] After Phaëton's death, his lover, Cycnus, underwent metamorphosis into a swan whose song lamenting the loss of his beloved is the origin of the term "swan song."[147] The initiate of the sixth grade sings a swan song for the entire world.

One thing relevant here is the difference between the initiate as *Sol*, at this stage, and *Sol Invictus*, which is Mithra in all his glory as The Father, namely Perseus. The Romans used the Persian epithet *Nabarze* or "victorious" for Mithra to express the same idea that is conveyed by the more common *Sol Invictus*.[148] The military salute has its origin in the Mithraic symbolism of shielding one's eyes from the brilliance of Mithra, the general and Invincible Sun.[149] *Sol Invictus* or "Unconquerable Sun" is not the sun in the sky that passes through the twelve zodiacal constellations in the 26,000 year cycle of precession. It is an invisible Sun, a light that shines even in the darkness of night as the power over stellar fate and fatality. This is significant because the grade of solar charioteer also involves the perishability of this world, of everything under the conquerable Sun that rises and sets.

After the banquet the initiate in the guise of *Sol*, naked except for a cape covered in stars and the seven planets, would lead the Father into his solar chariot, whip in hand ready to crack it on the four horses of the Apocalypse — another symbol that Christians misappropriated from Mithraism.[150] He carries a torch to set the world on fire.[151] This conflagration, referred to as the *Frashgard* in Middle Persian texts, takes place at the end of the Great Year culminating the cycle of world ages.[152] So in esoteric symbolism, the Statue of Liberty is the torch-bearing female version of Mithra, ready to set fire to the entire earthly realm that is divided into various sovereign territories. This is significant in terms of Lady Liberty being a watcher over the harbor, since the waters of the world are stateless and pirates are the true kings of the seas. Julius Caesar learned this first hand when he was captured by the Cilician pirates and only released for a very large ransom.

5.4 Mithra as the Gnostic Christ

By the end of the Parthian period, Mithraism was the dominant religion within the Roman military and even counted a few Caesars among its initiates. Roman centurions were stationed in places other than their region of origin, and moved often, so that any one legion of them was "a sort of microcosm of the empire."[153] These included soldiers who were natives of countries where Mithraism was dominant, for example, Cappadocia, Pontus, Commagene, Syria, and Cilicia.[154] Besides recruiting centurions from territories often governed by the Parthians, the Romans on occasion even recruited defeated Parthian cavalry into their own ranks.[155] These recruits formed brotherhoods to preserve their Mithraic religion, and owing to the humanistic character of Mithraism, these brotherhoods were open to their fellow Roman soldiers, men who no doubt found the mysteries of the Orient alluring — especially when the god in question was believed to secure martial victory.[156] When these converts were transferred, they themselves recruited others to the faith in a realm of Roman military power extending from the Black Sea to the Scottish highlands and the Sahara desert.[157] Aside from the Cilician pirates, there were Mithraic initiates in the Roman Navy itself and these spread Mithraism across Europe through the river systems that ran through Rome's continental empire.[158] No less than 420 Mithraea have been unearthed, from the Middle East to northern England.[159]

Throughout the Roman Empire, Mithra was unequivocally referred to as "the Persian god" and Romans, often suspiciously, saw Mithraism as "the Persian cult."[160] Firmicus Maternus, writing circa 350 CE, sees Mithraism as a Persian fifth column, and he also makes interesting observations about the Gorgonic goddess figure in Mithraism:

> The Persians and all the Magi who dwell in the confines of the Persian land give their preference to fire and think it ought to be ranked above all the other elements. So they divide fire into potencies, relating its nature to the potency of the two sexes, and attributing the substance of fire to the image of a man and the image of a woman. The woman they represent with triform countenance, and entwine her with snaky monsters. ... The male they worship is a cattle rustler, and his cult they relate to the potency of fire, as his prophet handed down the lore to us, saying: *mysta booklopies, syndexie patros agauou* (initiate of cattle-rustling, companion by hand-clasp of an illustrious father). Him they call Mithra, and his cult they carry on in hidden caves. ... Him whose crime you acknowledge you think to be a god. So you who declare it proper for the cult of the Magi to be carried on by the Persian rite in these cave temples, why do you praise only this among the Persian customs? If you think it worthy of the Roman name to serve the cults of the Persians, the laws of the Persians...[161]

Firmicus Maternus was a devout Catholic and his book on *The Error of Pagan Religions* looks back on Mithraism as a diabolical invention. Caesar Julian, "the Apostate" (336 AD), was a Mithraist who attempted to disestablish Christianity and establish Mithraism as the official religion of the Roman Empire.[162] From this it is clear that Mithraism was very close to becoming the dominant religion of the Roman Empire, rather than Christianity. Moreover, although it was never a state religion, the religious influence of Mithraism in Rome was as institutional as that of the Church as it rose to power. Like Churches today, Mithraic communities were juridical bodies capable of holding property.[163] Private benefactors would put up the cost of digging the subterranean chambers, or would volunteer their own cellars.[164] The similarities of Mithraism to Christianity frightened the Christian writers who became aware of them, and they resorted to claiming that the devil, who had the demonic power to attain foreknowledge of the coming of Christ, had imitated elements of what would become Christianity and introduced them into the world so as to denigrate Christ's gospel and misguide people.[165]

Mithra was born on December 25th and, according to some traditions, especially in Eastern Iran, his was a virgin birth. Anahita is both Mithra's *virgin* mother and his partner.[166] Anahita is the Lady of the Lake who conceives of Mithra by submerging in Lake Hamun, Sistan, where legend has it that the seed of Zarathustra was preserved.[167] This earthly incarnation of Mithra, comparable to the Trinitarian earthly incarnation of God as Jesus, lived from 272 BC to 208 BC, and after these sixty-four years ascended to Heaven. Mithra was born from his Immaculate (Anahid) mother, and his father Ahura Mazda, in the middle of the night of December 24th to 25th, celebrated by the winter solstice holiday of *Yalda*.[168] He is the *only* begotten son of Ahura Mazda. This myth dates from *at least* the third century BC, at the start of the Parthian dynasty.[169]

The Mithraic Communion feast was the prototype of the Christian sacrament of the Lord's Supper, with sacred wine and circular loaves of bread marked with an equilateral cross.[170] The equilateral cross inside of a circle (what is contemporarily known as the Celtic cross) was probably the main symbol or standard of the religion. The Mithraic Communion was a banquet held with Mithra to celebrate his imminent ascension. Mithra is the "savior and conductor of the soul," who assists the ascension of the soul just as he does the rising sun.[171] Sunday, or the day of the sun, was the holiest day of the week for Mithraists. Each of the seven planets was associated with a day of the week, with a particular metal, a degree of initiation, and a certain potency.[172] The planet of the day of the week was invoked in front of its effigy in the crypt on that day.[173]

The egalitarian spirit that later became characteristic of socialistic and progressive movements in European civilization, and which is mistakenly believed to have begun with Christianity in the late Roman period, is actually a legacy of Mithraism. Merchants were on an equal footing with upstanding citizens, who treated slaves as their equals and in this occult order even a common soldier who had attained the highest rank of initiation could be looked up to by an emperor.[174] So-called "aristocracy" based on wealth was replaced by a spiritual aristocracy wherein all brothers pledged loyalty to one another, and a slave could even be a wealthy man's superior depending on their respective grades of initiation.[175] The mitre (Latin *mitra*) worn by Christian bishops and abbots, and derived from the Phrygian cap, is another element of Mithraism adopted by Christianity.[176] It survives in popular culture as the red Santa Claus hat and even as the hat of the smurfs, who not accidentally live amongst mushrooms.

The evergreen tree ornamented with red and white, which became the Christmas tree, was originally a Mithraic symbol as well. The evergreen tree was a symbol of Truth in ancient Iran (especially the *Sarv*). It hosts the psychedelic mushroom *Amanita muscaria*, which is red and white.[177] As mentioned above, this mushroom was ingested by Mithraists, particularly admixed with wine, as crushed psychedelic mushrooms still are today in the rural parts of Iran.[178] The tricolor of the Iranian flag shares the green, white, and red commonly associated with the Christmas season on account of this common origin. White, red, and green also stand for the three main castes in ancient Iranian society: royalty, the warrior caste, and the farming peasantry.[179] One finds this color scheme on the flags of many nations of ethnically Iranian origin, including Tajikistan, Kurdistan, Bulgaria, and Hungary. The legacy of Mithraism in Rome is to account for its also having become the flag of Italy.

One of the major sources of Mithraic influence on the formation of Christianity must have been Paul (formerly Saul), who was from Tarsus. According to Plutarch, Mithraism entered the Roman world in Tarsus, the capital city of the province of Cilicia, from which the Cilician pirates get their name.[180] The lion attacking the bull was an important symbol of the city of Tarsus.[181] According to Strabo (64 BC–21 AD), Tarsus had "surpassed Athens, Alexandria, or any other place" in terms of its educational system, and the influence that Philosophy or the sciences had on social order and political administration.[182] Two of the chief administrators of the University of Tarsus, Athenodorus and Nestor, became political leaders of the city. It is fair to characterize it as a city-state that was ruled by a university. Stoicism was the predominant philosophical school in Tarsus, and one of the main beliefs of the Stoics is that a conflagration will engulf the world at the end of a Great Year.[183] It should go without saying that the Stoics, for whom Heraclitus was an intellectual wellspring, adopted this idea under Persian influence in the first place. This idea can be seen reflected in numerous Gospel passages. For example:

> I am come to send fire on the earth, and what will I, if it be already kindled? (Luke 12:49)

> Jesus said, 'I have cast fire upon the world, and behold, I am guarding it until it blazes.' (Thomas 10)[184]

> Jesus said, 'The heavens and the earth will roll up in your presence, and whoever is living from the living one will not see death.' Does not Jesus say, 'Whoever has found himself, of that person the world is not worthy.' (Thomas 111)[185]

> Whoever is near me is near the fire, and whoever is far from me is far from the kingdom. (Thomas 82)[186]

The global conflagration or *Frashgard*, which acts as an alchemical furnace for the entire earth, is clearly one that only a very select and transformed few will survive:

> Jesus said, 'I shall choose you, one from a thousand and two from ten thousand, and they will stand as a single one.' (Thomas 23)[187]

> Jesus said, 'I disclose my mysteries to those who are worthy of my mysteries. Do not let your left hand know what your right hand is doing.' (Thomas 62)[188]

> Jesus said, 'Blessed are those who are alone and chosen, for you will find the kingdom. For you have come from it, and you will return there again.' (Thomas 49)[189]

> Jesus said, 'There are many standing at the door, but those who are alone will enter the wedding chamber.' (Thomas 75)[190]

These elect were souls purified by many lifetimes of sometimes brutally instructive experience in this fallen world and vale of tears. The writings of Eubolos and Porphyry, among other Greco-Roman authors, attest to the belief in reincarnation as an element of the Mithraism of the Parthian period. Both of these authors claimed that certain Magi practice vegetarianism on account of their view that the process of metempsychosis can, in the worst instances, bring a human soul to be reincarnated as an animal.[191] One is reminded of the Pythagorean belief in both reincarnation and vegetarianism, which, as suggested in Chapter 2, Pythagoras learned from Magi in the period when Gautama himself was a member of the Magian Order in Babylon and before he became the Buddha, following his exile by Darius the Great to northern India. This cryptic passage of the Gospel of Thomas features a Mithraic Christ who, like Gautama Buddha, warns initiates of the burden of bearing awareness of one's deeds and personality in previous lifetimes: "When you see your likeness, you are happy. But when you see your images that came into being before you and that neither die nor become visible, how much you will bear!"[192]

Many Mithraic ideas besides that of an apocalyptic global conflagration were appropriated by Christianity in its formative phase. For example, the third grade of Mithraic initiation, the grade of *Miles* or the soldier, is the basis for the Christian rite of confirmation and the chrism of Ash Wednesday.[193] Its symbols are the lance and the helmet, and its astrological sign is the planet Mars.[194] The initiate, decked out in leather military attire and a breastplate, is conscripted to serve as a soldier of Mithra on the cosmic battlefield.[195] The crown of earthly kingship and worldly power is presented to the initiate on the point of a sword in the form of a wreath. He places this on his head, but then throws it off as he proclaims "Mithra is my Crown; my Crown rests with my god."[196] At this point the initiate's face is slapped and he is given a brand on the forehead by his immediate superior, a brother of the grade Leo.[197] This brand or seal takes the form of an ashen X and represents the *xvarneh* or *farr*, the divine royal glory, flaming from the forehead of Mithra. We see on the sarcophagus of the Emperor Hostilian, Trajan's youngest son, that he was a Mithraic initiate branded on the forehead with this X.[198] Thereafter the soldier of Mithra (Christ) would refuse to wear a crown of any kind, including a wreath crown at banquets, phrasing his refusal to whomever wanted to bestow him with one in the following terms: "It belongs to my god."[199] The Christian theme of Christ resisting the temptations of the devil for ruling the kingdoms of this world, and his later statement in the course of being questioned by Pilate, namely "My kingdom is not of this world" (John 18:36), probably have this Mithraic rite as their true origin.[200] We could add to that injunction these sayings of the same spirit from the Gospel of Thomas:

> Jesus said, 'Whoever has come to know the world has discovered a carcass, and whoever has discovered a carcass, of that person the world is not worthy.' (Thomas 56)[201]

> Jesus said, 'Let one who has become wealthy reign, and let one who has power renounce it.' (Thomas 81)[202]

The other main symbol of Christianity besides the cross, and the one that was used by the earliest Christians at least as much as the cross, if not more, is also Mithraic in origin. The geometric symbol of the *Vesica Pisces*, stylized by early Christians as a fish, evokes at least two powerful ideas that connect it to Mithraism. First of all, recall that Mithra is the Lord of Precession. The tauroctony image is a legacy of Mithraism at its historical origin, in the epoch of the transition between the Age of Taurus and the Age of Aries. By the first century AD, Mithraists would have needed a new symbol that would appropriately signal Mithra shifting the star globe of Zorvan's body, the *Sepehr*, from a spring equinox in Aries to a spring equinox in Pisces. What better symbol of the astrological age of Pisces than the fish? Secondly—though perhaps on a metaphysical level, this is even more important—the *Vesica Pisces* also symbolizes a mediation between two opposed spheres, in other words Mithra as the mediator between Ohrmazd and Ahriman.

This brings us to the most radical teaching attributed to Christ, which makes little sense in a Judeo-Christian context, against the backdrop of the Jewish Bible or "Old Testament," but makes perfectly good sense in the context of Mithraism. That is the set of maxims that includes "Resist not evil" (Matthew 5:39) and "Love your enemies" (Luke 6:27). Orthodox and Catholic Christians ensconced these sayings in the context of a Sermon on the Mount, which includes the servile and spineless injunctions to "turn the other cheek" and forgive every act of violence or injustice suffered at the hands of others. Of course, this did not stop them from carrying out brutal inquisitions and persecutory crusades. In their original Mithraic context, these maxims of not resisting evil and loving one's enemies mean something completely different, which can only be understood with a view to what has been revealed throughout this chapter as the hidden cosmological, metaphysical, psychological, and sociopolitical content of the Mithraic mysteries.

Moreover, the teaching needs to be placed in the context of other Gnostic sayings that kaleidoscopically reveal the light of the Unconquerable Sun of God, the light that continues to illumine the human mind even in the most encompassing heart of darkness. Not resisting evil and loving one's enemies would be the most ruinous maxims imaginable, *if* the objective were to secure a merely "human" life in *this* world. They take on another significance altogether against the backdrop of a doctrine that rejects the family, overcomes the gender binary, has utter contempt for political power and worldly wealth, even intends to watch the entire earth burn, and to see the end of all human life on it, with only those who surmount the human condition saved.

Members of a Mithraic secret society were bound together by oaths of loyalty that demanded greater devotion to one another than to their own kin, and the soldiers — or pirates — who became initiates were often far away from their families and even from their native country. In this case, water *was* actually thicker than blood. Those baptized into a Mithraic way of life were born again of a different mother. This ought to be considered as the context for understanding the following words put into the mouth of "Jesus," despite their evidently radical contradiction of Judeo-Christian "family values." Luke 12:49–53, which is mirrored by Saying 16 in the Gospel of Thomas, reads:

> Perhaps people think that I have come to impose peace upon the world. Little do they know that I have come to set the earth on fire, that I bring the sword of division, conflict, and war. For there will be five in a house that is divided, with three of them against the other two, and vice versa: The father will be divided against his son, and the son against his father, the mother against her daughter, and the daughter against her mother, mother-in-law and daughter-in-law against one another, and each of them will stand alone.[203]

The significance of setting the earth on fire has been addressed above, so let us focus on the destruction of the family. The same message is repeated over and over again in the Gospels. Luke 14:26 reads, "If any man come to me, and hate not his father, and mother, and wife, and children, and brethren, and sisters, yea, and his own life also, he cannot be my disciple." Saying 55 of the Gospel of Thomas employs an almost identical turn of phrase, "Whoever does not hate father and mother cannot be a disciple of me, and whoever does not hate brothers and sisters and bear the cross as I do, will not be worthy of me."[204] The cross that is being referred to here is not the one on which Jesus was crucified. This is clear both from the fact that the Christ saying this has yet to be crucified, and from the fact that Thomas is a Gnostic gospel and the Gnostics do not even believe that Jesus died on the cross. "*The* cross" that the Gnostic savior is referring to — rather than the formulation "his" cross, which is a corruption of this saying in the later, canonical gospels — is *the* one and only cross that there is to bear in this world: the crossing of the celestial equator by the ecliptic, which was the main symbol of Mithraism and, as we have seen, was represented by the crossed bones beneath a skull. It is Time and Death.

As the Lord of Time and primordial progenitor of both the first-born Ahriman and the late-comer Ohrmazd, Zorvan is an androgynous deity. This is an idea that we have only touched on in this chapter and that will be explored at greater length and in greater depth in the next chapter.

However, for the moment, it is significant to point out that restoring the shattered unity of the godhead through a Mithraic mediation between Ahrimanic and Mazdean forces also requires the devotee of Mithra to overcome the gender binary. We saw this in the initiation rite for the second degree in a Mithraic secret society, the degree of the Nymph or the Veiled One, wherein the male initiate becomes a transvestite. In this connection, note Saying 22 from the Gospel of Thomas:

> Jesus saw some babies nursing. He said to his disciples, 'These nursing babies are like those who enter the kingdom.' They said to him, 'Then shall we enter the kingdom as babies?' Jesus said to them, 'When you make the two into one, and when you make the inner like the outer and the outer like the inner, and the upper like the lower, and when you make male and female into a single one, so that the male will not be male nor the female be female, when you make eyes in place of an eye, a hand in place of a hand, a foot in place of a foot, an image in place of an image, then you will enter the kingdom.'

Mithraism has been accused of being an all-male religion, and Franz Cumot claimed that the alleged exclusion of women from Mithraic "brotherhoods" put the cult at a disadvantage in terms of its proselytizing power as compared to early Christianity.[205] First of all, if this were true, it would only be true of the shape that Mithraism took in the more patriarchal Roman Empire, as compared to its original Iranian form—both among the Parthians and their Achaemenid predecessors, and especially among the northern Iranians. The feminine or, at the very least, androgynous aspects of Mithra "himself," which are preserved in Roman iconography, are traces of a primordial tradition in which *Mitra* was a goddess figure—one and the same as the Sarmatian or "Amazon" archetype of Artemis or Satana. As suggested in the preceding chapter, when this *Mitra* was appropriated by the somewhat more patriarchal Persians, the feminine aspect of the deity was split off and recast as the mother and companion of Mithra, namely Anahita. The cult of Anahita is as integral to the classical Iranian form of Mithraism as Mithra and Zorvan.

Furthermore, in point of fact, there is ample reason to question the claim that women were not part of Mithraic "brotherhoods" even in the Roman Empire. First of all, a burial inscription concerning a woman named Aelia Arisuth, which was found in a Roman tomb in North Africa, uses phrases to honor her that suggest she was a Mithraic initiate.[206] In *De Abstinentia*, Porphyry mentions female initiates who were counterparts of male Mithraists of the lion grade.[207] These counterparts of the "lions" (Persian *shiré mardân*) were called "hyenas." This is because the hyena species is matriarchal and female hyenas have suggestively male genitalia. As Robin M. Weare observes:

> It is true that the female hyena's genitals look just like the male's; she has a huge clitoris she can erect at will and even has a sack of fibrous tissue that looks like testicles. This has led to the notion that hyenas can change sex!
>
> … The notion that hyenas changed sex from male to female and back again and again dates back at least to ancient Greece, although Aristotle refuted it. The idea probably comes from the fact that the genitals of the two sexes look nearly identical. In fact, Europeans often associated hyenas with sexual 'perversion,' especially homosexuality. … [T]here are cultures that believe some witches can turn themselves into hyenas.[208]

It is in the context of such beliefs that we should read the otherwise cryptic Saying 114 of the Gospel of Thomas, which is the last saying in the book, and should be placed alongside Saying 22 above. The passage begins with the misogynistic Simon Peter remarking, in reference to the presence of Mary Magdalene among the first rank and inner circle of the male disciples of Christ, "Let Mary leave us, for females are not worthy of life." In response to this Jesus says, "Behold, I shall guide her to make her male, so that she too may become a living spirit resembling you males. For every female who makes herself male will enter the kingdom of heaven." While seeming to be patriarchal on the face of it, this passage ought to be interpreted in the context of the metaphor of sex-changing matriarchal hyenas as well as the injunction in Saying 22 *for males to become female just as* females become males—so that the gender binary is alchemically overcome in a superior and trans-human form of embodiment. What is meant here by Mary being guided to "become male" is a maleness defined by what is called *Javânmardi* or *mardânegi* in Persian, a quality that the Sarmatian women of the northern Iranian realm had in equal or even greater measure than their male counterparts.

This calls to mind an apparently disparaging remark that Friedrich Nietzsche makes about women in *Thus Spoke Zarathustra*. It is a reflection on friendship that is quite relevant to understanding the character of Mithraic communion and camaraderie:

> Are you a slave? Then you cannot be a friend. Are you a tyrant? Then you cannot have friends. All-too-long have a slave and a tyrant been concealed in woman. Therefore woman is not yet capable of friendship: she knows only love.
>
> Woman's love involves injustice and blindness against everything that she does not love. And even in the knowing love of a woman there are still assault and lightning and night alongside light.
>
> Woman is not yet capable of friendship: women are still cats and birds. Or at best, cows.
>
> Woman is not yet capable of friendship. But tell me, you men, who among you is capable of friendship?
>
> Alas, behold your poverty, you men, and the meanness of your souls![209]

The first thing to be borne in mind about this passage is what the last line suggests: that hardly any *men* are capable of true friendship. Before passing an overly harsh judgment on Nietzsche for denigrating the qualities of women, one ought to ask oneself what kind of relationship between men — between comrades — would constitute friendship in the real and robust meaning of the word that Nietzsche wants to defend in this section of *Thus Spoke Zarathustra*. Friendship can only be forged beyond all of the most human emotions, such as envy, lust, avarice, greed, wrath, and vengeance. These demonic passions will become a focus of contemplation in the next chapter.

For now it suffices to ask what *man*, let alone what woman, would be capable of completely overcoming these passions in the kind of camaraderie that binds him to his friends. After all, a man should be nothing less to his friend than "an arrow and a longing for the overman."[210] Now when one considers the wording "not yet" and the time when Nietzsche wrote this passage, in the late nineteenth century when Western women were just barely starting to be recognized as more than the mere property and chattel of men (chattel as in cows), things start to become clearer. The significance of this passage for understanding Mithraism becomes even clearer when we contextualize the view against the backdrop of the Roman Empire. In such a context, a woman capable of true friendship would have been a "female who makes herself male" like the "hyena" initiates of the Mithraic secret societies.

The question remains how Mithraism, which was the dominant religion of the Roman Empire, could have been displaced by Christianity, which misappropriated so much from it on the way to becoming the official and exclusive state religion of Rome. Moreover, the Christianity that was institutionalized in Rome identified the teaching of the Gnostic Christ, which most clearly reveals Christianity's debt to Mithraism, as its greatest enemy, initiating inquisitorial persecutions of Gnostics in Alexandria and eventually a crusade against Gnostics in France. The answer to this riddle of history, namely Constantine's transformation of a nearly Mithraic Rome into an Orthodox or Catholic Rome (the two were not yet distinct), lies in the overthrow of Rome's centuries-long rival superpower to the East. In the early third century AD, the Parthian dynasty was toppled by a militant usurper from a priestly clan in Pars, the Persian heart of Iran. It is to the deeds of Ardeshir Babakan that we must look for an answer to how, first, Christianity, and then even Islam, shattered a Mithraic realm that had stretched from the Indus to Britain and rose up over the ruins of Ancient Iran as a specter that still haunts us.

CHAPTER 6

FROM PERSIA WITH LOVE

As we have seen, the Iranian cultural conquest of the Roman Empire through the spread of Mithraism was nearly victorious. It was undone, not by the Romans, but by Ardeshir Babakan, the founder of what can be seen as a Second Persian Empire. Ardeshir's suppression of Mithraism and invention of an Orthodox Zoroastrianism as the ideological foundation of the Sassanian state is the point of departure for this chapter. It ultimately focuses on the inquisitorial persecution of those who resisted this orthodoxy, especially the followers of a certain Zaradusht (the Middle Persian form of "Zarathustra") who was based in Pars — the same heart of Persia from out of which Ardeshir emerged to overthrow the Parthians.

Together with his grand inquisitors, Tansar and Kartir, Ardeshir attempted to eradicate Mithraism. He also stated an intention to re-conquer all of the lands of the first Persian Empire that had, for centuries, become part of the Roman Empire. Presumably he aimed, as part of this prototypical Crusade, to impose his totalitarian Zoroastrian Orthodoxy on Syrian, Anatolian, and Egyptian parts of Rome that had grown accustomed to a relatively tolerant and cosmopolitan pagan society. The first major claim of this chapter is that the institutionalized form of Christianity was invented by the circle around Constantine in order to erect a defensive cultural barrier between Romans and the puritanical Zoroastrian zealots of *Irânshahr*. This eventually resulted in a destruction of the Alexandrian high culture of a Roman Empire that, but for Ardeshir, had been on the verge of becoming spiritually Mithraic and socially integrated with Iran.

Ardeshir's son, Shapur the Great, who styled himself "King of Kings of Iran (the Aryan Realm) and the Non-Aryans" (*Shâhanshâhé Irân va Anirân*), breaks with his father's puritanical policies and backs the prophet

Mani's attempt to unify the East and the West with a single world religion based on an integration of the teachings of Zarathustra, Buddha, and the Gnostic Christ. Following the death of Shapur, the persecution faced by Mani and the Manicheans at the hands of Kartir becomes a template for the inquisitorial policies of those who had remained loyal to the Zoroastrian Orthodoxy of Ardeshir. Their most significant target ends up being the movement of Zarathustra of Persia. Originally known as the *Dorost Dînân* ("Those of Just Conscience"), this movement is rebranded as "Mazdakite" when Mazdak, Prime Minister of Emperor Kavad I, uses Sassanid state power to implement a revolution from above.

The Mazdakite redistribution of wealth and encouragement of free love was based on a fascinating Neo-Mithraic metaphysics and psychology. The reason that possessiveness with respect to wealth and women must be overcome is that the human mind is assailed by envy, vengefulness, anger, lust, and greed. These five demonic forces are all expressions of Concupiscence or *Âz*, the feminine arch-demon whose seduction of *Zorvân* — the androgynous deity of Time — is responsible for the premature birth of Ahriman before the birth of Ohrmazd. This is meant to signify first that the root of evil is the unconsciousness of God, and second that God only becomes good over the course of time and only on account of a dialectic that requires evil. Various prophets appear in successive historical epochs, beginning with Zarathustra and including Christ. Whereas these messengers publicly preach an exoteric doctrine for the sake of social evolution, they also initiate an elect of sagacious guardians into an esoteric secret doctrine that holds the key to the purpose and end of this divine evolution. At the apocalypse, Mithra or *Mehr Yazd* will ultimately force *Âz* to devour the demons that assail the hearts and minds of men. This will happen through revelation of the secret doctrine guarded by the initiates.

The Mazdakite Revolution was a failed attempt at this apocalyptic revelation. That it lasted as long as it did — an entire generation — is astounding when one considers how radically it dynamited all of the pillars of any traditional society: vast inequalities in the possession of private property, monogamous marriage and the patriarchal family, inquisitorial religious hierarchy, and the political persecution of dissidents. This chapter will place particular emphasis on the extreme misogyny of the Zoroastrian Orthodoxy, as evidenced by scriptures such as the *Vendidâd*. The Neo-Mithraist views that the Mazdakites had about the role of *Âz* in creation and God's evolution toward self-consciousness and the overcoming of his/her own inner evil surely also lent itself to the relatively egalitarian role of Iranian women in Mazdakite communities.

In the end the orthodox clergy backed the rise of Khosrow Anushiravan, who massacred up to 100,000 leading Mazdakites and authorized public book burnings to stamp out their "deviant" and "degenerate" Mithraic ideas about the evolution of God and the perfection of Man. Although Khosrow ironically later comes to be known as a Platonic "Philosopher King" on account of his having taken in Greco-Roman academicians after the Christian closure of the last of the academies in the West, he was the patron of a pacified court "philosophy" with no social implications — and, moreover, an *imported* scholasticism as compared to the revolutionary *native* philosophical movement that he tried to stamp out.

6.1 Ardeshir and Totalitarian Theocracy

The pre-Islamic period of Iran's history culminates in the reign of the Sassanian dynasty (224–651 AD), whose founder, Ardeshir Babakan, staged a coup against the Parthians. Like Caesar Marcus Aurelius, Ardeshir Babakan was a thinker in addition to being a statesman. Ardeshir advocated centralization of the Iranian form of government and the establishment of a theocratic Zoroastrian orthodoxy as the basis for his authoritarian regime.

Ardeshir named the Sassanian realm *Irânshahr*, a Middle Persian contraction of the ancient Persian words, *Aryâna* and *Khashatra*, meaning "Aryan Imperium." The contemporary usage *Irân* is a shorthand reference to this Sassanian-era terminology. Ardeshir was from a priestly clan of Pars (Arabized *Fars*), the province where Persepolis, the ceremonial capital of the Achaemenid Empire, had been located, and on the basis of which Westerners coined the term "Persia" to refer to all of Iran. Given the ruthlessness with which he lashed out from Pars to unify all of Iran under his centralized authority, Ardeshir can rightly be seen as the founder of a Second Persian Empire.[1]

The medieval historian Masoudi tells us that Ardeshir was accused of innovations in the religion of Zarathustra that broke with the understanding of previous kings (probably both the Parthians and the earlier Achaemenids).[2] Ardeshir thought that no one should be allowed to become more religious or zealous than the state, and that the greatest deceptions are those promulgated by religion. Consequently, in his view, the monarch has a duty to stand against these sects and protect people from being misled by them.[3] Ardeshir considered the execution of heretics a legitimate means of punishing them for their sins.[4] Tansar explains that Ardeshir extinguished the fires of most of the temples of Iran, because just anyone cannot be allowed to set up a fire temple and take advantage of people.[5] It is worthy of note that these temples were, and still are, referred to as *daré Mehr* (door of Mithra or door of "light and love"). The original fire temples were probably Mithraic and were adopted by Zoroastrians as their institutional buildings. After all, Zarathustra himself was originally a *Zaotar* or priest at one of these Mithraic temples. During the Parthian period, when Mithraism, albeit fused with elements of Zoroastrianism, had reemerged as the *de facto* (unofficial) religion of Iran, the majority of fire temples would have been Mithraeums.

We know that the fire temples that survived to the end of the Sassanian period were also repositories for sacred texts written and preserved by the Magi. Most of what we have from Pahlavi literature emerged from out of them. We also know that the *Avestâ* we have now is much shorter than the many-volume work that ancient sources describe. In this context, we would be remiss if we did not ask ourselves how it could be that the Parthians, whose art and architecture are at least at the level of the Sassanians in terms of technical competence and stylistic sophistication, could have produced no literature? In fact, it is patently false that there was no Parthian literature, because the extensive Manichean corpus, whose depth and breadth can be inferred from the few fragments of it that survive, is (from a stylistic, rather than a historical standpoint) an example of Parthian rather than Sassanian literature. Like these writings of Mani and his successors, much of Parthian literature may have been in languages other than Parthian Pahlavi (an earlier cousin of Sassanian Pahlavi), such as Syriac, and it would probably have been written using the Aramaic or Greek scripts.

Moreover, scholars of the Mazdakite heresy agree that it can be traced to a period much earlier than the famous (or infamous) Mazdak. As we shall see, it originated in the movement of a certain Magus by the name of Zaradusht (or Zarathustra) Khurragan who lived and taught in Pars, the Persian heart of Iran, *during the period of Ardeshir and his grand inquisitors, Tansar and Kartir.* If Manichaeism had not yet appeared in the public sphere — since the first mention of Mani is in the reign of Shapur, Ardeshir's successor, and since, despite Kartir's aims in carrying forward Ardeshir's theocratic project, Shapur actually endorsed Mani and members of his family became Manicheans — then who are all of these heretics that Ardeshir and Kartir are suppressing?

The Mazdakites had extensive scriptures that we know were totally destroyed during the reign of Khosrow I. How old were these? Did they date from the time of Zaradusht Khurragan or earlier? Were they Parthian literature? Persecutors of the Mazdakites refer to these texts as *Zand* or esoteric "interpretations" of the *Avestâ*, to the extent that *Zandiq* became synonymous with "heretic." What happened to the voluminous Parthian-period *Avesta* that these esoteric texts were commentaries on? Could it be that, while extinguishing all those fire temples, Ardeshir burned these books? Book burning and puritanical theocracy go hand in hand. What follows in this chapter is an attempt to reconstruct what was lost, or rather, what was censored and suppressed.

Ardeshir Babakan is the true originator of the so-called "Erastian" doctrine of the inseparability of religion and state, the fundamental statement of which we can see in this famous instruction that he gave to his successor, Shapur the Great:

> O my son … know that religion and kingship are two brothers, and neither can dispense with the other. Religion is the foundation of kingship, and kingship protects religion. For whatever lacks a foundation must perish, and whatever lacks a protector disappears.[6]

Unlike the Parthians, who were open to Greek cultural influence, Ardeshir had a xenophobic and exclusionary conception of Persian identity. Ardeshir anachronistically held the Romans responsible for Alexander's conquest of Iran, and from the outset he stated his intention to re-conquer all of the territories of the first Persian Empire that had become part of the Roman Empire. Given his puritanical monotheism and the mercilessness with which he was attempting to eradicate Mithraism in his own country, by closing down the majority of fire temples (*daré Mehr*) in Iran on account of their being too pagan, the Romans must have seen his rise to power as a grave threat — not only from a military standpoint, but from a sociological one as well.

Their reaction was to fortify the Roman state against the orthodox Zoroastrian crusaders of the Sassanian Empire by adopting a hierarchical and totalitarian state religion of their own. Given the national security threat from Iran, this could not be "the Persian religion" of Mithraism, and there was no pagan Greco-Roman religion structurally suitable to play such a role. So the social engineers of Constantine's time discovered a Jewish cult that could do the job, and incorporated many Mithraic ideas, symbols, and rituals into this universalist form of Judaism so as to placate those Romans who were already Mithraists. After all, it was not as if the Jews of Roman Palestine had the capability of taking over the Roman Empire through the Roman adoption of some version of their religion, in the way that Mithraism could be used as a fifth column for a Persian takeover of the Roman Empire — one that might be followed by a replacement of Mithraism with puritanical Sassanid Zoroastrian orthodoxy.

After conquering the Buddhist Kushans of Northern India, who backed Artabanus IV and fought to help keep the Parthians in power, and enforcing his brand of Zoroastrianism on Baluchistan, Kabul, and Punjab, Ardeshir turned to the West.[7] Both classical Roman and Islamic historians agree that Ardeshir's explicitly stated aim was to take back the Western lands of the Achaemenids with which he wanted to associate himself.[8] Ardeshir considered his victory over the last Parthian king as a kind of revenge against Alexander, and he also vengefully and illogically held the Romans, as standard-bearers of the West, responsible for the Greek conquest of the first Persian Empire.[9] He announced his intention to take back everything from the Euphrates to the Aegean Sea, Roman territory that had not been governed by Iran for five hundred years![10]

According to the *Letter of Tansar*, the founder of the Sassanian dynasty even planned to so decisively defeat the Romans that they would be forced to pay reparations for Alexander's conquest and the damage that all of his Hellenistic successors caused during their hundreds of years of occupying Iran.[11] By instituting compulsory military training for all male children whose parents could afford to train their sons, and requiring their registration as reserves, Ardeshir pushed for total mobilization and took Iran from a defensive to an offensive military posture.[12] Iran was the aggressor in most of twenty-two military battles, wars with Rome which were initiated by Ardeshir and inherited by his successors.[13]

It might be appropriate to call this a "crusade." After all, what did the pagan Romans have to look forward to from this puritanical theocrat? Even though federalism was invented by the Achaemenids, his supposed idols, and despite the fact that Alexander and his heirs adopted it from the Persians, Ardeshir Babakan and his advisors considered the federal government of the Parthians to be a legacy of the accursed Alexander and of Hellenism.[14] Ardeshir considered the establishment of a centralized and hierarchical state to be inseparable from his project of forming an orthodox Zoroastrian regime.[15] One could consider the latter a vehicle for accomplishing the former.[16] The freedom of religion in both Achaemenid and Parthian Iran was connected to the federal and quasi-feudal character of the governing system during these two dynasties. The Parthian feudal houses, such as the House of Karen, confronted Ardeshir's centralizing reforms with armed force.[17] Part of the reason for his establishment of a professional standing army was that the Parthian knights could not be counted on to fight for Ardeshir. So the Romans were facing militantly monotheistic, centralizing totalitarianism.

It would be concerning enough if, at a time when the Iranian religion of Mithraism was about to build a bridge between pagan Rome and Mahayana Buddhist northern India, Ardeshir's intention was to turn Zoroastrianism into a vehicle for a kind of national unity that shields itself against outsiders. But it would hardly have escaped the notice of the cosmopolitan Romans that Ardeshir was now claiming to be the rightful ruler of the entire Aryan world, which, at that time, besides Iran, included northern India and Europe. By explicitly defining his state as *Irânshahr* or "*the* Aryan Imperium," the founder of the Sassanian regime was equating Zoroastrianism with Aryan identity.

The Roman elite was terrified and reacted by erecting their own barrier. Ardeshir was persecuting Mithraists in Iran itself, forcibly transforming pagan and syncretistic Mithraism into his brand of Zoroastrian monotheism. So it was quite clear that if Mithraism went on to become the state religion of Rome — a development in long-term psychological warfare that would have handed Europe over to Iran with relatively little bloodshed — the Roman way of life would not go on as it would have under the *laissez-faire* Parthians. There was no pagan religion that could have fulfilled for Rome the function that Zoroastrianism was fulfilling for Ardeshir, so as to defensively match it with the same degree of hierarchical conformism and doctrinal rigidity. So the Roman elites settled on a modified version of a non-European religion to do the job. At the same time, they rejected and eventually persecuted the Gnostic form of this religion because its anti-authoritarian and antinomian bent was exactly the opposite of what they needed from a doctrine that had to serve as an imperial state religion.

The Roman Caesar Constantine's reign began in 306. He did not convert to Christianity until after the Battle of Milvian Bridge in 312. Constantine did not announce the toleration of Christianity until the Edict of Milan in 313. It was only between 324 and 330 that he built the new capital of Byzantium (later named Constantinople after him). He was still unbaptized when he called the Council of Nicaea in 325 to establish a cannon and doctrine for the Catholic or Orthodox Church (they were the same back then). It was only in 380 with the Edict of Thessalonica that Christianity was declared the official religion of Rome and all others made illegal. This was decades after the end of Constantine's reign in 337, and 138 years after the death of Ardeshir Babakan (who was born in 180 and reigned from 224 to 242). Note this key passage from Shahin Nezhad's study of Ardeshir Babakan:

> Ardeshir's plan of action for unifying the country also proved beneficial in Rome. About a hundred years after Ardeshir, Eastern Rome also announced that it was backing Christianity as the official religion of its empire. Medieval Europe followed the same procedure (or method) of the companionship of religion and government until the Renaissance period of thought (the European Renaissance) went on for a while.[18]

The establishment of Christianity as the official Roman religion was hardly "beneficial to Rome" and to "Medieval Europe." Actually, it was the greatest catastrophe in recorded human history. We lost 99% of the literature and scientific knowledge of classical antiquity when Christian mobs backed by Church authority set fire to the Library of Alexandria and eventually shut down other universities, libraries, and scientific institutions. But, yes, Shahin Nezhad is right that Ardeshir Babakan can take credit for the rise of the Roman Church, together with all of its consequences, like the eradication of cosmopolitan Alexandrian Humanism, which was replaced by over a thousand years of barbaric ignorance and brutal persecution. What a different world we would have if Rome had still been pagan, perhaps with Mithraism as its dominant but tolerant faith, when the Germans and Alans revolted and seized control of the Empire. We would likely have seen the starburst of German science in the library and laboratories of Roman Alexandria and conditions comparable to the Industrial Revolution around 800 AD. Except that this true Enlightenment would have come into being without the materialist and mechanistic delusions of modern science, which were framed against the Holy Inquisition of Alchemists who heretically studied the occult as part of Nature.

6.2 Mani and the Grand Inquisitors

Already in the Parthian period, Ahura Mazda or Ohrmazd, as he is called in Middle Persian, was deformed almost beyond recognition until he began to assume the aspect of Zeus, with which he was often analogized in bi-lingual Greek and Pahlavi inscriptions. Ardeshir Babakan demonized the Parthians and equated his conquest of them with the will of Ahura Mazda. The rock carvings at Naqshe Rajab show the coronation of Ardeshir. He takes the ring of legitimate sovereignty from Ahura Mazda. The latter is also holding a *barsom* or fasces. This is significant because Parthian reliefs depict Mithra in this fashion, so identification of the would-be Mithra as Ahura Mazda is an attempt to assert pure monotheism. Two children can be seen between Ahura Mazda and Ardeshir.[19] The one who is raising his hands in respect to Ardeshir is his son and Crown Prince, Shapur the Great, who would break with Ardeshir's theocratic project.[20] A damaged inscription nearby reads: "The religion of Zarathustra had perished in our midst, I who am King of Kings founded it anew."[21] In another rock carving that Ardeshir left us at Naqshe Rostam we see Ahura Mazda handing a large ring or wreath to Ardeshir, with both of them riding on horseback. It is suggested that Ardeshir owes his victory to no one other than Ahura Mazda. Ardavan (Artabanus IV), the last Parthian emperor of Iran, is under the hooves of Ardeshir's horse, while Ahriman is being trampled by the horse that Ahura Mazda is riding.[22] The inscription accompanying the carving reads: "This is the image of Mazda-worshipper, born of the Lords [*khodâvandgâr*] Ardeshir, King of Kings of Iran, who is of the race of the gods, son of the Lord Babak, king." Above the horse of Ahura Mazda we find inscribed, in three languages, a text that identifies this anthropomorphic figure as Ahura Mazda, with the Greek version reading: "This is the image of the Lord Zeus." In Pahlavi it reads: *In ast peykare khodâvand Ahurâmazdâ*.[23]

This is terribly significant. According to Shahin Nezhad, Ardeshir demonizes the Parthians for being Hellenized (*Younâni-zade*) and he wants to reestablish "a pure Iranian culture."[24] Yet the founder of the Sassanian dynasty equates Ahura Mazda with Zeus — the serial rapist, pathological liar, and sadistic tyrant of the Greek pantheon! The closest Greek equivalent of Ahura Mazda would have been Prometheus, the arch-rebel against Zeus. I suppose one could hardly expect a totalitarian theocrat who wants to secure law and order on the basis of uniform religious doctrine to admit this, even if the reverence for Truth is supposed to be the bedrock of Zoroastrianism. If Ahura Mazda is Zeus, then what is the Greek name of the *Ahriman* under the hooves of his horse, mirroring the trampled body of Ardavan? It is Prometheus. This is a total inversion.

Ardeshir's reconstruction of Zoroastrianism into an orthodox religious doctrine that could serve as the basis for an ultra-conservative, xenophobic, and totalitarian state was devised and implemented in collaboration with two Grand Inquisitors, Tansar and Kartir. The latter of these, Kartir, far outlived Ardeshir, and his son Shapur, eventually rising to the rank of High Priest (*mobedân-mobed*) and seeing through an inquisitorial campaign that persecuted and ultimately aimed to eradicate all "heretics." One group of these heretics were the Manicheans, whose founder, Mani, began his prophetic mission during the last years of the reign of Ardeshir Babakan.

Ardeshir entrusted his high priest, Tansar, with the formation of a religious canon.[25] In the fourth book of the *Dînkard* we read that Ardeshir had his *hirbadâné hirbad* (or high priest), a man named Tansar, gather together all of the Avestan scriptures from every corner of the country "and selected one and left the rest out of the canon."[26] During the period when he was assembling the Sassanian *Avesta*, Tansar held the office of *mobedân-mobed.*[27] After this selective reconstruction, or censorship, of the *Avesta* Tansar decreed, "The interpretation of all the teachings from the Mazdayasnian religion is our responsibility: for now there is no lack of certain knowledge concerning them."[28] In the Epistle of Tansar (*Nâmeyé Tansar*) it is stated that Sassanian government policy was to imprison heretics for a year, during the course of which they would be subjected to "instruction" by priestly inquisitors. The heretic who relented would be released, but the recalcitrant heretic was warned more threateningly, and then finally liquidated.[29] This is clearly the template for the later Holy Inquisition of the European Middle Ages.

Ardeshir's ideology did not go unchallenged. Shapur the Great follows in his father's footsteps when he brings Rome to its knees as one of the greatest conquerors in Persian history, but at the same time he tolerates the proselytizing of Mani. Under Shapur's protection, if not with his support, Manichaeism spreads both to the East, as far as China, and deep into the West (where the brand "Manichee" would eventually become synonymous with "heretic" during the Medieval Inquisition). The core of Manichean belief, that every "hearer" (or common believer) was expected to comprehend and accept, was the doctrine of "the Two Principles and the Three Times (or Epochs)."[30] The two principles were Light and Darkness, conceived of as radically distinct from, and opposed to, each other. The Three Times were the epoch before the entanglement of the two substances, the present epoch of the imprisonment of the light in the darkness of matter, and the final epoch of the ultimate state of their permanent separation.

In his synthesis of the teachings of Zarathustra, Buddha, and Jesus in the *Shabuhragan*, Mani was addressing himself to his patron, Shapur the Great, as a visionary who could develop a world religion suited to governing all of the Eastern and Western subject peoples that Shapur was intent on integrating into the second Persian Empire.[31] At that time Jesus was worshiped in the Roman provinces of Palestine, Egypt, and Greece, while Buddha was revered in northern India and northwestern China. These were all territories into which Shapur had sent the Sassanian military. Mani would recruit polyglots from different ethnicities and send them to proselytize in "the four regions of the world."[32] Mani was a visionary poet who composed hymns using Syriac metrical forms.[33] He encouraged his disciples to do the same, but in their own native languages, so that the teachings could spread to as many different ethnic and linguistic communities as possible in an idiom that was most familiar to them.

Even more unique than its dualism, the greatest innovation of Manichaeism is that Mani was the first person to *explicitly* advocate a universalist or Unitarian unification of diverse prophetic messages.[34] The idea of a "seal of the prophets," namely an individual whose spiritual message is a culmination, summation, and synthesis of all previous divine messengers, an idea which would later be incorporated into Islam in a perverse fashion, begins with Mani.[35] He claimed to be the Holy Spirit whose coming Jesus prophesied, as well as the arrival of Maitreya, the Buddha of the future, and of course, the Saoshyant or world savior that the followers of Zarathustra expected to appear at the apocalypse.

What is important here is not the specific content or evaluation of these particular claims, but *that* Mani made them at all. For the first time in recorded history, we are seeing a self-conscious will to unify all of humanity on the basis of a single worldwide religion supported, if not enforced, by an Imperial Iranian state that, for the second time, spanned the continental divides between Asia, Europe, and Africa.[36] In one surviving Middle Persian fragment of Manichaean writings, Mani gives this reason for why his religion is superior to that of all of his predecessors: "The preceding religions were [spread in] a single land and a single language. But my religion is such that it is manifest [*paydag*] in every land and in every language and is taught in distant lands."[37] This view is echoed in the Coptic *Kephalaia*:[38]

> He [Jesus] who elected his church in the West, his church has not reached the East. He [Buddha] who elected his church in the East, his election [*eklogé*] has not come to the West. My hope is to administer [my church] in such a way that it reaches the West and that it may be carried at the same time to the East. And the voice of its preaching will be heard in every language, and it will be announced in every city. My church is superior, in this primary respect, to preceding churches, for the preceding churches were elected only for particular places and particular cities. I administer my church in such a way that it comes to all cities and that its good news reaches all countries.[39]

Mani successfully converted the Buddhist king of Turan by performing a feat of public levitation.[40] Upon witnessing this the *Turânshâh* fell to his knees, but the Iranian prophet was able to levitate the Buddhist king who rose into the air, kissed Mani, and proclaimed: "You are the Buddha!" Mani, "the Buddha of Light," sought to synthesize the teaching of Buddha with that of the Gnostic Christ, whose Gospel he endeavored to bring to the East in the guise of "Mani, Apostle of Jesus Christ."

The example of Thomas, the "twin" of Jesus who was tasked with spreading the gospel by means of journeys to the East, up to and including India, was paradigmatic for Mani.[41] He closely studied the Gospel of Thomas, and it is the esoteric teaching of the Gnostic Jesus whose sayings were purportedly preserved by Thomas that Mani endeavored to synthesize with the wisdom of Zarathustra and Gautama Buddha. Mani's commentary on the Gospel of Thomas was in the fifth section of the eighteen section work *The Book of Mysteries*, entitled "Account of Jesus Regarding His Soul as Given to Judas."[42] The "Judas" referred to here is Didymos Judas Thomas, Jesus's "twin."

Shapur saw, in this synthesis of Zoroastrianism, Gnostic Christianity, and Buddhism, the potential for forming a world religion that could shore up the unity of an Indo-European empire stretching from northern India to eastern Rome. According to the Coptic *Kephalaia* (1:15–16), Mani was not present at the coronation of Shapur the Great, and so he never met Ardeshir Babakan. Rather, he journeyed back from India, where he had been preaching, to seek an audience with Shapur in Susa only after he received news of the death of Ardeshir.[43] In addition to their initial meeting in Susa, Shapur summoned Mani to counsel him at the main royal court of Ctesiphon on at least three occasions.[44] Manichean texts describe Mani's entrance into the audience hall of Shapur "as that of a radiant Buddha."[45] Mani established a close rapport with Shapur's brother Peroz. By gaining the trust of Peroz, Mani was granted security clearance to enter the Sassanian palace in Ctesiphon with the aim of converting members of the royal family and the governing elite.[46] Mani deeply penetrated and thoroughly infiltrated the imperial administration.[47] During this time he was living at Veh-Ardaxshir on the Tigris river, a suburb of Ctesiphon, where he composed the *Shabuhragan* for his patron and protector.[48]

Unfortunately, following the death of Shapur, the Grand Inquisition resumed. Mani immediately moved to secure his position in the wake of Shapur's death in 273.[49] However, his intrigues in the court of Hormozd came to naught when the latter's reign ended after only a few months and Bahram I assumed the throne. On account of a lust for power combined with irresoluteness, Bahram cut deals with the orthodox Zoroastrian clergy, and above all, with that grand old inquisitor, Kartir.[50] Under Bahram, Kartir had himself promoted from *herbed* to *mobed* or High Priest.[51] In the inscription that he left on the so-called "Kabeyé Zartosht" structure located at Naqshé Rostam, whose cliffs overlook Persepolis and contain the rock-hewn tombs of the Achaemenid emperors, Kartir boasts:

> As for heretical or degenerate men in the body of the magi who led an unsuitable life, I made them submit to punishment and reprimand. They mended their ways and I drew up charters and patents for many fires and magi ... and many of those who held the doctrine of the demons, thanks to my action, abandoned the doctrine of the demons, and adopted the doctrine of the gods.[52]

It is in the face of the persecution by Kartir that Mani's dualism begins to be radicalized in a really pessimistic direction.[53] Mani sets about writing his own version of the *Book of Giants*, so as to draw an analogy between the earthly tyrants persecuting his community and the *nephilim* who defiled the earth before being overthrown in an apocalypse.[54]

Mani's conversion of Bat, a prince of Kholasar (located between Baghdad and Dastagerd), was the catalyst for his arrest.[55] Kartir was incensed that this vassal of Bahram had turned away from orthodox Zoroastrianism and he gave orders for Mani and his close associates to be apprehended by the police and brought to the royal court.[56] Bahram, having just returned from a hunting expedition, with his Scythian queen on his arm, and in lockstep with Kartir, confronts Mani with a tirade that begins, "You are not welcome!" In response to Bahram's claims that Mani is a good-for-nothing who, in addition to being worthless as a soldier and hunter, is not even a proficient druggist and healer, Mani reads Bahram a letter that his father, Shapur, had very respectfully addressed to Mani, praising his service to the Sassanian royal family.[57] Thusly rebuked by his own father from beyond the grave, Bahram succumbs to a fit of rage and, presumably to the great satisfaction of Kartir, who is witnessing the entire scene, orders Mani to be imprisoned in the dungeon and bound around the neck, ankles, and wrists in iron chains that weighed an excess of a hundred pounds.[58] The plan was for him to be subjected to long inquisitorial tortures by Kartir, but he expired after only a few days. Outraged at having been cheated by Mani's premature departure from his body, the inquisitors tried to make up for the lost opportunity to torture him by having his corpse flayed, dismembered, and stuffed with straw, with his severed head being displayed above a city gate of Ctesiphon and his other body parts nailed to the gate.[59]

The martyred Mani was a visionary poet and artist, the inventor of both the Persian miniature painting and calligraphy traditions. Mani was a very accomplished painter who would illuminate his own manuscripts.[60] His lines were said to have been so fine that a stroke of his brush on a piece of white silk could no longer be seen after a single thread was removed.[61] He was also a calligrapher who invented a more phonetically accurate "Manichaean alphabet" for expressing Middle Persian, Sogdian, and other Iranian languages.[62] The Pahlavi script of his period only had thirteen signs and so scribes would resort to ideograms in order to express the meaning of a text that they were copying. This meant low fidelity in transmission and difficulties in comprehension. Mani's script, developed on the basis of Syriac, and therefore a predecessor of the Arabic-based script used to express Persian in the Islamic period, was one that had a letter for almost every sound, so that Middle Persian could be written as it was pronounced.

Mani's reputation as an artistic genius extended well into the Islamic period.[63] His book of illustrations called *Arzhang*, whose only text consisted of small calligraphic captions, was particularly popular and there are records of a few copies of it surviving in treasuries of the early Islamic period.[64] This was perhaps the earliest form of the graphic novel, particularly considering the fantastically mythic content of cosmic battles, demonic sex, preternatural monsters, and miraculous manifestations. Coptic Manichean texts use the Greek name *Eikon* to render the title of this book of "icons."[65] It is quite clear that both the Persian miniature painting and calligraphy crafts often mistakenly categorized as "Islamic art" actually begin in this period, particularly with Mani, and that any seemingly "Asian" elements in them have to do with the fact that Mani traveled through the Silk Route and preached extensively in Iranian Central Asia, as far east as Uighur parts of China. One Chinese Manichean manuscript found at Turfan is called *Compendium of the Doctrines and Styles of the Teaching of Mani, the Buddha of Light*.[66] This catechism was composed for the religious authorities of the T'ang imperial government of China. Among its contents are "Rules Concerning His Corporeal Representations," in other words, "rules for representing Mani as a Buddha of Light" and "Rules Concerning the Canon of the Scriptures and *Image*."[67] One can only speculate what influence this might have had on the history of Chinese painting, or in what way it accounts for the affinities between Chinese painting and the iconographic style of Persian miniatures—including in their portrayal of landscapes and nature in general.

Mani's doctrine was complex, if not convoluted, and it would be outside the scope of our study to enter into all of its elements. There is, however, one vision expressed in his writings that is particularly relevant to understanding the Mithraic mystery at the core of Iran's occult history. That is the role that Mithra or *Mehr Yazd* plays as a seducer of the Archons during the primordial creation of human life and also at the end of time, in the *Frashgard* or apocalyptic Renovation of Existence. One of the most interesting aspects of this appearance of Mithra is that it explicitly acknowledges the androgyny of the deity, which, as suggested in the last chapter, may originally have been feminine (with *Mitra* remaining an exclusively female name in Iran).

In the *Shabuhragan* version of his apocalypse, Mani claims that at the *Frashgard* "Mihryazd," i.e. the *yazata* or deity Mithra, will descend to the earth riding the chariot of the sun in order to set this world ablaze and free the trapped particles of light so that they can reassemble in the celestial realm as a "new paradise" [*wahishté nog*] awaiting the elect.[68] Mithra also tried to free the light particles during the primeval creation. In Mani's text titled *The Treasure of the Living* we meet with the scene known as "the seduction of the archons," wherein the Third Messenger exploits the "deadly unclean lust" of the celestial archons controlling the earthly realm by so exciting them with the masculine and feminine versions of his/herself that the male archons ejaculate the light particles trapped within them and the female archons emit them through miscarriages.[69] In Middle Persian texts this Third Messenger, who can make himself appear as either a man or a woman of the most seductively perfect beauty is the "Mihr Yazd" or the god Mithra.[70]

The two greatest demons, the son of the King of Darkness, namely the Prince of Darkness or Ashaqlun, and his consort, Nebroel (Namrael) devour the aborted fetuses (according to their respective sex), and thusly nourished they engage in a fornication through which Adam and Eve are conceived and born of Nebroel.[71] In the Middle Persian Manichaean texts, Nebroel is called *Âz* or the wife of Saclas.[72] Deciphering the demonization of the divine feminine in the guise of *Âz*, the mother of all demons, is central to understanding the psychological basis for the implosion of Sassanian society.

6.3 Demonization of the Divine Feminine

The persecution of the Manicheans was not the most significant element of the inquisition that aimed to establish the orthodox Zoroastrian state first envisioned by Ardeshir. It is a different group of heretics that will be our main concern in this chapter, a rebel movement in the Persian heart of Iran, one that originated in the very same province of Pars (*Fars*) where Ardeshir initiated the Sassanian coup. Its enigmatic founder, about whom we know next to nothing thanks to Tansar and Kartir's erasure of "heresy," was a man by the name of Zaradusht from a district called Fasa.[73] In other words, he was the Second Zarathustra, the Zarathustra of Persia. Zaradusht taught that the cultivation of Discernment, Understanding,

Recollection, and Joy leads to perfect enlightenment and freedom from bondage to arbitrary rules and regulations that mediate one's relationship with the divine.[74] The Magi who followed him accused Ardeshir and his inquisitors, Tansar and Kartir, of perverting the teachings of the original Zarathustra — the message of the *Gathas*. They called their version of Zoroastrianism, which owes a great debt to Parthian Mithraism, *Dorost Dîn* or "the Just Conscience."

The *Gathas* of Zarathustra are devoid of even the slightest trace of moralism, let alone litigious religious prescriptions. In fact, Zarathustra had explicitly preached against "the mumbling priests," as he called them. The alliance between them and the "wrathful warlords," which he lamented, is exactly what Ardeshir Babakan attempts to recreate and what Zaradusht of Pars initiates a movement to resist. Zaradusht taught that an inner knowing that comes about through an enlightenment with respect to esoteric truth, or *batin*, absolves one from *zâher*, the superficial facades of all exterior religious observances and allegorical doctrines. (The Arabic terms *zâher* and *batin* here were used by subsequent Islamic-period authors to describe a dichotomy that we have lost the original Sassanian-period, Middle Persian terms for.) This echoes the distinction between inner conscience and outward ritual, which was first expressed by Zarathustra in the *Gathas*.

The inner knowledge of *batin* was conceived of by the *Dorost Dinân* as the universal Truth at the heart of every right-minded religion or philosophy throughout history. In each age there is an attempt to define it in terms of words and concepts. Zaradusht taught that a given doctrine arises in this manner but is ultimately fated to lose its vitality or relevance, petrify and then be destroyed in order to clear the way for a fresh re-envisioning of the same Truth. These ideas are rooted in a belief that letters, words, and concepts are facets that manifest God as the "divine verb." A line of prophets extends throughout history to perform this periodic renovation. This succession will continue until enough people are enlightened so that there is no longer a need for outward practices and allegories, whereupon a final prophet will come to abolish all religions and liberate the esoteric knowledge to its fulfillment in the social and political world without the need for any exoteric façade.[75]

What we see in the *Dorost Dîn* is the Promethean spirit of the original teaching of Zarathustra, with its emphasis on personal conscience and creative individuation, reasserting itself in an adaptation of the figure of Mithra, a guarantor of free will who lies beyond good and evil. This Mithraic way of thinking was radicalized by the Second Zarathustra, in a manner that can be instructively contrasted with the Manichean heresy. Whereas Manichaeism threatened Ardeshir's Zoroastrian orthodoxy by radicalizing the dualism of good and evil into a metaphysical opposition of pure spiritual light and utterly corrupt material darkness, with life-negating ascetic consequences, Zaradusht's life-affirming teaching endeavored to overcome moralizing dualism altogether — since the duality in the teaching of the *Gathas* opposes cosmic forces of evolution and constraint, or intelligence and stupidity, not any puritanical definition of "good" vs. a demonized "evil." Friedrich Nietzsche's critique of Zarathustra as "the inventor of the moral world order" is based on an orthodox Sassanian distortion of Zarathustra. Nietzsche's perspective is actually, unbeknownst to him, quite Mithraic in nature.

One teaching that the *Dorost Dînân*, later known as Mazdakites, did share in common with the Manicheans was the belief in reincarnation.[76] According to Zaradusht, and as affirmed later by Mazdak, souls are reborn into this world countless times in different bodies and under different circumstances based on their degree of understanding and righteousness in previous lives. What others have called "Heaven" and "Hell" are merely projections of the joy and suffering that one's soul has endured amidst various circumstances in this world during one or another lifetime. When considering the awesome burden of the task of overcoming the demonic influence of unconscious passions that, as we shall see momentarily, was at the core of the *Dorost Dîn* teaching, it should be borne in mind that Zaradusht and the Mazdakites after him expected that attaining this spiritual liberation would take many lifetimes working to elevate one's consciousness.

The selective reconstruction of the Avesta carried out by Tansar and Kartir yielded a text full of the most oppressively patriarchal and overbearingly moralizing religious laws and ritual prescriptions. Those that demonize women are particularly abhorrent to the free-spirited ethos of Zarathustra and the humanistic Achaemenid culture that first brought Ahura Mazda onto the world stage. The *Vendidâd* is the only one of the twenty-one *nasks* of the Avesta that has come down to us totally intact.[77] It is the Zoroastrian law book, with its litigious injunctions and ritualistic prescriptions framed as "purifications" for exorcizing demons. The book's title is a corruption of *Vidaevo-dâtem* or "the anti-demoniac law." What was particularly audacious of the Sassanian-era priests who put this text together is that they composed it in the form of a series of responses on the part of Ahura Mazda to a variety of questions posed by Zarathustra.[78] In other words, the Zoroastrian Orthodoxy created by Ardeshir not only grossly distorts the authentic teaching of Zarathustra that survives in the *Gathas*, but the authors of Middle Persian texts such as the *Vendidâd* did so while claiming the authority of Zarathustra himself and effectively authoring a false revelation received by Zarathustra from Ahura Mazda. This is particularly appalling given the views on women that we are presented with in this text.

Presaging the Muslim obsession with what is *harâm* versus *halâl*, the *Vendidâd* is full of superstitiously fearful definitions of what is permissibly "clean" as opposed to the "unclean" and therefore forbidden. This book of the Avesta expresses utter horror at the menstruation of women as the supremely "unclean" calamity inflicted on human life by demonic forces.[79] Zoroastrians literally believe that a menstruating woman is demonically possessed, and on this account she is put in isolation for the duration of her period, with her food — meager rations, intended to starve out the demons — being passed to her at a distance in a long leaden spoon.[80] She is forbidden from even looking in the direction of any fire, including the hearth fire of her own home let alone a sacred perpetual fire, since it is believed that the holy element would be defiled by her very gaze. The place to which the menstruating woman is confined is called a "*Dakhmeh* for the living," a reference to the circular enclosures that Zoroastrians built beyond the edge of a town or city, where vultures would pick clean the unclean corpses of the dead, which means that a woman having her period was categorized together with a rotting dead body.[81] Other classes of people confined to this pseudo-*Dakhmeh* were lepers and those who have handled corpses.

The *Vendidâd* not only lays out prescriptions, this law book of the Avesta also defines sadistically harsh punishments for violating the codes of ritual purity allegedly revealed by Ahura Mazda to Zarathustra. A woman who suppresses her period so that she will appear clean when she is supposed to be unclean is dealt the punishment of *Peshotanu* or "paying with one's body" by receiving *two hundred lashes with a horse whip*![82] A woman who drinks water, and thereby defiles this sacred element, after just having given birth and therefore being unclean, is also subjected to the same two hundred lashes.[83] *Peshotanu* is the highest penalty save for the death sentence, which the *Vendidâd* prescribes for prostitutes and sodomites who are caught in the act.[84] Whether or not these punishments were always implemented, they certainly do represent the ideal set forth by the type of Zoroastrianism contrived by Ardeshir Babakan, Tansar, and Kartir as the Sassanian state orthodoxy.[85]

The *Vendidâd* is by no means the only text that reveals an orthodox Zoroastrian hatred of women and disgust at femininity. Note the extreme misogyny of the following passage in the *Bundahishn*, which takes the form of a soliloquy of Ohrmazd regarding his regretful creation of womankind:

> I created thee, thou whose adversary is the whore species, and thou wast created with a mouth close to thy buttocks, and coition seems to thee even as the taste of the sweetest food to the mouth; and thou art a helper to me, for from thee is man born, but thou dost grieve me who am Ohrmazd. But had I found another vessel from which to make man, never would I have created thee, whose adversary is the whore species. But I sought in the waters and in the earth, in plants and cattle, in the highest mountains and deep valleys, but I did not find a vessel from which righteous man might proceed except woman whose adversary is the whore.[86]

Add to this the following passage from Zatspram, which also demonizes women:

> When Ahriman rushed into creation, he had the brood of the demon Whore of evil religion as his companion even as a man has a whore woman as his bed-fellow; for verily the whore is a demon: and he appointed the demon Whore queen of her brood, that is the chief of all the whore demons, the most grievous adversary of the Righteous Man. And [the demon Whore] of evil religion … for the defilement of females she joined herself to him, that she might defile females; and the females, because they were defiled, might defile the males, and [the males] would turn aside from their proper work.[87]

The *Bundahishn* and Zatspram both refer to "Jeh, the Primal Whore."[88] Only she is able to rouse Ahriman again after his initial defeat at the hands of Ohrmazd. It is she who seduces him, and goads him on, to assault the creation of Ohrmazd, and it is she who defiles the entire human race.[89] She is the demonized chthonian goddess of the moist and fertile earth.[90] Jeh is the primordial woman and Primal Whore who appears in the *Selections of Zâtspram* and in Chapter 4 of the *Bundahishn*.[91] Menstruation began when, having related her evil deeds to Ahriman in minute detail, he relishes them and kisses her on the head.[92] "The appearance of the body of the Destructive Spirit was in the form of a frog."[93] As Ahriman's primeval companion, Jeh represents the entire female sex on the stage of the cosmic drama as it begins to unfold.[94] All subsequent females are prototypically defiled through her, and men are only defiled through interaction with womankind.[95]

In order to understand the metaphysical basis for this demonization of the feminine we need to study a heretical version of Zoroastrian cosmology that can only be reconstructed from between the lines of surviving Middle Persian texts from the Sassanian period. In these fragments of an earlier view that gestated in the Mithraic milieu of Parthian Iran, the Lord of Light and the Lord of Darkness were twins born of an androgynous deity whose primordial doubt and unconsciousness with respect to himself is personified by a feminine deity, the mother of all demons. In the Mithraism of the Parthian period the idea developed that Zorvan (Chronos) gave birth to Ahriman before bringing Ohrmazd into the world, and that, consequently, kingship over this world was handed down, as promised, to the first-born. What caused this miscarriage (a miscarriage of justice) was a doubt and hesitation within the mind of the lord of Infinite Time, who, being pure potentiality, did not yet know himself. This doubt can also be conceived of as a condition of primal desire, a profoundly insatiable need, called *Âz*.

We have four very similar accounts of the genesis of Ohrmazd and Ahriman from the Armenian writers Elishe and Eznik, and the Syriac works of Yohannân bar Penkaye and Theodore bar Konai.[96] Zorvan is a hermaphroditic deity, described as both the father and mother of Ohrmazd.[97] Zorvan is not asexual. He is both bisexual and also beyond the limitations of the sexual dichotomy.[98] In all of the Mithraic statues of Zorvan-Chronos, his sex is concealed or rendered ambiguous by a serpent entwining her body.[99] Zorvan promises to bequeath her kingdom to whoever is her firstborn, and since Ahriman is born first, the Satanic Lord of Darkness is the one who is made king of this world.[100] Zorvan appears as a seven-headed beast in the Persian *Rivâyats*, with each three-eyed head having its own name. One of these names is the most recognizable epithet of Ahriman — namely *Padyâr* or "the adversary."[101] In other words, Satan. As we shall see, Satan is an aspect of the godhead.

In his version of the Zorvanite cosmology, Theodore bar Konai renders the name of Ahriman as "Satan."[102] He also tells us that, contrary to what the Middle Persian texts of the Zoroastrian orthodoxy claim, Zorvan made Ahriman king of the world for a period of nine thousand years or three-quarters of the total timeframe for the cosmic war.[103] As Shahrestani recounts in a parallel narrative to that of Theodore bar Konai, "Ahriman went forth and mastered the world [*dunyâ*] and" — this is the really significant part — "Ohrmazd was without power over him."[104] Shahrestani's use of *dunyâ* for "world" suggests that Ahriman is only the king of the material world, and that his rule does not encompass the *giti* or spiritual world.[105] This is also suggested by the fact that when Shahrestani wants to refer to the entire cosmos he uses the word *âlam*, rather than *dunya*.

In this respect, the Mithraic conception of Zorvan is in agreement with the most pessimistic of the Gnostic sects who believed that Earth is a realm delivered over to evil and ruled by the Devil.[106] Unlike the Neoplatonists of the time, they did not put as many intermediary states or stages as possible between a perfectly remote One and the often miserable world of multiplicity. The gradation scheme of the "great chain of Being" is an attempt to evade their Gnostic recognition of a violent rupture in the very nature of things that radically alienates us from the source of our being.[107]

That Zorvan is in the amoral darkness of pure potentiality before the creation of Ohrmazd, and that Ahriman is born before Ohrmazd, suggests that the Lord of Light is forced to fashion his world from out of the substance of darkness and in a remedial, rather than prototypical, fashion.[108] So the work of the creator is fundamentally flawed. The aforementioned primordial darkness before the fiery birth of Ohrmazd is often also conceived of as an elemental wetness, which is essentially feminine and is demonized as evil.[109] It is the pre-cosmic void, which is prior to and devoid of the celestial luminaries. *Vây* was the Middle Persian term usually employed to refer to this primordial chasm or void of Space that is the womb for the seed of *Sepehr*.[110]

Zorvan herself forms heresy from her self-will, and she is also the creator of the demons, on account of which her cosmic body is rendered even more evil than it would be merely because of its material nature.[111] This primordial evil, essential to the very being of the godhead, is the desire that birthed both Ohrmazd *and Ahriman*, albeit with Ahriman being the firstborn and Crown Prince of the Cosmos.[112] The creation and the cosmic war over it is a process whereby a God who was *not* all good *becomes* good in time.[113] Unlike the radical dualism of the orthodox Zoroastrians, which averts the problem of evil, this Mithraic worldview sees the problem of evil as one located in the very heart of God.[114] The purpose of the separation of good and evil in finite time is to eliminate evil by means of a process of distillation. This is, as Zaehner notes, "a long-term plan with very unpleasant consequences for the powers of light in the earlier phases."[115] By contrast, "Mazdean Zoroastrianism destroys the unity of the godhead by positing two independent and eternal principles, and thereby gives man absolute freedom of choice between black and white alternatives."[116]

The doctrine of the essential defect in God, namely Zorvan's doubt, was "heavily censored in the Pahlavi books."[117] This doubt or deficiency is still visible as a trace in Pahlavi books that refer to a "single inconsistency *in potential*" with the Middle Persian word for "inconsistency" being *apattokih*.[118] As Zaehner reconstructs it, "Ahriman represents the actualization of an essential imperfection in the godhead hitherto concealed in the potential (*nerok*). Ahriman's birth precedes that of Ohrmazd as in the *Dînkard* text falsehood appears before God's true realization of his own nature."[119] The following passage from the conclusion of Zaehner's study of the idea of Zorvan makes the dialectical nature of this metaphysical system even more clear:

> God, the One, is a pure potentiality. Since this is so, neither good nor evil can be predicated of him *sub specie aeternitatis*. In the process of actualization, however, evil conceived as 'desire' or 'doubt' comes to light along with God's wisdom which is one of His eternal attributes. From a state of pure nescience the deity 'comes to know'; but there being as yet no object for his knowledge, knowledge turns to doubt, and the doubt gives rise to a separate principle which is the Devil. The contrast provided by this unwelcome intruder brings about self-realization within the deity. This self-realization manifests itself as Ohrmazd, the divine Wisdom. … God must be limited in order that he may become good. … Had there been no desire, the imperfection would have remained latent: there would have been no actual imperfection at all. Hence the desire was as evil as the unworthy doubt that followed it.[120]

Ahriman arises from Zorvan's lack of awareness of herself, and only once Zorvan is confronted with Ahriman in the guise of the Aggressor does s/he attain self-knowledge as hypostatized by the birth of Ohrmazd.[121] In this way limitation and cosmic order (*Ashâ*, *dâtastân*) are produced from out of negatively infinite chaos.[122] According to the Middle Persian text *Shikandé Gomâni Vazâr*, the genesis of Ahriman is a necessary consequence of God's ignorance of himself on account of his unfathomably infinite being in the primordial state before chronological Time and its unfolding of finite space.[123] Ahriman and Ohrmazd emerge in the twilight zone between eternity and temporality.[124] What the *Shikand* refers to as Zorvan's failure to fathom himself in eternity is what Eznik and other preservers of expunged Zervanite beliefs in the Sassanian period refer to more colloquially as "Zorvan's doubt."[125] By the time God attains self-awareness, Ahriman already exists and the self-aware God's power is de-limited by this adversary. In the *Pandnâmak* of the Sassanian period, it is written that Ahriman tries to turn time backwards in order to return to the primeval state before Ohrmazd's conscious action.[126]

The doubt of this androgynous supreme being is hypostatized (takes an anthropomorphic form) as the female demon *Âz*, a Concupiscence or primordial Desire, whose seduction of Zorvan — as a dissociated aspect of his own psyche — is responsible for Ahriman being the firstborn prince of this world. *Âz*, in turn, becomes the mother of five demons: lust, avarice, greed, wrath, and vengeance. In the *Bundahishn* and in the writings of Zatspram, Zorvan bestows a weapon to Ahriman, which is coal-like, "black and ashen," "like unto a fire, blazing, harassing all creatures" and fashioned "from the very substance of darkness."[127] This weapon is *Âz* or the personification of Concupiscence, that primordial need (*niyâz*) which manifests as acquisitiveness, gluttony, lust, and every other form of desire.[128] She is not only the greatest of the demons, *Âz* is the mother of them all and thus "the totality of evil" or "the principle of evil."[129] She even takes precedence over Ahriman, who is born from out of Zorvan on account of her.[130] Ahriman is born of the desire and doubt of Zorvan, and *Âz* is this primordial doubt as much as she is the hypostasis of the primal desire within the godhead.[131] That Zorvan hands *Âz* over to Ahriman, means that he is divesting himself of an evil that was part of his own nature — or, as Shahrestani notes, it suggests that "there was always something evil with God."[132]

Âz plays a significant role in the Middle Persian scripture *Dînkard* and in the writings of Zatspram, where she is "concupiscence on a cosmic scale."[133] Even if she were to consume all that is in the world she would still not be satiated.[134] In the *Dînkard,* the concept of *kherad* or "wisdom" has the strict sense of "reason," which ought to be the "directing faculty in man," and this rational faculty is explicitly contrasted with *Âz* in the guise of the irrational.[135] Note the following passage of the *Dînkard*: "Man who is the object of [diabolic] aggression, is tainted with aggressive concupiscence which is intent on destroying his *xvarr* [soul, or spiritual destiny]. Reason was created by the Creator to protect the *xvarr* from concupiscence. Concupiscence is first cousin to desire. There is a limit set to desire. So long as desire for wealth and power is fulfilled, concupiscence is greatly strengthened and reason is gravely impaired…"[136]

This, contrary to "reason," expresses itself as "self-will" or "choosing for oneself" or "wrong-headedness" which produces "error" and "heresy."[137] One could translate this into Christian terms as the sin of "intellectual pride."[138] It is most interesting that, rather than claiming that *Âz* is always entirely without logic, the irrational is also characterized as "the *logos* [*vâkhsh*] of evil."[139] So while *Âz* may be gluttony and other physical desires on the material plane, she manifests as a "misuse of the intellect" on the spiritual plane.[140] She personifies chaos to the extent of being the antithesis of cosmic order (*dâtastân*).[141] The chaos of *Âz* is destructive of Order both in the sense of *logos* and in the sense of *nomos*.[142] Someone who serves *Âz* is an agent of chaos.

In accordance with the Zoroastrian faith in an apocalyptic end of history, it was believed that *Âz* would be defeated by Mithra or *Mehr*, and forced to devour her own demonic progeny and even Ahriman himself. Ahriman warns his demon-spawn that at the end of the appointed period for the cosmic war, she will devour all that is his before starving to death herself.[143] Even the orthodox Zatspram condemns "the yearning for whatever good thing one sees or hears," subdividing the vices it yields into "hoarding by robbery and refusing to give through avarice."[144] Starving *Âz* forces her to resort to devouring the evil creation of Ahriman in a futile effort to stay alive a little longer.[145]

According to the account of Zatspram at the end of days, *Âz* will be engaged in a battle with the Mean, also referred to as Order. In this context, the *Sraosha* or angelic *Soroush* of Zarathustra's *Gathas*, namely the divine "inspiration" that moved him to sing his poems, is perverted into the all-too-conformist and conservative concept of *patmân* or "the Mean" between excess and deficiency.[146] In the apocalypse, "Âz is the genius of disorder."[147] According to the *Minouyé Kherad*, she is ultimately overthrown by Mithra acting in concert with Zorvan.[148] Mithra is the helper of Zorvan in the guise of the god of Justice.[149]

6.4 The Mazdakite Revolution

How could the primordial desire personified by *Âz* be turned on itself and become a means of fiery transcendence of this fallen world? This brings us to the heart of the mystery, the "heretical" mysticism of the Persian Zarathustra of the Sassanian period that was almost completely erased from our historical record by Ardeshir's grand inquisitors. Zaradusht taught that sexual possessiveness and conflicts over material goods were the two great snares by means of which the demon-spawn of *Âz* possessed and afflicted human beings. In other words, the Ahrimanic demons must be appeased — but at the same time neutralized — by practicing free love and communal property holding.[150]

On account of their having held these beliefs, contemporaneous Christian commentators in the West described these "Magi" as "devil worshipers." Plutarch's description of the religion of "Zoroaster, the Magus" aligns with the account of wicked "sorcery" that we are given by the *Dînkard* insofar as both describe a religion in which appeasing sacrifices and thanksgiving offerings were made to *both* Ohrmazd *and Ahriman* or, as Plutarch calls them, "Oramazes" and "Areimanios."[151] These "devil-worshipers" offering sacrifices to Ahriman are described by the Middle Persian text *Yavishté Friyân* as "prowling around in great secrecy" and carrying out their rites under the cover of darkness.[152] Clement of Alexandria also claims that "the Magians worship angels and demons."[153] These "Magians" may have seen themselves as followers of "Zoroaster, the Magus" but they are clearly not Zoroastrians in the orthodox sense that this designation would go on to develop in the Sassanian period. They are Mithraists who recognize evil as a necessary cosmic force. In the pantheon of the Mithraic mysteries Zorvan (Chronos) is second only to Mithra himself, and offerings are made to Ahriman as well as to Ahura Mazda.[154]

Theirs was a libertine doctrine of unbinding Desire, not by denying sensuality as the Manicheans did, but by liberating it. It was not only libertine, but also antinomian. *Dorost Dinân* communes lacked institutionalized buildings for religious observance and individuals were free to choose their own form of reverence and hold their own interpretations of the Truth, as long as they were fundamentally rooted in the movement's communistic and egalitarian vision of social justice.[155] The *Dorost Dînân* had absolutely no religious laws or moral prescriptions whatsoever, except one: live and let live, do what you will so long as you harm no one who is not an oppressor.[156] Now the other meaning of *Mehr* or Mithra, "the friend," becomes evident. The savior is not only "light," in the Persian language the deity's name also means *love* in exactly the same sense as the Greek term *agape*. Mithra is the god of true friendship. This religion of love was, however, at the same time a call to revolutionary war.

In the early sixth century AD, the *Dorost Dîn* movement gained ground to the point where one of its leaders, a man named Mazdak who, on account of being "eloquent and knowledgeable and possessed of great abilities," was appointed "chief minister and treasurer" of the Persian Emperor Kavad I.[157] Under Mazdak's influence Kavad even adopted vegetarianism, a practice rooted in the *Dorost Dîn* belief in reincarnation and the possibility of being reborn, not just in another human body, but in that of a suffering animal as well.[158] Ferdowsi expresses the pith of the *Dorost-Dîn* teaching in this passage of the *Shâhnâmeh* that he puts into the mouth of Mazdak, addressing Shahanshah Kavad or Qobad (as he is referred to in the Islamic period):

> There are five things that lead us away from justice, and the wise cannot add another to them. These five are envy, the longing for vengeance, anger, desire, and the fifth, which becomes a man's master, greed. If you can conquer these five demons, the way to God lies open to you. It is these five that make wom-

> en and wealth the ruin of the true faith throughout the world. If women and wealth are not to harm the true faith, they must be held in common. It is these two that generate envy, greed, and desire, and secretly they link up with anger and a longing for vengeance. Then demons corrupt the wise, and to prevent this these two must be held in common.[159]

The second major challenge to the Sassanian state doctrine of Ardeshir comes in the form of this Mazdakite Revolution which, from the top down, redistributed private property, opened the royal granaries to the poor, and targeted the Sassanian caste system and hereditary aristocracy by breaking up harems and promoting a promiscuity that would degrade bloodlines.[160] The revolutionaries raised the red banner or *Sorkh Alam* as their symbol of revolt, and they sometimes also wore red shirts on account of which they came to be known as *Sorkh Jâmegân*.[161] Given that Karl Marx believed Persian ought to be the International language of the future communist utopia, it is reasonable to speculate that the adoption of the Red Flag as the symbol of the International was an homage to the Mazdakites. In his *Siyâsatnâmeh*, the eleventh century Persian Prime Minister Nizam ul-Molk preserves this account of the radical Mazdakite policies regarding sex and wealth:

> If any man feels desire for a woman let him come together with her. There is no jealousy or intolerance in our religion and nobody is deprived of the pleasures and lusts of the world. The doors of satisfaction are open to everybody.
>
> Then by reason of the sharing of women, people were more eager to adopt his religion, especially the common people. And he laid down the custom that if someone invited twenty men to his house not only would he provide bread and meat and wine and minstrels and other amenities, but all the guests would get up one by one and make use of his wife; and they thought it no wrong.[162]

Written in a rearview Muslim mirror and from a hostile and patriarchal perspective, Nizam ul-Molk and other defenders of the Caliphate make it appear as if the Mazdakites themselves were objectifying women in the way that they "shared" wives and lovers. This could not be further from the truth. If anything, Mazdakite men were being subjected to cuckoldry by their wives, rather than their wives being forced to endure gangbanging. Women were shoulder to shoulder with men as the highest leaders of Mazdakite communities.[163]

Patricia Crone has argued at length that what is being described through a distorting patriarchal lens by hostile Muslim heresiarchs, is not "guest prostitution" but an essentially Tantric-type ritual orgy practiced *in the context of a quasi-Matriarchal culture.*[164] Men were not engaging in "wife sharing"; it is Iranian women of Mazdakite persuasion who were practicing polyandry—a practice that, as was noted in Chapter 1, ancient Greek historians had already observed in the Scythian or Sarmatian (i.e. northern Iranian) societies, whose women the patriarchal Hellenes mythologized as "Amazons."[165] In isolated rural areas of northern Iran, such as Gilan on the Caspian coast, such a situation, where women "wore male clothes, rode horses, were served better than the men by their slaves and slave girls, and slept with both their slaves and foreigners without being afraid of their husbands, who regarded their wives as their masters" endured for many centuries after Mazdak's revolution.[166] Even today, in contemporary Iran, jokes about shameless women of the Caspian region cuckolding their husbands are infamous.

It is astounding that practices such as these prevailed as official Sassanian state policy in Iran for nearly thirty years before the Zoroastrian orthodoxy and their financial backers were able to stage a conservative coup! This is as incredible as if the Carpocratian Gnostics of Alexandria were to have converted a Caesar and seized control of the Roman Empire for an entire generation. In fact, there have been some suggestions of a connection between the Gnostic school of Carpocrates in Alexandria (d. 215 AD) and the teachings of Zaradusht of Fasa later in the same century.[167] The Mazdakites were eventually crushed by Khosrow I, known to orthodox Zoroastrians as *Anushiravân* or "He of the Immortal Spirit." Despite being open-minded enough to take in Greek philosophers and scientists fleeing the Christian closure of the last pagan academies in the West, Khosrow shored up dogmatic Zoroastrianism by putting his stamp of approval on the doctrine of Aturpât (or Âzârpâd), a latter-day Kartir-type figure, as the unquestionable Sassanian state orthodoxy. Azarpad, son of Mahraspand, from the province of Makran, had come to power during the reign of the notoriously sadistic Shapur II (309 AD), known as "Zolaktav" and famous for his grotesque methods of impaling and skewering his opponents' bodies as if they were kebabs. After Azarpad submitted to the ordeal of trial by molten metal in order to be fully vindicated in his demand for a return to orthodoxy, Shapur Zolaktav issued a royal decree that Azarpad's doctrine should be exclusively recognized as the religion of the state and the true form of Zoroastrianism.[168] Azarpad resumed the orthodox and persecutory policies of Kartir with even more zeal than his predecessor.[169]

The reigns of Shapur II and Khosrow I, bookending the Mazdakite catastrophe under Kavad, are depicted by the *Dînkard* as model periods in Persian history.[170] Azarpad and Khosrow are idolized in the Pahlavi writings from the period immediately after the fall of the Sassanians, and *andarzes* or "wise sayings" are attributed to both of them.[171] The state orthodoxy of Azarpad and Khosrow was based on a pure dualism of the primeval antagonists, Ohrmazd and Ahriman, fundamentally separate and totally opposed to one another, with Ohrmazd as the absolutely good Lord of Light and Ahriman as the absolutely evil Lord of Darkness.[172]

Using Azarpad's fundamentalism as his justification, Khosrow initiated a horrific persecution and brutal suppression of the "Mazdakites" or *Zandiks* (heretical "interpreters") as the *Dorost Dinân* now came to be known. The Mazdakites were ruthlessly massacred after having been invited to a so-called "debate" with the orthodox priesthood at the royal court.[173] It is actually Kavad (Qobad) himself who presides over this sham, after regaining the throne by the use of foreign mercenaries and by making assurances to the orthodoxy that he would authorize the destruction of the Mazdakites before handing power over to Khosrow — the son who had always despised Mazdak and stood with the clergy against his father's folly. In the *Shâhnâmeh*, Ferdowsi preserves the following account of the demise of Mazdak and his leading comrades:

When the sun displayed its crown on the following morning, and the ground became like a sea of ivory, the king's son and the priests and sages he had summoned arrived at the king's palace, talking the matter over as they came. Mazdak delighted Qobad's heart with his words, and then a Zoroastrian priest addressed Mazdak in front of the assembly and said, 'You are a seeker after knowledge, but the new religion you have made is a pernicious one. If women and wealth are to be held in common, how will a son know his father, or a father his son? If men are to be equal in the world, social distinctions will be unclear; who will want to be a commoner, and how will nobility be recognized? If a laboring slave and the king are the same, when a man dies, who is to inherit his goods? This talk of yours will ruin the world, and such an evil doctrine should not flourish in Iran. If everyone is a master, who is he to command? Everyone will have a treasure, and who is to be its treasurer? None of those who established religions have talked in this way. You have secretly put together a demonic faith; you are leading everyone to hell, and you don't see your evil acts for what they are.'

When Qobad [Kavad] heard the priest's words, he sprang up and shouted his approval. Kesra [Khosrow] added his support, and Mazdak's impious heart was filled with apprehension. The assembly rang with voices saying, 'Mazdak should not sit next to the king, he is destroying our religion, he has no place in this court!' The king turned away from Mazdak's teachings in disgust, and his mind was filled with regret for what he had done. He handed Mazdak and his followers, who included a hundred thousand men of good standing, over to Kesra, and said, 'Do with these men as you will, and never mention Mazdak to me again.'

In Kesra's palace there was a garden with a high wall around it. It was dug up from end to end, and Mazdak's followers were planted there head down, with their feet in the air, like trees. Kesra said to Mazdak, 'Go to my garden and see there trees of a kind no one has ever seen or heard tell of before.' Mazdak went to the garden expecting to see fruit trees, but when he saw what was there, he gave a cry of despair and fainted. Kesra had a tall gallows built, and the impious Mazdak was strung up alive and head down. He was killed with a shower of arrows. If you have any sense, you will not follow Mazdak's way.

The nobility were once more assured of their wealth, their women folk, children and splendid gardens.[174]

After the grotesque execution of Mazdak and his closest collaborators in the royal gardens of Ctesiphon, Khosrow and his backers in the Zoroastrian priesthood murdered as many as 100,000 leading Mazdakites and he ordered home invasions to seize writings in private libraries. The "heretical" books were publicly burned in huge bonfires.

Khosrow's decree demanding the liquidation of the Mazdakites is preserved in the *Dînkard* passage that claims "the truth of the Mazdayasnian religion has been recognized" but only "after he had put down irreligion and heresy."[175] As a condition of deferring to them on religious matters, Khosrow required the Magians to precisely formulate the orthodox doctrine.[176] In another passage of the *Dînkard*, Khosrow demands the total destruction of the doctrines of all heretics in favor of an enforcement of the dogma of Azarpad, son of Mahraspand.[177] He also calls for the orthodox to have a monopoly on religious knowledge, which should be jealously denied to would-be heretics.[178] So much for the "philosopher King" of late Sassanian Iran.

It is true that, when Caesar Justinian closed the last of the pagan academies in Europe in 529 AD, a handful of European academicians fled to the court of Khosrow and were warmly received by him. They were mostly Platonists and, despite his official orthodoxy, Khosrow was interested in Platonist ideas such as reincarnation, which had already been introduced into Sassanian court culture in the period when Shapur I attempted to incorporate numerous Greco-Roman texts on philosophy and science into the *Avesta*. Khosrow set up these Byzantine scholars at academies such as Gondeshapur, which had been founded by Shapur I, and they set about translating Greek philosophical and scientific texts into Pahlavi and Syriac.[179] However, a number of these scholars found the atmosphere of the Sassanian court to be stifling and so they left Iran.

A look at what purports to be a compendium of thought from the late Sassanian period leaves us with little doubt as to why these Greco-Roman thinkers could not stomach the patron whom they, as frightened refugees, initially praised as an embodiment of the Platonic philosopher-king. The compendium is a book titled *Jâvedân Kherad* or what a Greek thinker would have titled *Sophia Perennis*. In other words, "The Perennial Philosophy." It is authored by Ibn Miskawayh (pronounced *Ibn-e-Meskouyeh* in Persian), who was an Iranian scholar from Rey, i.e. present-day Tehran, writing during the Buyid period. He was born in 932 to a family that had only recently converted from Zoroastrianism, which accounts for his intense interest in Sassanian thought. Miskawayh characterizes the latter as the Tradition of *Khosravâni* wisdom and virtue. The term *Khosravâni* is an adjectival form of the name Khosrow, although it refers not primarily to Khosrow I, but to Key Khosrow, a primordial Iranian king and sage whose teachings were supposed to have been preserved and promulgated by the would-be philosopher king of the late Sassanian period.

Jâvedân Kherad claims to preserve a Sassanian book of wise sayings and judgments by the primordial ruler Hushang Shah, a letter from Bozorgmehr to "Kasra," i.e. Khosrow I, and most importantly, "words of wisdom" from Khosrow *Anushiravan* ("he of the immortal soul").[180] There are indeed many fine (*nikou*) words of wisdom here, in the sense of sayings of a sage that the Chinese might neatly wrap up inside of a fortune cookie. Some of them are more insightful than others, which must be considered platitudes of the kind one would find in a nineteenth-century European handbook on morals and proper etiquette. Even the most profound and penetrating of these sayings are not connected to each other by any systematic thought process that could, on account of its principles and logical structure, enter into a fundamental conflict with a rival system. One would be hard pressed to find anything in here that a person might die for or that might drive him to kill another. Compare this to the zeal of the Manicheans and the martyrdom of around a hundred thousand Mazdakites at the hands of Khosrow I.

CHAPTER 7

EVERYTHING IS PERMITTED

THE MAZDAKITE REVOLUTION IS AN enigma. How could such a radically antinomian religious movement have seized control of the Sassanian state for an entire generation? This chapter begins by venturing an answer to that question. The Mazdakites had help from the Parthian houses, the feudal lords sidelined beginning with Ardeshir's centralization of the Sassanian state. As we saw in Chapter 5, these Parthians were Mithraists, and as Chapter 6 suggests, the religious movement that came to be known as "Mazdakism" actually had roots in Ardeshir Babakan's own time and place, namely third century Pars, and was probably a Mithraic resistance to his puritanical purge of the Magi and invention of a Zoroastrian orthodoxy.

The present chapter ventures the view that these Parthian feudal elites and what remained of their Mithraic magicians conspired against the Sassanian state and its Zoroastrian orthodoxy. Once their attempt at a coup under Mazdak and Kavad was met with such brutal massacres and inquisitorial persecution under Khosrow, they decided that no internal solution was possible. So they created a fifth column in the part of Arabia near Yemen, then an Iranian colony, together with a doctrine designed to act as a psycho-social inoculant that would destroy the Orthodox Zoroastrianism at the foundation of the Sassanian state.

The Lords of House Karen ruled Hyrcania (or "Wolf Country"), the only region of Iran that is spared from the Arab conquest—as if a deal had been struck with the invaders. Their knights wore green over their shining scale armor, including green face veils, and they rode into battle with the standard of the crescent moon and the star. This is the "angelic army" that intervenes in the Battle of Badr to turn the tide in favor of

Muhammad. More significantly, a Mithraic Magus operating under the name of "Salman, the Persian" had been sent some years earlier to "reveal" Islam to Muhammad in the first place. After the successful toppling of the Sassanian state through a combination of the Mohammedan armies and the Parthian knights' betrayal of the Sassanian military, Salman is given governorship of the former capital district of Iran. Almost immediately, Neo-Mazdakite revolts against the Arabian Caliphate began, including the revolt of Babak Khorramdin in Azerbaijan. Within a century, these revolts led to the emergence of semi-autonomous fiefdoms governed by Parthian feudal houses. Then, two centuries after the defeat of the Sassanids, the Iranian Buyid dynasty had managed to turn the tables and basically reduce the Baghdad Caliphate to vassal status beneath it.

This period of a post-Sassanid Iranian Renaissance, beginning in about 850, becomes the zenith of science and literature in Iran's history. It is the focus of the second section of this chapter. The lack of a centralized Iranian state cannot be counted against the glory of this epoch, which was truly a Golden Age — not of Islam — but of Iran, any more than the lack of a central government in Italy can be counted against the artistic splendor and intellectual genius of the Italian Renaissance. Furthermore, the Iran of this epoch was even more free thinking and secular in a humanistic sense than Renaissance Italy, where the Catholic Church had far more influence than Islam did in Buyid Iran. There was a renaissance of Persian literature, epitomized by the *Shâhnâmeh* of Abolqasem Ferdowsi — which preserves the Pre-Islamic folk history of Iran and becomes the Iranian national epic. This period is, however, best known for scientific discoveries and technological innovations that have been misattributed to Arab Muslims.

The vast majority of the scientists and inventors of this so-called "Islamic" Golden Age were actually Persians. These included such giants as Ibn Sina (Avicenna), Al-Farabi, and Abu Rayhan Al-Biruni. Iran became one of the few nations that have, at a certain period in history, led the world in scientific research and technological innovation. Iran was preceded in this by Greece and Roman Italy, then followed by Britain, France,

Germany, and America. During this period, Khwarizmi developed Algebra, Yahya ibn Abi Mansur (aka Bizist Pur-e-Firuzan) made the most sophisticated astronomical tables of the time, Haly Abbas wrote encyclopedic medical treatises that remained influential in Europe for centuries, Zakariyya Razi discovered kerosene and alcohol in addition to founding the fields of pediatrics and ophthalmology, and Omar Khayyam, who perfected Algebra, also devised the most sophisticated calendar that the pre-modern world had ever seen. Although most of these Persians wrote in Arabic, both the Buyid takeover of the Baghdad Caliphate and the later Assassin adoption of Persian as the liturgical language of Islam in place of Arabic strongly suggest that Persian, which underwent a fantastic literary flourishing at this time, would also have replaced Arabic for scientific works.

The Parthian aristocracy and their Mithraic magicians who engineered this Iranian Renaissance could not have known that it would only last a couple of hundred years, because the blood-lusting Turks would invade in 1050, followed shortly thereafter by the even more barbaric Mongols. Despite these invasions, the afterglow of that Renaissance shone at least into the 1300s both in poetic literature and the sciences. Nevertheless, as heirs to the Arabian Caliphate, which they took over in the Seljuk period, and by zealously embracing Islam and tyrannically forcing it upon the Iranian people just when they were getting out from under the Caliphate, the Turks destroyed the conditions for freedom of thought and expression in Iran. This was compounded a century later when, around 1200 AD, the Mongol hordes followed the Turks into Iran and genocided as much as half of the Iranian population. The most dramatic episode in the Mongol conquest was the siege of Assassin fortresses, such as Alamut.

The third and final section of this chapter, which is the most extensive, addresses the Order of Assassins. The title of the chapter as a whole is based on the motto legendarily ascribed to Hassan Sabbah, the leader of the Assassin fortress of Alamut, who purportedly held as his maxim: "Nothing is true; everything is permitted" (*Hich chizi haghighat nadârad, hame chiz halâl ast*). The esoteric meaning of this motto is multi-dimensional and, whether or not Hassan ever actually employed it, the saying does epitomize the Assassin Creed. On a metaphysical level the maxim reaches back to the Scythian sage Gautama's critique of Zoroastrian Idealism. It is a critique of the idea that the things (*chiz*) of this world could ever constitute an objective Reality that would be mirrored by the Truth of one's own thoughts, words, and deeds. On a socio-political level, this echoes Heraclitus' view of political power. It means that any regime that claims its authority is based upon instantiating the macrocosm of cosmic order in the microcosm of human society is either zealously deluded or engaging in deliberate manipulation of the population that it governs. The Sassanian state was such a regime.

The *sharia* or laws that discipline a body politic, and on the basis of which people are punished for engaging in forbidden acts, are not laws justified by an attempt to bring earthly affairs into line with cosmic order—what the Zoroastrians refer to as the Truth of *Ashâ* or *Artâ* and take to be the pattern for sovereign Justice or *Khashatra Vairya*. Things in this world are not Good or Evil, they are permitted (*halâl*) or forbidden (*harâm*) by a sovereign authority for the sake of its own Power. There is a Truth, but this singular Truth or *Haghighat* lies beyond the multiplicity of this world's phenomenal appearances. The only *Haghighat* is the *Vahdâniyat* or absolute unity of God, and those who attain *towhid* by becoming one in the recognition of this veiled reality are also thereby released from *sharia*. This does not simply mean the abrogation of Islamic law. Since the Quran is the guardian over all other books of law, it means liberation from the need for any and all external authority and imposed social order. At this point there is also no need for continued "dissimulation" or *taqiyya*, a practice central to Shi'ite Islam.

The Neo-Mazdakite followers of Babak Khorramdin, who revolted against the Arabian Caliphate, and the Buyids who eventually seized Baghdad and brought that Caliphate under Iranian control, thereby inaugurating the Iranian Renaissance, were both Shi'ite movements. As the most radical of the Shi'ites, the Assassins who resisted the demise of that Renaissance at the hands of the Turks and Mongols, also saw themselves as guardians of the esoteric secret concerning the true origin of Islam. Whereas other Shi'ites saw succession from Muhammad, or Imamate, as proceeding from Ali, the Nizari Ismailis revered Salman the Persian as the true first Imam and they even held that Imamate was above Prophet-hood—meaning that Salman was above Muhammad and his successors in the esoteric leadership of the Imamate were likewise above the Quran.

The most fundamental schism between the Shi'ites and the Sunnis is that the latter see the Quran itself as the absolute authority, with *hadith* or traditions of the sayings and deeds of the Prophet used only to interpretively augment Revelation—including and especially its legal and political dimension, i.e. *sharia*. By contrast, the Shi'ites believe in the interpretive authority of the Imams who are guardians of an esoteric teaching passed on to them from the first Imam, who was the closest companion of Muhammad. The most radical form of this Shi'ite doctrine can be seen in the Ismailism of Alamut, where Hassan Sabbah takes the idea of *ta'lim* or mystical authority of the Imam to the point that it is sufficient to negate the *sharia*—something that other Shi'ites believe can only happen under the guidance of the hidden and final Imam, when he emerges from out of occultation at the Apocalypse (*Qiyâmat*). While Hassan Sabbah did not claim to be this figure, his successor, Hassan II of Alamut did do so in 1164 when he declared the arrival of the Apocalypse and abolished the *sharia*.

What we glimpse at Alamut is a culmination of the occult project of the Mithraic movement that began in the Parthian period under the standard of the Skull and Crossed Bones—the movement that resisted its persecution and marginalization at the hands of the Sassanian state through the Mazdakite coup within that regime under the reign of Kavad. The esoteric teachings about the nature of God, prophet-hood, occult initiation, social evolution, and an apocalyptic conception of history that are expressed by Ismaili scriptures, or before that in practices of earlier radical Shi'ite movements such as the Khorramdinân, are ideas completely on a continuum with Mithraism or Mazdakism.

7.1 Salman the Persian and the Hyrcanian Origin of Islam

Given how radical Mazdak's revolutionary program was, the fact that it was backed by the Shah is not sufficient to account for how Kavad himself was able to implement such policies for several decades — in effect, to raise an entire generation of Iranians under a Mazdakite state! A Western reader ought to try and conceive of the enormity of this imperious transgression by imagining the Carpocratian Gnostics successfully converting a Caesar and seizing control of the Roman Empire for thirty years. It is, quite frankly, impossible to imagine. What happened in Sassanid Iran, Rome's rival world superpower, with no less sophisticated a society and economy, was an impossible revolution. Unless — there were elements within the highest levels of the state apparatus that, for some reason, wanted to destabilize the Sassanian state or perhaps even shatter it. Who would those individuals be? The heads of the Parthian feudal houses.

When Ardeshir Babakan toppled the Parthian regime, he also sidelined the Parthian feudal houses by centralizing the administration of *Irânshahr* and developing a conscripted national military. The Parthians had a feudal system, with significant power delegated to fiefdoms administered by various houses and a national military policy dependent on the mutual cooperation of the knights of each of the houses, who swore to defend the King of Kings. Yet, despite Ardeshir's attempts to totally centralize power, the Sassanian state wound up depending on the knights of the old feudal houses, such as Soren-Pahlav and Karen, for increasingly ambitious military campaigns to expand the Second Persian Empire and secure newly conquered territories while maintaining order back at home.[1]

These chivalric elites had remained Mithraists.[2] Lord Sukhra of the House of Karen had been the hidden power behind the reign of Kavâd, the Sassanid monarch under whose aegis the Mazdakite revolution took place.[3] This Parthian noble forcibly deposed the Sassanid Shah Bilash and installed Kavâd or Qobâd in his place in 488, remaining the occulted executive authority of the Sassanid Empire during the entire period wherein Mazdak acted as the front man for a Mithraic social justice project.[4] The House of Karen was one of a number of Parthian feudal houses that had been displaced by the rise of the Sassanians. By the late Sassanian period, they had ruled the Hyrcania region in northern Iran on the coast of the Caspian Sea for centuries.[5] This heavily forested region, which includes the Gilan, Mazandaran, and Golestan provinces of contemporary Iran, is verdantly green — one of the two colors most closely associated with Mithra (the other being red, the color of the Mazdakites). The Karenids wore green both as camouflage and in honor of Mithra.[6]

As late as the eighth century, the revolts of Bihafarid Mahfarvardin (from 747–749) and Sunbâd (in 755) against the encroachment of the Arabian Caliphate, which both take place in the Hyrcanian realm of the House of Karen, are clearly Mithraic in their ideology and symbolism.[7] For example, both movements established the Sun as their *qibla*, believed in reincarnation (*tanâsokh*), and featured ecstatic rites of intoxication.[8] What is most significant in this regard is that both of these movements were vehemently rejected by the surviving Zoroastrians of the region, who in these instances actually went so far as to side with the Arab Muslims against their fellow Iranians seeking freedom and independence from the Caliphate.[9] According to the Medieval scholar Shahristani, these crypto-Mithraists were even considered "the deadliest enemies of the *Zamzami Majus* [a derogatory term for Zoroastrians meaning "mumbling Magi" in a reference to Zoroastrian ritual incantations]."[10] It has never been properly considered, as it ought to have been, whether the strange mixture of Islamic and Pre-Islamic Iranian motifs in these movements — *so early in the Islamic period* — rather than attesting to a hybridization of Islam with the beliefs of Iranians who remained staunchly anti-Arab, actually reveals the occult Mithraic origin of Islam itself. Why, for example, was the rebel Sunbâd so intent on marching from Hyrcania to Mecca, where he planned to destroy the Kabba and replace it with the Sun as the *qibla*?[11] That seems like an awfully personal axe to grind against Islam. One does a thing like that when something that one has created oneself has been perverted or diverted to a purpose other than the one intended. More interesting still is Sunbâd's claim that *Mazdak is in occultation together with the Shi'ite Imâm Mahdi*, and that they will return to the world together.[12]

The Parthians had ruled Iran for about 400 years before Ardeshir Babakan, as the founder of the Sassanian dynasty, overthrew them and dislodged them from the prominent role that they played both in the bureaucracy of the nation and also in its military. The Parthians did not have a strong conscript military. They relied on knights in the service of various houses to form coalitions that would go and fight their enemies — for example, the Romans. As we saw in the preceding chapter, Ardeshir replaced this feudal system with a conscript military. He thereby sidelined the knights of the various Parthian houses. There were, however, occasional interventions by these knights, who apparently maintained a high level of military skill and preparedness.

In the late Sassanian period, during the reign of Khosrow Anushiravan, there was an attempted Turkic invasion of Iran. By this time, the Turks had come down into Central Asia, and they were impinging on the borders of *Irânshahr*. (Note that these were Turk*ic* people, not Turk*ish* people. They had not reached Anatolia yet, and "Turkey" as a nation dates to 1924.) The Sassanian military, led by Khosrow himself, was facing a possible defeat at their hands. The battle, which took place in the area around Gorgan (Jorjan), was not going well. In his *Târikhé Tabaristân*, Ibn Isfandiyar records that all of a sudden chainmail-clad horseback riders descended onto the battlefield, and both their scale armor and their horses were covered with green fabric.[13] Their faces were also covered with green veils, with only their eyes visible. They turned the battle in favor of Khosrow, and the Turks were defeated. Khosrow wanted to thank whomever was responsible but the mysterious green riders refused to identify themselves.[14] Finally, Khosrow forced the head of this army to grudgingly confess that he belongs to the House of Karen.[15] Presumably the green fabric covering the scale armor of their riders and horses was camouflage designed for fighting in their native element, the Hyrcanian Forest overlooking the Caspian Sea.

The leader of the troops of the House of Karen did not want to identify himself because he probably despised Khosrow and had only intervened so that Iran, and in particular Hyrcania, would not fall to the Turks. In addition to sidelining the knights of the Parthian houses, Ardeshir Babakan had developed a type of administrative bureaucracy at Ctesiphon that marginalized the Parthians. The puritanical form of Zoroastrianism that was upheld by some of the Sassanians who were ideologically in line with Ardeshir had wrecked Parthian society, marginalized Parthian feudal houses, and destroyed their long-term project of culturally conquering Rome through the spread of Mithraism. That is a rather large axe to grind on the part of the Parthian elite.

The Mithraic religion that the Parthians took into Rome was quintessentially a religion of secret societies and secret initiations, much more so than the orthodox Zoroastrianism of Ardeshir. As we have seen, it was an esoteric, occult form of religiosity inseparable from sophisticated astrological and alchemical practices. We are talking about a group of occultists. The Magi of the Parthian period, whose fire temples Ardeshir shut off — the most sacrilegious thing that one could possibly do — were magicians and leaders of secret societies. They were people adept in the occult arts. According to certain oral traditions or *hadith* concerning the companions of the prophet Muhammad, one of these Parthian Magi was a man named Ruzbeh Khoshnudân, who became more widely known under his pseudonym, Salmâné Fârsi.

"Salman, the Persian" was one of the companions of the prophet Muhammad — one of his very earliest companions. There are a number of conflicting oral traditions about just who this man was when he met Muhammad, and exactly what role he played in the formative stages of Islam. We have *hadith* or oral traditions from the companions of the Prophet that are not always in sync with one another. But there is one very curious passage in the Quran itself, Surah 16, Ayeh 103, which makes reference to the fact that people are promulgating the rumor that a certain *Ajam* is responsible for the composition of the Quran. *Ajam* is the word that the Arabs use to refer to the Aryans to the north, namely the Iranian people.

The Quran, which is the voice of Allah and always speaks of Muhammad in the third person, even though it is being recited by Muhammad, states: "We hear that they say that this *Ajam* is the composer of these verses, but this glorious Quran is composed in the Arabic tongue."[16] The *Ajam* in question could only be Salman, Muhammad's sole constant companion who was an "Aryan" or Iranian. It is preposterous for the Quran to suggest that Salman could not be its composer simply because his native language is not Arabic. Salman knew Arabic quite well. In fact, oral traditions suggest that he fluently spoke a number of different languages besides his native Persian tongue.[17]

According to these traditions, the man with the alias "Salman," namely Ruzbeh Khoshnudân, was a Persian Magus who tended a sacred fire in Esfahan, but he was a Magus of the Mazdakite rather than the Orthodox Zoroastrian persuasion.[18] Then he converted to Christianity.[19] In the process of doing so, he surely would have learned a great deal about the Abrahamic traditions — Judaism and Christianity, as Islam did not yet exist. It is also worthy of note that the Christians of the time were rather ascetic, at least in Iran. How curious then that after converting to Christianity, Ruzbeh becomes an international businessman involved in trade — particularly with Arabia. This is what brings Ruzbeh to Mecca, where he operates under the alias "Salman, the Persian" and seeks out the wife of the prophet Muhammad, Khadija, who is a very powerful businesswoman.[20] Salman's study of Judeo-Christianity would also have prepared him for this, since Khadija was from a tribe of Jewish descent and she had a number of Christian friends. It is by this means that Salman befriends Muhammad, and they become so close that there are rumors circulating that Salman is putting the Quran into Muhammad's mind.[21]

Some eyewitnesses of the prophetic career of Muhammad left *hadiths* to the effect that Gabriel was an actual cloaked man who would stealthily come into Muhammad's presence in order to convey the verses of the Quran to the prophet, who would studiously repeat and memorize them.[22] This has led to speculation, among some radical Shi'ite Gnostics, that the "angel" Gabriel was actually Salman, the Persian in disguise.[23] In that case, their first meeting would have been in the cave where Muhammad had been meditating when he was suddenly *grabbed in a stranglehold* from behind by *a man who did not allow himself to be seen* and who keep shouting "Recite!"[24] An exclamation that becomes the first "revealed" word of the Quran.

Salman subsequently becomes most famous for teaching advanced military tactics to Muhammad, which help him to prevail in battles against other Arabian tribes — in the face of tremendous odds. He advises Muhammad, for example, on how to conduct trench warfare — a Sassanian military tactic.[25] Who is this man who is a member of the order of the Magi, then converts to Christianity, then becomes an international businessman, and who, by the time he winds up in Arabia, becoming one of the first converts to the obscure cult of Islam (which he is also rumored to have created), somehow has enough knowledge of advanced military tactics to be teaching them to Muhammad and his commanders — a man who moreover speaks a number of foreign languages, including fluent Arabic? One has to wonder if Salman is a military intelligence operative of some kind. Then the question becomes: On behalf of whom? With what motive? With what objective?

Besides the Battle of the Trench, where Salman played a decisive role, there is another incident in Muhammad's combat with other Arabian tribes that is relevant in this regard. At the Battle of Badr an alleged "army of Angels" gallops onto the battlefield.[26] They are very strangely garbed according to the witnesses. They are the ones who turn the battle in favor of Muhammad. Again, the odds were that he should easily have been defeated. What was the strange garb that these angelic warriors were wearing? Could they have been the green-clad riders of the House of Karen? Remember that these knights wore green clothes and green face veils and rode horses covered in green, and both they and their horses were clad in shining scale armor, an Iranian invention and novelty that would have seemed mysterious to Arabs, perhaps even angelic. Green becomes the holy color of Islam, and the green face veil becomes standard in Muslim depictions of prophets, angels, and saints. Could this be because the "angelic army" that appeared at the Battle of Badr was dressed in the fashion of the knights of the House of Karen?

Among the elements of the feudal, chivalric culture that were transmitted to Europe by the Alans — Iranian tribesmen related to the Parthians — were animal or nature symbols for various houses. These would appear on their shields or standards (war banners). No trace has remained of the standard or coat of arms of the House of Karen in Iran. However, as part of the mass migration of northern Iranians into Europe, at the time of the fall of the Roman Empire going into Medieval Europe, the Alans and other Scythians (the Parthians branched off of the Scythians) carried the standard or *Tamgas* of various houses with them. The coat of arms of the House of Karen turns up in Saxony, and it is indeed the crescent Moon and the star.

So, when these green-clad horseback knights entered the Battle of Badr and bailed out Muhammad in one of the first great "miracles" of Muslim history, they were probably not only clad in green over their "angelically" shimmering scale armor, they were probably also carrying a green banner with the crescent Moon and the star on it — the standard of the House of Karen. This is how that symbol, which is neither Abrahamic nor even Mohammedan in origin, wound up being appropriated by Muslims. In fact, as we saw beginning in the first chapter, the star in this symbol is in fact not a star at all. It is the planet Venus, which in its guise as the morning star is referred to as Lucifer. Chapter 1 discussed how the cult of Artemis was closely associated with the crescent and the star.

Many pagan gods and goddesses were syncretized with one another. Artemis was syncretized with Cybele or *Kybele*.[27] She is the goddess that some archeologists have associated with the original meteorite at the *Kabba*, which they think may be a shortened form of the name of *Kybele*.[28] There have also been suggestions that it is the origin of the word *Kabbalah*. This meteorite that the Muslims subsequently turned into the core of their mosque at Mecca, and for which they built a cubic enclosure, actually has a vulva engraved in it that is filled with silver.[29] The original ritual was to circumnavigate the stone and kiss it in the place where this mark had been made. So it was part of a goddess cult, and particularly the cult of a goddess syncretized with Artemis, whose cult symbol is the crescent Moon and the star. This is another interesting layer in this whole puzzle of the secret origins of Islam and the possible Parthian conspiracy to engineer Islam in the Arabian peninsula, to unify the various tribal Arabs and pit them against the Sassanids, in order to shatter and overthrow the Sassanian Empire, presumably to open up a space for the return of the Parthian feudal houses.

There was, however, another even deeper motive at work than merely political machinations. The House of Karen was seeking to create a psycho-social inoculant. Islam was engineered by the Magian elite, the last remnant of Parthian Mithraism, in order to present hierarchical, patriarchal, theocratic totalitarianism in the most concentrated form possible and inject it into a society that, after all, did profoundly value innovation, free-spiritedness, and tolerance — so that, metaphorically speaking, the immune system of Iranian society would reject this *in essence*. That also meant rejecting orthodox Zoroastrianism and Christianity, which was on the march in a militarized form through the Byzantines. Thanks to Ardeshir, the Byzantines were now coming at Iran with their armies, trying to convert Iran to Christianity.

Meanwhile, a government upholding an orthodox form of Zoroastrianism had just massacred hundreds of thousands of Mazdakites in the mid-500s — only a century before the Islamic Conquest of Iran. As we have seen, "Mazdakism" may actually have been a form of Parthian Mithraism. After the Islamic Conquest it morphed into the Khorramdinan movement, whose stronghold against the Arabian Caliphate was the area in northern and northwestern Iran around the Caspian Sea. *Khorramdin* means "Joyous Religion" and is an epithet that Babak assumed from the movement that he inherited. Some scholars think that it derives from the name of Mazdak's widow, Khorramiya, and that it was a name adopted by the Mazdakites after they went underground following the massacre they suffered under Khosrow I. "Babak" was his assumed name. He was born "Hassan" and his three brothers, Abdallah, Muawiya, and Ishaq also had Muslim names.[30] They were Shi'ites, and although the Khorramdinân (or Khurramites) were suspected to be Mazdakites (and rightly so), they presented themselves as Shi'ites.

Hassan met Jâvidân Shahrak in the course of being the latter's delivery boy.[31] The aristocrat was so impressed with him, and the two became so close, that although Jâvidân had a young son of his own, he entrusted Babak with the management of his estate.[32] Medieval historians and heresiarchs who wrote of the Khorramdin movement described Jâvidân as Babak's *ostâd* or spiritual "master."[33] Jâvidân was the leader of a Khorrami organization based in the Caucasus mountains, 145 kilometers northeast of Ardebil — in other words, on the present border between what remains of Azerbaijan within Iran and what has become the Republic of Azerbaijan.[34] The Khorramdin movement was not limited to Azerbaijan but extended from the Caucasus mountains through the Zagros mountain range all the way down to Fars, where Mazdakism had begun in its original form of the *Dorost-Dîn*.[35]

Jâvidân had a rival, another Khorrami leader named Abu Imrân, and these two aristocrats would feud during the months when the deep snow covering the mountain passes did not force peace between them.[36] According to certain narratives, Jâvidân was killed in one of these feuds. According to others, he was poisoned by his wife who, although she had become something akin to Babak's adopted mother, was also rumored to have been carrying out an affair with him.[37] In any case, Jâvidân's widow married Babak and had the authority to force her late husband's followers to transfer their allegiance to Babak.[38] The Khorramdinân, having been Mazdakites, not only believed in reincarnation but also in forms of reincarnation that were indistinguishable from possession. Jâvidân's widow alleged that her departed husband's spirit has possessed Babak in furtherance of his mission to "possess the earth, slay the tyrants, restore Mazdakism, make the humble among you mighty and the lowly high."[39] The two were married in what is unmistakably a Mithraic wedding ceremony. It involved sacrificing a cow and using its flayed hide as a *sofreh* for a ritual communion meal of bread and wine, with the widow offering Hasan a sprig of *rayhân* or fragrant herbs symbolizing the green aspect of Mithra.[40] It has been surmised that Hasan only assumed the Persian name "Babak" on this occasion.[41]

Babak's followers were also referred to as *Sorkhjâmegân* or "the red-clothed ones", in another allusion to their having been Mazdakites.[42] Babak called his soldiers "the Army of the Immortals" (Persian *Sepâhé Jâvidân*).[43] This may, however, have been a reference to his master and godfather *Jâvidân* (whose name means "the Immortal"), since his band of brigands and partisans engaging in guerrilla warfare was hardly reminiscent of the Ancient Persian "Immortals" of the epoch of Darius and Xerxes.[44] Armenian Christian, Arab Muslim, and Iranian sources vary in their estimates of just how many people were killed by Babak and his soldiers, but these estimates seem to average in the hundreds of thousands, with some claiming up to one million.[45] Even the lowest estimates would translate into millions of casualties when scaled up to the population of today's world as compared to that of Babak's epoch. This is all the more disturbing when we consider that the Khorramdinân indiscriminately killed civilian women and even children who were linked to the men that fought against them.[46] Babak even burned monasteries full of women and children, so as to make a point that there was absolutely no place of refuge for Iranian traitors — or their family members — who, even if only out of cowardice, sided with the Arabian Caliphate that was occupying Iran.[47]

Babak Khorramdin, who is often hailed as the greatest Iranian freedom fighter in the early revolts against the Arab Caliphs of Baghdad, was undoubtedly a terrorist.[48] Actually, his tactics were an exemplary form of terrorism — the use of asymmetrical psychological warfare — as a means of legitimate resistance against foreign occupying forces *and even more so* against those elements of *the native population that submit to colonizers.* For example, it is clear that the spectacular violence that Babak *sometimes even inflicted on his would-be allies* was intended to terrorize the peasant population within his domain to dissuade them from siding with the Caliph's forces during any number of the Arab incursions into his territory, out of the fear that, once the Arabs were driven out again, these turncoat

Iranians could be subject to terrifying reprisals.[49] Babak's main targets were not Arab overlords, very few of whom had actually penetrated Azerbaijan. Rather, his main targets were those of his fellow Iranians who did not have the backbone to seek freedom and independence.[50] Scaled to today's population, *he killed millions of his own countrymen* — together with their children — *because they were complacently treasonous*. If Babak is a hero, that is why. Comparisons to Pol Pot are not entirely unwarranted, especially considering the communistic character of the Neo-Mazdakite provincial partisan guerrillas that he led.

From 816 to 837, Babak ruled over an autonomous Iranian territory that, at the zenith of his rebellion, extended from the Muqan plain in the Caucasus to Zanjan, with the Byzantines and Armenians to his west and the Iranian princes of the Caspian to his east.[51] Some have suspected links between Babak's movement and those of these Caspian nobles, especially Maziyar, the prince who staged his own revolt against the Caliphate in Tabaristan in 839, and who allegedly maintained a secret correspondence with Babak.[52] In 835 the Caliph appointed the Transoxanian prince Haydar bin Kavus, known as the Afshin, as a General of the forces ordered to march against Babak.[53] More conspiratorial minds have theorized that, unbeknownst to the Caliphate, both Mazyar and Afshin were actually in league with Babak, which would explain Afshin's repeated delays in the campaign against Babak's forces as well as his having somehow eventually allowed Babak and his upper echelon to escape.[54]

As he was facing defeat, Babak attempted to convince the Byzantine ruler Theophilus to attack the Caliphate in Baghdad.[55] When his fortress at al-Badhdh fell to Afshin's troops, Babak and those closest to him, who fled westwards, accepted an invitation to take refuge with an Armenian prince named Sahl bin Sunbât.[56] It was a trap. While hunting with falcons on prince Sunbât's estate, Babak was captured by soldiers of the Caliphate who had been tipped off by the Armenian in exchange for a ransom.[57] Babak's retort to the Armenian prince is interesting. He basically accuses Ibn Sunbât of being a Judas when he says, "you have sold me to these Jews for a trifling amount."[58] Babak and his followers considered the Arab Muslims that they were revolting against to be contemptible "Jews."[59] Babak's one-eyed mother, his sister, and his wife (in other words, Jâvidân's widow) were all raped by this Armenian noble in front of Babak's own eyes before they were handed over to the caliph's forces.[60] His daughter, who was still a virgin, was left for the Caliph al-Mutasim to deflower.[61] The caliph is alleged to have praised Allah that he was able to take her virginity, together with that of the captured daughters of the Iranian rebel Mâzyâr and the Byzantine emperor, in only a single hour.[62]

After witnessing such atrocities committed against those near and dear to him, Babak was executed by the Caliphate in a spectacularly brutal fashion at Samara in 838.[63] His last desire was to at least be killed by a nobleman, a *dehghân*, since Babak considered himself a king. In fact, some years earlier, he had disowned one of his sons who had come to him with a peace offering from the Caliph, yelling at the young man in rage, "One day as a king is better than forty years as an abject slave!"[64] In the end, all of his sons would wind up being forced into the military service of the Caliph who had Babak executed, the same Caliph who had forced their mother and sister into sexual slavery.[65]

The revolt of Babak and the Khorramdinân in Azerbaijan aside, the only part of Iran that remains free and independent of the Caliphate is the Hyrcania region (Greater Gorgan) which was ruled by the house of Karen when the Sassanid Empire fell. Did they cut a deal with the Arabian Caliphate? Is this why Afshin of Tabaristan betrayed Babak Khorramdin, who had been fighting the Arabs to maintain independent Persian rule in the neighboring Azerbaijan province?[66] After the initial victory of the Arabs in the Islamic Conquest of Iran, Salmâné Fârsi, or Rouzbeh Khoshnudân, was given control of the governorship of the former capital district of the Sassanian Empire.[67] Had some arrangement been reached between Salman, the House of Karen, and the Arabian conquerors in order to maintain the independence of their fiefdom in the north of Iran? Did some of the revolts against the Caliphate in northern Iran take place because, intoxicated by power and an insatiable lust for total control, the Arabian Caliphate went back on this deal? It is high time for Iranian patriots to ask themselves these hard questions about Iran's true history.

7.2 The Iranian Renaissance

Within the span of two hundred years after the Arabian Conquest, various semi-autonomous Iranian fiefdoms arose, and by about a thousand AD, they had undercut the Arabian Caliphate to the point that they were effectively self-governing and were promulgating an Iranian Renaissance in science and literature. Foremost among these was the Buyid Dynasty (circa 950–1050) who were Shi'ites that originated in Daylam, a mountainous part of the Caspian Sea coastal region of Hyrcania.[68] Under the reign of Azod al-Dawla Fanna Khosrow (949–983), the Buyid realm went from being a powerful semi-autonomous fiefdom to becoming a vast Iranian state that encompassed most of contemporary Iran and managed to seize control of Baghdad, the capital of the Caliphate, turning the former Arab master into an Iranian vassal by 975.[69] Instead of destroying the Sunni Caliphate, Khosrow decided to use its machinery in order to turn the Sunni Arab majority governed by it into vassals of his Shi'ite Iranian state. Meanwhile, he became the first ruler since the Sassanian period to adopt the title *Shâhanshâh of Iran*. It is well known that 90% of the scientists of the so-called Islamic "Golden Age" of science and technology were actually Iranians; the Buyid seizure of Baghdad meant that these scientists, who had hitherto been forced to pen their treatises in Arabic under the oppressive "patronage" of the Caliphate, would soon have been able to research in their native Persian.

Musa Khwarizmi (780–850), known in the West as Algoritmi, was a Persian from Khwarazm in the greater Khorasan region (part of present-day Uzbekistan). The historian Al-Tabari gives his full name as Mohammad ibn Musa al-Khwarizmi *al-Majussiyy* or "the Magian." So it seems that, despite the pious forward to his *Algebra*, necessitated by his being in the court of the Caliph Al-Mamun, Khwarizmi was known to have been an Iranian heathen. He arrived at the first systematic solution of linear and quadratic equations.

Khwarizmi, the Magian, called one method that he used for this *al-Jabr*, the source of the word "Algebra."[70] It is "restoration" or adding a number to both sides of an equation in order to consolidate terms.[71] For example, $x^2 = 40x - 4x^2$ is consolidated into $5x^2 = 40x$. Another method, *al-muqâbala*, puts the same type of quantities on the same side of an equation, as in the case where $x^2 + 14 = x + 5$ is elegantly transformed into $x^2 + 9 = x$. Algebra is a unifying theory allowing rational numbers, irrational numbers, and geometric magnitudes (which the Greeks handled separately) to be abstracted as algebraic objects. This is the beginning of the development of equations so elemental that they can define an infinite class of problems, rather than Greek mathematics that begins from a definite set of problems to be solved. But it also had wide practical applicability to problems of trade, surveying, and legal inheritance. "Algorithm" is a term derived from Khwarizmi's Latinized name.[72]

Khwarizmi's *Concerning Hindu Numbers* popularized the Hindu or "Arabic" numeral system.[73] Khwarizmi also revised Ptolemy's geographical data for the parts of Earth under the Caliphate's control. He wrote about the mechanics of devices such as the astrolabe and sundial, and oversaw seventy geographers to determine Earth's circumference for Mamun's world map.[74] The *Zij al-Sindhind* or "astronomical tables of Sind and Hind (India)" produced by Khwarizmi is a turning point in so-called "Islamic" astronomy, from mere re-discovery and book learning to direct observations resulting in tables for movements of the sun, moon, and planets.[75] The book also contains tables for the trigonometric functions of sine and cosine. A treatise on spherical trigonometry is also attributed to him.[76]

By no means was Khwarizmi the only *Al-Majusi* or "Magian" of the so-called "Islamic Golden Age." We also have the Persian author of influential and encyclopedic medical treatises, Ali ibn al-Abbas al-Majusi (fl. 983), who actually had a Persian (rather than an Arab) patron, and is known to Europeans as Haly Abbas.[77] Then there is Yahya ibn Abi Mansur (d. 832), a Persian originally named Bizist Pur-e-Firuzan.[78] He was also born and raised as a Zoroastrian, and only converted to Islam in his own lifetime in order to serve the Caliph and teach at the *Beyt al-Hikmat* (the House of Wisdom in Baghdad). He worked in the court of al-Mamun, and at his observatories in Baghdad and Damascus, where he created the first "Arabic" *zij* (astronomical tables) that are independent of Greek originals. Yahya ibn Abi Mansur became a close "boon companion" of the Caliph, offering him astrological advice on a regular basis.[79]

Abu Bakr Muhammad ibn Zakariyya al-Razi (854–925) was a Persian from the city of Rayy (Ragha), in other words, pre-modern Tehran. He was a critic of Galen and Aristotle, and a defender of the banned theory of atomic physics. The author of more than 200 manuscripts, Razi was a polymath who made fundamental contributions to scientific fields as varied as Physics, Chemistry, and Biomedical science. He pioneered experimental medicine as a practicing physician in the hospitals of Rayy and Baghdad, where he provided free health care to poor patients.[80] He wrote the first book that clinically delineates the diseases of smallpox and measles.[81] As a chemist (alchemist, al-Kimiya) he discovered compounds like kerosene and alcohol, as well as their uses.[82] He is the father of pediatrics and ophthalmology. Some of his works, which were translated into Latin, became part of the Western European medical curriculum in the late medieval period and paved the way for the scientific revival of the European Renaissance.[83] His most revolutionary work is his analytical destruction of Galen's theory of the four humors and Aristotle's theory of the four elements in *Shukuk 'ala alinusor*, because of the independent-minded and boldly inquisitive revolt against Scholasticism and rejection of appeals to authority that it represents.

Razi's character as a free-thinker, a genuine philosopher (lover of Wisdom) and an uncompromising scientific genius can also clearly be seen in his estimation of Islam, the Quran, and the prophet-hood of Muhammad. In his *Mahariq al-anbiya* or "The Prophets' Fraudulent Tricks," Razi wrote:

> You claim that the evidentiary miracle is present and available, namely the Koran. You say, 'Whoever denies it, let him produce a similar one.' Indeed, we shall produce a thousand similar, from the works of rhetoricians, eloquent speakers, and valiant poets, which are more appropriately phrased and state

> the issues more succinctly. They convey the meaning better and their rhymed prose is in better meter. By God what you say astonishes us! You are talking about a work which recounts ancient myths, and is at the same time full of contradictions and does not contain any useful information or explanation. Then you say, 'Produce something like it'?![84]
>
> If the people of this religion [Islam] are asked about the proof of the soundness of their religion, they flare up, get angry and spill the blood of whomsoever confronts them with this question. … They [Muslims] forbid rational speculation, and strive to kill their adversaries. This is why truth became silenced and concealed.[85]

In view of such statements it is obviously a travesty to glorify Islam with the works of this Persian scientist. At the same time, there is nothing particularly Zoroastrian about Razi's writings either. It is not as if his scientific thought, or that of any of the other Iranian freethinkers of the Buyid Renaissance, was based on Zoroastrian principles. Actually, such absolute ideals and perfect principles would have hindered their research.

Conceptual distinctions are grounded on nothing other than complex social and linguistic practices.[86] This is what determines the appropriateness of certain concepts depending on their intentional context, such as what is considered metaphorical versus literal depending on whether the context is fiction or nonfiction. Our everyday thought, with a view to action, never really involves absolutes—let alone requires them.[87] This does not mean science is impossible. Rather, it means that we have to acknowledge that science is a practical endeavor and that it is a science of perceived phenomena—not a mirror to fundamental but invisible structures.[88] As Christopher Beckwith explains:

> [T]here are by definition *differences* in precision, including differences of *quality* of the differences, such that some data (or samplings of things) can be more consistent than other data, and the judgments that some people make can be more consistent and conform more closely to the data than those made so far by another group of people, [which] can have more consistency than the totality of judgments made by another group, and so on.[89]

A practical science of phenomena is possible because, even without absolutes as criteria, things are relatively gradable in terms of their precision and internal coherence. Such practical standards of evaluation can be applied to groups of scientists doing research. In phenomenological science, we should neither look for absolutes nor expect to find them. This also means abandoning the baseless assumption that perfection exists somewhere veiled from us, namely in the mind of God.[90]

That imperfect scientific knowledge would in any way be problematic is an idea that would never have occurred to anyone who was not, in the first place, laboring under the delusion that certain knowledge of perfect things is even possible.[91] Imperfect science is no problem at all, because *it is the only kind of knowledge* that there is. A scientific theory is "valid" when it *works well enough* in application. It is never replaced by a theory that is more "true," but by one that *works better* for certain purposes (although perhaps not for all purposes and in all cases addressed by the former theory). In domains where high precision is required, practicality will demand preferring scientific theories that, when applied, yield higher precision data or more precise technical control.[92] At no point do we need to employ absolutes to make this evaluation, nor are we ever pressed to make indefensible claims about "the ultimate nature of reality." Science, in actual practice, is about methods and protocols for producing higher precision data and, to the best of our ability, more replicable results.[93] It is not a body of knowledge, let alone a canon or catechism of absolute truths, about "Reality."

The hypothetical "Science" (Arabic *Elm*, Persian *Dânesh*) produced in an alternate history wherein the Sassanian orthodoxy survived for long enough to cross the threshold of scientific research and technological development that was eventually attained in Iran from 900–1100 (and that could have been attained sooner had the Sassanids remained in power), would have produced an even more totalitarian rationalism than that of the European Enlightenment. Zoroastrian Science would have been absolutely self-assured in its absolutist "knowledge" of the nature of Reality, whether that involves biological processes or the inner workings of the human mind. By contrast, under the weakened Abbasid Caliphate, in a world where Zoroastrianism had been displaced and Iranian scientists did not take Islam seriously, there was no absolutist underpinning to Iranian science that could be defended with total sincerity and in as rigorously rational a fashion as Zoroastrians would have defended scientific theories. Had the Turks and Mongols not invaded, Science in Iran would have proceeded on a healthier basis than it did in the West after Descartes.

The Parthian elite's engineering of Islam would have been trying to accomplish a number of objectives at once. They were trying to inoculate the Iranian psyche against puritanical theocracy and totalitarianism, and they were also trying to make sure that the form of consciousness that arose from this would not be conquered by Byzantine Christianity; they wished to achieve here what they had been trying to accomplish in the first place with Rome, namely, that Iranians would spread a form of spirituality back into Europe that would lead to social enlightenment. The Golden Age of Islam has nothing to do with Islamic theology in a positive sense. In fact, it has to do with Islamic theology in a negative sense in that when one looks at the work of someone like Zakaria Razi, one sees an extremely humanistic, secular, skeptical thinker, who has been freed from Zoroastrian orthodoxy to think as an Iranian free-thinker. That characterized the whole culture of this period, which, in a real travesty, is described as a "golden age of Islam." The point is that Islam the inoculant, inoculated the Iranian psyche against any form of religious totalitarianism.

These schemers in the House of Karen could not have known that the Turks would wind up coming in around 1100 and adopting Islam of their own accord, taking over ruler-ship of the Caliphate from the Arabs, whom they defeated, and re-imposing Islam in an even more totalitarian form on the Iranian people. They were closely followed by the Mongols, who adopt the same strategy of seeing in Islam a perfect means of governing an empire in a totalitarian fashion — a great basis for a totalitarian state ideology. This the House of Karen did not foresee, and these unexpected developments turned Islam into something completely different from the purpose it may have been meant to have: a purpose designed specifically for the Iranian people, to act on the Iranian psycho-social system as a catalyst. It was not designed for Turks.

The House of Karen and these Parthian aristocrats in Hyrcania only thought of the Arabs as vehicles. They never *dreamed* that a bunch of Arabian tribesmen who had been busy slitting each other's throats for hundreds of years before that, who had no literary culture, who had no organized political life, would be able to maintain the cohesion of this caliphate and actually rule over Iranians. They probably did not even think that the Arabs would make it nearly as far north as Azerbaijan or the Caspian coast of Iran. They were simply bringing about a temporary unity of Arabian tribes for the purpose of unseating the Sassanids and returning to power themselves. This worked — for a while.

The courts that were patrons of these scientists and that were becoming increasingly independent of the Caliphate in Baghdad, were also the patrons of the revival of Persian literature — most significantly the *Shahnameh* of Ferdowsi. This renaissance was taking place in the same northern part of Iran that encompassed the realm of the House of Karen. As noted above, after numerous insurgencies and revolts, including that of Abu Muslim Khorasani in the region in which Ferdowsi was raised, by the ninth century the power of the Caliphate had been sufficiently weakened such that Iranian dynasties were able to start asserting limited regional autonomy.

One of these were the Samanids. They traced their lineage to the Sassanian-period general Bahram Choubin, who was actually a Parthian.[94] The Samanids used New Persian as their court language rather than the official Arabic of the Caliphate.[95] This *Dari* or *Parsi* language was the next stage in the evolution of the Persian language after *Pahlavi* or Middle Persian. To foster the resurgence of the Persian language, and with a view to the preservation of Iran's national consciousness, the Samanids became patrons of Persian poets such as Rudaki and Daqiqi.[96] The latter was commissioned to compose the *Shâhnâmeh* based on fragments of surviving pre-Islamic Iranian sagas and chronicles. Daqiqi was murdered after just barely beginning the project, and Ferdowsi took over.[97] As we saw in Chapter 2, the name *Sâmân* of the Samanids is the origin of the word "Shaman" and designated the Mithraic spiritual tradition of Scythians such as Zaal and Rostam. It is no wonder then, that Rostam the *Sâmâni* becomes the greatest hero of the *Shâhnâmeh*.

Abolqasem Ferdowsi (940–1020) was from Tous, an ancient city near present-day Mashhad in the Khorasan region of Iran. "Ferdowsi" is an Arabized pronunciation of *Pardisi* or "from Paradise" (recall that the ancient Persian word *Paridaeza*, which became *Pardis* in Middle Persian, is the source for the English word "paradise"). On account of being the author of the Persian national epic, which is the world's longest poem composed by a single author, he is referred to as "The Lord of the Word." Since he composed it in nearly pure Persian at a time when the Persian language was in danger of perishing under Arab colonization, Iranians also refer to him as "The Savior of the Persian language."

Scholars have divided the epic poem of Ferdowsi into three distinct types of material. The first third is mythological. The second third is epic and quasi-historical. The final third, which begins with the Parthians, presents a poetic history of Sassanian Iran up to the Arabian conquest that can be closely correlated with known facts. Ferdowsi uses the epic material, which apparently has Scythian origins, to exemplify and preserve certain chivalric values that define an Iranian worldview. This material is, to this day, recited in the *Zurkhâneh* or "Houses of Strength" where Mithraic martial arts are practiced in every city, town, and hamlet of Iran. The *zurkhâneh* or "Houses of Strength" are underground and cave-like, just as the Mithraea of antiquity, and Mithraic ethics can be seen in the chivalric (*jâvânmardâne*) code of conduct (*âdâb*) adhered to by the *pahlavâns* (martial arts "heroes").[98] The fundamental values that form the core of the ethos of the *Shâhnâmeh*, and have roots in ancient Iran, are: (1) the worship of wisdom, or *Setâyeshé Kherad*; (2) Justice, or *Dâd*; (3) charitableness, or *Daheshmandi*; (4) chivalric free-spiritedness, or *Âzâdegi*; and, (5) beautification, cultivation, and development of the living world, or *Âbâdsâzié Giti or Giti-ârâyi*.

The closest Western points of comparison to this epic are the works of Homer or the Norse sagas, with the very great difference that the *Shâhnâmeh* was written a couple of centuries after the Arab conquest of Iran and with the explicit aim of preserving both the Persian language and the Aryan heritage of Iran. The epic ends with the Islamic conquest, which is portrayed as a cosmic tragedy that breeds Luciferian contempt for the wheelwork of the heavens. Ferdowsi puts these words into a letter putatively penned by Rostam Pur-e-Hormozd, the general fated to lead the Sassanid military into defeat at the battle of Qadesiyya: "My grave is Qadesiya's battlefield. … The heavens will this. … The day comes soon when heaven's sphere will be, / Like Ahriman, our bitterest enemy."[99]

In fact, unlike in the case of Greek epic, which is a distinct genre from tragic drama, many if not most of the core stories of the epic portion of the *Shâhnâmeh* are tragedies: the legend of Siyavash, Rostam and Esfandiyar, or Rostam and Sohrab. This is psychologically and sociologically noteworthy, since the *Shâhnâmeh* also preserves exceedingly ancient lore about the earliest formative stages of the Aryan community of nations, with the division of the one realm of Fereidun into the realms of Iraj (Persia), Salm (Sarmatia), and Tur (Turan) — a subject that was already broached in the first chapter of this study. In this context the stories about the magical powers of the civilization of Jamshid, with his all-seeing goblet and throne that is flown through the sky by *divs*, parallels the Greek legend of Atlantis and Indo-Aryan material in the *Mahabharata* and *Ramayana*. Tragically, Ferdowsi was never properly paid for writing the *Shâhnâmeh* and he died in poverty.[100]

This is because the Samanids were overthrown by Turkic invaders who entered Khorasan and the Caucasus, on the two sides of the Caspian Sea, around the year 1050. The first prominent Turkic conqueror of Iran, Mahmud of Ghazna, was born of a Samanid slave soldier, a Turk named Sebuktegin, and a Persian woman.[101] There were different waves of Turkish invasion and the states established by each of these rivaled one another until the Seljuq Turks consolidated control over the entire Caliphate. For example, it is the Qara-Khanid confederation attack on Khorasan that allowed Mahmud's father Sebuktegin to overthrow the Samanids and establish the Ghaznavid Sultanate that he passed on to Mahmud, and then shortly following Mahmud's death the Ghaznavid state was conquered by the Seljuks who rode in from Central Asia.[102] The Turks originated in Eastern Siberia and were known both to the ancient Persians and their ancient Chinese neighbors as uncivilized raiders who would occasionally loot and pillage the Central Asian borderlands of both highly cultured empires.[103] The Turks brought the Iranian Renaissance of 850–1050 to an end by breathing new life into Islam and the totalitarian structure of the Caliphate that had been subsumed by Iranian dynasties such as the Buyids and Samanids.

7.3 Assassin Apocalypse

It is in the most radical form of the nativist Persian resistance to the Seljuq Caliphate of the Turks that the true nature of Islam reveals itself. From the outset, there was significant resistance to the Turkic takeover of the last remnant of the Arabian Caliphate in Baghdad. The latter had already yielded most of its authority and territory in the northeast to the semi-autonomous Persian fiefdoms of Hyrcania and Khorasan who fielded the Golden Age of Persia. An noted above, the Baghdad Caliphate had been so weakened by Persian resurgence that, from 934 to 1062, the Shi'ite Buyid family had been controlling the core of the Islamic world.[104] The Turks promised to restore orthodox Sunni Muslim rule and they used the fact of Shi'ite political dominance in Iran and in Egypt, under the Fatimids, as a goad to gain supporters among the Sunni majority populace of these territories.[105] The Seljuks took Baghdad from the Buyids in 1055.[106]

The battle to prevent the incoming Seljuq Turks from perverting the esoteric purpose and hidden destiny of Islam was a war which, in its initial stages, was mostly fought in the southwestern territories of *dâr al-Islam*. The Fatimid Ismailis established a rival center of power in Cairo, with strong backing from within Iran, with the aim of rivaling the Baghdad Caliphate, newly vitalized by the Turks, for control of the holy cities of Mecca and Medina in the Arabian peninsula. As the Shi'ite Fatimid

Caliphate competed with the Sunni Seljuq Caliphate for mainstream legitimacy, a shift toward conservatism for the sake of mass appeal catalyzed an internal reaction within the Ismaili Shi'ite form of Islam. These reactionaries—or perhaps it is more appropriate to term them revolutionaries—unveil an Islam that is essentially identical to the Neo-Mazdakite Khorramdin movement of Babak. In its most extreme form, as the Order of Assassins headquartered at Alamut fortress, the Nizari Ismaili sect of Shi'ism discloses the truth about the noble lie of Islam for the last time before Turkic barbarity is compounded by Mongol brutality in a way that perverts the purpose of the Parthian inoculant administered to Iran's sophisticated society.

The schism with Fatimid power in Egypt erupted in the late 1090s, shortly after Alamut was taken.[107] The Fatimid Caliph Imam al-Mustansir had appointed his son Nizar as his successor, and the latter had the backing of Hassan Sabbah who had come to Egypt as a representative of the Ismailis of Iran. Upon al-Mustansir's death in 1094, a military coup staged by an Armenian Vazir, Al-Afdal, installed the Caliph's younger son, Al-Musta'il on the Fatamid throne instead of Nizar. After a failed attempt to stage a comeback from Alexandria, Nizar was captured and executed by Al-Afdal's military regime. The more mainline Fatamid Ismailis of Egypt accepted the military coup because they accused the Nizaris of too much *ekhtiyâr* or free personal choice at the expense of established doctrine.[108] So a personal attachment to Nizar was not the basis of the Persian breakaway from the Fatamid Ismailis.[109] That having been said, there were legends that a son of Nizar was secreted away to Alamut where he was kept to legitimize the Assassin claim to leadership of the Ismaili community.[110]

The idea of "the Egyptian throne" with its Pharaonic legacy remained a part of the Persian Ismaili tradition, thereby infusing the heritage of Iran with that of alchemical Egypt for the second time in Iranian history since Cambyses became the Pharaoh.[111] For some time, the Persian Nizaris continued to struggle for power in the Fatamid capital of Cairo itself—including by means of assassination.[112] The tale of the Assassins could justly be described as the tale of two Hassans. The first of these is

Hassan Sabbah, and the other is Hassan II who, although not as widely known in the West, was the more radical of the two—the Messiah for whom Sabbah was a herald.

The followers of Hassan Sabbah, the most radical Nizari Ismailis, were known as *Sabbâhiyya*.[113] "Assassin" is an epithet that was applied to them largely by Westerners who became familiar with the Order through their key role in the Crusades. In Persian, the language of Nizari Ismailism, *Az Hasan* means "from Hassan"—as in an "assassin" sent from Alamut. Be that as it may, in the early nineteenth century the scholar De Sacy claimed that the word "Assassin" was a corruption of the Arabic *hashishiyya* or *hashishiyyun*, a laced and intoxicating form of hemp or "hashish."[114] Members of the order were allegedly drugged with this substance and were then carried, while sleeping, into a garden within Alamut fortress, which had been made to resemble Paradise, complete with delightful female and male attendants.[115] Having awoken in the garden, the dupe was told that he was getting a foretaste of the reward that he would receive for becoming a martyr for the cause. Then he would be drugged again and wake up back in the house of the Assassin who was recruiting him.[116] Marco Polo brought back this and other Assassin tales to the West.

Another of these is the legend of the three schoolmates (*se yâré dabestâni*). This tale was popularized by Fitzgerald's preface to his edition of Omar Khayyam. Supposedly, Hassan Sabbah had both Omar Khayyam and Nizam ol-Molk as his two schoolmates and closest companions. They had made a promise to each other that whichever of them became successful and powerful would support and raise up the other two. When Nezam ol-Molk became the grand vizier of the Seljuq Sultan, Omar Khayyam was happy to be given a pension for his scientific research. However, Hassan eventually locked horns with Nezam in the struggle for political power, with one becoming the greatest resistance fighter against the Seljuq Caliphate and the other its Prime Minister.[117]

Nizam ol-Molk considered the Assassins to be nothing more than a cloaked continuation of the Mazdakite movement, hell-bent on "a communism of property and of women" and "primarily interested in the expropriation of wealth, and in general license."[118] The Seljuq Prime Minster was not alone in believing, and promulgating, stories that portrayed the Assassin agenda as "the conspiracy of adherents of the old Persian faith … plotting how they could … introduce atheism and other evils."[119] The assassin who murdered Nizam ol-Molk was disguised as a Sufi offering him a petition.[120] The Ismailis claimed that they were avenging the death of an innocent carpenter that the Prime Minister had ordered to be executed. The Sultan himself was assassinated a few weeks later, which convinced the Seljuqs to abandon plans to attempt a siege of Alamut.

Before the legendary years in Alamut, Hassan Sabbah mainly worked in Rayy (Tehran) and Isfahan.[121] He was born in Qom to a Twelver Shi'ite family.[122] He studied in Rayy (Tehran) to enter the clergy. During his early years as a devout student of theology, he "supposed that the sect of the Ismâilis was Philosophy, and the ruler of Egypt [the Fatimid Caliphate] a Philosopher."[123] Sometime after the age of seventeen, in 1077, Hassan went to live in Isfahan and then set off for Egypt from there, in a round about way, which also took him through Azerbaijan.[124] The duration of his stay in Egypt was a year and a half.[125] He then returned to Isfahan and used it as a base of operations for missionary expeditions to Yazd, Kerman, Khuzestan and Irâqé Ajami — all of them power nodes of the Seljuq Caliphate.[126]

The Ismaili emphasis on *ta'lim* or "authoritative teaching" was considered a particularly grave threat to religious law.[127] Hassan Sabbah adopted and developed the doctrine of *ta'lim* as compared to the democratic argumentation by analogy or *ra'y* and *qiyâs*.[128] Hassan claimed that pure reasoning is circular and remains nothing more than justification for a knowledge ultimately grounded on authority, an authority that any honest seeker recognizes that he desperately needs.[129] His scathing skepticism regarding any beliefs that transcend evident matters of common sense was actually rooted in a will toward attaining and embodying a universal divine truth that is occluded by people's petty conventional justifications for customary living.[130] The Assassins had utter contempt for the psychological needs of the common mass of humanity, and yet, ironically, the Assassin Creed could actually be characterized as a form of ultra-humanism, on a metaphysical or cosmological as well as a sociopolitical level, one wherein all creation becomes humanized for the truly mature. Combining the idea of *hudud* as representing cosmic principles with the idea of the microcosmic man representing the world, the doctrine proceeded in an all-consuming symbolical anthropocentrism.[131]

The Cosmos of the Assassins is *ensâné kabir*, whereas the human being is *ensâné saghir*.[132] Marshall Hodgson notes the universalist spirit of this mirroring of the Macrocosm in the Microcosm of Man when he writes of the Assassin Creed, "The whole universe is made rational and familiar; so that no helplessness is felt before the most awesome attempt at orientation; men are to be grown up, and at home beyond all horizons. To be an Ismâ'îlî is to be of the elite of the universe."[133] The Nizaris saw the human form as so perfect that all things must pass through that form before achieving spiritual perfection.[134] They even held a humanistic view of superhuman beings, so "that angels or devils or fairies are simply certain kinds of men."[135] In the *Haft Bâb*, the view is stated that *Parîs* ruled the Earth in the time before Adam.[136] These putatively preternatural *Parîs* (fairies), who are also called *Jinn* (genies), are actually a certain kind of human being—neither as good as angels nor as wicked as *divs* (demons).[137]

Within the human race itself, the Nizari Ismailis drew a tripartite distinction between human types. This is a categorization reminiscent of the one employed by Plato and the Pythagorean Order of which he was a member.[138] Recall, from Chapter 2, that the so-called "Pythagorean" Order actually originated in Achaemenid Babylon. The masses, who are all opponents of the imâm, are referred to as *ahlé tedâd*. They are ignorant brutes without even the will to ascertain truth. Also referred to as *'âmm* or the "common people," they are bound to an externality or *zâhir* of merely apparent form (*shekl*), and cannot live without some kind of *sharia* or ritual law determined by *tanzil* or "outer revelation." The limit of their comprehension is reasoning (*nazar*) based on *mushâbaha* or analogical similarities, i.e. allegory. They are submitters (*moslemin*) to this world (*dunyâ*). The second category of people are *khvâss* or an "elite" who are capable of *ta'wil* or esoteric interpretation of the *ma'nié bâtin* or "inner meaning," and of drawing proper distinctions (*mubâyana*) according to their discernment, albeit under the *ta'lim* or guidance of the imâm. The imâm puts them on a spiritual path (*tariqat*) that leads through and beyond the *sharia*. The third and final human type, whose exemplars transcend the merely human, are the *akhassé khvâss* or "the super elite" who recognize the ultimate nature of reality, namely *haqiqat*, as the *vahdâniyyat* or "unity" of God through "direct inspiration" (*ta'yid*) rather than the *ta'lim* of an imâm outside of themselves. This super elite is already living from out of the Apocalypse (*qiyâmat*) in a state of total unity (*vahdaté kolli*). The *akhassé khvâss* are of the *âkherat*, "the last world," not this world (*dunyâ*).

In the Nizari scripture *Haft Bâbé Sayyid-nâ*, Hassan Sabbah predicts the coming of the *Imâmé Qâ'yem* in whom the entire line of the imamate culminates and who establishes perfect truth and justice through the apocalypse (*Qiyâmat*).[139] Hassan himself was understood to be the "proof" or *hojjat* of the hidden imam.[140] In turn the imam himself is, in and through his own existence, the *hojjat* of God (i.e. *hojjat' allah*).[141] No imam is bound by the decisions of a previous imam regarding any matter.[142] In taking this view, Hassan was effectively insisting on the immediacy and spontaneity of the imam's divine inspiration and manifestation of God's will through his *ta'lim*.[143] This reveals an understanding of the relationship between truth and *power*.[144] The *Haft Bâb* goes so far as to claim that "knowledge is power."[145] Hassan, who was himself a mathematician and an alchemist, understood that there can be no pure pursuit of knowledge, or philosophical learning or scientific research, apart from or outside of power relations.[146] This is why he forbade even the learned from having access to certain types of knowledge, and altogether prohibited the dimwitted rabble from studying Philosophy.[147] Those who seek knowledge can only be allowed to do so within a structure supported and sustained by the *fada'i*—the assassin who is willing to sacrifice himself.[148]

The doctrine of Alamut is that of recognizing "truth" and "justice" as the will to power.[149] The Assassins were enemies of what any traditional and conservative culture considered the "social good" insofar as the "policy of the state"—to the extent that we are dealing with a "state" at all—was "a diabolically consistent ... assassination of the pillars of society and asylum for its renegades."[150] The Assassins were committed to an "all-out attack against the established regime by any means available, including terrorism."[151] The Nizari Ismailis considered all those who were not totally devoted to them to be their enemies, and moreover enemies deserving of no decency.[152] On the other hand, the precisely targeted tactic of assassination can be seen as compassionate by comparison to waging a war in which innocents inevitably become "collateral damage."[153] This is especially the case in view of the fact that most of the targets of assassination were mighty and corrupt men, rather than downtrodden commoners. The Ismailis themselves considered their assassinations to be humane and just acts of heroism.[154] The Ismaili adoption of assassination as an official policy terrified the rest of the Muslim community, which, like national governments today, are loathe to openly admit to using such a tactic.

Around 1090 Hassan decided to turn the Qazvin (Caspian) region into his headquarters, and he orchestrated the siege of what was already a rudimentary fortress in Alamut from the woods of Mazandaran to the north.[155] The English word "Caspian" comes from the name of an Iranian tribe who lived in this region of central Hyrcania, south of the Sea and toward the western Alborz mountains. These Iranian folk were, from very ancient times, called *Caspi*—the plural of which, in Persian, is Caspi*ân*.[156] In their own local dialect, the term *Caspi* refers to the dark "green-blue" hue of the Sea named after them, a color popular with craftsmen of Persian ceramic tiles. This dialect is as exceedingly archaic as the people who speak it. The *Caspi* or "Caspians" may even be the oldest Indo-Europeans to have migrated to the Iranian plateau and are identified by some scholars with the Kassites, whose invasion of what is now Iraq led to the rise of Babylonian high culture under the influence of an Indo-European and Proto-Iranian elite.[157] The term *Qazvin* is an Arabic corruption of the Persian *Caspiân*, so that in Arabic the Caspian Sea—or as it was once named the Sea of Hyrcania—is called *Bahr al-Qazvin*, the Sea of Qazvin. All of this is to say that Alamut, the nerve center of the Assassin movement, was situated in Greater Hyrcania — the old stronghold of the Mithraic Parthian nobility.

Alamut fortress was located in a heavily forested rocky mountain terrain along the shortest route from the then-significant city of Qazvin to the Caspian Sea.[158] The Shi'ite Buyid dynasty had originated in the area south of the Caspian Sea, as had the Zaydi sect of Shia.[159] So by the time the Assassins took over large parts of this area, including towns such as Qa'en and Tabas, their rise to power reiterated the partisan spirit of local independence that was characteristic of northern Iran in the years and decades immediately following the Arab invasion of the Sassanian Empire. Operating under the false name "Dehkhoda," Hassan was perceived to be a very abstinent and pious individual, which qualities of character inspired the devotion of a great many of the local folk.[160] Hassan Sabbah was probably competent in Arabic, having been trained in theology and having spent some time in Egypt, but he wrote almost exclusively in his native Persian language.[161] Persian — the same form of it that still survives today — is the language of the Assassins.

The name "Alamut" is a contraction and corruption of *Aluh Âmut*, which means "the eagle's nest" in Persian.[162] Interestingly, the Persian word "Alamut" written in Arabic, in other words without its short vowels expressed, reads as *al-mawt* or "death."[163] Despite having marshaled the capability to take the mountain stronghold by force, Hassan Sabbah paid for the fortress of Alamut fair and square by writing a check for the sum of three thousand gold dinars.[164] Hassan is reputed to have gone outside of his fortress at Alamut on only two occasions, not counting the two other times that he went out onto the rooftops.[165] While directing operations from within his lair, he also hid his fatal illness throughout his life. He had a wife and daughters, which he sent away to a more secure and distant fortress once Alamut was threatened with scarcity due to an embargo by those besieging it.[166] They became spinsters in that other fortress; he never brought them back home. Alamut was no place for a respectable wife, or for daughters guarding their chastity. Marshall

Hodgson captures something of the atmosphere of Hassan's lair when he writes:

> The thrill of hashish and dagger offered to the sober and proper world a terrified gaze into fantastic possibility. All those things farthest beyond the daring of the ordinary man, yet most appealing in their perversity, could be believed of the astounding Nizaris ... [including] an irresponsible freedom where ties of past and future disappeared ... the exquisite horror of a dread deed and a devoted death.
>
> In the power of Alamut was thought to be all the wild malice and destruction a soul could dream of: at a word the dagger was ready, at a word were kings and lords laid low. No fear of earthly punishment or divine displeasure: only a total immersion in the power of death, as in the delight of sense. Of this atheistic devotion the ordinary citizen must hardly think: yet he was permitted a glimpse in the stories of the secret master of such men. A god to all about him, he owned no god beyond. At his command, the company would assemble at night in forbidden orgies, celebrating the rites and the rights of sex with any to hand in the covering darkness, to the nearest and most forbidden; or at his glance, fifty men would leap from the turrets about him to a death far below.[167]

Hassan Sabbah's followers understood his imamate to mean that he was above the law.[168] In the *Haft Bâb* we read that, "God in His essence has no attributes; but for the sake of revelation he can adopt any attributes he may choose — appearing one time as an infant, another time as an aged man, another time as the embryo in a womb."[169] The ultimate beatific form taken by God in this world is, however, the imâm who is the *hojjat allah*.[170] To truly penetrate the metaphysical or mystical significance of the person of the imâm is to see God.[171] What the Sufi shaykh did for the mystics that were his disciples was a pale reflection of the annihilation of the petty ego experienced by Nizari devotees of the *Imâmé Zamân*. The metaphysical centrality of the idea of imamate in Shi'ite cosmology can be gleaned from the maxim that "if for a moment there should not be an imâm, the world would cease to exist."[172] We can better understand the honorific *Qibleyé Âlam* or "Axis of the Cosmos," which was eventually bestowed upon certain of the Shahs of Iran during the Qajar period, when we consider how the "role of the imâm not only as uniquely visible revelation of the Divine but as objective focal point of existence, allowed him to provide what no shaykh could provide, bound as he was supposed to be within the Sunni framework: a concrete cosmic center for a man's whole religious life."[173]

The Nizari state was not formed deliberately, but was a function of strategic consolidation and organization in the face of the Seljuq attempt to eradicate Ismailis.[174] This is an important point to grasp in terms of the anarchical character of the Assassin Creed. The power network of which Alamut became the central node under Hassan Sabbah was a *de facto* structure developed through sheer tactical necessity, and it was sustained by a kind of religious devotion categorically different from that of subjects governed by a monarch or a normal theocratic orthodoxy. The Assassin system was such that each fortress was supposed to be able to endure on the basis of its own resources, including its scientific and technical resources, seeking aid from others only in the case of exceptionally serious emergencies, such as the outbreak of epidemics.[175] This decentralized system, when combined with loyalty to the Imam, meant that no enemy force—whether the Western Crusaders, the Seljuq Caliphate, or the Mongol hordes—could conquer some centralized nexus and bring the entire Ismaili network under their control (in a fashion comparable to conquering the administrative capital of a vast empire). In this way as well, the Assassins were anarchic partisans. Despite the anarchic and partisan quality of the Ismaili movement, especially the Nizari branch, the emphasis on authority did ultimately mean a drive toward centralization and hierarchy, with Alamut eventually emerging as the pinnacle of Assassin power.[176]

Hassan Sabbah, as *da'i* of Alamut, became the unquestioned leader of the entire Nizari Ismaili community.[177] On his death bed Hassan appointed Bozorgomid of the Lammasar fortress to be his successor, with three of his most experienced lieutenants at Alamut as assistants.[178] After Sabbah's death, Abu Ali had to make visits to the various fortresses to renew oaths of allegiance to Hassan's successor, Bozorgomid, at Alamut.[179] By the reign of Hassan II, the grandson of Bozorgomid, the Ismaili community at large had accepted the fortress of Alamut as its high command. Nevertheless, Isfahan remained an important center of Nizari Ismaili activity—albeit one more vulnerable to Seljuq counter-attack than Alamut and other remote fortresses. Ultimately, the leaders of all other Ismaili communities in both Persia and Syria were being appointed at, and sent out from, Alamut.[180] Hassan Sabbah was seen as the forerunner or herald of Hassan II in his guise as *Imâmé Qâyem*, and the Assassin reign of terror was interpreted as aiming to materialize the conditions of the Apocalypse.[181] Hassan II was about thirty-five years old when he replaced Muhammad as the leader of Alamut, initially claiming only the title of *da'i* before going on to proclaim himself the imam after only two and a half years.[182] At least in the secret epistles that he conveyed to his key lieutenants, Hassan II claimed to be the imam in truth (*dar haqiqat*), even if not after the manner of bloodline succession.[183]

This was an imamate apart from the lineage of Ali ibn Abu Talib.[184] As the Imam of the Apocalypse, Hassan II was also judge of the Resurrection or *Qâyemé Qiyâmat*.[185] From an Ismaili standpoint, this gave him an even higher standing than the Prophet Muhammad—let alone Imam Ali.[186] In the Nizari Ismaili creed, Salmâné Farsi takes the place that Imam Ali ibn Abu Talib has for other radical Shi'ites, those who already see Ali as greater than Muhammad.[187] The text *Haft Bâb* repeatedly praises Salmân in terms that rival the status of Muhammad, and at times through *hadith* attributed to the Prophet:

> On this subject, Hadrat Rasûl (peace be upon him) states in a hadith, 'As-Salmân is one of the gates of Paradise.' If the gate of Paradise is a man, then its court will also be a man. And in another hadîth Hadrat Prophet (bless him) said, Salmân is the life of Paradise. … Sayyid-nâ [i.e. Hassan Sabbah] states, When they punish the black stone they will make it second so that it stands opposite to the lord, and then they will punish it. And they will give a reward to the white stone when they make it the person of Salmân, so that it be the chosen of its lord."[188]

This passage draws on the imagery of the ritual stoning of Satan during the *Hajj*. The text goes on to draw a diametric opposition between Salmâné Farsi and Omar ibn Khattab, the tyrannical Rashidun Caliph who oversaw the invasion and occupation of Iran, with the Persian governor of Mada'in being seen as the legitimate successor of Muhammad: "It is said that Hadrat Salmân reached God, and whoever reaches God will be the Salmân of the age. In general one must be with Salmân or with Sukkad ['Umar]."[189]

Hassan II declared the *Qiyâmat* on the 17th of Ramadan in the year 559 Hijra. The festival of the *Qiyâmat* was deliberately held in the month of Ramadan, so that the abolition of the *sharia* — together with the need for *taqiyya* — could be celebrated by a drunken orgiastic feast that breaks the mandatory fast.[190] Hassan gathered his community together at Alamut, where white, red, yellow, and green banners were unfurled atop the mountain stronghold.[191] (Yellow was the Fatamid color.) As he mounted the pulpit that was also his throne, Hassan II greeted those on his right, center, and left-hand sides, corresponding to followers from Khorasan, Daylaman, and Iraq. Then he began his address with this extraordinary declaration, which makes it clear that he was addressing extraterrestrials in addition to terrestrial humans: "O inhabitants of the worlds, jinn, men, and angels!"[192] Note that he addresses the jinn before addressing humans. The same transhuman audience ought to be conceived of as the addressees in Hassan's mind when he closes his speech with the following:

> The imâm of our time [*emâmé zamâné mâ*, meaning himself] sends you blessings and compassion, calling you his specially selected servants. He has lifted from you the burden of the obligation of the shari'a [ritual law], and has brought you to the Resurrection [*qiyâma*].[193]

The provisional hierarchy of the Order of Assassins, which had been developed for tactical purposes, was also dismantled in Mazdakite fashion, with all of the faithful — rather, all of the Gnostics — banded together on an egalitarian basis under the guidance of the *Imâmé Qâyem*.[194]

Hassan not only claimed to be the imam, but even adopted the language of the Caliphate and proclaimed himself "caliph" of the Apocalypse.[195] At the core of his proclamation was the idea that the apocalypse is *now*, which is as much as to say that linear, chronological time, had come to an end in the sense of being broken open to God. Hassan II was clear about the fact that this apocalyptic disclosure meant that the esoteric relationship that Sufis secretly had with God could now be open to all, a direct relationship with the divine unmediated by doctrines, allegories, and signs:[196]

> Now men could see God directly, with their spiritual eyes, as was appropriate to Paradise; and at the same time those who still refused to accept the truth were condemned in their willful ignorance for ever. This was the great Resurrection toward which all lesser searchings, all partial truths, all former prophecies had been tending. This was the culmination of the ages.[197]

There was a certain tendency toward Pantheism in Assassin thought, which inclined to the view that in *haqiqat* "all things are spirit, and nothing is to be distinguished from the Divine."[198] There is also this passage from the *Haft Bâb*: "[I]f one sees the multitude of creatures with the eye of haqiqa, he will have seen the Unity of the lord. And of all opposites one must know similarly that whoever holds to the haqiqa in place of himself becomes free of the conceptions and fancies of this world..."[199] The Nizaris certainly rejected any metaphysical duality of matter as opposed to spirit, seeing no substantial difference between what the unenlightened perceive to be crude matter and what the illumined recognize as a manifestation of God.

Together with the abolishing of *sharia* came the dispensability of *taqiyya*.[200] Nor is *taqiyya* meant here in the narrow sense of Shi'ite dissimulation in order to avoid persecution at the hands of Sunnis, in other words the abolition of all outward forms of ritual practice and legal doctrine that Shi'ites superficially shared with Sunnis, but even the dissimulation of subscribing to *any* rigid moral laws or social norms.[201] It was understood that "there will be no laws in Paradise."[202] To the pure of heart, who know (*aref*) that nothing but God is true or objectively real, everything is "permitted" (*halâl*).

The Ismaili practice of *taqiyya* was so well known that captured or convicted Ismailis were not afforded the same opportunity of confession and repentance for certain crimes that other Muslims were afforded; rather, they were given the death penalty because it was believed that "the most explicit declaration could be construed in the Ismâ'ili's mind to mean its opposite."[203] Certain scholars of Islamic theology have come to the paradoxical conclusion that the Assassin threat from within Islam was actually the catalyst for a persecutory sharpening of the definition of being a proper Muslim as opposed to a deviant, since the Ismailis outwardly "accepted the forms, and claimed the privileges of membership [in the *Ummat*], while working for the total overthrow of the Sunni interpretation of Islam."[204] The Nizaris did not just consider other Muslims to be misguided, they believed themselves to be the only ones illuminated from among "the other seventy-two sects" of every known religion on Earth.[205]

Within a year and a half of his declaration of the *Qiyâmat*, while visiting the castle of Lambasar (in the Alborz mountains north of Tehran), Hassan II was stabbed to death by his brother-in-law, Hussain-i Nâmâvar, who was descended from the Twelver Shi'ite Buyid dynasty that had ruled Khorasan contemporaneously with the Fatamid rule of Egypt.[206] Hassan's son, Muhammad, had the entire Buyid family executed in reprisal. Although only nineteen when he came to power in 1166, he was able to secure recognition of himself as the Imâm and worked to elaborate on his father's vision of an apocalyptic imamate.[207] In fact, judging by the writings that he left behind, and by the testimony of his father's subordinate, Rashid ad-Din Sinan, who kept Syria under the command of Alamut as "the Old Man of the Mountain," Imam Muhammad was even more extreme than his father — who was in turn more radical than Hassan Sabbah.[208] Muhammad ibn Hassan's main contribution was to develop the vision of *Qiyâmat* into a sustainable way of life, a breakaway culture "not of this world" already living after the Apocalypse.[209]

While in one sense this could be seen as a declaration of independence and assertion of sovereign authority, the Assassin Apocalypse also meant an abandonment of the attempt to infiltrate the wider Islamic world by means of dissimulation with the aim of transforming it from within.[210] Sunnism was no longer a rival in the Shi'ite battle for hearts and minds, but an enemy to be eradicated through total war — no matter the cost — even if that cost was every single other person on Earth besides the Ismaili elect, and even including the nonhuman beings beyond the confines of the Earth, such as jinn and angels. The world had already ended, anyhow.

At this point in history, in the twelfth century AD, the vanguard of Iranian society had already developed the ultimate bunker mentality. What we saw from Adolf Hitler and other die-hard Reich's officials in the last days of the Second World War does not even come close in terms of its apocalyptic zeal. Hassan II directed that all those who refused to relinquish the *sharia* be subjected to the death penalty.[211] In a world where Islam has monopolized law and order, a sociopolitical sphere wherein Christians, Jews, and other tolerated minorities have legal and ritual norms nested within the system of *sharia*, this amounts to universal anarchy enforced by merciless authority. Had the Mongols not invaded Iran and zealously reaffirmed Islam as an instrument of their totalitarian brutality, this head-on confrontation with the Sunni Caliphate may have liberated Iran and the world from Islam as we know it.

During a brief period between 1250 and 1295, the potential existed for the Mongol Empire to act as a conduit for the return of Mahayana Buddhism to Iran through the Silk Route that had been used by Iranian missionaries to bring the teachings of the Iranian Buddha to Eastern Asia in the first place.[212] Chinese scholars came to Iran at Hülegü's invitation, and under his successor, the Buddhist Il-Khanid ruler Gaykhatu, who introduced paper money from China into Iran (wherefrom it entered the West), Buddhists along with Christians began to occupy the most distinguished and influential positions in the Mongol regime.[213] This quickly came to end, though, when in 1295 resentful Muslims installed his nephew, Ghazan Khan, who was a convert to Islam and saw its totalitarian ideology as a more effective basis for ruling a vast empire.[214] All non-Muslims, with the exception of Jews, immediately faced severe reprisals.

The Mongols ultimately saw in Islam an ideology that, if appropriated, would greatly assist them in governing Central Asia and the Middle East. Meanwhile, the Muslim elites that they conquered all seemed to agree that the Nizari Ismailis were the greatest menace from within the Islamic world. Kings and courtiers would reveal to their new Mongol overlords the chainmail armor that they were forced to always wear under their clothes for fear of assassination.[215] While the Mongols saw in Sunni Islam a pacifying force par excellence, they came to recognize the violently anarchical Assassins of Alamut as the epitome of the supreme danger to their totalitarian rule.[216] In this case, the enemy of their enemies was their own worst enemy. Destruction of the Ismailis became the Mongols' primary objective. Hulagu Khan sent his general Kitubuqa ahead of him to wage a lightning war against the Nizaris, before coming in to mop them up himself.[217] Hulagu Khan began his march on Iran in 1252, arriving in Samarqand in 1255 and in Khorasan by 1256.[218]

The Mongols were experts in the destruction of seized territories, but their wrecking crews were totally unprepared for what they encountered at Alamut and other Ismaili fortresses. The structures were impregnably titanic, with both water and food storage tanks hewn out of solid rock, with the water being channeled through the stone and vast stores of food that had been well-preserved from as early as the time of Hassan Sabbah.[219] As Marshall Hodgson recounts:

> Alamut proved the marvel of the Mongols; Hulagu himself climbed up and wondered at it. Presumably this lent all the more charm to its destruction. Except for what the garrison had been permitted to take away, or certain books that Juwayni salvaged, the Mongols managed with zeal and much hard labor to destroy all else that had been created in a hundred and sixty years of vision and resourcefulness.[220]

The Mongols found that the Nizari Ismaili strongholds were equipped with vast libraries and technocratic experts that consulted these.[221] Lamentably, some of these surrendered to the Mongols and entered the service of their court. The Mongols would kill all of the inhabitants of an area, with the sole exception of skilled artisans who were willing to serve them.[222] Although Nizari Ismailism did survive the Mongol conquest, this catastrophe certainly brought an end to the Assassin ambition to challenge the Sunnis for control of the entire Muslim world through an "Islamic revolution."[223]

CHAPTER 8

PERSIAN TONGUE OF THE INVISIBLE

Just when the Assassins were beginning to prevail in their asymmetrical warfare against the Caliphate of the Seljuk Turks, the Mongols invaded Iran with a genocidal force that resulted in the massacre of half of Iran's population — especially in Khorasan, which had up to that point remained the most ethnically Iranian (i.e. Aryan) part of Iran. The Mongols made the destruction of the Nizari Ismaili mountaintop fortresses their first order of business. These were, in many cases, dismantled stone by stone. The Mongols were from the same part of Siberia as the Turks, and shortly after the Mongol colonization, certain of the Turks made common cause with the Mongols and hybridized with them. Such was the genesis of Tamerlane (*Teymour*) and his Timurid successors. Tamerlane massacred so many Iranians that, in cities such as Isfahan, he was able to build tens of minarets out of their severed heads. He also became a zealous champion of Islam, which the Mongols, like the Turks before them, eventually came to see as a perfect ideological platform for totalitarian control of their empire.

What is astonishing is that amidst the horrific brutality of the Mongol conquest, the Mithraic spirituality of Iran not only endured, it further evolved into a full-blown "Religion of Love" (*Diné Eshq*, *Ayiné Mehr*). The present chapter takes the Persian poetry of Rumi and Hafez as exemplary of this mystical faith. Both men lived lives marked by the Mongol colonization of Iran. Rumi wound up in Anatolia because his family was forced to flee from his hometown of Balkh, and then to flee again and again, traveling Westwards across Iran with the Mongols at their rear. During Hafez's lifetime, after the initial Mongol Empire disintegrated, the Turkic warlord Tamerlane sought to reunify it by hybridizing the Turks and

Mongols — peoples who already shared a common origin and a long history of intermarriage in Siberia. Hafez met Tamerlane when the latter's armies finally arrived as far south as Shiraz, and brought all of Iran under their heels with tactics that included terrifying cities into submission by building minarets out of severed heads and throwing Iranian children into bonfires.

As already indicated, the Mongols had made the Order of Assassins their primary target on account of a suspicion, reinforced by all of their other subjugated informants, that the Nizaris were some kind of inscrutably paradoxical authoritarian anarchists who would never willingly submit to the Mongols, any more than they had to the Turks. Rumi has been claimed by the Nizaris as a secret initiate of what survived from the Assassin underground after the Mongol assault on Alamut and other fortresses. Shams of Tabriz was, in all likelihood, the man who initiated this nominally Sunni scholar and theologian, since at that time the Azerbaijan region of Iran was already rife with radical Shi'ism. The term *Mawlana*, which Persian speakers most commonly use to refer to Rumi, does not generically mean "Our Master." It was the specific title of the *Imâmé Zamân* or "Imam of the Present Time," the commander-in-chief and guru in the Nizari Shi'ism of Alamut and other Assassin strongholds. Hassan Sabbah used this title, as did his successor who nullified the *sharia*.

The first section of this chapter identifies five core ideas in Rumi's teachings that appear to reflect the Assassin Creed. The first of these is the idea of the absolute unity of God qua Being — God as a reconciliation of all opposites, whose opposed attributes allow for the manifestation of a hidden divine abundance through the apparent strife in the multiplicity of the realm of becoming. The second of these ideas, which is very closely related to the first, but worth distinguishing, is Rumi's specific insistence on the ultimate non-duality of Spirit and Matter and his affirmation of a *spectral* metaphysics that encompasses the most ethereal and the most earthly dimensions as phenomenological aspects or experiential polarities on the continuum of a singular Existence. The third idea that Rumi shares in common with the Nizari Ismailis is that the human being is not just a microcosm of God, but that Humanity is the *raison d'être* of the entire divine creation. This does not, however, mean that all human individuals are equal. A hierarchical differentiation of human beings into three types based on their relative degree of spiritual evolution is the fourth idea that Rumi shares with the Nizari Ismailis, and, in fact, the classification criteria for these types are identical. Of course, they are also basically identical to those used by the Pythagorean Order, an esoteric society, which, as we saw in Chapter 2, had its origin in Achaemenid Iran. The fifth and final reflection of the Assassin Creed in the poetry of Rumi is the most heretical from an orthodox Muslim standpoint: the idea that the only true faith is the Religion of Love, which lies beyond every religion including Islam, rendering anything like *sharia* null and void. Beyond these five specific ideas, we also see a reverence for the Divine Feminine in Rumi, up to the point of an occasional reference to God as female rather than male, which has a precedent in Nizari Ismailism and the entire current of Mithraic spirituality in Iran.

The Religion of Love so vividly portrayed by Rumi's poetry became paradigmatic for Persian Sufi poets in general. We see it in Sanai, Attar, and Hallaj. It is also more broadly characteristic of Persian literary humanism, the kind of humanism that Sa'adi of Shiraz so eloquently expresses both in his poetry and prose works. One of Sa'adi's humanistic verses is particularly famous, since it is stitched into a Persian carpet on display at the Hall of Nations in the United Nations headquarters. Sa'adi is not the greatest poet of the Religion of Love from Shiraz, that world-renowned Persian city whose name is inseparable from this creed. That distinction belongs to Hafez of Shiraz (1315–1390), an interpretation of whose poems is the focal point of the second section of this chapter.

The section on Hafez, which is in a sense the zenith of this entire study, begins with a reflection on the pen name that Shams al-Din Muhammad Shirazi adopted for himself. He was not just any *hafez* or memorizer of the Quran. Hafez not only memorized every "lection" or variant interpretation of the Quran's text, he also taught them all as a professor of theological exegesis. Anyone who dismisses the place of Islam in Hafez's poetry is a self-deluded idiot or a misguided ignoramus who has failed to really read the *Divân*. The imagery and symbolism in Hafez's poems would be even more inconceivable without Islam than the *Divine Comedy* of Dante would be without Roman Catholicism as its background—albeit a background that also disappears into the deeper and darker caverns of pagan antiquity. Indeed, Hafez draws on the entire tradition of Abrahamic revelation, with figures such as Noah, Abraham, Moses, Joseph, and especially Jesus Christ—depicted as a Messiah no less—making repeated appearances in his poems.

The reason that some of the more secular and modernist interpreters of Hafez have felt a need to dismiss all of this as "lip-service" to the religious establishment is that few have been able to make sense out of how Hafez could sincerely be both drowned in the Quran and also the most exemplary free-spirited libertine in the entire history of Persian poetry—perhaps even in human literary history as a whole. Hafez would never have written anything in his poems just to pay lip-service to social customs. The heroic figure around which his corpus revolves is the *rendé qalandar*, a roguish vagabond who is a model of inspired libertinage. In medieval Shiraz, the *rendân* were a cross between fiercely independent chivalrous desperados and Mafioso gangster types who protected taverns, brothels, drug dens, and casinos—all establishments deemed *harâm* or "forbidden" by the Muslim clerics and rulers under their sway. One can imagine the *rendân* constituting a kind of rebel alliance against the ruling religious and political authorities. One is reminded of the Mithraic pirates of the Parthian period infiltrating the Roman Empire and their Assassin successors undermining the social order of the Seljuk Caliphs. Actually, the point is that this is more than a mere resemblance.

Hafez takes the extant psycho-social type of the *rend* and turns him into a metaphor for the *ensâné kâmel* or "perfect human being" of Islamic mysticism. The *rend* of Hafez is also the *qalandar* who appears to deliberately destroy his own good name and courts infamy so as to become God's fool. It is actually God who, out of jealousy, singles out the *rendân* as His (or Her) true friends. Subjecting the *rendé qalandar* to ostracism in order to isolate him from the world of the rabble affords God the opportunity to receive all of the love of this greatest of all lovers. This love is conferred through a practice of reverently contemplating the divine beauty in an incarnate form, such as that of a weirdly beautiful and strangely compelling woman, recognized—and worshiped—as a *Bot* or "idol" of God. This contemplation is referred to as *shâhed-bâzi* or "the play [game] of witnessing" and it ends with the *rendé qalandar* becoming a *shahid* or "martyr" for the divine Beloved. In Persian poetry in general, chivalric martyrdom is symbolized by a red tulip. A parallel is drawn between this element in Hafez's *Divân* and the troubadour tradition of Grail Mysticism that was brought to Europe by the Sarmatians (Amazons, Alans), a subject which has been broached in Chapter 1. Even more so than for the Christianized Grail mystics of Europe, in Hafez there is absolutely no distinction whatsoever between erotic and divine love, what in the West has been defined as an *eros* that falls short of *agape*. In Hafez, they are one. Even God is prone to seduction. In imagery that is more than reminiscent of *Âz* seducing *Zorvân*, Hafez writes of how a feminine force of Chaos erotically moved God to create.

The image of the Holy Grail or *Jâmé Jam* in Hafez's poetry is drawn from the legend of Shah Jamshid, an Iranian iteration of the primordial Indo-European figure that the Greeks portrayed as the antediluvian King Atlas of Atlantis. The Grail of Jamshid, *Jâme Jamshid* (usually shortened to *Jâmé Jam*), is a goblet or chalice inside of which one may behold images of what is transpiring at any place in space or time—like a crystal ball. Jamshid is famous for having forced *divs*—the *daevas* worshiped as "gods" by the Hindus—to carry his throne into the heavens. The term *Takhté Jamshid* or "Throne of Jamshid" is the native Persian name for the place the Greeks called "Persepolis."

This is not an incidental association, since that ceremonial capital of Achaemenid Iran was primarily used to celebrate Nowruz (whereas the administrative capital was Babylon). According to ancient Iranian mythology, it is Jamshid's attempt to storm heaven by subjugating the gods under his own throne that inaugurates Nowruz—and this, rather than just the arrival of the Spring Equinox, is the titanic event that Iranian New Year is meant to commemorate. On such a reading the seven items on the *Haft Sin* altar are emblematic of both the qualities of character needed to attain a state of being higher than that of the gods — namely the qualities symbolized by the *Ameshâ Spentâs* — but also perhaps the seven heavenly spheres of the visible planets that would have to be traversed on the way to the apex of creation where Mithra's wheel gives one leverage to tilt the *axis mundi* and move the stars rather than being fatefully moved by them.

Whether it is in the imagery of Pre-Islamic Iranian mythology or the Abrahamic narrative of the Bible and the Quran, Hafez makes the divine potential of the human being a main theme of his poetry. He depicts the angels as having genetically engineered human beings, even though the latter were intended by God to supersede the angels. Satan or Iblis is chastised for the self-righteous pride that blinds him from recognizing what makes humans superior to the angels — the capacity for true love. Angels lack this. So did the puritanical inquisitors who forwarded Ardeshir Babakan's loveless Zoroastrian Orthodoxy.

When Hafez uses the term *Mazhabé Piré Moghân* as a synonym for *Mazhabé Eshq* he is referring, not to Zoroastrian *mobeds*, but to the Mithraic Magi who were Ardeshir's primary target and who really reemerged only with the fall of the Sassanids. In Chapter 5 it was noted that *Eshq* or *Arshk*, the root of the term *Ashkâniân* (the Parthians' name for their dynasty) and usually translated as "love," is one of the terms for Mithra. Another Persian synonym for *Mazhabé Eshq*, namely the Religion of Love, is *Ayiné Mehr* or "the Religion of Mithra." When the "Tongue of the Invisible" (*Lessân al-Qeyb*, Hafez's epithet) intimates that he knows an unspeakable secret (*serr, râz*) about the Quran, one directly revealed to him by God, it is the secret that was revealed in Chapter 7: that Islam was created by Mithraists with a view to catalyzing an evolution of human consciousness beyond even the psychological constraints that still apply to the angels.

The most shocking thing about this occulted teaching of Hafez, which is also the secret guarded by Rumi and every other partisan of the Religion of Love, is that until the nineteenth century, the *Divân* of Hafez and the *Masnavi* of Rumi had a status on par with that of the Quran itself in a geographical expanse from Ottoman Southeastern Europe to Mughal northern India. From childhood onward, Muslim children would memorize not only the Quran, but also Hafez and Rumi. It is only with the assault of European colonial powers in the 1800s, particularly the British, that what could be described as a Persianate World was transformed into a doctrinaire Islamic World. That is not to say that intolerant fundamentalism was not rife in Muslim lands from the time that the Turks and Mongols shattered the culture of the Iranian Renaissance of 850–1050, for it certainly was. However, the ultra-romantic Persian soul, particularly the mystical spirit of Persian poetry, was so strong that it continued to resist this exoteric Islamic orthodoxy — not just in Iran, but also in the Ottoman Caliphate and the Mughal Empire.

Devlate Hatun, a woman belonging to the Mevlevi Order founded by Rumi's son and successor, Baha al-Din Walad, married Sultan Bayezid I (1389–1403), who consequently gave state backing to Sufism of the Persian type. In addition to fostering a Persian literary culture at their court, the Ottomans also used Persian rather than their native Turkish as the administrative language of their Caliphate. Meanwhile, in Northern India, the Mughals had also adopted Persian as both their official governmental language and the tongue of all high culture — including and especially literature. Akbar the Great had all of the classics of Hindu literature, including all of the Hindu and Buddhist sacred texts, translated from Sanskrit into Persian. There were far more commentaries on Hafez in Mughal India than in Iran itself. The first editions of Hafez to reach Europe by sea were printed on the printing presses of the Dutch East India company. The India of the Taj Mahal, the masterwork of an Iranian architect, was a thoroughly Persianate India — including the territory of what is Pakistan today. The British destroyed this culture, and their presence in both India and Eastern Iran (i.e. Afghanistan) laid the groundwork for the rise of Islamic fundamentalism by cutting these regions off from the heartland of Iran. This chapter concludes with a third section that looks at the Persianate world encompassing the two great rivals of Safavid Iran, namely the Ottoman Turks and the Mughals of India. It was a world whose ethos was based on a Religion of Love that transcended all sectarian divides.

8.1 The Persian Religion of Love

Jalal al-Din Rumi was born in Balkh (present-day western Afghanistan) in 1207 AD (604 AH) to Baha Walad, a renowned preacher, jurisprudent and Sufi whose work influenced Rumi's style. Rumi was trained in all the exoteric disciplines from an early age. During Rumi's adolescence, the Mongol hordes rushed into Khorasan, forcing his family to flee from Balkh in 1219 and head westwards across Iran, moving each time the Mongols advanced further. Entire cities were razed. Ultimately the Mongols would be responsible for a genocide of half—yes, half—of the Persian population. The half that survived was subjected to plunder, rape, and forced miscegenation. Rumi ultimately wound up in Anatolia, which is where Mowlana Jalaluddin Balkhi picked up his nickname. *Rum* (pronounced *Roum*) is the Persian name for "Rome," including the Eastern Roman Empire or Byzantium—so *Rumi* means "the Roman." Konya, where Rumi settled, was hardly Turkish when he arrived there. Eastern-most Anatolia, the home of the Kurds, has always been ethnically and linguistically Iranian. This region, and the more central part of Anatolia in which Rumi's family settled, had only been conquered by the Seljuq Turks (which the Ottomans broke off of later on) for a little over a century.

Those Nizari Ismailis who survived the destruction of Assassin fortresses, such as Alamut, claimed, and still do claim today, that Rumi—or Mawlana, as they call him—was secretly a member of their order and a preserver of their revolutionary movement. In fact the title *Mawlânâ*, which is the name that Jalaluddin Rumi or Jalaluddin Balkhi comes to be most widely known by in Iran, is not a generic honorific. During the period of Alamut it was used, in particular, by the Nizari Ismailis as a synonym for their *Imâmé Zamân*. The phrase appears most frequently in those passages of Assassin scriptures that refer to the annulment of the *sharia* in favor of divine grace.[1] The title *Mawlânâ*, first used in retrospect as an honorific for Hassan Sabbah, was intended to indicate the singular person who incarnates the divine will in such a way as to lead men beyond all idolatry.[2]

If *Mawlânâ* was secretly recruited into the remnants of the Assassin Creed, this may have occurred during his time in Azerbaijan, the old stronghold of the Khorramdinân or Neo-Mazdakites. Rumi met Shams of Tabriz in 1244 and was intoxicated by divine love. Shams inspired the poetry which now poured out of him. Shams left Konya after two years of companionship with Rumi, perhaps on account of his disciples' jealousy. Rumi persuaded him to return, but shortly thereafter he disappeared for good in 1247, and was probably murdered by Rumi's jealous students. Rumi dedicated much of his poetry to Shams, who symbolizes the divine Beloved. After the disappearance of Shams, Rumi abandoned his career of preaching to the public, and focused only on his Sufi disciples. Until he died in 1273, he incessantly sang volumes of inspired poetry, which others often wrote down and read to him. An assessment of Rumi's teachings lends credence to the Ismaili claim that, despite his scholastic Sunni veneer, Rumi was secretly a Nizari. A handful of the principal cosmological, psychological, and ethical precepts expressed in Rumi's poetry have their precedents in the Assassin Creed.

Let us begin with his cosmology or ontological theology. One of the most scandalous Nizari positions is the emphasis on how the *vahdâniat* or unity of God overcomes and reconciles all of the opposite qualities or characteristics that can be discerned in this world. Rumi teaches that there is an essence of God-in-itself in which there is no duality whatsoever, but there are also the attributes of God that manifest themselves in his acts.[3] These attributes, such as the "merciful," the "living," or the "All-Powerful," which comprise the ninety-nine names of God, can be further divided into two categories. There are attributes of God that have no opposites in the nature of God (i.e. those which are purely positive), and there are attributes that have opposites. The latter category can also be further subdivided into God's attributes of gentleness and those of severity.

According to Rumi the former take precedence in God's nature and the negative attributes only exist in order to make the positive ones manifest by contrast. The reason for the world of appearances is that God wanted to make his hidden inner abundance manifest, in a sense to testify to his glory through the creation's submission to him. This manifestation can only come about through the contrast and even apparent strife of opposites: joy and suffering, light and darkness, peace and violence, etc… because in the absence of opposition finitude collapses into an infinite oneness, and thus into nothingness.[4] Together in interaction with each other, these apparent opposites structure the world of *forms*, which articulates and gives shelter to God's *meaning*.

As we have seen, the Nizari Ismailis went so far as to deny the distinction between spirit and matter, seeing the material world as a materialization of spiritual ideas. This affirmation of the spectral in a way that overcomes metaphysical dualism is also reflected in Rumi's poetry. At times he envisages the transmutation or transubstantiation of matter into spirit, rather than imagining that spiritual perfection consists of liberation from material substance: "So the saints have not said this lightly: the bodies of the purified ones become untainted, exactly like the spirit. Their words, their psyche, their outward form — all become absolute spirit without trace."[5]

A third Nizari idea that is central to the poetry of Rumi is an understanding of Man as not just the microcosm, but even the *raison d'être* of the divine creation. According to Rumi, a human being can be the mirror of all creation or the "mirror of God" only because the entire universe was brought into being to "set the stage" for human consciousness. The original purpose of Creation is Man, though temporally man may seem to be the last being to come into existence. However, he is not simply one being amidst others; all beings have their existence through man — and it is this transcendence of the human spirit which is God. Man is the complete manifestation of God, who would otherwise remain a "*hidden* treasure."[6] Man's descent brings all the stages into manifestation as objectifications whereby he forgets his own nature. Once man's spirit reaches the mineral state there is a reascent back to the origin.[7] It can be seen as a progressive realization of each stage as within oneself. This *miraj* takes a conscious form when one enters the spiritual path as a human being. The ultimate meaning of this descent and reascent is as the means of self-realization of the "Hidden Treasure" that is God.

Just because Man or humanity-in-general is a microcosm of God, does not mean that all human beings are on the same spiritual level. A fourth conception in Rumi's thought, which we met with above when surveying the worldview of Alamut, is the tripartite distinction between three human types. Rumi also hierarchically classifies human beings into three distinct types: those dominated by intellect, the prophets or saints, ordinary believers who struggle towards intellect but occasionally fall pray to sensuality, and finally the bestial human beings who are slaves of their senses.[8]

Fifth, and finally, there is the idea of the annulment of *sharia* through an unmediated relationship with God characterized by divine love. "Love" is at the very heart of Rumi's spiritual vision and doctrine.[9] God created the world out of a lover's longing for His Hidden Treasure to be known; He in turn becomes the Beloved of the Creation, whose purpose is to come to know Him. All beings are in love with each other and with God—this is the force which makes the planets revolve around the Sun and growing trees and budding flowers branch up and outwards towards its light. Though in this vein all love is ultimately love for God, the Sufi realizes true love (*ishqé haqiqi*) once the illusory objects of his love all fail to fulfill his desires and needs and he sees that in the end only God can provide true sustenance and fulfillment to a lover. While Rumi stresses the importance of the Universal Intellect in transcending the partial intellect throughout the Sufi path, the disciple who is to attain union with God must ultimately pass beyond the Universal Intellect as well. Only Love will bring one into God's presence; even Gabriel cannot complete the *Miraj*. Love is not simply another one of God's attributes, like Knowledge and Mercy and all His other attributes. At least at times, Rumi's poetry does express the insight that Universal or True Love is the same as God, and that He is "a coincidence of opposites" of all the other attributes *because He is Love*, or the reconciliation of all opposites.

Rumi speaks of his Sufism as a "Religion of Love," not a "Religion of Knowledge" or "Religion of Mercy," and so forth. This notion of the Religion of Love is also problematic from the Islamic standpoint, for Rumi clearly states that: "Love's creed is separate from all religions: the creed and denomination of Lovers is God."[10] In the *Divân* he writes: "Love's valley is beyond all religions and cults. … [H]ere there is no room for religions or cults." These passages do suggest that "the Religion of Love" *is not Islam*, just as it is not Christianity, Judaism or Buddhism. In a similar tone Rumi often suggests that a follower of the Religion of Love does not need to observe the *sharia* of Islam or of any other organized religion for that matter. When he is poetizing in this most inspired of all modes, Rumi even expresses the idea that God is female rather than male. Note the following verses from his *Divân* and *Masnavi* regarding the Divine Feminine:[11]

> Water prevails over fire because fire dreads it; but when fire is veiled, it brings the water to a boil. When a pot comes between them, oh king, the fire naughts the water and changes it to air. If, like water, you outwardly dominate over woman, inwardly you are dominated by her and seek her.
>
> … The Prophet said that women totally dominate men of intellect and Possessors of Hearts, but ignorant men dominate women, for they are shackled by the ferocity of animals.
>
> They have no kindness, gentleness, or love, since animality dominates their nature.
>
> Love and kindness are human attributes, anger and sensuality belong to the animals.
>
> She is the radiance of God, she is not your beloved. She is the Creator — you could say that she is not created.
>
> O' you men who claim to be mystics and call your Beloved 'He' — 'What kind of manliness is this, letting Iblis hump you like a pederast?'

Both before and after Rumi, *Diné Eshq* or *Mazhabé Eshq* was regarded by Persian mystical poets as the only true religion.[12] As early as 940 Rudaki of Samarqand wrote:

> What use is it to serve one's turn to face
> The Mihrab in your prayers, when all your heart
> Is set upon the idols of Taraz and of Bukhara?
> What God accepts from you are love's transports,
> But prayers said by rote He won't admit.[13]

Sanâ'i of Ghazna (d. 1131) writes: "Why do you ask about my creed and faith tradition? It's clear. My creed is *Eros. Amor* is my canon."[14] Ayn al-Quzât Hamadani, a follower of Mansur Hallaj who, like his master, was executed for heresy in 1132, equated the Religion of Love with "the Religion of God" while drawing a sharp distinction between this faith and the doctrines of other warring sects: "The lovers follow the religion and the community of God. They do not follow the religion and creed of Shâfi'i or Abu Hanifa or anyone else. They follow the Religion of Love and the Religion of God [*mazhabé eshq va mazhabé khodâ*]."[15]

At times this religion of love becomes synonymous with a Persian literary humanism of the kind exemplified by Sa'adi of Shiraz (1209–1291), who was a contemporary of Rumi. Best known for his *Bustân* (1257) and *Golestân* (1258), the first in poetry and the second in prose, Sa'adi had a tumultuous life in the course of which he traveled as far West as Damascus, where the Frankish Crusaders arrested him, as far East as India and Central Asia, and as far south as Yemen, before returning to his native Shiraz.[16] Such extensive travels and encounters with people as different from one another as Franks crusading in Syria, the Muslims of Yemen, and the Hindus of India must have lent themselves to Sa'adi's humanist perspective, which is most famously epitomized by these verses prominently displayed in the Hall of Nations at the United Nations building in New York City:

> Human beings are members of a whole,
> In creation of one essence and soul.

> If one member is afflicted with pain,
> Other members uneasy will remain.
> If you have no sympathy for human pain,
> The name of human you cannot retain.

What is often lost on liberals who quote these verses is the criterion posited by the last two lines: *To kaz mehnat-e digarân bi-ghami, Nashâyad keh nâmat Âdami.* "You who are indifferent to the miserable misfortune of others, / Are unworthy of being named among Humanity." In other words, not just any member of *Homo sapiens* qualifies as a "human" being. One must *earn* the right to be considered human. One *becomes* human through cultivating one's heart and mind. This is the same sense that *humanitas* had in the Italian Renaissance, a sense retained in the phrase "humanities" when it is used to refer to the study of history, literature, the arts, and all other humanizing disciplines. As we saw in Chapter 2, this is an ancient Persian idea that migrated to Greece and the West at large.

It is not the only aspect of his worldview that Sa'adi inherits from the Achaemenids in the foundational epoch of Cyrus and Darius. His humanism is complemented by an embrace of the Mithraic, and very un-Zoroastrian, concept of the noble lie. We see this especially vividly in a vignette from *Golestân*.[17] A foreign slave hurls a tirade full of vulgar insults at a king who has just condemned him to death. Two courtiers are present who both know the condemned man's foreign tongue. Upon the king's request for a translation, one vizier steps forward and claims that the condemned man was quoting verse 3:134 in the Quran: "Your Majesty, he says: 'Those who spend in prosperity and in adversity, who repress anger, and who pardon men; verily, Allah loves the good-doers.'" This lie enjoins the king to consult his conscience and retract his order for the slave's execution. Inspired by the deceptive "translation" of the vizier, he magnanimously pardons the man. However, the other vizier who spoke the slave's language, and was engaged in a rivalry for influence with the first courtier, turned and said to the king: "People of our rank and position should never lie to His Majesty. This man was not praising you or asking for forgiveness; he was cursing His Majesty and abused His Most Royal name." This saddened the monarch who, by means of the first courtier's noble lie, had already realized the harsh injustice of his initial death sentence. Thus the king chastises the second vizier in these lines that deliver the moral of Sa'adi's story: "That lie was far more appeasing to me than this truth, for that lie was meant to solicit a good deed, while the source of your truth was to do evil, and wise men have said, 'a judicious lie is better than a seditious truth.'"

8.2 Hafez as the Zenith of Iranian Civilization

Sa'adi is not the greatest of the poets of the Religion of Love to grace Shiraz, that Persian heart of Iran where Zaradusht of Fasa initiated the Mithraic movement that would eventually spawn Mazdak and become synonymous with his revolution. That distinction belongs to the Persian poet known by the pen name "Hafez," who was born in Shiraz in 1315 and died there in 1390. The epithet *Khwâjeh* or "Esquire" that is attached to his name, Khwajeh Shams al-Din Muhammad Shirazi, identifies Hafez as a member of the gentility or nobility.[18] Hafez's major work is known as the *Divân*, and it took him no less than fifty years to compose the five hundred poems contained in that volume.[19] The perfection of the product of such painstaking labor is not lost on him when he boasts:

> Each verse that Hâfiz pens is a masterpiece
> of gnostic lore and sapience.
> Let's praise his fetching turn of phrase
> and his stunning power of speech.[20]

The definitive Persian edition of Hafez's *Divân* consists of the 486 *ghazals* assessed to be authentic by Parviz Nâtel Khânlari in the mid-twentieth century, which is the basis for the most widely accepted contemporary French and English translations of Hafez's oeuvre.[21] In "Hafiz dar farhang-i mâ u farhang-i mâ dar Hâfez," a study heavily indebted to the depth psychology of Carl Gustav Jung, Khurramshahi describes Hafez as "the veritable spokesman of the Collective Unconscious of the entire Persian race," which is an assessment echoed by Zaryâb Khoi in *Â'yine-ye Jâm* where he claims that "Hâfiz is a compendium of our [Persian] culture and the symbol and archetype of the Persian spirit."[22] Hafez even earned the epithet *Lesân al-Qayb* or "Tongue of the Invisible."[23]

As in the case of "Will I Am Shake Spear" — also undoubtedly a pen name — many legends are woven around the man, but we know almost as little for certain about Hafez's personal life as we do about Shakespeare's authentic biography. For example, the lore that he was married to an adored wife who predeceased him is a yarn spun almost entirely out of a single ambiguous verse in his *Divân*:

> That friend whose presence made my house
> Seem a faery kingdom — of all faults she was free,
> Herself of faery substance head to toe.[24]

Although on account of the structural features of the Persian language the gender of the beloved is ambiguous in such poems in general, in the poetry of Hafez it is possible to infer from other descriptive characteristics that the beloved revered by the poet is almost always female.[25] Be that as it may, if a eulogy for his wife is the correct interpretation of this verse, then we have to ask ourselves what to make of passages in the *Divân* wherein Hafez boasts: "I'm well known throughout the whole city / For being a wild-haired lover…"[26] It is doubtful that this was written in old age. Perhaps he had an open marriage. Or maybe his live-in faery woman was just a very tolerant wife, as the wives of geniuses often have to be — since geniuses, whether in the arts or sciences, tend to be scoundrels:

> Don't expect obedience, promise-keeping, or rectitude
> From me; I'm drunk. I've been famous for carrying
> A wine pitcher around since the First Covenant with Adam.[27]

What we do know is that Hafez was a native-born denizen of Shiraz, a city that he portrays in his poems. Hafez refers to Shiraz eleven times in his *Divân*, offering us descriptions that are not meant to be literal but are intended to evoke "the topography of the *mundus imaginalis* of this cosmopolis of *Eros*."[28] The atmosphere of Shiraz and of Pars during the time of Hafez was comparable to that of Florence and Tuscany during the Italian Renaissance, when it was home to Cosimo and Lorenzo de Medici, Marsilio Ficino, Botticelli, Michelangelo and Pico della Mirandela.[29] Like Renaissance Florence, in this epoch Shiraz was "both hotly decadent and a hotbed of religious fervor."[30]

We are not engaging in an orientalist flight of fancy if we imagine the city as home to gardens filled with the songs of nightingales, opulent private palaces, romantic public promenades, bordellos (*bayt al-lutf*) and taverns (*kharâbat*).[31] The last of these locales is the inspiration for world-renowned "Shiraz" wine, which, in the form of "Syrah" (a French mispronunciation of the Persian city's name), was first brought from Iran to the West by Marco Polo. Hafez offers us a fascinating insight into how great cities are exteriorizations of a people's collective unconscious, a materialization of that spectral stairway to heaven soaring up from out of their heart's hidden striving with and against the element of earth:

> Our cities are incomplete copies from what lies in our heart;
> And all man's Babylons strive but to impart
> The grandeurs of his Babylonian heart.[32]

One particular episode in the long life of the city of Shiraz affords us an insight into Hafez's social and political orientation. The most anticlerical phase of Hafez's poetry is catalyzed by the reign of Mubariz al-Din (1353–1358), whose name literally means "Holy Warrior for the Faith."[33] Mubariz put his weight behind fundamentalist Sharia-enforcing clergy and only tolerated the most puritanical ascetics among the mystics.[34] This Islamist dictator earned the sobriquet "the Policeman" (*muhtasib*) by censoring poets, rounding up musicians, boarding up wine taverns, bordellos and other dens of "vice," all while enjoining the population of Shiraz to practice "virtue."[35] Hafez has nothing good to say about him. In fact, when Mubariz is blinded and deposed by his son, Hafez rejoices:

> The cop is gone! How great the news! Oh heart, oh God,
> The world's full of wine and ale-drinking demigods.[36]

Shah Shuja, who replaced his intolerant father, was actually an admirer of Hafez's poetry to the extent that some have speculated that he gave Hafez a post in his government.[37] He certainly used his power to help spread Hafez's verses across the Persianate world. Even if Hafez did accept a governmental position, he retained his profound contempt for political power as compared to the power of love:

> For kingship's pomp and glory are not worth
> A mite in Love's precinct. — Confess yourself
> A slave and acknowledge your servitude.[38]

Hafez did not just have contempt for political power, the intoxicated lover in him felt fearless if not invulnerable in the face of its coercive machinations: "the lover does not fear any judge, nor tremble before state police."[39] Hafez is acutely conscious of the political subversion involved in his inspired libertinage:

> What bliss! — That instant of disassociation,
> When blessed by license of intoxication,
> I exorcise my ties from both vizier and prince.[40]

This is that "intellectual liberty, which is a certificate of profound thought" and is granted "by the grace of the bounty-of-*Amor*" that Emerson saw at the heart of Hafez's poetry.[41] The only regime that Hafez really has faith in is *dawlat-e eshq* or "the government of love."[42] This cannot but raise the question of what he must have thought about the political content of the Quran that he so eruditely mastered in its multiplicity of exegeses.

The *nom de plume* of Shams al-Din Muhammad Shirazi, namely "Hafez," of course denotes a person — any person — who has memorized the Quran. But Hafez was not just any Hafez. As he tells us himself, he had committed all fourteen lections of the Quran to memory:

> *Eros* come to your rescue, even if you,
> Like Hâfiz, can chant the Qur'ân by heart
> In all its fourteen different lections.[43]

The Caliph Uthman had standardized the consonantal text of the Mohammedan revelation as early as 650. However, since the original manuscripts of the Quran written in primitive Kufic script lacked vowel signs, the choice of where to place these signs and which of them to use produced a variety of divergent readings of the Arabic scripture.[44] Hafez had memorized all fourteen of these "lections."[45] Hafez even goes so far as to confess:

> All I've done has come from the grace
> And *embarras de richesse* of the Qur'an.[46]

There is also this positively cosmic estimation of the significance of Islam's revelation:

> No reciter of a scripture who stands in the *mihrâb*
> Of the Firmament has ever enjoyed such delight
> As I have received from the wealth of the Qur'ân.[47]

The centrality of the Quran to Hafez's poetic endeavor is clear from numerous verses:

> I swear, Hafiz, by that Qur'ân you have by heart,
> I've found no poetry that's as sweet as yours.[48]

> Oh Hafiz in the darkness of poverty and in
> The solitude of the night, as long as you can sing
> And study the Qur'ân, do not sink into sadness.[49]

The hidden biographical context for this last verse is that Hafez enrolled in classes taught by Qiwam al-Din Abdullah, which covered theology in the predawn hours after midnight and then dealt directly with the Quran as dawn broke.[50] Within his own lifetime Hafez was known to have been adept at Quranic commentary or theological interpretation (*tafsir*) of the revelation, not just for setting the standard in its recitation.[51] A study by Dâryush Âshuri contends that the *Divân* is replete with influences from the massive Quran commentary of Meybodi, which it appears that Hafez studied inside and out.[52] He may even have taught it, since we know that as a member of the *ahl-i 'ilm* or "men of learning" he received a government stipend for working as a professor.[53]

It is not just the Quran. The Abrahamic revelation is inextricably entangled in Hafez's poetry. Abrahamic prophets such as Moses and Abraham make regular appearances in the poetry of Hafez and Sa'adi. Hafez pens these verses on Moses' encounter with the *Elohim* in the illuminated thicket:

> Here's pitch black night, there lies the Valley of Peace
> Before my feet, so where's Moses' light,
> Mt. Sinai's Burning Bush and the promised light?[54]

Noah also appears in the poetry of Hafez:

> Don't desert your mates and quit the ark
> Of Noah, Hâfiz, else this typhoon of
> Vicissitudes shall blow your ship to bits.[55]

But the Abrahamic prophet most prominent in Persian mystical poetry, including in Hafez, is the figure of Jesus. Christ inevitably appears not just as a prophet but as a Messiah (*masih*):

> Love's physician is compassionate and endowed
> With the breath of Jesus [*damé masih*],
> But whom should he assuage
> If you are without pain?
> To whom may I relate such a subtlety?
> She killed me — my stony-hearted mistress,
> Yet possessed the life-giving breath of Jesus.[56]

What makes Hafez's apparent embrace of the Quran, and his acknowledged debt to the Islamic revelation, so peculiar is that Hafez is an irredeemable libertine and a shameless advocate of the most antinomian libertinage. Literati well qualified to judge such matters have even regarded Hafez as "the supreme decadent and hedonist poet, leader of the world's grand debauchees."[57] Hafez positively portrays not just the *ibâhati* or "pursuer of libertine ways" but also even "the *mubâhi*, a wild libertine who is utterly outside the pale of all Islamic faith and piety."[58] *Ibâhat* was the term for libertinism among the early radical Shi'ites, and a variety of antinomian types were thought to exemplify this *Ibâhat*, including the *rend* (inspired libertine), the *qalandar* (vagabond, wildman), *qallâsh* (knave), *mubâhi* (libertine), *divâne* (lunatic) and *lâ-ubâli* (daredevil or desperado).[59] The last of these terms suggests an "I couldn't care less" attitude toward conduct that society considers immoral.

The Persian term *rendi* is the source of the English word "randy." The more racy elements of Hafez's portrayal of praiseworthy inspired libertinism or *rendi* were influenced by the poems of the pornographer and satirist, Ubayd-i Zâkâni (d. 1371).[60] Dariush Shayegan explains the concept of *rendi* or inspired libertinage, and the character of the *rend* or roguish vagabond mystic, in the following terms:

> In this concept we find a sense of immoderacy, a behavior out of the ordinary, shocking, scandalous, able to disorient the most composed spirits, a non-conformity which derives not so much from ostentation as from the explosive exuberance of a vision so rich, so full, that it cannot manifest itself without doing violence to everyday banality and without breaking the limits defined by the normality of things. This term expresses, further, a predilection for the uncertain, for language that is veiled and masked, for hints and insinuations, which in the authentic *rend* are expressed in inspired paradoxes [*shathiyât*]... Finally, there is in this concept a boundless love of the divine such as we see in the great thinkers and mystics of Iranian spirituality; but detached from its mystical content, it is transformed into fanaticism and, steered by *homines magni*, to the psychology of the mob.[61]

In other words, the *rend* is not just a psycho-spiritual type, but also a socio-political phenomenon.[62]

Before being adapted as a mystical symbol, the *tâyife-i rendân* or "gangs of hoodlums" in medieval Iran were Mafioso thugs who vied for control of metropolitan quarters in cities such as Shiraz, comparable in many ways to the Sicilian Mafia in New York and Chicago.[63] Hafez's native Shiraz, in particular, was known as *shahré rendân* or "the city of rogues."[64] The princes and politicians lived in fear of these Mafiosi's hired assassins, while the clergy (*mullahs*) and pious ascetics (*zâhed*) were checked in their attempts to act as morality police on account of the protection and patronage that the *rendân* offered to Shiraz's many wine taverns (*maykhâneh*), brothels (*beyté lotf*), opium dens (*bângkhâneh*), and casinos (*qomarkhâneh*) — all institutions that were, and are, *haram* ("forbidden") under Islamic *sharia* law.[65] Leonard Lewisohn aptly describes the unorthodox and renegade power that the *rendân* projected throughout the city from these various dens of iniquity, when he notes that they "were known for sensational adventurism (*mâjarâ-ju'i*), contempt for conventional religious morality, along with a devil-may-care attitude (*lâ-ubâligari*), and their deliberate courting of infamy and notoriety."[66]

The *rend* of Hafez's poetry is not simply the roguish libertine and notorious gangster of medieval Persian society, but a mystic whose enigmatic *ethos* is best described by analogy to this well-known sociological type.[67] Although Hafez's *rend* is a radical individualist in the way that he defies social customs and even breaks civil laws, that *rendân* is employed in the plural explicitly affirms a close analogy to the Mafioso gangster — who is a member of a renegade band of chivalrous desperados.[68] When he writes of *rendâné Pârsâ* or the "rogues of Persia," Hafez is envisioning a rebel alliance on a spiritual level: a mafia of mystics that defies both those who wield earthly power and the morality police who enforce religious orthodoxy, but a mafia whose defiance is characterized by a gracious chivalry that people do not receive from the authorities. Commenting on this seemingly paradoxical chivalric honor of the dishonored and infamous *rend* in Hafez's poetry, Leonard Lewisohn writes:

> Transforming their badge of infamy and dishonor and shame into acclaim and fame, the inspired libertine cuts a dash through his poems as a kind of

> revolutionary religious intellectual in society, an iconoclastic rebel who adhered to the religion of *Eros* as a counter-faith to the prevailing hardline fundamentalist version of orthodoxy and the moribund Islamic puritanism of the day.[69]

At one point Hafez even describes the inspired libertines as the only authentic "saints" (*wali*) and as the true "Friends of God."[70] Interestingly, a special class of rogues known as *rendâné madrasa*, namely the "schoolman libertines" or "rogues of the college," are thought to possess "insight into the reality of religion [*haqiqat-i din*] and morality beyond ... pretensions and falsehoods."[71] On the crassest and most superficial level, this imagery even heralds something reiterated by gangsta-rap and the Hollywood cowboy tough-talking through his gun barrel.[72] The type of the *rend* can even degenerate into that of the confidence man.[73] However, by contrast with the common con-man, the antics of the *rend* qua trickster exposes this entire world as a con: "The inspired libertine on the other hand reveals the world's deceit: 'wise-to-the-bait' of its charms, his actions serve to subvert and unmask the pretensions of the entire materialist mentality in both its religious and secular forms."[74]

That the religion of love is a "counter culture" comes across clearly in many of the main tropes of Hafez's poetry.[75] Provoking public rebuke and even infamy (*bad-nâmi, Nâm-o Nang*) is indispensable to the divine fool who enters into the path of love's religion.[76] Being reputable or having a good name (*Nâm-dâr*) counts against one who would embrace the religion of love as his own faith.[77] *Burhân al-Qâti* or "Decisive Argument," a most highly esteemed Persian literary dictionary, defines *rendân* (singular *rend*) as persons who are "crafty, deceitful, clever, fearless, reprobate, desperados with a devil-may-care attitude about them [*lâ-ubâli*]."[78] The dictionary entry adds that they "are called *rendân* because they repudiate all norms of society and reject the restraints of religious piety." The term *'ayyâr* or "brigand" is also associated with the *rend* and *qalandar*.[79] It is another term that was commonly taken to have only a negative value and that undergoes a radical inversion and revaluation by Persian poets.

What is most fascinating is the idea that "they are people who outwardly behave in a blameworthy manner and although they incur blame [*malâmat*], inwardly they are of sound character [*salâmat*]." The "perseverance in endurance of blame is renunciation of security and safety."[80] This is a spiritual practice that is intended to free the *rend* from the need for a social safety-net of collective affirmation and reliance on group-think rather than one's own divine inspiration and inner conscience, and it even aims to place the rogue mystic in a situation of financial ruin and physical danger:

> As a purificatory experience, the self-abasement generated by being reviled publically turns the *malâmati* ... from the vulgar mob towards God. Blame thus strengthens faith, being much more efficacious than praise in directing the mystic's attention to the Supreme Cause and away from secondary causes.[81]

As far as Hafez is concerned, the divine lover's life is dangerous without exception and no love affair that is more than merely human "is ever safe from public blame and slander."[82] In the *Divân* we read:

> I serve the will and *esprit* of that one
> Who commits to flames his own security,
> Who wears the rags of beggary, yet knows the lore of alchemy.[83]
>
> In a nook safe from blame, how can we stay
> Secluded when your dark eye reminds us
> Always of the joy and mysteries of drunkenness?[84]

Hafez and other Persian poets of the Religion of Love employ an entire lexicon of terms relevant to alcoholic intoxication, particularly wine-drinking, which is of course *harâm* or forbidden in Islam—the faith founded on that Quran that Hafez holds dear. These terms include *sâqi* (cup-bearer), *sâghar* (goblet), *khum* (wine-vat), *masti* (drunkenness), *maykhâne* (wine house), *kharâbât* (tavern), *piré kharâbât* (tavern master), *parishân* (the lover as a witlessly drunk wanderer) who is *bi-sar o pâ* (rendered a headless and footless vagabond), *mast* (a drunkard), or even *masté modâm* (one who is constantly intoxicated), and thereby in a state of *be-khishi* (ecstatic transcendence of the self through rapture) and *zowqé masti* (the bitterness of tasting drunken rapture), and who ultimately succumbs to *bihoushi* or acting from out of unconsciousness by being liberated from self-consciousness.[85] The Tavern of Ruin (*kharâbât*) is the abode of *rendân*.[86]

In its original meaning, *rend* connotes either "a clever, cunning and crafty person — an 'artful dodger' in Dickens' sense, or a 'rogue' in the Shakespearean sense" or "a person with a reckless, nonconformist, devil-may-care attitude unrestrained by any ties of the conventional social morality."[87] Hafez characterizes *rendi* as an art or "virtue" in the Renaissance sense of *virtù*, in other words what Persians call *honar* — a skill or perfectible craft, in this case of self-cultivation.[88] *Rendi*, as an art practiced by the *fedeli d'amore*, involves the practice of *shâhed-bâzi* and *nazar-bâzi*.[89] A *shâhed* is a seer or witness, and in a Sufi context its connotation is to bear witness to the divine amidst the mundane. This involves identifying and devotionally contemplating icons of divine beauty within the realm of what, at first glance, appears to be the merely human.[90] One is right to surmise that, from an orthodox Islamic standpoint, this practice would be considered idolatry. The proponents of this practice would defend themselves by claiming that it is not the heresy of *hulûl* or "incarnationism," but rather the highest achievement of *etehâd* or divine oneness — i.e. God having no other — and the ultimate aim of *mazhabé mohaqeqân* or "the religion of the truthful (or of those devoted solely to Truth or Reality, i.e. *Ahlé Haq*)."[91]

In fact, the term *bot* or "idol" is often used by Hafez and other Persian mystical poets to refer to the object of such contemplation, for example a mortal woman who is recognized, not just as a goddess, but as God incarnate. Interestingly, Hafez makes a point of noting the fact that the most appropriate idol for contemplation of the divine through earthly or human beauty is not necessarily the woman (or man) who is the closest approximation to some conventional standard of beauty or sexual attractiveness.

Rather, the *bot* of the *shâhed* is one who has "a certain ineffable *je ne sais quoi*" that renders her mysteriously or enigmatically beautiful in a *weird* way (with *Wyrd* understood in its oldest sense).[92] *Shâhed-bâzi* is not mere *jamâl-parasti* or "beauty-worship," even in the sense that Plato employs that as a preliminary stage to contemplation of the form of Beauty in his *Symposium*.[93]

The idea is ultra-humanist in that it ultimately concerns the reflection of the divine within the human being, or the divinity of humanity.[94] Leonard Lewisohn puts it this way: "*to be human is to 'regard' human beauty*, the measure of humanity lying in the capacity to love and to experience the erotic in all its degrees human and divine, according to the Religion-of-Love poets."[95] It is distinct from modern Western humanism, however, insofar as the identity of the witnessing mystic (*shâhid*) is believed to eventually melt into, and meld with, that of witnessed incarnate divinity (*mashud*).[96] The *shâhed* thereby becomes a *shahid* or martyr, symbolized by the red tulip, who has born witness for his faith, in the sense of "witness" that is employed by a "Jehovah's Witness."[97] The adept contemplator of divinity is also referred to as a *mashâhid*, an "observer."[98]

The term *nazar-bâz* is closely associated with the *rend* and *âsheq* (lover) in Hafez's poetry.[99] In fact, Hafez makes *âsheqi* or the state of being a true lover synonymous with *rendi*.[100] This equation of *rendi va âsheqi* can also be seen in Shah Nimatullah Vali: "Since the faith and creed of *qalandars* consists in taking lovers / And libertines as examples, we too take *qalandar* ways."[101] *Nazar-bâzi* means "the game of glances."[102] At one point Hafez even boasts:

> I am a lover and a libertine, a player of
> The game of glances with eyes that gaze in love.
> Such myriad arts and skills are my ornament:
> I say it plain — in fact, I show it off.[103]

More than mere flirtatious "making eyes" at an object of seduction, *Nazar-bâzi* also encompasses what the Indians call the *darshân* or blessing-conferring mystical gaze of the sage or guru. The "moon-faced ladies" thusly contemplated are referred to as such because they reflect the light of the divine Sun, or the one true God.[104] Hafez was among those who considered contemplating beautiful faces to be a legitimate devotional practice.[105] The *rend* is a Persian *fideli d'amore* and "an *extreme romantic*."[106] That is certainly true of Hafez:

> Should you pass by my shrine when I am gone
> Ask for soul-power, spirit-force and *esprit*,
> For all the world's pious rakes and holy reprobates
> Will be pilgrims to my tomb.[107]
> Become a lover; if you don't, one day the affairs of the world
> Will come to an end, and you'll never have had even
> One glimpse of the purpose of the workings of space and time.[108]

There is a close parallel between this tradition and that of the troubadours of late medieval France and Renaissance Italy, which also renders the erotic indistinguishable from the metaphysical.[109] This should be no surprise and it is not really a mere parallel, since the troubadour tradition was brought to Europe by Iranian cousins of the Persians—the "Alans" or that branch of Scythians/Sarmatians who mass migrated into the continent from the Caucasus, and intermarried with the Goths, during the "barbarian invasions" of the collapsing Roman Empire. The "Holy Grail" of Arthurian mysticism is originally an ancient Iranian symbol, the grail of Jamshid, the antediluvian emperor of the world—an Iranian King Atlas—who forced the gods (*div*, *daevas*) to raise his throne into the heavens—an event that inaugurates Nowruz and becomes the namesake for the endonym of Persepolis, namely *Takhté Jamshid* or "the Throne of Jamshid." In the poems of Hafez, Emperor Jamshid's Holy Grail or *jâm* symbolizes the celestial bowl or the dome of heaven inverted in the Cup.[110] Jamshid was the first "confidant of the Cup" to read this holy grail like an astrolabe and decipher its mysteries. Charles-Henri de Fouchécour writes: "Through the intoxication bestowed by its wine, the Cup also grants one access to the secret of the world marked out in the stars."[111]

In both grail traditions of Iranian origin, the Scytho-Sarmatian (i.e. Arthurian) and the Persian, the sacred vs. profane dichotomy is seen as being ultimately unreal.[112] However, unlike in the case of the Christian theological terms that eventually become basic to mystical discourse in the West, for Persian poets of the religion of love there is in the end no distinction at all between *eros* and *agape*.[113] *Eros* becomes a medium for the grace of *agape*, and *agape* is embodied and experienced through *eros*. From this authentically Persian perspective, "Fuck me, Jesus!" or "Grace me with your divine thighs, and let me suck on your holy tits, oh Mary, Mother of God!" are perfectly appropriate ecstatic exclamations. If Hafez were writing in today's world, his poetry would be full of such heretical expressions. He would sound a lot more like Alan Ginsberg or Jim Morrison than conservatives and antiquarians would like to imagine. What Hafez expressed with regard to the profanity of the sacred in the imagery of intoxication, drug-use, sex and seduction, within the psycho-social parameters of his own epoch, was at least equally scandalous. Judged against the background of the literary Persian of his time, Hafez's writing is full of lewd phrases and plebian vocabulary.[114]

One of the ironic terms used to refer to the libertinage often characteristic of those who practice the religion of love is *shari'at-e 'eshq* or "the Sharia (Cannon Law) of Love."[115] Hafez's poetry is the loftiest and most profound expression of the "religion of love"—an idea expressed by at least three synonymous phraseologies in the original Persian: *mazhabé eshq*, *diné eshq*, or *ayiné mehr*.[116] The last of these can be translated into English, not only as "the religion of Light" in addition to "the religion of Love," but more explicitly as "the religion of Mithra" since, as we saw beginning in Chapter 2, *Mehr* is the Pahlavi or Middle Persian form of the name of Mithra (Old Persian *Mitra*). The central Mithraic mystery that we discovered in Chapters 5 and 6, namely the seduction of Zurvan by Âz, is esoterically encoded at the core of Hafez's erotic theology:

'Âlam az shur-o sharé eshq khabar hich nadâsht
fetne-angizé jahân ghamze-yi jâdou-yi tow boud.

> The world knew naught of love's tumult and commotion:
> The chaos-causer of the world was the witchery of a wink from you.[117]

This is a clear allusion to the seduction of a hitherto unconscious God by the primordial seductress, namely the deity of chaos, Âz, so that this eternal Beloved moves the Creator to create the cosmos by becoming increasingly conscious of himself.

Hafez refers to the Religion of Love as *mazhabé eshq* or "Love's Creed" and *mazhabé rendân* or "the Religion of Rogues," i.e. the "creed of inspired libertines."[118] Despite his contempt for ascetic Sufis (*zahedân*), he sometimes also calls it *mazhabé ahlé tariqat* or "the faith of the Sufi Path." There are times when he just owns it as "our creed" (*mazhabé mâ*). Finally, and most significantly, he refers to it as *mazhabé piré moghân* or "the creed of the Elder Magus." It has mistakenly been assumed that the repeated appearance of the Magus in his *Divân* identifies Hafez as a kind of Crypto-Zoroastrian. Such an interpretation has been bolstered by the contrast between the Magi and Islamic orthodoxy. *Piré Moghân*, namely the Elder Magus or "Magian Master," is one of the most prominent and recurring tropes in the poetry of Hafez, who uses this character to stand for the initiator into a secret libertine faith that is considered heresy or apostasy from the orthodox Islamic standpoint, and even from the point of view of the more ascetic and puritanical Sufis:

> 'To wear the darvish robe and then to drink wine,
> That's not a rite of true doctrine.'
> I said. 'Indeed,' she said, 'but in the Magian
> Master's rite of faith, that's all holy doctrine.[119]

> From the hierocosmic heaven I've come — a Sufi who's doomed
> To dwell down here in the temple with the Magians.[120]

The *mogh-bache* or "Magian child" is a symbol positively contrasted with the puritanical Muslim in Hafez's poetry:

> Just when the Magi's child strolled along (the thief
> of hearts and wrecker of belief)

> At once the Muslim puritan was carried off,
> from all his friends divorced himself.[121]

However, such a Crypto-Zoroastrian interpretation loses sight of the painful historical reality that has been unveiled in Chapter 1 and 2 of this book, namely that the Order of the Magi (*Anjomané Moghân*) were essentially Mithraists. In Chapter 3 we saw how, when he engineered orthodox Zoroastrianism, Ardeshir Babakan considered these Mithraic Magicians to be his greatest enemy. He destroyed their fire temples together with the libraries at these locales, persecuting adherents of their teachings. The founder of the Sassanid Persian Empire attempted to reconstitute the entire Magian order, in a sanitized form, from out of a small, puritanical nucleus in the vicinity of Shiraz and under the totalitarian control of his inquisitorial henchmen, such as Tansar and Kartir. As recounted in Chapter 4, the Mithraic engineering of Islam and the Arab conquest was the ultimate consequence of the puritanical Sassanid state policies that reached their zenith in the coup against the revolutionary regime of Mazdak and Kavad.

We can only understand how a consummate libertine like Hafez can reverently write of his debt to the Quran, and at that after having deeply studied and taught theological exegesis, when we remember that the Mithraic Magus known as "Salmân, the Persian" was the author of the putatively "Mohammedan" revelation for which Muhammad himself was merely a medium. Read exoterically, the Quran itself has no philosophical content to speak of, but Hafez is pointing to an esoteric truth regarding the Quran's composition and purpose. Hafez is fairly forthright about the philosophical character of his relationship with the text of the Quran:

> Many there are who are *Hâfiz*, who preserve the holy book
> But none like me the world through who can collect
> The minutiae of philosophy with the Qur'ân's text.[122]

Hafez knows a shattering secret about the Quran, a secret of the greatest consequence for the Muslim creed founded upon that "revealed" book.

Hafez takes turns using both the Persian word *râz* and its Arabic synonym *serr* in order to designate the great "mystery" or supreme "secret."[123] It is at the discretion of the secret keepers to whom they deign to reveal this secret, and from whom they wish to continue to conceal it. The secret is a *vad'eh* or divine deposit vouchsafed into the guarded vault of the initiate's heart.[124] Hafez, who earned the sobriquet "Tongue of the Invisible" is an esoteric writer through and through, one whose verses are revelations precisely because they are at least as often aiming at artful concealment of what he knows based on intensely intimate and confidential communications with God: "Last night with my own ears I heard from His lips such words as one should not ask."[125]

This secret has to do with the reason why God created Humanity (*Âdami, Bani Âdam*) as a race that was intended to supersede the angels and jinn who inhabited the heavens and the earth long before Adam. Hafez is making reference to the angels when he writes of *sabokbârâné sâhelhâ*, since the angels lack both the troubled conscience and potentially divine consciousness of human lovers of God:

> *Shab-e târik-o bim-e mowj-o gerdâbi chenin hâyel*
> *Kojâ dânand hâl-e mâ sabokbârân-e sâhelhâ?*
>
> A dark night, the fear of the waves and such a dreadful whirlpool:
> What can the lightly burdened ones on the shore know of our situation?[126]

The relative ignorance and inferiority of the angels to humans is a persistent theme in Hafez:

> *Fereshte eshq nadânand ke chist ay sâqi!*
> *Bekhâh jâm-o golâbi be khâké Âdam riz.*
>
> O cup-bearer, angels do not know what love is.
> Ask for a beaker and pour rosewater on Adam's clay.[127]

There is also this verse:

Jelve-i kard rokhat did malak eshq nadâsht
'ayné âtash shod a-zin ghayrat-o bar âdam zad.

When Your countenance was revealed, it saw that angels had no love,
Its honour offended, it became all fire, and struck Adam's soul.[128]

Ghayrat means the offended honor of a jealous lover. In this case, God is offended by the fact that the angels do not love him — so he creates human beings as a new order of beings who, despite their earthly element and apparent frailty, are superior to the angels in the depth of their passionate hearts and tortured souls.

This *ghayrat* brings us back to the aim with which God renders His most ardent lovers notorious and disreputable. This path of deliberately incurring blame, the *malâmati* way, is characteristic of a genre of Sufi "Wildman poetry" or *qalandariyeh*.[129] The *qalandar* is a term used by a particularly rebellious strain of Sufis to refer to someone who, in their heart and soul, is liberated from the tyrannical demands of social convention and the hypocrisy of forced adherence to religious orthodoxy.[130] Before making its appearance in Hafez's *Divân*, this figure is fleshed out in the poetry of Sanâ'i, Attâr, and Rumi.[131] For example, Farid'ud'din Attar writes:

My work is turned all inside out
With people. For the worst slur
I think that ever I could incur
Is commendation by the crowd.[132]

The *qalandar* "endeavored to overturn and destroy established customs" all the while secretly performing "acts of devotion and piety," thereby being an unrecognized saint.[133] Hafez sometimes uses the term *rendé qalandar* to distinguish this mystical *rend* from the common Mafioso, vagabond, or desperado. He writes of this type of *rend* as a spiritual monarch and king-maker who alone has the right to confer legitimate sovereignty upon any earthly emperor and who, if need be, can remove a king's crown by inspiring righteous revolt:

Around the tavern door
The reprobates of God — *qalandars* — swarm
They withdraw and they bestow
The diadems of Empire."[134]

In a study of the *malâmati* path in Hafez's poetry, Khurramshahi identifies these elements of the *qalandar* character in the *rendân* figures portrayed in the *Divân*:

> Submitting oneself to public censure and blame, while not fearing — indeed, not being offended at — the accusations and slander… Being reckless vis-à-vis political conciliations conventionally made to protect one's reputation, along with disregard for fame and name. … Having a critical outlook on all conventional social institutions: religious, academic, governmental, mystical (e.g. mosque, madrasa and *khânaqâh*). … Affecting shamelessness, feeling impiety, irreligiosity, perversity and blasphemy. … Salvation through love.[135]

Blame incurred from the vulgar (*malamute khalq*) is a test of one's fidelity in *amor* and an expression of God's *qeyrat* or jealous possession, which places the *rend* qua lover (*âsheq*) in a state of spiritual isolation (*tajrid*) that divests him of his lower self (*tafrid*) and allows the *ma'shoqe-ye majazi* who is the object of his *shahed-bâzi* to bring him up to the level of committing *kufré haqiqi* or "real infidelity" as in the legendary love of Sheikh San'ân for a Christian girl who becomes his idol and on account of which he commits apostasy by converting from Islam to Christianity.[136] In the *Divân* Hafez recounts this story, which was first made famous by Attar in his *Conference of the Birds*:

If you profess yourself a devotee of
The highway of most noble Love
Never give a second thought for name
Or what men say is all 'ill-fame',
Recall the cap and gown
Of great Shaykh San'ân…"[137]

The final stage in the religion of love is *towhid* or divine unity.[138] To attain this stage the self-righteous pride of the puritan or orthodox ascetic has to be totally purged from one's psyche by "the carpenter's plane [a Masonic symbol] of self-obliteration and self-annihilation [*randahé mahv va fanâ*]":

> The ascetic had too much pride so could never soundly
> Traverse the Path. But the rake by way of humble entreaty
> And beggary at last went down to the House of Peace."[139]

Excessive pride was the sin of those angels—and jinn—who followed Lucifer in his rebellion against the Elohim. The indispensable context for this titanic insubordination is the engineering of human beings by the angels, on God's orders, with a view to humans superseding their angelic engineers. Hafez writes:

> *Doush didam ke malâyek daré meykhâne zadand*
> *Gelé Âdam besereshtand-o be paymâne zadand.*

> Last night, I saw the angels were knocking on the door of the wine-house
> Kneading the clay of man and drinking wine.[140]

In this verse we see that, although humans are being created because God is disappointed with the incapacity of the angels to love him, from the standpoint of efficient causality, it is the angels who are tasked with engineering human beings, even though the latter are intended to supersede them.[141] They may even be unaware of what God has in mind. This makes more sense out of the fact that archangel (*malak al-moqarrab*) Iblis, known as *Satan*, became the rebel angel and Adversary by refusing to bow before God's new creation—protesting that the angels are made of fire whereas man is made merely of clay, and that the angels only have a duty to bow before God, not to commit idolatry by bowing before some other authority and moreover submitting themselves to an inferior class of beings.[142] On account of his defiance Iblis is characterized as a quarrelsome egoist who worships himself and is not initiated into the intimacy of God's company (*nizâ'ju-ye khod-parast-o nâ-mahram*).[143] Hafez considers Iblis an imposter on account of his claim to be the only true monotheist:

> *Modda'i khâst ke âyad be tamâshâ-gâh-e râz*
> *dasté ghayb âmad-o bar sine-ye nâ-mahram zad.*
>
> The pretender wanted to come to see the secret spectacle:
> an invisible hand appeared and struck the chest of the outsider.[144]

> *Bâ modda'i magouyid asrâré eshq-o masti*
> *tâ bikhabar bemirad dar dard-e khod parasti.*
>
> Do not tell the pretender the secrets of love and drunkenness,
> that he may die not knowing, in the torture of self-worship.[145]

The pith of titanic hubris is believing that one has reason on one's side against what is perceived to be divine capriciousness, but what is in truth a trial to prove oneself worthy of the Beloved's company. The self-righteousness of the rationalist is a form of petty egotism that must be overcome if one is to become intimate with God. Hafez writes:

> Why should the inspired rogue who sets the world on fire
> Bother himself with wise counsel and advice? This world's
> Labours it is that require reflection and deliberation.[146]

That other great poet of Shiraz, Sa'adi also counsels us to abandon the "reason" of the "reasonable" if we wish to make the religion of love our own faith: "The reasoner [*'âqel*] is a thinker and a sere prudent deliberator over what's wise. Come, profess the Religion of Love [*mazhabé eshq*], and free yourself from both thinking and deliberation."[147]

One of the gravest sins committed by Ardeshir Babakan and those of his heirs who promulgated orthodox Zoroastrianism is their emphasis on Reason (*Aql*) and the equivalence that they draw between Reasonableness (*Aqlâniat*) qua Common Sense (*Âqel boudan*) and Wisdom (*Kherad*). Acting unwisely or *be-kherad-âne* is equated with both unreasonableness and being unethical (*qeyr-akhlâqi*), whereas ethical conduct or *niki* is misinterpreted as "propriety" in the sense of sensible conduct. *Niki*, which is etymologically related to the Greek *Nike* (Victory), originally meant *virtù* in the Renaissance sense of "excellence"—what Aristotle called *arete* (a cognate of the Old Persian *Artâ*). To misunderstand *goftâré nik* as speech within the confines of propriety, rather than as "excellent" speech—which may include the excellent profanity and eloquent blasphemy of the *rendé qalandar*—is to disinherit oneself from the spiritual heritage of the divinely mad soul of Iran.

Zoroastrians in the style of Ardeshir Babakan profess that their religion is *Mazdâyasnâ* or "Wisdom Worship," whereas in Hafez's view, Wisdom is only worthy of the name if it initiates one into the Religion of Love:

> The friend of wisdom who receives
> This wine that steals sleep is a traitor to love (*kâfaré eshq*)
> If he doesn't worship that same wine.[148]

There is a distinct strain of anti-scholasticism, if not anti-intellectualism in Hafez:

> Above homage and obeisance to lunatics
> Do not seek more from us, for our sect's master
> Professed all intellectualism to be wickedness.[149]

The Sassanid-style Zoroastrian conflates Wisdom (*kherad*) with a learned scholasticism of the schoolman (*elm-o dânesh dâneshmand*) that is ethical because it is based on a Canon approved by inquisitors, so that reason is under the umbrella of ethics (*aql ziré chatré akhlâqe*). In stark contrast with this pathetically impoverished conflation of Wisdom with the perfection of a moralistic scholasticism worthy of Confucius, Hafez identifies the *ensâné kâmel* or "Perfect Man" of Sufi mysticism with the *rend*.[150] He was not alone in this view. In a text titled *Marâtebé Rendân* or "Spiritual Degrees of the Inspired Libertines," Shah Nimatullah Vali (d. 1431) portrays erotic theology as a theology of liberation wherein ultra-romantic devotion paradoxically liberates one who is enslaved by love—liberates him from himself, which is to say, for most people, from a mass of internalized societal expectations, beginning with those acquired in childhood from one's own family.[151] The founder of the Nimatullahi Order of Persian Sufis writes:

> In our creed the inspired libertine is subject to no veil whatsoever, whereas the hapless puritan ascetic [*zâhed*] is veiled by dint of his own abstinence and devotion. … Since the inspired libertine is not subject to anything, how should he be fettered by learning and books? … The words of the inspired libertines [*qawlé rendân*] reflect their cognizance of the fact that the entire world consists of God's Beauty [*jamâl Allâh*], since 'God is Beautiful and loves beauty.' Therefore, the lover who is fond of the world through the love he harbors for God, in reality loves God alone through God's own love, for the beauty of the product in reality returns back to the Producer Himself. What a subtle matter![152]

Shah Nimatullah Vali was a generation younger than Hafez, but was well-known to the latter in his old age.[153] Even though Hafez called into question the spiritual claims of the founder of the Nimatullahi Sufi order, the latter's foremost disciple, Shah Qasim Anvar, became one of the most prominent admirers of Hafez's poetry, and he professed to be preaching the same religion of love found in the *Divân*.

8.3 The Persianate World

In the form in which it exists today, Hafez's *Divân* was first compiled and edited from out of five hundred different manuscripts collected from the four corners of what can be considered a "Persianate world" stretching from Azerbaijan and Iraq to Tajikistan and India.[154] Hafez's poetry had already penetrated throughout this vast geographical expanse in his own lifetime, as these verses from the *Divân* bear witness without exaggeration: "This itinerant Persian verse / sent errant on Bengal ways / is delicious and rich enough / for Indian parrots to crunch / its luscious, sugary chunks.[155] Those Samarqandi Turks / and black-eyed girls of Kashmir / All dance and flaunt their charms / to Hâfiz of Shirâz's verse."[156]

Toward the very end of his life, Hafez purportedly met with Tamerlane.[157]

According to a popular legend, Tamerlane chastised Hafez for his verse, "If that Turkish beauty would take our heart in hand / For the black mole on his (or her) cheek we would exchange Bukhara and Samarkand."[158] Tamerlane supposedly told Hafez that these cities were not his to give away, whereupon Hafez replied that "It is that very arrogance that has brought me to the lowly state in which you see me now."[159] This was after Tamerlane had just erected twenty-eight "minarets" in Isfahan made of the severed heads of the 200,000 Persians that he massacred there.[160] Then he and his Turkic berserkers turned on Shiraz and arrived in December of 1387. It was not, however, until two years after this vanguard expedition that Tamerlane returned to invade Shiraz in earnest—by which point, Hafez had already passed away. Fortunately, he was never forced to bear witness to the execution of the entire Muzzafarid administration and the brutal Turkic takeover of his beloved Shiraz together with the rest of southern Iran.[161]

Timur or Tamerlane (Persian *Teymour* or *Teymouré Lang*) was a Turk who aimed to restore the Mongol Empire of Genghis Khan.[162] In order to gain Mongol legitimacy, this warlord of the Turkic Barlas tribe married a Chinggisid princess, so that his half-Turkic heirs would also be of the bloodline of Genghis Khan.[163] He took the title of *göregen* or "son-in-law" of Genghis Khan. Like Mahmud of Ghazna before him, Tamerlane declared himself a *ghazi* or "holy warrior" for the cause of Sunni Islamic orthodoxy.[164] Everywhere he went, Tamerlane "threw children upon the fire as if burning incense" and built "towers out of the severed heads of his victims."[165]

It is true that he built up Samarkand with monumental architectural projects such as the Bibi Khanom, named after his wife, and his own mausoleum of Gur-i Amir.[166] However, these ill-conceived projects are also a testimony to Timur's tyrannical megalomania, which in this case drove him to disregard the counsel of his Persian architects who advised that the scale of the structures he had in mind exceeded the technical capabilities of the time. Both the dome of the Bibi Khanom mosque and the main entry arch of his palace at Shahr-i Sabz collapsed almost as soon as they were built.[167] Nevertheless, European traders and traveling merchants were impressed with the plundered wealth of Samarkand, and Tamerlane was memorialized as the epitome of opulent Oriental Tyranny by Occidental novelists, playwrights, operatic composers, and poets such as Christopher Marlowe, Nicholas Rowe, Georg Friedrich Handel, Antonio Vivaldi, Josef Myslivecek, Giacomo Puccini and Edgar Allan Poe.[168]

Tamerlane wanted to restore the shattered unity of the Mongol Empire. As in the case of Alexander's conquest of Iran, within a few decades of Genghis Khan's death the vast Mongol Empire that he established had already disintegrated into four khanates.[169] When Russia was ruled by the Golden Horde and China was under Kublai Khan's Yuan Dynasty, Greater Iran was divided between the Chaghatay Khanate that occupied Eastern Iran and Iranian Central Asia while Western Iran was the domain of the Il-Khanid dynasty based in Tabriz.[170]

Although the Mongol language is unrelated to that of the Turks, their blood-lusting and semi-nomadic tribal cultures were very similar and they shared a common geographical point of origin in Eastern Siberia.[171] Many Turkish clans joined Genghis Khan when he united the Mongol tribes in 1206, so that what he was really leading was a Mongol-Turkic confederation that invaded China in the East and Iran in the West.[172] Consequently, the Turkization of Tabriz continued when Hülegü Khan, the grandson of Genghis Khan, who conquered Iran, made it the capital of his Il-Khanid Dynasty, which lasted until 1335.[173] Most of the steppe nomads who took part in the Mongol invasion remained in Azerbaijan and filled both Tabriz and the countryside with brigandage, overgrazed the lands with their livestock, and did serious damage to local Iranian farms.[174] These issues continued into the twentieth century, with a distinct divide between the lowland Turkic dwellers in Azerbaijan and the ethnically Aryan Iranians — both Scytho-Sarmatian and Persian — who are industrious enough to endure in the harsh south Caucasus mountains.

The Mongol invasions devastated Marv, Balkh, and Nishapur, which never recovered.[175] Attar was killed during the Mongol invasion of Nishapur, Rumi's family fled from Balkh and Jalaluddin eventually wound up having to go as far east as Anatolia in order to escape their brutality. Known for their whirling dervish dance or *Samâ* ceremony, the *Mawlaw'iyya* or Mevlevi Order of Sufism traces its origin to Rumi himself. He is supposed to have established the order in Konya, which became the capital of the Seljuk Sultanate of "Rum" (Rome) in Anatolia once the Mongols had conquered the rest of the Seljuq Caliphate to the East. However, it was only after Rumi's death that his followers were really organized into a Sufi Order in any formal sense by Rumi's son, Baha al-Din Muhammad-i Walad, who is known among his devotees as Sultan Walad (Persian and Persianate Sufis have a tradition of referring to their spiritual masters with royal titles such as Sultan or, more commonly, Shah). The Mevlevi Order deeply impacted the development of Turkish culture during the Ottoman Empire, when a woman named Devlet Hatun, who was descended from Sultan Walad, married the Ottoman Sultan Bayezid I. Their son, Sultan Mehmet Chelebi, essentially gave Ottoman state backing to Rumi's Sufi order. This means that not only was the administrative language of the Ottomans Persian and their courtly high culture derived from Iran, but their spiritual orientation was Persianate as well.

The Turks who had settled in Anatolia were not the only ones who would wind up adopting Persian culture and expanding the geographical boundaries of what has been called a "Persianate World," which centered on an Iran formed in the fifteenth century and which began to disintegrate only with the intensification of European colonialism in the region during the nineteenth century. A major development in the formation of this Persianate World or renewed sphere of Iranian Civilization came when the Uzbek Turks brought an end to Timurid rule in Central Asia. In 1505, they expelled Babur, the governor of Samarkand, who consequently and very consequentially fled to Kabul where he organized a conquest of northern India.[176] This is ironic, since the government of Uzbekistan today views Tamerlane as the "father of the Uzbeks." It is doubly ironic because Tamerlane himself was not of the Uzbek tribe of Turks and his official chronicles record his view that the Uzbeks were among the most backward people that he had conquered, in need of being severely subjugated.[177]

Babur victoriously arrived in Delhi in 1526 and decided to make it his new capital, thereby founding the Mughal dynasty that endured until the British Raj ended it in 1857.[178] Babur's memories, titled the *Babur-nâmeh*, are written in Chaghatay Turkish.[179] In them, the founder of the dynasty in which both contemporary Pakistan and India take so much pride wrote this about the land he conquered and its native inhabitants: "Hindustan is a place of little charm. There is no beauty in its people, no graceful social intercourse, no poetic talent or understanding, no etiquette, no nobility or manliness."[180] Babur's grandson, Akbar the Great, remedied this perceived lack of culture by aggressively Persianizing Northern India, in what would become the third period of significant Iranian culture colonization of "Hindustan" (a term of Persian origin for the area now comprising Pakistan and Northwestern India).[181] Most of the Mughal administrative and literary elite, as well as the most skilled architects and craftsmen of the realm, were in fact ethnically Persian immigrants from Iran.[182] All governmental business of Mughal India was done in the Persian language. Even after the British colonization, Persian remained the language of administration in India under the Raj until well into the nineteenth century.[183] Court poetry was also composed in Persian, and it is musicians from Iran that developed the "Hindustani music" style that continues to be considered classical in Pakistan and northern India today.[184]

Within a couple of centuries of his lifetime, the most sophisticated and extensive commentaries on Hafez's poems were being written by Persian-speaking literati in Ottoman Turkey and Mughal India.[185] The Turkish commentaries extended as far to the West as that written by Sudi of Bosnia (d. 1597), which became the basis for most of the early European interpretations of Hafez.[186] Many more commentaries were written on Hafez by Persianate elites in India than in Iran, including the most monumental multi-volume work of Abdul-Hasan ʿAbd al-Rahmân Khatmi Lâhuri (d. 1507), which, as far as exegeses of Persian poetry are concerned, is comparable only to the Ottoman Turkish exegesis of Rumi's *Mathnawi* by Ismail Anqaravi (d. 1631).[187] Here is an example of the kind of insights that fill Lâhuri's grand exegesis of the Religion of Love:

> That Transcendent Beloved Being then spoke, stating that any gnostic who is a confidant of the arcane mysteries, who recognizes the true face of such an affair, when given such a wine — that is, beauty and loveliness decked out in the garb of the veiled presentment of a figurative mortal sweetheart — will only end up veiling and concealing this display of God, this divine theophany, unless he does become a worshipper of beauty [*husn-parast*]. This is because it is through the forms of mortal beauty [*suwari-i husniyya*] that God-as-Absolute in reality attracts the hearts of lovers to Himself.[188]

The first book-bound editions of Hafez to roll off of a modern printing press — in the original Persian — were published in 1791, not in Iran, but in Calcutta by the East India Company.[189] It is such Indian editions, shipped back to Europe and translated by early modern linguists, that granted Goethe, Nietzsche, Emerson, and other Western literary figures access to the Persian poet whose lyrical genius they would revere as an exemplar above all others. Hafez was so influential in India that the so-called *sabk-i Hindi* or "Indian style" of writing Persian poetry, which flowed back into Iran itself, is actually synonymous with the style defined by Indian poets under the influence of Hafez's *Divân*.[190]

It is well known that in medieval Islamic societies memorization of the Quran was a precondition to pursuing other studies.[191] What is less known is that up until the 1950s, it was almost as commonly expected, across the entire Persianate world, that grammar-school children memorize the poetry of Hafiz.[192] This was as true in Ottoman Turkey and Mughal India as it was in Timurid Central Asia and the core of Iran during the Safavid and Qajar periods.[193] Consequently, even in those periods when they were at war with the nation-state of Iran under the rule of the Safavids or Qajars, these Mughal, Ottoman, or Timurid cultures in India, Turkey, and Central Asia, could all be described as part of a "Persianate Civilization" that extends far beyond Persia itself to the East and West, and that is decidedly "Hafizocentric."[194] At least, that remained the situation until the late nineteenth or early twentieth century. One of the most impressive aspects of this Hafizocentrism of the Persianate World or Iranian Civilization is that it totally transcends, not only ethnic distinctions between Indians, Turks, and others within the Iranian orbit, but also the religious divide between Shi'ite and Sunni Muslims. Reverence for Hafez endured in a sphere that went beyond the constant warfare between Safavid Iran and Ottoman Turkey, and that encompassed non-Muslims within the Persianate world as well, such as Punjabi Sikhs, the Jews of Bokhara, and Persian-speaking Armenian Christians.[195]

In the following chapter we will see how Iran regained its political independence with the rise of the Safavid Dynasty and its institutionalization of Shi'ism. However, what ought to be borne in mind is that when Safavid Iran is considered as one of only three empires where the Persian language and culture reigned supreme, together with the Ottoman Empire to the west of it and the Mughal Empire to the east, we witness the contours of a Persianate World that stretched as far east as the Bay of Bengal, as far south as Yemen and as far north as the Caucasus, before ending on the coasts of the Mediterranean Sea in Southeastern Europe.[196] This revitalized sphere of Iranian Civilization was, until the nineteenth century, an expanse that included Delhi, Agra, Mecca, Medina, Jerusalem, and Athens.

CHAPTER 9

"I AM ZAHHAK AND ALEXANDER!"

The political reunification of Iran, after a period of 800 years, was accomplished by Shah Ismail of the Safavid clan in the Caucasus. The astounding accomplishments of Shah Ismail are the point of departure for this chapter. Emphasis will be placed on the esoteric Shi'ite origins of Shah Ismail and his debts to occult currents of spirituality that may have the Assassin Creed and Mazdakism as their fountainhead. It will be argued that his establishment of Shi'ism as the state religion was indispensable to restoring Iran's independent political existence for the first time since the Arab invasion. This also entrenched an institution that eventually took over the country in 1979. The roots of the Islamic Republic lie in Safavid Iran.

Beginning with Shah Ismail, a number of developments had the potential to restore Iran's rightful place as a global superpower. This came very close to materializing, but its various social and political preconditions failed to align in the proper order and sequence for Iran to enter the modern age as a superpower capable of playing a major role in shaping the World Order of humanity. This potential existed because, as we will have seen in the preceding chapter, in addition to the rise of the Safavid Persian Empire in the 1500s, the two main rivals of Safavid Iran had also adopted Persianate courtly cultures. In the early to mid 1700s, Nader Shah Afshar led a military coup against the Safavids and then proceeded to expand their empire to the greatest extent that Iran's borders had reached since the Sassanian period. The decline of the Safavids and the brief resurgence of Iran as an imperial world power under Nader Shah Afshar are the subject of the second section of this chapter. While an Afsharid triumph over both the Mughals and the Ottomans was at hand, and Nader's disestablishment of Shi'ism could have helped integrate the population of these realms into Iran, Nader failed to replace Safavid Shi'ism with any ideology strong enough and sufficiently dynamic to form the doctrinal foundation for an Iranian superpower entering modernity.

Such an ideology did eventually arise, but far too late. The revolutionary Babi and Bahai religious movement of the mid to late nineteenth century was yet another Iranian attempt to establish one world religion unifying all of humanity. A substantive consideration of the Babi and Bahai movements is the concern of the third and final section of this chapter. Viewed in hindsight, after the rude awakening of four decades under the Islamic Republic, we can recognize that the Bahai Faith seeks to reconcile Islam and the Abrahamic revelations as a whole with the Zoroastrian roots of Iranian Civilization in far too facile a fashion.

More significantly still, while the Bab began his movement in Shiraz as a Shi'ite apocalyptic and antinomian radical quite akin to the Nizari Ismailis before him, when he and the Bahais who followed in his wake invented a new set of "more progressive" religious laws and dogmas, they betrayed the messianic promise of Shi'ism. Islam is the final revelation in the sense that when the *Imâmé Zamân* or the *Mehdi* annuls the *sharia*, there is to be no replacement for it whatsoever. That is why this can only take place during the *Qiyâmat* or "Apocalypse." Normal society could not continue to function after such a disclosure event. For the Bahais to claim that the Quran is not the final revelation, and that prophetic history continues on indefinitely into the future, is to miss the point.

9.1 Shah Ismail Safavid

The Safavid Sufi brotherhood was established in the late thirteenth century.[1] The Safavid form of "Shi'ism" has been traced back to the Khorramdinân and related movements of the eight and ninth centuries.[2] The clan takes its name from Shaykh Safi al-din, a Kurd of Ardebil who founded the family and its initiatory line back in the thirteenth century.[3] Like most Kurdish mystics, Safi al-din and the first few generations of his Sufi clan had been nominally "Sunni."[4] They redefined themselves as Shi'ites in order to take control of the *Aq Qoyunlu* and use them as a partisan force against the Ottomans. *Aq Qoyunlu* or "white sheep" was a totemic clan name of Turkmen who had taken over Tabriz after the Seljuks were displaced by the Mongols.[5] The Turkmen tribes of Western Azerbaijan and Eastern Anatolia were generally hostile to any centralized authority, and they were devotees of Ali — in fact, they deified him in a way that was considered total heresy by the Sunnis.[6] Shaykh Ishaq Safi al-Din died in 1334.[7]

It is not hard to see how the unquestioning obedience of the members of a Sufi order to their *pir* or spiritual master would have a great military value in the case of an armed movement such as that of the Safavids.[8] The early Safavid partisan fighters went into battle without wearing any armor other than the spiritual armor of their faith.[9] The *Aq Qoyunlu* and other Turks that the Safavids brought under their command were given the epithet *Qezelbâsh* or "red heads." The red Safavid turban also had a pyramid jutting out of the center of it, which pyramid was marked with twelve triangles one inside the other.[10] The tombs of the early Safavid Sufi shaykhs are pyramidal in structure, recalling the *kurgans* of the Scythians, many of whom were redheads.[11]

Ismail Safavid succeeded his older brother Ali Mirza, following the latter's assassination.[12] At the time of this succession the danger to the teenager was such that he was forced to hide in the forests of Gilan, *where there were still many Ismaili strongholds.*[13] This, taken together with the fact that his poetry was canonized and considered sacred by the *Ahl-e Haq*, has led some scholars to suspect that Ismail himself was a crypto-Ismaili and latter-day Assassin.[14] The *Ahl-e Haq*, also known as the Yaresan, is a Kurdish esoteric group whose founder, Sultan Sahak, intended it as a continuation of the Nizari Ismaili initiatory lineage.[15]

The Yaresan or *Ahl-e Haq* is one of two Kurdish mystical sects that form the matrix from out of which the "Shi'ism" of Shah Ismail emerged. The other is the Yezidi or *Izadi* group.[16] The Kurds, as one of the most ancient Iranian people, have preserved traditions that are even older than Zoroastrianism.[17] The Yezidis have an annual bull-slaying ritual, and they also pray facing the sun.[18] These and other elements of their spiritual tradition have led scholars to conclude that what they practice is essentially a survival of Mithraism.[19] Certain themes in their myths, such as the serpent-slaying hero who releases water from a rock, are exceedingly ancient Aryan beliefs that predate Zoroastrianism.[20] The most important Yezidi festival, the *jezna jema'iyye* or "Festival of the Assembly," takes place in late September, around the Autumn Equinox, and is clearly the remnant of an ancient version of Mehregan or *Mithrakânâ*—the festival of Mithra.[21] The bull sacrifice is held on the fifth day of this festival, amidst music and dancing.[22]

The Yezidis refer to the Divine Heptad that become the Amesha Spentas in the teachings of Zarathustra as the *haft sirr* or "Seven Mysteries."[23] Yezidis refer to reincarnation, which is one of their core beliefs, as a "changing of the shirt."[24] The perfection of the world at the end of time is a belief that Yezidis share with Zoroastrians. They have a curious image for this state, which the Zoroastrians refer to as *Frashgard*; they say that after a final struggle the world will be made "smooth like an egg." What is fascinating is that the Yezidis do not see this perfection of the world as a victory of the Good, but as the outcome of a dialectical tension between two opposed forces that are equally worthy of reverence. The most fundamental teaching of the Yezidis, and the most shocking, is that good and evil are equally necessary and mutually interdependent.[25] The Yezidis believe that the fallen angel, Satan, did not prostrate himself before the Lord because he is actually the ultimate lover of God, one who refuses to commit idolatry by bowing before man (i.e. Adam) or any other created being.[26] They so revere Satan that, like Jews who refuse to speak the name of God, or devout Christians who refuse to take God's name in vain, the Yezidis have a taboo according to which the sacred name of Satan is unspeakable.[27] The Yaresan share with the Yezidis the view that, while there is a duality of opposed forces at work in the cosmos, both are equally necessary and, consequently, evil is as praiseworthy as good.[28] They venerate Satan in the form of *Malak Tâvus* or "the Peacock Angel."[29] Zoroastrians associated the peacock with Ahriman.[30]

Given that the Yezidis preserve a form of religion that predates Zoroastrianism and was viewed with hostility by Zoroastrians, even before the advent of Islam, it is odd that quite a number of Yezidis in northern Iraq are now attempting to present themselves as "reverts" to Zoroastrianism.[31] This development has met with skepticism, cynicism, and even outright hostility from Parsis and other hereditarily orthodox Zoroastrians.[32]

Whereas the Yezidis do not claim to be Muslims, the Yaresan, who share much of their beliefs, do consider themselves Shi'ites.[33] This, despite the fact that they do not observe *any* Muslim rituals or even have mosques in their communities.[34] The Yezidis are based in northern Iraq, while the Yaresan are concentrated in Kermanshah and Luristan — parts of Kurdistan that have remained inside Iran.[35] Their numbers have been estimated at anywhere from one to seven million people, which on the higher end of the estimate would be around 8% of the population of Iran.[36]

Unlike the Yezidis, who do not accept converts, and who also prohibit intermarriage, the Yaresan or *Ahl-e Haq* do accept initiates who are willing to "entrust their head" (*sar sepordan*) to a master of the community.[37] The ritual for this initiation is referred to as a "renewal of the contract," a phrase which, given the primary function of Mithra as the lord of contracts, is another indicator of the Mithraic character of the sect. The Yaresan share many of the same characteristic features of other Sufi orders, from absolute devotion to one's master to the practice of *zekr* or mantras, to ritual music and ecstatic dance, and especially, the idea of attaining spiritual perfection through a series of successive stages.[38] However, unlike other Sufi orders, who have more thoroughly assimilated themselves to Islamic orthodoxy, the Yaresan have retained the Mithraic belief that this process of spiritual perfection takes many lifetimes.[39] The *Ahl-e Haq* think that it may take as many as a thousand successive reincarnations in order to become a perfect person or *ensâné kâmel*.[40]

Shah Ismail and his predecessors in the Safavid mystical lineage believed in reincarnation, especially in the case of great historical figures such as Abu Moslem Khorasani.[41] The *Qezelbâsh* highly esteemed Abu Moslem and used his legacy as a means to garner support for their cause.[42] Ismail identified himself as a reincarnation of Abu Moslem Khorasani.[43]

As we have seen in previous chapters, the Mazdakites, the Khoramdinân, and the Ismailis (not just the Nizaris but also the Qarmatis and Horufis) all believed in reincarnation.[44]

The Yaresan and *Ahl-e Haq* have both preserved an origin myth that predates Zoroastrianism, according to which the Creator made a pearl that contained all future creation before bringing the Divine Heptad into being and making a contract (*Mithra*) that establishes the foremost of these seven as responsible for the affairs of this world.[45] Two of these seven beings are portrayed as a lion and a bull.[46] Whereas Zoroastrians attribute the bull or cow sacrifice to Ahriman, both the Yaresan and the Yezidis preserve the original version of the myth according to which Mithra carries out the sacrifice, which sacrifice is a positive act that is seen as the fountainhead for the creation of all other earthly life.[47] The Yaresan refer to this sacrifice as a "making green," thereby associating it with one of the two sacred colors of Mithra.[48]

The bull sacrifice, veneration of the Divine Heptad in a form other than the Zoroastrian one, and belief in reincarnation, which both call "changing the shirt," are among the common features of the Yezidi and Yaresan forms of surviving Kurdish Mithraism.[49] Both groups use musical instruments that they consider sacred as an accompaniment to the chanting of their liturgies.[50] The Yaresan also share in common with the Yezidis a strange belief that each member of the group ought to establish a contract with a spiritual brother or sister who will vouch for him or her during the last judgment.[51] This seems to hark back to Manichaean Gnostic ideas of the spiritual twin or *syzygy*.

The Yaresan sect, which still exists in the Kurdish parts of Iran today, was organized into its present form by Sultan Sohak in the late fourteenth and early fifteenth century.[52] His devotees alleged that he was an incarnation of God. His real name was Eshâq. The name "Sohak" is a Kurdish pronunciation of Zahhak or *Azhi-Dahâka* (*ezhdehâ*), the tyrannical "dragon" who ruled in ancient times according to the Avesta, Iranian folklore, and *Shâhnâmeh* of Ferdowsi.[53] The *Ahl-e Haq* consider *Azhi-Dahâka* to have been the same King of the Medes known to the Greeks as "Astyages"

(*Azdyaka*), or in other words, the grandfather of Cyrus the Great.[54] Recall that the Kurds consider themselves descendants of the Medes. In their view, this Median King was demonized by Persians who adopted and institutionalized Zoroastrianism.[55] This sheds light on the esoteric meaning of some of the most fascinating verses in all of Shah Ismail's poetry. The founder of Safavid Iran writes:

> Today I came down to earth: I am lord and king! Know as true that I am Hadar's son!
>
> I am Fereydun, I am Khosrow, I am Jamshid and I am Zahhak, I am Rustam son of Zal, I am Alexander!
>
> The mystery of *ana'l-Haqq* is hidden in this heart of mine, for I am the Absolute Reality and Reality is that which I do utter![56]

The pen name that Shah Ismail used to write such verses was *Khatai* or "the Sinner."[57] His references to figures in Ferdowsi's *Shâhnâmeh* are not instances of superficial name dropping. Shah Ismail revered the Iranian national epic as a sacred text. Prior to battles, he would recite the *Shâhnâmeh* to his troops — mostly in Turkish translation, since the majority of them did not speak Persian.[58] Shah Ismail gave all of his own children proper Persian names from out of the *Shâhnâmeh*, rather than the Arabic and Muslim, or even Turkic, names that had become common by that time (and which he himself had).[59] Shah Ismail commissioned the famous masterpiece of Persian miniature painting, the *Shâhnâmeh* that would come to be known as *Tahmâsebi* because it was completed, after Ismail's death in 1524, under the reign of his successor Tahmasp.[60] Art historians consider this illuminated manuscript to be the peak of Persian painting.

The Turkic tribes that supported Shah Ismail Safavid in his rise to power are known as the *Qezelbâsh* ("red heads") or the *Shâh-sevân*, and they included the Shamlu, Rumlu, Ustajlu, Tekelu, Afshar, Qajar, and Zulqadar tribes.[61] *Qezelbâsh* villages had neither mosques for a congregation to gather in, nor minarets from which there could be a call to prayer.[62] Instead, the *Qezelbâsh*, who freely consumed alcohol, had a form of ritual worship inside the privacy of their own homes. Under the cover of night, their ecstatic dancing to mesmerizing music would culminate in drunken sexual orgies.[63] Such was the atmosphere in which Shah Ismail was raised.

Ismail conquered the old Seljuq capital of Tabriz in 1501.[64] Two years later, at the tender age of sixteen, Ismail had himself proclaimed the first *Shâhanshâh* of Iran in many centuries.[65] *At the same time*, he declared Shi'ism the official state religion of his resurrected "Iran."[66] Shah Ismail even demanded that his followers curse the three Sunni caliphs that preceded Ali.[67] His declaration of Shi'ism as the official religion of Iran isolated Iranians from two groups of Turks, the Ottomans to the West in Anatolia and the Turkmens and Uzbeks to the East in Central Asia, in a way that made it possible for Shah Ismail to carve out the political boundaries of a cohesive Iranian state along the lines of a religiously charged friend-enemy distinction.[68]

Shah Ismail's declaration of Shi'ism as the state religion of Iran must have significantly facilitated the Iranian reconquista of Iraq, since the cities of southern Iraq were Shi'ite but the Ottomans attempting to rule them were Sunnis.[69] This was, of course, the second Iranian reconquista of Iraq under the banner of Shi'ism, following the short-lived subjugation of the Baghdad Caliphate by the Buyids in the tenth century, which was discussed in Chapter 7. Within a decade of establishing himself at Tabriz, Shah Ismail conquered all of the core territories that had been part of the Sassanid Empire—including the former Caliphate's capital at Baghdad and the Mesopotamian region (present-day Iraq) that had been the administrative district of the Sassanids and the Parthians and Achaemenids before them.[70] After his successful conquest of Baghdad in 1508, Shah Ismail sat on a boat in the Tigris river drinking as he watched the mass executions of his defeated enemies along the riverbank.[71]

He drank out of the skulls of his enemies. When he defeated Muhammad Shaybani Khan, Shah Ismail had the Uzbek ruler's skull crafted into his drinking cup in the old Scythian fashion.[72] Shah Ismail would on occasion dig up the graves of his enemies, or of the enemies of his clan, that had escaped his vengeance, so that he could burn their defiled corpses and ensure that they would not "rest in peace."[73] When he seized Daylam from Amir Husayn Kia Kolavi, who was a conservative Shi'ite, the latter committed suicide before Shah Ismail could lay hands on him. So the frustrated Safavid god-father had two of Kolavi's lieutenants captured and brought to Isfahan, where Ismail skewered and roasted them as rotisserie kebabs.[74] His followers had to eat the kebab to prove their loyalty to Ismail.[75] Shah Ismail demanded that his followers fully prostrate themselves before him, despite the fact that in Islam prostration even before a prophet, such as Muhammad, is considered a sin and partial prostration (with bent knees) is supposed to be reserved for Allah and to be performed only in the direction of the Ka'ba.[76] Of the Ka'ba, Shah Ismail had this to say in one of his poems: "My name is Shah Ismail. I am God's mystery. ... I am the Pir of the Twelve Imams... I am the Alexander of my contemporaries... I am free from the Ka'ba of hypocrites."[77]

In tactics reminiscent of the Assassin sleeper cells, the Safavids were able to infiltrate sensitive positions within the state apparatus of the Ottoman Caliphate.[78] This infiltration was so extensive that the Ottoman Sultan Selim I was forced to execute most of his own family, along with a great many of his courtiers, who were not beyond the suspicion of being Safavid secret agents.[79] This was only tolerable for so long before the Ottoman Sultan struck back hard.

Selim I engaged Shah Ismail on the plain of Chalderan in 1514.[80] Before the Safavid and Ottoman forces met at Chalderan, Shah Ismail had adopted a scorched earth strategy in the region that he projected would be the territory that Sultan Selim's forces were marching into.[81] By the battle of Chalderan in 1514, the Ottoman military had been somewhat modernized on account of its encounter with European military forces during the Caliphate's conquest of the Balkans.[82] A need to keep up with the Europeans on their Western flank forced the Ottomans to better equip and organize their military in ways that the Iranians had failed to do.[83] To be fair, *for centuries there had been no Iranian state at all* before Shah Ismail himself re-founded it — only thirteen years earlier.

Shah Ismail's forces at Chalderan were blown to bits by the Ottoman cannons, a technical innovation that overpowered the fanatical faith of his

Qezelbâsh partisans. Ismail was left venting his frustration by slashing at one of the Ottoman cannons with his sword, which left a deep gash in its barrel.[84] Two of Ismail's wives were captured by the Ottomans at Chalderan.[85] The Shah himself was wounded and barely escaped alive. Following the defeat at Chalderan, Shah Ismail took to always wearing black from head to toe.[86] The young Shah, only twenty-seven years old, never quite reemerged from the mourning and alcoholism that he descended into after the battle.[87] He was dead by thirty-seven. Some have suspected that his premature death in 1524 was due to alcoholism.[88]

However, he did not give up on forging a grand alliance against the Sunni Caliphate with the Continental European powers, and to this end he continued to exchange letters with the kings of the West.[89] This did result in a strategic partnership that endured for the reign of most of his successors, an arrangement that saw the Safavids attacking the Ottomans on their Eastern flank every time the Turks attempted to expand Westwards into Europe.[90] Frankly, had it not been for this support from Iran, the Ottomans may have been able to advance far enough into the European continent to nip the Renaissance in the bud to the point that it never would have yielded the Enlightenment and modern industrial society. (This is a complex counter-factual thesis that would demand an entire, highly speculative historical study in its own right.)

It is noteworthy, in the context of this speculation, to point out the extensive connections between the Safavids and Crypto-Byzantines.[91] Beginning with the fall of Constantinople to the Ottoman Turks, a number of the Safavid Sufi cult leaders married Byzantine royal women, such that Shah Ismail himself was rumored to have been of the bloodline of Caesar Andronikos III Palaiologos.[92] That would certainly shed a different light on his identification with Alexander. Also interesting in this regard is that one of the two most famous European portraits of Shah Ismail, the one made by André Thévet in 1584, depicts the founder of Safavid Iran making the specific gesture that would come to be known as the "Hand of the Mysteries" among the Freemasons.[93]

9.2 The Safavid and Afsharid Empires of Iran

Two structural problems intrinsic to the construction of the Safavid state would eventually undermine it and go on to plague Iran for a long time afterwards, perhaps even until the present day. One of these was the unruliness of the *Qezelbâsh* partisans that Ismail used to come to power, and the other was the forced integration of Turkic tribes with Persians — or "Tajiks" as the former liked to derogatorily refer to the Persians who Shah Ismail had made their masters.[94] The unruly *Qezelbâsh* can be compared to the *Hezbollahis* or *Basijis* of today, and the Turkic-Persian rivalry remains fierce today — not only in Iran, especially Iranian Azerbaijan, but also in former parts of Iran that have since become the artificial nations of the Republic of Azerbaijan, Afghanistan, Tajikistan, and the Tajik-dominant parts of Uzbekistan. Shah Abbas employed severe resettlement policies to break up local tribalism and enlist Kurds and Turkmen to defend the borders of the nation-state of Iran, which borders he had expanded to include all of Iraq by defeating the Ottomans to the West and much of Central Asia by defeating the Uzbeks to the East.[95] He also routinely reassigned regional governors in order to preempt any secessionist plots on their part.

One has to grasp that by the time Shah Ismail rose up with the aim of reunifying Iran, this country, which had once been Iranian with a sophisticated metropolitan population dwelling in world cities of the stature of Rey during the Buyid period, had been completely overrun by uncivilized nomads — mostly of Turkic stock.[96] The Mongol invasion of the thirteenth century had opened the floodgates for these Turkic tribesmen, so that even when the Mongols themselves withdrew, Iran was subsumed by tribal barbarism. Whereas, prior to the Mongol invasion, the Assassins had done a decent job of resisting Turkic encroachment into Iran and were close to toppling the Seljuk (i.e. Turkic) Caliphate, after the Mongols destroyed the political power of these radical Ismailis there was nothing to stop Turkic barbarity from pouring into Iran through both sides of the Caspian Sea, from Central Asia into Khorasan, and from the Caucasus into Azerbaijan. From the Seljuq period onward most of the rulers of Iran were either nomads themselves or had been brought to power by nomads, and none of them were native speakers of Persian.[97] They all did, however, make use of a Persian bureaucratic class. Shah Ismail penned poetry in Turkish as often as his rival, the Ottoman Sultan Selim wrote in courtly Persian.[98]

The Safavids were strategic allies of the Continental Europeans who were resisting the expansion of the Ottoman Caliphate into southeastern Europe.[99] The Ottomans, who already had regions such as Greece, Bulgaria, Romania, and Hungary under their control, came awfully close to capturing Vienna. The European desire for an ally against the Ottomans sustained the Safavids in terms of international trade.[100] Shah Abbas Safavid (1587–1629) built many roads, caravansarais, and workshops to accommodate and exploit this market for exports of silk and other products to Europe.[101] Shah Abbas not only moved the capital from the northwest of Iran southward to Isfahan, he also brought large numbers of Caucasians, such as Georgians and Armenians, to Isfahan in order to serve as the administrative and military elite of the Safavid Empire.[102] The emphasis on an elite drawn from the then still Iranian Caucasus region, especially from Georgia (*Gorgestân*, including *Irestoon* or Ossetia), and diffused throughout Imperial Iran remained characteristic of the Safavids all the way to the end of their reign in the 1720s.[103]

The Maydâné Naqshé Jahân with its Shah and Lotfallah mosques, the Ali Qapu and Chehel Sotun palaces, and the Allahverdi Khan bridge were all architectural marvels built—or at least commissioned—during the reign of Shah Abbas.[104] These monumental building projects turned Isfahan into a world city. In 1616, Shah Abbas played the British East India Company off against Portuguese colonialists in a way that allowed him to ultimately take back Iran's ports on the Persian Gulf from Portugal—especially the port of Bushehr.[105] However, lest one mistakenly imagine an overly idealized portrait of the man, it should be noted that the same Shah Abbas, who had come to power by deposing his own father, feared his sons to the extent that he not only had them all imprisoned, he eventually blinded one of them and killed another.[106] One of his grandsons had to succeed him.

It is Shah Abbas who, in order to build the institutions of a stable state, began propping up the conservative Shi'ite *Ulema* or "clergy" in order to fill the vacuum of power opened up by his sometimes brutal suppression of both *Qezelbâsh* partisans and decentralized Sufi orders.[107] On one occasion, Shah Abbas spent twenty-eight days walking across the desert from Isfahan on a pilgrimage to the tomb of Imam Reza in Mashad.[108] Such antics significantly increased the *Awqaf* (plural of *vaqf*) or "endowments" being received by the Ayatollahs and other clergymen for their seminaries and mosques.[109]

All Sufi orders except for the Safavid one were suppressed by the state.[110] Up to this point, Sufi orders had been the dominant religious influence in the Iranian countryside. The establishment of Shi'ism as Iran's state religion, and the Safavid crackdown on all Sunni Sufi orders, afforded an opportunity for the rise of two Shi'ite Sufi orders that have remained influential in Iran even until today — the Nematollahis and the Nurbakhshis.[111] It is ironic that the word *Sufi*, which early in the rise of the Safavids, had come to be almost synonymous with "supporter of the Safavids," eventually became a term of opprobrium under the reign of the dynasty's later monarchs.[112]

As the Safavids suppressed the Sufi orders, *tasavvof* gave way to *erfân*.[113] This also involved the transformation of the Illuminationist *hekmaté eshrâqi* into a *hekmaté elâhi* by Safavid era philosophers such as Mir Damad and Mullah Sadra.[114] Mir Damad and Shaykh Bahai who, together with Mir Fendereski, were members of the school of Isfahan, became the teachers of Mullah Sadra of Shiraz (born 1572).[115] Mullah Sadra studied with these men in Isfahan, and also spent some time in both Qazvin and Qom, before returning to his native Shiraz where he became a teacher of Philosophy in his own right.[116] His major work is *al-Afsar al-arba'a* or "The Four Journeys," which is a synthesis of Avicenna, Neo-Platonism, the Sufism of Ibn Arabi and the Illuminationist thought of Suhrawardi in the context of Shi'ite theology.[117]

Mullah Sadra inspired Azar Kayvan, who emigrated to Patna, India, where his philosophical vision informed the Persian poetry of Mirza Bidel.[118] This assimilation of a wide range of mystical Philosophy into the Shi'ism of the Safavid *madrasas* was dubbed *erfân* or "Gnosis."[119] The same Gnostic milieu was the matrix for the Mughal Emperor Akbar the Great's *Din-e Elâhi*.[120] It is this strain of Iranian mysticism that is the hidden source for the Kabbalistic works of Isaac Luria (d. 1572), such as *Esh Hayyim* ("The Tree of Life"), as well as certain writings of his disciples, for example, *Emeq ha-Melek* ("The Valley of the Kings").[121]

This philosophical revival of esotericism was, however, targeted by the clergyman Mohammad Baqer Majlesi (1627–1699), who was the single figure most responsible for institutionalizing conservative clerical Shi'ism in Iran.[122] Mohammad Bagher Majlesi suppressed Sufi orders and philosophers of the Illuminationist school, just as he banned gambling, public music and dancing, sodomy and opium smoking, and ordered the closure of brothels, taverns, and even cafés.[123] Treasury officials were ignored when they warned that losing the revenue from taxation of brothels, taverns, opium dens, and other entertainment and recreation institutions that were considered *harâm*, would be ruinous to the income of the Safavid state.[124] The new edicts were loudly proclaimed from the minarets of mosques and in some cases engraved above their doors, with an emphasis on the fact that these fundamentalist policies applied just as much to viziers and governors as they did to common folk.[125] All of the bottles from the royal wine cellar were brought out into the square in front of the palace where they were smashed and emptied.[126] Instead of a Sufi buckling the sword of the sovereign onto his belt during the coronation ceremony, as had been customary for the Safavids given their Sufi roots, Shah Sultan Hossein gave this honor to Majlesi.[127] The Madar-e Shah *madreseh*, which was built in Isfahan during this otherwise dark period, is the last gem of Safavid architecture.[128] Unfortunately, this beautiful *madreseh* would not be graced by the same quality of philosophical thought that had been characteristic of the earlier Safavid period.

Even as Philosophy had experienced a resurgence under the patronage of the early Safavids, philosophers such as Mir Damad and Mullah Sadra were seen as Hellenizing heresy-brewers by the orthodox clergy who tended to attack them and suppress their writings.[129] This despite the fact that these Safavid-era philosophers were Shi'ite mullahs themselves. Persecution in the name of religious orthodoxy was not limited to thinkers. Despite being ostensibly protected "peoples of the book," Jews and even Christians were persecuted by the Safavids along with the Zoroastrians.[130] The worst persecution was faced by the Jews. Mohammad Baqer Majlesi, who also penned voluminous texts against the Sunnis and Sufis, wrote a tract called *Lightning Bolts Against the Jews.*[131] By the mid to late Safavid period, from 1642 onward, Jews were forced to wear patches that would identify them as *najes* or "unclean."[132] They were prohibited from wearing elegant clothes and they had to wear mismatching shoes so that they could be mocked publicly. Jews were expected to remain silent in the face of this mockery or of any verbal abuse whatsoever that they were subject to by a Muslim.[133] They were forced to hold their ceremonies, including weddings, in secret. They were not allowed to enter Muslim shops lest they touch items that were for sale and render these unclean.[134] Jews were not allowed to walk in the middle of the street or walk past Muslims.[135] Worst of all, the word of a "dirty Jew" was almost worthless in court.[136]

An Italian who visited Iran at the beginning of the Safavid period remarked on how egalitarian the relationship was between men and women, with wives even joining their husbands in battle "in the same way as those ancient Amazons."[137] Another European traveler of the same period recounts how Persian women wear colorful "robes of silk" and only diaphanous "veils on their head" that partly cover their hair and "show their faces openly."[138] This matches the pictorial evidence from the *Tahmâsebi Shâhnâmeh*, which had been commissioned by Shah Ismail. This fashion of clothing is preserved in some rural parts of Iran today, although it must be a pale reflection of what was common attire for upper class ladies in the great cities of Iran, such as Tabriz and Isfahan, at the outset of the Safavid period. Yet, by the end of the Safavid era, in the late 1600s and early 1700s, women were clothed in a manner comparable to the early years of the

Islamic Republic of Iran and women of the upper class were sequestered and idle.[139]

Following Shah Tahmasp, who like Ismail was also considered divine, the Safavid state began to move toward the conservative Shi'ite theology of a largely imported *Ulema*.[140] Initially, these theologians were dependent on the monarchy for financial support and political influence.[141] However, once the Safavid Shahs gave them the ability to establish a system of *vaqf* or charitable "endowment" collection to run their schools, hospitals, mosques, and shrines, they became increasingly independent of the crown and, eventually, they even became the largest property holders in the country.[142] Specifically, they finagled a system whereby the *khums* and *zakat* payments of the faithful would go directly to the Ayatollahs without passing through the hands of the Safavid state bureaucracy or the national treasury.[143] Charitable contributions were, in theory, supposed to support the poor, but since it could be argued that religious students and teachers were among these, and clerical institutions were serving the poor, including hospitals, in the end such contributions enriched and empowered the conservative Shi'ite clergy. This development ultimately allowed the mullahs to bite the hand that fed them.

The situation was even more dire considering the fact that Shi'ite clergy have a much more significant role in the lives of their religious community than Sunni imams do. As long as it rested in the hands of antinomian mystics like the Assassins, the Shi'ite belief in the need for a broad scope of interpretation of Islam, including the Quran itself, served to foster a free-spirited society. However, once the conservative clergy assumed this power of constantly delivering interpretive *fatwas* on every matter of personal and social conduct, the opposite became the case.[144] Add to this the fact that, in a country wrecked by mass nomadic migrations, rampant tribalism, and the lack of a strong centralized authority, along with the difficulty of communication over vast distances (in a realm, in that period, five times the size of France), the local influence of the clergy posed a significant threat to the sociopolitical authority of the Safavid state.[145] As Iran entered the eighteenth century, it became increasingly the case that the Ayatollahs expected the Shahs to govern in line with their rulings — at least where social and political matters affected *sharia* — and they left only military affairs to the crown.[146] As they saw it, the Shah of Iran was there *to defend a Shi'ite Ummat.*

Shah Sultan Hossein (1694–1722), the last of the Safavid monarchs, basically instituted an Islamic theocracy comparable to that of Ayatollah Khomeini. Orthodoxy was enforced and the state suppressed both Sufis and philosophers, even when the latter were mullahs.[147] Actually, to be fair to Khomeini, who, as we shall see shortly, was himself a mystic and had seriously studied Philosophy with great interest, the final form of the Safavid state was in some ways an even more conservative Shi'ite theocracy than the Islamic Republic of Iran in its most orthodox early phase.[148]

While the last of the Safavid Shahs initially seemed like he would be the executive authority behind Majlesi's fundamentalist policies, Sultan Hossein eventually withdrew into a life of heavy drinking and harem sex, turning all effective control over to his aunt and her circle.[149] He was so interested in sex that he had the entire Safavid Empire scoured for women of all ethnicities (except Jews) to fill his harem.[150] While the royal wine cellar may have been re-stocked, for the rest of the country this meant more effective power in the hands of Majlesi and his *Usuli* circle of conservative clerics — from whom the contemporary term *usul-garâ* derives.[151] Majlesi died in 1699, but he would leave a legacy that would continue to impact the Islamic Republic of Iran to this day.[152]

The eventual displacement of overland trade routes by European colonial sea-based and ocean-going trade by the eighteenth century was a disaster for the Safavid economy.[153] The collapse of the Safavid economy due to the change in European trade routes was one of the factors that facilitated the rebellion of Afghan nomads and their brief occupation of large parts of Iran, including the former Safavid capital of Isfahan, from 1722 to 1730.[154] Whereas the Safavids were defeated by Afghan nomads, their Ottoman rivals lasted until they were taken down by a modern mechanized European military in World War I.[155] It is the rebellion by predominately Sunni Afghans that caused many of the leading Shi'ite clergy to flee to the holiest cities of Shi'ism in Ottoman Iraq, rather than to remain in Iran.[156] This was even more ruinous to the development of an Iranian national state, since these Ayatollahs continued to rule Iran on a social and religious level from outside of the borders of the country and beyond the authority of the crown. Such became the situation during the Qajar period and beyond, up to the time when Ayatollah Khomeini founded the Islamic Republic of Iran and re-centralized Shi'ite authority in Qom. Until then, the clerics of Qom were subservient to those of Najaf and Karbala — inside enemy territory. The Shah was, moreover, a hostage of these second-rate clergymen. One effect of the increasingly orthodox institutionalization of Shi'ism under the later Safavids was a revolt of Sunnis in the most peripheral parts of Safavid Iran, such as in Shirvan, Baluchistan, Herat and Kandahar.[157] The Sunni Afghans were particularly resistant.

The Sunni Afghan Mir Veis of the Ghilazi tribe went on a *hajj* to Mecca, with the Safavid Shah's approval, where he secured a Sunni *fatwa* legitimizing, not only an Afghan revolt but an attempt to overthrow the Shi'ite Safavids.[158] The Safavids had a Georgian governor running Kandahar.[159] The revolt began with this Georgian governor being murdered by Mir Veis in 1709. Mir Veis himself died in 1715, but his son Mahmud took up the mission that had been given the blessings of Mecca by leading the Afghan rebels into central Iran in 1719.[160] By 1721, he had recruited Baluchis and other secessionists into his tribal army.[161]

The Afghan army laid siege to the Safavid capital of Isfahan in 1722.[162] The Afghan assault on Isfahan began on March 8, and involved an eight-month long blockade of the city from March to October of 1722.[163] The conditions in Isfahan during the months-long Afghan blockade were absolutely appalling. As starvation set in people turned to boiling shoe leather to eat.[164] Once this became untenable they turned to devouring the corpses that lined the city's streets, secretly cutting the thighs off of them before they rotted.[165] Half-starved children were also abducted and cannibalized before they died of the famine.[166]

The population of Isfahan was reduced to one-tenth of what it had been during its zenith as the capital of Safavid Iran.[167] A city that had been comparable to London, the seat of the rising British Empire of the time, was reduced to a ghost town largely inhabited by owls and other wild animals.[168] Iran's international trade collapsed to one-fifth of what it had been under Shah Abbas.[169] On October 23, Sultan Hossein finally emerged from the city's gates in tears and surrendered in person to the Afghan Mahmud Ghilazi.[170] Mahmud the Afghan let him ride off to his pleasure gardens at Farahabad on a borrowed horse.[171] Sultan Hossein only returned from his "retirement" in 1725 to plead with Mahmud to stop slaughtering the entire Safavid royal family.[172] Mahmud had butchered nearly all of them by his own hand inside Chehel Sotun palace before the former Shah intervened.[173]

Meanwhile, the Ottomans moved on the Western frontier in a war against the Shi'ite "heretics" of Iran.[174] The Turks occupied Tabriz, Kermanshah, and Hamadan, annexing them to the Ottoman Empire.[175] Peter the Great was not willing to see his Ottoman enemy make gains in Iran without keeping pace, so he sent Russian forces to seize the Caspian coast of northern Iran.[176] The Russians eventually withdrew on account of the intolerably humid climate of Gilan, where many of their troops had succumbed to disease.[177]

The occupying Sunni Pashtun Afghans severely persecuted the Shi'ite Persians.[178] Mahmud's successor, Ashraf the Afghan, went so far as to issue an edict that Persians—despite being the majority of Iran's population—should be treated as if they were at the bottom of a hierarchy of persecuted and marginalized groups, such as Armenian Christians and Jews.[179] Despite having initially promised to protect the abdicated Sultan Hossein, Ashraf eventually beheaded the last Safavid ruler when he learned of an Ottoman plot to restore him to the throne in what they hoped would be the founding of a Safavid client state much smaller than the former Safavid Empire that had been their rival.[180] One of Shah Sultan Hossein's children, Tahmasp II, managed to survive while constantly fleeing the Afghans and other potential enemies. He would be used as a pawn by an ambitious military officer who would rival Shah Ismail in the extent of his superhuman will to reestablish Iran as a world power during the Islamic period.

Nader Gholi Beg of the Turkic Afshar tribe was a *Qezelbâsh*.[181] Nader was tall, handsome, and had a very loud voice.[182] He was renowned for being inseparable from his horses and for his eagle-like grace when performing feats of archery on horseback.[183] In the 1720s, this young warrior formed a tribal coalition that managed to seize control of Khorasan and its capital of Mashad.[184] Nader initially came to power by promising to bring the Safavids back to power and to serve Tahmasp II, the son of Shah Sultan Hossein, who gave Nader the name Tahmasp Qoli Khan or "the Lord who is a slave of Tahmasp."[185] He would not remain a "slave" for long.

Nader tirelessly trained his military forces in complex maneuvers, to the point where observers of the time noted that he could command them on the battlefield as if they were almost extensions of his own mind.[186] He expelled the Afghans from Isfahan in 1729.[187] After this success, Nader's first major move toward the seizure of power was to force Tahmasp to give him the right to directly collect taxes that would be used for developing his military.[188] In this way Nader was able to establish a militaristic state within the state.[189] The last straw came when, during a campaign in Herat, Nader learned that Tahmasp II had marched against the Ottomans on his own authority and been so badly defeated by them that he signed a peace treaty full of concessions on the Western front.[190] Nader issued a manifesto nullifying the treaty and marched back toward the capital, stating to everyone along the way his intention to seize sovereign power and enjoining them to back him.[191] Nader Afshar crowned himself Shah of Iran in 1736.[192]

Nader Shah's forces took the Mughal (i.e. Neo-Timurid) capital of Delhi in 1739.[193] The booty that he seized from India included the Peacock Throne and the Kuh-e Noor, the world's largest diamond.[194] The Central Asian territories of Iran, including the jewels of Samarkand and Bukhara, which remain Persian-speaking cities to this day, were recaptured by Nader from the Uzbek Turks and their Neo-Mongol Khanate in 1740.[195] Persian was the administrative language and literary tongue of high culture in the entire geographical expanse from the Mughal court of Delhi in India to the Ottoman court in Istanbul.[196] During the Safavid period, when the Ottoman court used Persian as its administrative language, so much more Persian poetry was written in India than in Iran that the Persian literary production of the epoch is referred to as work in "the Indian style" (*sabké Hendi*).[197] Many Persian poets were lured by the wealth of the Mughal court, where they knew they would receive more generous patronage than among the Safavids.[198] Persian was the lingua franca of a vast geographical expanse from the Ottoman court in Istanbul to the Mughal court in Delhi and the Tajiks of Samarkand.[199]

This meant that, despite his own ethnic Turkic origin, Nader's conquests could potentially have had a Persian cultural-linguistic backbone that would have allowed him to forge an Iranian superpower capable of speaking for Islam on Earth.[200] In the 1740s he seemed well on his way to becoming the Peter the Great of Iran, with military modernization spearheading a modernization of the country as a whole during the course of building a vast colonial world empire.[201]

Nader Shah disestablished Shi'ism, a move that was in large part motivated by the presence of large numbers of Sunnis in his army.[202] He did not seek to convert the Persian core of Iran out of Shi'ism, but in the Sunni periphery of his empire Nader Shah did misleadingly present himself as a converter of Iran to Sunni Islam — to the point that he had a serious chance of rivaling the Ottoman Empire for the legitimacy of leading the entire Islamic World.[203] Nader Shah was the first ruler in centuries to have established an Iranian Navy in the Persian Gulf, with a view to challenging the Portuguese and British colonialists who had been encroaching into the region during the Safavid period.[204] The construction of this Navy was also intended to secure Nader's control over India and expand the scope of his conquests there, which in theory could eventually have turned all of the Indian subcontinent into Iran's equivalent of Spain's territories in America.[205]

It is noteworthy in this regard that, especially after the severe drop in population that Iran suffered during the Afghan revolt, the proportion of Iran's population per the population of vast territories such as India that were under its imperial control is a ratio comparable to that of the domestic population of the major European colonial powers of the time as compared to the population of their colonies in the Americas, Africa, and Asia. The Iranian population of 1740 was around six million, but Nader had conquered Mughal India with a population of 150 million and was making headway in conquering an Ottoman Empire with a population of 30 million.[206] At the peak of his power, Nader's military force consisted of no fewer than 375,000 soldiers, which made it the largest military force on Earth in its own time.[207] Scaled to the world population of today, that would be an Iran with a larger military than China—a force many times the size of the American military at present, albeit some thirty-five years before the United States of America declared their independence from the British Empire.

Nader Shah saw himself as a second Tamerlane.[208] He compared himself to Timur in numerous addresses, repeatedly stressed his Turkic ancestry, and expressed admiration for his Timurid predecessors.[209] Nader even had Tamerlane's tombstone brought from Samarkand to his own mausoleum (it was broken before later being returned).[210] His brutal conduct upon his return from the Indian campaign certainly did fit the Timurid mold. For example, local tribal revolts broke out in response to the increasingly heavy taxation that was needed to raise funds for Nader's never-ending military campaigns.[211] Nader Shah responded to these revolts by building white towers with niches in them, which held the severed heads of hundreds of executed countrymen.[212] Mutilations became as common as executions, and those who witnessed Nader's increasing sadism noted that his acts of cruelty would not assuage his bloodlust but only drive him into an ever more uncontrollable frenzy of violence.[213] By the time he was assassinated, he was widely considered to be a madman.[214]

Upon his return from the subcontinent, already afflicted by malaria-induced delusions, Nader Shah was told that his son, Reza Qoli, was plotting to depose him.[215] Despite the young man's denials, Nader first stripped his son of his position as crown prince and then proceeded to have him blinded.[216] His guilt over this rash act proceeding from paranoia drove him into heavy drinking, which combined with his malaria to bring about a mental and physical breakdown.[217] In June of 1747 he was relieved of his command by officers who assassinated him while he was laying in a tent of his harem. As Nader raised his hand to stop them, they severed it while he was still gripping his sword, then they proceeded to decapitate him.[218] Nader was succeeded by his nephew, Ali Qoli, who renamed himself Adel Shah.[219] Far from being *âdel* or "just" as he claimed to be, Ali Qoli sent soldiers to Nader's stronghold in Khorasan, where they murdered all of Nader's other surviving heirs, and even cut developing fetuses out of the wombs of all those women Nader had impregnated.[220]

After Nader's assassination two of his officers would go on to become the rulers of large parts of what had been the Empire of Iran during the Safavid and Afsharid periods.[221] One of these was the Pashtun Ahmad Khan Abdali of the Durani tribe, who crowned himself Ahmad Shah Durani of the Afghans in what had been Eastern Iran.[222] The other was Karim Khan Zand, a Lor or Kurd from the Fars region, who had also been one of Nader's former generals.[223] Unlike his Afghan counterpart, Karim Khan never crowned himself Shah but preferred to be recognized as *vakil or-ra'ya* or "the People's Advocate."[224]

It is no wonder that Iran descended back into civil war and anarchy following the death of Nader Shah, since at that time as much as half of the country's population consisted of tribal nomads.[225] The Afshar, Zand, and Qajar tribes all vied for control of the country, each faced with the task of reunifying an Iran shattered by ethnic separatists and regional secessions.[226] This protracted Iranian Civil War defined the mid to the late eighteenth century, with a brief respite during the reign of Karim Khan Zand.[227] It ended only with the rise of Agha Mohammad Khan in the 1780s, a Qajar tribesman who had been castrated while being held as a prisoner of Adel Shah Afshar from 1747–1748.[228] Agha Mohammad Khan, the first Shah of the Qajar dynasty, succeeded in reunifying Iran only by being the most brutal and sadistic monarch in the entire history of the country.[229] How much of his sadism can be attributed to his never having been able to come to terms with the loss of his manhood remains a question for historians and psychologists to ponder. He was succeeded by his nephew, Fath Ali Shah Qajar.[230] The latter is notorious for having had a thousand wives or concubines, thereby producing hundreds of children.[231]

Fath Ali Shah's heirs, the Qajar monarchs of nineteenth-century Iran presided over a dramatic decline of Iran's national standing vis-à-vis the rising European colonial powers of the time. Both the Bukharan Khanate and Afghanistan became chess pieces in the nineteenth-century colonial Great Game between the Russians and the British, with the latter seeing what had been Iranian Central Asia as key to guarding their colonial project in India.[232] At the opening of the nineteenth century, the modernizing European-style military of Russia attacked the province of Georgia and seized it from Iran.[233] Qajar Iran retaliated in 1804. The first of the Russo-Persian Wars lasted until 1813, when the Qajars were forced into signing the Treaty of Golestan, wherein they ceded most of Iran's territory in the Caucasus to Russia in exchange for a Russian withdrawal from Tabriz.[234] When Iran attempted to regain these territories in 1826, a second round of the Russo-Persian Wars also ended in defeat and the transfer of the rest of Iran's remaining territories in the Caucasus, with the exception of the part of the south Caucasus that is still inside the Iranian province of Azerbaijan. The 1828 Treaty of Turkomanchay was so humiliating and devastating to Iranians that the nation of Iran would not attempt any offensive military campaign thereafter, even to this day.[235] Iran has not attacked another nation in 193 years.

9.3 The Babi Movement and Bahai Faith

Although Iran's military and economic decline seemed irreversible, a fascinating social phenomenon manifested during the reign of Fath Ali Shah's successor, Mohammad Shah Qajar, who was his grandson. It is this Qajar monarch who was faced with the advent of the Babi movement.[236] The roots of this movement, and of the Bahai Faith that ultimately arose from out of it, can be traced back to a Shi'ite theological school that resisted the fundamentalism of Majlesi and his *Usuli* clergy. This Shaykhi school also reached back to some of the radical forms of Shi'ism that, as we saw in Chapters 7 and 8, preserved ancient Iranian esotericism.

Ismaili esotericism, together with Illuminati Wisdom (*hekmaté eshraq*), was a major source for the thought of Shaykh Ahmad Ahsa'i (1756–1825).[237] Charismatic leadership played as significant a role in the Shaykhi school that took shape around his teachings, as it did in the various Sufi orders that had been suppressed by the Safavid state.[238] The Shaykhis explicitly elevated the personal insight of their spiritual leader over and above the legalism characteristic of the Usulis.[239] The decentralized and weak authority of the Qajar monarchs allowed charismatic spiritual movements such as this to fill the void, despite the hostility with which they were viewed by the Usuli clergy.[240]

One of the ideas that Ahsa'i adopted from the Illuminists was that of *barzakh* or an interzone between this world of sensuous phenomena and the realm of pure ideas.[241] According to Ahsa'i this is not just a place where the soul would be purified of all earthly stains after death and before being reunited with its celestial archetype, it is also a place that could be visited during earthly life — at least by adepts skilled in astral travel. From a Shi'ite theological perspective, this was particularly significant insofar as Ahsa'i and other Shi'ite thinkers influenced by Illuminati Wisdom believed that the Hidden Imam was dwelling in the *barzakh* — that this was the abode of his occultation (*gheybat*).[242] Consequently, someone able to travel to the *barzakh* while still alive would be capable of directly communicating with the Twelfth Imam, whereas the Shi'ite clergy depended on very indirect directives transmitted through a thousand years of scriptural and interpretive tradition.[243]

The Shaykhi community became the spiritual matrix for the revival of radical Shi'ite esotericism by Seyyed Ali Mohammad of Shiraz. He was born into a *bâzâri* or merchant class family in 1819 and became acquainted with the Shaykhi school of thought when he traveled to Karbala at the age of twenty, where he attended classes by Seyyed Kazem of Rasht — who was the successor to Shaykh Ahsa'i.[244] The Shaykhis of Karbala were so impressed with him that, even though he returned to Shiraz after only a year, Seyyed Ali Mohammad was chosen to be the successor to Seyyed Kazem when the latter died in 1844 without having designated a successor.[245] This, despite the fact that Seyyed Ali Mohammad had no formal legal training. The Shaykhis proclaimed him the *Bâb* or "gate" between the earthly realm and the occulted abode of the Hidden Imam.[246]

The year 1844 also marked a lunar millennium since the occultation of the Twelfth Imam. This may have been a factor in the Bâb's considerations when he ultimately proclaimed himself to be, not just the gate to the Hidden Imam, but the Mahdi himself.[247] As in the case of the Assassin Apocalypse at Alamut so many centuries earlier, this meant his claiming the right to abolish the *sharia*, and it also released Shi'ites from any need to follow the *Ulema*—Usuli or otherwise—who had, up until that time, been legitimately acting as the Imam's visible vice-regents.[248] Since the crown was, beginning from the Safavid period, predominately viewed as the Guardian (*Vali*) of the Shi'ite faith, the authority of the Shah and the monarchical regime of Iran would also be called into question.

As could have been expected, the Usuli clergy issued *fatwas* to the effect that the Bâb was a heretic—more than a heretic, actually an apostate—who should be put to death.[249] The Qajar authorities were slow to act on this "recommendation," but by 1848 the Ulema got their way and Bâb was tried for blasphemy in Tabriz.[250] It is in the course of this uproarious and widely publicized trial that the Bâb for the first time publicly declares that he considered himself to be the Mahdi or *Imâmé Zamân*.[251]

The Bâb taught that revelation did not end with the Quran but is continuously progressive, with the prophets of past and future revelations each meeting the needs of people in their respective period.[252] The two most important texts written by the Bâb are *Qayyum al-Asma* or "The Resurrection of Holy Names," which he wrote in scholastic Arabic, and the *Bayân*, which he composed in his native Persian.[253] Bâbis claim that, between these two scriptures, he received more than a million verses of revelation.[254] The concept of *Qiyâmat* was reinterpreted by Bâbis to indicate the period that had been ushered in by the Bâb's revelation, rather than a Resurrection of the dead at the end of time.[255]

Although he abrogated Islamic law, the Bâb did introduce certain rituals, rules, and regulations of his own, such as a nineteen-day fast period, prayers particular to his sect, a ban on smoking, and other laws set forth in his *Bayân*.[256] He allowed the charging of interest in business dealings.[257] The Bâb was not averse to occultism; he himself made special talismans and expected his followers to carry these around with them.[258] While Bâbis stopped making a ritual pilgrimage to Mecca, they replaced this with an expected pilgrimage to the house of the Bâb in Shiraz.[259]

Fatemeh Begum Baraghani (1814–1852), an Iranian woman known to Bâbis as *Tahereh* ("the Immaculate One") or as *Qurratol-'Ayn* ("Solace of the Eyes") and a disciple of Seyyed Kazem in Karbala (who had given her the latter of the two titles) became the leading advocate for Seyyed Ali Mohammad Shirazi during his apostasy trial.[260] At a meeting of Bâbis that took place in the village of Badasht during the summer of 1848, Solace of the Eyes removed her hijab in front of all of the men in the gathering.[261] Although this *kashfé hejâb* has since been interpreted in feminist terms, that is an anachronistic and inappropriately Westernized interpretation. Fatemeh Baraghani intended, by this act, to symbolically affirm the annulment of the *sharia* as a whole and thereby recognize Seyyed Shirazi's claim to being the Mahdi himself and not just the Bâb.[262]

Following the Badasht conference, and very much inspired by the Immaculate One, the Bâbis began to march en masse from Mashad to Azerbaijan, where they planned to free the Bâb.[263] However, they were intercepted by an angry mob that had been riled by the conservative clergy. After taking refuge in a local shrine dedicated to Shaykh Tabarsi during a seven-month-long siege, they were lured out by deceptive machinations and instead of a promise of safe passage they received martyrdom at the hands of the proto-*Basijis* and *Hezbollahis* who had surrounded the shrine for months just waiting to massacre them.[264]

Following this massacre, and fully in line with the Shi'ite roots of their worldview, the Bâbis initiated an armed uprising in the name of the martyrs.[265] This rebellion against both the clergy and the Qajar government endured for a year and a half, with especially intense fighting in Yazd, Zanjan, and Nayriz.[266] The end result was that, in July of 1850, the Qajar regime finally arrived at a decision to execute the Bâb by putting him in front of a firing squad in Tabriz.[267] Up to 2.5% of Iranians were Bâbis at this dramatic peak of the movement in 1850.[268] In 1852, the Bâbis retaliated for the massacre with an assassination attempt against Naser al-din Shah Qajar, which failed and only garnered them more severe persecution.[269] Fatemeh Baraghani and many other leaders of the movement were martyred, after which the Bâbis were forced to employ *taqiyya* or the Shi'ite practice of "dissimulation" in order to conceal their true beliefs so that they could continue their struggle as an underground movement.[270]

From out of no less than twenty-five Bâbis who came forward to try to fill the void left by the demise of their leader, two of these, who were half-brothers, secured the largest following as potential successors of Seyyed Shirazi. These were Mirza Yahya Nuri (1831–1912), also known as *Subh-e Azal* or "Morning of Eternity" by his followers, and Mirza Hossein Ali Nuri (1817–1892), who would come to be known as *Bahâ'ullah* or the "Glory of God" — founder of the *Bahâi* faith.[271] The followers of Bahaullah forced Subh-i Azal into exile in Cyprus in 1868.[272] Christian missionaries in Iran during the years of the rise of the Bahai faith perceived it as a much more powerful evangelical firestorm than their own efforts, and they projected that it would eventually supplant Islam as the official religion of Iran.[273]

The renowned patriotic Prime Minister Amir Kabir offered Mirza Hossein Ali a position in the Qajar government in an unsuccessful attempt to appease and co-opt him.[274] One wonders how progressive Qajar Iran could have become with him playing a major role, together with Amir Kabir, in determining reformist policies of a state that was at that time considering modernizing in the style of Peter the Great. In his *Ketâbé Aqdas*, Bahaullah forwards a number of progressive social policies with respect to women, such as the idea that girls and women ought to be afforded an education equivalent to that of their male counterparts, and monogamous marriage rather than polygamy.[275] His treatment of inheritance law does still favor men and broadly reaffirm patriarchy. Nevertheless, Bahaullah believed that women could be future prophets, and that anyone who did not recognize such women as God's appointed bringers of revelation simply because of their sex would be committing apostasy.[276] When he refused to work with the Qajar state, Iran's government banished Bahaullah to Iraq. Later, it was believed that too many Shi'ites in southern Iraq would be potential converts for his cause, so he was forced to relocate from there to the Palestinian port city of Acre that has become today's city of Haifa in Israel.[277]

Bahaullah claimed that Zarathustra was the first prophet in the same line of "revelation" as Abraham, Moses, Jesus, Mohammad and, following the prophet of Islam, the Bâb.[278] In other words, according to Bahais, the Abrahamic revelation has two Iranian book ends, Zarathustra and Bâb, and then continues indefinitely on into the future, including Bahaullah himself. This further eroded — in fact, it actually abolished — the apocalyptic conception of history that Shi'ites had inherited from the Pre-Islamic Iranian worldview — not just of Zoroastrianism, but also of Mithraism and Manichaeism.[279] Instead of conceiving of a catastrophic end to world history, wherein a final fulfillment of revelation or an ultimate disclosure of the divine reality would take place, Bahaullah and his Bahai followers believe in progressive evolution tending toward world peace.[280] Part of this vision of world peace is the establishment of One World Religion and One World Government.[281]

Unlike the Babis who — akin to the Mazdakites, Khorramis, and Assassins before them — believed in accomplishing their goals through political violence — the Bahai adopted an essentially pacifistic attitude of non-involvement in direct political struggle.[282] Bahaullah enjoined his followers to be dutiful subjects and exemplary citizens of whatever political state they found themselves born and raised into, while working on that basis for greater spiritual and political unity on the Earth.[283] Yet, despite this explicit disavowal of rebellion and "render-unto-Caesar" attitude that Bahai citizens were supposed to have toward their existing nation-states, Bahaullah nonetheless developed and attempted to implement a vision of global governance. He wrote letters to the Shah of his own Iranian fatherland, the Ottoman Sultan whose territory he was settled in, the Tsar of Russia, the Queen of Great Britain, and other world leaders, proposing a league of united nations that would ultimately usher in world peace through global governance.[284] His son and successor, Abdu'l-Baha (1844–1921) further elaborated and more explicitly articulated this vision of a "union of nations" in his 1875 book *The Secret of Divine Civilization*, which was addressed to the Shah of Iran.[285] This shows that, as late as the decline of Qajar Iran, at a time when Iran was suffering huge territorial losses to an expansionist Russian Tsar, the leading Iranian spiritual figure of the epoch still saw Iran as the nation that could, and should, play the key role in forming a planetary regime that would be God's government.

Bahaullah's proposal, as developed by Abdu'l-Baha, was the first version of what eventually became the League of Nations, which, after it failed to prevent World War II, was transformed into today's United Nations.[286] As in ancient times with the Achaemenid Empire, Iran was once more the forerunner of the modern idea of world government. The Bahai faith was also yet another expression of the originally Iranian vision of one world religion, which as we saw in Chapter 6, was an explicit aim of the prophet Mani. Bahaullah explicitly saw his message as aimed at people of all races in "the international community."[287] At a time when the Bahai faith was substantially expanding its proselytizing in India, his great-grandson Shoghi Effendi went so far as to claim that Bahaullah had been an incarnation of the Hindu god Krishna.[288] Today there are Bahai communities on every continent except Antarctica, and Bahais remain the largest religious minority inside Iran. This, despite facing severe persecution by the Islamic Republic.

In 1979 the house of the Bâb in Shiraz was destroyed by the Islamic Revolutionary Guard Corps and Bahai cemeteries were dug up and desecrated around the country.[289] Following the demolition of the house of the Bâb in Shiraz, the main pilgrimage site and *qibla* of the Bahai faith has become the Shrine of Bahaullah in Israel.[290] Local Israelis call the magnificent gardens at this shrine, as well as those at the majestic Shrine of the Bâb in Haifa, *ha-ganim persan* or the "Persian gardens."[291]

The Islamic Republic of Iran seized all of the considerable assets of the community, but this was the least of their troubles. Within the first few years of the Islamic Republic hundreds of the most prominent Bahais in Iran were executed by the new regime, including two rounds of the entire leadership of the Bahai National Spiritual Assembly of Iran.[292] Even today, there is no compensation for relatives of Bahais who are executed by the regime, usually on charges such as attempting to convert Muslims to their cause.[293] Bahais are denied public funeral ceremonies.[294] The most significant reason for this is the Bahai belief that prophecy and divine revelation can continue after Muhammad, who is considered by all Muslims to be the Seal of the Prophets who brought the final revelation in the form of the Quran.[295] Other causes for this persecution have been suspicions that Bahais are agents of Zionism, Freemasonry, or an Illuminati plot to establish a New World Order.[296]

One interesting difference between Bahaullah's vision for world government and what eventually took shape in the West is that the Iranian prophet conceived of his League of Nations as a union of monarchs, with a kind of King of Kings who would be the "Shadow of God on Earth" leading it.[297] This is indeed very close to the Achaemenid vision of realizing a *Khashatra Vairya* or "Desirable Dominion" that would bring earthly affairs in line with *Arta* under the King of Kings. It is worth noting that, unlike the subsequent United Nations, the original League of Nations was not that far away from this ideal, since some of its core constituting members were monarchical colonial powers controlling vast regions of the Earth. What it did lack, however, was a single charismatic world monarch leading a council of kings.

The internationalism — or, rather, *cosmopolitanism* — of the Bahais does not stop them from having a special reverence for Iran as "the Cradle of the Cause of God" (*mahdé amrullah*).[298] Bahais have incorporated many Iranian cultural elements into their universalist religion. These include: the Iranian New Year holiday of Nowruz celebrated not just as a holy day but as the universal New Year, the consideration of Persian as a sacred language, a proclivity for Persian music and cuisine at Bahai gatherings worldwide, and the adoption of Iranian etiquette and politesse (*ta'arof*).[299]

We need not endorse the Bahai faith today to admit that in its own time it represented not just the most advanced religious vision in Iran but one of the most visionary spiritual movements on Earth. If it could have secured the backing of a strong Iranian regime, perhaps the Bahai Faith would have at least supplanted Islam by now in all of the lands that were part of Nader's empire. Unfortunately, the Bahai Faith came too late to spread through the vast expanse of the Afsharid Empire.

Nader Shah tried, and failed, to turn Shi'ism into a fifth orthodox Sunni school of law.[300] If, instead of attempting to disestablish Shi'ism, Nader Shah had reaffirmed the Shi'ite character of Safavid Iran and used the social cohesion that would have provided the country to build a stable empire until the Babi revolution could take place in the context of a Shi'ite Iranian superpower controlling the entire core of the Islamic world, then Iran would probably be a more powerful nation than India today. After all, the Shaykhi school of Shi'ite theology that set the stage for radical Babi thought was already being developed in the eighteenth century as a rival of late Safavid clerical orthodoxy.[301]

As we have seen, the Afshar and Qajar tribes, who were both part of the *Qezelbâsh* confederation led by Ismail, each went on to successively rule Iran after the fall of the Safavids.[302] When the Afsharid and Qajar dynasties are taken together as successors of the Safavids, it becomes apparent that the esoteric *Qezelbâsh* cult was modern Iran's occulted backbone for 424 years, from the founding of a modern Iranian nation-state by Shah Ismail Safavid in 1501 until Reza Khan deposed the last Qajar monarch in 1925.

It would be mistaken to think that Shah Ismail is "too medieval" to be compared with modern political and military leaders. There *certainly* were comparable leaders in the twentieth century, but they are the likes of Adolf Hitler and Mao Zedong. Not even Mussolini or Stalin qualify, because Mussolini was nowhere near brutal enough and Stalin was an iron-willed maintainer, not a conquering founder, of the Soviet Empire. Scaled to the sociopolitical context of the twentieth century, Ismail's tyrannical ruthlessness matches that of Hitler, and only Mao's conquests to re-unify China were as impressive in their scope and defiance of the odds as Ismail's re-constitution of an Iranian nation-state after a hiatus of centuries. The policies of the Nazi Germans and Maoist Chinese are also the only adequate points of comparison for what a radical cultural revolution was forced upon Iranian society by Shah Ismail and his Safavid Shi'ite cult. The bottom line is that from 1500 to the present, Shi'ism has been inseparable from Iranian *national* identity conceived of in a political and juridical sense—so much so that, for a majority of Iranians, the latter is *still inseparable from the former* and, at least until 1989, the former was considered *more important than the latter.*[303]

CHAPTER 10

THE LEVIATHAN OF IRAN

THE FIRST SECTION OF THIS chapter covers the Persian Constitutional Revolution of 1906–1911, which established a modern parliamentary regime in Iran. This was already deep into the period of British and Russian colonial aggression in the face of the decadent Qajar dynasty, long after the fall of Nader Shah and the destruction of the Safavid imperial establishment. Had these reforms taken place around 1750 rather than around the year 1900, Iran would have entered the industrial epoch as a major geopolitical player. At a minimum Iran would be on the level of the BRIC nations right now, and within this context would be more closely comparable to Russia than to India or Brazil.

Despite the disastrously missed opportunity for social and political modernization at the height of Persian imperial expanse in the Islamic period, and leaving aside the harsh reality of racial decline, Qajar rule was not entirely lacking in cultural development. One constructive project of the period was the systematization of Persian Classical Music. The system of the *radif* with its various *dastgahs* and *gushehs* represents an auditory monument to the moods and modalities of the Persian spirit itself. If music is the soul of a nation, this Qajar contribution is certainly noteworthy and even on a par with the Safavid perfection of Persian art and architecture. Still, the Iranian Resurgence only really resumes with the rise of the Pahlavi Dynasty.

The second section of this chapter considers the legacy of Pahlavism. Reza Khan, a military officer from Mazandaran, led a coup against the Qajar dynasty in 1924. In 1935 he requested that foreign countries stop referring to his country as "Persia" rather than by its native name, Iran. Based on an authoritarian nationalist ideology, Reza Shah Pahlavi centralized the power structure of Iran and rapidly industrialized the country. He also promoted a return to the pre-Islamic ideals of Iran's ancient civilization. This was one reason for his lean toward the Axis Powers, especially Germany, which had recognized Iran as a fellow Aryan nation. Iran featured prominently in World-War-II-era German plans for creating an Eastern Aryan sphere that would have an India "liberated" from the British. Reza Shah's lean toward Hitler cost him when the Allied Powers invaded Iran, exiled him to South Africa, and held the Tehran Conference in 1943. Ultimately, his son, Mohammad Reza Shah Pahlavi, was allowed to become his father's successor. His first dramatic act, in 1946, was the expulsion of Soviet troops from Iranian Azerbaijan and the crushing of the Soviet-backed Mahabad Kurdish secession attempt.

In 1963, the Shah initiated an aggressive economic reform and social welfare program called "The White Revolution" (*Enghelâbé Sepid*). By the time he hosted the world's heads of state in the most spectacular party of all time, celebrating the 2,500th anniversary of the Persian Empire in 1971 at the ruins of Persepolis and the tomb of Cyrus the Great in Pasargadae, the White Revolution had given Iran the fastest economic growth rate of any nation. This emboldened the Shah, as the leader of OPEC, to drastically increase the price of oil in 1974, scaling it to the inflation rate in Western countries. When confronted about this policy he insisted that he was doing the West a favor by helping to wean Westerners off their dependency on petroleum, which would run out before long and should be saved for derivative industrial uses (such as petrochemical agriculture, plastics, pharmaceuticals, etc.). He promoted the switch over to nuclear energy, vowing to match France and Japan with an Iranian energy sector mostly based on nuclear power by the year 2000. The Shah also built up the fifth most powerful military force on Earth, and there were concerns that his atomic energy program would be used to produce nuclear weapons. This self-styled "King of Kings and Light of the Aryans" envisioned a culmination of Iran's resurgence in terms of a "Great Civilization" (*Tamadoné Bozorg*) reemerging at the crossroads of the Earth and rivaling the American-led West for world leadership.

Like the Constitutional Revolution, this project ended in a catastrophic failure. Pahlavi Iran did not follow the developmental trajectory of Japan, let alone that of Russia or China. Instead, the White Revolution and the Great Civilization project were rejected by the vast majority of Iranians, who overthrew the entire Pahlavi regime in the Islamic Revolution of 1979. Mohammad Reza Shah was driven into exile like his father before him and, as in the case of Reza Shah, most of his major contributions to Iran's development were nullified.

The third and final section of this chapter engages in a Mithraic monarchist critique of the confused policies and equivocating ideology of the Pahlavi regime. It begins with the suggestion that, instead of abandoning his commitment to the traditional Iranian monarchical tradition, Mohammad Reza Shah, who had after all styled himself *Shâhanshâh Âryâ-Mehr*, meaning "King of Kings and Light of the Aryans" or "Emperor and Friend of Mithra," could have appealed to arguments as cogent and convincing as those that Thomas Hobbes deploys in favor of Absolute Monarchy in his *Leviathan*. Then the concept of "the divine right of kings" that Hobbes appears to be defending in *Leviathan* is traced back to the introduction of Mithraism into the West under Iranian influence.

Once it has been made clear that the kind of sacred monarchy that became institutionalized in the West beginning with Rome is really Iranian in origin, the section will conclude with a critique of Hobbes on the basis of this original Iranian tradition. Particular emphasis will be placed on the cynical and at least tacitly materialistic attitude that the Leviathan of Hobbes takes toward occult ideas, such as the aura of divine royal glory (*Xvarneh*, *Farr*), which are at the foundation of sacred kingship. This magical conception of the miraculous nature of sovereign power, which enters the history of civilizations with the rise of Mithraism, is fundamentally at odds with "the rule of law." Consequently, the kind of constitutional monarchy proposed in Iran beginning with the Persian Constitutional Revolution of 1906 is even more confused than Hobbes would have argued it to be from the perspective of his defense of Absolute Monarchy in *Leviathan*.

10.1 The Persian Constitutional Revolution

In the late nineteenth century, with Iran plunging headlong into a catastrophic implosion, a Persian newspaper simply titled *Qanun* or "Law," published in London by the exiled Qajar court minister Malkam Khan, became one of the most prominent platforms for the constitutionalist advocacy in favor of "the rule of law" (*qânoun-madâri*).[1] The following is typical of the kinds of editorials that were published in *Qanun*, which was widely disseminated in Tabriz, Tehran, and other major cities beginning in 1889:

> Iran is full of divine gifts. What has left all of these gifts unused is the absence of law. No one in Iran owns anything, because there is no law.
>
> We appoint rulers without law. We remove officers without law. We sell what rightfully belongs to the government, without law. We imprison God's subjects without law. We tear open bellies without law.
>
> … There is no one who knows what amounts to an offense and what constitutes a service. What law did they use to exile such and such a *mojtahded*? What law did they use to stop such and such an officer's salary?
>
> What law was the basis of the removal of such and such a minister?
>
> What law was the basis of the title that was given to such and such an idiot?
>
> *There is not a single governor or prince who can feel secure about his conditions of life as much as the foreign [i.e. European] ambassadors' slaves.*[2]

Other newspapers that later contributed to creating and sustaining the atmosphere of the Constitutional Revolution included *Ruh al-Qodos* (The Holy Spirit), *Mosavat* (Equality), *Nassimé Shomâl* (Breeze of the North), and *Suré Esrafil* (The Trumpet of Esrafil), all of which sometimes featured stories deemed heretical, obscene, and libelous by conservative critics.[3] *Suré Esrafil*, especially its satirical column, was the first public platform of Dehkhoda, who went on to become one of the most widely respected writers of twentieth-century Iran and the creator of what is still regarded as the most extensive Persian language dictionary.[4] His fresh style was so influential that the late Modern Persian of twentieth-century metropolitan Iran was deeply shaped by it. The editor of *Suré Esrafil* was executed by Mohammad Ali Shah after his June 1908 coup.[5]

The late nineteenth and early twentieth century was a time of social turmoil and political implosion in Iran. Mirza Reza Kermani shot and killed Naser al-Din Shah near the shrine of Shah Abdol'azim in Tehran, as he prepared to celebrate the fiftieth anniversary of his rule in May of 1896.[6] It was suspected that he was taking vengeance on the crown for the state's treatment of his mentor, Seyyed Jamal al-Din Afghani, although Kermani himself had also been jailed and tortured by the Qajar regime.[7] The first few years of the twentieth century saw a spate of anti-Bahai pogroms or *Bâbi-koshis* carried out by the Qajar government at the behest of the Shi'ite clergy, especially in cities such as Isfahan and Yazd.[8] By 1903, this cleansed the Qajar regime of all Babi and Bahai sympathizers. Local lords in Khuzestan and Qashqai and Bakhtiari territories were refusing to pay taxes to the central government, whose mounted troops were scared away after suffering only a few casualties at the hands of armed tribesmen.[9] The worst kind of nomadic tribal savagery prevailed in a vast area from the Turkmen of the northeast to the Lors of the southwest, including looting, routine highway robbery, mass rape, and even a slave trade based on kidnappings.[10] Meanwhile, there was widespread corruption and increasingly arbitrary rule on the part of the royals — with especially hedonistic and sadistic behavior on the part of the many princes born from out of the vast Qajar harem.[11]

Mirza Fath'ali Akhundzadeh (d. 1878), who despite his name (*akhound* means clergyman) was a radically secular writer on religious, social, and literary matters, and an early advocate for the Westernization of Modern Iran.[12] Mirza Aqa Khan Kermani and Sheikh Ahmadi Ruhi were two prominent disciples of his that went on to directly participate in the Constitutional Revolution.[13] They had been part of the Babi movement, but later re-defined themselves as free thinkers.[14] Sometimes these ideas were also expressed in the context of novels, such as *The Travelogue of Ebrahim Beg* by Zeinol'abedin Maraghehi or the various novels of Abdorrahim

Talebof Tabrizi.[15] We see revolutionary constitutionalism fused with patriotism — or even an early form of modern Iranian nationalism — in the writings of all of these late nineteenth-century and early twentieth-century Iranian intellectuals. Critics of the constitutionalist movement responded to the effect that so-called *estebdâd* or putatively oppressive and allegedly arbitrary rule was really equivalent to stability, whereas the revolutionaries were inviting *fetneh*, *âshub*, and *enqelâbât* — in other words, lawless chaos by so many names, rather than their beloved "rule of law."[16]

The Russian Revolution of 1905 was a major catalyst for the rise of constitutionalist discourse in Iran. The decision of the Czar to accept a constitutional limitation of his powers inspired an Iranian proposal for what was called *hokoumaté mashrouteh*.[17] This roughly translates as "constitutional government," and indeed, at times, it was alternatively referred to as *qonstitusiyun*.[18] The Japanese victory in the Russo-Japanese War was taken as evidence of the superiority of a constitutionalist regime to an absolute monarchy, such as that of Russia just before its Constitutional Revolution.[19] Just as the Russian Revolution of 1905 had been catalyzed by national humiliation in the face of this defeat, the Persian Constitutional Revolution of 1906 was also catalyzed by the humiliating state of affairs in Iran, including the loss of vast stretches of Iranian territory to the Russians only a few decades earlier. A number of the main contributors to the Constitutional Revolution were from Iran's former territories in the Caucasus, which were now under Russian rule. These Iranians, such as Taqizadeh, Dawlat-Abadi, and Mosavat, relocated from the former provinces of Georgia, Armenia, and the northern part of Azerbaijan to Tabriz in the still-Iranian southern part of Azerbaijan.[20] They brought with them direct knowledge of how to organize a revolutionary program like the one that had just achieved a result in Russia.

In 1905 mosques began to become the scenes of political protest on the part of dissident sermonizers, such as Seyyed Mohammad Tabataba'i, Seyyed Abdollah Behbahani, and especially Seyyed Jamal al-Din Isfahani.[21] In 1906, Seyyed Jamal al-Din Isfahani preached: "People! Nothing would develop your country other than subjection to law, observation of law, preservation of law, respect for law, implementation of the law, and again law, and once again law."[22] He went on to argue that both religion and the crown ought to emphasize the rule of law, which law he takes to be the sovereign authority — rather than any particular monarch, whose power is limited by that of an independent legislature and judiciary:

> Children must from childhood read and learn at schools that no sin in religion and the *shari'a* is worse than opposing the law. … Observing religion means law, religion means law, Islam, the Koran, mean God's law. My dear man, *qanun, qanun*. Children must understand, women must understand, that the ruler is law and law alone, and no one's rule is valid but that of the law. The parliament is the protector of law. … The legislative assembly and legislature is the assembly which makes law, the sultan is the head of the executive which implements the law. The soldier is defender of the law, the police is defender of the law, justice means law, riches means implementing the law, the independence of the monarchy means rules of the law. In a word, the development of the country, the foundation of every nationality, and the solidarity of every nation arises from the implementation of the law.[23]

One interesting characteristic of the Persian Constitutional Revolution is that it was not a classist revolution. As many people among the aristocracy, such as Mokhber al-Saltaneh and Vosuq al-Dawleh — and even within the royal regime itself, such as Farmanfarma, Ehtesham al-Saltaneh, and Abolhasan Mirza — supported the constitutionalist program, as those within the peasantry opposed it and backed advocates of the persistence of absolute rule. The Shi'ite clergy was likewise internally divided between conservatives and progressives.[24] Hajj Mirza Hosein Tehrani, Akhund Mullah Kazen Khorasani, and Sheikh Abdollah Mazandarani, whose power in the clerical establishment was even greater than that of cardinal archbishops in the West, were among the staunchest supporters of the revolution and, consequently, were able to secure a significant place for the Shi'ite state religion within the framework of the new constitution that was written in August of 1906 and signed in December of that year.[25] Of this situation, the British diplomat Walter Smart observed that "in Persia religion has, by force of circumstances, perhaps, found itself on the side of Liberty, and it has not been found wanting."[26]

Despite this classless character of the Constitutional Revolution, the first *Majles* or parliament of Iran represented six distinct classes of citizens: the clergy (*Ulema*), royals (*Shazdehs*), the aristocracy (*a'yan*), magnate-level merchants, ordinary traders or shopkeepers, and finally, artisans.[27] As in the West at that time, neither women nor peasants were represented nor did they have the right to vote for representatives.[28] Not incidentally, the Qajar aristocrat Mohammad Mossadegh, who would later become the most infamous Prime Minister of Pahlavi Iran, was elected to the first parliamentary assembly, but his entry was barred on account of his not meeting the new constitution's minimum age requirement for representatives.[29]

Mohammad Ali Shah Qajar aimed to retain as much executive power as possible, and he looked for every opportunity to reverse the revolution.[30] The reactionary party relied upon a popular support base of religious fundamentalists, ruffians who marched through the streets chanting: "We follow the Koran, we do not want *mashruteh*; we want the Prophet's faith, we do not want *mashruteh*."[31] Artillery Square was filled with tents pitched by this mob when the Shah threatened to kill Prime Minister Naser al-Molk (the first Oxford-educated Iranian), dismissed and arrested his cabinet, then proceeded to subject the parliament building, with representatives protesting inside, to an artillery bombardment led by the Russian officered Cossack Brigade.[32] This coup of June 1908 included the arrest and execution of numerous intellectual advocates for, and political leaders of, the Constitutional Revolution.[33]

The crackdown ultimately met with a massive uprising in Tabriz, led by the populist Sattar Khan, who was able to rally the people of Gilan, Isfahan, and Fars to the constitutionalist cause.[34] In July of 1909, this combined force, which notably included Mohammad-Vali Khan Tonokaboni, Fathollah Khan Akbar of Gilan, and Yephrem Khan of Gilan on the Caspian coast, and numerous militiamen from the Caucasus, as far north as Baku, marched against the Shah in Tehran.[35] The revolutionary forces, which were about 10,000 men strong, quickly seized control of the capital. Mohammad Ali Shah Qajar took refuge in the Russian embassy compound and was given safe passage across the Caspian Sea to exile in Russia.[36] The victorious constitutionalists executed Sheikh Fazlollah Nuri, whose public sermons had characterized the constitutionalists as "free thinkers, Babis, nihilists, anarchists and socialists ... advocates of licentious and irreligious agendas."[37] He had openly endorsed Mohammad Ali Shah's military assault on the parliament.[38]

The internal division of Iran between constitutionalists and their conservative opponents allowed the already declining country to be divided into two colonial spheres of influence, with the Russians in the north and the British in the south. Such was the situation of Iran during World War I, despite the official neutrality of the Qajar regime. The Ottoman Empire, which was an enemy of Czarist Russia during the Great War, made incursions into the Russian-occupied part of Iran, and found Iranians powerless to protect their territory from the Turks.[39] Unlike the Turks, who were already modernizing and waging a World War with major European colonial powers, Iran was everybody's bitch. The Ottomans even became patrons of the pathetic constitutionalists, who were grateful to the Turks for setting up a protectorate in Kermanshah, where they could experiment with parliamentary democracy on a small scale—albeit as traitors to their own country and proxies of a Caliphate that was waging war on the heart of Europe.[40] Meanwhile, in the south of the country, the British set up their South Persia Rifles to protect the oil fields that they had recently discovered and were beginning to develop. By 1918, they gained the upper hand against the Russians.[41] It was at this time that, under British domination of Iran, the worldwide influenza pandemic of 1918–1919 hit the country, and the British presided over the deaths of millions of Iranians from disease and famine.[42] This deplorable situation persisted from the end of World War I until the rise of Reza Khan in the 1920s. This bold and shrewd military officer would adopt the ancient name "Pahlavi" and found a dynasty that attempted an Iranian national resurgence.

10.2 Pahlavi Iran: Resurgence of the Great Civilization?

Reza Khan was born in the village of Elasht, which is at an altitude of 6,000 feet in the Savadkuh district of the Alborz Mountains region of northern Iran, in other words, in Greater Hyrcania.[43] It was not far from here that Hassan Sabbah, the Old Man of the Mountain, had set up his Assassin stronghold at Alamut.[44] Hyrcanian by paternal descent, Reza Shah was also a Caucasian by maternal descent. His mother, Nush-Afshin Khanom, hailed from a family that had lived in Yerevan before the Russians seized the northern Caucasus from Iran in the nineteenth century.[45] His father had died months after his birth, and the infant Reza almost froze to death while being carried by his widowed mother through the snowy mountain passes in the winter.[46] Reza Khan was very tall, publicly aloof and brusque, with a well-hidden but boisterous sense of humor, and a notorious temper that he used to terrify people into dutiful obedience.[47] He first distinguished himself by his competence in the field of machine gunnery, a technology that had just been introduced into Iran through the Russian-officered Cossack Brigade that he served in.[48]

The Cossack Brigade had its origins in a Russian offer to train a personal bodyguard for Naser ad-Din Shah, an offer that was extended to the Qajar monarch during his second trip to Europe and which the Shah gladly accepted.[49] As it turned out, the 10,000 man cavalry and infantry force was not just trained by the Russians but was also led exclusively by Russian officers.[50] Even its lower ranks were hardly filled by native Iranians. One wonders how this could ever have been considered a royal bodyguard rather than a foreign power's potential hostage-taking force surrounding the Iranian sovereign.

Reza Khan began his rise in the Cossack Brigade with no greater ambitions than helping to remove Russian officers sympathetic to the Bolshevik cause and replacing them with loyal Czarists.[51] In 1920, the idea of an Iranian actually commanding the only competent Iranian military force was still unthinkable. It is not as if Reza Khan had any vision of an Iranian Renaissance as he was rising up the ranks of the Cossack Brigade, or that he ever imagined that he would depose the Qajar dynasty when he took over command of the Brigade.[52]

Britain and Russia both wanted to keep the Iranian government as weak as possible without this weakening leading to a total collapse that would require a deeper commitment to securing their interests than either colonial power was willing to make.[53] In other words, they each saw the weak Iranian government as an institution that would be allowed to have only enough power to secure their interests.

Ahmad Shah Qajar's government had virtually no authority beyond the city limits of Tehran and a few other metropolitan areas.[54] The Turkmens in northeastern Iran, the Kurds in northwestern Iran, the Bakhtiari and Qashqai tribes of the south, the Arabs of Khuzestan in the southwest, and the Baluch in the southeast were all basically governing their own territories and conducting independent dealings with foreign powers.[55] Even Gilan, on the coast of the Caspian Sea, was in a state of secessionist revolt backed by Bolsheviks who already wanted to absorb northern Iran into the nascent Soviet Union.[56] Reza Khan commanded military forces operating against Soviet proxies in Gilan in the lead up to the February 1921 Soviet-Iranian treaty, under the terms of which the Russians withdrew their troops from Iranian territory.[57] Ahmad Shah Qajar was wined and dined in London until he gladly accepted handing his country over to *de facto* control by the British.[58]

The Iranian national military of the time consisted of 600 men based in Tehran, which by today's standards would be insufficient even as a municipal police force.[59] The only other notable military forces in Iran during the period of the rise of Reza Khan were also foreign forces. There were the South Persia Rifles, a 6,000 man force staffed by British officers, and a Swiss-officered Gendarmerie.[60] The British managed to consolidate control over all of the armed forces in Iran, including the formerly Russian Cossack Brigade, bringing the South Persia Rifles and the Gendarmerie under its command.[61]

Lord Curzon, who had been the British Viceroy in India from 1899 to 1905, designed a British imperial policy toward Iran that was based on the containment of Russia.[62] This was the idea that Iran should act as a buffer state defending British interests in India from further Russian expansion driven by Bolshevik ideology. Iran essentially became a plaything in the "Great Game" between European colonial powers, including Russia. The Anglo-Persian Treaty signed on August 19, 1919, whose most important element was British control over development of the recently discovered oil resources of "Persia," essentially placed large parts of Iran under quasi-colonial British rule.[63] Throughout his entire reign, Reza Shah would prove unable to gain national control of Iran's oil from the British Empire.[64] British "advisors" were in charge of all important military and financial decisions. The fact that, even today in Iran, the British are blamed for almost everything, is a legacy of this traumatic period of utter Iranian subservience to British interests.[65] Lord Curzon wished to ensure a stable Iran that would not be conquered by Russia after an eventual British withdrawal of military forces.[66]

The British Major General Sir Edmund Ironside and Colonel Smythe noticed that the Hamadan division of the Cossack Brigade was outperforming others, and they looked to its leader, Reza Khan, to take command of the Cossacks as a whole.[67] Ironside and Smythe both claimed responsibility for the *coup d'état* of February 1921 that brought Reza Khan to power as a military dictator.[68] Reza Khan had obtained their explicit permission to organize and carry out, first a coup within the Cossack Brigade, and then the seizure of Tehran by the Cossack Brigade under his command, provided that Reza Khan stopped short of officially deposing Ahmad Shah Qajar.[69] Reza Khan engaged in a great deal of political intrigue and manipulation.[70] In addition to dealing with the British, he also bribed his officers in the Cossack Brigade to earn their loyalty before carrying out this operation.[71]

From his establishment of martial law in Tehran in 1921 until 1924, bearing the title *Sardâré Sepâh* that was forcibly given to him by Ahmad Shah Qajar, who was still abroad in Europe, Reza Khan made a reputation for himself by crushing various regional secessionist movements and re-establishing the territorial integrity of Iran under the central government of Tehran.[72] First he moved against Mirza Kuchek Khan in Gilan and Mazandaran in November of 1921, then against the Kurds led by Ismail Aqa Simitqu from September through October of 1922. Then in 1923 he pacified the Qashqai and Bakhtiari brigands and highway robbers. His greatest challenge from the middle of 1923 through 1924 was the reintegration of Khuzestan, then still called Arabestan province, which had been turned into a semi-autonomous shaykhdom by the Arab Shaykh Khaz'al, who hoped to court British protection against the Tehran government in exchange for British control of the area's newly discovered oil resources. Reza Khan's military campaign against the secessionist Arabs ended in victory on November 28, 1924, following which Reza Khan crossed the border of Khuzestan with Iraq to make a pilgrimage to the Shi'ite holy cities of Najaf and Karbala, returning to Tehran thereafter on January 1, 1925.[73] In December of the same year, the Majles voted to depose the Qajar dynasty and recognize Reza Shah Pahlavi as the new monarch of Iran and as the founder of the Pahlavi dynasty.[74]

Reza Khan took his oath as the Shah of Iran before the parliament on December 15, 1925. His statement on that occasion is particularly noteworthy on account of the repeated references that he makes to the protection of Islam, especially in light of his just having returned from a pilgrimage to the Shi'ite holy cities in Iraq:

> As God is my witness, I swear on the Word of God and on all that is revered in the eyes of God that I will devote all my efforts to the preservation of the independence of Iran, and will preserve and defend the territorial integrity of the kingdom and the rights of the nation. I will guard the Fundamental Laws of the Constitution of Iran and reign in accordance with those laws. I shall strive for the propagation of the Ja'fari Ithna'ashari Faith, and recognizing that God Almighty is watching over all my actions, I shall hold no purpose but the welfare and greatness of the state and nation of Iran. I pray to God Most High for success in the service of the advancement of Iran, and I seek the aid of the righteous spirits of the saints of Islam.[75]

This Shi'ite Islamist discourse is even more evident in the speech that he gave at his ceremonial coronation in Golestan Palace on April 25, 1926:

> Firstly, my particular attention has always been and always will be directed to the preservation of the principles and foundations of religion, for in my opinion one of the most effective means of ensuring national unity and strengthening the spirit of community of the Iranians is the fortifying of the bases of religious faith.
>
> Secondly, I have under God Most High and with the support of the Immaculate Emams always preferred action to speech, and any position that I may have achieved in the task of reforming our country has only been the result of work and effort.[76]

To some extent, Reza Shah's deference to the Shi'ite clergy can be seen as a debt that he owed them for their support for him during his initial rise to power. In 1924, there had been wide-ranging discussions in the Iranian press concerning the establishment of a Republic in Iran, along the lines of Ataturk's transformation of the Ottoman Caliphate. Although Reza Khan was seen as the only viable candidate for the Presidency of such a Republic, the clergy was vehemently opposed to the Republican idea and so they rallied behind the idea that Reza Khan should be installed as the new Shah of Iran, with the monarchy remaining a protector of the Shi'ite state religion, which would be threatened with disestablishment under a secular republic.[77] During the height of this push for an Iranian Republic amongst intellectuals and journalists, Reza Khan issued the following statement regarding Islam's place in Iran on April 1, 1924:

> At the same time my own policy from the very first has always been confined to the preservation of the majesty of Islam and the independence of Iran, and the furthering of the interests of the nation and the people.
>
> … I have in mind … the maintenance of security and order and sound government. From the first day, I and every man in the armed forces has held before him the high ideal of the preservation of the splendor of Islam. We have always striven to ensure that Islam thrives and spreads, and that the status of our religious leaders is respected and honored. Recently I visited Qom and spoke with the divines of that holy city. We discussed the present

> situation, and in consequence we came to the decision to recommend to our fellow countrymen that they should cease all talk of a republic.[78]

In addition to his endorsement of Islam, Reza Shah was an ultra-conservative moralist who believed in the most paternalistic attitude of the state toward what the citizenry was exposed to that might corrupt the morals of young men and women.[79] Censorship laws were so extreme that it was prohibited to discuss or depict anything frivolous, trivial, sensational, or criminal in any medium, including newspapers, radio broadcasts, cinema, and literature.[80] It is on account of such policies that the intelligentsia of the time, including thinkers on the level of Sadegh Hedayat and Bozorg Alavi, who could really have spearheaded an Iranian Renaissance, became harsh critics of Reza Shah, who they saw as an uneducated brute.[81] Hedayat was so disgusted by Reza Shah that he effectively exiled himself from Iran in India and Paris. Reza Shah was even against a foreign free press, and he threatened to sever diplomatic relations with both Germany and France over unfavorable newspaper articles about him, apparently unable to grasp the concept that the governments of these countries had little control over what privately owned newspapers published.[82]

As compared to Kemal Ataturk, the Freemason who was capable of delivering erudite seven-day long speeches expounding novel and complex political theories, Reza Khan was an uneducated illiterate who only later taught himself to read and write.[83] He left Iran only twice before his forced abdication and exile in 1941, once to make the aforementioned pilgrimages to the Shi'ite holy cities of Iraq and once on a state visit to Turkey where he was hosted by Ataturk.[84] Unlike Ataturk, who broke with the Ottoman heritage, Reza Shah made the legacy of the Achaemenids, Parthians, and Sassanids the backbone of his program for national resurgence.[85] Of course, he was able to do so because Iran, unlike Turkey, is a real nation with an ancient heritage far predating Islam.

Reza Shah owed his awareness of his country's glorious Pre-Islamic past to the works of foreigners such as the American art historian Arthur Upham Pope and those of his advisors that had actually kept abreast of such scholarship.[86] His main motive for emphasizing the greatness of the

Achaemenid, Parthian, and Sassanian periods was to inspire Iranians to take pride in their country and believe in its potential for greatness despite the present state of humiliating backwardness.[87] This is why he adopted Achaemenid motifs in his monumental building projects and inaugurated celebrations such as that of the birth of Ferdowsi. He had no inclination whatsoever to replace Islam with a restoration of Zoroastrianism, which had been proposed by a small fringe of ultra-nationalist intellectuals and writers of the period.[88] Rather, in his speech to the parliament on March 1, 1937 Reza Shah made it clear that he saw Islam as fully compatible with his "revolution from above" for the sake of national development. He chastised those who, whether from a secular Westernizing position or in the name of Neo-Zoroastrianism, were arguing that

> reform and the acceptance of the civilization of the world today mean the abandonment of the principles of the faith and of the religious law, or that there is any conflict between reform and modernization on the one hand and religion and faith on the other. If the Great Lawgiver of Islam were alive today to see the progress of the world, he would confirm the complete harmony of his true teachings with the basis and institutions of the civilization of today. Unfortunately those noble and lucid ideas have with the passing of time been misused by certain people, and in consequence our country has fallen into decline. For thirteen centuries, in each of which the country ought to have taken a great leap forward, it has remained motionless and backward. We are now faced with the consequences of this neglect, and must make amends for the torpor of the past.[89]

So Reza Shah Pahlavi saw the Prophet Muhammad as a great man who would have fully endorsed all of his modernizing reform policies, and moreover he considered himself a humble servant of Allah and a protector of Muhammad's prophetic mission.

Reza Shah's main motivation in championing women's rights to vote, to receive equal education, and to participate in various fields, was to liberate the labor potential of half of the country.[90] It was the effect of this move on industrial and economic development that really motivated him, not a progressive Western outlook. Reza Shah endeavored to turn Iran into a meritocracy where competence, rather than wealth or connections, determined one's capacity to contribute to national development and be recognized for that accomplishment.[91] He replaced the medieval *madrasseh* system, i.e. the theological seminaries of the *mullahs*, with a modern education system centered on the University of Tehran, which opened in the 1930s.[92] Some would wish to compare Reza Shah's rise to imperial power from the ranks of being a common soldier to that of Napoleon Bonaparte.[93] His emphasis on a synergy of nationalism and modernization also elicited comparisons to Czar Peter the Great of Russia.[94]

The authoritarianism of Reza Shah was partly a function of his historical milieu, which included Kemal Ataturk in Turkey, Benito Mussolini in Italy, and Adolf Hitler in Germany.[95] The first two of these men were in power early enough to act as explicit models for Reza Khan as he became Reza Shah, and then Hitler's rise to power encouraged and validated this approach on the part of the first Pahlavi monarch.[96] In 1935 Reza Shah demanded that foreigners officially refer to his country by its endonym of Iran, a cognate of "Aryan," rather than by the then internationally accepted appellation of "Persia."[97] This emphasis of the Aryan identity of Iran was certainly related to the increasingly close relationship between Pahlavi Iran and Nazi Germany.[98]

When its contents were later revealed, it became apparent that the secret accord that had been arrived at between Molotov and Hitler on November 26, 1940, before Hitler broke the agreement with the launch of Operation Barbarossa in June of 1941, was an agreement that included a plan to partition Iran—with the Nazis taking the Western part of the country, including its oil resources, and the Soviet Union integrating the rest of Iran all the way down to the Persian Gulf.[99] The Nazi invasion of Russia created the condition for an alliance between the two great colonial powers that had competed for control of Iran in the nineteenth century, namely the Russian and British Empires.[100] During World War II, Iran was the only overland route whereby Western military supplies would be able to reach Russia from ships docked in the Persian Gulf.[101]

The Allied Invasion of Iran began on August 25, 1941, on the pretext that despite Iran's official neutrality in the war, Reza Shah was leaning toward Hitler and the Nazis by inviting so many German technicians into the country to contribute to his industrial and infrastructural development programs.[102] After a very brief resistance, Reza Shah's tiny Navy in the Persian Gulf was totally wiped out.[103] It took only three days for the allies to seize Iran from Reza Shah. Following the entry of allied forces into Iran, the man who had been Reza Shah's Minister of War voluntarily disbanded Iran's 200,000-strong army without even making any attempt to resist the foreign occupation.[104]

When Reza Shah formed his small standing army it was with the intention of guaranteeing internal security, as a kind of National Guard; he never even imagined that it would find itself in a position of having to guard against a foreign invasion, let alone one led by three world powers: Britain, America, and Russia.[105] Reza Shah Pahlavi resigned on September 16, 1941, in a letter addressed to his Prime Minister Mohammad Ali Forughi, in which he wrote:

> As I have during these past years devoted all my powers to the affairs of the country and am exhausted, I feel that the time has come for a younger strength to take charge of the affairs of the country, which require constant attention, and thereby to ensure the well-being and prosperity of the nation. I have therefore handed over the sovereign power to my heir and successor and retired from active life. From today, Shahrivar 25, 1320 [September 16, 1941], let the whole people, military and civil, recognize my legal heir and successor as sovereign, and offer to him in furtherance of the interests of the country what they have offered to me.[106]

The Iranian national railway, the construction of which had been the accomplishment of which Reza Shah was most proud, was taken over by the occupying British and American military forces to transport supplies to the Soviet Union.[107] The only real resistance to the joint Allied-Soviet occupation of Iran was from far right-wing groups sympathetic to Nazi Germany, such as the paramilitary forces known as the *Anjoman* that later became the kernel for the formation of the SUMKA or National Socialist Workers Party of Iran and which were, even later, absorbed into the Pan-Iranist Party.[108]

In early 1942, the British Foreign Secretary Anthony Eden took a dig at the exiled Reza Shah when he declared that Iran would be henceforth known as "Persia" again in all Western announcements and communications.[109] Iran was forced to declare war on Germany on September 9, 1943.[110] The cost of living increased sevenfold as the Iranian economy was destroyed by inflation between the Fall of 1941 and the Spring of 1944.[111] From his exile in South Africa, Reza Shah was appalled to hear that famine had broken out in Tehran under the Allied occupation and that he was being blamed for it.[112] Unscrupulous self-seeking and treasonous double-dealing characterized the attitude of many people in Iran during the war years, especially those in positions of power.[113] Everything built up over the preceding twenty years by Reza Shah Pahlavi was destroyed by the British, American, and Russian occupying forces.[114] It was not until 1950 that Reza Shah was retrospectively honored with the sobriquet "Great" (*Kabir*) by the parliament, and his corpse was brought from Cairo to Tehran were a monumental tomb had been prepared by his son for his interment.[115] Soviet expansionism in Iran from 1945–1946 was an important factor in the formulation of the Truman doctrine of containment in 1947, which ended the wartime American strategic alliance with the Russians and formally initiated the Cold War.[116] There was a possibility in Iran for the rise of a type of nationalism that was fused with communism through an anti-colonial and anti-Western discourse, similar to Chinese, Cuban, or Vietnamese patriotism.[117]

Mohammad Reza Pahlavi was just barely twenty-two years old when he succeeded his father as the Shah of Iran on September 16, 1941.[118] The first crisis that Mohammad Reza Shah Pahlavi had to deal with was the Soviet-backed Kurdish and Azeri secessions of 1945–1946, beginning with the Kurdish declaration of the Republic of Mahabad led by the Russian-puppet Mustafa Barzani.[119] Following his successful expulsion of the Soviets from Iran, the Shah banned the use of the Kurdish language and he executed Ghazi Mohammad, the President of the Mahabad Republic.[120] Barzani, its founder, fled to exile in the Soviet Union and was elected, *in absentia*, as head of the Kurdish Democratic Party (KDP) of Iraq. The Tudeh Party became increasingly popular in 1950s Iran, no doubt with the clandestine backing of the Soviet Union, to the point where the United States took very seriously the prospect of a communist takeover of Iran.[121]

It is in this atmosphere that the United Kingdom was able to convince the American CIA to orchestrate a coup against Iranian Prime Minister Mohammad Mossadegh who, the British argued, would embolden and empower leftist party politics in an Iran that was, at the time, relatively democratic. After weeks of failed negotiations with Britain in March of 1951, in April, with the backing of the Iranian Parliament, newly appointed Prime Minister Mohammad Mossadegh of the National Front (*Jebhe Melli*) Party nationalized Iran's oil resource, which had been owned by the Anglo-Iranian Oil Company, formerly known as the Anglo-Persian Oil Company, and rebranded as British Petroleum after its expulsion from Iran.[122] The Shah, who opposed what he considered a reckless move by the National Front, was driven out of the country by the populist Mossadegh. Mohammad Reza Pahlavi spent his brief exile in Italy "on vacation." This, despite the fact that, under the Iranian constitution of the time, the Prime Minister, while suggested by a democratic parliament, had to be approved by the Shah and he officially served at the pleasure of the monarch. So, from a legal standpoint, it is actually Mossadegh who carried out the coup. Nevertheless, the infamous CIA-orchestrated and funded Operation Ajax, widely known as the August 1953 American *coup d'état* in Iran, succeeded in toppling Mossadegh, who was first jailed and then put under house arrest.[123] This would be the first of many subsequent US "regime change" operations. Fazlollah Zahedi, the general that the CIA put in charge of boots on the ground, was appointed Prime Minister by the Shah upon his return to Iran.

The CIA immediately moved to create an espionage organization and secret police in Iran, a royal intelligence service known as SAVAK, which also received training from the Israeli Mossad, with which SAVAK had a long-standing secret intelligence sharing relationship.[124] The Shah's deference to the United States of America, which was partly a function of the need to reconstruct the oil industry that had been destroyed by Mossadegh's attempt at nationalization, gained him many outspoken political opponents. Among these were Jalal Al-e Ahmad, an intellectual who authorized a popular 1962 book with the catchy title *Gharbzadegi* ("Westoxification"), a firebrand Shi'ite cleric who would go on to become world-famous (or infamous), namely Ayatollah Khomeini, and Ali Shariati, a revolutionary sociologist trained in Paris who sought an intellectual synthesis of Shi'ism with Leftist post-colonial thought in the mold of the black thinker Frantz Fanon, whose *Wretched of the Earth* Shariati had translated into Persian.[125] The 1960s and 70s also saw a continued rise of militant leftist groups, some of them armed, which ran the spectrum from the rabidly secularist Fadayan-e Khalq to the Islamist-Marxist hybrid Mojaheddin-e-Khalq (MEK). While some of these groups occasionally carried out terrorism, and Shariati's lectures at the Hosseiniyeh Ershad were quite popular among the more intellectually minded young, dissident religious believers, it was Khomeini who represented the most serious threat to the Pahlavi regime.

The first flashpoint between him and the Shah came in 1963 when Khomeini led mass demonstrations against the Shah's new bold reform program. The protests intensified when Khomeini was arrested in June of 1963, and hundreds of demonstrators were eventually killed by the regime's security forces. In this context, Khomeini, not yet an Ayatollah, was promoted by his senior colleagues in the clergy to the rank of *Marja ot-taghlid* (Source of Emulation), which prevented the Shah from executing him or even giving him any sentence harsher than house arrest.[126] Mohammad Reza Pahlavi opted to exile Khomeini to the Shi'ite holy city of Najaf in Iraq, where the cleric would go on to rise up the Shi'ite ranks. From the safety of his refuge, Khomeini was able to regularly deliver sermons that were tape-recorded and smuggled back into Iran.

The reforms that pitted Khomeini against the Shah were partly a Pahlavi regime response to the communist threat of a Red Revolution. In 1963 the Shah began a six-point social and economic reform program known as the White Revolution (*Enghelâbé Sepid*).[127] Throughout the 1960s and 1970s, this program yielded a level of industrial development in Iran that was faster-paced than that of almost any other developing nation. The only comparable models were those of Japan and Korea. Iran had exceeded Turkey in terms of its development and was expected to rival Japan as the most rapidly developing non-Western country.[128] In the early 1970s, under the Shah of Iran's leadership of OPEC, the economic development of the White Revolution was augmented by an aggressive increase in the price of petroleum exports, scaling these to the runaway rate of Western inflation and the consequent rise in the price of commodities produced in America and Europe.[129] By 1975, Iran had achieved military hegemony in the Persian Gulf region and the Shah's Imperial Navy was the uncontested escort "protecting" petroleum tanker shipping that passes through the Strait of Hormuz.[130] Mohammad Reza Shah celebrated the fiftieth anniversary of the Pahlavi dynasty in 1976.[131]

The 1970s were a period of extreme political contradiction in terms of the policies of the Pahlavi regime. In the early to mid 1970s, emboldened by international recognition of the resurgence of Iran after the 2,500th anniversary of the Persian Empire in 1971 and a successful dramatic increase in the price of petroleum under the Shah's leadership of OPEC from 1973 to 1974, Mohammad Reza Pahlavi transformed what had nominally been a constitutional monarchy into a one-party Fascist state.[132] In 1975, the Shah dismantled the two-party parliamentary system, banned all outlying opposition parties that had still been socially active, and established a single party known as *Rastâkhiz* or "Resurgence." In this period, the Shah authored a book titled *Toward the Great Civilization*, wherein he envisioned the resurgence of Imperial Iran as a world power second only to America by the turn of the millennium. His plans included an atomic energy program on par with that of France and Japan, and speculation was rife that he was secretly pursuing the development of nuclear weapons.

With a view to the socialistic elements of the White Revolution program, it would be fair to call the kind of regime that emerged from out of the transformations of 1971–1975 National Socialist in nature. Nazi Germany in the 1930s and Fascist Italy in the 1920s would be the closest modern points of comparison. Just as this period began with the fascist pageantry of the 2,500th anniversary of the Persian Empire in 1971, it came to a culmination with the equally fascistic commemoration of the Golden Jubilee or fiftieth anniversary of the Pahlavi Dynasty in 1976. When confronted about his increasingly authoritarian, not to say totalitarian, style of governance, and especially the alleged abuses of SAVAK, the Shah of 1971–1976 would consistently tell foreign reporters that Iran was not a democracy, that democracy was a Western political form and that Iran had its own political tradition, an ancient tradition in the context of which his people saw him as the Father of their nation. He spoke often of his God-given responsibility and divinely ordained destiny, the latter idea having been reinforced in the Shah's mind by his miraculous survival of a point-blank assassination attempt.

Then, with an almost schizophrenic degree of contradiction, from later 1977 through 1978 the Shah suddenly became a liberal social democrat. He ended censorship, legalized political parties opposed to his regime, freed political prisoners, and promised that entirely free and fair elections would be held by 1979.[133] In interviews with foreign journalists he vowed that his ambition was to transform Iran into a country as democratic as France within the foreseeable future. Instead of appeasing those who had begun protesting in the streets after an economic downturn in 1977, the Shah's concessions emboldened the demonstrators, and by the Fall of 1978 the nation was faced with widespread labor strikes that required the imposition of martial law.[134] After an initial violent exchange between protesters and security forces led to the death of sixty-four unarmed civilians, the Shah repeatedly called for restraint from the army, so much so that by November of 1978, there was anarchy in the streets.[135] In early December, the Shi'ite holiday of *Ashura* became an opportunity to transform the mourning processions for Imam Hussein into mass demonstrations against the Pahlavi regime. Millions of people filled Shahyâd Square (later renamed Freedom Square) on December

2, 1978, and the Shah, who overflew the masses in his helicopter, was shocked and horrified.

On December 6, 1978, Mohammad Reza Shah spoke his famous last words in a televised address to the nation that began, "I have heard the voice of your revolution."[136] He proceeded to apologize for past mistakes and vowed to work with opposition parties to enact revolutionary democratization, and he also made major concessions to Islamists—even beyond his closure of casinos and nightclubs earlier in the Fall of 1978. After a series of mass arrests of government officials, including the scapegoated longtime Prime Minister Amir Abbas Hoveyda, the Shah formed a new administration led by former dissident Shapur Bakhtiar, who had been the head of the National Front, the party of Mohammad Mossadegh.[137] Then, on January 16, 1979, the Shah left Iran on a "vacation" from which he would never return.

The caretaker Bakhtiar government, which made the mistake of letting Khomeini back into the country, collapsed within eleven days of the Ayatollah's return to Iran on February 1, 1979. Militants who seized the US Embassy in Tehran on November 4, 1979 and took its staff hostage demanded the return of the Shah, and so Mohammad Reza Pahlavi was denied cancer treatment in the United States, which would have been his preferred place of exile. From his exile first in Panama and then Egypt, the broken Shah, wasting away from cancer and depleted by increasingly futile attempts to treat him, watched everything that he and his father had built up over half a century be destroyed by the Ayatollahs and the Leftists who, at that time, were still an integral part of the revolutionary coalition. This included the destruction of the magnificent military that he had built up, which the founders of the Islamic Republic divested of any competent command and control capability by executing nearly the entire officer corps of every branch. Fortunately, his death on July 27, 1980 spared the Shah from having to witness the invasion of Iran by Saddam Hussein in September of the same year.

10.3 "Light of the Aryans"? A Mithraic Monarchist Critique of Pahlavism

There is plenty of room for speculation as to why the Shah caved in so easily to those demanding democracy in Iran. For one, few who witnessed this about-face knew that the Shah had been diagnosed with cancer in the mid 1970s. For a long time, this information had been hidden even from Empress Farah Diba. So it is possible that either the cancer itself, or the increasingly aggressive treatments that the Shah began to receive for it in the late 1970s, had seriously impaired his judgment. Whether this, or other related factors (regarding which I will presently remain silent), played a part in the Shah's radical change of approach to governance, it is clear that he did not have a monarchical ideology substantive enough to guide his decision-making based on firm principles despite such contingencies. Pahlavism remained a vague and general tendency toward a certain style of governance, not a well-developed political ideology comparable to Turkish Kemalism. The deficit of Pahlavism as the state ideology of Iran for fifty-three years — or rather for fifty years, since after 1976 the Shah basically abandoned it — can be seen very clearly when we compare it to philosophical arguments for Absolute Monarchy.

The most insightful and sophisticated of these arguments remains that of Thomas Hobbes in his book *Leviathan*. It is quite possible that Mohammad Reza Shah read *Leviathan* during his university studies in Switzerland, but he would probably have encountered it only in the context of arguments against Hobbes' vision of the social contract — especially the arguments of that most famous Swiss social contract theorist, and advocate of democracy, Jean-Jacques Rousseau. That is a pity, because many of Hobbes' arguments for a strong sovereign authority could have been appropriated by the Shah, and they remain applicable even to the present situation of the Islamic Republic of Iran. If the Shah was going to adopt Western models, he adopted the wrong ones.

Hobbes makes explicit reference to the divine beast that is the namesake of his book on only three occasions throughout the text. The first of these is in the opening paragraph of the Introduction, where Hobbes immediately recognizes that the Leviathan is "an Artificial Animal."[138] Evidently noting the peculiar details in the description of the beast that we are presented with in the Book of Job, peculiarities that call to mind "*Automata* (Engines that move themselves by springs and wheels as doth a watch)", Hobbes describes the Leviathan as akin to a form of "artificial life" artfully designed by the rational faculty of man in order to imitate the work of Nature.[139] The Leviathan is, however, not just any automaton like the others designed by man, it is nothing less than "an Artificial Man … of greater stature and strength than the Natural."[140] Tasked with the protection of natural man, the Sovereign authority is "an Artificial *Soul* … giving life and motion to the whole body" of "that great Leviathan called a Common-Wealth, or State."[141]

After a discussion of how representations or carved or manufactured metal idols of chimerical ideas in the mind come into being, Hobbes makes the titanic claim that "an earthly Sovereign may be called the Image of God."[142] This is a particularly controversial statement, coming as it does in the lead-up to a definition of idolatry.[143] Hobbes' explicitly unstated worry here is that some will allege that he is advocating an idolatrous cult of the Leviathan.

The second reference to the Leviathan is in Part II, toward the end of Chapter XVII on "the Causes, Generation, and Definition of a Common-Wealth."[144] Here Hobbes describes the sovereign power as one man, or an assembly of men, that represents the reduction of the plurality of wills and voices in a society to one univocal and unequivocal will. "This," he says, "is more than Consent, or Concord; it is a real Unity of them all, in one and the same Person."[145] This unity in plurality of the sovereign is depicted on the original frontispiece illustration for *Leviathan*. Hobbes describes the Person of the sovereign as constituted of the plurality of men who, by their social contract with one another, mutually relinquish their natural right of self-governance to this artificial man and thereby authorize his actions.[146] It is in this context that the name of the divine beast appears for the second time in Hobbes' text:

> This done, the Multitude so united in one Person, if called a Common-Wealth, in Latin Civitas. This is the Generation of that great Leviathan, or rather (to speak more reverently) of that *Mortal God*, to which we owe under the *Immortal God*, our peace and defense.[147]

Here the depiction of the commonwealth or the state as "that great Leviathan" reaches back to the Biblical imagery of the Book of Job insofar as it characterizes the Leviathan as a mortal God. Hobbes goes on to explicitly identify this mortal God as the head of state: "And he that carryeth this Person, is called Sovereign, and said to have *Sovereign Power*; and every one besides, his Subject."[148] The same paragraph ends with a comparison of the sovereign to a man who subjects his children to his authority "as being able to destroy them if they refuse."[149] Although he contrasts this patriarchal "Common-wealth by *Acquisition*," which is characteristic of a family, with "a Common-wealth by *Institution*," which is the constitution of the state, the fact that he can draw this analogy at all, and that he describes a father's subjection of his children in such tyrannical terms, means that Hobbes' conception of sovereign power is very paternalistic.[150] It would have fit very well with Mohammad Reza Shah Pahlavi's insistence, in the early 1970s, that he was the Father of the Iranian nation.

On the other hand, there are some fascinating passages in *Leviathan* where, contrary to what one might expect of a putatively patriarchal and ultra-paternalistic text, Hobbes imagines the absolute sovereign power being wielded by female monarchs; he even envisions a matriarchal form of Absolute Monarchy.[151] He may have had Queen Elizabeth in mind, but as we saw in Chapter 1, this fits very well with the Sarmatian and Scythian types of Iranian society that always resisted the patriarchal Persians and Medes. Note the following:

> We find in History that the *Amazons* Contracted with the Men of the neighboring Countries, to whom they had recourse for issue, that the issue Male should be sent back, but the Female remain with themselves: so that the dominion of the Females was in the Mother.
>
> If there be no Contract, the Dominion is in the Mother. For in the condition of mere Nature, where there are no Matrimonial laws, it cannot be

> known who is the Father, unless it be declared by the Mother: and therefore the right of Dominion over the Child dependeth on her will, and is consequently hers. Again, seeing the Infant is first in the power of the Mother, so as she may either nourish, or expose it; if she nourish it, it oweth its life to the Mother; and is therefore obliged to obey her, rather than any other; and by consequence the Dominion over it is hers. But if she expose it, and another find, and nourish it, the Dominion is in him that nourisheth it.
>
> … If the Mother be the Fathers subject, the Child, is in the Fathers power: and if the Father be the Mothers subject, (as when a Sovereign Queen marrieth one of her subjects,) the Child is subject to the Mother; because the Father also is her subject.[152]

The third and final instance in which Hobbes makes explicit reference to the Biblical Leviathan is the only one where he explicitly identifies Chapter 41 of the book of Job as his source for "that comparison" of God's "King of the Proud" to the sovereign power of the state.[153] This passage, which is the last of Chapter XXIX of Part II, reiterates the mortality of the Leviathan and signals Hobbes' intention to discuss, in the following chapters, the various marks of this mortality and the earthly vulnerabilities of the state conceived of as a Leviathan. His main point is that, while the Leviathan is earthly and therefore perishable, God has declared that: "*There is nothing … on earth, to be compared with him. He is made so as not to be afraid. He seeth every high thing below him and is King of all the children of pride.*"[154] A formulation of this kind, based on Job, turns state power into an intermediary in the relationship between God on the one hand, and everything—and everyone—earthly on the other. So far as anyone on Earth is concerned, the Sovereign is God—or the closest anyone will ever get to God. To think otherwise is to be guilty of excessive pride, which is a sin that will lead to crime.

Hobbes places himself in the tradition of political philosophers such as Plato, Aristotle, and Cicero when he proposes to analyze, not any particular laws relevant to one or another place and time, but the philosophical foundation of law as such.[155] He draws a distinction between "Counsel" and "Command," identifying law as the latter, and then further defines

"Civil Law" as consisting of commands issuing from the "*Persona Civitatis*, the Person of the Common-wealth," in other words, from the Leviathan.[156] The most significant implication of this is that the sovereign himself is not bound by the civil law, since in Absolute Monarchy the king is not just the executive power of the state but also the chief legislative and judicial authority (at least by means of absolute veto power over any legislature or judiciary).[157] The sovereign is the only absolutely free man with respect to the law, which he has the authority to change at any time, and which binds all of his subjects: "For he is free, that can be free when he will: Nor is it possible for any person to be bound to himself; because he that can bind, can release; and therefore he that is bound to himself only, is not bound."[158] On the absoluteness of the sovereign power, Hobbes writes:

> He cannot be Accused by any of his Subjects, of Injury: He cannot be Punished by them: He is Judge of what is necessary for Peace; and Judge of Doctrines: He is the Sole Legislator; and Supreme Judge of Controversies; and of the Times, and Occasions of War, and Peace: to him it belongeth to choose Magistrates, Counselors, Commanders, and all other Officers, and Ministers; and to determine of Rewards, and Punishments, Honor, and Order.[159]

Hobbes argues for Absolute Monarchy in a very elegant fashion. First, he makes his case for why the sovereign power of the state is needed at all. Then, he makes a convincing case that there are basically only three types of states. Finally, he argues that of these three it is monarchy, in its pure form, that is the most authentic type of sovereign power and the one best able to meet the need for government to secure a society from internal strife and external threats.

Sovereign power is needed, because without it, in the state of nature, we would be subjected to a war of all against all. In the state of nature, even the weakest person can kill the strongest if he put his mind to it.[160] Interestingly, as a reader of Descartes, Hobbes notes that the only thing that really introduces a dramatic and insurmountable disproportion of power between individuals is the possession of science and scientifically advanced technology by some and not by others. He claims that this is not relevant to most people, though, and certainly not to theorizing the state of nature or the primordial condition of war that we would be in without the state, since without the social stability afforded to us by the state there would be no scientific innovation either.[161] Without the security of the state, nothing that one cultivates or builds would be safe from the avarice and ambition of others who might, singly or with their combined force, come to seize it.[162]

Hobbes distinguishes three sources of potential conflict in the general state of war that would afflict a stateless society. The first of these is when men attack their fellows for the sake of "Gain" of another's property or control over the life of another man or the lives of his wife, children, and kinfolk, the second when anyone uses violence to defend himself and secure "Safety" from such an attack, and the third when a person's expectation that others value him in the same way or to the same degree that he values himself causes him to do violence against others in order to "extort" from them respect for his "Reputation" or to punish any perceived disrespect to his "Kindred, their Friends, their Nation, their Profession, or their Name."[163]

By the state of nature being a state of war, Hobbes does not mean a state of perpetual warfare but a condition comparable to inclement weather, with dark storm clouds hanging over head and liable, at any moment, to erupt into thunder and lightning.[164] In this sense, for so long as "men live without a common Power to keep them all in awe," we are confronted with the prospect of a condition of war that is not even a conflict between groups but of "every man, against every man."[165] What is most lamentable in this condition of generalized enmity is that there is never enough security for the development of industry, commerce, culture, science, and technology.[166] Constantly preoccupied with mere survival, and divested of all the hallmarks of civilization, this barely human life is "solitary, poor, nasty, brutish, and short."[167]

Hobbes counsels those who are skeptical of his characterization of human nature in the absence of the overseeing power of the state to consider their own behavior, which, despite what they would like to think, is rife with suspicion of their fellows and even their family.[168] Why, he asks, do people go on journeys armed or at least well-accompanied, why do they lock their doors when they go to sleep, why do they lock their chests even when they are in their own homes, if not out of suspicion that their very own children, let alone their fellow citizens, might mishandle or misappropriate what is theirs?[169]

One of the most profound philosophical statements in *Leviathan* is the claim made by Hobbes that, in the absence of "a Law that forbids them" none of the impassioned acts of any individual are sinful or wrong by nature.[170] Crime only comes into being through a definition of the prospect of punishment, which is the prerogative of the sovereign power.[171] In the absence of the state, or in the event of its total failure, "nothing can be Unjust."[172] Hobbes is unequivocal in his groundbreaking claim that wherein the "war of every man against every man" prevails, the "notions of Right and Wrong, Justice and Injustice have there no place."[173] "Where there is no common Power," he says, "there is no Law: where no Law, no Injustice."[174] Then, to sum it up, he drops this bomb of a maxim: "Force, and Fraud, are in war the two Cardinal virtues."[175] Without laws, and the state's capability of enforcing them, there is also "no Propriety, no Dominion, no *Mine* and *Thine*," so that property means only that which is "every mans" insofar as "he can get" it "and for so long, as he can keep it."[176]

According to Hobbes the only three forms that a commonwealth can take are Monarchy, Democracy, and Aristocracy.[177] In a monarchy, only one man is the representative of the collective will, whereas in a democracy the people represent themselves through an "Assembly of All," and in an Aristocracy they are represented by "an Assembly of a Part" of the population — consisting of some elite, however the criteria for belonging to this governing elite might be determined (whether on the basis of merit or money, or both, or some other criteria, such as military authority in a timocracy or military dictatorship).[178] Hobbes insists that the supposed other forms of government that have been delineated by certain political philosophers, such as Tyranny, Oligarchy, and Anarchy, are actually nothing more than the three aforementioned types of sovereign power in either a degenerate state or when viewed critically by an opponent of any one of them who is an advocate for one of the others.[179] So, for example, a democrat might characterize any Monarchy as a Tyranny, and an aristocrat may see a Democracy as mere Anarchy, while someone aspiring to be a just monarch could make an appeal to his people that a reigning Aristocracy is actually an Oligarchy of corrupt moneyed men who ought to be put in their place by him. *Tyranny* originally meant nothing more than Monarchy, without any necessarily negative evaluation.[180] By extension Aristocracy became "*Tyranny of the Few*," also known as *Oligarchy*.[181]

Hobbes gives six reasons why Absolute Monarchy is superior to other forms of government.[182] The first reason is that, of all forms of government, the public and the private interest are closest to being absolutely unified, and all the more absolutely, the more absolute the monarchy.[183] A division of the sovereign power into an assembly constituted either by all or by part of the people actually multiplies the number of individuals who are vulnerable to personal corruption and the abuse of power on account of nepotism, in other words to enrich their family and friends.[184] The more the representatives, the less any one of them is held accountable for harm done to the society on account of political corruption. A single sovereign, who is recognized as absolutely responsible for matters of state, is most likely to see his own interest as identical to the interests of his people, since, as Hobbes puts it: "The riches, power, and honor of a Monarch arise only from the riches, strength and reputation of his Subjects."[185] There is no honor in being the king of a poor, downtrodden, and backward nation.

The second reason is that, unlike in a Democracy or even an Aristocracy, the sovereign of a Monarchy can receive counsel from anyone he wishes, on whatever subject he needs guidance, whenever he wishes, *and in total confidentiality*.[186] In an Aristocracy, only the elite are admitted to advise the aristocrats, and whatever advice is given to them that may guide state policy, is known by all of them. A Democracy is even worse. First of all, among the parliamentarians themselves the "counsel" that they give one another really consists of a demagoguery driven by the passions, which aims to "dazzle" rather than to truly enlighten anyone's understanding.[187] Furthermore, whatever advice is given to the Parliament by expert testimony is so prone to being leaked to the press that it is practically a public matter. This means that the sovereign authority cannot deliberate conscientiously without being subjected to pressure from ignorant masses or fearing a scandal for even considering certain policies rather than others, or for seeking advice from one or another unpopular person whose guidance may nonetheless be vitally informative in a particular situation.[188] Only in an Absolute Monarchy can the king summon whomsoever he believes he needs to consult with, privately, and however far in advance of a decision that needs to be made on a particular issue, without his deliberations being derailed either by unthinking rabble or self-interested elites. This also gives the singular Sovereign the prerogative to seek counsel, albeit in total secrecy, from individuals who may not be a part of the respectable elite but who may have expert knowledge in a field relevant to some matter that requires a sovereign decision that will affect the welfare of the commonwealth.

The third and fourth reasons that Hobbes gives for the superiority of Absolute Monarchy are so closely interconnected that they could be considered two clauses of a single proposition. It concerns the internal consistency of the sovereign's decision-making and the long-term stability of the policy arrived at thereby. Only in Absolute Monarchy can one rest assured that when important matters are resolved upon, the sovereign is able to carry a policy through until it bears fruit.[189] An Assembly constantly disagrees with itself, or at the very least future representatives disagree with their predecessors, and so important policies are often reversed before they have even been implemented for long enough to properly estimate their effectiveness.[190] As Hobbes puts it, this leads to a situation in which the dissent of those "of the contrary opinion, undoes to day, all that was concluded yesterday."[191] By contrast, a monarch as sovereign does not have any more inconsistency in his own mind and will than there is in human nature in general. However much he may disagree with himself on account of the latter, in other words, by changing his mind, in general this will yield far more consistency in long-term policy making on important matters of state than when such inconsistency in human nature is multiplied in number by however many members of an Assembly divide and paralyze the sovereign power.[192] An Assembly's disagreements with itself "out of envy, or interest" may be so severe as to even "produce a Civil War."[193]

The fifth reason why Absolute Monarchy is a choice-worthy regime is that one of the strongest arguments against it — namely that the monarch can be corrupted by flatterers — is actually an argument in its favor.[194] If a monarch can make poor decisions as a consequence of having his ego manipulated by those who would flatter him, who seek to become his favorites, and for whom he is willing to do personal favors that are at odds with the interests of the state and the welfare of the people, then the same is also true of each member of an Assembly — whether Democratic or Aristocratic — just *on a much larger and more ruinous scale.*[195] Each and every member of a Counsel, Parliament, or Congress has his own flatterers and favorites — or, to refer to them by today's terminology rather than that of Hobbes' era — the people's representatives allow themselves to be manipulated by special interests.[196] In the present time these include pharmaceutical corporations, defense contractors, oil companies, and others whose lobbyists promise to enrich not just these representatives but their families as well. If the royal family is vulnerable to bad policy making on account of nepotism, how much greater is the danger of nepotism when there is a prospect for each of the tens or hundreds of individuals who collectively constitute the sovereign power to enrich their own families, friends, and cronies at the expense of the nation?

The sixth and final reason that Hobbes gives to defend Absolute Monarchy is a response to critics that point to the problem of succession falling upon an Infant King (for example, in case of the assassination of his father). In such situations, the would-be king who is next in line of succession must be put under the guardianship and guidance of a Lord Protector. At least in an Absolute Monarchy, it is the former king who has himself chosen who will be his heir's Lord Protector in the event that he meets an untimely demise and his son is still underage.[197] In a constitutional monarchy, the Assembly is likely to choose this Lord Protector, so that all of the aforementioned incoherence and potential for corruption that exists in the Assembly is reflected into the character of the young king being raised by this tool of the Assembly. In an Aristocracy or, worst of all, in a Democracy, there is a vast multiplication of Lord Protectors whose guidance will be permanently needed, since — as Hobbes observes through the lens of his characteristic cynicism — the constantly conflicted representatives are like a giant infant king who is always violently moody, recalcitrantly rebelling, *and can never be expected to grow up*.[198] The members of this Assembly will then, in actual fact, need a much larger number of custodians to watch over and temper their otherwise rash decision-making and protect them from harming themselves, that is, from harming the people. This larger number of custodians is what we today call the Deep State, and it is even more amenable to corruption and abuse of power than a Lord Protector who has been chosen by a monarch to be the ward of his heir for a fixed period of time and only in the event of an emergency that would require succession while the successor is underage.

The very idea of a limited monarchy rather than "a Sovereign absolute" is incoherent, since this would subject the sovereign to others who appoint or elect him, at least by virtue of being able to dismiss him, should he overstep the limits that they have placed on his executive, legislative, and judicial authority.[199] Sovereign is he who is sovereign, not one who is subjected to a group of persons who actually turn out to be sovereign.[200] The king of a constitutional monarchy is not truly a sovereign. Rather, in such a system, whether democratic or aristocratic, the true sovereign power always rests in the parliament or counsel that has the power to reprimand or even remove the king for overstepping his authority. In other words, constitutional monarchy is a farce. A nation with such a system might as well just become an Aristocracy or a Democracy.

This critique obviously applies to the Constitutionalist movement in Iran as well. Those who spearheaded the Persian Constitutional Revolution of 1906 were really either advocates of Aristocracy or of Democracy.

This remains true of the contemporary proponents of the restoration of constitutional monarchy in Iran. Most of them are democrats, including the Crown Prince himself, who is an ultra-liberal democrat. To be fair, Reza Pahlavi II is really picking up where his father left off in 1978 when Mohammad Reza Shah seemed to stop believing that he was the "Light of the Aryans" or the "Aryan Mithra" (*Âryâ-Mehr*) and rebranded himself as a champion of democratization — with disastrous consequences. It was certainly not on the basis of a constitutionalist conception of monarchy that, seven years earlier, in 1971, Shâhanshâh Âryâ-Mehr Pahlavi stood at the tomb of Cyrus the Great in Pasargadae and, before the eyes of tens of top-tier foreign dignitaries and a global television audience, proclaimed: "From my person, and on behalf of my nation, to you, Oh Cyrus, King of Kings, King of the Achaemenids, I say: Sleep soundly, for we have awakened and will remain vigilant!" What happened to this vigilance when the same Shah became a democrat in 1978? What happened to the respect that he, and his father before him, showed for the Achaemenids?

Ascribing a transcendent and divine character to the statesmen was not a part of the classical Greek tradition of democracy nor of the early Republicanism of Rome.[201] In fact, it was anathema to the Greco-Roman spirit, and men who were suspected of having pretensions of godlike qualities of character or who aspired to something like divine kingship found themselves before the juries of a Greek polis or beheaded by defenders of the Roman Republic.[202] Even Spartan kingship did not have this quality to it. Such a monarchical tradition first appears in the West when the West assimilates itself to the Iranian East and Alexander of Macedon goes native by attempting to portray himself as the legitimate Shâhanshâh of Iran. Imperial Rome adopted *this* Hellenistic-Iranian model, not the monarchical traditions of the Etruscan Italians themselves, nor those of the Celts or other peoples that their empire encompassed who had a tradition of kingship.[203]

Prior to this period, the title "Imperator" had only been granted to victorious generals by the Roman Senate and their "imperial" power could only be exercised on military campaigns outside of Rome.[204] The idea of generalized *Imperium* in Rome, and by extension in the Western World at large, is an inheritance from Iran under the direct influence of the spread of the ideology of Mithraism in the late Roman Republic and early Roman Empire, complete with the bird of prey — the Eagle, as in the case of the standard of Cyrus the Great — symbolizing the divine royal glory.[205] Nero, Commodus, and Julian were all Roman Caesars who received Mithraic initiation.[206] By the time of Caesar Aurelian in 274, Mithraism had been so thoroughly embraced that the emperor was seen as enjoying the patronage of the solar deity and came to be known as the Sun King — a Mithraic title that would be retained by the French monarchical tradition long after the collapse of the Roman Empire.[207] It is in this period that the date of December 25 was adopted as *Dies natalis Solis Mithrae* or "the nativity day of the solar Mithra."[208] It would be another century before Christians would adopt this holiday and claim, falsely, that Jesus of Nazareth was born on this day. Sun Day, or the holiest day of the week in Mithraism, was likewise adopted by them when they Christianized Pagan Rome. In 288, Diocletian introduced the Iranian custom of *proskynesis* or full prostration to the Emperor, a most distasteful rite from the Greco-Roman perspective, but one which was ultimately adopted from Mithraic Rome into the rites of the Vatican where the cardinals and bishops give such honor to the Pope.[209]

This Mithraic tradition of divine royal glory was preserved by the Holy Roman Empire, an attempted resurrection of Imperial Rome, which was established in the year 800 by the French Emperor Charlemagne in league with Pope Leo III.[210] At his coronation ceremony, Charlemagne is said to have worn Mithraic red and white clothes similar to those worn by Magi in Roman mosaic depictions of the Iranian magicians.[211] He had the Pope fully prostrate to him before placing the crown on his head.[212] Such a tradition would endure all the way to the concordat between General Bonaparte and the Vatican, which brought the French Revolution and its nascent Republic to an end when, with the full authorization of the Pope, Napoleon crowned himself as the Sun King on December 2, 1804 in Notre-Dame Cathedral.

Napoleon, who was part Italian and who also ruled Italy, handled two crowns at his coronation, the golden laurel wreath of the Roman Empire and also the French crown of Charlemagne and his Holy Roman Empire. Having already placed the first on his head, Napoleon held the second one over his head before crowning his Queen Josephine with it. To this day, in the *Interregnum* between the death of one Pope and the appointment of another, a red and white stripped Mithraic banner (the esoteric basis for the pattern of the American flag) is raised over the Vatican together with the sacred crossed keys, which, as mentioned in Chapter 5, have the same meaning as the crossed bones of the Skull and Crossbones: the celestial equator crossed by the zodiac at 23°, a Mithraic symbol for the precession of the equinoxes through the series of world ages that will eventually bring to an end this world of time and death.

What all of this amounts to is the realization that the divine right of kings that Thomas Hobbes is putatively defending in *Leviathan* is actually an Iranian idea that entered the West through the spread of Mithraism. So, had the last Shah of Iran adopted the arguments of Hobbes in order to defend his sovereign right, he would actually have been re-appropriating his own monarchical tradition — the one that he so explicitly aligned himself with during the 2,500th anniversary of Imperial Iran as the Shâhanshâh Âryâ-Mehr Pahlavi. In fact, a deep reading of *Leviathan* reveals just how badly Hobbes misunderstood the metaphysical foundation of this Iranian tradition, which he is attempting to defend in its very late and far-removed British form. Hobbes is a cynic who dismisses the occult underpinnings of sacred monarchy.

As a reader and contemporary of Descartes, he was seduced by early materialism and modern mechanistic reductionism. Read as a defense of the divine right of kings, *Leviathan* is insincere at best — if not downright hypocritical. This comes across very clearly in the parts of the text where Hobbes forwards a rather cogent critique of the idea of freedom of religion, which was just becoming popular among some of the more liberal intellectuals of his time. Reading between the lines of his argument for the state's control of religion or, put another way, a conception of sovereign power as the viceroy of God, we see that Hobbes is only feigning belief in religious ideas that are supposed to consecrate state power. He barely conceals his rejection of the magical or miraculous qualities traditionally ascribed to royal glory.

Hobbes argues that no one anywhere is allowed to believe in a religion that conflicts with the fundamental precepts and dogmas of the state: "Besides, there is no place in the world where men are permitted to pretend other Commandments of God, than are declared for such by the Common-wealth."[213] It would be an ignorant objection to claim that such an observation has been superseded by the political reality of freedom of religion in liberal democratic Western countries, since not one of these nations would tolerate a religion that, for example, holds as a commandment that it is pious to kidnap certain people and use them as human sacrificial victims. This shows that, at least tacitly, the state does expect to define the range of acceptable religious belief *and practice*, and whereas proponents of freedom of religion in Western liberal democracies are naïve hypocrites in this regard, Hobbes is as clear-sighted—albeit cynical—as he is with regard to most things. While it may no longer be the case that, "Christian States punish those that revolt from Christian Religion," in the Islamic world it is certainly still true that "other States" do so with respect to "those that set up any Religion by them forbidden."[214] Hobbes would see the position of Islamic states as more consistent and authentic than that of modern Western liberal democracies, which are just waiting for the "Commandments" of some religion, most probably Islam, to explicitly conflict with the civil laws of the state.[215]

Hobbes admits at least the negative authority of scripture in shaping the legal system of any commonwealth. The laws made by "every Christian King" may not be determined by the Biblical canon, but certain laws may be proscribed by the latter.[216] This follows from one of the most profound axiomatic statements in *Leviathan*: "God is the Sovereign of all Sovereigns."[217] That being the case, there is the danger that someone might feel directly addressed by God in such a manner that, as a subject of God, he feels compelled to disregard the fact that he is also a subject of the state and he may even take this insubordination to the point of rebelling against the Sovereign on the grounds that he has been tasked to do so by the Sovereign of Sovereigns.

The only solution to this serious challenge to the power of the state is to recognize that the earthly Sovereign, as the Leviathan, is the only authority who legitimately defines both what counts for canonical scripture *and what may be considered the proper interpretation of it.*[218] This includes the power to put to death those who wrongly interpret scripture, especially if this misinterpretation threatens state power.[219] For example, Hobbes asserts that in his own British context, such authority is vested in the Church of England under the aegis of the King. Period. Unless a man claims direct revelation from God, the Sovereign is the sole authority that determines in what way scripture is to be translated into law, heavenly commandment into earthly order.[220] Hobbes claims that it is not possible, using one's natural reason alone, to know for certain whether another person has had a supernatural revelation from God or manifested some miracle; rather, the best that he can do is believe or disbelieve in this to varying degrees.[221]

The state also decides what counts for true Miracles, also known as Wonders, Portents, and Signs that are given by God to impress the legitimacy of a revelation upon the faithful.[222] (In Latin such signs are referred to as *Ostenta*, which is the root of the word ostentatious.) The whole point of miracles is to substantiate the authority of messengers, prophets, and other ministers of God, by making their revelations more believable to men precisely by demonstrating the unbelievable.[223] Hobbes defines a miracle as a kind of event that is both a rare occurrence and one that we cannot imagine to have been produced by Nature.[224] However, he argues that our conception of the limits of natural phenomena has been repeatedly broadened, so that much of what was once considered miraculous is now considered part of the natural order not a deliberate intervention of God into earthly affairs.[225] In sum, Hobbes offers this concise definition: "A Miracle, *is a work of God, (besides his operation by the way of Nature, ordained in the Creation,) done for the making manifest to his elect, the mission of an extraordinary Minister for their salvation.*"[226]

Hobbes is insistent that miracles must be the direct effects of God's action, without even the will or ability of a prophet acting as an intermediary cause.[227] The latter would open the door to contemplating the possibility that men could effect something akin to miracles, namely occurrences outside of the natural order, *by their own will alone*. To admit this is, for Hobbes, unconscionable, as it is likewise unacceptable to think that there is *any power at all* that is independent of the will of an Almighty God. As far as Hobbes is concerned "no Devil, Angel, or other created Spirit, can do a miracle."[228]

Hobbes dismisses the practice of Demonology, still alive and well in his time, because no such thing as daemons actually exist; in other words, those who "have feared them, as things of an unknown, that is, of an unlimited power to do them good, or harm" have empowered Demonology by blaspheming against the Almighty power of God with the claim that there are superhuman wills other than His own divine will.[229] He alleges that those apparently possessed by demons in olden times were simply the same kind of people found in the madhouses of his day, and that existence of discarnate spirits with the power to interfere in this world should not be inferred from the conduct of mere madmen.[230]

Ungodly occult power seems, to the mind of Hobbes, to be the most unspeakable monstrosity: "For it must either be by virtue of some natural science, or by Incantation, that is, virtue of words. For if the enchanters do it by their own power independent, there is some power that proceedeth not from God; which all men deny."[231] Hobbes is so concerned with this because in the Bible itself there are passages of scripture that suggest practicing "Magick" outside—or even against—the will of God is possible, for example the serpents conjured by Pharaohs magicians, and other wonders that they performed, in their magical contest with Moses:

> There be some texts of Scripture, that seem to attribute the power of working wonders (equal to some of those immediate Miracles, wrought by God himself,) to certain Arts of Magick, and Incantation. As for example, when we read that after the Rod of Moses being cast on the ground became a Serpent, *the Magicians of Egypt did the like by their Enchantments*.[232]

It is not just the Old Testament, but the casting out of demons and other magical practices of Jesus that also pose a problem for Hobbes in this regard.[233] He has no good answer for why Christ did not assert that all magicians are charlatans or speak against others who performed healings and wonders of a similar kind as his own. It is especially problematic that Jesus tells his disciples that they can perform the same miracles as he does if they put their hearts and minds to it. The best that Hobbes can do to explain away such statements in scripture is to claim that while God may have endowed men in the company of Christ with such supernatural powers, this special dispensation was ended after the time of Christ.[234]

Hobbes goes so far as to claim that every instance of such apparent "power of Magick, Witchcraft, and Enchantment" must actually be "Imposture, and delusion, wrought by ordinary means; and so far from supernatural" that all the "Imposters" need to study to perform such feats is "the ordinary ignorance, stupidity, and superstition of mankind."[235] Manipulation of this kind he puts on a par with the sleight of hand practiced by jugglers and ventriloquists or, in the best case, scientifically informed frauds, as are seen for instance in the manipulation of masses ignorant of natural phenomena on the part of royals who used their astronomers in order to predict eclipses in advance and then claimed, on this basis, that they or their priesthood had miraculous insight or power because they accurately "prophesied" a darkening of the Sun — or even caused it.[236] This is *a very revealing passage*, because concealed in it is an admission of the kind of thing that would be fundamentally destructive of Hobbes' theory of the state's sovereign power.

The lamest and most pathetic line of argument that Hobbes pursues with regard to this matter, is the claim that even genuine miracles just do not take place any more. Hobbes has the audacity to assert that neither he nor anyone he knows has ever witnessed "any such wondrous work" that even a person endowed "but with a mediocrity of reason, would think supernatural."[237] Miracles may have been performed by God in Biblical times, but not any longer — and if, perchance, one should take place, only the Sovereign could determine this in his capacity as the "Lieutenant of God, and Head of the Church."[238]

Whatever any man might wish to believe in the silent depth of his own heart or mind, his public professions of faith must be in line with state policy.[239] By the same token, however, Hobbes comes down against Inquisitions.[240] "Conformity of their Speech and Actions" should be sufficient for the magistrates, who ought not to torture men in order to investigate their hidden beliefs.[241] The roots of a man's recognized legal right not to make statements that incriminate himself may extend back to passages such as this one in *Leviathan*.[242]

Hobbes lays great emphasis on Christ's injunction to his followers to obey the civil authorities even if they are pagans, and he argues from this that obedience is therefore all the more due by Christians subjects to their Christian king.[243] He also quotes St. Paul on the duty of children to obey their parents, without any recognition of how this conflicts with at least some of Christ's sayings that, as we saw toward the close of Chapter 5, call on the true children of God to disown and even hate their earthly parents.[244] Hobbes quotes line after line of Christian scripture that enjoins subjects of a state to submit themselves "to every Ordinance of Man, for the Lord's sake."[245] For anyone who sees Paul as a Gnostic, the passages from Paul quoted by Hobbes ought to give them pause, such as: "*Put men in mind to be subject to Principalities, and Powers, and to obey Magistrates.*"[246] In other words, obey the archons.

It is especially revealing of Hobbes' true aim that he goes to the length of demanding obedience to the Sovereign even if the latter should demand that people renounce their faith in Christ.[247] He argues that such a renunciation can only be "Profession with the tongue" which "is but an external thing" and that no one can really expunge a sincere faith from the recesses of a person's heart.[248] In other words, the government of the Antichrist ought to be obeyed. But one may secretly still have faith in Christ, albeit with no way to express this in one's actions.

In response to those who criticized submission to state power even if it contradicts one's heartfelt faith, Hobbes does make the good point that, if the Christian subject were to be substituted with someone who is "in his heart of the Mahometan Religion," no one living in a Christian

Commonwealth would expect a Muslim to be justified in defying the civil authority in order to practice his religion in ways inconsistent with the law.[249] If one were to argue that a man of faith, such as the Muslim in question, ought to prefer death to feigned obedience, then the person arguing for this would be inciting people to rebellion against their lawful governments.[250]

When confronted with the objection of whether, according to this logic, the Christian martyrs have to be seen as having "needlessly cast away their lives," Hobbes has no good answer.[251] He says that only those who personally bore witness to the ministry of Jesus and were then unjustly put to death are true martyrs, because the idea of martyrdom involves testimony to the power of God and only these could testify based on direct experience.[252] Again, this is similar to his position on miracles: they may have happened once, long ago, but God does not do such things these days, just as he does not call for martyrs to prove their faith by resisting what seems to be an unjust state. This could not be further from the place that martyrs have had in the sacred tradition of Iran, all the way from the chivalric heroes of the ancient Iranian epic tradition to the martyrs of the Shi'ite faith—including those still valorized in the Islamic Republic of Iran.

Hobbes tears into the Catholic Church both for its religious doctrines, which are threatening to the authority of any Sovereign other than the Pope, and also for its scholastic preservation of Aristotelian metaphysics, which he thinks prevents the proper development of Reason and what we would now call Science.[253] Of the Church he asks *Cui bono?* and concludes no one other than the Vatican—which, in Hobbes' view, is certainly not the one true Kingdom of God on Earth.[254] Rather, *Leviathan* describes the Catholic Church hierarchy as the "Kingdom of Darkness."[255] He even compares their institution to "the *Kingdom of Fairies*" from "the old wives *Fables* in England, concerning *Ghosts* and *Spirits*, and the feasts they play in the night."[256]

Even if one is a proponent of Catholicism in its most Traditional form, one ought to at least recognize the astuteness of Hobbes' insight into the pagan substrate of the Church of Rome—as compared, say, to Hobbes' own Church of England, let alone to certain puritanical or rationalistic forms of Protestantism. This insight culminates in the shockingly definitive and unequivocal statement of Hobbes, that, "the *Papacy*, is no other, than the *Ghost* of the deceased *Roman Empire*, sitting crowned upon the grave thereof … [as it arose] out of the Ruins of that Heathen Power."[257] Even their language is a Ghost of the Old Roman one.[258] As we have seen, the Caesarian power of pagan Rome itself, which Hobbes still sees in the Papacy, is actually a ghost or spectral shadow cast by the Mithraic monarchical tradition of ancient Iran. Everything magical that Hobbes rejects about the tradition of the Roman Catholic Church is a legacy of Mithraism and Zoroastrianism. It is a gift of the Magi who went in search of their expected sacred king.

In ancient Iran it was believed that the *Saoshyant* or expected savior at the end of history would bear "in one person" (Pahlavi *pat evak tan*) both the "kingly glory" or *Farré Kiâni* (*khvarrah-e khvatayih* in Pahlavi) and also the "divine glory" known as *Farré Izadi*.[259] We see this in the following passage of the Pahlavi scripture *Dinkard*, the original version of which dates from the Sassanian period:

> The event against which the Evil Spirit is most stubbornly opposed is the conjunction in one single person and with the utmost intensity of the kingly *khvarrah* and the Good Religion: for it is this conjunction that will drive him to destruction. Because, should the kingly *khvarrah* in its utmost degree of intensity, as it was in Yam [Jamshid], be joined with that of the Good Religion, or should the *khvarrah* of the Good Religion in its utmost degree of intensity, as it was in Zartusht [Zarathustra], be coupled with that of the kingship in its utmost intensity, as it was in Yam, then the Evil Spirit would have perished and the creatures could have been preserved from the assault, and the Renovation of Existence would have taken place.[260]

The traditional titles of the Iranian monarch attest to the fact that kingship or imperium was a sacred institution—albeit one that transcended the distinction between a variety of Iranian religions, including Mithraism,

Zoroastrianism, Manichaeism, and Shi'ite Gnosis.[261] For example, as we saw in Chapter 5, the Parthian monarchs struck their coins with the Greek phrase *Epiphanes* or "manifestation of God," which appeared together with the title *Shâhanshâh of Âryânâ* around their portraits (or images of Perseus/Mithra that stood in for them). Mithradates was the first of the Parthian kings to use this phrase. Roman chronicles record that

> when Mithradates Eupator, the King of Pontus who claimed to be a descendant of the Achaemenian royal family, was born, a star was shining with such radiance that all the heavens seemed to be ablaze for seventy days: the same event was repeated when the coronation of this king took place, some twenty years later (112–111 BC).[262]

The very name Mithra-dâtes or *Mehr-dâd* in Middle Persian indicates the divinity of the monarch insofar as it means that he has been "given by Mithra" or is the representative of "Mithra's Justice."[263]

The Pahlavi or Middle Persian title *haft keshvar khvatay* or "Lord of the Seven Climes" was employed in the Sassanian period, when Shapur the Great, the patron of Mani and Manichaeism, described himself as "King of Kings, partner with the stars, brother of the Sun and the Moon."[264] In Manichaeism the righteous king was also described as *amud as-subh* or "The Column of Light" or "Pillar of Glory" linking heaven and earth.[265] The title *Shâhé Zamân* was a precursor of the Shi'ite title *Imâmé Zamân*, or the Imam of Time (namely the occulted Imam who will appear at the Apocalypse), as the culmination of a line of leaders who are each guardians of the esoteric truth in their own time and place—a Mazdakite idea in origin.[266] It was also the basis for the heads of Sufi orders being referred to as Shah, as in the case of Shah Nimatullah Vali or Shah Ismail before he actually founded the Safavid dynasty. The Sufis conceived of such a Shah as the *Ensâne Kâmel*, "the Perfect Man" or "the Whole Human Being."[267] The most divine of the various kingly titles from the Islamic period is probably *Qebleyé 'Alam* or "Pivot of the Cosmos."

The latest of these many titles was that adopted by Mohammad Reza Pahlavi, namely *Âryâ-Mehr*, which could be translated as "Light of the

Aryans" but also literally gives the meaning "Sun or Friend of Mithra."[268] This Pahlavi title was supposed to signal the unique association of Mithra with the divine royal glory, which descends upon a man destined to be a legitimate monarch in the form of a winged solar halo.[269] It also took the form of a winged hawkish or phoenix-like fire bird, usually equated with the griffin, and known as *homâ-ye homâyoun* in New Persian.[270]

Natural phenomena, whether beneficently bounteous or catastrophically destructive, were seen as falling within the control of the monarch and inextricable from his virtue or lack thereof.[271] The Achaemenid term *vazraka* is used in inscriptions in which, for example, Darius is warding off drought and famine at the same time as he is described as *khshayathiya vazraka* or *Shâhé Bozorg* in New Persian. This term *vazra-ka* is an adjectival form of the noun *vazra*, meaning "club" or "thunderbolt," in other words, the thunderbolt scepter wielded by the sky father of primordial Indo-European religion, which the Hindus call Indra and the Greeks call Zeus, the thunderbolt of Thor in the Norse religion, and the *Vajra* of Bodhisattvas and Buddhas.[272] Thus this title points back to the prehistoric epoch of Indo-European society in which, as in the case of primitive or aboriginal cultures that still survive, the Shaman-King was believed to be capable of commanding nature, most dramatically by hurling lightning-bolts against his enemies or the foes of his tribe. The double thunderbolt symbol of the Nazi German SS knightly order had the same meaning. It is common knowledge in Iran that the primordial King of the World, Jamshid, forced *divs* or Daevas to carry his throne into the heavens, but it is less well known that this is an expression of the more general magical power that Jamshid Shah wielded over all the forces of Nature. Note the following passage from the apocalyptic Middle Persian scripture *Abyatkaré Zhamaspik*:

> And Jamshid, the one of the fine cattle, was endowed with majesty, with glorious bravery, with splendid victory; and he took the seven climates under his sway, which was exerted on men and on devs during 616 years and 6 months. ... During his age, clouds, winds and rain were submitted to his will and he gave the devs and the paris as slaves to men; and the devs made ready the food

> for men, who lived therefore in peace and comfort. Under his domination, there existed no frost, no heat, no nuisance of old age, no death, no envy created by the devs.[273]

This is a fascinating description of the Iranian equivalent of the antediluvian world known as Atlantis in the lore of the Western branch of the Indo-European community, depicted by ancient Semites in Genesis and the Book of Enoch as the civilization of Noah that was governed by fallen angels. The ancient Iranians describe the capital of the world empire of Jamshid as having polar conditions, wherein "the whole year lasted but one day and one night."[274] The crown, the throne, the golden dagger, and the royal seal were all considered holy symbols from the time of the primordial world-governing Emperor Jamshid onward.[275] It was believed that after the fall of Jamshid, the *Farr* divided itself into three parts — each one corresponding to the proper task and destiny of one of the three social classes represented in the Mithraic tricolor of Iran.[276] It is believed that in the end times, these three bands of the *Farr*, namely the priestly white, the knightly red, and the agrarian green, will reunite into the single divine royal glory borne by the final Savior.[277]

Beginning at least with Darius the Great, who uses the term *frasha tya vainataiy* in his inscriptions, meaning "the regeneration *which is seen*," the holy aim of the Iranian sacred monarch has been to help bring about the *frasha-kereti*, or *Frashgard* as it was later known in Middle Persian.[278] This is a renewal of the primordial perfection that was lost when the divine royal glory flew away from Jamshid — in other words, when he lost his legitimacy on account of his hubris and will to storm heaven, which resulted in the overthrow of his World Empire by the demon-king Zahhak, whose caduceus-like symbolism we have repeatedly had occasion to contemplate throughout this study.

Suffice it to add only that when the hero Fereidun comes to liberate Jamshid's daughters who are being taught black magic by the demon-king in his fortress, the Mithraic knight smashes Zahhak's skull with a bull-headed mace that goes on to be the scepter of Mithraic (and then Zoroastrian) priests. As early as the *Gâthâs* of Zarathustra, the bull was a symbol of the Earth. This means that, in avenging Jamshid, Fereidun is claiming the scepter that had been wielded by Jamshid, namely the scepter of World Empire.[279] This fits very well with the lore of the Holy Grail of Jamshid or *jâmé jam*, which is also known as *jâmé jahân namây* or "the world-showing cup"—in other words, a magical device through which everything that is going on all over the planet can be observed.[280] Ultimately, what is being said in these myths and symbols is, not only that Iranian monarchy is sacred, but the Iranian monarch is really supposed to be a King of the World (*Jahân Shâh*).

Jamshid fell from such a status because instead of exercising this office as the viceroy of God, he forced the gods to raise his throne up into the heavens in an attempt to become the highest god. Darius the Great writes, "I am king by Ahura Mazda's will: I have put *the earth* in order."[281] Not "I have put Iran in order." No, the whole planet Earth. It is not an accident of history that the Achaemenid ceremonial capital of Persepolis, which was used to celebrate both Nowruz, inaugurated by Jamshid Shah, and Mehregan, which commemorates the defeat of Zahhak by Fereidun who avenges Jamshid, came to be called *Takhté Jamshid* or the "Throne of Jamshid." Not incidentally, when Fereidun defeats Zahhak and binds him inside Mount Damavand, the *Farr* or divine royal glory that had been lost by Jamshid is bestowed upon him from the depth of the Caspian Sea where it was supposedly safeguarded by a representative of Mithra after being lost by Jamshid.[282] As the freer of the Iranians from Zahhak's tyranny, Fereidun becomes the Free-dân, or Frei-donne to put it in Franco-Germanic, the "giver of freedom." The most ancient form of Fereidun's name is Thraetaona (Triton), the source for the name Trita.[283]

The divine royal halo, which is depicted around the heads of both prophets and kings, and which entered both European art and Indo-Buddhist Art under Iranian influence, was not seen as a mere poetic abstraction.[284] According to the *Dinkard*, the *khvarenah* or *khowraa*—the aura—is "a *visible energy* … strictly *bound to the destiny of each man* … [and] granted in accordance with his personal worth (*arzih*)."[285] The bearers of an aura are "the Holy Geniuses" whose light has been drawn from the Endless Light.[286] In the Iranian tradition, the original meaning of being a "king" as such meant being "a man capable of realizing, in full awareness, his own destiny by developing his inborn *khvarenah*," in other words, by following and actualizing that spark of the divine fire that is his own Genius.[287]

The term for the divine royal glory, namely *khvarenah*, which was shortened to *Farr*, has a fascinating and terrifying etymology. It comes from the phrase *a-khvaretem khvarenah*, with the *khvar* in it as the root of the contemporary Persian *khor* for "eat" or "devour."[288] *A-khvaretem khvarenah* means that Light so Victorious that it devours those who find themselves in its presence without itself ever being consumed by anything or running out of incandescent energy.[289] This ancient Persian phrase is undoubtedly the origin for that epithet of Mithra that became so prevalent in Rome, namely *Sol Invictus* or the Unconquerable Sun (*Mehré Nabarz* or *Khorshidé Shekast-nâ-pazir* in Middle and New Persian). That the gods of old were believed to be blindingly haloed in this way must be why they were referred to as *Daeva* in Sanskrit and *Elohim* in Hebrew, both of which terms literally mean the "shining." Again, this points us back to the God-King archetype at the fount of Iranian monarchy. By now it ought to be no surprise that the next person who would embody this archetype, after Mohammad Reza Shah disowned it, would be his greatest nemesis, the Ayatollah Ruhollah Khomeini — founder of the Islamic Republic of Iran and the inheritor of Shah Ismail Safavid's theocratic Shi'ite state.

CHAPTER 11

THE GOVERNMENT OF GOD

A STERN AND HANDSOME FACE, engraved with charisma by the sands of time and wearing the white beard of wisdom, shone in the midday sun. Black turban and black cloak blew starkly against the pure blue dome of the sky. His piercing gaze surveyed them slowly — four million strong — men, women, children — crying, shouting, reaching to touch his hands. They called him *Bot-Shekan* — the "Idol Smasher," destroyer of illusion...

Ayatollah Ruhollah Khomeini, the founder of the Islamic Republic of Iran, is one of the most enigmatic figures in modern political history. His life and character are the focus of the first section of this chapter. Outside of Iran, and even to an extent within his own country, Khomeini has become synonymous with Islamic Fundamentalism. However, the man was a gnostic (*aref*) whose deep study of Mysticism and Philosophy was unconventional compared to the legalism of the traditional Shi'ite clergy. What he learned from such sages as Plato, Al-Farabi, Ibn Arabi, Sohrevardi, and Molla Sadra formed the foundation of his revolutionary political program. In particular, certain core structures of the Islamic Republic of Iran mirror the constitution of the ideal state that Plato delineates in his *Republic* governed by sagacious Guardians.

Imam Khomeini's mystical charisma and occult power over the Iranian people was not lost on the French philosopher Michel Foucault. Having observed the Iranian Revolution of 1978–1979 first-hand as a journalist reporting from Tehran, Foucault concluded that Khomeini was the most perfect embodiment of Jean-Jacques Rousseau's idea of the "general will" that had ever manifested in the history of nations. Foucault also saw the potential of Khomeini's vision to revolutionize not only Iran, but the entire Earth by becoming "the spirit of a world without spirit." The second section of this chapter examines Khomeini's revolutionary leadership through the lens of the German sociologist Max Weber's conception of charismatic authority.

The third and final section of this chapter is a meandering history of the Islamic Republic of Iran, highlighting various major challenges to the regime's establishment. The first of these was the rebellion of the Mojaheddin-e-Khalq (MEK, MKO) who founded the National Council of Resistance of Iran (NCRI) after being driven into exile by Ayatollah Khomeini. The conflict between Khomeini and Massoud Rajavi, the cultish leader of the Mojaheddin is analyzed in terms of a struggle between two claimants to charismatic leadership of the same revolutionary movement. The similarity in the form of their leadership and the way in which they were perceived by their followers, despite the differences in the content of their doctrines, reveals something important about the nature of charismatic leadership in an Iranian sociopolitical context that stretches back to Shah Ismail, Hasan Sabbah, and Babak Khorramdin.

Other major challenges to the establishment include the Islamic Reform Movement that was philosophically spearheaded by Abdolkarim Soroush and that President Mohammad Khatami attempted, and miserably failed, to turn into a political reality. In this context, Soroush's philosophical doctrine of Islamic Democracy is briefly explicated. The first flashpoint between the reformists and the establishment were the protests of July 1999, and the catastrophic crescendo of this movement was the Green Uprising of Summer and Fall of 2009, a protest movement sparked by allegations of an electoral fraud that prevented Mir Hossein Mousavi from becoming the President of the Islamic Republic of Iran. Discussion of this calamity becomes an opportunity to examine a few elements of the Constitution of the Islamic Republic of Iran with a view to understanding what exactly leaders of the so-called "Green Path of Hope" were trying to accomplish by insisting on strict implementation of the constitution.

11.1 Khomeini as a Mystic and Philosopher-King

Ruhollah Khomeini was a lover of poetry — especially that of the supreme Persian poet, Hafez of Shiraz, whose worldview was identified as the cultural and spiritual zenith of Iranian Civilization in Chapter 8. Almost immediately upon arriving in Qom as a young theological student he began to seek masters that could teach him *erfân* and *hekmat*. For various reasons, the images of Khomeini that are prevalent today in the West, and even in his own Islamic Republic, do not recognize that this period of passionate searching and attainment of mystical and philosophical knowledge in his early years is the key to Khomeini's life and mission. It is the key to understanding the regime that he founded as an attempt to establish a Platonic Republic of Virtue on earth in a conscious reaction to the rise of Western Nihilism. As Ahmad Sadri realizes that

> in opposing such liberal ideals as democracy in favor of an Islamic 'republic of virtue,' fundamentalism *also* follows a long antidemocratic Western tradition, expressed across the centuries from Thrasymachus's debate with Socrates. ... The right-wing clerical ideal of a true Islamic community of virtue is profoundly influenced by authoritarian interpretations of Platonic and Aristotelian thought. The elites who took over the reigns of power in Iran conceived of themselves more as 'enlightened despots' than as Shi'ite vice regents of the 'occulted Imam.'[1]

The Platonic inspiration for the Islamic Republic did not come to Khomeini directly from the work of Plato, although an Arabic translation of *The Republic* was one of Khomeini's most treasured books. Rather, it came through the traditions of *erfân* and *hekmat*. *Erfân* is Gnosticism and *hekmat* is analytic philosophy. *Erfân* is now exclusively a practice of the predominately Persian Shi'a sect of Islam. However, major contributors to its tradition were not Shi'a, and many were Sufis.

In the period from the ninth to the eleventh centuries, Al-Farabi's commentaries on Aristotelian texts developed an Arabic formal logic.

More importantly, Farabi wrote the first works on Islamic political philosophy, the substance of which was later refined by Avicenna. This political vision is decidedly Platonic: "the Virtuous City is invoked to describe divinely inspired just rule by the philosopher-ruler, the *jurist-guardian*."[2] Farabi's vision was, of course, inspired by Plato's *Republic* — but also by the monistic Neo-Platonist reformations of Plotinus, which were more metaphysically in line with Islamic eschatology. Shahab al-din Suhrawardi further developed the Islamic transfiguration of philosopher-kingship by fusing it to the Shi'ite concept of the succession of Imams when he called for "the enlightened rule of the divinely inspired, appearing in every age, who manifest signs indicating knowledge and power, and thus become authorities who serve as rulers or *Guardians of Justice*."[3] In lines mirroring Plato's basic requirement for the philosopher-king, Suhrawardi wrote that the Guardian of Justice must have "direct experience of the signs [Platonic *eidos*] from the divine realm."[4]

As we have seen, in the sixteenth to early seventeenth centuries the Safavid dynasty in Iran sought national cohesion vis-à-vis the Arabs and Ottoman Turks, by making Shi'ism the state religion. Initially, the Safavids provided an atmosphere of scholarly freedom and substantially endowed their centers of learning. The product was a major development of Shi'a philosophical thought. The clergy not only adopted Al-Farabi's Platonic political doctrine of the Virtuous City but they found a place for its jurist-guardians as interpreters of law and even for a single supreme knowledge-holder (Suhrawardi's Guardian of Justice), within the bureaucratic system that they now jointly administered with the Safavid monarchs. In Chapter 9 it was mentioned that the crowning achievement of the Islamic period of Iranian Philosophy comes with Molla Sadra of Shiraz (d. 1641), who tied together all the strands that had been developing since the ninth century in his magnum opus *The Four Intellectual Journeys*. This work, which defines Islamic 'metaphysical philosophy' by drawing together *erfân* and *hekmat*, was to be the other major source of inspiration for Khomeini along with Ibn Arabi.

Khomeini soon found three masters in Qom to teach him both *erfân* and *hekmat*, mainly in private. His first teacher was Akbar Yazdi, who was known for his deeply mystical approach rather than the run-of-the-mill formalism of other teachers. Khomeini then focused on ethics with Maleki Tabrizi and Rafai Qazvini. From these men Khomeini learned the fundamentals of Islamic philosophy. However, the man whom Khomeini would later call his "spiritual father and teacher" was Mirza Mohammad Shahabadi (d. 1950). Khomeini had to repeatedly beg Shahabadi to teach him the shady subject of mysticism. Finally, after four refusals he proved his worth and Shahabadi relented. In their years together, Khomeini plunged first into the work of Ibn Arabi and then that of Molla Sadra.

Ibn Arabi was profoundly influenced by the Neo-Platonic idea of *logos* as the Perfect Man. Ibn Arabi believed that while the macrocosm of the material universe is not God in its full essence, the microcosm of the soul of man *is* of the divine essence. Thus through the disciplining and refinement of the soul by the guidance of divine law, man can bring about a congruence between his inner perfection and his material existence in such a way that it comes to reflect the essence of God. The profound and controversial implication of this process of "opening" is that it is indeed possible to achieve divine perfection in this very life, rather than spending life in blind submission to religious law with the hope of redemption and understanding only after death.

The Perfect Man (*ensâné kâmel*) is "the center and animating principle of the whole created universe, the spirit and life of things." Ibn Arabi calls this Perfect Man the *vali* or "guardian", which the Shi'ites subsequently identified with the Imam. Thus in their interpretation of Ibn Arabi's work *Shahré Fusus*—which Khomeini studied with Shahabadi—the Shi'ite mystic can only gain *gnosis* through identification with the Imam of the Age. Each of these Imams who appear following the death of the prophet, are charged with "cosmic guardianship," and without them the world would fall into the darkness of Chaos. Khomeini's 1929 commentary on the prayer "The Dawn Supplication" exudes his fascination with the Sufi or Gnostic concept of the Perfect Man. He writes:

> [T]he Perfect Man is the holder of the chain of existence, with which the cycle is completed. It is the beginning and the end, it is the external and the internal, the totality of the Divine Book. He is God's greatest sign, created in God's image. Whoever knows the Perfect Man has known God.[5]

Once he had absorbed Ibn Arabi's concept of the Perfect Man, Khomeini turned to studying Mollah Sadra's grand synthesis of *erfân* and *hekmat*—the peak of Islamic Neo-Platonism. Molla Sadra's *Four Intellectual Journeys* outlines the following path of perfection:

> Before starting the journey, the traveler must have purged his soul of all earthly, carnal desire by practicing all the religious duties, immersing himself in piety and asceticism, and robing himself with total submission in certitude and love of the Almighty. It is only after this that he can leave the physical world and cross some of the metaphysical, spiritual barriers in order to reach God's essence. The second journey is with God in God, and that is when the traveler is acquainting with His essence, and having achieved certitude in Him begins his journey with God's help. He will submerge into oceans of secrets and mysteries to acquaint himself with the beauty of God's 'names' [the Platonic *forms*], witnessing their real manifestations, influence and governance [in the *substance* of the world]. The traveler will also learn from God the qualities of love, anger or disaffection and see them among the people. The third journey is one in which the traveler returns to the people, but is no longer separate from God, as he can now see His omnipotent essence. The fourth and final journey is one in which the traveler has acquired godly attributes with which he can begin to guide and help others to reach God. This is the crucial stage. It is here that *velâyat* [Guardianship] and prophet-hood are realized, giving the traveler the mission to preach God's word … [and] by establishing rightful policies, *the government of absolute Justice* and the reign of divinity, the Perfect Man will guide society towards absolute perfection.[6]

By the age of twenty-seven Khomeini had written voluminously on such subjects—though he chose not to publish most of these writings openly. His commentary on the prayer "The Dawn Supplication" is considered to have demonstrated the compatibility and interdependence of mysticism and *sharia*, arguing that there is no contradiction between the *gnosis* arrived at through the study of *erfân* and strict adherence to Islamic law. Meanwhile, in *The Ascension of the Traveler and the Prayer of the Mystics*, Khomeini implicitly reveals his view that the outward practices of religion, such as prayer, are only a "ladder" to the perfection of the Guardianship of Justice:

> [W]hen one has left the people and is in the presence of the Almighty ... [the] journey which is from the people to the people [i.e., the practice of religion] will end ... and this truth needs more explanation than I'm able to give and people are able to hear.[7]

While Khomeini himself never openly claimed to have achieved the final state of perfection that entitles one to Guardianship, this humble concealment is a characteristic virtue of mystics. Mehdi Yazdi, the son of Ayatollah Ha'eri, a former student of Khomeini and a leading Iranian scholar of both Western and Islamic Philosophy argues that "Khomeini, not unlike Hallaj, considered himself as having completed the fourth journey, which implies a belief in the words: I am the truth and the people [*ana al-haqq wa'l khalq*]."[8] Khomeini's son Ahmad also claims that he understood from his mother and close friends that his father "believed he had a special relationship with God with whom he was at one, often speaking with frightening enthusiasm about his beloved Lord."[9]

After completing his studies and receiving his diploma, Khomeini became a teacher of Jurisprudence and Philosophy in Qom. In the years of Reza Shah's erosion of the standing of the religious class in order to press on with his Westernization of Iran, Khomeini's outspoken lectures on ethics drew crowds of hundreds. In these lectures Khomeini interpreted Islam as inseparable from a commitment to political causes and social justice—not in some future paradise, but *here* and *now*. This message would bring him into several clashes with the Pahlavi regime over the following decades. These incidents, which form the outlines of the story of Khomeini's rise to power, include the protest of the Local Council Law of 1962 to the Moharram and Ashura speeches of 1963, his subsequent first term of imprisonment, release, and finally the reaction to the 1964 Status of Forces Law which sent him into exile in Turkey, then Najaf (Iraq), and his triumphant return to Iran via Paris.[10]

What is important to understand is why it is that in the comments and actions of all these years Khomeini did not appear to his peers in the political clergy, and the international press to which he was exposed in Paris, as the mystic that he in fact was. He had good reason to conceal himself. Khomeini's study of *erfân* and *hekmat* is by no means common among the clergy. Actually, the more orthodox Shi'a clergy view these practices with great suspicion and condescension as being influenced by the Greeks, and have historically marked their adherents as deviants or heretics. While in Islam, there are three paths to God, the majority of the clerical establishment reject the rationalism of philosophy (*hekmat*) and the illumination of mysticism (*erfân*) in favor of blind devotion and obedience to Quranic law (*sharia*). Mansur Hallaj was crucified for claiming attainment, Ibn Arabi suffered condemnation and imprisonment as a heretic, Sohrevardi was executed at thirty-seven, Ayn al-Qozat was hanged and his body burned with oil near Khomeini's hown town, Molla Sadra (Khomeini's hero) was driven out of his native city of Shiraz. These are the fates of members of the mystical tradition that Khomeini followed.

Thus it is understandable why Khomeini had to hide his dissatisfaction with the orthodox version of religion that was adhered to by the majority of the clergy. On the surface Khomeini took the posture of conforming to the disciplines of law, jurisprudence, and the Quran. He wrote on these subjects, but he also wrote much on mysticism, though he kept his mystical writings secret. However, enough of his aura of *gnosis* seeped through his concealment that by the time of his return to Iran the majority of people did in fact feel that he possessed the perfection of one of Suhrawardi's Guardians when they greeted him, not only as an Imam carrying the mantle of the Prophet—but initially, as the *Mahdi*.

The many comments that Khomeini made, both before and after he gained power, which rallied such popular support, also raise questions as to how he could have been a mystic. However, there is a rationale underlying Khomeini's notorious rhetoric on the conspiratorial ties between

Israel, America, and the West and Iran's Jewish and Bahai minorities, as well as his evocation of mythical imagery in this connection. Khomeini's great mentor in Qom, Shahabadi, had emphasized the use of calculative planning in order to organize Muslims. In his lectures, which Khomeini followed for seven years, Shahabadi advised his students not to hesitate in simplifying complex and difficult subjects for a wider public understanding, and to bring about an initial cohesion necessary for more far reaching aims. In his defense, he cited the saying of the Prophet Mohammad: "Talk to people according to the level of their intelligence."[11] One of the most brilliant philosophers of the West would witness the effectiveness of this policy first-hand, as Khomeini drew the Iranian people together in a wave of revolt.

11.2 "The Spirit of a World Without Spirit"

Michel Foucault was in Tehran in the fall of 1978. He was fascinated by the events unfolding in Iran and had consequently obtained a contract for a regular eye-witness column from the Italian newspaper *Corriere della Sera*. Even if more in the rapture that infected their author than in their predictive accuracy, Foucault's writings on Iran from this period are a powerful testament to the transcendent nature of a movement that sought nothing less than to resist and overthrow the hegemonic and soulless regime of Western Nihilism.

Foucault immediately recognized that there was something about the Iranian Revolution that made it unlike all other revolutions in modern history. It did not explode out of class struggle and was not led by a vanguard. Moreover, there were no objective factors at work sufficiently strong to produce such a massive revolt:

> There's a very remarkable fact in what is happening in Iran. There was a government that was certainly one of the best endowed with weapons, the best served by a large army that was astonishingly faithful. … [T]here was a police that was certainly not very efficient, but whose violence and cruelty often made up for a lack of subtlety: it was moreover, a regime directly supported

> by the United States; lastly, it had the backing of the whole world, of the countries large and small that surrounded it. In a sense, it had everything going for it, plus, of course, oil, which guaranteed the state an income that it could use as it wished. Yet, despite all of this, a crisis, of economic difficulties, etc., but the economic difficulties in Iran at that time were not sufficiently great for people to take to the streets, in the hundreds of thousands, in the millions, and face the machine-guns bare chested. That's the phenomenon that we have to talk about. …
>
> Now we recognize a revolution when we can observe two dynamics: one is that of the contradictions in that society, that of the class struggle or of social confrontations. Then there is a political dynamics, that is to say, the presence of a vanguard, class, party, or political ideology, in short, a spearhead that carries the whole nation with it. Now it seems to me that, in what is happening in Iran, one can recognize neither of those two dynamics that are for us distinctive signs and explicit marks of a revolutionary phenomenon. What, for us, is a revolutionary movement in which one cannot situate the internal contradictions of a society, and in which one cannot point out a vanguard either?[12]

Furthermore, Foucault refuted what has now become the common view, that the exoteric fact of the "Islamic Religion" acted as the cohesive force in the absence of the Western criteria of revolution that he saw as lacking above. He believed that "the religious opponents of the Shah were *not*, as they were often glibly portrayed in the Western media, 'fanatics'" and that "It was not the desire [of the Iranian people] to be ruled by a 'government of mullahs'":

> [T]his is perhaps the soul of the uprising: 'Of course, we have to change this regime and get rid of this man, we have to change this corrupt administration, we have to change the whole country, the foreign policy. *But above all, we have to change ourselves. Our way of being, our relationship with others, with things, with eternity, with God, etc., must be completely changed and there will only be a true revolution if this radical change in our experience takes place…*
>
> I believe that … Islam played a role … but above all, in relation to the way of life that was theirs, religion for them was like the promise and guarantee of finding something that would radically change their subjectivity. Shi'ism is

> precisely a form … that, with its … esoteric content, distinguished between what is mere external obedience to the code and what is the profound spiritual life. … [T]hey were looking to Islam for a change in their subjectivity. … [T]raditional Islamic practice was already there and already gave them their identity; in this way they had of living the Islamic religion as a revolutionary force there was something other than the desire to obey the law more faithfully, there was the desire to renew their entire existence by going back to a spiritual experience that they thought they could find within Shi'ite Islam itself. People always quote Marx and the opium of the people. The sentence that immediately preceded that statement and which is never quoted says that *religion is the spirit of a world without spirit…* Islam, in that year of 1978, was not the opium of the people precisely because it was the *spirit of a world without spirit.*[13]

Instead of "religion," Foucault saw the cohesive force of the Iranian Revolution as a transcendent *general will*, and the mystic "saint" Khomeini as its point of focus:

> Among the things that characterize this revolutionary event, there is the fact that it has brought out—and few peoples in history have had this—an absolutely collective will. The general will [*volonté générale*] is a political myth with which jurists and philosophers try to analyze or justify institutions, etc. It's a theoretical tool: nobody has ever seen the 'general will' and, personally, I thought that this collective will was like God, like the soul, something one would never encounter. I don't know whether you will agree with me, but we met, in Tehran and throughout Iran, the general will of a people. Well, you have to salute it, it doesn't happen every day.[14]
>
> No head of state, no political Leader, even with the support of all the media in his country, can claim today to be the object of so personal and so intense an affection. … Khomeini *is not a politician…* Khomeini is the point of fixation for a collective will.[15]

Foucault expressed the essence of this *volonté générale* in the French word *ivress* which can be translated as "rapture," "intoxication," or "ecstasy." He was deeply moved by apparently having seen this "inner experience" alive amongst the Iranian people. He said: "There was literally a light that lit up all of them and which bathed all of them at the same time." Foucault was convinced that once a movement is inspired by such rapture, "there is no power that is capable of making such a movement impossible."

Prime Minister Shapour Bakhtiar and others who briefly served in the short-lived last administration of the Pahlavi regime after the departure of the Shah, were deeply confused when, in January and February of 1979, they offered Khomeini a deal to form some kind of coalition with him and the revolutionary forces under his command, and he refused. In rejecting all rational economic considerations, charismatic leaders are never willing to "make a deal" for the sake of private gain.[16] Those who try to seduce a man like this into such a compromise have fundamentally misunderstood him. The determination and restraint of one who holds charisma — *who is held by it* and who holds others captivated by means of it — comes only from within himself, never on account of external constraints or pressures that might cause him to hold back or cave in.[17] Ayatollah Khomeini was a charismatic leader in exactly the sense that the sociologist Max Weber defines this type of person.

When viewed from a sociological perspective, beyond judgments of good or evil, the person with *charisma* — whether of the type of a hero or a sorcerer, or the judge or military leader — is someone seized by, and capable of seizing others with, a shamanic power.[18] In the most distant antiquity — as even today among the few remaining aboriginal societies — the charismatic person was usually a witch doctor, a tribal pathfinder, or the leader of big hunting expeditions.[19] In times of distress — whether that distress is of a psychic, physical, economic, ethical, or religious kind — it is not bureaucratic office holders with expert knowledge who can provide leadership. Rather, under such conditions it is a *charismatic* person who becomes a guide to the distressed society, a person whose special gifts are often even perceived to be of a supernatural character.[20]

In the eyes of his followers, "Imam" Khomeini was indeed believed to wield supernatural powers — as in the spectacular downing of the American helicopters that failed in their mission to rescue the hostages from the US Embassy in Tehran. Ayatollah Khomeini allowed his devotees to believe that, rather than simply being casualties of a sandstorm, the American choppers were smashed into each other and downed in the desert by Jinn that he had summoned to do his bidding against the Great Satan. In his *Theory of Social and Economic Organizations* Max Weber offers this most concise definition of "charisma" and the defining qualities of the charismatic leader:

> The term 'charisma' will be applied to a certain quality of an individual personality by virtue of which he is set apart from ordinary men and treated as endowed with supernatural, superhuman, or at least specifically exceptional powers or qualities. These are such as are not accessible to the ordinary person, but are regarded as of divine origin or as exemplary, and on the basis of them the individual concerned is treated as a leader. In primitive circumstances this peculiar kind of deference is paid to prophets, to people with a reputation for therapeutic or legal wisdom, to leaders in the hunt, and heroes in war. It is very often thought of as resting on magical powers.[21]

Shamans, founders of new religions, and intellectual demagogues are all different types of charismatic leaders.[22]

Appointment or dismissal for bureaucratic office according to certain technocratic criteria is as alien to the charismatic leader as a regular salary or an expectable path for career advancement.[23] A man with charisma is not elected or appointed to an office, nor can he expect regular compensation for performing the duties of such an office. Rather, he demands recognition from his followers by virtue of proving himself in the expression of a higher calling and in his furtherance of this mission.[24] Even if he is the most popular man in his society, the charismatic leader is not "elected" in a democratic fashion — or supposing that he is, he does not derive his legitimacy from this.[25] Rather, his "right" comes from the sense of duty that compels his followers from within as they swear their allegiance to him and look to his leadership.[26] One corollary to this is that his primary source of financial support will always be of the type of saints or pirates, never that of salaried bureaucrats.[27]

A charismatic leader whose mission is of a peaceful nature, or at least is still in a peaceful phase, may accept charitable contributions from individual patrons, which may take the form of charity, donations to a cause, or honorific gifts.[28] This need not necessarily take the form of large-scale foundations or honoraria, for the charismatic leader even bribery and begging are more acceptable means of securing financial survival than a routine job and economizing.[29] If such a leader is pursuing a more warlike or revolutionary cause, he may aggressively seek out booty in the course of struggle against his enemies, booty seized in a totally self-assured fashion for the purpose of carrying on that fight and obeying the genius that tasks him with his special mission.[30] What is clear is that any rational economic considerations or calibration of his behavior on the basis of concern for pecuniary gain is utterly foreign to the character of a charismatic leader.[31] Those who are outside the scope of such a man's mission will often think that he behaves with reckless disregard for his own economic welfare, and it will seem to them that he courts financial ruin.

Of course, charismatic leaders are almost inevitably also willing to die for their particular cause, so the idea that they might be unconcerned with suffering economic hardship ought not to be all that surprising. These men trust in divine providence to provide, perhaps by means of their devotees, whatever they require to single-mindedly pursue their mission. A charismatic leader might live in great austerity, or suddenly come into tremendous wealth, but neither of these conditions is relevant other than insofar as it allows him to stay on target. He would never seek out the wealth, nor would he be averse to the austerity so long as he still had sufficient means to continue his work as the kind of leader that he is.

During his years of exile in Iraq and, even in his villa outside Paris, Khomeini was known for sleeping on the floor in a room with little furniture. He lived very frugally, had few possessions, and was single-mindedly devoted to studying, writing, sermonizing, and organizing for his seizure of political power in Iran. That it has since been disclosed that Western intelligence agencies transferred funds to the bank accounts of some of his associates in order to support his movement, does not change the fact that he never allowed such funds to corrupt him or alter his way of life as a charismatic leader. These funds would be considered as booty by a leader of this kind and, as it turned out, booty seized from an enemy that would be shown for a dupe on account of handing it over to someone who would go on to bite off the hand that fed him.

The charismatic disregard of economy is not just a rejection of financial considerations, it is a rejection of the very principle of "economy" as such.[32] The basis of economic conservatism on a sociopolitical level is a deeper metaphysical principle of "economy" as conservation of energy. Charisma is the overflowing of energy into this world, as channeled by a particular person, from a source that almost seems to be out of this world. For the charismatic person, it makes no sense to operate according to a principle of the conservation of energy. As Weber writes, pure charisma "is the opposite of all ordered economy" and is in fact "the very force that disregards economy."[33] Even raising revenue based on inherited property holdings is not a revolutionary enough means of securing financial support.[34] Charismatic authority really is the antithesis to "rational economic activity" and it "can only tolerate … irregular, unsystematic, acquisitive acts."[35] "Economics is for donkeys," as Ayatollah Khomeini put it. This is what he meant when he said that. Khomeini never intended to suggest that donkeys are not needed—just that he was not a donkey, and so it ought not to be expected of him that he think like one.

What is most striking about Foucault's keen insight into the Iranian Revolution is his belief that it was not simply a struggle against monarchy and for national independence, Islamic values or any other "cause"; these were only "elements of a still more radical rejection: the rejection by a people, not only of foreigners, but of everything that had constituted, for years, for centuries, its political destiny."[36] Foucault dared to propose that the events of the Fall of 1978 represented no less than "the first great insurrection against the planetary system, the most mad and most modern form of revolt … [against] global hegemony … casting off the weight of the order of the entire world."[37] He believed that this revolt against the entire Western world order of late modernity and the centuries of thinking that had brought it forth was "the threshold of something new."[38] Moreover,

Foucault saw in the *volonté générale* of the Iranian Revolution not only the unleashing of "the latent … power of a people … to transfigure itself spiritually," but even "that rarest of historical phenomenon — the possibility of a total 'transfiguration of this world.'"[39] In his article "What Do the Iranians Dream of?" Foucault writes:

> What is the meaning for these people, is to seek out, at the price of their lives, the thing whose very possibility we Europeans have forgotten at least since the Renaissance and the period of the great crisis of Christianity — *a political spirituality*. I can already hear the French laughing at these words, but they are making a mistake.[40]

11.3 The Islamic Republic of Iran as God's Government

Ayatollah Khomeini's famous policy of "Neither East nor West" — i.e. neither Capitalist Europe and America nor Communist Russia and China — was not just another example of the Third World politics of non-alignment. Rather, it was the philosophical rejection of both the Liberal Capitalism and Hegelian-Marxism of secular enlightenment rationality, as leading inevitably towards the nihilistic profanation of everything. As an alternative, Khomeini proposed a two-phase vision for the spiritual redemption of mankind. First, a "Universal Islamic State" composed of the world's Muslims would have to be established.

The mandate of the elite Islamic Revolutionary Guard Corps (IRGC) established by Khomeini to safeguard his revolutionary program is not limited to Iran's borders. Article 11 within the body of the Constitution of the Islamic Republic of Iran, entitled "Unity of Islam Principle," explicitly states that "all Muslims form a single nation" so that the duty of the government of the Islamic Republic is to "bring about the political, economic, and cultural unity of the Islamic world." The sections of the Preamble on "An Ideological Army" and "Representatives" go even further, calling for the immanent "establishment of a universal holy government and the downfall of all others" and tasking the Islamic Revolutionary Guard Corps with "fulfilling the ideological mission of jihad in God's way; that is, extending the sovereignty of God's law throughout the world." This conflicts with the protection of the *national* sovereignty and territorial integrity of Iran [Article 9], as well as with the claim that the Islamic Republic seeks peaceful relations with all non-belligerent states and that it rejects both oppressive domination of others and dominant power over others [Article 152]. Article 154 attempts to resolve this tension, but it is completely self-contradictory. It reads:

> The Islamic Republic of Iran has as its ideal human felicity throughout human society, and considers the attainment of independence, freedom, and rule of justice and truth to be the right of all people of the world. Accordingly, while scrupulously refraining from all forms of interference in the internal affairs of other nations, it supports the just struggles of the freedom fighters against the oppressors in every corner of the globe.

The most obvious contradiction here is that if the IRI is to support freedom *fighters*, i.e. armed revolutionaries (Hezbollah, Hamas, etc.) seeking the overthrow of oppressive governments, then it cannot refrain from interfering in the internal affairs of other nations, let alone "scrupulously" refrain from doing so. Moreover, adding the words "rule of justice and truth" to the claim that the goal of the Islamic Republic is the liberation of all people the world over, is a very significant qualifier. As is patently clear from so many of the passages already discussed, for this Constitution "rule of justice and truth" can only be a euphemism for the *rule of Islam*. So the words "attainment of independence" only mean independence from non-Muslim Western or Communist colonial powers, not independence vis-à-vis the Islamic World State projected in Article 11 and in the sections of the Preamble on "An Ideological Army" and "Representatives."

Once the Muslims of the world were relatively united under the aegis of the Islamic Republic of Iran, Ayatollah Khomeini envisioned a *jihad*—a "holy war" or crusade against the West. He did not speak so much of a *jihad* against the East, because he foresaw the fall of the "little devil" of Soviet communism at the hands of the "Great Satan" of capitalism and its mass-media consumer culture. The successful completion of the *jihad* would be the submission of the enemy and the liberation of their oppressed in a global government based on the Guardianship of Justice. The Islamic Republic of Iran would be looked back on as the embryo of this regime. Foucault took this potential of Khomeini's revolution to transform the world very seriously when he warned the West that

> it will turn all the political facts in the Middle East upside down—hence doing the same for the strategic balance worldwide. Its singularity, up to now its strength, risks later becoming a power for expansion. It is certainly as an 'Islamic' movement that it can inflame the entire region, overturning the most unstable regimes and disrupting the most solid. On the scale of hundreds of millions of men, Islam, which is not simply a religion but also a way of life, the belonging to a history and a civilization, is liable to constitute a gigantic powder-keg. As of yesterday, any Muslim state can be revolutionized from within...[41]

The only reason that this elaborate program was not carried out was that it was consciously and willfully prevented by the American-supported Iraqi invasion of Iran immediately after the successful completion of the revolution. The West, particularly the United States, encouraged and supported the Iraqi invasion of Iran in order to checkmate what would have been Khomeini's first step toward *jihad*, or what Western analysts and media called his attempt at "exporting the revolution." The Iraqi cities of Najaf (where Khomeini was exiled) and Karbala are the two holiest cities of Shi'ism, along with Qom and Mashad in Iran. The southern region of Sunni Iraq has always been home to a population of Shi'a Muslims oppressed by the implicitly atheistic Bathist regime of Saddam Hussein, and they were extremely inspired by Iran's revolution. The Iran-Iraq War was designed by the West as a preemptive closure of Khomeini's road to Karbala (the place of the martyrdom of Imam Hussein and the birthplace of Shi'ism).

Despite the attempt to derail Khomeini's crusade, it was able to advance quite substantially in smaller ways. The assassination of Anwar Sadat in 1981 as part of an attempt to establish an Islamic Republic in Egypt was directly called for by Khomeini in an interview with Mike Wallace during the hostage crisis. The Islamic Revolution in Lebanon in 1981 saw the ascendancy of Hezbollah, which pledged its direct allegiance to Imam Khomeini. The subsequent arrival of the Iranian Revolutionary Guard and (the original Iranian) Hezbollah paramilitary forces (that served as the model for the Lebanese version), marked the virtual extension of Iran's Islamic Republic to Lebanon, and provoked the 1982 Israeli preemptive strike, which incited the violence that continues in the Middle East today (as well as the "peace process" aimed at ending it).

The successes of the *jihad* were not limited to the West. The Islamic Republic sent troops to Afghanistan, where it helped to successfully defeat the Soviet Union. Iran's revolution also incited nationalist sentiments in the tens of millions of Muslims living in the southern provinces of the Soviet Union, annexed from Iran in the late nineteenth century. The failure to capture Afghanistan and the loss of commitment and rise of rebellion in Central Asia firmly closed the Soviet Union's path to Persian Gulf oil. As high-ranking Soviet officials later admitted that the capture of the Persian Gulf and its oil reserves was always viewed as crucial to the Soviet Union's survival and triumph in the Cold War, Khomeini's jihad must be considered one of the factors leading to the fall of Communism.

Michel Foucault titled a May 11, 1979 article on Iran published in *Le Monde* "Is it Useless to Revolt?" A month earlier, in an open letter that he penned to Mehdi Bazargan, the first Prime Minister of the Islamic Republic of Iran, Foucault wrote: "You are called upon to make sure that this people never has to regret the unyielding force with which it has just liberated itself."[42] Within two years Bazargan himself fled Iran for his life. He was following in the footsteps of the Republic's first President, Abdol-Hassan Bani-Sadr who, only a few months earlier, had escaped the country disguised as a woman in a *châdor*.

The American-supported Iraqi invasion of September 20, 1980 forced Khomeini to consolidate the fragmented and quarrelsome revolutionary coalition through ruthless purges. His position as a symbol of the revolution and his religious aura allowed him the initial public support necessary for his fundamentalist Party of God to purge moderate leaders from the regime's ranks, and banish both the socialist Mojaheddin-e-Khalq (MEK) and the secular National Front from Iran. The dream of a liberating and just spiritual government began to unravel before the Iranian people's eyes.

The crackdown on the MEK proved to be particularly consequential. The *Mojâheddin-e-Khalq*, literally "the People's Holy Warriors," began in the 1960s as a guerrilla group opposing the Shah based on a bizarre hybrid of Shi'a Islamist and Marxist ideologies. Its brand of armed Liberation Theology sought to combat what it perceived to be the exploitative American imperialism and bourgeois capitalism of the old feudal landlords turned entrepreneurs of the Pahlavi era. However, the group's Marxist orientation rendered its Islamist position radically different from that of Khomeini's camp. Mojaheddin ideology interpreted early Shi'ism and the mission of its martyrs as a protest movement against exploitation and state oppression that opposed the Sunni Arab Caliphs because they had betrayed the Prophet's true cause of an egalitarian society. The Mojaheddin sought to synthesize Marxist social thought (social evolution, historical determinism, and the class struggle) with Islam, while rejecting the atheistic aspects of Marxist philosophy.[43]

According to their vision, God had set the dialectic of historical evolution in motion, with the ultimate goal of an egalitarian society, as promised in the Quran, when "the masses will inherit the earth." Thus the mission of the prophets sent by God was to continually provide examples of a "classless society free of poverty, corruption, war, injustice, inequality, and oppression." The future manifestation of the hidden Twelfth Imam, the Shi'a Messiah, was interpreted chiefly as the establishment of "the perfect society which, being classless, would be free of want, war, injustice, oppression, and alienation"—not simply the divinely just rule of a single Messianic figure as an end in itself.

Mojaheddin ideology also advocated a radical interpretation of the Quran. It argued that the essential revolutionary message of Islamic texts should be grasped by reading them in their historical socio-economic context, and that such texts have as their aim not only to interpret the world, but chiefly to change it in order to embody what they saw as the Quran's true essence: "absolute equality between masters and slaves; between men and women; between whites and blacks."[44]

As one can imagine, this radical socialist ideology did not sit well with the clerics who consolidated power after the Iranian Revolution of 1979 — Ayatollah Khomeini foremost amongst them. The Mojaheddin's disciplined organization and dedicated guerrilla attacks on Pahlavi-regime targets had been a driving force of the Revolution, without which Khomeini and his fellow clergymen would never have been able to overthrow the Shah. Despite this fact, Khomeini and his inner circle of clerics quickly set about fashioning a system that would exclude them from key posts in the government. The Mojaheddin responded in 1981 by assembling its hundreds of thousands of supporters in massive demonstrations against the nascent fundamentalist regime of Khomeini. A reign of terror ensued in which thousands of *Mojâheds* were executed on the orders of Khomeini.

As this crisis developed, Masoud Rajavi, the leader of the Mojaheddin, was a General commanding a tank division in the ongoing war with Iraq.[45] Rajavi defected to Saddam Hussein's side, taking 300 tanks, as well as artillery and some armed helicopters across the Iraqi border with him. There, joined by thousands of fleeing *Mojâheds*, he founded the National Liberation Army of Iran, which continued to fight to topple the Khomeini regime for the remainder of the eight-year war with Iraq. This act of treason cost the Mojaheddin almost all of the support that it had among the Iranian people, and over the course of the war it lent weight to Khomeini's frantic anti-Mojaheddin propaganda. While continuing to base the NLA in Iraq, Rajavi moved the Mojaheddin's political apparatus to Paris where, together with Bani Sadr, the aforementioned President who also had to flee, Rajavi founded the National Council of Resistance of Iran (NCRI) — a putative government in exile.

Following the Mojaheddin's failure to overturn the clerical regime during its initial phase of resistance throughout the 1980s, the exiled group began to withdraw into itself and become an authoritarian cult. In the early phases of movements based on pure charisma, the followers tend to live with or near the leader in a relatively communistic fashion — without any clear hierarchy of the kind that there would be in a traditionalist institution or a bureaucratic system.[46] They are collectively supported by gifts that have been voluntarily given by the wider community of supporters of their cause.[47] This was as true of the inner circle of Khomeini during his years of exile, as of the Mojaheddin as they went into exile after Khomeini consolidated control over the Islamic Republic at their expense.

Massoud Rajavi took on the persona of a messianic figure overlooking every aspect of the movement's activities. His sexual relations with the wives of various comrades were the subject of scandals, especially one that led to his marriage to Maryam.[48] As his powers grew vast and unchecked, Masoud Rajavi even came to be called *Imâmé Hâl* or "the Imam of the Present Time." An increasingly rigid hierarchy was set up within the organization, which demanded unquestionable fidelity. It developed its own icons, relics, ceremonies and rituals that were based on various bizarre distortions of Shi'a Islam, honoring its own martyrs and families of distinction. In addition to ideological handbooks it developed censorship indices for its various activities, especially its news and communications media. Most disturbing of all, the MEK's seething hatred of the clerical regime was matched by an extreme religious conviction that the Mojaheddin was privy to the only true interpretation of Islam.[49]

The conflict between Imam Khomeini and Imam Rajavi is a textbook case of conflict between claimants to charismatic leadership of the same revolutionary movement, as this is understood by Max Weber. The situation that takes place when two claimants of such authority come into conflict with each other is quite revealing of the nature of charismatic authority.[50] In such cases, unlike in legal battles or political disputes that can be mediated with a view to some framework of laws or procedures, "the only recourse is to some kind of a contest, by magical means or even an actual physical battle of the leaders."[51] No compromise is possible. Charismatic authority is of the nature that "In principle only one side can be right in such a conflict; the other must be guilty of a wrong which has to be expiated."[52]

Massoud Rajavi had not yet understood himself when he ran for President of the Islamic Republic of Iran in 1980. He could never have been a mere office-holding bureaucrat. He was a rival claimant of the same charismatic revolutionary leadership being exercised by Khomeini. As we have seen, the latter was not exactly a traditional Shi'ite theologian and he was in fact opposed by the more conservative clerical establishment. However, in the ideology of Rajavi's Mojaheddin we see an even clearer demonstration of Weber's thesis that charismatic leadership is as opposed to constraint by established tradition as it is resistant to any standards of legalistic or bureaucratic rationality.

The charismatic leader who is not a hereditary monarch must have his power legitimated in a "hierocratic" manner, in other words his personal charisma has to be perceived as that of an incarnation of the divine will.[53] Charismatic authority is sacred and as such its power emanates from a sphere outside that of the profane and mundane world.[54] The charismatic ruler is the "God-willed master" of his people, to whom he is responsible for as long as he has the "divine right of kings" — but responsible in a manner that is totally different from democratic accountability to an electorate.[55] While, on the one hand, this means that such a leader may rule for life, on the other hand, it also means that if he loses his charisma, he is not even assured the security of a single term in office, the way that a person whose legitimacy derives from his having been elected can bank on serving out the rest of his term despite how unpopular he becomes. When a charismatic leader loses his charisma and falls, his fall is often as fast as his meteoric rise. In primitive societies this means the abandonment of a shaman who no longer has the power to heal the sick of the community or make rain when they are facing a drought.

The judgments of a charismatic leader have the quality of the oracle of a sage or the revelations of a prophet; they are not bound by any external or preexisting standards.[56] Weber explicitly associates this kind of sovereign power with the Islamic *fatwa* of a person believed to be a representative of the divine will, and he adds:

> Genuinely charismatic justice always acts in this manner. In its pure form it is the polar opposite of formal and traditional bonds, and it is just as free in the face of the sanctity of tradition as it is in the face of any rationalist deductions from abstract concepts.[57]

The parallel negation of both religious tradition and rationalist abstractions that we see in this statement is also very noteworthy. It means that when Weber associates this with theocratic Islam he cannot have Sunni legalism in mind, but must be thinking in terms of the *fatwas* of a figure like Hassan Sabbah — or Massoud Rajavi.

Legitimate authority is either grounded on charisma, tradition, or rationality.[58] Whereas charismatic authority is based on a sanctification of the heroic or exemplary character of an individual, the traditionalist claims the sanctity of customs established from time immemorial as the source of his authority, and the rationalist sees only that authority as justified which is "legal" or in accordance with a pattern of normative rules and within the context of a procedural system.[59] The charismatic basis of sovereign power in its most primordial and originary form underlines the distinction between legitimacy and legality.[60] The charismatic ruler has legitimacy without being bound by any limits of legality and it is, in fact, only on the basis of his leadership as lawgiver — in the sense that Cyrus and Solon were lawgivers — that a legal order either comes into being or replaces one that he overturned.

Obedience to a legal order is totally impersonal in that it is due to an office holder by virtue of his office. By contrast, traditional authority is obedience to a person, but one who is bound by tradition and can have his legitimacy revaluated on the basis of this customarily accepted standard.[61] Only charismatic authority is of an entirely personal nature, where each follower of a leader with charisma feels personally addressed by, and magnetically bound to, that person *who is in turn not bound* by any external or pre-established criteria on the basis of which the legitimacy of his authority can be assessed.[62] Like a magnetic field, such authority fails only in practice. Its efficacy is its own justification. Up until that evident failure, no charismatic leader — whether prophet or king — questions or judges his own legitimacy on the basis of the attitude that the masses have towards him.[63] He is convinced of his mission long before he has any mass following, and will endure in his conviction through huge ups and downs in his popularity.

For the decade during the course of which Rajavi transformed from a rival claimant of the charismatic leadership of Iran's revolution into the leader of an exiled MEK cult, the pressures and grief of the war with Iraq demanded national unity in Iran. Then the war ended on July 18, 1988 and about a year later, on Saturday June 3, 1989, the Imam died. In the following days, as the government attempted to bury Ayatollah Khomeini's body, several million mourners poured into the streets in a sea of black that was probably the greatest display of grief in human history. Foreign observers called it "a sheer frenzy," "an orgy of emotion," and even "an emotional orgasm." This grief ran to hidden depths. Something much greater than leadership (*Rahbari*) had died with Khomeini — and even then, people already sensed this on a subconscious level. Their Messiah had come and gone, the *jihad*'s road to Karbala appeared to be closed, and a world without spirit had not been transfigured.

In the months and years following the end of the Iran-Iraq War, intellectuals, writers, and artists were the first dissenting voices to express rising grievances and disillusionment that had been silenced for a decade. Chief among them was the philosopher Abdolkarim Soroush, whose vision of an "Islamic Reformation" would come to spearhead an attempt at democratization within the parameters of an Islamic regime.

Dr. Abdolkarim Soroush has been hailed by some as the "Martin Luther of Islam." His rise to fame (and infamy) is on account of his view that the clergy should not hold a monopoly on the interpretation of religion or (more specifically) of *sharia* (religious law). The essence of Soroush's objection to absolute interpretation is a view of human nature as extremely imperfect. He believes that the tragedies of human history are a clear testament to this imperfect nature. This imperfection expresses itself in a variety of differing interpretations of historical events, of natural phenomena, and also of religious texts. While religion-in-itself, i.e. the Quran, is divine and absolute, religious knowledge is just another form of human knowledge that is as subject as others to fallibility, continuous evolution in expansion and contraction, and is also open to exchanges with other forms of human knowledge.

Soroush argues that his view that *a religion equals its history* (*of interpretation*), does not mean that the "essence of religion" condones the atrocities of that history, but that religion itself is a "seed" from which a "plant grows that acts as a canopy" for both good and bad alike. In the course of this elucidation, Soroush offers a very telling definition of the religious reformer and his task:

> Reformers have experienced and accepted not only the doctrine but the mundane history of religion. Although they have detected the gathering of the flies, they have not forsaken their taste for the sweetness of the *truth*.[64]

Soroush's view of the verifiability of the nature of a religious doctrine by the comparative study of its various historical interpretations became the basis of his magnum opus *The Hermeneutical Expansion and Contraction of the Theory of Shari'ah*. Soroush's great work parallels the Western tradition of *hermeneutics* in the conviction that we must understand a text both grammatically and psychologically. However, since we neither have complete understanding of language nor of the person of the author, we cannot gain a complete understanding of either of these aspects. This is even more profoundly true when the author is purported to be "God" or His "messenger." Furthermore, we cannot fully understand a text unless we understand its parts, and in turn we cannot understand the parts unless we understand the whole of the text. We are forever caught in circles of reciprocity between the part and the whole. Thus a religious text can never be understood in *the right* way—it can never be understood *absolutely*—rather, each and every different reading helps to bring us to a "second-order vantage point" that grants us ever-deepening knowledge.

Soroush believes this hermeneutical realization will bring about two transformations in the understanding of Islam.

The first transformation is the abandonment of ideology. According to Soroush, the conflation of religion with ideology, such as in the work of Ali Shari'ati, lends itself to absolute and authoritarian interpretations. Furthermore, such interpretations are often based upon an *idealism* that believes in the innate perfection of mankind and thus both in the possibility of an absolute interpretation and that its implementation will yield a perfect society. This is of course the view of Khomeini's treatise, *Velayat-e-Faqih*. Soroush believed that in light of grave human imperfection such a regime can only lead to disastrous projects of 'social engineering', exemplified by communist Russia and China, but also by Khomeini — though Soroush does not dare to openly criticize the latter. Such ideological and idealist interpretations represent an inflation of religion, or what Soroush calls its "swelling" and "obesity." That is, especially in the wake of the Islamic Revolution of 1979, the understanding of religion has taken on many responsibilities that it can and should not carry. Soroush sees the possibility of a more slender and purified faith. He looks back to "Islamic Mysticism" in his advocacy of "an individual religion based on personal experiences, whose teacher is Rumi."

The second transformation in the understanding of religion associated with Soroush's *hermeneutical* theory is his belief that "the Islam of identity should yield to the Islam of truth." Soroush believes that the idea of an Islamic *civilization*, and thus an Islamic cultural "identity," is a modern construct and has no basis in religion-in-itself. He argues that the prophets were not seeking to establish a cultural identity distinct from that of other peoples. The evolution of civilization and culture, like that of language, is the complex product of a web of social factors and actors over many generations. Rather, the prophets were trying to lead humanity towards a greater understanding of "truth," and so a "Muslim" should also be defined chiefly by this search for truth. While identities contradict each other and inherently lend themselves to conflict, Soroush believes that "truths" (when not conflated with identity or identification) cooperate with each other, as different subjective perspectives which help us to gain a greater understanding of the objective reality. Thus, such an understanding of Islam would be sincerely open to the "truths" of other faiths or civilizations, because its affinity with them in the common search for truth is more fundamental than the difference of its cultural conditioning.

Through these transformations of Islam, Soroush does not merely wish to prepare its place in a secular society. What is distinct about Soroush's reformist thought is his faith in the possibility of a "secularization without profanation," and thus of an "Islamic Democracy." Soroush believes that a democratic religious government is founded upon, and testifies to, the concordance of reason and religion. Soroush argues that freedom allows a dynamic whereby religious Truth is ultimately strengthened, by being scrutinized and shedding unnecessary pretensions, and falsehood is weakened: "the ascendance of the noble truths is worth the sacrifice of the occasional minor truth."[65] Thus freedom itself is a truth and those who argue that freedom is against truth only do so out of attachments to petty beliefs that are not essential to Truth and thus may be stripped from it by reason. Furthermore, while individual "reason" can be tainted by emotional prejudices, the use of collective reason will preserve only the universal in reason (i.e. its true essence). Such collective reason can only be fostered in a free society.[66]

However, this freedom would be a freedom *for* religion rather than *from* it. Soroush looks back to the ascetic and transcendental ideal of "Islamic Mysticism" in his critique of how the Western Enlightenment went wrong. Westerners were so concerned about the battle against external oppression that they neglected the battle against the internal oppressor, the ego and its selfish desires. Soroush writes:

> [To be] only concerned with inner challenges … is a worthy but incomplete enterprise because the external enemy can easily divert our attention from the internal battle. The inner battle is contingent upon overcoming the external enemy … living under tyranny plunges the whole society into such iniquity and … institutionalization of corruption that fighting the internal enemy becomes impossible.

> Conversely, the contemporary Westerners have entirely forsaken the internal battle. The battle against desires has vanished from their discourse. … "Liberty, Equality and Fraternity" was the slogan of the French Revolution. … Liberation from passions and ambitions were not at issue. The truth is that if the internal and external freedom are not combined, both will suffer. … Thus in the Western world we see injustice, colonialism, and arrogance … alongside the pursuit of liberty. There is external freedom, but no one is interested in internal freedom. Internal freedom can be achieved only by the light of submission and through following the guidance of the divine messengers. Those who are deprived from this beacon of guidance can not fully embrace either kind of freedom.
>
> What we desperately need today is to take our cue from the seekers of freedom [the West] and from our own religious and mystic culture, to combine external and internal freedoms: the freedom predicated on submission and the submission predicated on freedom. We must tie these two together and desire them at once. We must *not* elevate one at the expense of the other.[67]

An even greater departure from the Western conception of a secular society is Soroush's insistence that *sharia* (religious law) still govern the society of believers, but that it be open to transformation and refinement at the hands of rational citizens. Soroush argues that his critics fail to realize that *sharia* is not identical to the whole of religion, and that it derives its validity from something more fundamental, which is *the faith of the people in* divine law and their (evolving, changing) comprehension of it — in such a way that *sharia* is an expression of man's dynamic relationship with God. Thus religious law is not "impervious both to people's will and change." Critics also fail to see that "the expectation that the mission of the prophets include[s] [dictating] minute religious laws and regulations" is a limited view. Instead we may view the mission of the prophets as "involv[ing] accelerating human spiritual *evolution*. … Religion, in this interpretation will assume an entirely different character and mission that excludes methods (but not values) of government and endows religious law with an entirely new identity and trajectory."[68]

Soroush also applies his distinction between religion-in-itself and religious understanding in his view of *sharia*. If religious law is to operate in the world, then it has entered the world and is subject to fallibility in the hands of fallible human beings: these transformations of the traditional view of *sharia* are the foundation for Soroush's most radical proposition. He asks "What authenticity and ground would religious law have if it disregarded the freedom of faith and the humanity of understanding, refused to base its precepts upon these, and neglected to harmonize its regulations with them?"[69] He answers: "If it is established that the religious society, due to the nature of religiosity, the inherent freedom and irreducible plurality of faiths, and the dynamism of religious understanding is consistent with, even in need of, democracy, then religious jurisprudence should follow rather than compete with the above conclusions."[70] In sum, this would be the first principle of a "Democratic Islamic Republic of Iran":

> Surely, in the minds of the faithful, no religious edict could be unjust, contrary to public good, or vain. *Religious decrees that are so found will be corrected and revised in accordance with the lofty principles of justice and right or through careful and prudent deliberation.*[71]

Aside from his fundamental misunderstanding of Islam, its origin and purpose, Soroush's entire philosophical program betrays a failure to comprehend the charismatic basis and revolutionary character of the Islamic Republic of Iran. Soroush's political thought, and the Islamic Reform movement of Iran in general, represents a decline of charisma in the structure and function of political power. This generally proceeds from the desire of certain social classes (such as the aristocracy or priesthood), political functionaries (such as judicial officials who aspire to the independence of the judiciary from executive power), and economic forces (factory owners or agricultural laborers) for stable and officially recognized legitimacy in the form of acquired "rights."[72] In a political order based on pure charisma, no one has any rights against the sovereign. The charismatic hero who embodies sovereign power has a divine right to every*thing* and every*one* needed to fulfill his mission. That he runs the risk of losing his charisma if he abuses this power does not change the fact that he has it, and that charismatic authority does not recognize any such thing as a political "right" that would limit this power. So long as Imam Khomeini's successor, Ayatollah Ali Khamenei, has millions of Basijis and Hezbollahis ready to give their lives to follow his every *fatwa*, the Supreme Leader of the Islamic Republic of Iran will be assured of his own sovereign legitimacy.

This is why Soroush's theory was bound to fail when it was actually tested in practice during the presidency of Mohammad Khatami — a man who, like Soroush, held a doctorate in Philosophy. Khatami and others involved with his administration, such as Abdollah Nouri, attempted to democratize Iran's form of government by limiting the power of unelected supervisory institutions and, when they met with severe resistance, threatened to remove them altogether. Despite the support of a pro-reform Parliament, this program failed to even achieve its most minimal goal: protection of a free press. The clash between reformists and hardliners culminated in "six days of rage" in July of 1999, which were sparked by a paramilitary raid on dissident university students.

A decade later, in June of 2009, the Islamic reform movement was briefly revived by the presidential candidates Mir Hossein Mousavi and Mehdi Karroubi, but only to take its last gasp. Catalyzed by an apparent hardliner fraud in the presidential election that secured Mahmoud Ahmadinejad a second term in office, massive demonstrations rocked the country and met with a bloody crackdown. The collective face of those killed in the protests became that of Neda Agha Soltan, a twenty-six-year old girl who was a graduate student of Philosophy, and who died fearlessly, with open eyes, after being shot through the heart. The regime's hardline leadership and security forces saw this soft coup coming, and their decisive, preemptive, and sustained response dispelled the mirage of Islamic reformation conjured by Soroush.

Article 177:5 of the Constitution of the Islamic Republic of Iran reads: "The contents of the articles of the Constitution related to the Islamic character of the political system; the basis of all the rules and regulations according to Islamic criteria; the religious footing; the objectives of the Islamic Republic of Iran; … the holy principle; the Imamate of Ummah;

and the … official religion of Iran and the religious school are unalterable." Taken together, these two non-eliminable and non-revisable articles prevent any gradual secular democratization of the present regime. Even if, after somehow abolishing *Velâyaté Faqih*, parliament were to be given the power to elect members of the Guardian Council, the members of the Council would still have to be Islamic legal scholars who vet parliamentary legislation according to Islamic criteria. This means that the leadership of the Green Path of Hope would have liked Iran to remain an Islamic theocracy—albeit one whose friendlier face is plastered with a Khatami smile.

However, most of the followers of the Green Path probably had something else in mind when they continued to insist on "reform" or "referendum." Imagine amendments that reify and emphasize the few theologically unqualified civil rights that there are in the Constitution. All of these are negative rights; they have to do with norms governing arrest, prosecution, and the means of evidence collecting related to these. In other words, they presuppose already having violated the Islamic legal order or being in danger of so doing. The secrecy of private communications is protected against various types of state surveillance and censorship, except with specific judicial authorization (Article 25). This means all evidence used to prosecute a person must be culled from statements or actions of that person in the public sphere. No one may be arrested without charges and the reasons for accusation being immediately conveyed to the accused, and at that, in writing (Article 32). Due process also includes rights to timely sentencing (Article 36) and presumption of innocence (Article 37). All forms of torture are prohibited, forced confessions or compelled testimony are inadmissible in a court of law, and oaths obtained under duress are not to be believed and are without any value (Article 38). Article 38 article explicitly states that violations of it are punishable in accordance with the law. Article 39 goes far beyond forbidding of torture, demanding that "All affronts to the dignity and repute of persons arrested, detained, imprisoned, or banished in accordance with the law, whatever form they may take" be "forbidden and liable to punishment." Prison rapes were clearly in mind in the formulation of this article, but it is broad enough to demand extremely sensitive treatment of prisoners.

Articles 84 and 86 taken together seem to grant a special right, and even a duty, of parliamentary representatives to freely express their views in the Assembly, either verbally or by means of voting, without being prosecuted or arrested for so doing. One of the most important unqualified civil rights is the prohibition of anything resembling martial law in response to a state of emergency, including but not limited to war, for a period longer than thirty days, at least not without express authorization by the Assembly (Article 79).

If amendments to the Constitution were to protect these negative rights from conflicts with any other articles that might mistakenly be interpreted as rightfully overriding them, then this would increase the possibilities for private conspiracy and public dissent—including on the floor of Parliament by "protected" representatives. Furthermore, the *Basij* (a militant Muslim mercenary militia answerable to the IRGC) has no constitutional grounds and could be legally disbanded. It was initially intended to be a cannon fodder suicide strike (*kamikaze*) force during the Iran-Iraq War, when many of the "volunteers" were minors promised direct entrance to Heaven. Since the end of the war in 1988, it has been used *de facto* for domestic enforcement of Islamic principles, but there is no legal basis for this—unless the *Basij* were to be absorbed into the IRGC.

However, as noted above, for the IRGC to declare "martial law"—at least for a period longer than thirty days, would be illegal, which is why it has thus far allowed the *Basij* to confront demonstrators instead of intervening directly. The idea is that many more people would be willing to violate the law by opposing the theocratic Islamic Republic as a form of government, and eventually the sheer mass of those arrested and imprisoned—but under very respectful and dignified conditions—would become untenable. It would require turning the whole country into a prison, and in view of the absurdity of this, the system would collapse. This subversive tactic was the only remotely reasonable motivation for accepting Mousavi's insistence on impeccable adherence to the Islamic Constitution.

In holding this position, followers of *The Green Path of Hope* presumed that defenders of the establishment were stupid enough not to see the upshot of this, the long-term civil disobedience campaign that would be facilitated by following extant legal paths to a constitutional revision emphasizing the rights to private communications and dignified arrest and humane conditions of imprisonment. In fact, the hardliners *did* see this threat of subversion, and saw it from the moment that they declared, a few days before the June 12 election, that they would nip in the bud any attempt at a "velvet revolution" by the Greens. Even if Mir Hossein Mousavi and Mehdi Karroubi did not intend such a "*velvet* revolution," most of those who voted for one or the other of them certainly meant to use them in this manner.

If they were naïve for allowing this, those who believe that a velvet revolution remains possible are still more naïve. The brutally repressive response of the establishment to the peaceful mass demonstrations of the summer of 2009 precluded a "velvety" soft and slow revolution—just as the *Sepâhé Pasdâran* (IRGC) promised it would. In effect they have said: *If there is going to be a revolution to overthrow the system, it is not going to happen insidiously; everyone is going to know it is a revolution, and either the revolutionaries will win, or we will.* The IRGC decided not to allow an Iranian Gorbachev to set the conditions for a quiet internal collapse. Whereas they were right in their assessment that Khatami was not willing to play Gorbachev (a fact that became clear enough in July of 1999), they knew Mousavi was ideal for this role, and so they acted preemptively. The violent reaction of many demonstrators to the regime's second lethal crackdown, on December 27th, 2009, showed that, at least in this respect, the regime attained its objective. As soon as it became clear that only a violent revolution could bring down the system, protesters abandoned the streets and the final attempt at a democratic reform of the Islamic Republic of Iran came to an end.

CHAPTER 12

THE RENAISSANCE OF IRANIAN CIVILIZATION

THE PAST DECADE OF THE Islamic Republic of Iran, since the mass uprising of 2009, has been defined by a rise of imperial power abroad on the one hand, and an increasing loss of domestic legitimacy on the other hand. The American misadventures in Iraq and Afghanistan, especially the toppling of Saddam Hussein, have created conditions ripe for the resurgence of Iran as the regional hegemon, not just of the Middle East, but of the entire core of the Islamic World, including Central Asia. Iran's readiness and willingness to assume this responsibility, beginning with its role as the foremost defender of the Middle East and Central Asia from the Sunni fundamentalist Islamic State and Al-Qaeda in Iraq, Syria, Lebanon, Afghanistan, and Yemen, has in turn intensified efforts by Anglo-American neo-colonialists to resume the old British and Russian project of containing and crippling Iran. Meanwhile, like burning embers under the ashes, domestic dissent has only increased since 2009, even if has gone underground and a dream of democracy has transformed into populist outrage on the part of patriots and nightmarish aspirations for secession on the part of treasonous ethnic separatists. The latter have positioned themselves to become the useful idiots of Western powers, mainly American Neo-Conservatives and British Neo-Colonialists, who want to divide and conquer Iran — or rather, to control a rump state of Persia after they have balkanized Iran.

Crippling sanctions intended to inflame internal dissent are being coupled with the threat of a military intervention aimed at defanging the country, with a view to forcing Iran to become "a normal country." An attempt to disestablish the Persian language as the national language of Iran and a promotion of the idea of federalism on the part of proponents of democracy are two particularly insidious features of the existential threat to Iran. This threat to Iran's very existence as a cohesive and sovereign nation, and as the core state of a broader Iranian Civilization, will be the subject of the first section of this final chapter.

The best defense is a good offense, and any country that loses expansive energy immediately runs the risk of internal disintegration. This is particularly the case with Iran, where the sudden disestablishment of Shi'ite Islam as the religious cement of the society could lead to the inflammation of foreign-engineered ethnic separatism. This could begin in Azerbaijan, where the majority of the population are now Turkic speakers. These Azeris, who constitute something like 25% of Iran are, however, Shi'ite Muslims. As long as Shi'ism remains integral to the Iranian state and Iran leads the Shi'ite Muslim *Ummat*, not only will what is left of Azerbaijan within Iran's borders remain Iranian, the potential also exists, over the longer term, of reintegrating the northern part of Azerbaijan in the Caucasus, which was lost to the Russians in the Russo-Persian Wars of the nineteenth century. On the other hand, a loss of the rest of Iranian Azerbaijan to a larger Shi'ite-Turkic Republic of Azerbaijan on account of a sudden disestablishment of Shi'ism — or even a rabidly Neo-Zoroastrian attack on Shi'ism — would be the opening phase of a wider process of disintegration along ethnic and religious lines. Kurdistan, Al-Ahwaz, and Baluchistan could receive meddlesome foreign backing to follow Azerbaijan out of Iran. The current federalist discourse within the putatively "Iranian" so-called "opposition" to the Islamic Republic is nothing other than a preparation for the dismembering of Iran. The first responsibility of those forwarding an Iranian Renaissance is to resist this discourse and, at all costs, maintain the territorial integrity of Iran.

The second section of this chapter looks at a potential evolution of the strategic doctrine of the Islamic Republic of Iran to synthesize Shi'ism with Pan-Iranism. Under current geopolitical conditions, where the West, China, and Sunni Islam are vying to establish a new global order under their own hegemony, an Iranian entry into this struggle for World Order on the basis of the values and vision of Iranian Civilization demands the endurance of a strong and unified Iran at the core of this civilization. Iran's very survival is bound up with its capacity to project force in at least the core of the so-called "Islamic world" that has historically been the sphere of Iranian Civilization.

Unfortunately, however unpleasant the matter may be, an Iranian Renaissance will remain elusive unless we also confront the evident dysgenic decline of Iranian Civilization and need to reverse it through the use of emergent Neo-Eugenic biotechnology. Dysgenic decline is one major reason why the last Shah of Iran failed in his attempt at a resurgence of the Great Civilization, or why, for that matter, Safavid or Afsharid Iran was not able to achieve industrialization at a level and a pace even comparable to Russia or China, let alone the West. This has to do with the demographic shift that took place in Iran after the Turkic and Mongol invasions, the catastrophe that destroyed the Iranian Renaissance of 850–1050. In this connection, the third section of this chapter presents scientific evidence for a dysgenic decline of Iranian Civilization.

Recent genetic research reveals that different extinct hominids interbred with various, relatively geographically discrete *Homo sapiens* populations to different degrees, as can be determined from genetic markers that appear in certain contemporary ethnic groups and not in others. These extinct hominids had, among other variant characteristics, significantly different cognitive capacities, so that their differentiation on at least a sub-species level (as reflected in the inheritance of phenotypically distinct and geographically clustered populations) correlates to the well-established concept of human "racial" difference. There may have been elements of the genome of certain extinct hominids that correlate to psychological characteristics other than the mathematical and spatial reasoning measured by IQ tests. For example, some of the psychology of Neanderthals has been speculatively reconstructed from paleontological and archeological research, and we know that Africans do not have any Neanderthal genes, so they could not have inherited these psychological characteristics, whereas some Caucasians may have.

Iran (which literally means "Aryan") was not just linguistically and culturally Indo-European, the Persians, Medes, Scythians, and other Iranians were also genetically similar to their European cousins, which is unsurprising since Iranians are from Europe, specifically from Ukraine, and mass migrated both through the Caucasus and around the other side of the Caspian Sea, in various successive waves, to the plateau that they named "Aryana" (Ancient Persian) or "Iran" (Middle Persian) after themselves. The Turkic and Mongol invasions of Iran from 1050–1250 were genocidal in nature and the dramatic demographic shift that they brought about correlates to an eventual decline in the intellectual capacity and cultural brilliance of Iranian Civilization after 1300 AD.

The Turks and Mongols brought a Siberian mentality to Iran that is inimical to the daring dialectical debate and revolutionary intellectual discovery characteristic of Caucasians. This Promethean mentality has a genetic basis. You do not find it in Asians, Arabs, Africans, and other non-Aryan peoples. It is worthy of note that the Safavid elite who reinvigorated Iranian Civilization were, contrary to common misconceptions, not Turks but ethnically Indo-European Caucasians. It is quite possible that without this injection of fresh blood from the Caucasus in 1500, Iran would never have come back, even briefly, from the decline that set in after the Turkic and Mongol invasions ended the Renaissance of 850–1050. By comparison, the Qajars, who deepened Iran's civilizational decline, were ethnic Turks.

Fortunately, as will be suggested at the close of this third section, the dysgenic decline of Iranian Civilization can be reversed through the emergence of biotechnology with Neo-Eugenic potential, such as pre-implantation genetic diagnosis, embryo selection, and germ-line genetic engineering. These technologies are certainly going to be used for Neo-Eugenic purposes by countries such as China and Japan. There is no reason why Iran should not follow the lead of, or even preempt, these East Asian countries rather than sheepishly stand behind the West, which was traumatized by Nazi Eugenics.

The chapter ends with a fourth and final section that looks at the occulted roots of the most recent uprising against the establishment of the Islamic Republic of Iran, the protests of December 2017 to January of 2018. These protests were fueled not by a Westernized upper-class or upper-middle-class demand for democracy, as in the case of the Reformist protests of 1999 and 2009, but by working-class economic demands together with a new discourse of "Iranism" (*Irângarâi*) and the will to an Iranian Renaissance. For our purposes here, what is most relevant and intriguing is the apparent role that former President Mahmoud Ahmadinejad's closest advisor, dear friend, and personal guru played in organizing this challenge to the establishment. Esfandiyar Rahim Mashaei, Ahmadinejad's Rasputin, has been linked to a strange Neo-Zoroastrian Theosophical group whose beliefs in a coming savior are similar to his pronouncements, and those of Ahmadinejad himself, that the government of the Hidden Imam is coming very soon.

12.1 The Existential Threat to Iran

The German philosopher Martin Heidegger once insightfully described the language of a folk (Persian *mellat*) as "the house" or abode of their very existence. The subversive post-colonialist and cultural Marxist project, post-1979, to rebrand the name of the Persian language as "Farsi" has been driven by an attempt to falsely suggest that an ethnic group originating in the Fars (properly *Pârs*) province of Iran is somehow colonially imposing its language on the rest of Iran. In fact, ethnic Persians originated in an area between the Black Sea and the Caucasus, like many of their European cousins. They migrated to the plateau that they named "Iran" after themselves. Moreover, the contemporary form of the language originated in Khorasan, not in Fars.

The English and other international usage of "Farsi" has also been accepted and promoted by Islamists who want to cut the Islamic Republic of Iran off from its Persian imperial and literary heritage by conveying the false impression that "Farsi" is some kind of Arabic dialect. Even in the Persian language itself "Farsi" is an incorrect, Arabized pronunciation of

Pârsi. This corruption stems from the fact that the Arabs have no *P* in their language, and consequently all *Ps* are pronounced as *Fs*. No one speaking English refers to German as "*Deutsche*" or asks someone "Do you speak *Française*?" The name that has been accepted and used in literature for centuries for referring to *Pârsi* in the English language is "Persian," just as in the French language it is *Persan* — not "Farsi."

Persian belongs to the Iranian branch of the Indo-European language family that includes both Indian languages such as Sanskrit, Hindi, and Punjabi, as well as European languages such as Greek, Latin and all of the languages derived from it (Italian, French, Spanish, etc.), the Germanic languages (including German and English), Russian and other Eastern European languages. Today, Persian is the native language of 60% of the citizens of Iran, but it remains the official language of the entire country. Persian is also the official language of Tajikistan, where it is referred to as "Tajiki," and it used to be the official language of Afghanistan, where it is called "Dari" by the northern half of the country that speaks it. Other languages belonging to the Iranian branch of the Indo-European language family include all dialects of Kurdish, Baluchi, Pashtu, and the original languages of Azerbaijan, such as Tati and Talysh.

It is also very important to point out that, unlike the other colonial languages of the Aryan world, Persian was never imposed on any non-Persian population. The Achaemenids adopted Aramaic as the administrative language of their empire because it had already been in use by the Babylonians when Cyrus liberated Babylon and turned it into the capital of Imperial Iran. When the Parthians, who were Iranians but not Persians, and whose native language was the Scythian language, re-conquered the Iranian plateau and Mesopotamia from the Greeks, they voluntarily adopted the Persian language and manufactured false genealogies connecting themselves to Darius and other Achaemenids. In effect, they became Persians.

Although the Sassanians originated in the heart of Persia — in the province of *Pârs* where *Persepolis* (or "City of the Persians") had been built — they also deferred to the use of Syriac and other local Semitic languages in the Western parts of their empire. Even though Shapur the Great, the most domineering Sassanian Emperor, was himself the patron of the prophet Mani, the vast Manichean literary tradition that spread through the Silk Route consists mostly of works written in languages other than Persian — whether these are other Iranian languages, such as Sogdian, Semitic languages, or even Asian languages. Mani only composed a single great work in Persian, the *Shapurgân*, for his patron (not incidentally, he managed to thereby convert members of the Persian royal family to his proposed world religion).

Most dramatically, when the Turkic hordes invaded Iran and took over the leadership of the oppressive Caliphate from the Arabs, the Seljuks adopted the Persian language. Even once the Safavids carved out a sphere of political independence for Iran for the first time since the Islamic Conquest and in opposition to the Ottoman Caliphate, the Ottomans continued the Seljuk practice of promulgating a Persian literary and administrative culture rather than using their native Turkish language. Finally, the Mughals of Northern India also voluntarily adopted Persian as their imperial language of high culture. The point is that the Persian language has survived on the strength of its captivating cultural force. European scholars of the eighteenth and nineteenth centuries considered the Persian language as one of a handful of classical languages with world-historical significance, the others being Greek, Latin, Sanskrit, and Chinese.

In light of the above, when we hear today that Persian should be displaced as the language of standardized education and nationwide communication even within Iran, we must recognize that something is terribly wrong. Surely, after 2,500 years of accepting the Persian language as the core of their civilizational identity, and one used for administration even by non-Persians *and non-Aryans* (such as the Turks) who have lorded over Iran for centuries, Kurds, Azeris, Khuzis, and Baluchis did not suddenly come up with the idiotic idea of depriving their children of an education that would give them access to the treasure trove of Persian culture.

No, the displacement of Persian, with a view to the eventual eradication of Iran as a distinct civilization, has been a project of European colonial powers such as Britain and Russia. They feared the revival of the Persian Empire, or a politically re-unified Iranian Civilization, as a potential rival in a part of the world that they planned to loot for natural resources. This began in Central Asia and the Caucasus, where Persian was the *de facto* language until the British and Russian Empires divided and conquered these regions in the 1800s. It continued in the twentieth century with the suppression of Persian among the Tajiks of the USSR, Russian support for the Kurdish separatist "Republic of Mahabad" in Iran, the attempted Soviet military seizure of the rest of Azerbaijan in 1944–1946 (the northern part of which they seized from Iran during the nineteenth century), and the destruction of Persian as the official language of "Afghanistan," an artificial state carved out of Eastern Iran by the British. Most recently, Wahabi and Salafist organizations funded by the United States via Anglo-American Deep-State support for Saudi Arabia and Pakistan, have led to Sunni fundamentalist insurgencies among the Arab minority in Khuzestan (which they call "Al-Ahwaz") and the Baluch of Iran near the border with the Pakistani province of Baluchistan.

The issue of the Persian national heritage of Iran, the heritage of the four major Persian Empires, has been politicized by foreign conspirators and their fifth column amongst the various minorities of Iran with a view to using the Islamic Republic's loss of legitimacy as an opportunity to carve up Iran and loot the resources of microstates that secede from "Persia." With a view to the attempt to disestablish Persian as the national language of Iran, the proposal that Iran's system of government should be federalized amounts to the denial of a cohesive and coherent Iranian national identity. Proponents of federalism tend to view "Iran" as a geographical designator demarcating nothing other than a space within which a number of different "nations" or "peoples" (*melliat*) live alongside one another. With total disregard for the distinction between the Iranian languages and those imposed on the Iranian people (*mellaté Irân*, singular) by brutal and barbaric non-Iranian occupiers such as the Turks and Arabs, these federalists put Azeri (or as they say "Turk") and Ahwazi Arab aspirations for autonomy on the same level as calls for greater Kurdish self-determination.

The federalist ignorance with respect to, or resentful denial of, an Iranian national heritage revolving around the axis of the Persian language and the legacy of the Persian Empires will have, as its ultimate consequence, the destruction of any common cultural frame of reference as the background for effective political decision making—especially at the level of parliamentary legislation. As both Jean-Jacques Rousseau and Carl Schmitt recognized, a tacitly acknowledged national ethos is the ultimate basis for assessing the legitimacy of sovereign power. A nation (Latin *natio*, Persian *mihan*) in the proper sense presupposes the existence of a people (German *Volk*, Persian *mellat*). The discourse of Iranian Federalism is an inherently anti-Iranian discourse insofar as it denies the existence of an Iranian people (*mellaté Irân*). A federal Iran would be incapable of effective decision making on matters of major social development or geopolitical engagement, leading either to acceptance of the status quo or, if sufficient pressure is applied to urgently make such policies, to federalism serving as a precursor to territorial disintegration through referenda for regional autonomy and, eventually, secession and the dissolution of Iran.

It is true that the idea of federal government is actually Iranian in origin. The founders of the United States of America adopted it from their study of the Persian Empire and of elements of the Ottoman system of governance that were also Iranian in origin. However, the *satrapy* system of the Achaemenids or the feudal federalism of the Parthians is not even remotely applicable to the current nation-state of Iran. The preservation of a centralized government in Iran, with a strong Persian axis, but including numerous other Iranians, is indispensable to the project of politically re-unifying Iranian Civilization as a whole.

To use the language of Samuel Huntington's analysis in *The Clash of Civilizations*, the nation-state of Iran, in its current form, must play the role of "civilizational core state." If artificially engineered Kurdish separatism is allowed to achieve its goal of an independent Kurdish state that includes the Kurds in Western Iran, transnational corporate interests will ensure that this Kurdistan never rejoins Persia to form a federative Iran that would, in terms of territorial scope, encompass more of Iranian

Civilization than present-day Iran. It must be noted that Kurds also live in a certain pocket of northeastern Iran, totally removed from the rest of a proposed "Kurdistan." If the Kurds remain an integral part of Iran, then a Kurdish nation-state created in northern Iraq, and perhaps someday even in what is now eastern Turkey, could be connected to the core state of Iran in a federation that eventually includes all of Iranian Civilization.

In other words, it is not that federalism is necessarily bad for Iran — as a civilization. Federalism, which enfolds within itself an entire humanistic political philosophy that is opposed to tyranny, is one of the great inventions of Iranian Civilization. Without it, the Persian Empire, history's first true empire, would have been impossible, and the broader sphere of Iranian Civilization, or the Persianate World, would never have taken shape. However, it is not the current nation-state of Iran that ought to be artificially broken up by a federal government. Rather, Tajikistan, Iraqi Kurdistan, Ossetia, Bulgaria, and Croatia, among other countries that are part of Iranian Civilization, should rejoin the core state of Iran in a federative manner.

Those Azeri, Kurdish, and Baluchi traitors who are being manipulated by foreign powers do not just intend to walk away with Iranian territory, or afford foreign powers the opportunity to loot Iran's natural resources. They are also intent on misappropriating Persian culture. "Cultural appropriation" is a term that is often used these days in resentful anti-colonialist, and generally anti-Western discourse to refer to adoption and adaptation of the cultural practices of one ethnic group by others elsewhere in the world — for example, Americans of European ethnicity practicing Yoga or using acupuncture.

Contrary to what these idiots believe, cultural appropriation is very constructive in catalyzing innovation based on cultural mutation and furthering the evolution of consciousness rather than the stagnation of humanity in a ghettoized world full of regressively tribal cultures. The unique glory of Persian culture itself, and even more so Iranian Civilization as a whole, is highly syncretistic in origin and would not have evolved but for repeated appropriation, adaptation, and synthesis of elements originating in other cultures. The problem is not cultural appropriation, in cases where the people who are doing the appropriating respectfully and appreciatively acknowledge the national or ethnic origin of what it is that they are appropriating. No American who practices Yoga refuses to acknowledge that this tradition originates in India. No Frenchman who reveres the *Analects* tries to pass off Confucius as French, rather than Chinese. The problem is cultural misappropriation. That is, when a group of people steal a cultural treasure by falsely claiming that it is originally their own and coercing others in the world who do not know better to accept their claim.

Unfortunately, no one has suffered more from this than the Persians. One of the worst examples is in the so-called "Republic of Azerbaijan." The Azeri government has ripped the original tiles off of the tomb of the Persian poet, Nezami Ganjavi, which featured passages from his poems in beautiful *Nastaliq* calligraphy, and they have replaced these with Azeri Turkic translations. What is worse is that this physical erasure of history is being psychologically reinforced by government-authorized textbooks that claim Nezami was a Turk, whereas any competent scholar of literary history knows that he was a Persian or native Persian speaker from among the ethnically Iranian Azeris (Tat and Talysh). Nezami Ganjavi's works are among the masterpieces of Persian literature.

It is bad enough that the barbaric Turks invaded and occupied large parts of Azerbaijan beginning around 1100 AD. This tragedy ought not to be compounded by their claiming the cultural heritage of the highly civilized Persians who had to tolerate the sadistic brutality of these invaders. Of course, Azerbaijan was eventually liberated. As we have seen, in the early 1500s, it became the fountainhead of the political resurrection of Iran under the Safavids. The same chapter discussed how the Safavids were, both ethnically and phenotypically, Caucasian Iranians who probably descended from the Scythians or Sarmatians and who only spoke some Turkish and recruited Turks into their military. It bears repeating that Shah Ismail Safavid looked like a Celt or German. Azerbaijan went on to be the wellspring of the Persian Constitutional Revolution of 1906.

Large parts of this Iranian province were, however, lost to the Russians during the Russo-Persian Wars of the nineteenth century, and these northern parts were turned into the Soviet Socialist Republic of Azerbaijan, which declared independence in 1991.

The Russians, in particular, were adept at engineering artificial identities in the parts of Iran that they seized, so as to weaken the identification of the colonized population with the Persian heritage and thereby guard against the potential for revolt and reintegration with Iran. They did this in Tajik territories such as Samarkand and Bukhara as well, deliberately placing them within the Uzbek SSR, so that the Persians (Tajiks) would be drowned out by Uzbek Turks. Meanwhile, in the Tajik SSR they worked at fostering the absurd notion that "Tajik" is a language or that there is some Tajik identity distinct from the Persian identity of Iran. The proper name of the Persian dialect spoken in Central Asia, namely *Dari* (short for *Darbâri*) clearly identifies it as the language of the *Darbâr* or Persian royal court. In fact, it is an even purer form of Persian than Iran's *Pârsi*. Rudaki is not a "Tajik" national poet. He is an ethnic Iranian and native Persian speaker.

Note how communists, whose ultimate goal was to destroy national identity altogether, felt that they first had to invent false discourses of national identity for Russian-colonized peoples to identify with, before divesting them of any identity whatsoever. Leftists are still at this game today. The Persian identity was too strong to deconstruct, whereas "Azeri" or "Tajik" identity could simply become pawns in the discourse of "peoples' liberation movements," with the USSR's social engineers perversely framing the Persians as imperialist overlords and the Russian colonialists as "liberators."

They did this in Kurdistan as well. When the Soviet Union invaded Iran in 1941, together with the other Allied Powers of the Second World War, the Russians seized the rest of Azerbaijan and occupied it until Mohammad Reza Shah Pahlavi forced them out in December of 1946. As we saw in Chapter 10, during this same period, they attempted to expand the Soviet Union even further into Iranian territory by establishing the "Republic of Mahabad" in Iranian Kurdistan. For twelve months, from

January to December of 1946, Mahabad was an ostensibly "independent" state with Kurdish as its "national" language, but with the Soviet ruble as its currency. It was a Russian puppet government, undoubtedly slated to become another Soviet Socialist Republic.

The Kurdish region of Iran is home to two of the most important Persian cultural treasures. One is the Behistun Inscription of Darius the Great, carved into the rock cliffs of the Kermanshah region. I suppose it is ironic that this inscription depicts the Persian Emperor crushing secessionist rebellions and taking their leaders prisoner. Behistun has been described by archeologists as being to cuneiform what the Rosetta Stone is to deciphering the hieroglyphs of ancient Egypt. That is because the relief features the same proclamation of Darius in three different languages: the Emperor's native Old Persian language, as well as Elamite, and Babylonian. It is in this inscription that Darius famously, or infamously, affirms the Aryan identity of the Persian people. In addition to the titanic inscription of Darius, there are many other reliefs and archeological remains of the Median, Parthian, and Sassanian periods at Behistun. The 116 hectare site also features remains of the Achaemenid "Royal Road," the world's first highway (*Shâh Râh*). It is the site of the last traces of the palace of the Sassanian Emperor Khosrow II and the residence of his beloved Shirin, a heroine rendered immortal in Persian literary works, such as those of Nezami and Ferdowsi.

The other Persian cultural treasure in the Kurdish part of Iran is Taq-e Bostan, a large rock-carved Sassanian site whose magnificent reliefs and sculptures date from around the fourth century AD. It is one of the best, and one of the very few, surviving examples of Sassanian period Persian art in the medium of sculpture. The imagery includes a memorialization of the investitures of Ardeshir II and Shapur III, as well as scenes depicting beautiful ring-bearing female Zoroastrian angels and one of the few surviving images of the goddess Anahita that has not been defaced beyond recognition by Muslim conquerors.

Perhaps the most interesting image is the Sassanian Emperor Khosrow II (591–628) as a chainmail-clad knight mounted on his favorite horse,

Shabdiz. This is a very significant image from the standpoint of art history, since it has a medieval European aesthetic, centuries before the imagery of lance-wielding horseback-riding knights in shining armor pervades Europe. This emphasizes the Iranian origin of Chivalry, which was discussed in Chapters 1 and 5. There is also a relief sculpture of women playing harps, a popular instrument at the Sassanian court, although these women's faces, like the face of the goddess Anahita, have been smashed and gouged out by Muslims.

Taq-e-Bostan and Behistun are not the only major Iranian archeological sites that are in danger of being culturally misappropriated by Kurdish separatists. Lake Urumia, on the border between the Kurdish region of Iran and what is left of Azerbaijan, is reputed to have been the home of Zarathustra (Zoroaster). Consequently Zarathustra is claimed by both the Kurds and the Azeris, in an equally ridiculous and anachronistic fashion. In this connection it is important to note that the idea that the tribal Kurds are descendants of the Medes is highly questionable. The Kurds are more like Greater Iran's equivalent of the Bedouins in Arabia. The actual Medes intermarried with the Persian aristocracy and were likely absorbed into the Persian ruling class by the end of the Achaemenid period. At this point, Persians in Western Iran probably have at least as much Median blood as the Kurds — if not more.

Claiming that Zarathustra was a Kurd and that Zoroastrianism is a Kurdish religion, or for that matter that "Zoroaster was from Azerbaijan" is one of the most disgustingly pathetic attempts, not only to rob Iran of another cultural treasure, but to steal the genius who is the spiritual fountainhead of Iranian Civilization. That the Islamic Republic's disregard for ecology has led to the desiccation of lake Urumia, which should be sacred not only to Zoroastrians but to all Iranians, has not helped to put down Kurdish and Azeri separatists dwelling on the West and East banks of the lake.

In a nightmarish future where Tabriz is part of an even larger Azerbaijani state than the one that has already been carved out of the Iranian Caucasus, one can easily imagine that the Azeris, in addition to stealing

Zarathustra or at least fighting the Kurds to claim him, would join with the Turks of Turkey in attempting to claim Mowlana Jalaluddin Rumi. Of course, in this case, they would have to fight those in Iran's former eastern province of Herat, who already want to absurdly claim that Rumi, whom they refer to as Jalaluddin Balkhi, was an "Afghani" poet. Rumi is, of course, a Persian poet and an Iranian by ethnicity — even if his birthplace is presently in Afghanistan and his tomb is in what has become Turkey. That British colonial machinations used a local tribal revolt in Eastern Iran to carve out an "independent" state of Afghanistan hundreds of years after Rumi's lifetime is irrelevant to his identity. If Iran were to lose Tabriz, the finest Persian carpets are not the only cultural treasures that would suddenly become "Azeri" (i.e. Turkic). Rumi's Persian teacher, Shams of Tabriz, could also be misappropriated.

It is not impossible to imagine that Baluchi separatists would start claiming that Rostam, the greatest hero of the Persian national epic, Ferdowsi's *Shâhnâmeh*, is a Baluch simply because he was from Sistan and the Baluchistan province of Iran is amalgamated with Sistan, which would also be lost if an independent state of Baluchistan were carved out of Iran (and neighboring Pakistan). Imagine that: Rostam as the future "national hero of Baluchistan," which is currently the poorest and most backward province of Iran, full of anti-Persian Sunni fundamentalists of the kind that sheltered Osama bin Laden in neighboring Pakistan.

Finally, there is the question of what the secession of Khuzestan and its transformation into the Arab Republic of Al-Ahwaz would mean for the Persian Gulf. It is unlikely that the Elamite heritage at Chogha Zanbil (Elamite *Dur Untash*) ziggurat would become a point of pride for the Islamist Arabs who would be leading "Al-Ahwaz." In fact, one would have to fear for the safety of this monument, which is another UNESCO World Heritage Site in Iran. The Ahwazi Arab minority, direct descendants of the Arabs who conquered Iran in the seventh century AD, loathe Iran so much that they have threatened to kill the ethnically Iranian Bakhtiari tribesmen and take their wives as sex slaves. So they are likely to work with Saudi Arabia, Qatar, the UAE, and the other sheikhdoms to turn the

Persian Gulf into an "Arabian Gulf" recognized by those key players in first-world nations that these Arabs have bribed with oil and gas money. The longer "Arab" coastline along the Persian Gulf that an independent "Al-Ahwaz" would give them, together with the wealth-producing capacity of the single largest petroleum-rich region of what was Iran, could go a long way toward helping them to erase the *Persian* Gulf and to tactically dominate the new "Arabian" one. Apparently, the Arabs are not satisfied that they already have an entire sea named after them.

12.2 Iran as a Global Superpower and Hegemon of the Islamic World

The will to ensure that the Persian Gulf does not become Arabian, that Persian is not disestablished as the official language of Iran, and, in short, that Iranian Civilization does not disappear, is based on more than just patriotic sentimentality, let alone nationalistic chauvinism. Iran is certainly a civilization among only a handful of other living civilizations on Earth, rather than a lone state with its own isolated culture, like Japan — but Iran is even more than that. As we enter the era of the clash of civilizations, Iran's historic role as the crossroads of all of the other major civilizations cannot be overstated.

In this context it must also be recognized that Iran is not just another civilization, on par with the West, India, or China. In the event that it is allowed to return to its own heritage and reclaim its proper destiny, Iran could be the cosmopolitan nexus for a dialogue of civilizations with a view to their eventual convergence in the most constructive way imaginable. The first step toward that must, however, be the transformation of the core of the current sphere of so-called "Islamic Civilization" back into an Iranian civilizational sphere. This demands that Iran become what Samuel Huntington would call the "core state" of Islamic Civilization.[1]

Iran has seven potential rivals for the status of Islamic civilizational core state, namely: Saudi Arabia, Iraq, Egypt, Turkey, Pakistan, Malaysia, and Indonesia. Most of these countries are utterly incapable of leading the

Islamic world, and the few that are capable of doing so would never be able to make the case that they can transform so-called "Islamic Civilization" into something that would at least be benign, if not beneficent, when considered in terms of its implications for the human community at large and in view of the demographic dominance of Muslims on Earth by the mid to late twenty-first century. Let us briefly take a look at each of these potential rivals to Iran.

Saudi Arabia is the nation within the borders of which Mecca and Medina, the two holiest cities in Islam, are located. It is the territory of both Muhammad's own prophetic mission and the administrative capital of the Rashidun Caliphate, the first Caliphate in the history of Islam. In a world still largely dependent on oil for energy and transportation, Saudi Arabia also remains the Earth's leading oil producing nation and is, on that basis alone, among the wealthiest nations on Earth. Moreover, this key energy-production role in the global economy has garnered Saudi Arabia a valuable diplomatic and military ally in the United States of America.

These are, however, the only factors in favor of Saudi Arabia assuming the role of Islamic civilizational core state and, in light of the competition, they are far from sufficient. Although Islam as a religion appears to have originated in the Arabian peninsula, none of the great civilizational achievements commonly attributed to Islam took place there. Arabia, Saudi or otherwise, is culturally barren and backwards. The Saudis have the most barbaric and inhumane socio-political system of any major player on the world stage. This ought not to be surprising, since the Hejaz is a desert wasteland populated by camel herders. The country has no indigenous agricultural capacity and has never had any significant industrial capability. The Saudi "nation" is a totally artificial construction dating back to 1932. Prior to that, despite the status of Mecca and Medina, the uninhabitable peninsula was peripheral to the Islamic world for most of history. Saudi Arabia's entire mirage of wealth, and the purchased paper tiger of its military might, rests on a non-renewable energy resource discovered by Western colonialists in the twentieth century—a resource that will run dry within the next twenty years.

After the fall of the Arabian-peninsula-based Rashidun Caliphate, the administrative capital of the Islamic world moved to Baghdad under both the Umayyad and Abbasid caliphs. The nation-state of Iraq was formed in the same year as Saudi Arabia, namely 1932. Historically, both the names "Baghdad" and "Iraq" refer to parts of Iran. *Bogh-Dâd* means either "Given by God" or "God's Justice" in the Middle Persian language of the Parthian period, when the city was founded in what was then Western Iran.[2] The term *Erâq* is a geographical designator for the mountainous region of southwestern Iran, with the part that remains in Iran today being referred to as *Erâqé Ajami* or "Aryan Iraq."[3]

From October 29, 539 BC, when Cyrus the Great marched into Babylon until the Arab-Muslim conquest of the Sassanid state in 651 AD, Iraq was the administrative capital of Iran through three successive Iranian empires, that of the Achaemenids, the Parthians, and the Sassanians. By about 900 AD, semi-autonomous Persian fiefdoms in northern Iran had essentially reduced the Abbasid Caliphate in Baghdad into their own cat's paw. Even once the Seljuq Turks took over in the middle of the eleventh century, the administrative elite of the Caliphate remained Persian. Iraq then changed hands between the Ottoman Caliphate and Iran for a period of several hundred years under the Safavid and Afsharid dynasties. It is not until around the year 1800, relatively recently in the scope of Iran's history, that most of Iraq, including Baghdad, was lost — first to the Turks and then to Western colonialists aligned with the country's Arab majority. Even still, the Arabs of Iraq remained largely Shi'ite and thereby under the religious influence of Iran. Meanwhile, the Kurds in northern Iraq, while Sunni, are ethnically Iranian and speak an Iranian language.

All of this is to say that, in civilizational terms, Iraq is essentially an integral part of Iran and has been so for about twenty-five centuries. The one brief epoch of radically anti-Iranian politics in Iraq, the period of Saddam Hussein, is when Iraq came closest to assuming leadership of the Islamic world at large. Saddam Hussein's invasion of Kuwait and Saudi Arabia in 1990–1991, a few years after the failure of his eight-year long campaign to seize Iran's oil-rich Khuzestan province, was fated to be nothing more than a passing gleam. As an avowed secular Arab nationalist, Saddam would never have fooled anyone into believing that he had the legitimacy to hold Mecca and Medina and to speak as the vice-regent of Allah on Earth.

Ironically, it was only after the total destruction of Saddam's Arab nationalist regime in the 2003 American invasion of Iraq that the country became the base of operations for a ragtag group of partisans and mercenaries who claimed to constitute a new Sunni Caliphate, with a caliph named "Baghdadi." The actual government in Baghdad had become little more than a Shi'ite client state of the Islamic Republic of Iran. Meanwhile, the ethnically Iranian Kurds in the north began their march toward secession from an "Iraq" that had clearly become a failed state because nothing coherent or cohesive ever really held it together after it was severed from the Persian and Ottoman Empires. With the recent defeat of Islamic State forces within Iraq, albeit after the destruction of irreplaceable cultural treasures by those barbarians, it is clear that the reemergence of Iraq as a core state of Islamic Civilization is totally out of the question. Not now. Not ever. Iraq will continue to be dominated by either Iran or Turkey.

As much as Recep Tayyip Erdogan would like to be remembered as the founder of a New Ottoman Caliphate, Turkey's prospects for leading the Islamic world at large are rather grim. In a scenario where Iran were to lose what is left of Azerbaijan within its own borders, and a greater Republic of Azerbaijan comes to connect Turkey to the Caspian Sea and across to the Turkic lands of Turkmenistan and Uzbekistan, a Pan-Turkic federation of some kind is conceivable. This is, not incidentally, all the more reason for Iranians to insist on holding Tabriz and Ardebil, potentially even recapturing Baku, by any and all means necessary—including the reaffirmation of Shi'ite discourse.

However, these Turkic territories are peripheral to the Islamic world. The language barrier between Turks and Arabs, and the significant differences between their cultures, poses a nearly insurmountable barrier to any reassertion of Turkish control over Arabia. First of all, to do so, Sunni Turkey would have to pass through the most solidly Shi'ite among the Arab lands, namely Iraq and Syria, not to mention through the rest of Kurdistan—one third of which is already inside of Turkey's borders. These are all lands within the Iranian civilizational sphere—Iraq and Syria on account of Shi'ism and Kurdistan on account of its Iranian ethno-linguistic identity. Moreover, in a rivalry with Iran, both the Kurds and a sizeable Shi'ite minority in Eastern Anatolia could be mobilized against the government of Turkey. By contrast, the capacity of a Neo-Ottoman Turkey to mobilize self-identifying "Turks" in Iranian Azerbaijan against the government of Iran would be limited by the hardline Sunni stance of this Neo-Ottoman Calipahte as compared to the Shi'ite identity of the Azeris in Iran.

In short, Turkey is locked in. There is certainly no question of a Westward expansion of a Neo-Ottoman Caliphate. The countries of Eastern Europe, which have the bitterest memories of Ottoman rape and pillage, have been the first to reject European Union migration policies and erect a cultural barrier against the Islamization of Europe. The massive number of Turks in Germany poses a serious national security threat to that country, but they are separated from Turkey by this anti-Islamic firewall in the Visegrád region. The most likely outcome is that the continued degradation of German culture at their hands will eventually lead to their mass expulsion or internment by ethnic Germans. If anything, the Turkish threat to Eastern and Central Europe should be reason for the Visegrád Group, and ultimately Germany as well, to support Shi'ite Iran as a strong Eastern ally against Turks with an ambition of reestablishing a Sunni Ottoman Caliphate. Such an alliance existed between Safavid Iran and some European powers at war with the Ottoman Empire, and it would make a great deal of sense for this paradigm to be revived.

Pakistan was never the seat of the Caliphate. In fact, Pakistan was not even a nation until its secession from India in 1947. The discourse surrounding and justifying that secession was, however, an explicitly Islamist discourse and the Islamic Republic of Pakistan was consciously conceived of as a bastion for all of the Muslims of the world. Practically speaking, this served no real purpose other than to reinforce the artificiality and rootlessness of the so-called Pakistani "nation." At no point have Arabs, Turks, and others in the Islamic world ever come to consider Pakistan an exemplary Islamic State, let alone a country that would lead the Islamic world in a way comparable to America's leadership of the Western world. This, despite the fact that Pakistan is (as of the time of writing) the only Muslim country to have developed nuclear weapons, and there appears to be a tacit agreement between Pakistan and Saudi Arabia, who largely financed the Pakistani nuclear program, to provide the latter with these weapons in the event of a threat to Mecca and Medina. Even still, this Pakistan-Saudi Axis has never been tested by war, and if the war should prove to be one between Iran and Saudi Arabia, it is doubtful that Pakistan would risk war with Iran by coming to the aid of the Saudis.

Pakistanis are well aware of the fact that, as was discussed in Chapter 9, the closest thing that Pakistan has to a cultural heritage is the legacy of the Mughal Empire, which was a Persianate culture through and through. Pakistan is nothing other than Persianate India. The denial of this heritage, and the idiotic adoption of Urdu as a national language in an area where Persian had been dominant for hundreds of years until British colonization, has led to cultural rootlessness and the rise of Sunni fundamentalist ideology. The potential for a Taliban-style Islamist seizure of power in at least some parts of Pakistan cannot be dismissed, but given the Pakistani nuclear arsenal, this would pose such a grave threat both to India and to Western powers allied with India, including Israel, that such an Islamist toppling of Pakistan's central government and seizing of power even in a single province would mean a massive military intervention with only one final outcome: reintegration of a devastated Pakistan into India. Such a forcible reversal of the partition would probably result in a religious clash between Hindus, Muslims, and Sikhs on a genocidal scale and cripple the capacity of Pakistanis — or, in that event, North Indian Muslims — to lead the Islamic world. They will be busy enough defending themselves from Hindus and Sikhs within the borders of a re-unified India.

The neighboring Southeast Asian nations of Malaysia and Indonesia are so peripheral to the Islamic world that the potential for either of them to lead the Arab or Turkic peoples in the formation of a new Caliphate is, from a geographical and historical perspective, utterly preposterous. They merit mention only because the former is among the wealthiest nations in the Islamic world and the latter is among the most populous. Both countries have even been home to some of the most zealous support for Al-Qaeda, particularly, Malaysia, where Osama bin Laden is seen as a hero by many devout Sunnis. In short, Malay financial power and Indonesian military force could play a significant role in an intercontinental Sunni Caliphate *in the event that one were to be successfully established in some other, more central part of the Islamic world.* Another reason why both Western powers and the Chinese ought to back an Iranian Shi'ite dominance of the Islamic world is that under such a scenario, Sunni Malaysia and Indonesia would become so peripheral and irrelevant to the core of the Islamic world, as they were during the period of the classic Caliphates, that the archipelago would be left for China to dominate. This region is home to the second largest community of overseas Chinese in the world.

Of all of the countries that could potentially rival Iran for leadership of the Islamic world, Egypt is actually the most viable contender. As we have seen in Chapter 7, Iran and Egypt were closely connected during the one period when Egypt was the seat of the Caliphate, namely the Fatamid period, which is the only time that Shi'ites dominated the entire Islamic world. It is the Ismaili Fatamids of Egypt who finally stopped the Westward advance of the Mongols. Egypt has, of course, since become solidly Sunni. Like Saudi Arabia and Iraq, and unlike the remaining countries that we are about to address, its language is the Arabic language, which is authoritative for Islamic theology and is the language of the majority of Muslims in the historical core of the Islamic world. In fact, it is the Arabic of Cairo that has become standard for the entire Islamic world in modern times — not the Arabic spoken in the Arabian peninsula itself. Al-Azhar in Cairo remains the world's leading Muslim theological academy.

Said Qotb's ideology of Al-Qaeda and the organizational infrastructure of the Muslim Brotherhood took shape in the shadows of this conservative Sunni school of thought. In a scenario where the Al-Saud regime in

Arabia meets its demise, whether through internal upheaval or war with Iran (or both), there is a potential for Egypt to reemerge as the core of a Sunni Arab-Muslim Caliphate extending from Morocco to Oman and as far south as Sudan. Such a situation ought not to be conceived of in terms of the projection of conventional Egyptian military force, nor does it require Egypt to emerge as a major industrial power. Rather, the Cairo-based Caliphate scenario is one that has, as its precondition, the collapse of the Egyptian national state and the surrender of its secularist military to an Islamist movement that is radically transnational — or, at the very least, Pan-Arab in its ideological orientation.

This is exactly the kind of threat that ought to convince major world powers to at least tolerate, if not encourage, an Iranian dominance of the Islamic world. First of all, such a Caliphate would be taking shape on the doorstep of the State of Israel, and it is abundantly clear that its cohesion, even at any early stage, would have to involve the annihilation of Israel. Cooperation with Israel has been forced upon the succession of undemocratic but relatively secular Egyptian administrations since the 1970s precisely because this situation has been felt as such a serious long-term strategic threat. It is actually the main reason why, with the brief anomaly of Barack Obama's misadventure in Cairo, Western powers have not been keen on supporting democratization in Egypt. The brief Obama Administration experiment of supporting the Arab Spring, including in Egypt, yielded a democratic but fundamentalist Islamic regime led by the Muslim Brotherhood. Had it not been for General Al-Sisi's Western-backed *coup d'ëtat*, this democratic election would have put Cairo on track to becoming the epicenter of a new Caliphate.

One catastrophic danger that immediately became apparent during the crisis of the brief Muslim Brotherhood rule in Egypt was a Sunni fundamentalist threat to ancient Egyptian monuments and artifacts. The situation became so dire that, at one point, prime time Egyptian national television was hosting Mufti guests promising to blow up the Giza Pyramids. It became easy to imagine that one fine morning we would all wake up to scenes of the Great Sphinx having been decapitated with dynamite in the cover of night. It is true that in the early days of the Islamic Revolution in Iran, there were a few zealots within the rising regime who had similar ideas with regard to Persepolis or the tombs of the Achaemenid emperors. However, the traditional stance of Shi'ism prevailed and, as was the case in the Safavid period, let alone with the ultra-Persian Ismaili Shi'ites in the medieval period, the Pre-Islamic heritage of Iran was appropriated by the Shi'ite clergy to bolster their Imamate in a way comparable to the Romanness of the Catholic Church.

Oftentimes one's enemies have a clearer perception of one than one does oneself. So we ought to take very seriously the claims of surrounding Sunni Arab countries that contemporary expansionist Shi'ite militancy is actually a reassertion of Persian Imperialism (including in Turkic, but Shi'ite Azerbaijan). Unlike Iran, Egypt has no organic continuity with its ancient cultural heritage. There have been too many disruptions and changes of language in the country, from the ancient Persians to the classical Greeks and the Romans, all before the Arab-Muslim conquest, and followed by the Ottoman Turks later in the Islamic period. The native Egyptian language and culture did not even survive into the pagan Roman epoch, let alone into Islamic times. The contemporary nation of Egypt is an artificial British colonial construction from out of the ruins of the Ottoman Caliphate. It is so uprooted that Taliban-style destruction of ancient Egyptian cultural treasures is conceivable.

In the battle for hearts and minds, worldwide, an Iranian Shi'ite Imamate will trump an Egyptian Sunni Caliphate any day. Even Israel would align with a militantly Shi'ite Iran if it were to be presented with such a binary. Furthermore, if a Sunni Cairo-based Caliphate were to endorse or even condone vandalism committed against archeological sites, or destroy the extensive tourism industry of Egypt, it is likely that a significant enough segment of secularists in the country would align with Western powers to re-impose some type of colonial rule over Egypt — in whatever masked form that would need to take for the sake of salvaging an archeological heritage that belongs to all mankind. This could happen in the context of a broader NATO or European intervention on the North

African side of the Mediterranean. Israel could, under these conditions, recapture the Sinai peninsula.

All of that would be completely compatible with Iranian dominance further to the East—especially in Shi'ite parts of Syria, Iraq, the Kurdish territories, Azerbaijan, Shi'ite parts of the Persian Gulf, southwestern Yemen, and the Shi'ite and Tajik parts of Central Asia— especially Herat, Kabul, Badakhshan, Dushanbe, Samarkand, and Bukhara. Such a geopolitical strategy requires a fusion of the Shi'ite Muslim and Pan-Iranist discourses. The Pan-Iranist discourse would be more significant in Sunni parts of Iranian Civilization, such as Kurdistan, Afghanistan, Tajikistan, and relevant parts of Uzbekistan. In other words, a Renaissance of Iran's leadership of the Islamic world ought not to be considered solely in terms of a Shi'ite victory in a sectarian war with Sunnis. Continued Iranian dominance across all Shi'ite Muslim territories is a necessary but not a sufficient condition for the renaissance of Iran as a civilization, one that is at least geopolitically on par with China in the rivalry to define the World Order of the twenty-first century. This return to superpower status also requires Iran reaching into Sunni parts of its civilizational sphere on the basis of a renaissance of the Iranian heritage that Kurds share, as well as the Persian language and culture that endures in Sunni, but ethnically Iranian, parts of Central Asia such as Northern Afghanistan, Tajikistan, and the Tajik parts of Uzbekistan.

12.3 Dysgenic Decline and Neo-Eugenic Biotechnology in Iranian Civilization

Genetics should be considered as a factor in the absorption or reintegration of such large populations of Iranians who are currently living outside of the borders of the nation state of Iran. Even within Iran itself, population genetics cannot be ignored as a major factor contributing to the catastrophic decline of Iranian Civilization that any reader will have noticed in the narrative of the past couple of chapters. In Chapter 9, it was proposed that historical misalignment of the imperial conquests of Nader

Shah Afshar with the rise of the Babi movement, which came too late, was partly to account for the failure of Nader, or of the Safavids before him to enter the modern age on par with European colonial powers. However, even if Nader had not disestablished Shi'ism, and even if something like the Babi movement had materialized while the Safavids were still in power, it is highly unlikely that Iran would have been able to develop on the same trajectory as Russia, let alone the British imperial nemesis of Iran.

Once the Arab-Muslim invasion was compounded by the genocidal Turkic and Mongol conquests of Iran, a demographic shift took place that deprived Iran of the genetic basis for the kind of genius that produced the Achaemenid, Parthian, and Sassanid Empires, *and that we still saw flourishing in the sciences from the ninth through the eleventh century*. Geniuses are fewer than one in a million, even in a population with a predominately Indo-European gene pool. But their thinking goes on to impact millions in the broader intellectual culture of their nation.

After 1945 in the Western world it became politically correct to claim that "race" is a social construction that does not correspond to any biological reality. This is essentially a Marxist view that, for reasons having to do with the outcome of the Second World War, became just as culturally predominant in the West as it was among the Soviet allies of the West during the war. In the last five years, advances in gene sequencing technology and new archeological finds have destroyed this left-wing myth of human racial equality.

It turns out that there were multiple co-existing hominid species, which were vastly unequal in significant respects such as their cognitive abilities. So-called *Homo sapiens* did not neatly and cleanly follow these extinct species in evolutionary history. Rather, different groups of hominids that are now extinct mated with certain populations of *Homo sapiens* and not with others. For example, many Europeans have Neanderthal genes, but no Africans do. Many Africans and South Indians have genes from an extinct hominid called the Denisovan, but no Europeans have Denisovan genes. Racial difference is real, and it matters. That Africans have an average IQ of around 70 whereas whites have an average IQ of around 100, and Africans who have mixed with whites (for example in North America or South Africa) have an average IQ of around 80 has to do not with education or social conditioning, but with different genetic inheritances from extinct hominid species.[4] The average IQ of modern Iran has been measured at 84, as compared to an average of 100 in Europe and 105 in East Asia.[5]

On March 17 of 2016 *The New York Times* published an article entitled "Ancestors of Modern Humans Interbred With Extinct Hominins," which discusses the mainstream scientific studies demonstrating that Africans do not have the Neanderthal genes that Europeans inherited, whereas Europeans do not have the Denisovan genes inherited by Africans.[6] In April of 2008, neuroscientists Gary Lynch and Richard Granger published a book called *Big Brain: The Origins and Future of Human Intelligence*, which focuses on the significant cognitive differences between these extinct human sub-species.[7] Again, various ethnic groups have unequally inherited genes from these sub-species based on their relative geographic isolation. It is perfectly reasonable to argue that the significant differences in IQ, which correlate to the phenotypic concept of "racial" difference, are among these unequally inherited characteristics.

In their 2002 book *IQ and the Wealth of Nations*, psychologist Richard Lynn and political scientist Tatu Vanhanen presented overwhelming evidence of ethnic differences in cognitive capacities that correlate to the relative industrial productivity and socio-economic welfare of groups of nations that cluster along "racial" lines such as Caucasian, African, and Asian.[8] In 2006 they followed up with *IQ and Global Inequality*, which gave a detailed response to the scientific community's critical reception of their first book.[9]

There has been a lively contemporary debate over race and cognitive capacity in the scientific community ever since psychologist Richard J. Herrnstein and political scientist Charles Murray published *The Bell Curve* in 1994.[10] The work of Thomas Kuhn and Paul Feyerabend demonstrates that science is an ongoing revolutionary process of discovery, not a dogmatically established body of knowledge. Defenders of failing paradigms, who want to make it seem as if the latter are true, are always politically motivated and usually dishonest.

When liberals or socialists hostile to genetic explanations of human ability state that there is only a "slight genetic difference," and then deceptively add "between individuals," whereas ethnic *groups* are in question here, it is important to bear in mind that we share 50% of our genes in common with a banana and 99% with the average chimpanzee. Small fractions of less than 1% thus make a huge difference. The real problem is that thinking along these lines at all is now a "thought crime" in the West. This is not the case in China, where race is recognized as an undisputed reality and the political and scientific establishment embraces the New Eugenics to reaffirm presumed Chinese supremacy.[11] The politically incorrect reality of race has been recognized by leading geneticists, such as James Watson, who discovered DNA—albeit his recognition came at the cost of his being stripped of all of his honorary degrees and professional memberships.[12] Racial difference is real, and it matters. Islam stopped acting as a catalyst intended to provoke the sociological equivalent of an immune response, and was instead swallowed whole, only when the population of Iran began to be demographically dominated by very low-IQ people—people with an IQ on the same level as ethnic (Central Asian) Turks or native Arabs.

Before the Arab, Turkic, and Mongol conquests of Iran, or in other words up to the end of the Sassanian period, the majority of the Iranian elite were genetically identical to the Indo-Europeans who migrated into Europe from the same region that was the racial cradle of the Iranians. This view has been corroborated by recent genetic studies, which were published in leading journals from 2015 to 2018. The first of these is a 2015 study by Wolfgang Haak and his associates at Cold Spring Harbor Laboratory, which was published in *Nature* with the title "Massive migration from the steppe is a source for Indo-European languages in Europe."[13] The study traces the genes of the Yamnaya people, or as the late Lithuanian scholar Marija Gimbutas called them, the "Kurgans," who were the earliest Indo-Europeans that migrated from the Pontic-Caspian

Steppe (between the Black Sea and the northern Caspian Sea) into Europe from 5000–5400 BC. Harvard University geneticist David Reich has noted that this resulted in a 70% replacement of the native German population. Yamnaya DNA became the single most significant contributor to the genetic constitution of the Northern European or "Nordic" population. The so-called "Corded Ware" culture of Germany and Scandinavia was formed by a hybrid of the Yamnaya and the Neolithic native European hunter-gatherers of this region. Whereas Yamnaya men are carriers of the R1B haplogroup, the hybrid population that they bred together with the native Europeans in Germany developed what geneticists term the R1A haplogroup. The implications of this are unpacked in a study by Harvard's David Reich, together with Iain Mathieson and their associates, titled "The genomic history of southeastern Europe," which appeared in *Nature* in March of 2018.[14]

Tracing the R1A genes shows that the Germanic-Yamnaya hybrid population, which formed in Northern Europe and is known as the "Corded Ware" culture, spread eastwards into the North Caucasus, the northern part of the Caspian basin and the Eurasian steppe from 2800 to 1800 BC. The densest concentration of these people in Eurasia is found in the Sintashta and Andronovo cultures, located between the Caspian Sea and Tajikistan. This culture, wherein we find the oldest burials of chariots or wheeled vehicles, was the matrix for the Indo-Iranian branch of the Indo-European language family that came to include both Persian and Sanskrit.

Around 1500 BC this population came down around the Caspian Sea and entered the plateau that they named "Iranian" after themselves, settling in large numbers in the land that they turned into "Iran" by 1000 BC. The same stock of people "invaded" India around 1700 BC to become the Indo-Aryans, the progenitors of the Sanskrit high culture of the Indian subcontinent. In other words, the "Aryans"—as they called themselves—entered India slightly before they entered the country that they dubbed *Aryana* (i.e. Iran). In both cases, this was a Germanic population from Europe. The regions within Iran which have been longest inhabited by Aryans are the Caspian and Kurdistan, with the Mitanni culture of Kurdistan having been established by 1500 BC. In Chapter 1 we saw how this Proto-Iranian culture already invokes the holy name of Mithra on its seals.

It was once believed that the Aryans who named "Iran" were a hybrid population of native Bronze Age hunter gatherers and incoming Indo-Europeans — a hybrid that originated in the Bactria-Margiana Archeological Complex in present-day Turkmenistan. That theory has now been falsified by the latest genetic data, which shows the Aryans entering the plateau that they named "Iran" at a point to the West of the BMAC, along the coast of the Caspian Sea in the region that became known as Hyrcania. The same group traveled to India from a point to the east of the BMAC without passing through it. The genetic analysis of R1A carriers in Northern India supports this conclusion. Some Aryans of North India and Iran migrated into the BMAC, but not the other way around.

Harvard geneticist David Reich admitted that in *Who We Are and How We Got Here* he had to blunt the edges of this finding so as to appease his collaborators in India, who were threatening to pull out of their joint study if he straightforwardly reported their finding that ancient genes originating in Germany are present in northern India, including what has since become Pakistan.[15] He was forced to use deliberately obscure terminology in order to obfuscate what was clearly evidence for a Nordic-Aryan invasion of ancient India, one which resulted in the Swastika-revering Sanskrit high culture of that country. The often blond and blue-eyed Kalash people of Pakistan have nearly 50% Yamnaya DNA. Blond hair and blue eyes are genetic traits that evolved in Pre-Aryan Europe among the native hunter-gatherers in and around Germany. It was introduced into Indo-European or Aryan DNA by the hybridization of the Yamnaya and the native Northern European population. The pure Yamnaya were brunettes, but genetic studies of the Proto-Iranian Andronovo population has revealed many cases of blond hair and blue eyes.

Today this R1A genetic constitution is shared by 63% of people in Persian-speaking Tajikistan, 51% of people in Afghanistan (i.e., Eastern Iran until the nineteenth century), only 35% of people in Iran, as compared to 47% of people in Russia, where the earliest Pre-Slavic "Russians" were actually the Iranian Scythians, 48% of people in the old Sarmatian heartland of Ukraine, 51% in Poland, a nation whose genetic foundation was Sarmatian, a mere 16% of Germany, despite its being the place where this specific genome came into being, and 30% of Norway. 48% of people in the far-north of India, specifically in Kashmir, also share these genes.

When popular online DNA ancestry sites classify someone as 100% genetically "Iranian" what they are really doing is comparing that person's sample to a statistical average of the types of genes found across the entire population of the contemporary nation state of Iran. Consequently, if Iran is only 35% Iranian on a genetic level, someone who tests as 100% "Iranian" according to such criteria has actually been evaluated as being only about one-third Iranian. In other words, someone whose genes were only 35% "Iranian" by these standards might actually be the person who is 100% Iranian, depending on what 35% of Iranian genes their sample actually cluster together with. Unfortunately, this empirical data is occluded by the politically correct statistical leveling used to form the categories according to which such sites carry out their analyses.

The Nordic-Aryan elite of genetically authentic "Iranians," which formed the Achaemenid Empire after an original migration and then successive waves of Scythian invasions of the Median Kingdom, and which was replenished by the Parthians, may have consisted of only 10% of the population of Achaemenid, Parthian, and Sassanian Iran. However, considering the fact that leading lights in the realms of religion, science, art, and politics constitute far less than 1% of a population, when the Achaemenid royals identify themselves as "Aryans" and we read accounts of Sassanid rulers, such as Shapur the Great, being ruddy-cheeked and having auburn hair, we can reasonably assume that this elite of less than 1% was culled from that 10% of high-IQ ethnic Indo-Europeans — not from the other 90% of the population.

Although some Persian elites mixed with local non-Aryan Elamites and Assyrians, this was compensated for by repeated southward mass migrations of northern Iranian tribes such as the Scythians and Sarmatians, who looked—and thought—like Germans (recall Chapters 1 and 5). Their "white" phenotype (with fair skin, green or blue eyes, and red, light brown, or even blond hair) can still be seen in rural parts of Iran, particularly in the mountains of Kurdistan and Azerbaijan, as well as around the Caspian Sea, and even in isolated Persian-speaking towns in the desert around Yazd and Kerman.

There can be little doubt about two things: Firstly, if Germanic barbarians had not invaded the Roman Empire from the north around the time that Christianity was destroying the intellectual life of Rome, there would never have been a Renaissance or Enlightenment in Europe. This took place in Northern Italy, France, and Germany, all territories where the vast majority of the population are genetically Aryan. These movements did not take place in Sicily, and that is significant because hundreds of years earlier—in the time of Pythagoras and Plato, Sicily was actually one of the most intellectually sophisticated parts of Europe. Later Sicily had essentially become Arab despite remaining Christian. Without the barbarian invasions from the north, Italians today would be like the Christian Lebanese and Syrians or essentially like the majority of today's orthodox Greeks. There can also be little doubt that if Central Asia had still been Scythian during the period of the so-called "Islamic Golden Age," and instead of the Turkic and Mongol invasions, Iran had been invaded by Scythians, we would have seen the Enlightenment and Industrial Revolution take place in Iran instead of Europe.

This does not mean that Iran will never again produce thinkers on the level of Razi, Avicenna, or Farabi. With the emerging technologies of embryo selection and genetic engineering, it would be possible, with the right leadership and government planning, to restore the pre-Turkic and pre-Mongol genetic character of the majority of the Iranian population within only one or two generations. Bringing about an Iranian Renaissance in the near future would require, in addition to numerous cultural factors, use of such biotechnologies to restore relevant aspects of the ancient or even early medieval Iranian genetic constitution, such as those that correlate with IQ.

As Richard Lynn explains in his 2001 book *Eugenics: A Reassessment*, all of the leading nations of the Western world had Eugenics programs in the late nineteenth and early twentieth centuries.[16] The most aggressive programs were not in Fascist countries, they were in liberal or social democratic ones like the United States and Sweden.[17] Nazi Germany played catch up. Furthermore, advocates of eugenic uses of new biotechnologies are by far most numerous in East Asian countries. Nearly all of the Chinese scientific, medical, and political establishment is in favor of Neo-Eugenics using embryo selection and genetic engineering in order to, for example, increase the IQ of its population.[18] It should be noted that, together with Ashkenazi Jews, it is the Chinese who already have the highest IQ of any ethnic group in the world — not Caucasians. There is no reason why Iran's position on Neo-Eugenics should resemble that of the Western countries rather than the position of China. Iran should take the lead on this from China and resist all pressures brought to bear by the Western discourse of political correctness.

One can imagine a Neo-Eugenics program in Iran that consists of three simultaneous approaches. The first of these parallel tracks would be to legalize the elective use of In-Vitro Fertilization (IVF) and Pre-Implantation Genetic Diagnosis (PGD) by parents for the sake of selecting optimal embryos, thereby maximizing the IQ of their children as well as reducing hereditary diseases and other factors of disability. The second track would consist of filling Iran's sperm banks with sperm acquired from donors who have been identified as men of original Iranian ethnic stock, namely Caucasoid Indo-Europeans of high genetic worth in terms of their IQ and other properties such as the absence of hereditary diseases. An emphasis would be placed on donors from rural areas where a Caucasian phenotype endures, such as Kurdistan and among the ethnically Iranian Tat and Talysh of Azerbaijan. The children of all women in Iran receiving assisted reproduction would thereby be at least 50% pure Iranian. This policy would also mitigate the danger of secessionism, with Kurds and ethnic Azeris taking pride in being sperm donors for Persians and other Iranians. Finally, the third track of the Iranian Neo-Eugenics program would involve Iran's immigration policy with respect to surrounding countries that are a part of the sphere of Iranian Civilization. Tajiks from Tajikistan and Afghanistan, Talysh from northern Azerbaijan, and Kurds from Iraq and Syria who are of Caucasoid phenotype and whose genotype is screened for preferable traits, such as high-IQ, will be preferred over ethnic Arabs and Turks from the region.

Without any deliberate attempt at racial selection, and in the context of a meritocratic society and political system, such a program ought to yield at least a productive and directive elite of Iranian society that is genetically Aryan within a single generation. The emergence of such an elite of supermen is a *sine qua non* for vigilantly guarding the other Iranian Renaissance programs and guiding them through to their completion. The scale of the task that lies before Iran is, within the context of modern history, even more daunting than the resurrection of Germany from 1919 to 1939, and it must be accomplished within a time frame that is just as compressed if it is to happen at all. As demonstrated at length in *World State of Emergency*, by around the year 2050 the human community as a whole will be faced with a Technological Apocalypse, an evolutionary singularity that brings human history to an end in one way or another.[19] Iranians can only play a decisive role in determining the shape of post-human history if Iran manages to reestablish itself as a major world power, or even a superpower, by 2040. That is only twenty years from the time that these words are being written, which means the Iranian Neo-Eugenics program using emergent biotechnologies must begin immediately.

12.4 Homage To Hyrcania: Occulted Abode of the Once and Future Imam

If one constructive phrase ever came out of the Islamic Republic, it was the phrase "dialogue of civilizations." The dialogue of civilizations is not a utopian fantasy, at least not any longer. In the twenty-first century, it is a survival imperative. Convergent advancements in technology are bringing about a developmental singularity, like that of a black hole, which calls into question the human form of life as such and threatens us with the prospect of a Posthuman future. On the basis of what worldview or value system will humanity face unprecedented challenges such as genetic engineering, the fusion of human consciousness with drone robotic systems and virtual reality, ubiquitous surveillance and the encompassing of the "real world" by simulacra, as well as the expansion of the field of conflict over resource acquisition from the Earth to the Moon and interplanetary space? In *World State of Emergency* (Arktos, 2017) I argued that, taken together, these technological developments represent a state of emergency that is global in scope and that demands the formation of a world state by 2050.

If Iran is to play a determinative role in the formation of this world state and the character of its socio-political constitution, then Iran has to be in a position to rival America, Russia, and China no later than 2040. That is only twenty years from the time that this book is being written. If the Islamic Republic of Iran were to be totally shattered, even in the most optimistically unrealistic scenario Iran would not be able to return to its current position of nearly establishing hegemony over the Islamic World in such a short time frame — let alone surpass that and once again project its strategic influence on a planetary scale.

It ought to be obvious that the project of re-establishing Iran as a superpower in our time requires a certain degree of internal stability in that country. Even if it also demands a cultural revolution, the kind of Iranian Renaissance that could transform the Islamic World through Iranian hegemony over the Middle East and Central Asia certainly cannot take place if the Iranian state is fragmented by a violent revolution or, what would be even worse, if the Islamic Republic were to be overthrown in a foreign "regime change" war. In this light, the most recent round of demonstrations that rocked the Islamic Republic are alarming indeed. These took place in late December of 2017, nearly a decade after the uprising of 2009.

The violent protests that engulfed more than seventy Iranian cities and towns from December of 2017 through January of 2018 were fundamentally different from the Green Movement of 2009. Unlike in 2009, no one was asking "Where is my vote?" and not so much as a green handkerchief could be seen on the streets during this uprising. The slogans were not calling for democracy or demanding so-called "free elections." Instead, masses of protesters were yelling: "We are Aryans, we don't worship Arabs!" "Islam and the Quran, we sacrifice them both to Iran!" "Whether by cannons, guns, or tanks — the clergy have to go!" and "Reza Shah, may your soul rejoice!"

The last of these was probably the most popular slogan of the current uprising, and suggests that what protesters wanted in the Winter of 2017–2018 was not democracy but a transition out of the Islamic Republic under martial law. As we have seen, Reza Shah Pahlavi (d. 1944) was an authoritarian ultra-nationalist who came to power in a military coup. Slogans of "Reza Shah, may your soul rejoice!" should not be conflated with support for Crown Prince Reza Pahlavi, even if the latter's supporters inside of Iran are attempting to conflate the two. The Crown Prince has repeatedly and emphatically rejected the legacy of his father and his even more authoritarian and ultra-nationalist grandfather. He is an advocate of liberal democracy, neo-liberal economics, and a kind of "human rights" that entails federalism on an ethnic basis and the disestablishment of the Persian language (which we have not once heard come out of the mouth of his daughter and heir). In the summer of 2016 there was a revolt against him from among the ranks of the most elite proponents of a restoration of the Iranian Imperial tradition.

Those of us who signed the "Last Warning" statement of August 20, 2016 were particularly vexed by his close relationship with the Arab sheikhdoms of the Persian Gulf (which he has referred to as "the Gulf" in order to placate them). At a CFR meeting in Dallas on February 25, 2016, he went so far as to belittle the genocidal Arab invasion of Iran and mock Iranian nationalists. At the same meeting, Reza Pahlavi II relinquished a future post-Islamic Iran's right to nuclear weapons and suggested that Saudi Arabia should so deeply invest in Iran's economy and industry that war with the Wahhabi Kingdom would become inconceivable for Iranians. The Crown Prince has also gone on record saying that if the religious beliefs of Muslims are to be disrespected under a new regime, then it would be better for the Islamic Republic to remain in power.

Reza Shah adopted the Pre-Islamic identity of Iran as the backbone of Pahlavi state ideology. Protesters who chant, "We are Aryans, we don't worship Arabs!" are spearheading a renaissance of the Aryan heritage of Iran after centuries of Arab, Turkic, and Mongol colonization. Reza Shah came from the rural working class, and contrary to the peaceful nature of the 2009 upper-class protest movement, this working class uprising was a violent insurrection spread across the countryside rather than concentrated in large cities. People in the streets were not demanding a chaotic "democratic" revolution, one that would decimate the nation's industries and threaten its territorial integrity. Rather, they were inviting a military coup and removal of the Ayatollahs under martial law conditions. It is safe to say that it resembled a "color revolution" in no way whatsoever.

For some time leading up to the protests of *Dây Mâh* (December 2017 to January of 2018), a faction within the so-called "hardliners" of the Islamic Republic had been considering embracing the idea of an Iranian Renaissance in order to salvage some of the core structures of the Islamic Republic that protect Iran's banking system from globalist control and secure Iran's territorial integrity in the face of foreign-backed separatist agitators. This faction is centered around Esfandiar Rahim Mashaei, who briefly served as Mahmoud Ahmadinejad's Vice President and was unsuccessfully backed by Ahmadinejad to run against Rouhani, because the Guardian Council deemed Mashaei a "deviationist" for his nationalism. Mashaei's circle had been reading Iranian Renaissance texts such as *Aryan Imperial Political Thought* by Shahin Nezhad.

As part of the core structure of the Islamic Republic themselves, these hardliners were able to secure permits for demonstrations against worsening economic conditions and corruption. Ahmadinejad gave a speech threatening the regime's corrupt establishment shortly before the protests began, and in very short order he was arrested by the Islamic Republic for provoking unrest. The slogans of the Ahmadinejad-associated protests condemned the so-called "reformist" Rouhani administration for its broken promise that Iran's concessions in the nuclear deal would raise living standards. These legal demonstrations were organized in the city of Mashad, the hometown of Shahin Nezhad, which is also where the grand Shi'ite shrine of Imam Reza is located.

At the same time, the Iranian Renaissance planned a celebration for Ferdowsi's birthday. The event was originally scheduled for the 27th of *Âzar* (his actual birthday), but then Shahin Nezhad rescheduled it for the 2nd of *Dây* (the date that he gives for his birth, not adjusted to changes in the calendar system), or December 23, 2017. The tomb of the author of the Persian national epic, the *Shâhnâmeh*, is in Tous, just outside of Mashad. The idea was to replicate the Cyrus Day event, when hundreds of thousands gathered at the tomb of Cyrus the Great on October 29, 2016. Once busloads of ultra-nationalists arrived at the tomb, they were informed that their rally permit was revoked. These angry ultra-nationalists were diverted to Mashad where they encountered the legal hardliner demonstrations, and joined them, shifting the slogans in a nationalist direction. Then they went back home to the smaller cities and towns where the Renaissance has its largest following, rather than in more Westernized major metropolitan areas. The rest is history.

As in the case of 2009, the protests were ultimately suppressed by regime forces. Following this suppression, Esfandiyar Rahim Mashaei was arrested and, as of the time of this writing, remains in prison. Mahmoud Ahmadinejad has indignantly protested against the injustice of the regime's judiciary and intensified his accusations of systematic corruption in protest of the detention of a man that some claim is not only his friend, but his guru. Despite whatever formal charges were brought against Esfandiyar Mashaei by the regime, those in the know are aware that he is being detained for his key role in attempting a coup from within the structure of the Islamic Republic. (I have substantive information in this regard that I cannot yet publicly disclose.) Just what vision for Iran's sociopolitical future informed this aborted coup attempt remains enigmatic to the public, but one key to unlocking the esoteric project that was underway is the connection between Esfandiyar Mashaei and a theosophical group called Elmé Khoshnoom.

Elmé Khoshnoom is a Neo-Zoroastrian form of Theosophy that was formally founded by Behramshah Nowroji Shroff (1858–1927), a Parsi of Gujarat who claimed that, during a several-year-long pilgrimage to Iran in his youth, he studied with seventy-two hidden masters living inside of Damavand and other mountains in the Alborz range.[20] Shroff claimed that the occulted *sâheb delân* or "Big-Hearted Ones" had gone into hiding in their *vârs* — their secret mountain caverns — at some point during the late Sassanian period.[21] In 1910, Shroff founded the "Ilm-I Khshnoom Institute" with the stated purpose of passing on the ancient Iranian teachings of these hidden masters, which include a number of beliefs not typical to orthodox Zoroastrianism, but that we have come across repeatedly in the course of this study as part of Mithraic or Gnostic sects that competed with Zoroastrian Orthodoxy in Pre-Islamic Iran, among them: reincarnation, vegetarianism, astrology, and a cultivation of occult abilities, with an emphasis on psychic healing, telepathy, and precognition.[22] In this regard it is worth noting that *Elmé Khoshnoom*, which is supposed to translate into English as "Science of Ecstasy," sounds awfully similar to *Khorramdin*, "the Joyous Religion" that was the form Mazdakism took after the Islamic conquest of Iran.

Shroff claimed to be a John-the-Baptist-type herald figure, who was preparing the way for the coming of a Zoroastrian messianic king and spiritual leader, a *Rainidar* or "shower of the path" for the Aquarian Age, whose true name is Shah Bahram Varjavand.[23] These Neo-Zoroastrian (or Mazdakite?) theosophists now believe that he is already living among us, but has yet to reveal himself.[24] Although no one claimed that he was the expected savior, Meher Baba (1894–1969) did emerge from out of this Parsi Theosophical movement as a guru whose popularity peaked in the 1960s.[25]

Elmé Khoshnoom may actually have taken shape in British-colonized India under the influence of the school of Azar Kayvan, an Iranian Zoroastrian mystic who was influenced by the *eshrâqi* or Illuminationist theosophy of Suhrawardi and who immigrated to India in the 1570s.[26] From the time that Shroff founded the Institute, a number of nominally Zoroastrian publications in India have, over the years, successively served as journals espousing the theosophy of Elmé Khoshnoom. The first of these was *Frashogard* from 1910–1943, which was followed by *Parsi Avaz* from 1947–1974, and then *Dini Avaz* from 1976 to the present, *Mazdayasni Connection* from 1983 to the present, and *Parsi Pukar*, which was founded in 1995 and is also still in print.[27]

In 1986, a Parsi woman named Meher Master-Moos took over leadership of the Elmé Khoshnoom and, with the participation of academics from elsewhere in the Iranian world, such as Professor Rustom Fuzaylov of Khojand, she established a "Zoroastrian College" in Sanjan, Gujarat as the leading educational institution of the movement.[28] The institution describes itself, in the most New Age terms, as "A Spiritual White Light Center" and "a Universal Center for Development of Body, Mind, Aura, Halo and Soul."[29] What is fascinating is the list of prominent politicians involved with this college, including President Emamali Rahmon of Tajikistan and the Representative of Iran's Zoroastrians in the Parliament of the Islamic Republic of Iran, Kourosh Niknam.[30] On the occasion of the twenty-fifth anniversary of the college, the Embassy of Iran in India was among those to officially send their congratulations.[31] In fact, beginning in 2009, the cultural wing of the embassy of the Islamic Republic of Iran began collaborating with the college on projects that included a Persian language program under the direct supervision of the Consulate of Iran in Mumbai, who was awarded an honorary doctoral degree by the Elmé Khoshnoom.[32] This was followed, in April of 2010, by the college's president, Mehr Master-Moos, being presented with the Dara Shikoh Award by the Embassy of the Islamic Republic of Iran in New Delhi.[33]

What is most remarkable, however, is the visit of former Iranian President Mahmoud Ahmadinejad's would-be Vice President and closest advisor, Esfandiyar Rahim Mashaei. The enigmatic and mysterious Esfandiyar Mashaei, who has been rumored to be Ahmadinejad's spiritual guru and personal Rasputin, has been accused by his political opponents in the Islamic Republic of having connections with occultists who are believed to be hiding out in the Damavand mountain region to the northeast of the nation's capital.[34] The entrance to the city inside the mountain is supposed to be underneath the Iranian coastline of the Caspian Sea, which brings to mind the myths of Satana with which this book began in Chapter 1. Recall that the Sarmatian myths of Satana that became the inspiration for the Grail mysticism of Europe through the Alanic migration, legends that have survived in the Ossetian culture in the Caucasus along the Caspian Sea, depict Satana as the Lady of the Lake (after all, the Caspian so-called "Sea" really is a giant lake) training Mithraic heroes in a hidden realm underneath the waters before bestowing on them the sacred sword.

Not incidentally, it is astonishing that no one has noticed that the sacred sword, planted downwards in typical Sarmatian fashion and awaiting the Once and Future King to unearth it, is at the center of the Coat of Arms of the Islamic Republic of Iran. The red tulip is, after all, a symbol of martyred chivalric knights in Persian epic poetry. In light of the claims of Elmé Khoshnoom's founder, Nowroji Shroff, regarding the hidden masters dwelling in the same mountain range since the late Sassanid period, the allegations of Mashaei and his circle being in touch with a subterranean or submarine community in the Caspian-Alborz region is very curious indeed—especially considering the fact that Mashaei and Ahmadinejad have both come under severe scrutiny for repeatedly claiming that the coming of the Hidden Imam is imminent, which is the same thing that these Zoroastrian Theosophists say about their expected Shah Bahram Varjavand.

As we have seen throughout this study, the Caspian-Alborz region of Iran has been known since ancient times as Hyrcania (*Varkâna*) or "realm of wolves." Its oldest name, *Mâzandarân*—a corruption of *Mazâré Indra-yân* or "the place of Indra's people," referencing the ancient Aryan King of the Gods who wields the thunderbolt scepter, suggests that it may even be the cradle of the Aryan community. In the *Shâhnâmeh*, one of the knightly ordeals of Rostam, the Mithraic Scythian hero, is to rid the region of *Divs* or, as the Hindus still call their gods, the *Daevâs*. Mithra is, of course, an Ashura or titan. In Achaemenid times, the realm was already called Hyrcania, and it probably gained that name during the period when, as we saw in Chapter 2, the Median Kingdom extended to the eastern coast of the Caspian Sea, bordering on the Scythian realm. The Scythian invasion of the Median Kingdom likely led to the settlement of this region by Scythians whose totem was the wolf. The Hyrcanian Forest is home to some wolves, but Hyrcania was probably named after the dreaded wolf's head of the Scythian war banners.

The wolf's head has a fascinating history as a political symbol. As explained in Chapter 1, the Scythians are the ethnic basis of the Saxons of Germany whose name *Saka-son* means "Sons of the Saka (i.e. Scythians)." This explains the introduction of the *wulfsheud* or "wolf's head" into Anglo-Saxon political symbolism. Meanwhile, we have the Italian myth of Romulus and Remus, the founders of the city of Rome, being suckled by a she-wolf. It is not unreasonable to wonder whether this she-wolf, the mother of the fathers of Rome, is a veiled reference to Sarmatian warrior women. The Sarmatians, close cousins of the Scythians, are depicted in the *Shâhnâmeh* of Ferdowsi as the descendants of Salm or *Sarm* and as the founders of *Roum*, the Persian designation for a geographical expanse that stretches all the way from Kurdistan to Rome proper. Recall also the Mithraic tricolor of Italy, which the Romans share in common with other Iranian communities such as the Bulgarians, Kurds, Tajiks, and the Hungarians, who before the arrival of the Huns, were a nation constituted mostly by ethnic Sarmatians. The Transylvania Saxons of Hungary, bordering on Romania in the Carpathian mountains, are still ethnically Iranian. At any rate, just as in the case of the Sarmatian dragon — the one used both by King Arthur and the *Draculae* Kings of the Transylvanian Order of the Dragon, such as Vlad the Impaler (*Welâdé Zolaktav*), an Iranian legacy lies behind the wolf as a totemic theologico-political symbol in Europe.

As we saw in Chapter 10, in his *Leviathan* Thomas Hobbes argues that the sovereign power is justified because strong men in the state of nature are akin to wolves — *Homo hominis lupus* — who will tear everyone apart and turn on each other if they are not domesticated by the authority of the state.[35] Paradoxically, this also means that, in any lawful socio-political order, the state of nature survives in at least one person: the sovereign himself.[36] The force of his decisive action straddles the dichotomies between nature and culture, violence and law.[37] The Germanic peoples, including Scandinavians, represented the sacred sovereign as a wolf-man, a werewolf.[38] This sacredness of the wolf or *wargus/vargr* reaches back to the oldest strata of Indo-European society.[39] The *wargus* or werewolf, symbolized by a wolf's head or *wulfesheud*, is also a specter in as much as Germanic and Anglo-Saxon law considered such a person to be, not just banned from the city, but already dead.[40]

Presumed dead — like the Führer of the Third Reich — the spectral sovereign endures, outside the limits of the law, as a haunting figure. Edward the Confessor (1030–1035) writes of the arch bandit that "He bears a wolf's head [*wulfesheud*] from the day of his expulsion."[41] Latin authors called this *caput lupinem*.[42] This insignia signifies both sovereignty "and expulsion from the community."[43] Such symbolism is alive even today, as is not lost on any initiate who is capable of decoding the esoteric ending to the series *Game of Thrones*. The would-be bastard, John Snow, whose Dragon blood has been hidden from him, is exiled and condemned as only befits the true and sacred king whose castle is in the forest — in the True North — in Hyrcania by so many other names.

The Germanic term *ban* designates both an ostracism, namely an exclusion from the community, and also the insignia of the sovereign.[44] The one who is banned is not only cast outside of the law-governed realm, but is also a*ban*doned by the protective power of the law.[45] Exile has a duality similar to that of the sacred; some see it as a punishment, while others have understood it to be a right of taking refuge (rather than being killed).[46] For example, the classical Roman statesman and philosopher Cicero wrote: "Exile is not a penalty, but a haven and a refuge from penalty."[47] That sacred man or *homo sacer* who "is outside the hearth, the sacrament, and the law" is the ultimate form of the exiled individual.[48] In his treatise *On the Significance of Words*, Pompeis Festus discusses the figure of the *homo sacer* in archaic Roman law.[49] Festus writes:

> The sacred man is the one whom the people have judged on account of a crime. It is not permitted to sacrifice this man, yet he who kills him will not be condemned for homicide; in the first tribunitian law, in fact, it is noted that 'if someone kills the one who is sacred according to the plebiscite, it will not be considered homicide.' This is why it is customary for a bad or impure man to be called sacred.[50]

Although the "sacred man" could be killed by anyone with impunity, it was forbidden for him to be subjected to the ritual death entailed in becoming a sacrificial victim.[51] As Agamben puts it, "*Homo sacer* is unsacrificeable, yet he may nevertheless be killed by anyone."[52] In his *Saturnalia*, Ambrosius Theodosius Macrobius remarks on how peculiar it is that, whereas people are normally prohibited from violating the sanctity of anything that is deemed holy, it is permissible for anyone to kill the sacred man without being punished.[53]

The sacred man, like anything that is taboo, is both something—or rather, some*one*—who at the same time provokes terror and is worthy of veneration.[54] What this figure points us back towards is a twilight zone of awful power that precedes both the dichotomy of sacred and profane as well as that of the religious and the political.[55] This is a matter of what scholars of religion call "the ambivalence of the sacred," the idea that *the holy is not "good."* The holy, or what is truly sacred, always involves a mixture of veneration and horror.[56] Nothing good is sacred, and prophets or holy kings are never good men.

There are an abundance of examples of what is considered taboo but not holy, such as, in Semitic law, women after childbirth or men who have touched a dead body.[57] Moreover, contact with what is considered *herem* in Hebrew, or *harâm* in Arabic, is often considered contagious.[58] This is especially the case with things that are supposed to be destroyed as part of the holocaust of cities, when the latter is commanded by the Lord, as in the book of Joshua where Yahweh demands the total annihilation of everything and everyone in Jericho.[59] To seize what was supposed to be destroyed as booty is taboo, and bringing such items (or persons or animals) into one's home can render one contaminated by their impurity.[60]

In such holocausts, only metals could be salvaged *but only by passing them through fire.*[61]

The ambiguity of the sacred is also the propensity for what is impure, for a thing *or a person* who is banned as the most contaminated and contaminating creature, to be transmuted into the most holy person in this world—sacred insofar as he is a conduit for a power that seems otherworldly as it breaks through the crust of the mundane.[62] This capacity of the transmutation of the *harâm* into what is most sacred has its primordial basis in the subconscious dreamscape that lies deeper than the principle of contradiction at work in conscious cognition.[63] In profoundly meaningful dreams, the totemic and the taboo are often indistinguishable.[64] In archaic Roman times, *sacer esto*—"may it be sacred"—was considered a curse.[65] What was sacred was removed from the sphere of the profane and made to be taboo. The sacred was the accursedly untouchable.[66] As what is most dirty, filthy actually, it is liable to so badly contaminate a person who comes into contact with it that everything and everyone that he touches thereafter is likewise tainted. Among politicians of our nihilistic age, *so far* only Adolf Hitler has succeeded in becoming sacred. But someone else is coming. Ahmadinejad and Mashaei know this.

Perhaps it is by design that sufficient attention has not been paid to the concept of occultation in Iranian political thought. By being absent, or going missing, the true king is more powerfully present than any ordinary potentate. In *Game of Thrones*, we see the Once and Future King enter occultation or *gheybat* as Iranian Gnostics call it, over repeated images of the wolf's head—the Stark House standard, on the prow of Arya Stark's ship and banners of the Winterfell fortress ruled by her sister.

It is key that this figure is not simply a wolf, but a wolf-headed man or werewolf, in other words, someone who, as a man, is still related to civilization in a way that no wild animal can be, but at the same time, the *homo sacer* stands above or beyond or beneath the law—beneath in the sense of being deeper than it, and thus never under its authority.[67] He is a dweller on the threshold between the city and the wilderness. His castle is in the forest. The sovereign is "a survival of the state of nature at the very heart of the state..."[68] He is "the werewolf, the wolf-man of man, [who] dwells permanently in the city."[69] Sovereign power is a dance between beast and man, nature and culture.[70] That is one reason why this book was, deep in the process of writing, renamed *Iranian Leviathan* rather than *Iranian Civilization*. The savagery and wilderness of the Iranian soul is as important to the history of Iran as the crust of civilization that this volcanic barbarism has repeatedly broken through, and in whose lava the great works of Iranian genius have been formed and forged.

The classical Greek concepts of *Bia* and *Dike* are supposed to be opposites, since the latter, namely Justice, ought to be an impartial balance and proportionality that reins in the former, namely violence.[71] However, *Nomos* or the law of the state as incarnated by the decisive power of the sovereign, preserves the *Bia* that is characteristic of *Physis* or Nature in the violence of the ruler as he executes the law or governs effectively despite his having suspended it.[72] The Hobbesian state of nature is not an epoch *prior to* the foundation of the state, rather, it is the abyssal chaos that always underlies the state's seeming order and stability.[73] It is not temporally foundational; it is the perpetually *underground*. The state of nature is revealed whenever there is a state of exception, a state wherein, according to Hobbes, "man is a wolf to men."[74] The founding of the state is never something achieved once and for all, something secured through a legal constitution.[75] The sovereign decision is continually required to ensure that the state is not just an apparent order that appears for an instant from out of this chaos before dissolving back into it through civil war—the kind of civil war that was the context for Hobbes having written *Leviathan*, the prospect of civil war that faces Iran today.[76]

That any legal order emerges from out of chaos and can dissolve back into it, when taken together with the power of the sovereign to determine or dissolve a juridical order as the one who stands both inside and outside of the law, reveals that there is a "zone of indistinction" between the normal situation—i.e. a situation based on norms—and the state of exception wherein chaos reemerges.[77] Chaos (*Âz*) cannot be definitively excluded from any juridical order, but haunts it in the manner of both a specter and a primordial abyss seducing every state to destroy itself by returning to its womb. This zone of indistinction is also one that defies the difference between human and animal.[78] The fact that the sovereign decides what constitutes a state of exception, wherein he may suspend the entire constitution, means that he is both inside and outside the juridical order at the same time, and by extension it also means that there is a sense in which the law is ecstatically outside of itself.[79] No law or rules of any kind are applicable to a condition of chaos; insofar as the sovereign is the one who decides whether a sufficient order has been made out of this chaos so that a situation allows for the proper functioning of a legal system, all law is ultimately or fundamentally *situational* in nature.[80]

This also means that, despite itself, the juridical order refers back to the dynamic force of bare life.[81] The *nomos* or force of law is inextricable from the life force. This is a relation of the law to the non-relational.[82] In that the ban reaches most deeply into bare life, it is the most foundational political structure.[83] This relation "has constituted the essential structure of sovereign power from the beginning."[84] This is ecstatic and excessive in the same way as eroticism pushed to an extreme that seeks the sacred in the face of death.[85] Bataille, who sought this in the "pure and filth, repugnant and fascinating—and in the interiority of the subject, to which the experience of this life is always given in privileged or miraculous moments" was met with the accusation: "You are working for Fascism."[86]

In the situation of failing or failed states subject to disintegration, what is supposed to be a state of exception starts to become the rule.[87] The violent chaos of the state of nature reemerging through the disintegration of Yugoslavia, a phenomenon that was such an epitome that it yielded the word "balkanization," is also the herald of "the new *nomos* of the earth"—a post-national sphere of sovereign decision that could "soon extend itself over the entire planet."[88] It is certainly in danger of extending itself over a balkanized Iran if the Islamic Republic should become a failed state. Anyone familiar with the history of Hyrcania, with how it was the cradle of the resurgence of Iran during the Parthian period, and how it maintained its independence from the Caliphate after the fall of Sassanids and became the fountainhead of the Iranian Renaissance of the Buyid era, would wonder about what could yet come out of this region under the aegis of the wolf's head, if Iran were to be occupied or its central government were to collapse. Hyrcanian partisan warfare, always rooted in the Occult, reaches back to the Parthians.

Sacred monarchy will be restored in Iran when Neo-Zoroastrians and Shi'ites are ready to see Shah Bahram Varjavand and the Occulted Imam of Time in one and the same monarch, a man — or wolf-man — who will lead what is left of humanity into a new celestial reality beyond the end of this earthly life. Lord knows that no country has contributed more than Iran to the creation of culture and the cultivation of civilization on this Earth. Trust me, the Devil knows that too. The whole of Iranian history to date has merely been an overture or a preface, albeit a monumental preface. So far from being finished, the imperial idea of Iran still has the cosmos to conquer. Hail victory! May the Unconquerable Sun be the crown jewel of new constellations overlooking a new Earth.

NOTES

INTRODUCTION

1 Thomas Hobbes, *Leviathan* (New York: Penguin Classics, 2017), x.
2 Hobbes, xii.
3 Hobbes, xiv.
4 Hobbes, 315.
5 Hobbes, 315.
6 Hobbes, 315.
7 Hobbes, 373.
8 Hobbes, 376.
9 Hobbes, 376.
10 Hobbes, 376.
11 Hobbes, ix.
12 Hobbes, ix.
13 Hobbes, x.
14 Hobbes, ix.1

CHAPTER 1. THE MOTHER OF IRAN

1 Reza Zarghamee, *Discovering Cyrus: The Persian Conqueror Astride the Ancient World* (Washington DC: Mage Publishers, 2013), 527.
2 Ibid.
3 Ibid.
4 Ibid., 530.
5 Ibid., 388.
6 Ibid., 389, 526.
7 Ibid., 389.
8 Ibid., 525.
9 Ibid., 386.
10 Ibid.
11 Ibid.
12 Richard Foltz, *Religions of Iran: From Prehistory to the Present* (London: Oneworld Publications, 2013), 23.
13 Ibid., 20.
14 Ibid., 21.
15 Ibid.
16 Ibid., 27.
17 Ibid.
18 Ibid.
19 Reza Zarghamee, *Discovering Cyrus*, 468.
20 Foltz, *Religions of Iran*, 28.
21 Ibid., 26–27.
22 Ibid., 25.
23 Ibid., 28.
24 Ibid.
25 Ibid.
26 Ibid.
27 Ibid., 29.
28 Ibid., 28.
29 Ibid., 29.
30 Ibid.
31 Ibid.
32 Reza Zarghamee, *Discovering Cyrus*, 454.
33 Ibid.
34 Ibid., 159.
35 Ibid.
36 Ibid.
37 Ibid.
38 Ibid., 160.
39 Ibid., 146.
40 Ibid., 264.
41 Ibid., 452.
42 Ibid., 456.
43 Ibid.
44 Ibid., 458.
45 Ibid., 8.
46 Ibid., 263.
47 Ibid.
48 Ibid.
49 Ibid., 453.
50 Ibid.
51 Ibid.
52 Ibid.

53 Ibid., 454.
54 Kaveh Farrokh, "Exploring the Possibility of Relationships Between the Iranian Goddess Anahita and the Dame du Lac of the Arthurian Legends" in *Anahita: Ancient Persian Goddess & Zoroastrian Yazata* (London: Avalonia, 2012) 49.
55 Ibid., 49.
56 D.M. Murdock, "Was the Persian Goddess Anahita the Pre-Christian Virgin Mother of Mithra?" in *Anahita: Ancient Persian Goddess & Zoroastrian Yazata* (London: Avalonia, 2012), 97.
57 Reza Zarghamee, *Discovering Cyrus*, 473.
58 D.M. Murdock, "Was the Persian Goddess Anahita the Pre-Christian Virgin Mother of Mithra?," 98.
59 Ibid.
60 Ibid., 105.
61 Ibid., 94.
62 Ibid.
63 Ibid., 104.
64 Ibid., 100.
65 Ibid., 101.
66 Ibid., 102.
67 Ibid., 106.
68 Ibid.
69 Ibid., 114.
70 Ibid., 107.
71 Ibid.
72 Ibid., 108.
73 Ibid., 109.
74 Ibid., 105.
75 Ibid., 111.
76 Ibid., 109.
77 Ibid., 110.
78 Ibid.
79 Ibid., 109–110.
80 Ibid., 111.
81 Zarghamee, *Discovering Cyrus*, 468.
82 Ibid., 468.
83 Ibid., 471.
84 Ibid., 472.
85 Ibid.
86 Ibid.
87 Ibid., 468.
88 Ibid., 469.
89 Richard Stoneman, *Xerxes: A Persian Life* (New Haven: Yale University Press, 2015), 186.
90 Ibid.
91 Ibid.
92 Stoneman, *Xerxes*, 185.
93 Ibid.
94 Amélie Kuhrt et al., *The Persian Empire: A Corpus of Sources from the Achaemenid Period* (New York: Routledge, 2007), 132.
95 Ibid.
96 Murdock, "Was the Persian Goddess Anahita the Pre-Christian Virgin Mother of Mithra?," 96.
97 Zarghamee, *Discovering Cyrus*, 474.
98 Farrokh, "Exploring the Possibility of Relationships Between the Iranian Goddess Anahita and the Dame du Lac of the Arthurian Legends," 52.
99 Zarghamee, *Discovering Cyrus*, 503.
100 Ibid., 531.
101 C. Scott Littleton and Linda A. Malcor, *From Scythia to Camelot* (New York: Routledge, 2000), 27.
102 Zarghamee, *Discovering Cyrus*, 531.
103 E.V. Cernenko, *The Scythians: 700–300 BC* (Oxford: Osprey Publishing, 1983), 14–14.
104 Farrokh, "Exploring the Possibility of Relationships Between the Iranian Goddess Anahita and the Dame du Lac of the Arthurian Legends," 57.
105 Roman Ghirshman, *Persian Art 249 BC–AD 651: The Parthian and Sassanian Dynasties* (New York: Golden Press, 1962), 283–315.
106 Farrokh, "Exploring the Possibility of Relationships Between the Iranian Goddess Anahita and the Dame du Lac of the Arthurian Legends," 57–58.

107 Ibid., 58.
108 Ibid.
109 Ibid., 67.
110 Ibid.
111 Ibid., 59.
112 Ibid., 60.
113 Ibid., 61.
114 Ibid., 62.
115 Ibid., 65.
116 Ibid., 62.
117 R. Brzezinski and M. Mielczarek, *The Sarmatians: 600 BC–AD 450* (Oxord: Osprey Publishing, 2002), 38–39.
118 Littleton and Malcor, *From Scythia to Camelot*, 244.
119 Ibid., 248–249.
120 Ibid., 63.
121 Ibid., 244.
122 Ibid., 16.
123 Lyn Webster Wilde, *On the Trail of the Warrior Women: The Amazons in Myth and History* (New York: St. Martin's Press, 2000).
124 Murdock, "Was the Persian Goddess Anahita the Pre-Christian Virgin Mother of Mithra?," 98.
125 Zarghamee, *Discovering Cyrus*, 471.
126 Ibid.
127 Wilde, *On the Trail of the Women Warriors*, 86.
128 Ibid., 97–98.
129 Sorita D'Este, *Artemis: Virgin Goddess of the Sun & Moon – A Comprehensive Guide to the Greek Goddess of the Hunt* (London: Avalonia Press, 2005), 66. D'Este, *Hekate: Liminal Rites – A Study of the rituals, magic and symbols of the torch-bearing Triple Goddess of the Crossroads* (London: Avalonia Press, 2009), 169.
130 D'Este, *Artemis*, 48, 63, 103.
131 Ibid., 63–64.
132 Wilde, *On the Trail of the Women Warriors*, 72.
133 Herodotus, *The Histories* (New York: Barnes and Noble, 2004), IV, 104.
134 Zarghamee, *Discovering Cyrus*, 527.
135 Patricia Crone, *The Nativist Prophets of Early Islamic Iran: Rural Revolt and Local Zoroastrianism* (New York: Cambridge University Press, 2013), 401.
136 Zarghamee, *Discovering Cyrus*, 529.
137 Wilde, *The Amazons in Myth and History*, 92.
138 D'Este, *Artemis*, 56.
139 Ibid., 125.
140 Ibid., 105.
141 Ibid., 109. D'Este, *Hekate*, 56.
142 D'Este, *Artemis*, 97.
143 Ibid., 91–96.
144 D'Este, *Hekate*, 52.
145 D'Este, *Artemis*, 88, 115.
146 Farrokh, "Exploring the Possibility of Relationships Between the Iranian Goddess Anahita and the Dame du Lac of the Arthurian Legends," 67.
147 Ibid., 66.
148 Ibid., 52.
149 Ibid., 49.
150 Ibid., 50, 67.
151 Ibid., 48, 50.
152 Ibid., 67.
153 Ibid., 68.
154 Ibid., 49.
155 Ibid., 66.
156 Littleton and Malcor, *From Scythia To Camelot*, 79–124.
157 Ibid., 153–179.
158 Ibid., 181–194.
159 Ibid., 195–208.
160 Ibid., 216, 237–240.
161 Ibid., 70.
162 Farrokh, "Exploring the Possibility of Relationships Between the Iranian Goddess Anahita and the Dame du Lac of the Arthurian Legends," 54.
163 Ibid., 55.
164 Ibid.
165 Ibid.

166 Ibid.
167 Ibid.
168 Ibid., 60.
169 Ibid., 61–62.
170 Ibid., 61.
171 Ibid.
172 Ibid., 60.
173 Ibid., 61.
174 Ibid., 60.
175 Ibid.
176 Ibid., 58–59.
177 Zarghamee, *Discovering Cyrus*, 163.
178 Ibid., 165.
179 Ibid., 529.
180 Ibid., 148.
181 Ibid., 149.
182 Ibid.
183 Ibid.
184 Ibid., 460.
185 Ibid., 143.
186 Herodotus, *The Histories*, III, 34–35.
187 Kuhrt, *The Persian Empire*, 118.
188 Ibid., 127.
189 Ibid., 131.
190 Ibid.
191 Ibid, 141.
192 Ibid., 143.
193 Ibid.
194 Ibid., 142.
195 Ibid., 143.
196 Ibid., 142.
197 Ibid., 200.
198 Ibid., 8.
199 Ibid., 263.
200 Ibid., 472.
201 Ibid., 471.
202 Ibid., 473.
203 Ibid., 471.
204 Farrokh, "Exploring the Possibility of Relationships Between the Iranian Goddess Anahita and the Dame du Lac of the Arthurian Legends," 49.
205 Ibid., 50, 67.
206 Zarghamee, *Discovering Cyrus*, 471.
207 Ibid.
208 Ibid., 68.
209 Ibid., 145.
210 Ibid., 474.
211 Ibid.
212 Ibid., 41.
213 Ibid., 85.
214 Ibid., 72.
215 Ibid., 42.
216 Ibid., 64.
217 Ibid., 389.
218 Ibid., 387.
219 Ibid.
220 Ibid.
221 Ibid.
222 Ibid., 145.
223 Ibid.
224 Ibid., 529.
225 Ibid.
226 Ibid., 388.
227 Ibid., 388.
228 Ibid., 525.
229 Ibid., 530.
230 Ibid., 525–526.
231 Ibid., 526.
232 Ibid., 393.
233 Ibid.
234 Ibid., 393–394.
235 Ibid., 394.
236 Ibid.
237 Ibid., 392.
238 Ibid.
239 Ibid.
240 Ibid., 393.
241 Ibid.
242 Ibid.
243 Ibid., 393–394.
244 Ibid., 394.
245 Ibid.
246 Ibid.
247 Ibid.
248 Ibid.
249 Ibid., 398.
250 Ibid., 395.
251 Ibid., 395, 399–400.
252 Ibid., 400.
253 Ibid., 400–401.
254 Ibid., 400.
255 Ibid., 529.

CHAPTER 2. THE IRANIAN ORIGINS OF PHILOSOPHY

1 Muhammad A. Dandamayev, "Magi" in *Encyclopaedia Iranica.*

2 Abolqasem Ferdowsi, *Shahnameh: The Persian Book of Kings* (New York: Penguin Books, 2007), 397–398.

3 Reza Zarghamee, *Discovering Cyrus: The Persian Conqueror Astride the Ancient World* (Mage Publishers, 2013), 165.

4 Ibid., 529.

5 Ibid., 163.

6 Ibid., 526–527.

7 Ibid., 527.

8 Ibid., 526–527.

9 Ibid., 527.

1 Ibid., 527.

11 Christopher Beckwith, *Greek Buddha: Pyrrho's Encounter With Early Buddhism in Central Asia* (Princeton: Princeton University Press, 2015), 1.

12 Ibid.

13 Ibid.

14 Zarghamee, *Discovering Cyrus*, 533.

15 Ibid.

16 Ibid.

17 Ibid., 534.

18 Ibid., 166.

19 Ibid.

20 Ibid., 145.

21 Ibid., 533.

22 Ibid.

23 Ibid., 272.

24 Gustav Neckel, *Germanen und Kelten: historisch-linguistisch-rassenkundliche Forschungen und Gedanken zur geisteskrisis* (Heidelberg, 1929), 30–32; E. Herzfeld, *The Persian Empire: Studies in the Geography and Ethnography of the Ancient Near East* (Wiesbaden, 1968), 298.

25 C. Scott Littleton and Linda A. Malcor, *From Scythia to Camelot* (New York: Routledge, 2000), 17.

26 Sharon Turner, "Persian Origins of Anglo-Saxon Words," reproduced by *The Circle of Ancient Iranian Studies* (1827).

27 Richard N. Frye, *The Heritage of Persia* (Costa Mesa: Mazda Publishers, 1993), 30.

28 Ibid., 31.

29 M.L. West, *The Hymns of Zoroaster: A New Translation of the Most Ancient Sacred Texts of Iran* (New York: I.B. Tauris, 2015), 4–5.

30 Zarghamee, *Discovering Cyrus*, 385.

31 Ibid., 385–386.

32 Ibid., 386.

33 Ibid.

34 Ibid.

35 Ibid., 140.

36 Ibid.

37 Ibid.

38 Ibid.

39 Zarghamee, 141.

40 Ibid.

41 Ibid.

42 Ibid., 21.

43 Mary Settegast, *Plato Prehistorian: 10,000 To 5,000 B.C. Myth, Religion, Archeology* (New York: Lindisfarne Press, 1990), 211–235, 265–274.

44 Mary Settegast, *When Zarathustra Spoke: The Reformation of Neolithic Culture and Religion* (Costa Mesa: Mazda Publishers, 2005).

45 Ibid., 54.

46 Ibid.

47 Ibid.

48 Ibid., 8–9.

49 Ibid., 7.

50 Ibid., 64–65.

51 Ibid., 57.

52 Parvaneh Pourshariati, *Decline and Fall of the Sasanian Empire: The Sasanian-Parthian Confederacy and the Arab Conquest of Iran* (I.B. Tauris, 2008), 360.

53 P.O. Skjaervø, "Asha" in *Encyclopaedia Iranica* Vol. II, Fasc. 7, 694–696.
54 Mary Boyce, *Textual Sources for the Study of Zoroastrianism* (Chicago: University of Chicago Press, 1990), 9.
55 Skjaervø, "Asha," 694–696.
56 Ali Akbar Jafarey, *The Gathas, Our Guide: The Thought-Provoking Divine Songs of Zarathustra* (Cypress, CA: Ushta Publications, 1989), 46.
57 Piloo Nanavutty, *The Gathas of Zarathustra: Hymns in Praise of Wisdom* (Ahmedabad: Mapin Publishing, 1999), 83.
58 Jafary, *The Gathas, Our Guide*, 89.
59 Jaideva Singh, *Spanda-Karikas: The Divine Creative Pulsation* (Bombay: Motilal Banarsidass, 2012).
60 Nanavutty, *The Gathas of Zarathustra: Hymns in Praise of Wisdom*, 84.
61 Ibid., 109.
62 Jafarey, *The Gathas, Our Guide*, 44–45; Nanavutty, *The Gathas of Zarathustra: Hymns in Praise of Wisdom*, 109–112.
63 Henry Corbin, *Spiritual Body and Celestial Earth: From Mazdean Iran to Shi'ite Iran* (Princeton: Princeton University Press, 1989), 7–8.
64 Nanavutty, *The Gathas of Zarathustra: Hymns in Praise of Wisdom*, 98–99.
65 Boyce, *Textual Sources for the Study of Zoroastrianism*, 13.
66 Ibid.
67 Richard Foltz, *Religions of Iran: From Prehistory to the Present* (London: Oneworld Publications, 2013), 63–64.
68 Payam Nabarz [Editor], *Anahita: Ancient Persian Goddess & Zoroastrian Yazata* (London: Avalonia, 2013).
69 Jafarey, *The Gathas, Our Guide*, 83.
70 Boyce, *Textual Sources for the Study of Zoroastrianism*, 90; Jafarey, *The Gathas, Our Guide*, 33.
71 Ibid., 64–65; Michael Axworthy, *A History of Iran: Empire of the Mind* (New York: Perseus Books Group, 2010), 8–9.
72 Foltz, *Religions of Iran*, 67.
73 J. Duchesne-Guillemin, "Angra Mainyu" in *Encyclopaedia Iranica* Vol. II, Fasc. 1, 70.
74 Boyce, *Textual Sources for the Study of Zoroastrianism*, 35.
75 Aminrazavi, "Bundahishn" and "Greater Bundahishn" in *An Anthology of Philosophy in Persia* (New York: Oxford University Press, 1999).
76 Jonathan Barnes, *Early Greek Philosophy* (New York: Penguin Books, 1987), 55–56
77 M.L. Mills, *Early Greek Philosophy and the Orient* (Oxford: Clarendon Press, 1971), 203-204.
78 Ibid., 204–205.
79 Herodotus, *The Histories* (New York: Barnes and Noble, 2004), 1.131.
80 Ibid., 1.138.
81 Ibid., 1.136.
82 Ibid., 1.133.
83 Stanley Insler, *The Gâthâs of Zarathustra* (Tehéran-Liège: Bibliothèque Pahlavi; Leiden: diffusion E.J. Brill, 1975).
84 Ruhi Afnan, *Zoroaster's Influence on Anaxagoras, the Greek Tragedians, and Socrates* (New York: Philosophical Library, 1969), 71–71.
85 Ibid.
86 Ibid., 30.
87 Ibid., 31.
88 Iamblichus, "The Life of Pythagoras" in Guthrie, *The Pythagorean Sourcebook and Library*, 61.
89 Ibid.
90 Ibid.
91 Guthrie, *The Pythagorean Sourcebook and Library*, 37.

92 Iamblichus, "The Life of Pythagoras" in Guthrie, *The Pythagorean Sourcebook and Library*, 70.
93 Aminrazavi, "Bundahishn" and "Greater Bundahishn" in *An Anthology of Philosophy in Persia* (New York: Oxford University Press, 1999), 7–8, 12, 17, 20.
94 Ibid., 7.
95 Ibid., 6–7, 16.
96 Ibid., 8, 17.
97 Ibid., 11.
98 Ibid., 15, 21.
99 Ibid., 13–15.
100 Ibid., 14.
101 Ibid., 13.
102 Ibid.
103 Kenneth Sylvan Guthrie, *The Pythagorean Sourcebook and Library* (Grand Rapids: Phanes Press, 1988), 37–38.
104 Charles H. Kahn, *Pythagoras and the Pythagoreans: A Brief History* (Indianapolis: Hackett Publishing Company, 2001), 19.
105 Patricia Crone, *The Nativist Prophets of Early Islamic Iran: Rural Revolt and Local Zoroastrianism*, 233–252.
106 Heraclitus, *Fragments*, Diels 129, 81, Kahn XXV–XXVI.
107 Ibid., Diels 47, Kahn XI; Diels A23, Kahn XII; Diels 55, Kahn XIV; Diels 101a; Kahn XV.
108 Heraclitus, *Fragments*, Diels 5, Kahn CXVII.
109 Ibid., Diels 30, Kahn XXXVII.
110 Ibid., Diels 41; Kahn LIV.
111 Ibid., Diels 32, Kahn CXVIII.
112 Ibid., Diels 114; Kahn XXX; Diels 45, Kahn XXXV; Diels 2, Kahn III.
113 Ibid., Diels 28B, Kahn LXXXVII.
114 Ibid., Diels 16, CXXII.
115 Ibid., Diels 1, 34, 2, 17, 71–73, 89; Kahn I–VI.
116 Ibid., Diels 114; Kahn XXX.
117 Ibid., Diels, 40, 105, 38, 129, 81; Kahn XVIII, XXIII–XXVI.
118 Ibid., Diels 115, Kahn CI.
119 Ibid., Diels 116, 112, Kahn XXIX, XXXII.
120 Ibid., Diels 66, Kahn CXXI; Diels 28B, Kahn LXXXVII.
121 Ibid., Diels 100, Kahn XLIIIA.
122 Ibid., Diels 27; Kahn LXXXIV.
123 Ibid., Diels 96; Kahn LXXXVIII.
124 Boyce, *Textual Sources for the Study of Zoroastrianism*, 65.
125 Beckwith, *Greek Buddha*, 124.
126 Ibid., 15.
127 Ibid., 16.
128 Ibid., 13.
129 Ibid., 19.
130 Ibid., 168.
131 Ibid., 13.
132 Ibid., 10.
133 Ibid., 16.
134 Ibid., 16.
135 Ibid., 16, 20.
136 Ibid., 20.
137 Ibid., 24.
138 Ibid.
139 Ibid., 26.
140 Ibid., 139.
141 Ibid., 146.
142 Ibid., 158.
143 Ibid., 159.
144 Ibid., 27.
145 Ibid.
146 Ibid., 28.
147 Ibid.
148 Ibid., 36.
149 Ibid., 39.
150 Ibid., 2.
151 Ibid., 3.
152 Ibid.
153 Ibid.
154 Ibid., 2.
155 Ibid., 5.
156 Harvey Kraft, *The Buddha from Babylon: The Lost History and Cosmic Vision of Siddhartha Gautama* (New York: Select Books, 2014), xxix.
157 Ibid., xxix.

158 Beckwith, *Greek Buddha*, 6.
159 Kraft, *The Buddha From Babylon*, xv.
160 Ibid., xxviii.
161 Beckwith, *Greek Buddha*, 12.
162 Ibid.
163 Kraft, *The Buddha From Babylon*, xxx.
164 Ibid.
165 Beckwith, *Greek Buddha*, 165.
166 Ibid., 108.
167 Ibid., 169.
168 Ibid., 6.
169 Ibid., 169.
170 Ibid., 10.
171 Ibid., 177.
172 Ibid., 178.
173 Ibid., 8.
174 Ibid., 115.
175 Ibid., 70.
176 Ibid., 160.
177 Ibid.
178 Kraft, *The Buddha From Babylon*, xxix.
179 Ibid., xxix, xxx.
180 Ibid., xv.
181 Beckwith, *Greek Buddha*, 100.
182 Ibid., 95.
183 Ibid., 102.
184 Ibid., 103.
185 Ibid., 6.
186 Ibid.
187 Ibid., 117.
188 Ibid., 118.
189 Ibid.
190 Ibid., 121.
191 Ibid., 119.
192 Ibid.
193 Ibid., 120.
194 Ibid., 122.
195 Ibid., 123.
196 Ibid., 111.
197 Ibid., 121.
198 Ibid., 112.
199 Ibid., 124.
200 Ibid., 121.

CHAPTER 3. EMPEROR OF NOBLE LIES

1 Christopher Beckwith, *Greek Buddha: Pyrrho's Encounter With Early Buddhism in Central Asia* (Princeton: Princeton University Press, 2015), 9.
2 Richard C. Foltz, *Iran in World History* (New York: Oxford University Press, 2016), 1; Roman Ghirshman, *Persia the Immortal Kingdom* (New York Graphic Society, 1971), 41; Amélie Kuhrt et al., *The Persian Empire: A Corpus of Sources from the Achaemenid Period* (New York: Routledge, 2007), 149, 157.
3 Roland G. Kent, *Old Persian: Grammar, Texts, Lexicon* (American Oriental Society, 1953), 7, 8, 63.
4 Amélie Kuhrt et al., *The Persian Empire: A Corpus of Sources from the Achaemenid Period* (New York: Routledge, 2007), 149.
5 Foltz, *Iran in World History*, 19.
6 Ibid.
7 Ibid.
8 Ibid., 18.
9 Ibid., 19.
10 Ghirshman, *Persia the Immortal Kingdom*, 60.
11 Ibid.
12 Ibid., 60.
13 Ibid., 76.
14 Ibid., 60.
15 Ibid.
16 Foltz, *Iran in World History*, 23.
17 Homa Katouzian, *The Persians: Ancient, Mediaeval and Modern Iran* (New Haven: Yale University Press, 2010), 33.
18 Ibid., 34.
19 Foltz, *Iran in World History*, 19.
20 J.A. de Gobineau, *The World of the Persians*, 76.
21 Homa Katouzian, *The Persians*, 32.
22 Foltz, *Iran in World History*, 19.

23 Ibid., 26.
24 Reza Zarghamee, *Discovering Cyrus: The Persian Conqueror Astride the Ancient World* (Washington DC: Mage Publishers, 2013), 518.
25 Ibid., 517.
26 Ibid.
27 Ibid.
28 Ibid.
29 Ibid.
30 Ibid.
31 Ibid., 518.
32 Ibid.
33 Ibid.
34 Ibid.
35 Ibid.
36 Ibid., 519.
37 Ibid., 520.
38 Foltz, *Iran in World History*, 27.
39 Katouzian, *The Persians*, 33.
40 Ibid.
41 Ibid.
42 Foltz, *Iran in World History*, 19.
43 Katouzian, *The Persians*, 34.
44 Kuhrt, *The Persian Empire*, 195.
45 Ibid., 202.
46 Ibid., 194.
47 Beckwith, *Greek Buddha*, 7.
48 Kuhrt, *The Persian Empire*, 182.
49 Ibid., 183.
50 Ibid., 196.
51 Ibid.
52 Herodotus, *The Histories* (New York: Barnes and Noble, 2004), IV, 102, 120.
53 Ibid., IV, 122–123.
54 Ibid., 103–119.
55 Kuhrt, *The Persian Empire*, 199.
56 Ibid.
57 Ibid., 183.
58 Ibid.
59 Ibid.
60 Ibid., 182.
61 Ibid., 143–144.
62 Ibid., 144–147.
63 Kuhrt, *The Persian Empire*, 176; Herodotus, *The Histories*, III, 118–19; Kuhrt, *The Persian Empire*, 175.
64 Kuhrt, *The Persian Empire*, 184.
65 Ibid., 137.
66 Ibid., 149.
67 Harvey Kraft, *The Buddha from Babylon: The Lost History and Cosmic Vision of Siddhartha Gautama* (New York: Select Books, 2014), xxxvii.
68 Herodotus, *The Histories*, III, 67.
69 Ibid., III, 70.
70 Ibid., III, 68–69.
71 Ibid., III, 72–73.
72 Ibid., III, 127.
73 Ibid., III, 84.3–85; 87–88.3.
74 Allan Bloom, *The Republic of Plato* (New York: Basic Books, 199), 93, 138.
75 Harvey Kraft, *The Buddha from Babylon*, xxxi.
76 Ibid., xxxviii.
77 Beckwith, *Greek Buddha*, 173.
78 Ibid., 174.
79 Ibid., 175.
80 Kraft, *The Buddha from Babylon*, xv.
81 Ibid., xxxiii.
82 Ibid.
83 Ibid., xxxiv.
84 Ibid., xvi, xxxviii.
85 Ibid., xxx.
86 Ibid., xxxiv.
87 Ibid., xxxviii.
88 Ibid., xxxix.
89 Ibid., xxxviii.
90 Beckwith, *Greek Buddha*, 29.
91 Ibid.
92 Ibid.
93 Ibid., 30.
94 Ibid., 31.
95 Ibid.
96 Ibid., 92.
97 Ibid., 156.
98 Ibid.
99 Ibid., 82.
100 Ibid.
101 Ibid.

102 Ibid., 83.1
103 Ibid., 154.
104 Ibid., 63.
105 Ibid., 64.
106 Ibid., 63.
107 Ibid., 34.
108 Ibid.
109 Ibid., 34.
110 Ibid., 37.
111 Ibid., 34–35.
112 Ibid., 140–141.
113 Ibid., 142.
114 Ibid., 143.
115 Ibid., 144.
116 Ibid., 146.
117 Ibid., 152–153.
118 Ibid., 42.
119 Ibid., 140.
120 Ibid., 7.
121 Ibid., 10.
122 Ibid., 9.
123 Ibid.
124 Ibid., 133.
125 Ibid., 35.
126 Ibid.
127 Ibid., 155.
128 Ibid., 156.
129 Ibid., 155–156.
130 Ibid., 40.
131 Ibid.
132 Ibid., 154.
133 Ibid., 37.
134 Ibid.
135 Ibid.
136 Ibid., 169.
137 Ibid., 172.
138 Ibid., 158.
139 Ibid., 179.
140 Diogenes Laertius, *Lives of Eminent Philosophers* (New York: Oxford University Press, 2018), book 9, sections 13–14.
141 Ibid., Book 9, sections, 3–4.
142 Friedrich Nietzsche, *The Pre-Platonic Philosophers* (Chicago: University of Illinois Press, 2001), 53.
143 Heraclitus, *Fragments*, Diels 121, Kahn LXIV.
144 Ibid., Diels 104, Kahn, LIX.
145 Ibid., Diels 49, Kahn LXIII.
146 Ibid., Diels 110–111, Kahn LXVII.
147 Ibid., Diels 80, Kahn LXXXII.
148 Ibid., Diels A22, Kahn LXXXI.
149 Ibid., Diels 53, Kahn LXXXIII.
150 Ibid., Diels 70, Kahn LVIII.
151 Ibid., Diels 102, Kahn LXVIII.
152 Ibid., Diels 23, Kahn LXIX.
153 Ibid., Diels 52, Kahn XCIV.
154 James Darmesteter, *The Zend Avesta, Part 1 of 3: The Vendidad* (ForgottenBooks, 2008), 78.
155 Ibid., 143.
156 Heraclitus, *Fragments*, Diels 110-11, Kahn LXVII.
157 Ibid., Diels 61, Kahn LXX.
158 Ibid., Diels 9, Kahn LXXI.
159 Ibid., Diels 13, Kahn LXXII.
160 Ibid., Diels 1, Kahn I.
161 Ibid., Diels 2, Kahn III.
162 Ibid., Diels 89, Kahn VI.
163 Ibid., Diels 113, Kahn XXXI.
164 Ibid., Diels 21, Kahn LXXXIX.
165 Ibid., Diels 26, Kahn XC.
166 Ibid., Diels 75, Kahn XCI.
167 Ibid., Diels 62, Kahn XCII.
168 Ibid., Diels 88, Kahn XCIII.
169 Ibid., Diels 50, Kahn XXXVI.
170 Ibid., Diels 90, Kahn XL.
171 Ibid., Diels 12, Kahn L.
172 Ibid., Diels 91, Kahn LI.
173 Ibid., Diels 84a, Kahn LII.
174 Ibid., Diels 103, Kahn XCIX.
175 Ibid., Diels 60, Kahn CIII.
176 Ibid., Diels 126, Kahn XLIX.
177 Ibid., Diels 8, Kahn LXXV.
178 Ibid., Diels 51, Kahn LXXVIII.
179 Ibid., Diels 48, Kahn LXXIX.
180 Ibid., Diels 54, Kahn LXXX.
181 Ibid., Diels 67, Kahn CXXIII.
182 Ibid., Diels 10, Kahn CXXIV.
183 Beckwith, *Greek Buddha*, 63.
184 Ibid., 111.
185 Ibid., 112.

186 Ibid., 113.
187 Herodotus, *The Histories*, III, 79.
188 Beckwith, *Greek Buddha*, 177.
189 Red Pine, *Lao-Tzu's Tao Te Ching* (Port Townsend: Copper Canyon Press, 2009), Chapter 29, p. 58.
190 Ibid., Chapter 45, p. 90.
191 Ibid., Chapter 57, p. 114.

CHAPTER 4. *TEKEL TEKEL, MENE SHEKEL*

1 Herodotus, *The Histories* (New York: Barnes and Noble, 2004), VII, 1.1, 4; Amélie Kuhrt et al., *The Persian Empire: A Corpus of Sources from the Achaemenid Period* (New York: Routledge, 2007), 236.
2 Kuhrt, *The Persian Empire*, 237.
3 Richard Stoneman, *Xerxes: A Persian Life* (New Haven: Yale University Press, 2016), 122.
4 Ibid., 9.
5 Ibid., 126.
6 Ibid., 115.
7 Ibid., 129.
8 Ibid., 149.
9 Ibid.
10 Ibid., 134.
11 Ibid.
12 Ibid., 135.
13 Ibid., 135–136.
14 Ibid., 136.
15 Ibid., 132.
16 Ibid., 194.
17 Ibid., 184.
18 Ibid., 185.
19 Ibid., 123.
20 Ibid., 190.
21 Ibid., 144.
22 Ibid.
23 Ibid., 145.
24 Ibid., 196.
25 Ibid.
26 Ibid., 197.
27 Ibid.
28 Ibid., 145.
29 Ibid., 190.
30 Ibid., 198.
31 Ibid., 199.
32 Ibid., 198.
33 Ibid., 199.
34 Ibid.
35 Ibid., 140.
36 Ibid.
37 Ibid., 142.
38 Ibid., 141.
39 Ibid., 144.
40 Ibid., 143.
41 Ibid., 123.
42 Ibid., 124.
43 Ibid.
44 Ibid., 135.
45 Ibid.
46 Ibid., 122–123, 132.
47 Ibid., 132.
48 J.A. de Gobineau, *The World of the Persians* (Geneva: Minerva, 1971), 113.
49 Ibid.
50 Ibid., 116.
51 Ibid., 116–119.
52 Ibid., 119.
53 Ibid., 121.
54 Joseph P. Farrell, *Babylon's Banksters: The Alchemy of Deep Physics, High Finance and Ancient Religion* (Port Townsend: Feral House, 2010), 202.
55 Reza Zarghamee, *Discovering Cyrus: The Persian Conqueror Astride the Ancient World* (Washington DC: Mage Publishers, 2013), 473.
56 D.M. Murdock, "Was the Persian Goddess Anahita the Pre-Christian Virgin Mother of Mithra?" in *Anahita: Ancient Persian Goddess & Zoroastrian Yazata* (London: Avalonia, 2012), 98.
57 Zarghamee, *Discovering Cyrus*, 473.
58 Murdock, "Was the Persian Goddess Anahita the Pre-Christian Virgin Mother of Mithra?" 99.

59 Zarghamee, *Discovering Cyrus*, 185.
60 Ibid., 184.
61 Ibid., 185.
62 Ibid.
63 Gobineau, *The World of the Persians*, 121.
64 Ibid.
65 Ibid., 122.
66 Ibid., 123.
67 Ibid., 129.
68 Ibid.
69 Ibid.
70 Ibid.
71 Ibid.
72 Ibid., 130.
73 Ibid., 134.
74 Ibid.
75 Ibid.
76 Ibid., 137.
77 Ibid.
78 Ibid., 137–138.
79 Ibid., 138.
80 Richard C. Foltz, *Iran in World History*, (New York: Oxford University Press, 2016), 19.
81 Ibid., 2016, 19.
82 Roman Ghirshman, *Persia the Immortal Kingdom* (New York Graphic Society, 1971), 60.
83 Ibid., 58.
84 Ibid.
85 Ibid., 60.
86 Ibid.
87 Ibid., 58, 60.
88 Ibid., 60.
89 Farrell, *Babylon's Banksters*, 202.
90 Ibid.
91 Ibid., 203.
92 Ibid.
93 Ibid., 204.
94 Ibid.
95 Ibid.
96 Ibid., 203–205.
97 Ibid., 205.
98 Zarghamee, *Discovering Cyrus*, 229.
99 Ibid., 227.
100 Ibid., 230.
101 Ibid., 231.
102 Ibid.
103 Ibid., 237.
104 Ibid., 232.
105 Ibid., 237, 504.
106 Ibid., 504.
107 Ibid., 503–504.
108 Ibid., 504.
109 Ibid., 237, 505.
110 Ibid., 503.
111 Ibid.
112 Ibid., 106.
113 Ibid., 82.
114 Ibid.
115 Ibid., 183.
116 Ibid., 213.
117 Ibid., 193.
118 Ibid., 207.
119 Ibid., 208.
120 Ibid., 209.
121 Ibid., 211.
122 Ibid., 211, 215.
123 Ibid., 210.
124 Ibid.
125 Ibid., 210–211.
126 Ibid., 211.
127 Ibid., 210.
128 Ibid., 215.
129 Ibid.
130 Ibid.
131 Ibid.
132 Stoneman, *Xerxes*, 193.
133 Farrell, *Babylon's Banksters*, 37.
134 Ibid., 201.
135 Ibid., 202.
136 Zarghamee, *Discovering Cyrus*, 219.
137 Ibid., 231.
138 Ibid., 243.
139 Ibid.
140 Ibid.
141 Ibid., 232.
142 Ibid.
143 Ibid., 235.
144 Ibid.
145 Ibid., 232–233.
146 Ibid., 233.
147 Ibid.

148 Ibid., 146.
149 Ibid., 146, 458.
150 Ibid., 157.
151 Ibid.
152 Ibid., 151.
153 Ibid., 150.
154 Ibid., 209.
155 Ibid., 235.
156 Ibid.
157 Ibid.
158 Ibid.
159 Ibid.
160 Richard C. Foltz, *Spirituality in the Land of the Noble: How Iran Shaped the World's Religions* (London: Oneworld Publications, 2004), 49.
161 Zarghamee, *Discovering Cyrus*, 246.
162 Ibid., 224.
163 Ibid., 247.
164 Foltz, *Spirituality in the Land of the Noble*, 49.
165 Ibid., 49.
166 Ibid.
167 Zarghamee, *Discovering Cyrus*, 245.
168 Ibid., 246.
169 Ibid.
170 Foltz, *Spirituality in the Land of the Noble*, 49.
171 Ibid.
172 Ibid.
173 Zarghamee, *Discovering Cyrus*, 249.
174 Foltz, *Spirituality in the Land of the Noble*, 49.
175 Zarghamee, *Discovering Cyrus*, 507.
176 Ibid.
177 Ibid.
178 Ibid.
179 Ibid., 555.
180 Ibid., 555–556.
181 Ibid., 556.
182 Ibid., 510.
183 Ibid.
184 Ibid., 207.
185 Stoneman, *Xerxes*, 105.
186 Ibid., 132.
187 Parvaneh Pourshariati, *Decline and Fall of the Sasanian Empire: The Sasanian-Parthian Confederacy and the Arab Conquest of Iran* (New York: I.B. Tauris, 2008), 353.
188 Ibid., 350.
189 Ibid., 353.
190 Ibid., 352.
191 Ibid.
192 Ibid., 357.
193 Ibid., 356–357.
194 Ibid., 357.
195 Ibid.
196 Ibid.
197 Ibid., 356.
198 Ibid., 357.
199 Payam Nabarz, *The Mysteries of Mithras* (Rochester, VT: Inner Traditions, 2005), 170–171.
200 Stoneman, *Xerxes*, 107.
201 Richard Foltz, *Religions of Iran: From Prehistory to the Present* (London: Oneworld Publications, 2013), 21.
202 Ibid.
203 Ibid.
204 Ibid., 22.
205 Ibid., 21.
206 Ibid.
207 Ibid., 22.
208 Ibid.
209 Ibid.
210 Pourshariati, *Decline and Fall of the Sasanian Empire*, 358.
211 Ibid.
212 Ibid.

CHAPTER 5. THE SKULL AND BONE CROSS

1 Homa Katouzian, *The Persians: Ancient, Mediaeval and Modern Iran* (New Haven: Yale University Press, 2010), 40.
2 Michael Axworthy, *A History of Iran: Empire of the Mind* (New York: Perseus Books Group, 2010), 31.

3 Parvaneh Pourshariati, *Decline and Fall of the Sasanian Empire: The Sasanian-Parthian Confederacy and the Arab Conquest of Iran* (I.B. Tauris, 2008), 19.
4 Axworthy, *A History of Iran: Empire of the Mind*, 33.
5 Pourshariati, *The Decline and Fall of the Sasanian Empire*, 19.
6 R.C. Zaehner, *Zurvan: A Zoroastrian Dilemma* (New York: Biblio and Tannen, 1928), 29.
7 Pourshariati, *The Decline and Fall of the Sasanian Empire*, 20.
8 Ibid., 24–27.
9 Ibid., 20.
10 Axworthy, *A History of Iran: Empire of the Mind*, 34–43.
11 Ibid., 36.
12 Richard C. Foltz, *Iran in World History* (New York: Oxford University Press, 2016), 29.
13 Axworthy, *A History of Iran: Empire of the Mind*, 37.
14 Ibid., 38.
15 Ibid., 39–40.
16 Ibid., 39.
17 Ibid., 40.
18 Herodotus, *The Histories* (New York: Barnes and Noble, 2004), VII: 61,150.
19 David Ulansey, *The Origins of the Mithraic Mysteries* (New York: Oxford University Press, 1991), 28.
20 Ibid., 30.
21 Ibid., 38.
22 Ibid., 36–37.
23 Ibid., 37–38.
24 Foltz, *Iran in World History*, 29.
25 Ulansey, *The Origins of the Mithraic Mysteries*, 89.
26 Ibid., 90.
27 Ibid., 25.
28 Ibid., 30.
29 Ibid., 26.
30 Ibid., 26–27.
31 Ibid., 29.
32 Ibid., 32.
33 Ibid., 33.
34 Ibid., 34.
35 Ibid., 117.
36 Ibid., 120.
37 Ibid., 123.
38 Ibid., 120.
39 Ibid., 121.
40 Ibid.
41 Zaehner, *Zurvan: A Zoroastrian Dilemma*, 242.
42 Ibid., 239.
43 Ibid.
44 Ibid., 240.
45 Ibid., 111.
46 Ibid., 161.
47 Ibid., 122.
48 Ibid., 96–97.
49 Ibid., 67.
50 Ulansey, *The Origins of the Mithraic Mysteries*, 100.
51 Ibid., 101.
52 Zaehner, *Zurvan: A Zoroastrian Dilemma*, 101.
53 Payam Nabarz, *The Mysteries of Mithras* (Rochester, VT: Inner Traditions, 2005), 25.
54 Ibid., 26.
55 Ibid.
56 Franz Cumont, *The Mysteries of Mithra* (Chicago: Open Court, 1903), 19.
57 Ibid., 20.
58 Zaehner, *Zurvan: A Zoroastrian Dilemma*, 101.
59 Ibid., 102.
60 Ibid., 101.
61 Ibid.
62 Ibid., 151.
63 Ulansey, *The Origins of the Mithraic Mysteries*, 107.
64 Ibid., 110.
65 Zaehner, *Zurvan: A Zoroastrian Dilemma*, 102.
66 Ibid., 103.
67 Ulansey, *The Origins of the Mithraic Mysteries*, 76.
68 Ibid., 77.

69 Ibid., 83.
70 Ibid., 95.
71 Ibid., 96.
72 Ibid.
73 Ibid., 98.
74 Ibid.
75 Ibid., 82.
76 Ibid., 84–85.
77 Ibid., 86.
78 Ibid., 105.
79 Ibid., 78–79.
80 Ibid., 98.
81 Ibid., 88.
82 Richard Foltz, *Religions of Iran: From Prehistory to the Present* (London: Oneworld Publications, 2013), 24.
83 Ulansey, *The Origins of the Mithraic Mysteries*, 89.
84 Ibid., 89.
85 Ibid.
86 Cumont, *The Mysteries of Mithra*, 31, 35.
87 Ibid., 32.
88 Ibid., 35.
89 Carl A. P. Ruck, Mark A. Hoffman, Jose Alfredo González Celdrán, *Mushrooms, Myth, & Mithras* (San Francisco: City Lights Books, 2011), 213–214.
90 Ibid., 121.
91 Ibid., 119.
92 Ibid., 121.
93 Ibid., 119.
94 Ibid., 120.
95 Ibid., 122.
96 Ibid., 119–120.
97 Ibid., 120–121.
98 Ibid., 122.
99 Ibid., 120, 122.
100 Ibid., 120.
101 Ibid.
102 Ibid., 121.
103 Ibid., 211–212.
104 Ibid., 211.
105 Adrienne Mayor, *The Poison King: The Life and Legend of Mithradates, Rome's Deadliest Enemy* (Princeton: Princeton University Press, 2010).
106 Ruck, *Mushrooms, Myth, & Mithras*, 214.
107 Ibid., 123.
108 Ibid., 124.
109 Ulansey, *The Origins of the Mithraic Mysteries*, 94.
110 Ruck, *Mushrooms, Myth, & Mithras*, 123.
111 Ibid., 162.
112 Ibid., 126.
113 Abolqasem Ferdowsi, *Shahnameh: The Persian Book of Kings* (New York: Penguin Books, 2007), 10.
114 Ibid., 13.
115 Ibid., 5.
116 Foltz, *Religions of Iran*, 29.
117 Ruck, *Mushrooms, Myth, & Mithras*, 127, 130.
118 Ibid., 127.
119 Ibid., 126.
120 Ibid., 127.
121 Ibid., 129.
122 Ibid., 206.
123 Ibid., 128.
124 Zaehner, *Zurvan: A Zoroastrian Dilemma*, 157–158.
125 Ibid., 157, 160.
126 Ibid., 158.
127 Ibid., 160.
128 Ibid., 158.
129 Ibid.
130 Ibid., 159.
131 Ibid.
132 Ibid., 160.
133 Ibid., 162.
134 Ibid., 160.
135 Ibid.
136 Ruck, *Mushrooms, Myth, & Mithras*, 138.
137 Ibid., 220.
138 Ibid., 221.
139 Nabarz, *The Mysteries of Mithras*, 54–55.
140 Ruck, *Mushrooms, Myth, & Mithras*, 140.

141 Ibid., 142.
142 Ibid., 235–236.
143 Ibid., 237.
144 Ibid., 182.
145 Ibid., 136.
146 Ibid.
147 Ibid., 137.
148 Cumont, *The Mysteries of Mithra*, 100.
149 Nabarz, *The Mysteries of Mithras*, 26.
150 Ruck, *Mushrooms, Myth, & Mithras*, 174.
151 Ibid., 137–138.
152 Ibid., 135.
153 Cumont, *The Mysteries of Mithra*, 37.
154 Ibid., 38.
155 Ibid.
156 Ibid.
157 Ibid.
158 Ibid., 39.
159 Foltz, *Religions of Iran*, 26.
160 Cumont, *The Mysteries of Mithra*, 40.
161 Nabarz, *The Mysteries of Mithras*, 11.
162 Ibid., 18.
163 Ibid., 114.
164 Ibid.
165 Ibid., 13.
166 Ibid., 4.
167 Ibid., 19.
168 Ibid., 6.
169 Ibid.
170 Cummont, *The Mysteries of Mithra*, 109.
171 Foltz, *Religions of Iran*, 25.
172 Cummont, *The Mysteries of Mithra*, 85.
173 Ibid., 113.
174 Nabarz, *The Mysteries of Mithras*, 12.
175 Cumont, *The Mysteries of Mithra*, 115.
176 Foltz, *Religions of Iran*, 30.
177 Ruck, *Mushrooms, Myth, & Mithras*, 63.
178 Ibid., 236–237.
179 Pourshariati, *Decline and Fall of the Sasanian Empire*, 380.
180 Ulansey, *The Origins of the Mithraic Mysteries*, 68.
181 Cumont, *The Mysteries of Mithra*, 91.
182 Ulansey, *The Origins of the Mithraic Mysteries*, 68.
183 Ibid., 76.
184 Marvin Meyer, *Q Thomas Reader* (Santa Rosa, CA: Polebridge Press, 1990), 131.
185 Ibid., 153.
186 Ibid., 148.
187 Ibid., 136.
188 Ibid., 144.
189 Ibid., 141.
190 Ibid., 147.
191 Patricia Crone, *The Nativist Prophets of Early Islamic Iran: Rural Revolt and Local Zoroastrianism* (New York: Cambridge University Press, 2013), 303–304.
192 Meyer, *Q Thomas Reader*, 149.
193 Ruck, *Mushrooms, Myth, & Mithras*, 130–131.
194 Ibid., 131.
195 Ibid., 130.
196 Ibid.
197 Ibid., 131.
198 Ibid.
199 Cummont, *The Mysteries of Mithra*, 108.
200 Ruck, *Mushrooms, Myth, & Mithras*, 130.
201 Meyer, *Q Thomas Reader*, 142.
202 Ibid., 148.
203 Meyer, *Q Thomas Reader*, 133.
204 Ibid., 142.
205 Cumont, *The Mysteries of Mithra*, 116.
206 Nabarz, *The Mysteries of Mithras*, 45.
207 Ibid., 43.
208 Ibid., 44–45.
209 Friedrich Nietzsche, *Thus Spoke Zarathustra* (New York: Modern Library, 1995), 57.
210 Ibid., 56.

CHAPTER 6. FROM PERSIA WITH LOVE

1 R.C. Zaehner, *Zurvan: A Zoroastrian Dilemma* (New York: Biblio and Tannen, 1928), 7.
2 Shahin Nezhad, *Ardeshir Babakan* [Dissertation Draft], 20.
3 Ibid., 36.
4 Ibid., 37.
5 Ibid.
6 Zaehner, *Zurvan: A Zoroastrian Dilemma*, 36.
7 Shahin Nezhad, *Ardeshir Babakan* [Dissertation Draft], 12.
8 Ibid., 23.
9 Ibid., 66.
10 Ibid., 23–24.
11 Ibid., 67.
12 Ibid., 65.
13 Ibid., 11.
14 Ibid., 22–23, 64.
15 Ibid., 27.
16 Ibid., 37.
17 Ibid., 13.
18 Ibid., 27.
19 Ibid., 14.
20 Ibid., 15.
21 Ibid.
22 Ibid., 14.
23 Ibid.
24 Ibid., 22.
25 Zaehner, *Zurvan: A Zoroastrian Dilemma*, 35-36.
26 Ibid., 8.
27 Ibid., 44.
28 Ibid., 8.
29 Ibid., 49.
30 Ibid., 75.
31 Michel Tardieu, *Manichaeism* (Chicago: University of Illinois Press, 2008), 17.
32 Ibid., 23.
33 Ibid., 48, 75.
34 Ibid., 17–18.
35 Ibid., 13–14.
36 Ibid., 16.
37 Ibid., 24.
38 Ibid., 154.
39 Ibid., 25.
40 Ibid., 21.
41 Ibid., 32.
42 Ibid., 39.
43 Ibid., 22.
44 Ibid.
45 Ibid., 23.
46 Ibid.
47 Ibid., 26.
48 Ibid., 23.
49 Ibid., 25.
50 Ibid., 26.
51 Ibid.
52 Ibid., 27.
53 Ibid.
54 Ibid.
55 Ibid., 28.
56 Ibid.
57 Ibid., 29.
58 Ibid.
59 Ibid., 30.
60 Ibid., 32.
61 Ibid., 43.
62 Ibid., 33.
63 Ibid., 32–33.
64 Ibid., 43–44.
65 Ibid., 43.
66 Ibid., 56.
67 Ibid.
68 Ibid., 35.
69 Ibid., 37, 79.
70 Ibid., 85.
71 Ibid., 80.
72 Ibid., 82.
73 Richard Foltz, *Religions of Iran: From Prehistory to the Present* (London: Oneworld Publications, 2013), 153.
74 Ehsan Yarshater, "Mazdakism" in *The Cambridge History of Iran, Vol. 3(2)* (New York: Cambridge University Press, 1983), 106–108.
75 Yarshater, "Mazdakism," 107, 112, 116-117.

76 Patricia Crone, *The Nativist Prophets of Early Islamic Iran: Rural Revolt and Local Zoroastrianism* (New York: Cambridge University Press, 2013) 303–310.
77 James Darmesteter, *The Zend Avesta, Part 1 of 3: The Vendidad* (Forgotten Books, 2008), 70.
78 Ibid., 71.
79 Ibid., 78.
80 Ibid., 79.
81 Ibid., 80.
82 Ibid., 79, 84.
83 Ibid., 84.
84 Ibid., 86–87.
85 Ibid., 87.
86 Zaehner, *Zurvan: A Zoroastrian Dilemma*, 188.
87 Ibid., 190.
88 Ibid., 74.
89 Ibid., 74–75.
90 Ibid., 75.
91 Ibid., 183.
92 Ibid., 184.
93 Ibid.
94 Ibid., 191.
95 Ibid.
96 Ibid., 54.
97 Ibid., 62.
98 Ibid., 65.
99 Ibid.
100 Ibid., 66–67.
101 Ibid., 230.
102 Ibid., 69.
103 Ibid.
104 Ibid.
105 Ibid., 70.
106 Ibid.
107 Ibid., 267.
108 Ibid., 71.
109 Ibid., 71, 74, 77.
110 Ibid., 236.
111 Ibid., 114.
112 Ibid., 116.
113 Ibid., 183.
114 Ibid., 181.
115 Ibid., 238.
116 Ibid., 270.
117 Ibid., 248–249.
118 Ibid., 249.
119 Ibid., 270.
120 Ibid., 270–271.
121 Ibid., 234.
122 Ibid., 235.
123 Ibid.
124 Ibid.
125 Ibid.
126 Ibid., 236.
127 Ibid., 114–115.
128 Ibid., 115–116, 167.
129 Ibid., 167, 170.
130 Ibid., 167, 182–183.
131 Ibid., 175.
132 Ibid., 115.
133 Ibid., 170.
134 Ibid., 171.
135 Ibid., 172–173.
136 Ibid., 173.
137 Ibid., 174.
138 Ibid., 175.
139 Ibid., 174.
140 Ibid., 175.
141 Ibid., 174.
142 Ibid., 253.
143 Ibid., 114.
144 Ibid., 179.
145 Ibid., 178.
146 Ibid., 175.
147 Ibid., 175.
148 Ibid., 175.
149 Ibid., 239.
150 Ehsan Yarshater, "Mazdakism" in *The Cambridge History of Iran, Vol. 3(2)*, 999.
151 Zaehner, *Zurvan: A Zoroastrian Dilemma*, 13.
152 Ibid., 15.
153 Ibid., 20.
154 Ibid., 19.
155 Yarshater, *Cambridge History of Iran, Vol. 3(2)*, 1024.
156 Yarshater, "Mazdakism," 107, 112, 116-117.

157 Ferdowsi, *Shahnameh: The Persian Book of Kings*, 679.
158 Patricia Crone, *The Nativist Prophets of Early Islamic Iran: Rural Revolt and Local Zoroastrianism* (New York: Cambridge University Press, 2013), 254–255, 234.
159 Ferdowsi, *Shahnameh: The Persian Book of Kings*, 681-682.
160 Yarshater, "Mazdakism," 112, 120–121.
161 Yarshater, *Cambridge History of Iran, Vol 3(2)*, 1004.
162 Foltz, *Religions of Iran*, 154.
163 Yarshater, "Mazdakism" in *Cambridge History of Iran, Vol. 3(2)*, 999, 1001.
164 Crone, *The Nativist Prophets of Early Islamic Iran*, 265, 392–393.
165 Ibid., 392–393, 400–401.
166 Ibid., 430.
167 Ibid., 443–444.
168 Zaehner, *Zurvan: A Zoroastrian Dilemma*, 39.
169 Ibid., 11.
170 Ibid., 12.
171 Ibid., 12.
172 Ibid., 12–13.
173 Ibid., 48.
174 Abolqasem Ferdowsi, *Shahnameh: The Persian Book of Kings* (New York: Penguin Books, 2007), 682–683.
175 Zaehner, *Zurvan: A Zoroastrian Dilemma*, 48.
176 Ibid.
177 Ibid.
178 Ibid., 49.
179 A. Tafazzoli and A.L. Khromov, "Sasanian Iran: Intellectual Life" in *History of Civilizations of Central Asia: Volume III The Crossroads of Civilizations A.D. 250 to 750* (Paris: United Nations Educational, Scientific and Cultural Organization, 1999), 91–93.
180 Seyyed Hossein Nasr and Mehdi Aminrazavi [Editors], *An Anthology of Philosophy in Persia: Volume 1* (New York: Oxford University Press, 1999), 276–302.

CHAPTER 7. EVERYTHING IS PERMITTED

1 Parvaneh Pourshariati, *Decline and Fall of the Sasanian Empire: The Sasanian-Parthian Confederacy and the Arab Conquest of Iran* (New York: I.B. Tauris, 2008), 1–3.
2 Ibid., 350–395.
3 Ibid., 76–80.
4 Ibid., 384.
5 Ibid., 20, 76–81, 112–115.
6 Ibid., 380.
7 Ibid., 426.
8 Ibid., 433.
9 Ibid., 427–428.
10 Ibid., 436.
11 Ibid., 439.
12 Ibid.
13 Ibid., 380.
14 Ibid.
15 Ibid.
16 N.J. Dawood [Translator], *The Koran: With a Parallel Arabic Text* (New York: Penguin Books, 2006), 278.
17 Milad Milani, *Sufism in the Secret History of Persia* (Durham: Acumen Publishing Limited, 2013), 168.
18 Ibid., 157, 177, 179–180.
19 Ibid., 181.
20 Ibid., 177, 190–191.
21 Ibid., 163–165, 169, 171, 178.
22 Ibid., 169.
23 Ibid., 169, 171, 173, 178.
24 Ibid., 178.
25 Martin Lings, *Muhammad: His Life Based on the Earliest Sources* (Rochester, VT: Inner Traditions, 2006), 223.

26 Ibid., 151–152.
27 Lyn Webster Wilde, *On the Trail of the Woman Warriors: The Amazons in Myth and History* (New York: St. Martin's Press, 2000), 100–102.
28 Ibid., 99.
29 Ibid.
30 Patricia Crone, *The Nativist Prophets of Early Islamic Iran: Rural Revolt and Local Zoroastrianism* (New York: Cambridge University Press, 2013), 48.
31 Ibid., 49.
32 Ibid.
33 Ibid., 62.
34 Ibid., 49.
35 Ibid., 64.
36 Ibid., 49.
37 Ibid.
38 Ibid., 49–50.
39 Ibid., 50.
40 Ibid.
41 Ibid.
42 Ibid., 67.
43 Ibid., 66.
44 Ibid.
45 Ibid., 68.
46 Ibid.
47 Ibid.
48 Ibid., 69.
49 Ibid.
50 Ibid., 76.
51 Ibid., 65.
52 Ibid., 66–67.
53 Ibid., 71.
54 Ibid.
55 Ibid., 67.
56 Ibid., 71.
57 Ibid., 71–72.
58 Ibid., 61.
59 Ibid.
60 Ibid., 59.
61 Ibid., 60.
62 Ibid.
63 Ibid., 71.
64 Ibid., 72.
65 Ibid., 71–72.
66 Ibid., 66–67.
67 Miles Augustus Navarr, *Forbidden Theology: Origin of Scriptural God* (Xlibris, 2012), 124–125.
68 Tilman Nagel, "Buyids" in *Encyclopaedia Iranica, Vol. IV, Fasc. 6* (New York: Encyclopaedia Iranica Foundation, 1990), 578–586.
69 Ch. Bürgel and R. Mottahedeh, "Azod-Al-Dawla, Abü Sojâ' Fannâ Khosrow" in *Encyclopaedia Iranica, Vol. III, Fasc. 3*, (New York: Encyclopaedia Iranica Foundation, 1988), 265–269.
70 Seyyed Hossein Nasr, *Islamic Science: An Illustrated History* (Kent: World of Islam Festival, 1976), 84.
71 Ibid., 85.
72 Ibid., 79.
73 Ibid., 78–79.
74 Ibid., 40.
75 Ibid., 97.
76 Ibid., 84.
77 Ibid., 172, 177.
78 Benno van Dalen, "Yahyâ ibn Abi Mansûr: Abû 'Ali Yahyâ ibn Abi Mansur al-Munajjim in Thomas Hockey et al, *The Biographical Encyclopedia of Astronomers* (New York: Springer, 2007), 1249–1250.
79 D. Pingree, "Banu Monajjem" in Ehsan Yarshater [Editor], *Encyclopaedia Iranica, Vol. III, Fasc. 7* (Encyclopaedia Iranica Foundation, 1988), 716.
80 Nasr, *Islamic Science*, 155, 166.
81 Ibid., 177.
82 Ibid., 200–201, 204.
83 Ibid., 154.
84 Sarah Stroumsa, *Freethinkers of Medieval Islam: Ibn al-Râwandi, Abu Bakr al-Râzi, and Their Impact on Islamic Thought* (Boston: Brill, 1999), 103.
85 Tarif Khalidi, *The Proofs of Prophecy* (Brigham Young University, 2012).
86 Christopher I. Beckwith, *Greek Bud-*

dha: Pyrrho's Encounter with Early Buddhism in Central Asia (Princeton: Princeton University Press, 2017), 147.

87 Ibid.
88 Ibid., 148.
89 Ibid.
90 Ibid., 149.
91 Ibid.
92 Ibid., 150.
93 Ibid.
94 Pourshariati, *Decline and Fall of the Sasanian Empire*, 463.
95 Richard C. Foltz, *Iran in World History* (New York: Oxford University Press, 2016), 58.
96 Ibid.
97 Dick Davis, *Shahnameh: The Persian Book of Kings* (New York: Penguin Books, 2007), xix.
98 Richard Foltz, *Religions of Iran: From Prehistory to the Present* (London: Oneworld Publications, 2013), 31.
99 Davis, *Shahnameh*, 837.
100 Ibid., xxxii.
101 Foltz, *Iran in World History*, 62–63.
102 Ibid., 63.
103 Ibid., 61.
104 Ibid., 62.
105 Ibid.
106 Ibid., 63.
107 Marshall Hodgson, *The Secret Order of Assassins: The Struggle of the Early Nizârî Ismâʿîlîs Against the Islamic World* (Philadelphia: University of Pennsylvania Press, 2005), 62.
108 Ibid., 64.
109 Ibid.
110 Ibid., 66.
111 Ibid., 69.
112 Ibid., 70.
113 Ibid., 64.
114 Ibid., 134.
115 Ibid., 135.
116 Ibid.
117 Ibid., 137.
118 Ibid., 122.
119 Ibid., 123.
120 Ibid., 75.
121 Ibid., 69.
122 Ibid., 43.
123 Ibid., 44.
124 Ibid., 46.
125 Ibid., 47.
126 Ibid.
127 Ibid., 123.
128 53
129 Ibid., 58.
130 Ibid.
131 Ibid., 310.
132 Ibid., 308.
133 Ibid., 324.
134 Ibid., 310.
135 Ibid.
136 Ibid., 314.
137 Ibid., 313–314.
138 Ibid., 172–173.
139 Ibid., 67.
140 Ibid., 68.
141 Ibid., 56.
142 Ibid., 59.
143 Ibid., 59–60.
144 Ibid., 60.
145 Ibid., 321.
146 Ibid., 60–61.
147 Ibid., 60.
148 Ibid., 61.
149 Ibid., 119.
150 Ibid.
151 Ibid., 120.
152 Ibid., 84.
153 Ibid.
154 Ibid.
155 Ibid., 48.
156 Rüdiger Schmitt, "Caspians" in *Encyclopaedia Iranica Vol. V, Fasc. 1* (New York: Encyclopaedia Iranica Foundation, 1990), 62.
157 Ernst Herzfeld, *The Persian Empire* (Wiesbaden, 1968), 195–199.
158 Hodgson, *The Secret Order of Assassins*, 73.
159 Ibid., 74.

160 Ibid., 49.
161 Ibid., 325.
162 Ibid., 49.
163 Ibid., 138.
164 Ibid., 49.
165 Ibid., 50.
166 Ibid.
167 Ibid., 139.
168 Ibid., 147.
169 Ibid., 164.
170 Ibid., 165.
171 Ibid.
172 Ibid.
173 Ibid., 166.
174 Ibid., 110.
175 Ibid., 260.
176 Ibid., 81.
177 Ibid., 118.
178 Ibid.
179 Ibid.
180 Ibid.
181 Ibid., 154.
182 Ibid., 148.
183 Ibid., 152.
184 Ibid.
185 Ibid., 153.
186 Ibid.
187 Ibid., 175.
188 Ibid., 314–315.
189 Ibid., 319.
190 Ibid., 156.
191 Ibid., 148.
192 Ibid., 149.
193 Ibid., 149–150.
194 Ibid., 158.
195 Ibid., 150–151.
196 Ibid., 155.
197 Ibid.
198 Ibid., 167.
199 Ibid., 312.
200 Ibid., 155.
201 Ibid., 156.
202 Ibid.
203 Ibid., 125.
204 Ibid., 126.
205 Ibid., 116.
206 Ibid., 159.
207 Ibid.
208 Ibid., 160.
209 Ibid.
210 Ibid., 157.
211 Ibid., 158.
212 Richard Foltz, *Iran in World History*, 67.
213 Ibid.
214 Ibid.
215 Marshall Hodgson, *The Secret Order of Assassins*, 259.
216 Ibid.
217 Ibid., 260.
218 Ibid., 259.
219 Ibid., 260.
220 Ibid., 269.
221 Ibid., 260.
222 Ibid., 266.
223 Ibid., 263.

CHAPTER 8. PERSIAN TONGUE OF THE INVISIBLE

1 Marshall G. S. Hodgson, *The Secret Order of Assassins: The Struggle of the Early Nizârî Ismâ'îlîs Against the Islamic World* (Philadelphia: University of Pennsylvania Press, 2005), 302, 308.
2 Ibid., 322.
3 William C. Chittick, *The Sufi Path of Love: The Spiritual Teachings of Rumi* (Albany: State University of New York Press, 1983), 42–47.
4 Ibid., 47–53.
5 Ibid., 29–30.
6 Ibid., 61–71.
7 Ibid., 72–82.
8 Ibid., 86–87.
9 Ibid., 194–231.
10 Ibid., 213.
11 Ibid., 168–169.
12 Ghomshei, "The Principles of the Religion of Love in Classical Persian Poetry" in Leonard Lewisohn [Editor], *Hafiz and the Religion of Love in*

Classical Persian Poetry (New York: I.B. Tauris, 2015), 77.
13 Ibid.
14 Ibid., 78.
15 Ibid., 77.
16 Hamid Dabashi, *The World of Persian Literary Humanism* (Cambridge, MA: Harvard University Press, 2012), 3–4.
17 Ibid., 1–2.
18 Leonard Lewisohn, "Socio-historical and Literary Contexts: Hâfiz in Shiraz" in *Hafiz and the Religion of Love in Classical Persian Poetry*, 18.
19 Charles-Henri de Fouchécour, "Hâfiz and the Sufi" in *Hafiz and the Religion of Love in Classical Persian Poetry*, 154.
20 Ibid., 155.
21 Lewisohn, "Socio-historical and Literary Contexts: Hâfiz in Shiraz" in *Hafiz and the Religion of Love in Classical Persian Poetry*, 14.
22 Ibid., 58.
23 Ibid., 13.
24 Ibid., 19.
25 Leonard Lewisohn, "The Mystical Milieu: Hâfiz's Erotic Spirituality" in *Hafiz and the Religion of Love in Classical Persian Poetry*, 48.
26 Ibid., 41.
27 Ibid.
28 Lewisohn, "Socio-historical and Literary Contexts: Hâfiz in Shiraz" in *Hafiz and the Religion of Love in Classical Persian Poetry*, 5.
29 Ibid., 3.
30 Ibid., 4.
31 Ibid., 5.
32 Ibid., 6.
33 Ibid., 23.
34 Ibid.
35 Ibid., 23–24.
36 Ibid., 24.
37 Ibid.
38 Ibid., 25.
39 Ibid., 28.
40 Ibid.
41 Ibid.
42 Ibid.
43 Ibid., 17.
44 Ibid.
45 Ibid.
46 Ibid.
47 Ibid.
48 Ibid., 16.
49 Ibid.
50 Ibid.
51 Ibid., 18.
52 Ibid., 18-19.
53 Ibid., 19.
54 Husayn Ilahi-Ghomshei, "The Principles of the Religion of Love in Classical Persian Poetry" in *Hafiz and the Religion of Love in Classical Persian Poetry*, 100.
55 Ibid., 102.
56 Ibid., 101–102.
57 Ibid., 91.
58 Ibid., 93.
59 Ibid., 90.
60 Lewisohn, "Socio-historical and Literary Contexts: Hâfiz in Shiraz" in *Hafiz and the Religion of Love in Classical Persian Poetry*, 10.
61 Lewisohn, "The Mystical Milieu: Hâfiz's Erotic Spirituality" in *Hafiz and the Religion of Love in Classical Persian Poetry*, 31.
62 Ibid., 32.
63 Ibid., 33.
64 Ibid.
65 Ibid.
66 Ibid.
67 Ibid., 33–34.
68 Ibid., 34.
69 Ibid.
70 Ibid., 34, 43.
71 Ibid., 35.
72 Ibid.
73 Ibid., 36.
74 Ibid.

75 Lewisohn, "Socio-historical and Literary Contexts: Hâfiz in Shiraz" in *Hafiz and the Religion of Love in Classical Persian Poetry*, 9.
76 Ibid., 8.
77 Ibid., 9.
78 Lewisohn, "The Mystical Milieu: Hâfiz's Erotic Spirituality" in *Hafiz and the Religion of Love in Classical Persian Poetry*, 36.
79 Ibid., 39.
80 Ibid., 36.
81 Ibid., 40.
82 Ibid.
83 Ibid., 38.
84 Ibid., 40.
85 Ilahi-Ghomshei, "The Principles of the Religion of Love in Classical Persian Poetry" in *Hafiz and the Religion of Love in Classical Persian Poetry*, 96–98.
86 Lewisohn, "The Mystical Milieu: Hâfiz's Erotic Spirituality" in *Hafiz and the Religion of Love in Classical Persian Poetry*, 54.
87 Ibid., 43.
88 Ibid.
89 Ibid.
90 Ibid.
91 Ibid., 44–45.
92 Ibid., 46.
93 Ibid., 47.
94 Ibid., 44.
95 Ibid., 50.
96 Ibid., 44.
97 Ibid., 45.
98 Ibid.
99 Ibid., 49.
100 Ibid., 50.
101 Ibid.
102 Ibid., 49.
103 Ibid.
104 Ibid., 50.
105 Lewisohn, "Socio-historical and Literary Contexts: Hâfiz in Shiraz" in *Hafiz and the Religion of Love in Classical Persian Poetry*, 9.
106 Lewisohn, "The Mystical Milieu: Hâfiz's Erotic Spirituality" in *Hafiz and the Religion of Love in Classical Persian Poetry*, 50.
107 Fouchécour, "Hâfiz and the Sufi" in *Hafiz and the Religion of Love in Classical Persian Poetry*, 155.
108 Ilahi-Ghomshei, "The Principles of the Religion of Love in Classical Persian Poetry" in *Hafiz and the Religion of Love in Classical Persian Poetry*, 83.
109 Lewisohn, "The Mystical Milieu: Hâfiz's Erotic Spirituality" in *Hafiz and the Religion of Love in Classical Persian Poetry*, 46–47.
110 Fouchécour, "Hâfiz and the Sufi" in *Hafiz and the Religion of Love in Classical Persian Poetry*, 153.
111 Ibid.
112 Lewisohn, "The Mystical Milieu: Hâfiz's Erotic Spirituality" in *Hafiz and the Religion of Love in Classical Persian Poetry*, 47.
113 Ibid., 48.
114 Ibid., 52.
115 Lewisohn, "Socio-historical and Literary Contexts: Hâfiz in Shiraz" in *Hafiz and the Religion of Love in Classical Persian Poetry*, 9.
116 Lewisohn, "The Mystical Milieu: Hâfiz's Erotic Spirituality" in *Hafiz and the Religion of Love in Classical Persian Poetry*, 32.
117 Ali Asghar Seyed-Gohrab, "The Erotic Spirit: Love, Man and Satan in Hâfiz's Poetry" in *Hafiz and the Religion of Love in Classical Persian Poetry*, 112.
118 Ilahi-Ghomshei, "The Principles of the Religion of Love in Classical Persian Poetry" in *Hafiz and the Religion of Love in Classical Persian Poetry*, 85.
119 Ibid., 86.
120 Fouchécour, "Hâfiz and the Sufi"

in *Hafiz and the Religion of Love in Classical Persian Poetry*, 149.
121 Ilahi-Ghomshei, "The Principles of the Religion of Love in Classical Persian Poetry" in *Hafiz and the Religion of Love in Classical Persian Poetry*, 84.
122 Lewisohn, "Socio-historical and Literary Contexts: Hâfiz in Shiraz" in *Hafiz and the Religion of Love in Classical Persian Poetry*, 22.
123 Fouchécour, "Hâfiz and the Sufi" in *Hafiz and the Religion of Love in Classical Persian Poetry*, 151.
124 Ibid.
125 Ibid., 152.
126 Seyed-Gohrab, "The Erotic Spirit: Love, Man and Satan in Hâfiz's Poetry" in *Hafiz and the Religion of Love in Classical Persian Poetry*, 114.
127 Ibid., 115.
128 Ibid., 116.
129 Lewisohn, "The Mystical Milieu: Hâfiz's Erotic Spirituality" in *Hafiz and the Religion of Love in Classical Persian Poetry*, 36.
130 Ibid.
131 Ibid., 36–37.
132 Ibid., 37.
133 Ibid.
134 Ibid.
135 Ibid., 38.
136 Ibid., 53.
137 Ibid.
138 Ibid., 54.
139 Ibid.
140 Seyed-Gohrab, "The Erotic Spirit: Love, Man and Satan in Hâfiz's Poetry" in *Hafiz and the Religion of Love in Classical Persian Poetry*, 116.
141 Ibid.
142 Ibid., 117.
143 Ibid.
144 Ibid., 118.
145 Ibid.
146 Lewisohn, "The Mystical Milieu: Hâfiz's Erotic Spirituality" in *Hafiz and the Religion of Love in Classical Persian Poetry*, 52.
147 Ibid.
148 Ghomshei, "The Principles of the Religion of Love in Classical Persian Poetry" in *Hafiz and the Religion of Love in Classical Persian Poetry*, 84.
149 Ibid., 86.
150 Lewisohn, "The Mystical Milieu: Hâfiz's Erotic Spirituality" in *Hafiz and the Religion of Love in Classical Persian Poetry*, 43.
151 Ibid., 51–52.
152 Ibid., 52.
153 Lewisohn, "Socio-historical and Literary Contexts: Hâfiz in Shiraz" in *Hafiz and the Religion of Love in Classical Persian Poetry*, 10.
154 Ibid., 13.
155 Ibid.
156 Ibid.
157 Ibid., 26.
158 Richard C. Foltz, *Iran in World History* (New York: Oxford University Press, 2016), 70.
159 Ibid.
160 Lewisohn, "The Mystical Milieu: Hâfiz's Erotic Spirituality" in *Hafiz and the Religion of Love in Classical Persian Poetry*, 26.
161 Ibid., 27.
162 Foltz, *Iran in World History*, 68.
163 Ibid.
164 Ibid.
165 Ibid., 68–69.
166 Ibid., 69.
167 Ibid.
168 Ibid., 70.
169 Ibid., 68.
170 Ibid.
171 Ibid., 66.
172 Ibid.
173 Ibid.
174 Ibid.
175 Ibid., 67.
176 Ibid., 73.
177 Ibid., 68.

178 Ibid., 73.
179 Ibid.
180 Ibid.
181 Ibid.
182 Ibid.
183 Ibid., 60.
184 Ibid., 74.
185 Lewisohn, "The Mystical Milieu: Hâfiz's Erotic Spirituality" in *Hafiz and the Religion of Love in Classical Persian Poetry*, 14.
186 Ibid.
187 Ibid.
188 Husayn Ilahi-Ghomshei, "The Principles of the Religion of Love in Classical Persian Poetry" in *Hafiz and the Religion of Love in Classical Persian Poetry*, 85.
189 Lewisohn, "Socio-historical and Literary Contexts: Hâfiz in Shiraz" in *Hafiz and the Religion of Love in Classical Persian Poetry*, 14.
190 Ibid., 15.
191 Ibid., 16.
192 Ibid.
193 Ibid.
194 Ibid.
195 Ibid., 18.
196 Foltz, *Iran in World History*, 74.

CHAPTER 9. "I AM ZAHHAK AND ALEXANDER!"

1 Richard C. Foltz, *Iran in World History* (New York: Oxford University Press, 2016), 75.
2 Michael Axworthy, *A History of Iran: Empire of the Mind* (New York: Perseus Books Group, 2010), 130.
3 Richard Foltz, *Religions of Iran: From Prehistory to the Present* (London: Oneworld Publications, 2013), 198; Hamad Subani, *The Secret History of Iran: How Iran is the key to the both the survival & the destruction of the Islamic World* (Cabal Times, 2013), 171.
4 Foltz, *Religions of Iran*, 198.
5 Ibid., 197.
6 Foltz, *Religions of Iran*, 197–198.
7 Pio Filippani-Ronconci, "The Tradition of Sacred Kingship in Iran," in George Lenczowski [Editor], *Iran Under The Pahlavis* (Stanford: Hoover Institute Press, 1978), 79.
8 Axworthy, *A History of Iran*, 131.
9 Ibid., 131.
10 Subani, *The Secret History of Iran*, 171.
11 Ibid.
12 Ibid., 176.
13 Ibid.
14 Ibid., 176–177.
15 Ibid., 177.
16 Foltz, *Religions of Iran*, 218.
17 Ibid., 219.
18 Ibid., 221.
19 Ibid.
20 Ibid.
21 Ibid., 222.
22 Ibid.
23 Ibid., 221.
24 Ibid.
25 Ibid., 223.
26 Ibid., 222.
27 Ibid., 223.
28 Ibid., 226.
29 Ibid.
30 Ibid., 222.
31 Ibid., 227.
32 Ibid.
33 Ibid., 223.
34 Ibid.
35 Ibid.
36 Ibid.
37 Ibid.
38 Ibid., 224.
39 Ibid.
40 Ibid.
41 Ibid., 199.
42 Subani, *The Secret History of Iran*, 175–176.
43 Axworthy, *A History of Iran*, 133.
44 Foltz, *Religions of Iran*, 224.

45 Ibid., 225.
46 Ibid., 226.
47 Ibid.
48 Ibid.
49 Ibid., 225.
50 Ibid.
51 Ibid.
52 Ibid., 223.
53 Ibid.
54 Ibid.
55 Ibid.
56 Filippani-Ronconci, 80.
57 Subani, *The Secret History of Iran*, 176.
58 Ibid., 178.
59 Ibid., 179.
60 Foltz, *Iran in World History*, 75.
61 Filippani-Ronconci, 79.
62 Subani, *The Secret History of Iran*, 175.
63 Ibid.
64 Axworthy, *A History of Iran*, 131.
65 Filippani-Ronconci, 79.
66 Axworthy, *A History of Iran*, 132.
67 Ibid.
68 Filippani-Ronconci, 79.
69 Foltz, *Religions of Iran*, 197.
70 Axworthy, *A History of Iran*, 132.
71 Ibid., 142.
72 Foltz, *Iran in World History*, 75.
73 Subani, *The Secret History of Iran*, 178.
74 Ibid.
75 Ibid., 179.
76 Ibid., 177.
77 Ibid., 177.
78 Ibid., 174.
79 Ibid., 179.
80 Foltz, *Iran in World History*, 75.
81 Subani, *The Secret History of Iran*, 180.
82 Ibid.
83 Ibid.
84 Axworthy, *A History of Iran*, 133.
85 Subani, 180.
86 Ibid.
87 Axowrthy, *A History of Iran*, 133.
88 Ibid., 142.
89 Subani, *The Secret History of Iran*, 180.
90 Ibid., 181.
91 Ibid., 171.
92 Ibid., 173.
93 Ibid., 176.
94 Axworthy, *A History of Iran*, 134.
95 Ibid., 136.
96 Keddie, 13.
97 Ibid., 13.
98 Ibid., 12.
99 Subani, *The Secret History of Iran*, 170.
100 Nikki R. Keddie, *Roots of Revolution* (New Haven: Yale University Press, 1981), 13.
101 Ibid.
102 Axworthy, *A History of Iran*, 134–135.
103 Ibid., 150.
104 Ibid., 136.
105 Ibid., 135.
106 Ibid., 137.
107 Ibid.
108 Ibid.
109 Ibid.
110 Ibid., 134.
111 Foltz, *Religions of Iran*, 200–201.
112 Keddie, *Roots of Revolution*, 12.
113 Foltz, *Religions of Iran*, 201.
114 Ibid.
115 Axworthy, *A History of Iran*, 138.
116 Ibid.
117 Ibid.
118 Filippani-Ronconci, 80.
119 Axworthy, *A History of Iran*, 138.
120 Filippani-Ronconci, 80.
121 Ibid.
122 Foltz, 2013, 201.
123 Foltz, *Iran in World History*, 79.
124 Axworthy, *A History of Iran*, 147.
125 Ibid.
126 Ibid., 146.
127 Ibid.
128 Ibid., 148.
129 Keddie, *Roots of Revolution*, 19.

130 Axworthy, *A History of Iran*, 133–134, 144.
131 Ibid., 144.
132 Ibid., 140.
133 Ibid.
134 Ibid.
135 Ibid.
136 Ibid.
137 Keddie, *Roots of Revolution*, 14.
138 Ibid.
139 Ibid.
140 Ibid., 15.
141 Ibid., 16.
142 Ibid., 16–17.
143 Ibid., 17.
144 Ibid., 18, 21.
145 Ibid., 18.
146 Ibid.
147 Ibid., 20.
148 Ibid.
149 Foltz, *Iran in World History*, 79.
150 Axworthy, *A History of Iran*, 147–148.
151 Ibid., 147.
152 Ibid.
153 Keddie, *Roots of Revolution*, 13.
154 Ibid., 20.
155 Subani, *The Secret History of Iran*, 170.
156 Keddie, *Roots of Revolution*, 21.
157 Axworthy, *A History of Iran*, 147.
158 Ibid., 149.
159 Ibid.
160 Ibid.
161 Ibid.
162 Foltz, *Iran in World History*, 79.
163 Axworthy, *A History of Iran*, 150.
164 Foltz, *Iran in World History*, 80.
165 Ibid.
166 Ibid., 80.
167 Ibid., 20.
168 Axworthy, *A History of Iran*, 167.
169 Ibid.
170 Foltz, *Iran in World History*, 80.
171 Axworthy, 150.
172 Ibid.
173 Ibid.
174 Foltz, *Iran in World History*, 20.
175 Axworthy, 150.
176 Ibid.
177 Ibid., 155.
178 Foltz, *Iran in World History*, 80.
179 Axworthy, 151.
180 Ibid.
181 Foltz, *Iran in World History*, 20.
182 Axworthy, 151.
183 Ibid., 151, 153.
184 Foltz, *Iran in World History*, 80.
185 Axworthy, 151.
186 Ibid., 152–153.
187 Foltz, *Iran in World History*, 20.
188 Axworthy, 153.
189 Ibid.
190 Ibid., 154.
191 Ibid.
192 Foltz, *Iran in World History*, 81.
193 Ibid.
194 Ibid.
195 Ibid.
196 Axworthy, 159.
197 Ibid., 139.
198 Ibid.
199 Ibid.
200 Ibid., 159.
201 Ibid., 162.
202 Foltz, *Iran in World History*, 81.
203 Axworthy, 157.
204 Foltz, *Iran in World History*, 81.
205 Axworthy, 159.
206 Ibid., 160.
207 Ibid.
208 Foltz, *Iran in World History*, 81.
209 Axworthy, 161.
210 Ibid.
211 Foltz, *Iran in World History*, 81.
212 Axworthy, 163.
213 Ibid., 164.
214 Ibid., 165.
215 Ibid., 159.
216 Ibid., 159–160.
217 Ibid., 160.
218 Ibid., 163.
219 Ibid., 165.
220 Ibid.

221 Foltz, *Iran in World History*, 82–83.
222 Ibid., 82.
223 Ibid., 83.
224 Ibid.
225 Ibid., 81.
226 Axworthy, 167.
227 Ibid., 167–168.
228 Ibid., 169.
229 Ibid., 170–175.
230 Ibid., 176.
231 Foltz, *Iran in World History*, 86.
232 Ibid., 83.
233 Ibid., 84.
234 Ibid., 85.
235 Ibid.
236 Ibid., 86.
237 Foltz, *Religions of Iran*, 231.
238 Ibid.
239 Ibid.
240 Ibid., 232–233.
241 Ibid., 232.
242 Ibid.
243 Ibid.
244 Ibid., 233.
245 Ibid.
246 Ibid.
247 Ibid.
248 Ibid., 233, 236.
249 Ibid., 234.
250 Ibid.
251 Ibid.
252 Ibid., 235.
253 Ibid.
254 Ibid.
255 Ibid.
256 Ibid., 236.
257 Ibid.
258 Ibid.
259 Ibid.
260 Ibid., 234.
261 Ibid.
262 Ibid.
263 Ibid.
264 Ibid., 235.
265 Ibid.
266 Ibid.
267 Ibid.
268 Ibid., 234.
269 Ibid., 235.
270 Ibid.
271 Ibid., 236.
272 Ibid., 237.
273 Ibid., 241.
274 Ibid., 237.
275 Ibid., 239.
276 Ibid.
277 Ibid., 237–238.
278 Ibid., 238.
279 Ibid.
280 Ibid.
281 Ibid., 238–239.
282 Ibid., 245.
283 Ibid., 240.
284 Ibid., 239.
285 Ibid., 241.
286 Ibid., 239.
287 Ibid., 240.
288 Ibid., 238.
289 Ibid., 243.
290 Ibid., 240.
291 Ibid., 246.
292 Ibid., 243.
293 Ibid., 244.
294 Ibid.
295 Ibid., 245.
296 Ibid., 244.
297 Ibid., 239.
298 Ibid., 245.
299 Ibid.
300 Keddie, *Roots of Revolution*, 22.
301 Ibid.
302 Subani, *The Secret History of Iran*, 175.
303 Keddie, *Roots of Revolution*, 23.

CHAPTER 10. THE LEVIATHAN OF IRAN

1 Homa Katouzian, *The Persians: Ancient, Mediaeval and Modern Iran* (New Haven: Yale University Press, 2010), 175.
2 Ibid., 175.
3 Ibid., 188–189.

4 Ibid., 188.
5 Ibid.
6 Ibid., 170.
7 Ibid.
8 Ibid., 177.
9 Ibid., 173.
10 Ibid.
11 Ibid.
12 Ibid., 176.
13 Ibid.
14 Ibid.
15 Ibid.
16 Ibid.
17 Ibid., 174.
18 Ibid., 181.
19 Ibid.
20 Ibid., 178.
21 Ibid., 174.
22 Ibid., 170.
23 Ibid., 180.
24 Ibid., 181.
25 Ibid.
26 Ibid., 188.
27 Ibid., 182.
28 Ibid.
29 Ibid.
30 Ibid.
31 Ibid., 184.
32 Ibid., 184.
33 Ibid., 185.
34 Ibid.
35 Ibid., 186.
36 Ibid., 186–187.
37 Ibid., 187.
38 Ibid., 188.
39 Michael Axworthy, A *History of Iran: Empire of the Mind* (New York: Perseus Books Group, 2010), 213.
40 Ibid.
41 Ibid., 214.
42 Ibid.
43 L.P. Elwell-Sutton, "Reza Shah the Great: Founder of the Pahlavi Dynasty" in George Lenczowski [Editor], *Iran Under The Pahlavis* (Stanford: Hoover Institute Press, 1978), 4.
44 Ibid.
45 Ibid., 5.
46 Ibid.
47 Ibid., 45.
48 Ibid., 5.
49 Ibid., 6.
50 Ibid.
51 Ibid., 8.
52 Ibid., 14.
53 Ibid., 7.
54 Ibid., 8.
55 Ibid., 9.
56 Ibid.
57 Lenczowski, "Introduction" in *Iran Under The Pahlavis*, xvii.
58 Elwell-Sutton, "Reza Shah the Great" in *Iran Under The Pahlavis*, 10.
59 Ibid., 9.
60 Ibid.
61 Ibid., 10.
62 Ibid., 9–10.
63 Ibid., 10.
64 Ibid., 31.
65 Ibid., 14.
66 Ibid., 11.
67 Ibid., 13.
68 Ibid., 16.
69 Ibid., 16–17.
70 Ibid., 14.
71 Ibid., 18.
72 Ibid., 21–25.
73 Ibid., 26.
74 Ibid., 27.
75 Ibid., 27–28.
76 Ibid., 28.
77 Ibid., 23–24.
78 Ibid., 24.
79 Ibid., 36–37.
80 Ibid., 37.
81 Ibid., 40–41, 47.
82 Ibid., 43.
83 Ibid., 6, 44.
84 Ibid., 6.
85 Lenczowski, "Introduction in *Iran Under The Pahlavis*", xvi.
86 Elwell-Sutton, "Reza Shah the

Great" in *Iran Under The Pahlavis*, 37.
87 Ibid., 37.
88 Ibid., 40.
89 Ibid., 39.
90 Ibid., 34.
91 Lenczowski, "Introduction" in *Iran Under The Pahlavis*, xviii.
92 Ibid., xviii.
93 Ibid., xvi.
94 Ibid., xvi.
95 Elwell-Sutton, "Reza Shah the Great" in *Iran Under The Pahlavis*, 12.
96 Ibid., 48.
97 Ibid., 43.
98 Ibid., 44.
99 Lenczowski, "Introduction" in *Iran Under The Pahlavis*, xix.
100 Elwell-Sutton, "Reza Shah the Great" in *Iran Under The Pahlavis*, 49.
101 Lenczowski, "Introduction" in *Iran Under The Pahlavis*, xix.
102 Elwell-Sutton, "Reza Shah the Great" in *Iran Under The Pahlavis*, 49.
103 Ibid., 2.
104 Ibid., 2–3.
105 Ibid., 29.
106 Ibid., 1.
107 Ibid., 2.
108 Ibid., 3.
109 Ibid., 3.
110 Ibid., 3.
111 Ibid., 3.
112 Ibid., 2–3.
113 Lenczowski, "Introduction" in *Iran Under The Pahlavis*, xix.
114 Elwell-Sutton, "Reza Shah the Great" in *Iran Under The Pahlavis*, 3.
115 Elwell-Sutton, "Reza Shah the Great" in *Iran Under The Pahlavis*, 50.
116 Lenczowski, "Introduction" in *Iran Under The Pahlavis*, xxi.
117 Ibid., xxi.
118 Lenczowski, "Introduction" in *Iran Under The Pahlavis*, xx.
119 Richard C. Foltz, *Iran in World History* (New York: Oxford University Press, 2016), 99.
120 Ibid., 99.
121 Ibid., 100.
122 Ibid.
123 Ibid.
124 Ibid., 102.
125 Ibid., 102–103.
126 Ibid., 103.
127 Lenczowski, "Introduction" in *Iran Under The Pahlavis*, xxii.
128 Ibid., xv.
129 Ibid., xxii.
130 Ibid., xxii.
131 Ibid., xv.
132 Foltz, 2016, *Iran in World History*, 106.
133 Ibid., 108.
134 Ibid.
135 Ibid.
136 Ibid.
137 Ibid., 109.
138 Thomas Hobbes, *Leviathan* (New York: Penguin Classics, 2017), 7.
139 Ibid., 7.
140 Ibid.
141 Ibid.
142 Ibid., 543.
143 Ibid., 544.
144 Ibid., 140.
145 Ibid.
146 Ibid.
147 Ibid.
148 Ibid.
149 Ibid., 141.
150 Ibid.
151 Ibid., 164–165.
152 Ibid., 165.
153 Ibid., 263.
154 Ibid.
155 Ibid., 216–217.
156 Ibid., 217.
157 Ibid., 218.
158 Ibid.

159 Ibid., 163.
160 Ibid., 100.
161 Ibid.
162 Ibid., 101.
163 Ibid., 102.
164 Ibid., 102–103.
165 Ibid., 102.
166 Ibid., 103.
167 Ibid.
168 Ibid.
169 Ibid.
170 Ibid., 103–104.
171 Ibid., 104.
172 Ibid.
173 Ibid.
174 Ibid.
175 Ibid.
176 Ibid., 105.
177 Ibid., 151.
178 Ibid.
179 Ibid.
180 Ibid., 570.
181 Ibid.
182 Ibid., 152–157.
183 Ibid., 153.
184 Ibid., 152–153.
185 Ibid., 153.
186 Ibid.
187 Ibid., 154.
188 Ibid., 153.
189 Ibid., 154.
190 Ibid.
191 Ibid.
192 Ibid.
193 Ibid.
194 Ibid.
195 Ibid., 154–155.
196 Ibid., 154.
197 Ibid., 155.
198 Ibid., 156.
199 Ibid., 157.
200 Ibid.
201 Pio Filippani-Ronconci, "The Tradition of Sacred Kingship in Iran," in George Lenczowski [Editor], *Iran Under The Pahlavis* (Stanford: Hoover Institute Press, 1978), 64.
202 Filippani-Ronconi, "The Tradition of Sacred Kingship in Iran," in *Iran Under the Pahlavis*, 64.
203 Ibid., 64–65.
204 Ibid., 65.
205 Ibid., 65–66.
206 Ibid., 67.
207 Ibid., 66–67.
208 Ibid., 66.
209 Ibid., 67.
210 Ibid., 68.
211 Ibid.
212 Ibid.
213 Thomas Hobbes, *Leviathan*, 237.
214 Ibid.
215 Ibid.
216 Ibid., 310.
217 Ibid., 311.
218 Ibid., 311, 322.
219 Ibid., 322.
220 Ibid., 320–321.
221 Ibid., 235.
222 Ibid., 360–361.
223 Ibid., 262.
224 Ibid., 361.
225 Ibid.
226 Ibid., 364.
227 Ibid.
228 Ibid.
229 Ibid., 534.
230 Ibid., 539.
231 Ibid., 364–365.
232 Ibid., 365.
233 Ibid., 535.
234 Ibid., 539.
235 Ibid., 365.
236 Ibid., 366.
237 Ibid., 368.
238 Ibid.
239 Ibid.
240 Ibid., 571.
241 Ibid.
242 Ibid.
243 Ibid., 413.
244 Ibid.
245 Ibid., 414.
246 Ibid.

247 Ibid.
248 Ibid.
249 Ibid., 415.
250 Ibid.
251 Ibid., 415–416.
252 Ibid., 416.
253 Ibid., 578–579.
254 Ibid., 579.
255 Ibid., 582.
256 Ibid.
257 Ibid., 583.
258 Ibid.
259 Filippani-Ronconi, "The Tradition of Sacred Kingship in Iran," in *Iran Under the Pahlavis*, 56.
260 Ibid.
261 Ibid., 58.
262 Ibid.
263 Ibid.
264 Ibid., 57.
265 Ibid., 58.
266 Ibid.
267 Ibid.
268 Ibid., 57.
269 Ibid.
270 Ibid., 63.
271 Ibid., 59.
272 Ibid.
273 Ibid., 60.
274 Ibid., 62.
275 Ibid., 57.
276 Ibid., 63.
277 Ibid.
278 Ibid., 60.
279 Ibid., 62.
280 Ibid., 52.
281 Ibid., 61.
282 Ibid., 63.
283 Ibid.
284 Ibid., 62.
285 Ibid.
286 Ibid.
287 Ibid., 63.
288 Ibid.
289 Ibid.

CHAPTER 11. THE GOVERNMENT OF GOD

1 Abdolkarim Soroush, *Reason, Freedom, and Democracy in Islam* (New York: Oxford University Press, 2002), xv.
2 Nikki R. Keddie, *Roots of Revolution* (New Haven: Yale University Press, 1981), 420.
3 Ibid.
4 Baqer Moin, *Khomeini: Life of the Ayatollah* (New York: Thomas Dunne Books), 2000, 41.
5 Ibid., 48.
6 Ibid., 49.
7 Ibid., 50.
8 Ibid., 51.
9 Ibid., 52.
10 Shaul Bakhash, *Reign of the Ayatollahs: Iran and the Islamic Revolution* (Basic Books, 1986), 24–44.
11 Moin, *Khomeini*, 43–44.
12 Michel Foucault, "Iran: The Spirit of a World Without Spirit" in *Politics, Philosophy, Culture: Interviews and Other Writings 1977–1984* (London: Routledge, 1988), 213–217.
13 Ibid., 217–218.
14 Ibid., 215.
15 Didier Eribon, *Michel Foucault* (Cambridge, MA: Harvard University Press, 1991), 287.
16 Weber, 21.
17 Ibid., 20.
18 Ibid., 19.
19 Ibid., 19.
20 Ibid., 18–19.
21 Ibid., 48.
22 Ibid., 49.
23 Ibid., 20.
24 Ibid., 20.
25 Ibid., 20.
26 Ibid., 20.
27 Ibid., 21.
28 Ibid., 21.
29 Ibid., 52.
30 Ibid., 21.

31 Ibid., 21.
32 Ibid., 21.
33 Ibid., 21.
34 Ibid., 53.
35 Ibid., 53.
36 Foucault, "Iran: The Spirit of a World Without Spirit", 215.
37 James Miller, *The Passion of Michel Foucault* (New York: Simon and Schuster, 1993), 309.
38 Ibid.
39 Ibid.
40 Michel Foucault, *The Essential Works of Michel Foucault 1954–1984, Vol. 1: Ethics, Truth, Subjectivity* (The New Press, 1997), xxii-xxiii.
41 Eribon, *Michel Foucault*, 288–289.
42 Michel Foucault, *Essential Works of Michel Foucault 1954–1984, Vol. 3: Power* (The New Press, 2000), 442.
43 Ervand Abrahamian, *The Iranian Mojahedin* (New Haven: Yale University Press, 1989), 92–97.
44 Ibid.
45 The Shah's loyal national military was completely purged of its commanders and general staff after the revolution, just before Iraq invaded. Thus the Islamic Republic was forced to make up a mock military leadership out of various heads of opposition groups that had helped to overthrow the Shah, and fill their divisions with their own devoted guerrilla commanders.
46 Weber, 50–51.
47 Ibid., 51.
48 Abrahamian, *The Iranian Mojahedin*, 251–253.
49 Ibid., 260–261.
50 Max Weber, *On Charisma and Institution Building* (Chiacgo: University of Chicago Press, 1968), 51.
51 Ibid.
52 Ibid.
53 Ibid., 40.
54 Ibid., 51.
55 Ibid., 23.
56 Ibid., 24.
57 Ibid.
58 Ibid., 46.
59 Ibid.
60 Ibid., 41.
61 Ibid., 46.
62 Ibid., 47.
63 Ibid., 49.
64 Abdolkarim Soroush, *Reason, Freedom, and Democracy in Islam* (Oxford University Press, 2000), 86-87.
65 Ibid., 91.
66 Ibid., 92-94.
67 Ibid., 103-104.
68 Ibid., 151.
69 Ibid., 144.
70 Ibid., 146.
71 Ibid., 148.
72 Weber, *On Charisma and Institution Building*, 39.

CHAPTER 12. THE RENAISSANCE OF IRANIAN CIVILIZATION

1 Samuel Huntington, *The Clash of Civilizations and the Remaking of World Order* (New York: Simon and Schuster, 2003), 174–182.
2 H. Kennedy, "Baghdad" in *Encyclopaedia Iranica, Vol. III, Fasc. 4*, pp. 412–415 (New York: Encyclopaedia Iranica Foundation, 1990).
3 Michael Morony, "Iraq" in *Encyclopedia Iranica*, Vol. XIII, Fasc. 5, pp. 543–550 (New York: Encyclopedia Iranica Foundation, 2006).
4 Richard Lynn and Tatu Vanhanen, *IQ and the Wealth of Nations* (Praeger, 2002), 87–158.
5 Ibid., 61–62.
6 Carl Zimmer, "Ancestors of Modern Humans Interbred With Extinct Hominins" (*The New York Times*, March 17, 2016).
7 Gary Lynch, and Richard Granger, *Big Brain: The Origins and Future of Human Intelligence* (Griffin, 2009).

8 Richard Lynn and Tatu Vanhanen, *IQ and the Wealth of Nations* (Praeger, 2002).
9 Richard Lynn and Tatu Vanhanen, *IQ and Global Inequality* (Washington Summit Publishers, 2006).
10 Richard J. Herrnstein and Charles Murray, *The Bell Curve: Intelligence and Class Structure in American Life* (Free Press, 1996).
11 Richard Lynn, *Eugenics: A Reassessment* (London: Praeger, 2001), 312–315.
12 Megan Solly, "DNA Pioneer James Watson Loses Honorary Degree Titles Over Racist Comments," in *Smithsonian* (January 15, 2019).
13 Wolfgang Haak et al., "Massive migration from the steppe is a source for Indo-European languages in Europe" in *Nature* doi:10.1038/nature14317.
14 David Reich and Iain Mathieson, "The genomic history of southeastern Europe" in *Nature Vol. 555*, 197–203 (08 March 2018).
15 David Reich, *Who We Are and How We Got Here: Ancient DNA and the New Science of the Human Past* (Pantheon, 2018).
16 Richard Lynn, *Eugenics: A Reassessment*, 18–43.
17 Ibid., 24–28.
18 Ibid., 312–315.
19 Jason Reza Jorjani, *World State of Emergency* (London: Arktos, 2017).
20 Richard Foltz, *Religions of Iran: From Prehistory to the Present* (London: Oneworld Publications, 2013), 211.
21 Ibid.
22 Ibid.
23 Ibid.
24 Ibid., 212.
25 Ibid., 211.
26 Ibid..
27 Ibid.
28 Ibid., 212.
29 Ibid.
30 Ibid.
31 Ibid., 213.
32 Ibid.
33 Ibid.
34 Ibid.
35 Giorgio Agamben, *Homo Sacer: Sovereign Power and Bare Life* (Stanford, CA: Stanford University Press), 1998, 35.
36 Ibid.
37 Ibid.
38 Ibid., 104–105.
39 Ibid., 104.
40 Ibid., 105.
41 Ibid.
42 Ibid., 106.
43 Ibid., 111.
44 Ibid., 28.
45 Ibid.
46 Ibid., 110.
47 Ibid.
48 Ibid.
49 Ibid., 71.
50 Ibid.
51 Ibid., 72.
52 Ibid., 113.
53 Ibid., 72.
54 Ibid., 73.
55 Ibid., 74.
56 Ibid., 77.
57 Ibid., 76.
58 Ibid., 76–77.
59 Ibid., 76.
60 Ibid., 77.
61 Ibid., 76.
62 Ibid., 78.
63 Ibid.
64 Ibid.
65 Ibid., 79.
66 Ibid., 79–80.
67 Ibid., 105.
68 Ibid., 106.
69 Ibid., 107.
70 Ibid., 109.
71 Ibid., 35.

72 Ibid.
73 Ibid., 105.
74 Ibid., 105–106.
75 Ibid., 109.
76 Ibid.
77 Ibid., 19.
78 Ibid., 107.
79 Ibid., 15.
80 Ibid., 16.
81 Ibid., 28.
82 Ibid., 29.
83 Ibid., 109.
84 Ibid., 111.
85 Ibid., 112.
86 Ibid., 113.
87 Ibid., 38.
88 Ibid.

INDEX

A

B

C

D

E

F

G

H

I

J

K

L

M

N

O

P

Q

R

S

T

U

V

W

X

Y

Z

BIBLIOGRAPHY

Abrahamian, Ervand, The Iranian Mojahedin (New Haven: Yale University Press, 1989).

Afnan, Ruhi, Zoroaster's Influence on Anaxagoras, the Greek Tragedians, and Socrates (New York: Philosophical Library, 1969).

Agamben, Giorgio, Homo Sacer: Sovereign Power and Bare Life (Stanford, CA: Stanford University Press), 1998.

Aminrazavi, Mehdi, "Bundahishn" and "Greater Bundahishn" in An Anthology of Philosophy in Persia (New York: Oxford University Press, 1999).

Axworthy, Michael, A History of Iran: Empire of the Mind (New York: Perseus Books Group, 2010).

Bakhash, Shaul, Reign of the Ayatollahs: Iran and the Islamic Revolution (Basic Books, 1986).

Barnes, Jonathan, Early Greek Philosophy (New York: Penguin Books, 1987).

Beckwith, Christopher, Greek Buddha: Pyrrho's Encounter With Early Buddhism in Central Asia (Princeton: Princeton University Press, 2015).

Benoist, Alain de, The Indo-Europeans: In Search of a Homeland (London: Arktos, 2016).

Bloom, Allan, The Republic of Plato (New York: Basic Books, 199).

Boyce, Mary, Textual Sources for the Study of Zoroastrianism (Chicago: University of Chicago Press, 1990).

Brzezinski, R. and M. Mielczarek, The Sarmatians: 600 BC – AD 450 (Oxord: Osprey Publishing, 2002).

Bürgel, C. and R. Mottahedeh, "Azod-Al-Dawla, Abü Sojâ' Fannâ Khosrow" in Encyclopaedia Iranica, Vol. III, Fasc. 3, (New York: Encyclopaedia Iranica Foundation, 1988).

Cernenko, E.V., The Scythians: 700–300 BC (Oxford: Osprey Publishing, 1983).

Chittick, William C., The Sufi Path of Love: The Spiritual Teachings of Rumi (Albany: State University of New York Press, 1983).

Corbin, Henry, Spiritual Body and Celestial Earth: From Mazdean Iran to Shi'ite Iran (Princeton: Princeton University Press, 1989).

Crone, Patricia, The Nativist Prophets of Early Islamic Iran: Rural Revolt and Local Zoroastrianism (New York: Cambridge University Press, 2013).

Dabashi, Hamid, The World of Persian Literary Humanism (Cambridge, MA: Harvard University Press, 2012).

Dalen, Benno van, "Yahyâ ibn Abi Mansûr: Abû 'Ali Yahyâ ibn Abi Mansur al-Munajjim in Thomas Hockey et al, The Biographical Encyclopedia of Astronomers (New York: Springer, 2007).

Dandamayev, Muhammad A., "Magi" in Encyclopaedia Iranica.

Darmesteter, James, The Zend Avesta, Part 1 of 3: The Vendidad (Forgotten Books, 2008).

Dawood, N.J. [Translator], The Koran: With a Parallel Arabic Text (New York: Penguin Books, 2006).

D'Este, Sorita, Artemis: Virgin Goddess of the Sun & Moon – A Comprehensive Guide to the Greek Goddess of the Hunt (London: Avalonia Press, 2005).
————, Hekate: Liminal Rites – A Study of the rituals, magic and symbols of the torch-bearing Triple Goddess of the Crossroads (London: Avalonia Press, 2009).
Duchesne-Guillemin, J., "Angra Mainyu" in Encyclopaedia Iranica Vol. II, Fasc. 1, 70.
Eribon, Didier, Michel Foucault (Cambridge, MA: Harvard University Press, 1991).
Farrell, Joseph P., Babylon's Banksters: The Alchemy of Deep Physics, High Finance and Ancient Religion (Port Townsend: Feral House, 2010).
Farrokh, Kaveh, "Exploring the Possibility of Relationships Between the Iranian Goddess Anahita and the Dame du Lac of the Arthurian Legends" in Anahita: Ancient Persian Goddess & Zoroastrian Yazata (London: Avalonia, 2012).
Ferdowsi, Abolqasem, Shahnameh: The Persian Book of Kings (New York: Penguin Books, 2007).
Filippani-Ronconci, Pio, "The Tradition of Sacred Kingship in Iran," in George Lenczowski [Editor], Iran Under The Pahlavis (Stanford: Hoover Institute Press, 1978).
Foltz, Richard C., Spirituality in the Land of the Noble: How Iran Shaped the World's Religions (London: Oneworld Publications, 2004).
————, Religions of Iran: From Prehistory to the Present (London: Oneworld Publications, 2013).
Foltz, Richard C., Iran in World History (New York: Oxford University Press, 2016).
Foucault, Michel, "Iran: The Spirit of a World Without Spirit" in Politics, Philosophy, Culture: Interviews and Other Writings 1977–1984 (London: Routledge, 1988).
————, The Essential Works of Michel Foucault 1954–1984, Vol. 1: Ethics, Truth, Subjectivity (The New Press, 1997).
————, The Essential Works of Michel Foucault 1954–1984, Vol. 3: Power (The New Press, 2000).
Fouchécour, Charles-Henri de, "Hâfiz and the Sufi" in Hafiz and the Religion of Love in Classical Persian Poetry, (New York: I.B. Tauris, 2015).
Frye, Richard N., The Heritage of Persia (Costa Mesa: Mazda Publishers, 1993).
Ghirshman, Roman, Persian Art 249 BC– AD 651: The Parthian and Sassanian Dynasties (New York: Golden Press, 1962).
————, Persia the Immortal Kingdom (New York Graphic Society, 1971).
Ghomshei, Husayn Ilahi, "The Principles of the Religion of Love in Classical Persian Poetry" in Leonard Lewisohn [Editor], Hafiz and the Religion of Love in Classical Persian Poetry (New York: I.B. Tauris, 2015).
Gobineau, J.A. de, The World of the Persians (Geneva: Minerva, 1971).
Guthrie, Kenneth Sylvan, The Pythagorean Sourcebook and Library (Grand Rapids: Phanes Press, 1988).
Haak, Wolfgang et al., "Massive migration from the steppe is a source for Indo-European languages in Europe" in Nature doi:10.1038/nature14317.
Herodotus, The Histories (New York: Barnes and Noble, 2004).
Herrnstein, Richard J. and Charles Murray The Bell Curve: Intelligence and Class Structure in American Life (Free Press, 1996).
Herzfeld, E. The Persian Empire: Studies in the Geography and Ethnography of the Ancient Near East (Wiesbaden, 1968).
Hobbes, Thomas, Leviathan (New York: Penguin Classics, 2017).

Hodgson, Marshall, The Secret Order of Assassins: The Struggle of the Early Nizârî Ismâ'îlîs Against the Islamic World (Philadelphia: University of Pennsylvania Press, 2005).
Huntington, Samuel, The Clash of Civilizations and the Remaking of World Order (New York: Simon and Schuster, 2003).
Insler, Stanley, The Gâthâs of Zarathustra (Tehéran-Liège: Bibliothèque Pahlavi; Leiden: diffusion E.J. Brill, 1975).
Jafarey, Ali Akbar, The Gathas, Our Guide: The Thought-Provoking Divine Songs of Zarathustra (Cypress, CA: Ushta Publications, 1989).
Kahn, Charles H., Pythagoras and the Pythagoreans: A Brief History (Indianapolis: Hackett Publishing Company, 2001).
Katouzian, Homa, The Persians: Ancient, Mediaeval and Modern Iran (New Haven: Yale University Press, 2010).
Keddie, Nikki R., Roots of Revolution (New Haven: Yale University Press, 1981).
Kent, Roland G., Old Persian: Grammar, Texts, Lexicon (American Oriental Society, 1953).
Khalidi, Tarif, The Proofs of Prophecy (Brigham Young University, 2012).
Kraft, Harvey, The Buddha from Babylon: The Lost History and Cosmic Vision of Siddhartha Gautama (New York: Select Books, 2014).
Kuhrt, Amélie et al., The Persian Empire: A Corpus of Sources from the Achaemenid Period (New York: Routledge, 2007).
Laertius, Diogenes, Lives of Eminent Philosophers (New York: Oxford University Press, 2018).
Lenczowski [Editor], George, "The Tradition of Sacred Kingship in Iran," in Iran Under The Pahlavis (Stanford: Hoover Institute Press, 1978).
Lewisohn, Leonard, "Socio-historical and Literary Contexts: Hâfiz in Shiraz" in Hafiz and the Religion of Love in Classical Persian Poetry, (New York: I.B. Tauris, 2015).
Leonard Lewisohn, "The Mystical Milieu: Hâfiz's Erotic Spirituality" in Hafiz and the Religion of Love in Classical Persian Poetry, (New York: I.B. Tauris, 2015).
Lings, Martin, Muhammad: His Life Based on the Earliest Sources (Rochester, VT: Inner Traditions, 2006).
Littleton, C. Scott and Linda A. Malcor, From Scythia to Camelot (New York: Routledge, 2000).
Lynch, Gary and Richard Granger, Big Brain: The Origins and Future of Human Intelligence (Griffin, 2009).
Lynn, Richard and Tatu Vanhanen, IQ and the Wealth of Nations (Praeger, 2002).
————, IQ and Global Inequality (Washington Summit Publishers, 2006).
Mayor, Adrienne, The Poison King: The Life and Legend of Mithradates, Rome's Deadliest Enemy (Princeton: Princeton University Press, 2010).
Meyer, Marvin, Q Thomas Reader (Santa Rosa, CA: Polebridge Press, 1990).
Milani, Milad, Sufism in the Secret History of Persia (Durham: Acumen Publishing Limited, 2013).
Miller, James, The Passion of Michel Foucault (New York: Simon and Schuster, 1993).
Mills, M.L., Early Greek Philosophy and the Orient (Oxford: Clarendon Press, 1971).
Moin, Baqer. *Khomeini: Life of the Ayatollah* (New York: Thomas Dunne Books, 2000).

Murdock, D.M., "Was the Persian Goddess Anahita the Pre-Christian Virgin Mother of Mithra?" in Anahita: Ancient Persian Goddess & Zoroastrian Yazata (London: Avalonia, 2012).

Nabarz, Payam, The Mysteries of Mithras (Rochester, VT: Inner Traditions, 2005).

Nabarz, Payam [Editor], Anahita: Ancient Persian Goddess & Zoroastrian Yazata (London: Avalonia, 2013).

Nagel, Tilman, "Buyids" in Encyclopaedia Iranica, Vol. IV, Fasc. 6 (New York: Encyclopaedia Iranica Foundation, 1990).

Nanavutty, Piloo, The Gathas of Zarathustra: Hymns in Praise of Wisdom (Ahmedabad: Mapin Publishing, 1999).

Nasr, Seyyed Hossein and Mehdi Aminrazavi [Editors], An Anthology of Philosophy in Persia: Volume 1 (New York: Oxford University Press, 1999).

Navarr, Miles Augustus, Forbidden Theology: Origin of Scriptural God (Xlibris, 2012).

Neckel, Gustav, Germanen und Kelten: historisch-linguistisch-rassenkundliche Forschungen und Gedanken zur geisteskrisis (Heidelberg, 1929).

Nietzsche, Friedrich, Thus Spoke Zarathustra (New York: Modern Library, 1995).

————, The Pre-Platonic Philosophers (Chicago: University of Illinois Press, 2001).

Pine, Red, Lao-Tzu's Tao Te Ching (Port Townsend: Copper Canyon Press, 2009).

Pingree, D., "Banu Monajjem" in Ehsan Yarshater [Editor], Encyclopaedia Iranica, Vol. III, Fasc. 7 (Encyclopaedia Iranica Foundation, 1988).

Pourshariati, Parvaneh, Decline and Fall of the Sasanian Empire: The Sasanian-Parthian Confederacy and the Arab Conquest of Iran (I.B. Tauris, 2008).

Reich, David and Iain Mathieson, "The genomic history of southeastern Europe" in Nature Vol. 555, 197–203 (08 March 2018).

Reich, David, Who We Are and How We Got Here: Ancient DNA and the New Science of the Human Past (Pantheon, 2018).

Ruck, Carl A. P., Mark A. Hoffman, Jose Alfredo González Celdrán, Mushrooms, Myth, & Mithras (San Francisco: City Lights Books, 2011).

Schmitt, Carl, The Leviathan in the State Theory of Thomas Hobbes: Meaning and Failure of a Political Symbol (Chicago: University of Chicago Press, 2008.

Schmitt, Rüdiger, "Caspians" in Encyclopaedia Iranica Vol. V, Fasc. 1 (New York: Encyclopaedia Iranica Foundation, 1990).

Settegast, Mary, Plato Prehistorian: 10,000 To 5,000 B.C. Myth, Religion, Archeology (New York: Lindisfarne Press, 1990).

Seyed-Gohrab, Ali Asghar, "The Erotic Spirit: Love, Man and Satan in Hâfiz's Poetry" in Hafiz and the Religion of Love in Classical Persian Poetry, (New York: I.B. Tauris, 2015).

Singh, Jaideva, Spanda–Karikas: The Divine Creative Pulsation (Bombay: Motilal Banarsidass, 2012).

Soroush, Abdolkarim, Reason, Freedom, and Democracy in Islam (New York: Oxford University Press, 2002).

Stoneman, Richard, Xerxes: A Persian Life (New Haven: Yale University Press, 2015).

Stroumsa, Sarah, Freethinkers of Medieval Islam: Ibn al-Râwandi, Abu Bakr al-Râzi, and Their Impact on Islamic Thought (Boston: Brill, 1999).

Subani, Hamad, The Secret History of Iran: How Iran is the key to the both the survival & the destruction of the Islamic World (Cabal Times, 2013).

Tafazzoli, A. and A.L. Khromov, "Sasanian Iran: Intellectual Life" in History of Civilizations of Central Asia: Volume III The Crossroads of Civilizations A.D. 250 to 750 (Paris: United Nations Educational, Scientific and Cultural Organization, 1999).

Tardieu, Michel, Manichaeism (Chicago: University of Illinois Press, 2008).

Turner, Sharon, "Persian Origins of Anglo-Saxon Words", reproduced by The Circle of Ancient Iranian Studies (1827).

Ulansey, David, The Origins of the Mithraic Mysteries (New York: Oxford University Press, 1991).

Weber, Max, On Charisma and Institution Building (Chiacgo: University of Chicago Press, 1968).

West, M.L. The Hymns of Zoroaster: A New Translation of the Most Ancient Sacred Texts of Iran (New York: I.B. Tauris, 2015).

Wilde, Lyn Webster, On the Trail of the Warrior Women: The Amazons in Myth and History (New York: St. Martin's Press, 2000).

Yarshater, Ehsan, "Mazdakism" in The Cambridge History of Iran, Vol. 3(2) (New York: Cambridge University Press, 1983).

Zaehner, R.C., Zurvan: A Zoroastrian Dilemma (New York: Biblio and Tannen, 1928).

Zarghamee, Reza, Discovering Cyrus: The Persian Conqueror Astride the Ancient World (Washington DC: Mage Publishers, 2013).

Zimmer, Carl, "Ancestors of Modern Humans Interbred With Extinct Hominins" (The New York Times, March 17, 2016).

OTHER BOOKS PUBLISHED BY ARKTOS

Sri Dharma Pravartaka Acharya	*The Dharma Manifesto*
Joakim Andersen	*Rising from the Ruins: The Right of the 21st Century*
Winston C. Banks	*Excessive Immigration*
Alain de Benoist	*Beyond Human Rights*
	Carl Schmitt Today
	The Indo-Europeans
	Manifesto for a European Renaissance
	On the Brink of the Abyss
	The Problem of Democracy
	Runes and the Origins of Writing
	View from the Right (vol. 1–3)
Arthur Moeller van den Bruck	*Germany's Third Empire*
Matt Battaglioli	*The Consequences of Equality*
Kerry Bolton	*Revolution from Above*
	Yockey: A Fascist Odyssey
Isac Boman	*Money Power*
Ricardo Duchesne	*Faustian Man in a Multicultural Age*
Alexander Dugin	*Ethnos and Society*
	Ethnosociology
	Eurasian Mission
	The Fourth Political Theory
	Last War of the World-Island
	Political Platonism
	Putin vs Putin
	The Rise of the Fourth Political Theory
Edward Dutton	*Race Differences in Ethnocentrism*
Mark Dyal	*Hated and Proud*
Koenraad Elst	*Return of the Swastika*
Julius Evola	*The Bow and the Club*

OTHER BOOKS PUBLISHED BY ARKTOS

	Fascism Viewed from the Right *A Handbook for Right-Wing Youth* *Metaphysics of War* *The Myth of the Blood* *Notes on the Third Reich* *The Path of Cinnabar* *Recognitions* *A Traditionalist Confronts Fascism*
Guillaume Faye	*Archeofuturism* *Archeofuturism 2.0* *The Colonisation of Europe* *Convergence of Catastrophes* *A Global Coup* *Sex and Deviance* *Understanding Islam* *Why We Fight*
Daniel S. Forrest	*Suprahumanism*
Andrew Fraser	*Dissident Dispatches* *The WASP Question*
Génération Identitaire	*We are Generation Identity*
Paul Gottfried	*War and Democracy*
Porus Homi Havewala	*The Saga of the Aryan Race*
Lars Holger Holm	*Hiding in Broad Daylight* *Homo Maximus* *Incidents of Travel in Latin America* *The Owls of Afrasiab*
Richard Houck	*Liberalism Unmasked*
A. J. Illingworth	*Political Justice*
Alexander Jacob	*De Naturae Natura*
Jason Reza Jorjani	*Prometheus and Atlas* *World State of Emergency*

OTHER BOOKS PUBLISHED BY ARKTOS

Roderick Kaine	*Smart and SeXy*
Peter King	*Here and Now* *Keeping Things Close* *On Modern Manners*
Ludwig Klages	*The Biocentric Worldview* *Cosmogonic Reflections*
Pierre Krebs	*Fighting for the Essence*
John Bruce Leonard	*The New Prometheans*
Stephen Pax Leonard	*The Ideology of Failure* *Travels in Cultural Nihilism*
William S. Lind	*Retroculture*
Pentti Linkola	*Can Life Prevail?*
H. P. Lovecraft	*The Conservative*
Norman Lowell	*Imperium Europa*
Charles Maurras	*The Future of the Intelligentsia & For a French Awakening*
Michael O'Meara	*Guillaume Faye and the Battle of Europe* *New Culture, New Right*
Brian Anse Patrick	*The NRA and the Media* *Rise of the Anti-Media* *The Ten Commandments of Propaganda* *Zombology*
Tito Perdue	*The Bent Pyramid* *Lee* *Morning Crafts* *Philip* *William's House* (vol. 1–4)
Raido	*A Handbook of Traditional Living*
Steven J. Rosen	*The Agni and the Ecstasy* *The Jedi in the Lotus*

OTHER BOOKS PUBLISHED BY ARKTOS

Richard Rudgley	*Barbarians* *Essential Substances* *Wildest Dreams*
Ernst von Salomon	*It Cannot Be Stormed* *The Outlaws*
Sri Sri Ravi Shankar	*Celebrating Silence* *Know Your Child* *Management Mantras* *Patanjali Yoga Sutras* *Secrets of Relationships*
George T. Shaw (ed.)	*A Fair Hearing*
Fenek Solère	*Kraal*
Oswald Spengler	*Man and Technics*
Richard Storey	*The Uniqueness of Western Law*
Tomislav Sunic	*Against Democracy and Equality* *Homo Americanus* *Postmortem Report* *Titans are in Town*
Hans-Jürgen Syberberg	*On the Fortunes and Misfortunes of Art in Post-War Germany*
Abir Taha	*Defining Terrorism* *The Epic of Arya* (2nd ed.) *Nietzsche's Coming God, or the Redemption of the Divine* *Verses of Light*
Bal Gangadhar Tilak	*The Arctic Home in the Vedas*
Dominique Venner	*For a Positive Critique* *The Shock of History*
Markus Willinger	*A Europe of Nations* *Generation Identity*
Alexander Wolfheze	*Alba Rosa*

Printed in Great Britain
by Amazon

20015965R00333